U.S. HISTO
DOCUMENTS COLLE
TO ACCOMPANY

VOLUME **II** SINCE 1863

AMERICAN PASSAGES

A HISTORY OF THE UNITED STATES

PREPARED BY
ROBERT WEISE
EASTERN KENTUCKY UNIVERSITY

EDWARD AYERS
UNIVERSITY OF VIRGINIA

AYERS   GOULD   OSHINSKY   SODERLUND

THOMSON
WADSWORTH

Australia • Canada • Mexico • Singapore • Spain • United Kingdom • United States

ISBN 0-15-506761-3

COPYRIGHT © 2000 Wadsworth, a division of Thomson Learning, Inc.
Thomson Learning ™ is a trademark used herein under license.

ALL RIGHTS RESERVED. No part of this work covered by the
copyright hereon may be reproduced or used in any form or by any
means — graphic, electronic, or mechanical, including photocopying,
recording, taping, Web distribution, or information storage or retrieval
systems — without the written permission of the publisher.

Wadsworth/Thomson Learning
10 Davis Drive
Belmont CA 94002-3098
USA

For information about our products, contact us:
Thomson Learning Academic Resource Center
1-800-423-0563
http://www.wadsworth.com

For permission to use material from this text or product,
submit a request online at http://www.thomsonrights.com

Any additional questions about permissions can be
submitted by email to thomsonrights@thomson.com

Printed in the United States of America
10 9 8 7 6 5 4 3 2

Table of Contents

Chapter XV – Blood and Freedom, 1863–1867 319

    92. Mattie Griffith on the New York Draft Riots, 1863 319

    93. Clabe Jones's Civil War Experience in Kentucky, 1863 320

    94. John Dooley, Gettysburg Diary, 1863 324

    95. James F. Legate on Quantrill's Raid on Lawrence, Kansas, 1863 327

    96. Letters on Emancipation 330

        A. Missouri Slaveholder to Abraham Lincoln, 1863 330

        B. Jourdan Anderson to His Former Owner, 1865 332

        C. Alice Dabney to Her Former Owner, 1867 333

Chapter XVI – Reconstruction Abandoned, 1867–1877 335

    97. The Mississippi Black Code, 1865 335

    98. The Address of Alabama Colored Convention, 1867 338

    99. Thaddeus Stevens on Negro Suffrage, 1867 341

    100. George Washington Plunkitt, Plunkitt of Tammany Hall 342

    101. A New Orleans Editor on Colfax, 1873 347

    102. *The Nation* and the Panic of 1873 351

    103. The Destruction of the Plains Buffalo, 1870s 355

        A. Old Lady Horse 355

        B. Pretty Shield 356

Chapter XVII – An Economy Transformed: The Rise of Big Business, 1877–1887 357

    104. William Graham Sumner, "On a New Philosophy: That Poverty is the Best Policy," 357

    105. Chief Joseph, "An Indian's View of Indian Affairs," 1879 360

    106. Edward Bellamy, *Looking Backward, 2000–1887* 371

Chapter XVIII – Urban Growth and Farm Protest, 1887–1893 377

    107. Hon. William C. Oates, George Curtis, and T. V. Powderly, Chairman, The Homestead Strike, 1892 377

108. Michael Gold, *Jews Without Money*   387

109. The Populist Party, The Omaha Platform of the People's Party, 1892   392

110. Tom Watson and Anthony Wilson, The *People's Party Paper*, 1892   395

111. Elizabeth Cady Stanton, "Solitude of Self," 1892   403

Chapter XIX – A Troubled Nation Expands Outward, 1893 – 1901   405

112. Woman's Suffrage Convention, "The Colorado Campaign," 1893   405

113. Albert Beveridge, "The March of the Flag," 1898   407

114. Mark Twain, "To the Person Sitting in Darkness," 1901   410

115. Booker T. Washington, *Up From Slavery*, 1901   419

116. W. E. B. DuBois, *The Souls of Black Folk*, 1901   424

Chapter XX – Theodore Roosevelt and Progressive Reform, 1901 – 1909   431

117. Roosevelt, Panama and Colombia   431

118. Mary Antin, *The Promised Land*, 1904   434

119. Upton Sinclair, *The Jungle*, 1906   443

Chapter XXI – Progressivism at High Tide, 1909 – 1914   449

120. Gifford Pinchot, *The Fight for Conservation*, 1910   449

121. John Muir, *The Yosemite*, 1912   455

122. Edward A. Ross, "American and Immigrant Blood," December 1913   459

Chapter XXII – Over There and Over Here: The Impact of World War I, 1914 – 1921   467

123. Margaret Sanger, *My Fight for Birth Control*, 1915   467

124. Woodrow Wilson, An Address to the Joint Session of Congress, 1917   473

125. George Norris, "A Speech in the Senate," 1917   478

126. Mother Jones, "The Steel Strike of 1919"   480

127. John Dos Passos, "The Scene of Battle," 1919   485

Chapter XXIII – The Age of Jazz and Mass Culture, 1921 – 1927   489

128. Sinclair Lewis, "Boosters — Pep!," 1922   489

129. Ernest Hemingway, "Soldier's Home," 1925   497

130. H. L. Mencken, "Was Bryan Sincere?," 1925   500

131. W. B. Riley, "The Fundamentalists' Point of View," 1927   503

Chapter XXIV – The Great Depression, 1927–1933   509

132. Beatrice M. Hinkle, "Against the Double Standard," 1930   509

133. Woody Guthrie, "Hard Hitting Songs for Hard Hit People"   513

134. Nate Shaw, *All God's Dangers,* ca. 1933   517

135. Studs Terkel, *"Campus Life in the Depression"*   532

Chapter XXV – The New Deal, 1933–1939   535

136. Ralph Shaw, "The New Deal: Its Unsound Theories and Irreconcilable Policies," 1935   535

137. C.P.U.S.A., Central Committee Statement, The Communist Party on the Results of Elections, 1936   542

138. John Steinbeck, *The Grapes of Wrath,* 1939   547

Chapter XXVI – The Second World War, 1940–1945   551

139. Steve Weisman, "Pearl Harbor in the Mind of Japan"   551

140. Studs Terkel, *The Good War*   557

141. Leo Szilard, "Chicago Scientists' Petition to the President," July 17, 1945   559

142. President Truman, White House Press Release on Hiroshima, August 6, 1945   560

143. Paul Fussell, "Hiroshima: A Soldier's View"   562

144. Robert S. Abbott, "Splitting the Atom of Race Hate," August 18, 1945   566

Chapter XXVII – Postwar America, 1946–1952   569

145. George Kennan, "The Sources of Soviet Conduct," July 1947   569

146. *The Charlottesville Tribune,* "Are We Ready for Total Abolition of Racial Segregation?" January 6, 1951   577

147. Anne Moody, *Coming of Age in Mississippi*   579

148. Lillian Hellman, *Scoundrel Time*   586

Chapter XXVIII – The Eisenhower Years, 1953–1960   591

    149. Dwight D. Eisenhower, Eisenhower Explains the Domino Theory, 1954   591

    150. Chief Justice Earl Warren, *Brown v. Board of Education*, 1954   592

    151. *Newsweek,* "The Big Surge. . . . The New America," 1955   597

    152. William H. Whyte, Jr., *The Organization Man:* "A Generation of Bureaucrats," 1956   619

    153. Southern Representatives and Senators, "The Southern Manifesto: Declaration of Constitutional Principles"   622

Chapter XXIX – Turbulent Years, 1960–1968   625

    154. Michael Harrington, *The Other America: Poverty in the United States,* 1962   625

    155. Rachel Carson, *Silent Spring,* 1962   632

    156. Students for a Democratic Society, "The Port Huron Statement," 1962   636

    157. Betty Friedan, *The Feminine Mystique,* 1963   639

    158. Malcolm X, Malcolm X Explains His Ideas, 1964   647

    159. Lyndon B. Johnson, "Why Americans Fight in Vietnam," 1965   650

    160. Ho Chi Minh, President Ho Chi Minh's Reply to U.S. President Lyndon B. Johnson, 1967   652

    161. Robert F. Kennedy, Kennedy Attacks Johnson's Policy on Vietnam, 1968   653

Chapter XXX – Crisis of Confidence, 1969–1980   657

    162. Michael Smith, "Selling the Moon"   657

    163. William Sullivan, "Was the Vietnam War Inevitable?"   674

    164. 93rd Congress, Impeachment of Richard M. Nixon, August 20, 1974   676

    165. NBC, Richard M. Nixon on "Meet the Press"   679

Chapter XXXI – The Reagan-Bush Years, 1981–1992   681

    166. Jerry Falwell, "Can We Forget the Little Ones?," 1986   681

    167. David Stockman, *The Triumph of Politics: How the Reagan Revolution Failed,* 1986   687

168. Stephen L. Carter, "Racial Preferences? So What?," 1991   696

169. John Tenula, "Voices from Southeast Asia," 1991   703

170. *U.S. News and World Report,* "Triumph Without Victory: The Unreported History of the Persian Gulf War," 1991   708

Chapter XXXII – Toward the New Millennium   717

171. The Republican Party, "The Contract with America," 1994   717

172. Brent Schlender, "Microsoft: First America, Now the World," 1997   719

173. Debra Dickerson, "Crazy as They Wanna Be," 1999   722

CHAPTER XV

Blood and Freedom, 1863–1867

92. MATTIE GRIFFITH ON THE NEW YORK DRAFT RIOTS, 1863

The Enrollment Act of March, 1863, did not go over well with the working people of New York. Mostly Irish and firmly attached to the Democratic Party, New York's manual laborers considered the new draft law an act of tyranny and a violation of their civil liberties. White workers also opposed the Emancipation Proclamation, which they feared would bring a flood of ex-slaves to Northern cities to compete for jobs. The draft, it appeared, would force poor workers to fight a war to free slaves, who would then take workers' jobs. As the names for the draft were beginning to be called, New York's workers rioted in the streets, lynching a dozen black residents and destroying the homes of prominent Republicans. President Lincoln responded forcefully, sending in troops who put down the rebellion by killing over one hundred of the participants.

" . . . I am so excited by the recent outrageous Irish Mobs which has Just disgraced this city of the Free North. . . . For four days this entire city was under the rule of the most boisterous, noisy, riotous, murderous mob that ever disgraced barbaric let alone civilized times.

Source: Letter from Mattie Griffith, New York, to Mary Estlin, England, July 27, 1863. Mary Estlin Papers, Dr. Williams's Library, London. Courtesy of Dr. Kerby Miller, University of Missouri.

The Conscription was made the pretext; but really it was the outbreak of the sympathizers with the Southern rebellion. That I live to tell you the story is a Marvel; for the Mob threatened to burn our house, because the American Freedman's Commission office is under this roof, and we lived in momentary expectation of an attack. . . . We had no police in the Streets They had all been detailed to the more immediate Scenes of violence. Murder and Arson stalked abroad. Men entered houses and demanded money from ladies—at the point of the bayonet. The Mob burnt any house they fancied—one Telegraph wire was destroyed; railway tracks torn up; the fire engines were not allowed to work—Plunder and Murder went on by the wholesale. Through the bowed blinds of my windows, I watched the Strange, wretched, abandoned creatures that flocked out from their dens and lairs. They Stood under my window, defied the Government, cursed the draft and used all sorts of wicked language. I was heart-sick The Negroes—the poor Negroes! they have been the worst sufferers—no one helped them. They were recklessly shot down, hanged, burned, roasted alive—every device and refinement of cruelty practiced upon them & no one dared interpose on their behalf. God knows my heart bleeds when I attempt to recount the atrocities to which, in their friendless, helpless condition, they were forced to submit. A child of 3 years of age was thrown from a 4th story window and instantly killed. A woman one hour after her confinement was set upon and beaten with her tender babe in her arms and driven, on peril of her life, to the woods where she remained during a pelting storm and was found dead next morning. Children were torn from their Mother's embrace and their brains blown out in the very face of the afflicted Mothers. Men were burnt by slow fires—Mutilated, arms, limbs cut off—and they

319

forced to meet death in this slow manner! All sorts of barbarities were practiced for four long, bloody days. Each one of us silently waiting our own call.

"Yet [when she visited them and dispensed food and clothes to them at the police station] they were humble and modest, never asking for any thing or preferring claims. . . . There was one old man of 80 years; blind and Lame—whom the rioters cruelly beat—there was one little boy of six years old, who was ill, with a low bilious fever at the time the Mob broke out. They took him from his bed—beat him and hung him to a tree; he was cut down before Life became extinct, by a humane fireman and brought to Police Headquarters in an old starch box, such was the violence of the Mob that the child could not be publically or openly rescued! I think he will die in the course of a few days. I sat down beside his little bed and took his little, thin brown hand in mine; it was burning with fever and the pulse exceedingly rapid. He turned his large, sad eyes to me and I saw the tears slowly gather under the lid—the little dry lips attempted to move; but could not for the grateful heart was too full— Ah gentle and kindly race! I thought 'twas one of you who succored my Childhood and rendered me the most affectionate services as nurse good, old nurse, and now it is a profound pleasure to me to return all those acts in, even, so poor a manner as this—Quite a Large sum of money has been subscribed by the New York Merchants for the relief of the Colored sufferers; but there is so much 'red tape' about it that the fund is almost inaccessible to ordinary applicants I had to go, in person, to the Relief Association on Saturday last, before I could obtain the paltry sum of two dollars for a poor sick Negro man, so rigid is the examination &c. . . ."

93. Clabe Jones's Civil War Experience in Kentucky, 1863

While the state of Kentucky voted to remain with the Union, its people were heavily divided on the issue. James Clayborn ("Clabe") Jones led a Union guerrilla unit in the mountains of eastern Kentucky. Jones's unit, and those he fought against, were not closely linked to the national armies and official purposes of either side. Instead, these were irregular bands that fought to settle personal scores, in the process devastating the countryside and terrorizing the inhabitants.

The great Civil War had now begun and I was a Democrat in politics, but I cast my fortune with the Union cause and this compelled me to leave home or be killed. A man lived near me by the name of Coburn who had a son that had joined the Rebel army and coming home the old man Coburn reported me as a Yankee. I took to the brush and began dodging for my life. The Coburns robbed my house, took everything I had and then burned the house and left my wife and children homeless. I sent my wife to one of her sisters whild I stayed in hiding. One day I met up with one of the Coburns. He was carrying off some of my household goods he had stolen from my house. We had some hot words. He made at me with a large knife and I knocked him down with my gun and pulling my knife gave him a stroke or two, and left him lying in the road. I then went to Perry County and soon there was a man sent into Perry by the name of Tom Johnson from the United States army to raise a battalion of soldiers, and I enlisted with the Federal forces. We went to work and soon had enough men to organize a batallion. We met together in Harlan county to organize. Johnson and a Mr. Blankinship were candidates for major. Blankinship was elected and we were mustered into the Union army October 13, 1862, and were mustered out of Harlan Batallion January 13, 1863.

I was first lieutenant under Captain Morgan of Company A. I was patrolled to do all the scouting, hardly a raid was made without sending for me to get my advice. I went to Floyd county after my wife and mother, and was captured by Col. Caudill who took me to Letcher county. Caudill's company was ordered to Richmond, Va. They camped on the Rock House and

Source: "Life of James Claybourn Jones" (n.p., 1915), 6–11.

stayed there three days and nights. They guarded me closely. I learned when they were going to start for Richmond and I made up my mind to not go with them quite so far. The weather was very cold and they made a big log fire at the mouth of our camp. I lay down on the outside in order to be able to work the stakes loose, and I saw one of the guards lay his pistol on the end of a log of wood, and as soon as the guards had all fallen asleep I eased up and got the gun, and lay back on the ground and raising the tent cloth I rolled outside. I was about the middle of the camp, but I made my way out without being observed. I went up the hill to the top of the ridge and it was so cold I had to run up and down the ridge to keep from freezing till daylight. About eleven o'clock in the day I came to the Old Life Breeding farm and saw a boy hauling wood and following the haul road to where Breeding was chopping wood. I told him I was hungry and he sent the boy back to the house after my dinner. The boy brought me a good dinner. Breeding was a Union man. I then went to a moonshine still Breeding had told me about and got a canteen of whiskey—a half pint would have made a jack rabbit spit in the face of a bull dog—I then left the woods and took the road, and hadn't gone a mile until I met Col. Ben Caudill himself. He at once drew his sword and ordered me to turn my course. I threw my gun on him and told him to hit the road and not to look back; if he did I would kill him. He took me at my word, and I was glad of it for I didn't know whether my gun would fire or not. The colonel then put a reward of $500 for my capture, but he never had the pleasure of getting me, but I did help capture him at Gladeville, Va.

In a few days after this I took two men and made a raid on the rebel camp about five miles below Whitesburg. I hadn't gotten to the place I wanted to before I saw the rebels coming. I got the first fire on them and made one of them leave his horse and stick his nose in the mud. His name was Mitchell.

Captain Stamper had moved about fifteen miles below Whitesburg, having a good time drinking apple jack, and, as I used to love to drink myself, I concluded to take my men and meet the captain and help him drink the brandy. We started one evening and marched all night. Next morning about day we came in sight of old Aunt Cynthian Boggs' apple orchard. I placed my men in the brush to watch the rebels. In the evening we saw some men in the road, all afoot. They left the road and went to the woods, and after awhile I saw a man coming on a horse. It proved to be the captain himself. He had two large jugs under him and was headed for Aunt Cynthian Ann's to get some of her apple jack. I watched the place awhile and in a short time we heard a big racket down at the house. I took two men, went to the house, stepped in the door and threw my gun on the captain and told him to surrender. I told Aunt Cynthian to fill the captain's jugs for him as I knew he would like to have a dram the next morning. After paying her for the brandy, I told the captain I would treat him white. He sent a girl to his men with a note telling them that he was a prisoner and for them to go back to camp. I told him if we were fired on before we got to our camp I would kill him. I got on the rebel's fine horse, put the jugs across the saddle, took the captain up behind me and started for camp. When we got to camp I learned that Col. Caudill had captured a federal captain belonging to the thirty-ninth by the name of Webb. We sent in a flag of truce asking to exchange captains, the next day the rebels brought Captain Webb and exchanged him for Captain Stamper.

In a few weeks Major Blankinship let his men go home on a five days furlough. We went home and on the day we were all to report at camp, the rebels had placed themselves on all the roads and had captured every man that had went to camp. I stayed at home and in the evening I heard our men were all captured. Col. Caudill had placed himself on the road which he thought I was to come to kill me, to get rid of paying the reward he had offered for my capture, but the Old Grey Fox, as he called himself, didn't get me. This was one time the rebels got the best of us. It was dark when the rebels crossed the mountains and while crossing they met a company of their own men and got into a fight with them and most of all our men got away and returned to camp. Major Blankinship was hot and in making a raid on the rebel camp lost two men in the attack and then returned to camp.

In a few weeks the rebels went from Whitesburg to the salt wells in Perry County. Captain Morgan and myself concluded to drive the rebels out of Perry and on our way we met and engaged them in battle at Leatherwood Creek and surprised them while they were stealing a deaf and dumb man's watermelons. There was one man killed on each side. The rebels were commanded by Captain Jesse Caudill, a brave man. He was on one side of the creek and I was on the other. He was standing behind a small tree. I was watching him closely and as he turned to give a command to his men I give him a yankee pill from Shampee some where in his hind quarters. We had a hot time for awhile. I was unusually mad, not because we had met the Rebels, for we had defeated them, but I had gathered an armful of ripe pawpaws and had to drop them when the fight began. We captured the watermelons also from the deaf man and all their grub. We got the biggest pone of corn bread I ever saw. It would have weighed more than fifty pounds. They had baked it in a salt kettle and were carrying it in a coffee sack.

The next battle I was in while I belonged to the Harlan Battalion was with the Georgia Ann Tigers, who were in camp near Harlantown. We went to them one morning before day and surrounded them, fired on their camp and the fight began. They formed line of battle and fired several round. We were dropping them so fast they fell back behind the creek bank. We had it there for about three hours. We had nothing to shoot at but their heads. They finally retreated in bad order; we captured everything they had and carried it to our camp. They left eighteen dead on the ground, we didn't learn the number wounded, but two more died of their wounds. We buried the dead soldiers and returned to our camp.

Our next trouble was with Col. Slemp from Virginia. He had too many men for us, but we gave him the best we had in our shop, but he drove us out of camp and stayed one night. We fought him going and coming from the brush. I could hear the boys firing on them day and night. The most of our men had been gone more than a week before they got back to camp. There lived a Mr. Eversole mear by who was a moonshiner. He had a barrell of brandy hid in the woods, so he fired on Slemp's men, they drove him off and found his brandy. They took it down in the road and all got drunk. I took my men down to the lower pickets, in a skirmish I killed three of the pickets and drove the remainder in the camp. Slemp then retreated into Virginia. The next trouble was with Lieutenant Bentley. We had a man with us by the name of Screech who lived on Mason's Creek near the salt wells. Major Cineworth, a rebel, was in camp at the salt wells. Henry Hall, Gilbert Screech and myself went over to Screech's house, and next day went to the rebel camp and finding that they were too many for us we passed them by and went about one mile up a creek and suddenly met a company of rebels in a short curve in the road. Both sides opened fire at the same time. I shot and wounded the lieutenant. The lower side of the road was very steep and covered with pine and laurel, the rebels went over into the pine for shelter. They had been out stealing and had a fine load of chickens which they dropped in the road. We carried the chickens up into the woods and cut them loose. The little roosters seemed to be very well satisfied and went to scratching and crowing like democrats. We were about eighteen miles from camp and had to leave all the spoils behind. Captain Shade Combs and myself were guarding some sick men at the mouth of Carr's Fork when the rebel captain, Ans Hays, thought he would cut a big dash by capturing the sick men. Hays attached our camp with several times our number. Rev. Ira Combs, myself and two other soldiers only had guns, but we held the rebels at bay until the sick men all got away and held the fort until the enemy retreated and left us the victors. After that were were ordered to camp to be mustered out of service. This was January 13, 1863. In a few days after we were mustered out Gen. John H. Morgan made a raid through Harlan County, captured our major and killed him, so that put an end to the Harlan Battalion.

We then went to Irvine, Kentucky, and joined the Fourteenth Kentucky Cavalry and stayed at Irvine about one week, then the Fourteenth moved to Richmond, Ky., and on examination I was pronounced a disabled bodied man and was left out. My men seem to all be dissatisfied about them not taking me in so Col. Lilly told me to stay with the command and he would give me work to do. He kept me out as a spy and very often with a bunch of men. I took two men and went to Perry County as a spy. William Mosely and Font Fuller went with me. We captured a man on Mason's Creek by the name of Cornett. I promised his wife that I would not hurt him if I could prevent it. I had a good horse and made the prisoner ride behind me to better protect him, for Mosely was mad because the rebels had run him off from his home and had broken up his house and took all he had, and he was swearing vengence against all the prisoners. I took Cornett with me to a small log cabin and made a good fire and after dark Mosely and Fuller came to the cabin and wanted in. I told them that I could not let them in, they flew mad and said they would break the door down. I told the prisoner to take my pistol and help me shoot if they tried to come in. Next morning I turned Mosely and Fuller off and took charge of the prisoner myself and started for Booneville. The next night I stopped on Goose Creek, there were three women at the house, all the men had gone to war. I was worn out for sleep and put two of the girls to guard the prisoner and gave them my arms and the girls said if the prisoner tried to escape they would kill him, for they wanted to kill a rebel anyway, for the rebels had killed one of the women's husbands and the other's brother a few weeks before. The girls proved to be good soldiers and kept their prisoner safe until morning. I took the prisoner on to Booneville and turned him over to Col. Lilly and the soldiers of the Fourteenth who had been with me in former raids, seized me and lifting me on their shoulders carried me all over the camp.

Next Col. Lilly sent me with a posse of men to Letcher County. We were on march two days, reaching Whitesburg. On Sand Lick we were fired upon by the rebels, but when we reached town the rebels had all retreated towards Virginia. We saw a wagon crossing the point above town so we went for it and fired on the men in charge of the wagon and they all broke and ran leaving the wagon in the road and when we came up we found the wagon loaded with dried apples and a barrel of apple brandy. After filling our canteens we concluded to bury the barrel of brandy. There was a man with us by the name of John Smith, so Uncle John preached the funeral of good old apple jack and we buried him in a sand-bar, then drove the wagon up a branch, took the fruit out and hid it and piled the wagon full of fence rails and firing them burned up the wagon. We captured a Mr. Sturdivant and he told us the rebels would be back, we marched down the river about a mile and I stationed my men in the gap of a ridge below a mill dam and waited their return. We let the rebels pass us, then fired on them. We sent the yankee pills so thick after them they had to swim the mill pond, we pursued after them and sent them back to Virginia. We then went back to the grave of Gen. Apple Jack, dug him up and carried him to camp and found a good excuse for staying a few days longer.

My men bantered me and my pet rebel for a game of poker, so me and Mr. Sturdivant fixed up our signs and went for all the greenback they had. We had a good old time courting the girls, playing cards and drinking brandy. After me and my pet rebel had won all the money the boys had, I swore to him to not take up arms against the Union and let him go home. I captured my brother-in-law, Miles Webb and a Mr. Williams. We went up a branch to rest a day or two. We killed a cow and put up with a man by the name of Caudill who was making cane molasses. We borrowed one of their kettles and hired the girls to kill us two chickens for me and the prisoner's supper. The boys were cooking supper on the outside. After we had all eaten supper, I failed to put out any pickets, for we still had some of the good old apple brandy and didn't care if it snowed. Immediately the guns began on the outside, the rebels had us surrounded, we quickly rallied in line and commanding the men to follow me we fired in front of us as we went, so we all got away safe with the prisoners except my brother-in-law Webb. As soon as we got through their lines we turned back and began pouring the lead to them. I heard Captain Hall order his men to hold their grounds until every man was killed. They fell back behind the houses and there was a hot time for a while. It soon became dark and the rebels retreated to Whitesburg. As soon as Col. Caudill had learned I had whipped his men over the body of General Apple Jack he took to the woods. Next day I swore the prisoners and sent them home.

I learned that Captain Hays was camping at the mouth of Lot's Creek, below Hazard, in Perry County. Col. Lilly ordered Captain Strong to take a company of men and break up the rebel den. Strong told the men as many as wanted to go with me, to fall in line. The order was soon filled. We marched on the rebel camp, surrounded them while they were cooking breakfast. I ordered them to surrender, they began to parley, I ordered the men to fire on them and then the fun began. The captain's men returned our fire and then took leg bail and fled to the woods. We captured all they had, even their guns and sent them to Dixie for amunition. We ate their breakfast, drank their Jeff Davis coffee and got several jugs of moonshine and put out for Letcher. On our way we run into Captain Cook's company on Carr's Fork. We made a charge on them and they were as brave as Captain Hays' men, they fled to the woods. In the fight I shot and killed Lieutenant Mays. We run on another posse of rebels commanded by the notorious Lige Hixs. Captain Hixs rather started to run from a house near by and we fired on him. He jumped behind a stump and threw up his hands. I knew him and running to him I commanded the men to cease firing. I had stayed at his house many years before while I lay wounded and I counld not have him hurt. When we got back to Whitesburg the rebels had all gone to Virginia. We then returned to Booneville. On this raid we killed and captured thirteen of the enemy without losing a single man.

Col. Lilly then sent me back to Letcher County with a few men and when we got to Whitesburg we couldn't hear of any rebels, but in going back to camp we captured two rebel deserters, and going up Mason's Creek I stopped at a house to buy some cucumbers and while I was talking to the young lady I heard shooting ahead of me. I put spurs to my horse and when I came up I found a man by the name of Calhoun had killed both of the prisoners. From Booneville we went to Camp Nelson and on our way Leslie Johnson and Calhoun fell out over killing the prisoners. Calhoun shot Johnson and then fled to Ohio. Captain Foster with a posse was in camp at Round Bottom doing a lot of robbing and stealing, and I took Captain Strong's men and marched on their camp. They were camping in a schoolhouse near the river. They had just left the camp and gone down the river. We captured a rebel spy and he told us that they would be back. We took up a position on both sides of the mountain and waited their return. They marched right up between us before we fired on them. They took shelter behind the river bank. We killed three at the house and two as they crossed the road and five more at a pass down the river while they were crossing and captured seventeen more. The captain and the rest of his men swam the river and escaped. On this raid we killed and captured twenty-seven of the grey coats without losing a single man.

While at Camp Nelson we learned that Gen. John H. Morgan was marching on Lexington, so we hurried to that point, but Morgan went by way of Cynthiana and crossed into Ohio below Cincinnati, and being eluded by Morgan, we learned that Col. Clay was in Eastern Kentucky, and was ordered to intercept his march. We met the rebels at the mouth of Puncheon Creek on Licking River. The enemy fought with great bravery until Col. Clay was slain and his men broke and fled in confusion. We were then ordered to Fort Nelson and the Fourteenth Kentucky was mustered out of service. This was the end of the great Civil War, and we all took a long breath, then breathed easily and thanking God that it was all over went to our homes. But when we got back home it was far from being the homes we had left a few short years before, for many of our dearest friends had answered the roll call on the other shore.

94. John Dooley, Gettysburg Diary, 1863

The battle of Gettysburg, Pennsylvania, marked the end of Robert E. Lee's invasion of the North and the turning point of the war. Captain John Edward Dooley, CSA, kept a diary of the campaign. Dooley apparently rewrote and expanded some of his entries in the years after 1863.

The Gettysburg Campaign

June 3rd. This morning we are marching towards Tappahannock. Resting upon the road side a courier rides by, and a little dog belonging to one of the soldiers flies at the horse's heels, all the while barking furiously. The courier, indignant at this unmannerly interruption, loses all patience, checks his horse's speed, and drawing his cavalry sword makes a gallant charge. The whole Division sets up deafening huzzas as they witness the act of bravery, and the unfortunate courier rides off completely crestfallen and the subject of numberless sarcasms from the laughing troops.

June 15th. Resume our march, passing through Culpepper [sic] C.H. The heat is frightful, and the road in many places is strewn with the *sunstruck*. I stand the sun better than some of the stoutest of my men; and perceiving one of my poor fellows in great distress on account of his gun and accoutrements, I give him my sword for his rifle and it helps him along very much.

June 24th, 1863. We are moving in the direction of Martinsburg and learn for the first time that Pennsylvania is our objective point.

June 25th. Pass through Martinsburg about 11 A.M. and perceive at once that we are not treading friendly streets. The Yankee citizens feel doubly aggrieved since their favourite butcher Milray has but lately fled ignominiously through these same streets, having lost his entire army and only escaping with a small body guard. Late in the afternoon we reach the Potomac and being disappointed in our pontoons prepare to wade this mighty stream which separated us from our beloved Virginia soil.

Terrible had been that march along the scorched and blazing plains of Virginia. Angry was the glare of the sun during those fearful days of June, as it flashed upon our ranks and fiercely smote again and again the burning temples of our fagged and fainting soldiers. Choking, blinding were the clouds of dust that rose from beneath the army's unsteady tread; parching was that unquenchable thirst which dried the tongue to its very roots. The men fell by tens, twenties, nay by hundreds along the

---

Source: Joseph T. Durkin, S. J., ed., *John Dooley, Confederate Soldier, His War Journal* (Washington: Georgetown University Press, 1945), 95–107.

dusty roadsides. Such days as these prove the true soldier, and he who falters not in the long and wearisome march will not be absent from the charge.

But now we stand upon the banks of the Potomac and prepare to cross. As we advance into Pennsylvania the road becomes almost impassable, so slippery is the mud; whilst a cold steady rain falls constantly upon our ranks.

The wheat fields are every where nearly ripe for harvesting, and all around plenty appears to bless the fertile land. We destroy nothing uselessly, but in self defence (on account of the roads) are obliged to cut a passage through these rich fields of wheat, which however is no larger than necessary; for our Generals are even more careful of the property of these Thrifty German Farmers than they were of the lands and houses of their own soil. And General Lee was so solicitous for the safety of the fences that he dismounted this morning (so we are told) and on the muddy road side made some of his staff officers assist him in putting up the portion of a rail fence which had been through negligence left down. We are further informed that several of the soldiers in the van of the army have already been shot by their generals for plundering the houses of these peace loving German Yankees.

DOOLEY IS IN THE REAR GUARD

Our Division (Pickett's) is the rearmost, and we are left in the vicinity of Chambersburg to cover the march of the main body advancing on Gettysburg, to protect the convoys of horses, cattle, etc., the spoils of our invasion, which with very frail guards were being constantly sent across the Potomac; and to be ready at a moment's warning to join the main army whenever the enemy might be found, for as yet we were ignorant of his position.

In and around the town of Chambersburg we found the people very sullen and maliciously disposed, and not a few maledictions were hurled at us from garret windows by croaking croans; and many young but frowning brows and pouting lips we saw in doorways and even on the sidewalks. But our boys laughed cheerfully, and when contempt and scorn were shewn them answered by jests and witticisms rather than with the bayonet, as so often did those Yankee ruffians in our Southern Cities. But here let me say that the inhuman barbarities and insulting ruffianism was not so often the action (perhaps was never so) of the veteran Northern soldier as of the low hirelings who skulked in forts and cities distant from the battle field and who continually fashioned their conduct on such leaders as Ben Butler.

Unpleasantly for myself, I am today in command of the rear guard, whose duty it is to urge forward stragglers and to keep up in fact all who desert their ranks under any pretense whatever. This is at times a painful duty, for frequently it happens—especially when the Division is moving rapidly, as today—that many soldiers leave their ranks through necessity, and, weakened by diarrhea, can scarcely with all their efforts rejoin the ranks. Others fall by the roadside either deadly sick or pretending to be so (and who can be sure that they are only pretending?); others are barefoot, and although they may have thrown away their shoes purposely so as to have an excuse for desertion and straggling, still their feet are bruised and even bleeding, and it is a hard thing to keep these men upon the move.

Many good persons during the war seem to have the idea that any man who wears the confederate uniform and hails from a confederate regiment must of necessity be the very essence of all that is truly brave and chivalrous; and they receive, as a general thing, all their accounts of battles and their knowledge of heroic deeds of war from men who, far from having performed the deeds of daring they so vividly describe, have never even witnessed the noble exploits of their brave companions in arms. For the true soldier has no time to stop by the wayside and recount his brave deeds to persons whom he does not know, and then devour their *buttermilk,* apple butter, and chickens in payment for the beautiful and thrilling tales he has fabricated. But he keeps in his ranks, is found in his camp, in the charge and the retreat, and leaves to the straggling coward the grateful task of glorifying his actions, who at the same time adopts them and makes them his own.

July 3rd. Before the day has fully dawned we are on our way to occupy the position assigned to us for the conflict of the third day. As we turn from the main road to the right, Gen. Lee, or better known as Uncle Robert, silent and motionless, awaits our passing by, and anxiously does he gaze upon the only division of his army whose numbers have not been thinned by the terrible fires of Gettysburg. I must confess that the Genl's face does not look as bright as tho' he were certain of success. But yet it is impossible for us to be any otherwise than victorious and we press forward with beating hearts, hundreds of which will throb their last today.

How long we take to gain our position, what delays, what suspense! We are soon passing over the battlefield of yesterday, and the details of burying parties are digging graves to receive the freshly fallen comrades, and, in many instances, they have only the ghastly and mangled remnants of their gallant friends to deposit in these hastily dug pits. I pass very close to a headless body; the boy's head being torn off by a shell is lying around in bloody fragments on the ground.

A little further we take temporary position in the hollow of a field. Before us is a rising slope which hides the Yankee position from view. To the right of our front some quarter of a mile is a brick house near which one of our batteries now and then opens on the enemy who are generally ready to respond to the harsh greeting. Around us are some trees with very small green apples; and while we are resting here we amuse ourselves by pelting each other with green apples. So frivolous men can be even in the hour of death.

Now Genls. Lee, Longstreet, and Pickett are advising together and the work of the day is arranged. Soon we are ordered to ascend the rising slope and pull down a fence in our front, and this begins to look like work.

Farther to our right is posted a division of North Carolina troops who should have charged simultaneously or immediately following us, thus overlapping our flank (right) and preventing our force from being surrounded in that direction. Unfortunately, owing to bad management (I am sure not to want of bravery) they were of no assistance to us in the charge; and, advancing either in the wrong direction or when too late, two thousand of them fell into the enemy's hands.

Again, orders come for us to lie down in line of battle; *that all the cannon* on our side will open at a given signal, will continue for an hour and upon their ceasing we are to charge straight ahead over the open field and *sweep from our path* any thing in the shape of a Yankee that attempts to oppose our progress. This order is transmitted from Regt. to Regt., from Brigade to Brigade, and we rest a long time awaiting the signal.

At last it sounds away to the right and the echoes have scarcely rebounded from the rocks of the mountain when the earth, mountains and sky seem to open and darken the air with smoke and death dealing missiles. Never will I forget those scenes and sounds. The earth seems unsteady beneath this furious cannonading, and the air might be said to be agitated by the wings of death. Over 400 guns nearly every minute being discharged!

We are immediately in rear of Genl. Dearing's batteries and receive nearly all the missiles intended for his gallant troops. In one of our Regts. alone the killed and wounded, even before going into the charge, amounted to 88 men; and men lay bleeding and gasping in the agonies of death all around, and we unable to help them in the least. Ever and anon some companion would raise his head disfigured and unrecognizable, streaming with blood, or would stretch his full length, his limbs quivering in the pangs of death. Orders were to lie as closely as possible to the ground, and *I like a good soldier* never got closer to the earth than on the present occasion.

Our artillery has now ceased to roar and the enemy have checked their fury, too. The time appointed for our charge is come.

I tell you, there is no romance in making one of these charges. You might think so from reading 'Charlie O'Malley,' that prodigy of valour, or in reading of any other gallant knight who would as little think of riding over *gunners and sich like* as they would of eating a dozen oysters. But when you rise to your feet as we did today, I tell you the enthusiasm of ardent breasts in many cases *ain't there,* and instead of burning to avenge the insults of our country, families and altars and firesides, the thought is most frequently, *Oh,* if I could just come out of this charge safely how thankful *would I be!*

We rise to our feet, but not all. There is a line of men still on the ground with their faces turned, men affected in 4 different ways. There are the gallant dead who will never charge again; the helpless wounded, many of whom desire to share the fortunes of this charge; the men who have charged on many a battlefield but who are now helpless from the heat of the sun; and the men in whom there is not sufficient courage to enable them to rise,— but of these last there are but few.

Up, brave men! Some are actually *fainting* from the heat and dread. They have fallen to the ground overpowered by the suffocating heat and the terrors of that hour. Onward—steady—dress to the right—give way to the left—steady, not too fast—don't press upon the center—how gentle the slope! steady—keep well in line— there is the line of guns we must take—right in front— but how far they appear! Nearly one third of a mile, off on Cemetery Ridge, and the line stretches round in almost a semicircle. Upon the center of this we must march. Behind the guns are strong lines of infantry. You may see them plainly and now they see us perhaps more plainly.

To the right of us and above the guns we are to capture, black heavy monsters from their lofty mountain sites belch forth their flame and smoke and storms of shot and shell upon our advancing line; while directly in front, breathing flame in our very faces, the long range of guns which must be taken thunder on our quivering melting ranks. Now truly does the work of death begin. The line becomes unsteady because at every step a gap must be closed and thus from left to right much ground is often lost.

Close up! Close up the ranks when a friend falls, while his life blood bespatters your cheek or throws a film over your eyes! Dress to left or right, while the bravest of the brave are sinking to rise no more! Still onward! Capt. Hallinan has fallen and I take his place. So many men have fallen now that I find myself within a few feet of my old Captain (Norton). His men are pressing mine out of place. I ask him to give way a little to the left, and scarcely has he done so than he leaps into the air, falling prostrate. Still we press on—oh, how long it seems before we reach those blazing guns. Our men are falling faster now, for the deadly musket is at work. Volley after volley of crashing musket balls sweeps through the line and mow us down like wheat before the scythe.

On! men, on! Thirty more yards and the guns are ours; but who can stand such a storm of hissing lead and iron? What a relief if earth, which almost seems to hurl these implements of death in our faces, would open now and afford a secure retreat from threatening death. Every officer is in front, Pickett with his long curls streaming in the fiery breath from the cannons' mouth. Garnett on the right, Kemper in the center and Armistead on the left; Cols., Lieut. Cols., Majors, Captains, all press on and cheer the shattered lines.

Just here—from right to left the remnants of our braves pour in their long reserved fire; until now no shot had been fired, no shout of triumph had been raised; but as the cloud of smoke rises over the heads of the advancing divisions the well known southern battle cry which marks the victory gained or nearly gained bursts wildly over the blood stained field and *all that line of guns is ours.*

Shot through both thighs, I fall about 30 yards from the guns. By my side lies Lt. Kehoe, shot through the knee. Here we lie, he in excessive pain, I fearing to bleed to death, the dead and dying all around, while the division sweeps over the Yankee guns. Oh, how I long to know the result, the end of this fearful charge! We seem to have victory in our hands; but what can our poor remnant of a shattered division do if they meet beyond the guns an obstinate resistance?

There—listen—we hear a new shout, and cheer after cheer rends the air. Are those fresh troops advancing to our support? No! no! That huzza never broke from southern lips. Oh God! Virginia's bravest, noblest sons have perished here today and perished all in vain!

Oh, if there is anything capable of crushing and wringing the soldier's heart it was this day's tragic act and all in vain! But a little well timed support and Gettysburg was ours. The Yankee army had been routed and Pickett's division earned a name and fame not inferior to that of the Old Guard of Bonaparte. I will not attempt to describe . . .

95. JAMES F. LEGATE ON QUANTRILL'S RAID ON LAWRENCE, KANSAS, 1863

William Clarke Quantrill led a Confederate guerrilla unit known as Quantrill's Raiders through Missouri and Kansas. In August of 1863, Quantrill's Raiders attacked Lawrence, Kansas, killing almost two hundred people. The attack on Lawrence was a continuation of the violence of Bleeding Kansas, and Quantrill's objective in part was to kill Senator James H. Lane, one of the leaders of the free-soil forces. Quantrill failed in that goal, and he was himself killed in 1865 in a raid on Kentucky. Members of the Raiders included Frank and Jesse James and the Younger brothers.

Special Correspondence of the *Globe-Democrat,* Leavenworth, Kan.

Several articles have appeared recently on "Quantrell's raid on Lawrence," but no one can tell a more thrilling story about it than James F. Legate, the noted Kansas politician, who was a resident of Lawrence at the time. Mr. Legate took a leading part in border ruffian troubles

Source: St. Louis Globe-Democrat, n.d. Reprinted in William Elsey Connelley, *Quantrill and the Border Wars* (Cedar Rapids, IA: The Torch Press, Publishers, 1910), 369–373 n7.

during the early territorial days, has served nine terms in the Kansas Legislature, and has passed through some exciting times, but he considers them tame compared with his marvelous escape from Quantrell's gang. It was Mr. Legate who brought the news to Leavenworth of the sacking and burning of Lawrence, and he told Gen. Ewing, then in command of Fort Leavenworth, the way to head off the guerrillas. Had his advice been acted on the outlaws would have been captured before getting out of the state. Mr. Legate nearly killed three horses in making the trip from Lawrence, and his story contains some historical points about the famous raid never published before.

Mr. Legate is quite old, and is becoming very feeble. He was called on at his home on Fifth avenue by a *Globe-Democrat* reporter, when he consented to tell the story, which follows:

On the night of August 20, 1863, we had a very large meeting at Lawrence, in which the people were very much excited concerning the Union Pacific Railroad. The excitement grew out of the fact that it was asserted that Senator Lane was indorsing the project of building the road about three miles north of town. Everybody was very much excited over it. During the meeting it was announced by Lane that he had information that a rebel spy was in town, but the excitement over the railroad and the charges against Lane led every one to conclude it was one of Lane's tricks. The meeting broke up about 12 o'clock. We all went home, not thinking anything about rebels or Quantrell or any one else excepting the railroad.

On the morning of the 21st, about daybreak, a little colored boy living with me came to my room with much excitement, saying "The rebels are in town." I said to him "Put on my hat and run to the woods." I got up and dressed and walked out of the house. I saw the town full of Quantrell's men, shooting and yelling, giving them the appearance of a great degree of ferocity. I put on my coat and walked right down among them about two blocks from my house. They were killing three men, and I never in my life heard such pleading for a moment of life as came from these men, yet I was so stupified that I was entirely unmoved by their prayers. I did not dare to run, lest I might attract their attention as not being of their number. I turned slowly around, walked up onto the hill where John Speer lived, went into the house of a Swede, which was filled with frightened women, who had gathered there, and they seemed to be of all nationalities. I was asked questions by each in their turn, but made no answer, walking straight through the house into the yard in the rear, where there were four rows of corn planted in the lot. I managed to find the center row, and I walked through to the fence, got over the fence and started on a run like a quarter horse, through the valley to a hemp field. Through fright and nerved to the quick, I performed a feat that $1,000,000 couldn't make me repeat. I made a jump over a ditch about 2 feet wide, over a four-rail fence, into the hemp lot.

About half way through the hemp lot I met John Speer and his deputy coming from his house. I told them rapidly of what I knew, and what I had seen, and turned and ran toward the timber. I ought to have said just as I jumped the fence a bevy of Quantrell's men fired a volley at me, and they seemed to hit everything and everywhere but exactly where I was. After speaking with John Speer I turned toward the timber, the grass was high, and there were little clumps of bushes. As I ran near one of the clumps of bushes I saw a movement and started directly toward the clump to see what it was. As I reached the clump I found Solon O. Thatcher, afterwards Judge Thatcher, hid in that clump of bushes. We were both equally frightened. He cried out "Oh, don't! don't, don't!" I jumped back, apparently very brave, and said, "Who are you, or I'll put a hole through you in a second?" He, recognizing my voice, in plaintive manner said, "Why, it's Solon; why, don't you know Solon?"

We conversed but a moment. I said that I was going to the river, and he followed me. We got down to the river and we heard the clatter of horses' feet coming pellmell toward us. He started back for the brush and I jumped into the river. They were so near to me I didn't dare to go into the river, so I backed up under a stump, under which the water had washed out. They came down, and seeing our footprints, waited but a moment, discussing what to do. Finally one of them discovered the footprints of Judge Thatcher going towards the brush. With a wild yell they all started in that direction.

As soon as they had gone I started to swim across the river. I swam, it seems to me, faster than any steamboat I had ever rode upon to that time. I was two-thirds over the river when they all came back, and they began to shoot at me. Their shots all went wide of the mark. I thought there was too much surface to my back to shoot at. I whirled over and swam on my back so that I could see them. One fellow got off his horse and says: "I can hit that Abolition son of a ———." He rested his musket against a tree—I presume this is imaginary on my part, but it seems entirely real—I imagined that I could see to the very bottom of that gun, and thought that he would certainly hit me. I turned my eye to see whether I should float down the river or strike a sand bar. I looked back before he had fired, and it seemed to me that when he pulled the trigger I could see the muzzle of the gun turn to the right, and I felt perfectly safe. The ball struck about 10 feet to my left, as I lay on my back, which convinced me that my sight was correct when I saw the movement of the gun. I had then got near the shore.

As I reached the shore I looked around and a Delaware Indian by the name of Half Moon said to me in Indian, "Give me your hand." I gave him my hand and he pulled me out of the river. He wanted to know who they were. I told him they were Quantrell's men, rebels. "Well," he said, "I'll take one shot at them." He had an old Kentucky rifle. He took one shot at the crowd and one man fell from his saddle. They immediately got off and put the man back in the saddle and slowly moved away toward town again.

I went from there to Old Pechaukee. I found there only the old lady, his wife, and the children. They had a horse and buggy all hitched up. I asked for the use of the horse and buggy. While she could speak English as well as I could, wouldn't utter a word in English, but said to me in the Delaware language, "No, Pechaukee has gone with the men and has bade me go to the bottoms with the children in the buggy. There is going to be a fight." I said to her, "All right, I want to ride up on the hill to see where the fight is going to be. Will come back again."

I started in the buggy for Leavenworth and made the horse run until he entirely broke down. It was a very hot day.

I rode to where Mr. McFarland, an old gentleman who formerly lived in Lawrence, was making hay, and he had a very fine-appearing horse hitched to the fence. He said, "Yes, sir, he is one of the finest buggy horses in the territory." I said to him, "I want to try him," and then stripped the harness off of the Indian's horse and put McFarland's horse in the buggy. I did it so quickly the old gentleman was much surprised and somewhat alarmed. I left him on a dead run. His son followed me to Nine-mile Creek. When his son overtook me and I told him the story he said, "All right, go ahead."

That horse broke down, or so near broke down that I rode up to the stage stable. There was a stage stable at Nine-mile Creek. I went in very cooly and asked the stable keeper if he had a good, swift buggy horse. He pointed out a horse to me and I walked in and unhitched the horse and took him out, when he, the stable boss, came out with a club and said, "What do you mean?" "I mean to swap horses." He began to show fight and I drew out a revolver that I carried through the Kaw River, but he didn't know it. I told him to change the harness and he complied. As soon as the horse was hitched to the buggy I jumped in and said, "The rebels are in Lawrence, and I want to get to Leavenworth. I'll bring your horse back."

I came on as fast as that horse could bring me from there to this city. I stopped at Col. Jennison's or Jim Brown's stable; they were both together then. I told him rapidly the story and asked for Gen. Ewing. He went post-haste to the fort for Gen. Ewing, telling the story up there. Gen. Ewing came in person to the Planter's House to see me.

I said to him that I had rode up on to the hill four miles from Lawrence, and that evidently the town was burned, for I saw it all on fire. I said to him the whole border was guarded with the exception of one place about ten miles south of Kansas City; that if he would press into the service three steamboats that lay at the wharf here and take his men to Kansas City he could intercept the entire gang.

He said that he thought that he could go across the country and intercept them better. So he started across the country by the way of De Soto, thinking that he could intercept them in that way. It was a long march, though a forced one, and he simply got behind them, and drove them out of the state, without harm to any of them.

In the middle or some time in the night of August 21 there came word from Lawrence that everything was burned up, with about 100 persons dead, without a coffin to bury them in. Early on the morning of the 22d every coffin in this town was taken, about 100 of them, in two wagon loads, and started for Lawrence. Gov. Carney, Nelson McCracken, L. T. Smith, and some others got together and made a donation of about $1500 in groceries and provisions, and started that to Lawrence.

Gov. Carney and myself, in his team, drove over. We found the town almost absolutely destroyed, most of the prominent men killed, and the stories of escape were wonderful. . . .

George W. Collamore was Mayor of the city. His house was surrounded, and, believing it was death to show himself, he was lowered into the well by his wife, and when the rebels had gone they found he was dead.

They went to my house and set it on fire. My wife pleaded with them, told them she was a widow, and it was all she had in the world, and she didn't want them to burn it up. Nellie, my daughter, who was little more than a year old, grabbed around the leg of one of the men and said: "You won't kill my papa, will you?"

There was an old colored woman who had two children, a little boy and girl. The little boy ran up to see the Free State Hotel burned, and one of the men grabbed and threw him into the flames.

Quantrell, as we knew him, lived there by the name of Charley Hart, and made his personal headquarters at the Lawrence Hotel kept by Mr. Stone. Quantrell guarded the hotel, and had it surrounded. Quantrell had a long fit of sickness there, and was tenderly nursed by the Stone family. Some of his men killed the old gentleman.

I knew Quantrell quite well when he lived in Lawrence under the name of Charles Hart. I was going East at the time he was sick at the hotel. I visited him, and left him $10 to buy medicine with. He was known among us as a noted Abolitionist from Ohio. He planned raids into Missouri to steal negroes. There was a band formed, of which he was the leader, for that purpose. They made several raids into Missouri, and brought to Lawrence quite a number of slaves that were shipped on to Canada. Finally, he made an arrangement for another raid into Missouri. Under the pretense of reconnoitering he went to a farm house near Independence, and selected the spot, told the man they were coming to steal his negroes that night. He said they were a gang of desperate Abolitionists from Lawrence. True to what he said, a band of fellows from Lawrence went there, and the farmer was well supplied with help. Four of them were badly wounded, and five of them escaped. From that hour Charley Hart became Quantrell, which was his real name, and soon became the leader of the most desperate outlaws in Western Missouri.

96. Letters on Emancipation

Emancipation came gradually and slowly for African-American slaves. Many created their own freedom, without legal sanction, by leaving their homes when the war weakened planters' power. Sometimes following Union troops, and sometimes heading for the North, ex-slaves valued mobility as a primary symbol of their freedom. These letters show some of the dimensions of ex-slaves' mobility. In the first, a white Missouri slave owner complains about the disappearance of slaves from his Missouri community. The second is an ex-slave's response to a request by his former master to return to the plantation and work for wages. The last letter shows some of the pain and misgivings slaves went through as they left people they loved and the only homes they knew.

A. Missouri Slaveholder to Abraham Lincoln, 1863

St. Louis March 24 *1863*
My Dear Sir, You ware aware that I have written to you several letters heretofore & in which I have shewn you that I have approved of your measures & especially do I refer to your suggestion or proposition to aid Missouri in emancipating slaves (which I fully indorse). That I have always been a loyal man faithful to the Union and the constitution of the U. States, & know not how to be any thing but a devoted Union man. To be any thing else I would of course have to stultify myself.

Having more fully stated all these things to you in my previous communications, to you, & having more fully given my views., I now proceed to the matter for which

---

Source: Ira Berlin, Barbara J. Fields, Thavolia Glymph, Joseph P. Reidy, and Leslie S. Rowland, eds., *Freedom: A Documentary History of Emancipation, 1861–1867* ser. I, vol. I: The Destruction of Slavery (New York: Cambridge University Press, 1985), 450–452.

this communication is more especially addressed. I live in Franklin County Mo, which I think is as loyal a county as perhaps any in the U. States, & most so of any in our State. It is the banner county for Loyalty & devotion to the Union. We were all getting along prosperously & unitedly until a few months ago, when by some construction of some order, the officers assigned us in our County came to the conclusion that all negroes who came into the camp then, & ever afterwards were free from their owners., & that no one could take them afterwards in the county without such person being arrested. Such being the case, the poor negro thought that he had nothing to do but to go to the camp & there be fed & clothed & do nothing & be free.

For a very long time under the operation of this construction of the order, my negroes remained quiet, until nearly evry other negro had left his owners & gone to Washington in Franklin County & took what they call free or Protection papers–

Mine having wives among some of those having free papers, of course would naturally become affected by it, & finally in my abscence at the hour of midnight when my wife & children were solitary & alone, nearly all of my negroes started off to Washington taking with them whatever they saw proper & are there now claiming to have free papers.

Even the nurse, that assisted in attending to my smallest child went off, a girl about 12 years old, leaving us without any one there to attend to the farm, or stock or any thing else. I have just passed through Washington & saw my negroes in a brick House, & they showed me what they call their free papers. The Capt intimated that he was sorry he could not do any thing– That he was under orders & would be removed, if he disobeyed. I told him that I did not wish him to disobey any order! but that I thought he was wrong in his construction of it. He said further that I could not get them, & that he would resist any & evry effort to retake them.

Evil by civil process. Now to be brief. Nearly all my negroes are there young & old, & nearly all of my best hands. My farm will go uncultivated, for there are no white men to get here. Is it right that I should be broken up. Last summer for being a Union man my horses were stolen from me & the only man in the neighborhood, who lost any thing that way was myself.

I have a large family, of helpless little children to support, & have got a farm to support them on, & if I cant cultivate it, it will be valueless to me. I make my appeal to you to grant me relief & that those professing to be agents of the Gov. should not destroy me.

Why cant Franklin Co be treated as well as Saline or Lafyette, where there are Southern sympathisers. Why cant the State Militia of Franklin Co attend to Franklin. Franklin is loyal to the backbone. Nearly all the slaves of Franklin County are now congregated at Washington. We can do nothing. And yet here there is no other earthly trouble. What shall I do? Were I a single man, & no family, I would not care, if my property was destroyed, And now if it was necessary to serve the interests of my country that I should sacrifice my property, I would submit without a murmur. I as a loyal man intending to stand by the Union & the Govermt of U. States, through evil as well as good report, I ask you to extend protection to me. My negroes are well treated well taken care of, & do less labor than any others in my county– A family of them that I purchased five or 6 years ago, who came to me to save them from being sold South, & whom I purchased more from sympathy than any other consideration, & who have never been taken to my residence, but lived on a farm near the County seat to themselves with evry comfort of life, they have taken up their abode in Washington.

I will not trouble you longer, but do again appeal to you to render me such assistance as may be proper; and command me for the Governmt in any way that I can be useful & I will give you any guantee that I will serve my country & Govt in any way in my power– I wish my rights to be protected in an open & substantial manner, that the people may see that there is property in being a loyal man, extending even to the protection of his property. I wish it to be effectual. I tell my slaves, that I know they are misled, and if they return not a hair of their heads shall be Hurt & no violence used. And such shall be the case– I want protection that in the open day, like an honest transaction I can have my rights redressed. If it cant be done effectually & substantially I dont care to have it done. For as an honest man, making my living honestly & fairly in evry way, I desire protection as my Governmt always has protected her citizens fully, effectually & substantially. *I am a Loyal American Citizen.* Now having said this much, I deem it unnecessary to say more, but as we are now in a ruinous condition unable to cultivate our farms, implore your intervention, & you can accomplish it at once–

Permit me, My Dear Sir, to say that sinking or swimming, surviving or perishing, I will be found to the last man standing if necessary solitary & alone *for the Union & the Constitution of the U. States.* With Sentiments of the very highest Consideration, I am Yours Most Truly

Charles Jones

B. Jourdon Anderson to His Former Owner, 1865

DAYTON, OHIO, August 7, 1865.

To my old Master, COLONEL P. H. ANDERSON, *Big Spring, Tennessee.*

Sir: I got your letter, and was glad to find that you had not forgotten Jourdon, and that you wanted me to come back and live with you again, promising to do better for me than anybody else can. I have often felt uneasy about you. I thought the Yankees would have hung you long before this, for harboring Rebs they found at your house. I suppose they never heard about your going to Colonel Martin's to kill the Union soldier that was left by his company in their stable. Although you shot at me twice before I left you, I did not want to hear of your being hurt, and am glad you are still living. It would do me good to go back to the dear old home again, and see Miss Mary and Miss Martha and Allen, Esther, Green, and Lee. Give my love to them all, and tell them I hope we will meet in the better world, if not in this. I would have gone back to see you all when I was working in the Nashville Hospital, but one of the neighbors told me that Henry intended to shoot me if he ever got a chance.

I want to know particularly what the good chance is you propose to give me. I am doing tolerably well here. I get twenty-five dollars a month, with victuals and clothing; have a comfortable home for Mandy,—the folks call her Mrs. Anderson,—and the children—Milly, Jane, and Grundy—go to school and are learning well. The teacher says Grundy has a head for a preacher. They go to Sunday school, and Mandy and me attend church regularly. We are kindly treated. Sometimes we overhear others saying, "Them colored people were slaves" down in Tennessee. The children feel hurt when they hear such remarks; but I tell them it was no disgrace in Tennessee to belong to Colonel Anderson. Many darkeys would have been proud, as I used to be, to call you master. Now if you will write and say what wages you will give me, I will be better able to decide whether it would be to my advantage to move back again.

As to my freedom, which you say I can have, there is nothing to be gained on that score, as I got my free papers in 1864 from the Provost-Marshal-General of the Department of Nashville. Mandy says she would be afraid to go back without some proof that you were disposed to treat us justly and kindly; and we have concluded to test your sincerity by asking you to send us our wages for the time we served you. This will make us forget and forgive old scores, and rely on your justice and friendship in the future. I served you faithfully for thirty-two years, and Mandy twenty years. At twenty-five dollars a month for me, and two dollars a week for Mandy, our earnings would amount to eleven thousand six hundred and eighty dollars. Add to this the interest for the time our wages have been kept back, and deduct what you paid for our clothing, and three doctor's visits to me, and pulling a tooth for Mandy, and the balance will show what we are in justice entitled to. Please send the money by Adams's Express, in care of V. Winters, Esq., Dayton, Ohio. If you fail to pay us for faithful labors in the past, we can have little faith in your promises in the future. We trust the good Maker has opened your eyes to the wrongs which you and your fathers have done to me and my fathers, in making us toil for you for generations without recompense. Here I draw my wages every Saturday night; but in Tennessee there was never any pay-day for the negroes any more than for the horses and cows. Surely there will be a day of reckoning for those who defraud the laborer of his hire.

In answering this letter, please state if there would be any safety for my Milly and Jane, who are now grown up, and both good-looking girls. You know how it was with poor Matilda and Catherine. I would rather stay here and starve—and die, if it come to that—than have my girls brought to shame by the violence and wickedness of their young masters. You will also please state if there has been any schools opened for the colored children in your neighborhood. The great desire of my life now is to give my children an education, and have them form virtuous habits.

Say howdy to George Carter, and thank him for taking the pistol from you when you were shooting at me.

From your old servant,
JOURDON ANDERSON.

Source: Lydia Maria Child, *The Freedmen's Book* (New York: Arno Press, 1968), 265–267. Reprinted in Leon F. Litwack, *Been in the Storm So Long: The Aftermath of Slavery* (New York: Vintage Books, 1980), 333–335.

C. Alice Dabney to Her Former Owner, 1867

Montgomery, February 10, 1867

My Dear Old Master,—I am anxious to see you and my young masters and mistresses. I often think of you, and remember with pleasure how kind you all ever were to me. Though freedom has been given to the colored race, I often sigh for the good old days of slave-times, when we were all so happy and contented. . . . I am tolerably pleasantly situated. I am hired to a Mr. Sanderson, who treats me very well. I am very well, and hope I may have an opportunity of coming to see you all next Christmas. I am still single and don't think much about beaux. I don't think the men in these days of freedom are of much account. If I could find one whom I think a real good man, and who would take good care of me, I would get married. Please, dear old master, ask some of my young mistresses to write to me.

My kind and respectful remembrances to all.

Your former servant and friend,
Alice Dabney

Source: Susan Dabney Smedes, *Memorials of a Southern Planter* (New York: James Pott, 1890). Reprinted in Leon F. Litwack, *Been in the Storm So Long: The Aftermath of Slavery* (New York: Vintage Books, 1980), 333–335.

Chapter XVI

Reconstruction Abandoned, 1867–1877

97. The Mississippi Black Code, 1865

Many Southerners, feeling sure that Negroes would work only under compulsion agreed with Howell Cobb that some substitute for slavery must be devised. Accordingly, at the sessions of 1865–66 the new state legislatures which Johnson had sponsored passed laws regulating the life and labor of the Negro. These laws were commonly known as **black codes.** *The Mississippi Black Code, one of the most comprehensive and most severe, even prohibited Negroes from owning their own farms. It consisted of a series of laws dealing with segregation, apprenticeship, vagrancy, legal rights, and disorderly conduct.*

Segregation

It shall be unlawful for any officer, station agent, collector, or employee on any railroad in this State, to allow any freedman, negro, or mulatto, to ride in any first class passenger cars, set apart, or used by, and for white persons; and any person offending against the provisions of this section, shall be deemed guilty of a misdemeanor; and on conviction thereof before the circuit court of the county in which said offence was committed, shall be fined not less than fifty dollars, not more than five hundred dollars; and shall be imprisoned in the county jail, until such fine, and costs of prosecution are paid: *Provided,* That this section of this act, shall not apply, in the case of negroes or mulattoes, travelling with their mistress, in the capacity of maids.

Apprenticeship

It shall be the duty of all sheriffs, justices of the peace, and other civil offices of the several counties in this State, to report to the probate courts of their respective counties semi-annually, at the January and July terms of said courts, all freedmen, free negroes, and mulattoes, under the age of eighteen, in their respective counties, beats, or districts, who are orphans, or whose parent or parents have not the means or who refuse to provide for and support said minors; and thereupon it shall be the duty of said probate court to order the clerk of said court to apprentice said minors to some competent and suitable person, on such terms as the court may direct, having a particular care to the interest of said minor: *Provided,* that the former owner of said minors shall have the preference when, in the opinion of the court, he or she shall be a suitable person for that purpose. . . .

If any person entice away any apprentice from his or her master or mistress, or shall knowingly employ an apprentice, or furnish him or her food or clothing without the written consent of his or her master or mistress, or shall sell or give said apprentice ardent spirits without such consent, said person so offending shall be deemed guilty of a high misdemeanor, and shall, upon conviction thereof before the county court, he punished as provided for the punishment of persons enticing from their employer hired freedmen, free negroes or mulattoes.

W. L. Fleming, ed., *Documentary History of Reconstruction,* 2 vols. (Cleveland, 1906), I, 281–90.

Vagrancy

... All freedmen, free negroes and mulattoes in this State, over the age of eighteen years, found on the second Monday in January, 1866, or thereafter, with no lawful employment or business, found unlawfully assembling themselves together, either in the day or night time, and all white persons so assembling themselves with freedmen, free negroes or mulattoes, or usually associating with freedmen, free negroes or mulattoes, on terms of equality, or living in adultery or fornication with a freed women, free negro or mulatto, shall be deemed vagrants, and on conviction hereof shall be fined a sum not exceeding, in the case of a freedmen, free negro or mulatto, fifty dollars, and a white man two hundred dollars, and imprisoned at the discretion of the court, the free negro not exceeding ten days, and the white man not exceeding six months. ...

All fines and forfeitures collected under the provisions of this act shall be paid into the county treasury for general county purposes, and in case any freedmen, free negro or mulatto, to any person who will, for the shortest period of service, pay said fine and forfeiture and all costs: *Provided,* A preference shall be given to the employer, if there be one, in which case the employer shall be entitled to deduct and retain the amount so paid from the wages of such freedmen, free negro or mulatto, then due or to become due; and in case said freedmen, free negro, or mulatto cannot be hired out, he or she may be dealt with as a pauper.

The same duties and liabilities existing among white persons of this State shall attach to freedmen, free negroes or mulattoes, to support their indigent families and all colored paupers; and that in order to secure a support for such indigent freedmen, free negroes, or mulattoes, it shall be lawful and is hereby made the duty of the county police of each county in this State, to levy a poll or capitation tax on each and every freedmen, free negro, or mulatto, between the ages of eighteen and sixty years, not to exceed the sum of one dollar annually to each person so taxed, which tax, when collected, shall be paid into the county treasurer's hands, and constitute a fund to be called the Freedmen's Pauper Fund, which shall be applied by the commissioners of the poor for the maintenance of the poor of the freedmen, free negroes, and mulattoes of this State, under such regulations as may be established by the boards of county police in the respective counties of this State.

If any freedman, free negro, or mulatto shall fail or refuse to pay any tax levied according to the provisions of the sixth section of this act, it shall be *prima facie* evidence of vagrancy, and it shall be the duty of the sheriff to arrest such freedmen, free negro, or mulatto or such person refusing or neglecting to pay such tax, and proceed at once to hire for the shortest time such delinquent tax-payer to any one who will pay the said tax, with accruing costs, giving preference to the employer, if there be one.

Legal Rights

All freedmen, free negroes, and mulattoes may sue and be sued, implead and be impleaded, in all the courts of law and equity of this State, and may acquire personal property, and choses in action, by descent or purchase, and may dispose of the same in the same manner and to the same extent that white persons may: *Provided,* That the provisions of this section shall not be so construed as to allow any freedman, free negro, or mulatto to rent or lease any lands or tenements except in incorporated cities or towns, in which places the corporate authorities shall control the same.

All freedmen, free negroes, and mulattoes may intermarry with each other, in the same manner and under the same regulations that are provided by law for white persons: *Provided,* That the clerk of probate shall keep separate records of the same.

All freedmen, free negroes, or mulattoes who do now and have hereberfore lived and cohabited together as husband and wife shall be taken and held in law as legally married, and the issue shall be taken and held as legitimate for all purposes; that it shall not be lawful for any freedman, free negro, or mulatto to intermarry with any white person; nor for any white person to intermarry with any freedman, free negro, or mulatto; and any person who shall so intermarry, shall be deemed guilty of felony, and on conviction thereof shall be confined in the State penitentiary for life; and those shall be deemed freedmen, free negroes, and mulattoes who are of pure negro blood, and those descended from a negro to the third generation, inclusive, though one ancestor in each generation may have been a white person.

In addition to cases in which freedmen, free negroes, and mulattoes are now by law competent witnesses, freedmen, free negroes, or mulattoes shall be competent in civil cases, when a party or parties to the suit, either plaintiff or plaintiffs, defendant or defendants; also in cases where freedmen, free negroes, and mulattoes is or are either plaintiff or plaintiffs, defendant or defendants, and a white person or white persons, is or are the opposing party or parties, plaintiff or plaintiffs, defendants or defendants. They shall also be competent witnesses in all criminal prosecutions where the crime charged is alleged to have been committed by a white person upon or against the person or property of a freedman, free negro, or mulatto; *Provided,* that in all cases said witnesses shall be examined in open court, on the stand; except, however, they may be examined before the grand jury, and shall in all cases be subject to the rules and tests of the common laws as to competency and credibility.

Every freedman, free negro, and mulatto shall, on the second Monday of January, one thousand eight hundred and sixty-six and annually thereafter, have a lawful home or employment, and shall have written evidence thereof as follows, to wit: if living in any incorporated city, town, or village, a license from the mayor thereof; and if living outside of an incorporated city, town, or village, from the member of the board of police of his beat, authorizing him or her to do irregular and job work; or a written contract, as provided in section six in this act; which licenses may be revoked for cause at any time by the authority granting the same.

All contracts for labor made with freedmen, free negroes, and mulattoes for a longer period than one month shall be in writing, and in duplicate, attested and read to said freedman, free negro, or mulatto by a beat, city or county officer, or two disinterested white persons of the county in which the labor is to be performed, of which each party shall have one; and said contracts shall be taken and held as entire contracts, and if the laborer shall quit the service of the employer before the expiration of his term of service, without good cause, he shall forfeit his wages for that year up to the time of quitting.

Every civil officer shall, and every person may, arrest and carry back to his or her legal employer any freedman, free negro, or mulatto who shall have quit the service of his or her employer before the expiration of his or her term of service without good cause; and said officer and person shall be entitled to receive for arresting and carrying back every deserting employe aforesaid the sum of five dollars and ten cents per mile from the place of arrest to the place of delivery; and the same shall be paid by the employer, and held as a set-off for so much against the wages of said deserting employe: *Provided,* that said arrested party, after being so returned, may appeal to the justice of the peace or member of the board of police of the county, who, on notice to the alleged employer, shall try summarily whether said appellant is legally employed by the alleged employer, and has good cause to quit said employer; either party shall have the right of appeal to the county court, pending which the alleged deserter shall be remanded to the alleged employer or otherwise disposed of, as shall be right and just; and the decision of the county court shall be final.

If any person shall persuade or attempt to persuade, entice, or cause any freedman, free negro, or mulatto to desert from the legal employment of any person before the expiration of his or her term of service, or shall knowingly employ any such deserting freedman, free negro, or mulatto, or shall knowingly give or sell to any such deserting freedman, free negro, or mulatto, any good, raiment, or other thing, he or she shall be guilty of a misdemeanor, and, upon conviction, shall be fined not less than twenty-five dollars and not more than two hundred dollars and the costs; and if said fine and costs shall not be immediately paid, the court shall sentence said convict to not exceeding two months' imprisonment in the county jail, and he or she shall moreover be liable to the party injured in damages: *Provided,* if any person shall, or shall attempt to, persuade, entice, or cause any freedman, free negro, or mulatto to desert from any legal employment of any person, with the view to employ said freedman, free negro, or mulatto without the limits of this State, such person, on conviction, shall be fined not less than fifty dollars, and not more than five hundred dollars and costs; and if said fine and costs shall not be immediately paid, the court shall sentence said convict to not exceeding six months imprisonment in the county jail.

It shall be lawful for any freedman, free negro, or mulatto, to charge any white person, freedman, free negro, or mulatto by affidavit, with any criminal offense against his or her person or property, and upon such affidavit the proper process shall be issued and executed as if said affidavit was made by a white person, and it shall be lawful for any freedman, free negro, or mulatto, in any action, suit or controversy pending, or about to be instituted in any court or law or equity in this state, to make all needful and lawful affidavits as shall be necessary for the institution, prosecution or defense of such suit of controversy.

The penal laws of this State, in all cases not otherwise specially provided for, shall apply and extend to all freedmen, free negroes and mulattoes.

Disorderly Conduct

No freedman, free negro or mulatto, not in the military service of the United States government, and not licensed or do so by the board of police of his or her county, shall keep or carry fire-arms of any kind, or any ammunition, dirk or bowie knife, and on conviction thereof in the county court shall be punished by fine, not exceeding ten dollars, and pay the costs of such proceedings, and all such arms or ammunition shall be forfeited to the informer; and it shall be the duty of every civil and military officer to arrest any freedman, free negro, or mulatto found with any such arms or ammunition, and cause him or her to be committed to trial in default of bail.

Any freedman, free negro, or mulatto committing riots, routs, affrays, trespasses, malicious mischief, cruel treatment to animals, seditious speeches, insulting gestures, language, or acts, or assaults on any person, disturbance of the peace, exercising the function of a minister of the Gospel without a license from some regularly organized church, vending spirituous or intoxicating liquors, or committing any other misdemeanor, the punishment of which is not specifically provided for by law, shall, upon conviction thereof in the county court, be fined not less than ten dollars, and not more than one hundred dollars, and may be imprisoned at the discretion of the court, not exceeding thirty days.

If any white person shall sell, lend, or give to any freedman, free negro, or mulatto any fire-arms, dirk or bowie knife, or ammunition, or any spirituous or intoxicating liquors, such person or persons so offending, upon conviction thereof in the county court of his or her county, shall be fined not exceeding fifty dollars, and may be imprisoned, at the discretion of the court, not exceeding thirty days. . . .

If any freedman, free negro, or mulatto, convicted of any of the misdemeanors provided against in this act, shall fail or refuse for the space of five days, after conviction, to pay the fine and costs imposed, such person shall be hired out by the sheriff or other officer, at public outcry, to any white person who will pay said fine and all costs, and take said convict for the shortest time.

98. The Address of Alabama Colored Convention, 1867

In May of 1867, very soon after the passage of the first Reconstruction Act, Alabama Negroes held a convention in Mobile and drew up an "Address of the Colored Convention to the People of Alabama."

As there seems to be considerable difference of opinion concerning the "legal rights of the colored man," it will not be amiss to say that we claim exactly *the same rights, privileges and immunities as are enjoyed by white men*—we ask nothing more and will be content with nothing less. *All legal* distinctions between the races are now abolished. The word white is stricken from our laws, and every privilege which white men were formerly permitted to enjoy, merely because they were white men, now that word is stricken out, we are entitled to on the ground that we are men. *Color can no longer be pleaded for the purpose of curtailing privileges, and every public right and immunity is enjoyable by every individual member of the public.*—This is the touchstone that determines all these points. So long as a park or a street is a *public* park or street the entire public has the right to use it; so long as a car or a steamboat is a public conveyance, it must carry all who come to it, and serve all alike who pay alike. The law no longer knows white nor black, but simply men, and consequently we are entitled to ride in public conveyances, hold office, sit on juries and do everything else which we have in the past been prevented from doing solely on the ground of our color. . . .

We have said that we intend to claim all our rights, and we submit to our white friends that it is the height of folly on their part to withhold them any longer. One-half of the voters in Alabama are black men, and in a few months there is to be an entire reorganization of the State government. The new officers—legislative, executive and judicial—will owe their election largely, if not mainly to the colored people, and every one must see clearly that the voters will then be certain to require and the officers to compel a cessation of all illegal discriminations. The question which every man now illegally discriminating

---

Source: The Address of Alabama Colored Convention. *Montgomery Daily State Sentinel,* May 21, 1867. Public Domain Reprint.

against us has to decide is, whether it is politic to insist upon gratifying prejudices during a few dull months, with the certainty by so doing, of incurring the lasting displeasure of one-half of the voting population of the State. We can stand it if they can, but we assure them that they are being watched closely, and that their conduct will be remembered when we have power.

There are some good people who are always preaching patience and procrastination. They would have us wait a few months, years, or generations, until the whites voluntarily give us our rights, but we do not intend to wait one day longer than we are absolutely compelled to. Look at our demands, and then at theirs. We ask of them simply that they surrender unreasonable and unreasoning prejudice; that they cease imitating dog in the manger; that they consent to allow others as well as themselves to prosper and be happy. But they would have us pay for what we do not get; tramp through the broiling sun or pelting rain, or stand upon a platform, while empty seats mockingly invite us to rest our wearied limbs; our sick must suffer or submit to indignity; we must put up with inconvenience of every kind; and the virtuous aspirations of our children must be continually checked by the knowledge that no matter how upright their conduct, they will be looked on as less worthy of respect than the lowest wretch on earth who wears a white skin. We ask you—only while in public, however—to surrender your prejudices,—nothing but prejudices; and you ask us to sacrifice our personal conduct, health, pecuniary interests, self-respect, and the future prospects of our children. The men who make such requests must suppose us devoid of spirit and of brains, but they will find themselves mistaken. Solemnly and distinctly, we again say to you, men of Alabama, that we will not submit voluntarily to such infamous discrimination, and if you will insist upon tramping on the rights and outraging the feelings of those who are so soon to pass judgment upon you, then upon your own heads will rest the responsibility for the effect of your course.

All over the state of Alabama—all over the South indeed—the colored people have with singular unanimity, arrayed themselves under the Republican banner, upon the Republican platform, and it is confidently predicted that nine-tenths of them will vote the Republican ticket. Do you ask, why is this? We answer, because:

1. The Republican Party opposed and prohibited the extension of slavery.
2. It repealed the fugitive slave law.
3. It abolished slavery in the District of Columbia.
4. It abolished slavery in the rebellious states.
5. It abolished slavery throughout the rest of the Union.
6. It put down rebellion against the Union.
7. It passed the Freedmen's Bureau Bill and the Civil Rights Bill.
8. It enfranchised the colored people of the District of Columbia.
9. It enfranchised the colored people of the nine territories.
10. It enfranchised the colored people of the ten rebel states.
11. It provided for the formation of new constitutions and state governments in those ten states.
12. It passed new homestead laws, enabling the poor to obtain land.

In short, it has gone on, step by step, doing first one thing for us and then another, and it now proposes to enfranchise our people all over the Union. It is the only party which has ever attempted to extend our privileges, and as it has in the past always been trying to do this, it is but natural that we should trust it for the future.

While this has been the course of the Republican Party, the opposition had unitedly opposed every one of these measures, and it also now opposes the enfranchisement of our people in the North. Everywhere it has been against us in the past, and the great majority of its voters hate us as cordially now as ever before. It is sometimes alleged that the Republicans of the North have not been actuated by love for us in what they have done, and therefore that we should not join them; we answer that even if that were true they certainly never professed to hate us and the opposition party has always been denouncing the "d—n nigger and abolitionist" with equal fervor. When we had no votes to give, the opposition placed us and the Republicans in the same boat, and now we reckon we'll stay in it. It may be and probably is true that some men acting with the Republican Party have cared nothing for the principles of that party; but it is also certainly true that ninety-nine-hundredths of all those who were conscientiously in favor of our rights were and are in the Republican Party, and that the great mass of those who hated, slandered and abused us were and are in the opposition party.

The memories of the opposition must be short indeed, to have forgotten their language of the past twenty years but we have *not* forgotten it.

But, say some of the members of the opposition party, "We intend to turn over a new leaf, and will hereafter give you all your rights." Perhaps they would, but we prefer not to put the new wine of political equality into the old bottles of "sectional animosity" and "caste feeling." We are somewhat fearful that those who have always opposed the extensions of rights are not sincere in their professions. . . .

Another fact should be borne in mind. While a few conservatives are making guarded promises to us the masses of that party are cursing us, and doing all they can to "make the d—d niggers stay in their place." If we were, therefore, to join that party, it would be simply as servants, and not as equals. Some leaders, who needed our votes might treat us decently, but the great majority would expect us to stay at home until election day, and then vote as our employers dictated. This we respectfully decline doing. It seems to us safest to have as little as possible to do with those members of the community who delight to abuse us, and they are nearly, if not quite, all to be found in the ranks of the opposition party. . . .

It cannot be disguised, however, that many men calling themselves conservatives are disposed to use unfair means to carry their points. The press of Mobile, and other parts of the State, contain numerous threats that those colored people who do not vote as their employers command, will be discharged; that the property-holders will combine, import white laborers, and discharge their colored hands, etc. Numerous instances have come to our knowledge of persons who have already been discharged because they attended Republican meetings, and great numbers more have been threatened. "Vote as we command, or starve," is the argument these men propose to make [use] of, and with it they expect to succeed.

In this expectation they will be mistaken, and we warn them before it is prosecuted any further, that their game is a dangerous one for themselves. The property which they hold was nearly all earned by the sweat of our brows—not theirs. It has been forfeited to the Government by the treason of its owners, and is liable to be confiscated whenever the Republican Party demands it. The great majority of that party is now opposed to confiscation, but if the owners of property use the power which it gives them to make political slaves of the poor, a cry will go up to Congress which will make the party a unit for confiscation.

Conservatives of Alabama, do you propose to rush upon certain destruction? Are you mad, that you threaten to pursue a policy which would only result in causing thousands of men to cry out to their leaders, "Our wives and little ones are starving because we stood by you; because we would not be slaves!" When the nation abolished slavery, you used your local governments to neutralize and defeat its action, and the nation answered by abolishing your governments and enfranchising us. If you now use your property to neutralize or defeat this, its last act, it will answer by taking away the property you are only allowed to retain through its unparalleled mercy and which you have proved yourself so unworthy of retaining. . . .

So complete, indeed, will be our victory, that our opponents will become disheartened unless they can divide us. This is the great danger which we have to guard against. The most effectual method of preserving our unity will be for us to always act together—never to hold separate political meetings or caucuses. It may take some time for us to get to pulling together well, but perseverance and honest endeavor will overcome all obstacles. In nominations for office we expect that there will be no discrimination on account of color by either wing, but that the most capable and honest men will always be put in nomination. We understand full well that our people are too deficient in education to be generally qualified to fill the higher offices, but when qualified men are found, they must not be rejected for being black.

This lack of education, which is the consequence of our long servitude, and which so diminishes our powers for good, should not be allowed to characterize our children when they come upon the stage of action, and we therefore earnestly call upon every member of the Republican Party to demand the establishment of a thorough system of common schools throughout the State. It will benefit every citizen of the State, and, indeed, of the Union, for the well-being of each enures to the advantage of all. In a Republic, education is especially necessary, as the ignorant are always liable to be led astray by the arts of the demagogue.

With education secured to all; with the old and helpless properly cared for; with justice everywhere impartially administered, Alabama will commence a career of which she will have just cause to be proud. We shall all be prosperous and happy. The sad memories of the past will be forgotten amid the joys of the present and the prospect of the future.

99. THADDEUS STEVENS ON NEGRO SUFFRAGE, 1867

At first, in 1865 and 1866, Thaddeus Stevens had hesitated to give Negroes the vote. There was the danger that this vote might be controlled by the former master class and used to strengthen the Democrats in the South. Besides, there was the risk of antagonizing Republican voters in Stevens' own state of Pennsylvania, where Negro suffrage was not possible. At that time Negroes could not vote in Pennsylvania nor in most of the Northern states (only in six of them; New York and all of New England except Connecticut). Nevertheless, by 1867 Stevens had decided that Congress must include Negro suffrage in its reconstruction plan. He gave reasons for this in a House speech on January 3, 1867.

Unless the rebel States, before admission, should be made republican in spirit, and placed under the guardianship of loyal men, all our blood and treasure will have been spent in vain. I waive now the question of punishment which, if we are wise, will still be inflicted by moderate confiscations. . . . Having these States . . . entirely within the power of Congress, it is our duty to take care that no injustice shall remain in their organic laws. Holding them "like clay in the hands of the potter," we must see that no vessel is made for destruction. Having now no governments, they must have enabling acts. The law of last session with regard to Territories settled the principles of such acts. Impartial suffrage, both in electing the delegates and ratifying their proceedings, is now the fixed rule. There is more reason why colored voters should be admitted in the rebel State than in the Territories. In the States they form the great mass of the loyal men. Possibly with their aid loyal governments may be established in most of those States. Without it all are sure to be ruled by traitors; and loyal men, black and white, will be oppressed, exiled, or murdered. There are several good reasons for the passage of this bill. In the first place, it is just. I am now confining my argument to negro suffrage in the rebel States. Have not loyal blacks quite as good a right to choose rulers and make laws as rebel whites? In the second place, it is a necessity in order to protect the loyal white men in the seceded States. The white Union men are in a great minority in each of those States. With them the blacks would act in a body; and it is believed that in each of said States, except one, the two united would form a majority, control the States, and protect themselves. Now they are the victims of daily murder. They must suffer the constant persecution or be exiled. . . .

Another good reason is, it would insure the ascendency of the Union party. . . . I believe . . . that on the continued ascendency of that party depends the safety of this great nation. If impartial suffrage is excluded in the rebel States, then every one of them is sure to send a solid rebel representative delegation to Congress, and cast a solid rebel electoral vote. They, with their kindred Copperheads of the North, would always elect the President and control Congress. While slavery sat upon her defiant throne, and insulted and intimidated the trembling North, the South frequently divided on questions of policy between Whigs and Democrats, and gave victory alternately to the sections. Now, you must divide them between loyalists, without regard to color, and disloyalties, or you will be the perpetual vassals of the free-trade, irritated, revengeful South. . . . I am for negro suffrage in every rebel State. If it be just, it should not be denied; if it be necessary, it should be adopted; if it be a punishment to traitors, they deserve it.

Source: Congressional Globe, 39th Congress, 2nd Session. January 3, 1867. Public Domain Reprint.

100. GEORGE WASHINGTON PLUNKITT, PLUNKITT OF TAMMANY HALL

A series of very plain talks on very practical politics, delivered by ex-Senator George Washington Plunkitt, the Tammany philosopher, from his rostrum—the New York County Court House bootblack stand.

The Curse of Civil Service Reform

This civil service law is the biggest fraud of the age. It is the curse of the nation. There can't be no real patriotism while it lasts. How are you goin' to interest our young men in their country if you have no offices to give them when they work for their party? Just look at things in this city today. There are ten thousand good offices, but we can't get at more than a few hundred of them. How are we goin' to provide for the thousands of men who worked for the Tammany ticket? It can't be done. These men were full of patriotism a short time ago. They expected to be servin' their city, but when we tell them that we can't place them, do you think their patriotism is goin' to last? Not much. They say: "What's the use of workin' for your country anyhow? There's nothin' in the game." And what can they do? I don't know, but I'll tell you what I do know. I know more than one young man in past years who worked for the ticket and was just overflowin' with patriotism, but when he was knocked out by the civil service humbug he got to hate his country and became an Anarchist.

This ain't no exaggeration. I have good reason for sayin' that most of the Anarchists in this city today are men who ran up against civil service examinations. Isn't it enough to make a man sour on his country when he wants to serve it and won't be allowed unless he answers a lot of fool questions about the number of cubic inches of water in the Atlantic and the quality of sand in the Sahara desert? There was once a bright young man in my district who tackled one of these examinations. The next I heard of him he had settled down in Herr Most's saloon smokin' and drinkin' beer and talkin' socialism all day. Before that time he had never drank anything but whisky. I know what was comin' when a young Irishman drops whisky and takes to beer and long pipes in a German saloon. That young man is today one of the wildest Anarchists in town. And just to think! He might be a patriot but for that cussed civil service.

Say, did you hear about that Civil Service Reform Association kickin' because the tax commissioners want to put their fifty-five deputies on the exempt list, and fire the outfit left to them by Low? That's civil service for you. Just think! Fifty-five Republicans and mug-wumps holdin' $3000 and $4000 and $5000 jobs in the tax department when 1555 good Tammany man are ready and willin' to take their places! It's an outrage! What did the people mean when they voted for Tammany? What is representative government, anyhow? Is it all a fake that this is a government of the people, by the people and for the people if it isn't a fake, then why isn't the people's voice obeyed and Tammany men put in all the offices?

When the people elected Tammany, they knew just what they were doin'. We didn't put up any false pretenses. We didn't go in for humbug civil service and all that rot. We stood as we have always stood, for rewardin' the men that won the victory. They call that the spoils system. All right; Tammany is for the spoils system, and when we go in we fire every anti-Tammany man from office that can be fired under the law. It's an elastic sort of law and you can get it will be stretched to the limit. Of course the Republican State Civil Service Board will stand in the way of our local Civil Service Commission all it can; but say!—suppose we carry the State sometime, won't we fire the upstate Board all right? Or we'll make it work in harmony with the local board, and that means that Tammany will get everything in sight. I know that the civil service humbug is stuck into the constitution, too, but, as Tim Campbell said: "What's the constitution among friends?"

Say, the people's voice is smothered by the cursed civil service law; it is the root of all evil in our government. You hear of this thing or that thing goin' wrong in the nation, the State or the city. Look down beneath the sur-

---

Source: Plunkitt of Tammany Hall (Excerpt), recorded by W. L. Riordon, pp. 11–16, 90–98. Copyright Penguin USA. Reprinted by permission.

face and you can trace everything wrong to civil service. I have studied the subject and I know. The civil service humbug is underminin' our institutions and if a halt ain't called soon this great republic will tumble down like a Park Avenue house when they were buildin' the subway, and on its ruins will rise another Russian government.

This is an awful serious proposition. Free silver and the tariff and imperialism and the Panama Canal are trifflin' issues when compared to it. We could worry along without any of these things, but civil service is sappin' the foundation of the whole shootin' match. Let me argue it out for you. I ain't up on sillygisms, but I can give you some arguments that nobody can answer.

First, this great and glorious country was built up by political parties; second, parties can't hold together if their workers don't get the offices when they win; third, if the parties go to pieces, the government they built up must go to pieces, too; fourth, then there'll be h———— to pay.

Could anything be clearer than that? Say, honest now; can you answer that argument? Of course you won't deny that the government was built up by the great parties. That's history, and you can't go back of the returns. As to my second proposition, you can't deny that either. When parties can't get offices, they'll bust. They ain't far from the bustin' point now, with all this civil service business keepin' most of the good things from them. How are you goin' to keep up patriotism if this thing goes on? You can't do it. Let me tell you that patriotism has been dying out fast for the last twenty years. Before then when a party won, its workers got everything in sight. Now, when a party wins and its men come forward and ask for their rewards, the reply is, "Nothin' doin', unless you can answer a list of questions about Egyptian mummies and how many years it will take for a bird to wear out a mass of iron as big as the earth by steppin' on it once in a century?

I have studied politics and men for forty-five years, and I see how things are driftin'. Sad indeed is the change that has come over the young men, even in my district, where I try to keep up the fire of patriotism by gettin' a lot of jobs for my constituents, whether Tammany is in or out. The boys and men don't get excited any more when they see a United States flag or hear "The Star-Spangled Banner." They don't care no more for firecrackers on the Fourth of July. And why should they? What is there in it for them? They know that no matter how hard they work for their country in a campaign, the jobs will go to fellows who can tell about the mummies and the bird steppin' on the iron. Are you surprised then that the young men of the country are beginnin' to look coldly on the flag and don't care to put up a nickel for firecrackers?

Say, let me tell of one case. After the battle of San Juan Hill, the Americans found a dead man with a light complexion, red hair and blue eyes. They could see he wasn't a Spaniard, although he had on a Spanish uniform. Several officers looked him over, and then a private of the Seventy-first Regiment saw him and yelled, "Good Lord, that's Flaherty." That man grew up in my district, and he was once the most patriotic American boy on the West Side. He couldn't see a flag without yellin' himself hoarse.

Now, how did he come to be lying dead with a Spanish uniform on? I found out all about it, and I'll vouch for the story. Well, in the municipal campaign of 1897, that young man, chockfull of patriotism, worked day and night for the Tammany ticket. Tammany won, and the young man determined to devote his life to the service of the city. He picked out a place that would suit him, and sent in his application to the head of department. He got a reply that he must take a civil service examination to get the place. He didn't know what these examinations were, so he went, all lightheaded, to the Civil Service Board. He read the questions about the mummies, the bird on the iron, and all the other fool questions—and he left that office an enemy of the country that he had loved so well. The mummies and the bird blasted his patriotism. He went to Cuba, enlisted in the Spanish army at the breakin' out of the war, and died fightin' his country.

That is but one victim of the infamous civil service. If that young man had not run up against the civil examination, but had been allowed to serve his country as he wished, he would be in a good office today, drawin' a good salary. Ah, how many young men have had their patriotism blasted in the same way!

Now, what is goin' to happen when civil service crushes out patriotism? Only one thing can happen: the republic will go to pieces. Then a czar or a sultan will turn up, which brings me to the fourthly of my argument—that is, there will be h———— to play. And that ain't no lie.

Strenuous Life of the Tammany District Leader

NOTE: This chapter is based on extracts from Plunkitt's Diary and on my daily observation of the work of the district leader.—W.L.R.

The life of the Tammany district leader is strenuous. To his work is due the wonderful recuperative power of the organization.

One year it goes down in defeat and the prediction is made that it will never again raise its head. The district leader, undaunted by defeat, collects his scattered forces, organizes them as only Tammany knows how to organize, and in a little while the organization is as strong as ever.

No other politician in New York or elsewhere is exactly like the Tammany district leader or works as he does. As a rule, he has no business or occupation other than politics. He plays politics every day and night in the year, and his headquarters bears the inscription, "Never closed."

Everybody in the district knows him. Everybody knows where to find him, and nearly everybody goes to him for assistance of one sort of another, especially the poor of the tenements.

He is always obliging. He will go to the police courts to put in a good word for the "drunks and disorderlies" or pay their fines, if a good word is not effective. He will attend christenings, weddings, and funerals. He will feed the hungry and help bury the dead.

A philanthropist? Not at all. He is playing politics all the time.

Brought up in Tammany Hall, he has learned how to reach the hearts of the great mass of voters. He does not bother about reaching their heads. It is his belief that arguments and campaign literature have never gained votes.

He seeks direct contact with the people, does them good turns when he can, and relies on their not forgetting him on election day. His heart is always in his work, too, for his subsistence depends on its results.

If he hold his district and Tammany is in power, he is amply rewarded by a good office and the opportunities that go with it. What these opportunities are has been shown by the quick rise of so many Tammany district leaders. With the examples before him of Richard Croker, once leader of the Twentieth District; John F. Carroll, formerly leader of the Twenty-ninth; Timothy ("Dry Dollar") Sullivan, late leader of the Sixth, and many others, he can always look forward to riches and ease while he is going through the drudgery of his daily routine.

This is a record of a day's work by Plunkitt:

2 A.M.: Aroused from sleep by the ringing of his doorbell; went to the door and found a bartender, who asked him to go to the police station and bail out a saloon-keeper who had been arrested for violating the excise law. Furnished bail and returned to bed at three o'clock.

6 A.M.: Awakened by the fire engines passing his house. Hastened to the scene of the fire, according to the custom of the Tammany district leaders, to give assistance to the fire sufferers, if needed. Met several of his election district captains who are always under orders to look out for fires, which are considered great vote-getters. Found several tenants who had been burned out, took them to a hotel, supplied them with clothes, fed them, and arranged temporary quarters for them until they could rent and furnish new apartments.

8:30 A.M.: Went to the police court to look after his constituents. Found six "drunks." Secured the discharge of four by a timely word with the judge, and paid the fines of two.

9 A.M.: Appeared in the Municipal District Court. Directed one of his district captains to act as counsel for a widow against whom dispossess proceedings had been instituted and obtained an extension of time. Paid the rent of a poor family about to be dispossessed and gave them a dollar for food.

11 A.M.: At home again. Found four men waiting for him. One had been discharged by the Metropolitan Railway Company for neglect of duty, and wanted the district leader to fix things. Another wanted a job on the road. The third sought a place on the Subway and the fourth, a plumber, was looking for work with the Consolidated Gas Company. The district leader spent nearly three hours fixing things for the four men, and succeeded in each case.

3 P.M.: Attended the funeral of an Italian as far as the ferry. Hurried back to make his appearance at the funeral of a Hebrew constituent. Went conspicuously to the front both in the Catholic church and the synagogue, and later attended the Hebrew confirmation ceremonies in the synagogue.

7 P.M.: Went to district headquarters and presided over a meeting of election district captains. Each captain submitted a list of all the voters in his district, reported on their attitude toward Tammany, suggested who might be won over and how they could be won, told who were in need, and who were in trouble of any kind and the best way to reach them. District leader took notes and gave orders.

8 P.M.: Went to a church fair. Took chances on everything, bought ice cream for the young girls and the children. Kissed the little ones, flattered their mothers and took their fathers out for something down at the corner.

9 P.M.: At the clubhouse again. Spent $10 on tickets for a church excursion and promised a subscription for a new church bell. Bought tickets for a baseball game to be played by two nines from his district. Listened to the complaints of a dozen pushcart peddlers who said they were persecuted by the police and assured them he would go to Police Headquarters in the morning and see about it.

10:30 P.M.: Attended a Hebrew wedding reception and dance. Had previously sent a handsome wedding present to the bride.

12 P.M.: In bed.

That is the actual record of one day in the life of Plunkitt. He does some of the same things every day, but his life is not so monotonous as to be wearisome.

Sometimes the work of a district leader is exciting, especially if he happens to have a rival who intends to make a contest for the leadership at the primaries. In that case, he is even more alert, tries to reach the fires before his rival, sends out runners to look for "drunks and disorderlies" at the police station, and keeps a very close watch on the obituary columns of the newspapers.

A few years ago there was a bitter contest for the Tammany leadership of the Ninth District between John C. Sheehan and Frank J. Goodwin. Both had had long experience in Tammany politics and both understood every move of the game.

Every morning their agents went to their respective headquarters before seven o'clock and read through the death notices in all the morning papers. If they found that anybody in the district had died, they rushed to the homes of their principals with the information and then there was a race to the house of the deceased to offer condolences, and, if the family were poor, something more substantial.

On the day of the funeral there was another contest. Each faction tried to surpass the other in number and appearance of the carriages it sent to the funeral, and more than once they almost came to blows at the church or in the cemetery.

On one occasion the Goodwinites played a trick on their adversaries which has since been imitated in other districts. A well-known liquor dealer who had a considerable following died, and both Sheehan and Goodwin were eager to become his political heir by making a big showing at the funeral.

Goodwin managed to catch the enemy napping. He went to all the livery stables in the district, hired all the carriages for the day, and gave order to two hundred of his men to be on hand as mourners.

Sheehan had never had any trouble about getting all the carriages that he wanted, so he let the matter go until the night before the funeral. Then he found that he could not hire a carriage in the district.

He called his district committee together in a hurry and explained the situation to them. He could get all the vehicles he needed in the adjoining district, he said, but if he did that, Goodwin would rouse the votes of the Ninth by declaring that he (Sheehan) had patronized foreign industries.

Finally, it was decided that there was nothing to do but to go over to Sixth Avenue and Broadway for carriages. Sheehan made a fine turnout at the funeral, but the deceased was hardly in his grave before Goodwin raised the cry of "Protection to home industries," and denounced his rival for patronizing livery-stable keepers outside of his district. The cry had its effect in the primary campaign. At all events, Goodwin was elected leader.

A recent contest for the leadership of the Second District illustrated further the strenuous work of the Tammany district leaders. The contestants were Patrick Diver, who had managed the district for years, and Thomas F. Foley.

Both were particularly anxious to secure the large Italian vote. They not only attended all the Italian christenings and funerals, but also kept a close lookout for the marriages in order to be on hand with wedding presents.

At first, each had his own reporter in the Italian quarter to keep track of the marriages. Later, Foley conceived a better plan. He hired a man to stay all day at the City Hall marriage bureau, where most Italian couples go through the civil ceremony, and telephone to him at his saloon when anything was doing at the bureau.

Foley had a number of presents ready for use and, whenever he received a telephone message from his man, he hastened to the City Hall with a ring or a watch or a piece of silver and handed it to the bride with his congratulations. As a consequence, when Divver got the news and went to the home of the couple with his present, he always found that Foley had been ahead of him. Toward the end of the campaign, Divver also stationed a man at the marriage bureau and then there were daily foot races and fights between the two heelers.

Sometimes the rivals came into conflict at the deathbed. One night a poor Italian peddler died in Roosevelt Street. The news reached Divver and Foley about the same time, and as they knew the family of the man was destitute, each went to an undertaker and brought him to the Roosevelt Street tenement.

The rivals and the undertakers met at the house and an altercation ensued. After much discussion the Divver undertaker was selected. Foley had more carriages at the funeral, however, and he further impressed the Italian voters by paying the widow's rent for a month, and sending her half a ton of coal and a barrel of flour.

The rivals were put on their mettle toward the end of the campaign by the wedding of a daughter of one of the original Cohens of the Baxter Street region. The Hebrew vote in the district is nearly as large as the Italian vote, and Divver and Foley set out to capture the Cohens and their friends.

They stayed up nights thinking what they would give the bride. Neither knew how much the other was prepared to spend on a wedding present, or what form it would take; so spies were employed by both sides to keep watch on the jewelry stores, and the jewelers of the district were bribed by each side to impart the desired information.

At last Foley heard that Divver had purchased a set of silver knives, forks and spoons. He at once bought a duplicate set and added a silver tea service. When the presents were displayed at the home of the bride, Divver was not in a pleasant mood and he charged his jeweler with treachery. It may be added that Foley won at the primaries.

One of the fixed duties of a Tammany district leader is to give two outings every summer, one for the men of his district and the other for the women and children, and a beefsteak dinner and a ball every winter. The scene of the outings is, usually, one of the groves along the Sound.

The ambition of the district leader on these occasions is to demonstrate that his men have broken all records in the matter of eating and drinking. He gives out the exact number of pounds of beef, poultry, butter, etc., that they have consumed and professes to know how many potatoes and ears of corn have been served.

According to his figures, the average eating record of each man at the outing is about ten pounds of beef, two or three chickens, a pound of butter, a half peck of potatoes, and two dozen ears of corn. The drinking records, as given out, are still more phenomenal. For some reason, not yet explained, the district leader thinks that his popularity will be greatly increased if he can show that his followers can eat and drink more than the followers of any other district leader.

The same idea governs the beefsteak dinners in the winter. It matters not what sort of steak is served or how it is cooked; the district leader considers only the question of quantity, and when he excels all others in this particular, he feels, somehow, that he is a bigger man and deserves more patronage than his associates in the Tammany Executive Committee.

As to the balls, they are the events of the winter in the extreme East Side and West Side society. Mamie and Maggie and Jennie prepare for them months in advance, and their young men save up for the occasion just as they save for the summer trips to Coney Island.

The district leader is in his glory at the opening of the ball. He leads the cotillion with the prettiest woman present—his wife, if he has one, permitting—and spends almost the whole night shaking hands with his constituents. The ball costs him a pretty penny, but he has found that the investment pays.

By these means the Tammany district leader reaches out into the homes of his district, keeps watch not only on the men, but also on the women and children; knows their needs, their likes and dislikes, their troubles and their hopes, and places himself in a position to use his knowledge for the benefit of his organization and himself. It is any wonder that scandals do not permanently disable Tammany and that it speedily recovers from what seems to be crushing defeats?

101. A New Orleans Editor on Colfax, 1873

Reconstruction in the South following the Civil War created a crisis of governmental authority in many areas. Fraud, corruption, and violence followed elections in almost every locality, as white Democrats tried to wrest power from black and white Republicans. In Colfax, a town in Grant parish, Louisiana, Republicans and Democrats contested the results of local elections. Supported by the Republican governor Kellogg, black Republicans in Colfax took possession of public offices by force. In response, whites from miles around organized a huge and well-armed posse to oust the Republicans from power. The resulting warfare left perhaps three hundred people dead, most of them black, and gave control of the city to white Democrats. The New Orleans Daily Picayune, a Democratic newspaper and staunch opponent of Reconstruction, supported the assault, claiming that the black Republicans of Colfax held their power illegitimately.

Mob Violence in Grant Parish.

What The Negroes Are About.

On Tuesday evening last, Judge Rutland, of Colfax, Grant parish, was accosted by a large mob of armed negroes, headed by one Flowers, a member of the Legislature, and the mob ordered Judge Rutland to leave the parish of Grant. He was given fifteen minutes to make his start—under the penalty of being killed if he refused to obey the order.

Source: New Orleans Daily Picayune, April 7, 9, 16, 18, 1873.

The judge quietly left within the time given, and his wife and family followed him as soon as they could get a small amount of wearing apparel together.

That night his house was broken open by the mob—his furniture broken to pieces and his household goods stolen.

During the night the mob were yelling and shouting all around. In the village they fired into the house of Mr. Richardson, endangering his life and the lives of his family.

On Wednesday morning the mob ordered Mr. Richardson to leave within ten minutes. He obeyed, and he and family crossed to the east side of the river. As soon as they were gone their house was broken open and robbed of its contents.

Another house was also broken open and robbed by the mob on Wednesday.

During the nights of Wednesday and Thursday guns were firing for several miles around the town by the negroes, killing the cattle and hogs of the whites.

On Friday, Butler, a freedman, who is a merchant, and bears a reputation above reproach, called on Register, the parish judge, to take measures to stop this rapine and outrage, and he declined to interfere in any way: whereupon Butler tried all his power of persuasion to stop their unlawful outrages, and the mob gave Butler a few minutes' notice to leave the country. About this time the steamer Marie Louise, from Shreveport, bound for this city, came along and took off Butler and his family, who are here now.

There was no white person seen at Colfax as the Marie Louise passed. A great many negroes, all armed with guns and six-shooters, were on the bank, and appeared in defiant and insolent attitude.

It was reported that the negroes were five hundred strong at the time; about two hundred armed.

A collision was looked for on Friday night, the whites, it was understood, being in the neighborhood.

The Marie Louise brought several families from below Colfax to Alexandria, who were fleeing for safety.

Upon particular inquiry we learned that there was no contest for office in that parish, and the Republicans were peaceably and without dispute in the possession of the offices claimed by them.

The Riot in Grant Parish. Statement of Judge W. R. Rutland.

THE CAUSE OF THE DIFFICULTY.

The Lynch Returning Board ignored the election of our parish officers, and Mr. Kellogg appointed a set of men to fill the vacancies, but who did not qualify according to law, and allowed the time to elapse in which they are required by law to do it in. Mr. Kellogg, at my instance, commissioned all officers who were elected, including both Republicans and Fusionists, white and colored, except a parish judge who had already qualified and was a Republican.

Ward, a member of the Dryades street Legislature, learning that Mr. Kellogg was going to issue these commissions, hastened to Colfax and took violent and forcible possession of the Court-House and offices with a mob. There was a proposition to hold a mass meeting of the people for the purpose of expressing their condemnation in a quiet way at the course pursued by these men, but when the day arrived for the meeting to have been called together there was such violent demonstrations made by Ward, Register and Flowers, and the armed band that was backing them, that the few white people who had the matter in hand did not pretend to do anything, but quietly returned to their homes without going near the court-house, or assembling anywhere. After this I was advised by friends to seek safety, as my life was in danger. I took their advice and started to cross the river to Mr. J. C. Moranline's place, but when I got to the river I was interviewed by another friend, who told me that it would not be safe for me to return to this side of the river that night. After crossing the river I was met again by persons who told me that there was a determination to assassinate me if I returned to the Colfax side of the river.

At 12 o'clock at night I found out that the mob had sacked my house, and that they were going to attempt to cross the river and arrest me. I made my escape by Mr. Morantini furnishing me with a horse and guide, and went to Montgomery, where I found my family, which had preceded me by boat. Since that time I have been quiet and have done nothing, remaining at Montgomery. I did not go out of town at all, until I got on board of the steamboat John T. Moore to come to this place. In passing Colfax last Monday morning I was discovered on board of the boat by the mob of negroes, and my ears were greeted with prolonged and terrific yells from the shore, and many, mounting their horses, got their guns and pursued after the boat for some distance, some even following a distance of over seven miles.

I will state also that on the way down, the boat was hailed to take a Mr. Calhoun on, but she could not make the landing, owing to a very violent wind that was blowing at the time. The steamboat La Belle came along directly after, and made the landing, and took Calhoun on board, and passed us before we got to Alexandria. When we got to Alexandria I learned that Calhoun had been arrested and had been taken off of the boat. The gentlemen who took him from the boat stated that they were going to take him to Colfax and make him quiet the mischief and restore the peace that he was the promoter and head cause of, as he was principally responsible for what had been. But I do not believe (although, of course, I did not see the persons who had him in custody) that any violence against him was meditated; but it is hard to say what an angry set of men will do under such circumstances. I have good evidence to believe that the destruction to my property resulted from the failure to assassinate me, which had been premeditated.

The white people in Grant parish and in adjoining parishes were assembling to resist the encroachments of these men. Ward and his desperadoes have been, and doubtless are now, prowling about the country taking horses, guns and whatever else they could lay their hands upon. Ward and his men, about a week ago, killed two peaceable colored men, and a perfect reign of terror is now instituted in Colfax. This is the first statement for any newspaper that I have made, except a letter I wrote the New Orleans *Republican*, which they refused to publish.

I will state that all of my personal property has been taken away and destroyed, that the coffin spoken of contained the body of a little girl, who died in Lake Charles, in 1867, which I had taken up and was going to re-inter in Red River; and that I learned in Alexandria, as I came through on Monday, that the negro mob had taken it out and burned it. A great many colored men were in Alexandria, who had run away from Colfax to keep out of the trouble.

The judge stated to us that he confidently believed that by this time the matter had reached its culmination, as both parties seemed determined to act, and that at once.

Fate of the Outlaws of Grant Parish.

In order that our readers may be informed of the origin and character of the tragical events, which within the past ten days have transpired in Middle Louisiana, we present a succinct resumé of the facts, as we have learned and understand them.

The parish of Grant, on Red River, has a population, white and black, of about 4500, which is nearly equally divided. In the election of November 4th, the declared return of the Forman board, composed of men of high character and in possession of all the returns, shows the vote to have been:

For Governor, McEnery (Fusion) 514—Kellogg (Rad.) 405; for Legislator, J. H. Hadnot (Fusion) 522—W. Ward (Rad.) 338; for Parish Judge, W. A. Lea (Fusion) 522—J. Osborn (Rad.) 404; for Clerk of Court, R. C. Register (Fusion) 424—R. Walker (Rad.) 589; and for Sheriff, D. W. Shaw (Fusion) 359—C. Nash, Rad.) 498.

Hadnot took his seat in the Louisiana Legislature, and Ward was admitted into the Bayonet Legislature.

The Lynch returning board, so-called, had no returns, and in this case did not assume to declare the election of the parish officers. Kellogg, however, undertook to appoint men to what he called vacancies, but they did not qualify according to law, and allowed the time stipulated by law to pass. Kellogg then commissioned officers who had really been elected, both Republican and Fusion, white and colored, except the Parish Judge, a Republican, who had already qualified.

It seems that Ward and other Radicals, being dissatisfied at not having all the offices, came down to New Orleans and remonstrated with Kellogg. Getting no satisfaction, they returned breathing threatenings, organized an armed company of negroes and took violent and forcible possession of the court-house at Colfax, a small village on the river and the county seat of Grant parish, and drove out the Sheriff, Nash. The Sheriff then attempted to collect a *posse comitatus* to recover possession of the public building thus lawlessly seized. A mass meeting of the white people was proposed to express in a quiet way their condemnation of this high-handed outrage, but in consequence of violent demonstrations of the armed negroes under Capt. Ward, Register, Flowers, Brantley, Snowden, Railey, Show, Green, etc., the assembly was given up. The posse failed to take the building or to disperse the mob. Threats were made by the ringleaders of organized negroes against those who were obnoxious—who had urged Kellogg to commission men not Republicans, or who become conspicuous in the effort to stop their lawless proceedings.

The negroes of Grant, having had their minds poisoned against the white people by the industrious inculcations of a few scalawags and carpet-baggers, malignant and bad men, were headed by turbulent and daring fellows. Ward and his gang had a short time before killed two of their own color with small provocation. Having occupied the village as a military post, they began to threaten the lives of political opponents, gave some of them a short time to leave the place on pain of death, shot at others, broke open and gutted dwelling houses, driving women out and robbing a female school teacher of her jewelry and effects, and even rifling the coffin of Judge Rutland's dead babe and flinging its body in the middle of the highway. They picketed the country for miles, seizing horses and firearms, and breathing threatening and slaughter, sought to inaugurate a reign of terror, to drive out their political opponents and white people, and to become masters of all they surveyed.

For a period these semi-barbarians had matters all their own way. But the white people, whom they had thus menaced, attacked and outraged in organized lawlessness, fortunately escaped to a safe distance.

Sheriff Nash got together a posse of armed men, to the number of a hundred and fifty, and returned to Colfax. The negroes meantime had fortified their ground with breast-works and prepared the Court-House for defense. When called on, last Sunday, to surrender the Court-House and disperse, they refused, and a fight followed. The result was, the entrenchments were taken, the Court-House was burned, and a number of negroes killed. Colfax is no longer a prey to the political desperadoes and marauders.

Unfortunately the authors and conductors of this nefarious business have so far escaped the condign punishment they deserve. The people of Louisiana are worn out with usurpation: Patience may cease to be a virtue. When it becomes established that there is sure danger to the plotters and managers of high-handed oppression, then affairs may be freed from pestilent and fraudulent interference. For the negro victims we feel sorry, and the occasion of this trouble is greatly to be deplored.

Grant Parish Troubles.

STATEMENT OF A CITIZEN.

Over fifty negroes were killed. Their bodies were lying around the field of action.

Previous to the engagement they had entrenched themselves and thoroughly fortified their position.

The battle with the people of the adjoining parishes lasted about four hours. At one time it was most severe.

It is believed that there were about ten white men killed and wounded.

The whites, before the fight took place, endeavored to avoid bloodshed. They raised a flag of truce. Mr. Nash, the sheriff of Grant parish, sent for L. Allen—a leader of the negroes—and begged him to disperse them. The reply of the latter was that they would fight to the last.

The white people then gave them an hour for the women and children to retire from the place of conflict, which they did.

Whilst the negroes were in possession of the town of Colfax, they committed many cruel acts against people of their own color. They sent different bodies of armed men to the plantations throughout the whole parish to compel the negroes to come into town and assist the revolutionists in defending the same. When resistance was made the leaders of the mutiny and their followers did not hesitate to resort to violence. Indeed, many of the poor, inoffensive field laborers, were unmercifully beaten.

The postmaster of Colfax—one Sam Cuney—a negro, formerly a member of the Legislature, was driven out of the town, and not allowed to attend to the duties of his office. The hostility against him arose from the fact that he would not assist the negroes in their work of violence.

All the negroes who sympathized with the whites were compelled to flee from the parish—their lives were threatened.

In the adjoining parish of Rapides the enmity of the negroes against the whites was so great that a war of races seemed to be inevitable. The most serious difficulties would have occurred there, had it not been for the defeat of the revolutionists at Colfax.

The negroes, since the reduction of this place, have confessed that they had a full military organization in Rapides. They were prepared to assist their friends in Grant parish. They even gave the names of some of their leaders.

Since the fight all the negroes belonging to the plantations in Grant parish have returned to work.

The Colfax Troubles.

WHAT THE SPECIAL CORRESPONDENT OF THE NEW YORK TIMES SAYS— A MALICIOUS SLANDER.

The following was received by telegraph this morning. It is a dispatch sent from this city to the New York *Times,* by its special correspondent. The American Press Association have circulated it. It would certainly be gratuitous on our part to stamp it as a malicious fabrication. That fact is too patent to the most casual reader:

NEW YORK, April 18.—The *Times* New Orleans special says late news from the scene of hostilities in Grant parish shows that the massacre of negroes in Colfax Court-House was more horrible and complete than first announced. It appears that not a single colored man was killed until all of them had surrendered to the whites, when one hundred unfortunate negroes were shot down in cold blood. After the butchery, the whites scattered in every direction. Many left for the Texas border. No arrests have yet been made. Grant parish being over two hundred miles from the mouth of Red River, and few boats leaving the city, the State authorities have great difficulty in procuring transportation to that region for the militia that has been ordered from this city. A small number of the State militia arrived at the scene the day after the massacre, and buried over sixty bodies of colored men.

Since the above was put in type the following was received:

WASHINGTON, April 18.—The following dispatch was received here last night:

"NEW ORLEANS, April 17,
"Hon. G. H. Williams, Attorney General:

Deputy Marshal De Klyne has returned from Colfax. He arrived there the day after the massacre. The details are horrible. The Democrats (white) of Grant parish attempted to oust the incumbent parish officers and failed, the Sheriff protecting the officers with a colored posse. Several days afterward, recruits from other parishes, to the number of three hundred, came to the assistance of the assailants, when they demanded the surrender of the colored posse. This was refused; an attack was made and the negroes were driven into the court-house. The court-house was then fired and the negroes slaughtered as they left the burning building. After resistance ceased, sixty-five negroes, terribly mutilated, were found dead near the court-house.

Thirty known to have been taken prisoners are said to have been shot after surrender and thrown into the river. Two of the assailants were wounded. The slaughter is greater than in the riot of '66, in this city. Will send report by mail.

G. R. BECKWITH,
United States Attorney.

102. *The Nation* and the Panic of 1873

The United States economy fell apart in 1873. Philadelphia financier Jay Cooke's Northern Pacific Railroad Company collapsed, taking Cooke's own bank and scores of others down with it. Many Americans, especially farmers, linked the panic with the revelations of corruption that involved railroad companies, state government, the federal government, and Ulysses Grant's administration. Farmers, workers, and reformers called for new public regulations on railroads and for an expanded currency to lessen the effects of the panic. Here, The Nation *cautions against those reforms.*

A Few Words to Railroad Moralists.

We hope the present crisis will not pass away without bringing back to their sober senses at least a considerable proportion of the gentlemen who have helped in the ravings of "The Farmers' Movement." We notice a good many of them just now among the number of those who are railing against the railroad builders and are ridiculing Jay Cooke for trying to construct the Northern Pacific, and Kenyon Cox for advancing money to the Canada Southern, and Sheppard Gandy and Francis Skiddy for helping the Missouri, Kansas, and Texas. They can hardly find language strong enough to show up the folly and wickedness of those who have been engaged in the construction of these new lines. The country did not want them, they say, and prudent men ought not to have risked their funds in them, and thus brought this ruin on us all. There are several newspapers, which ought to know better, engaged in the production of this rather senseless talk, and these we would remind of a few health-giving facts in this wise: When you engaged in the wild part of the farmers' movement and began to talk of railroads as if they were public property, and of confiscating all stock which you did not think was properly issued, and of completing the spoliation of the unfortunate stockholders, already begun by the directors, your attention was distinctly called to the fact that railroads were built in the main with private capital, and that they were highly hazardous enterprises, in which men would not enlist for the mere chance of the ordinary profits on capital. Even where they received grants of land, the land was not of any immediate value, and all return for the investment was sure to be remote and slow. But you were glad to get the roads built on any terms, and eagerly encouraged people to build them, or, in other words, to embark in what has to most of them proved a losing venture.

Now, those who took your advice did exactly what Messrs. Jay Cooke and Kenyon Cox have done. They incurred great risks for the chance of extraordinary gains, and you thought they had done right and had acted in a manly, public-spirited, and American way, for which you were very grateful; and it never occurred to you to call their railroads "wildcat" enterprises or denounce them as gamblers or squanderers of the public wealth. On the contrary, you honored them as great public benefactors. Far from trying to limit or define their interest in the railroads, too, you tried both by your oratory and legislation to make it as large and unrestricted as possible. So far from talking of arbitrarily restricting their profits, you tried to make them believe that their profits would go beyond the dreams of avarice, and, by way of assuring them against hostile State legislation, you flaunted the Dartmouth College Case in their faces, with some grateful reference to the immortal Webster who argued it.

You will, therefore, see at a glance that it does not do for you now to turn round and revile the men who have risked their all and lost it in following your foolish and uproarious advice. It is, in particular, highly unbecoming of you, to use a mild word, to dwell with so much solemnity on the fact that the new railroads which have brought these gentlemen down, run out into the wilderness, or to insist, as you are doing, that railroads ought not to be made except through populous districts, or made at all till they are sure to pay. You know perfectly well that every American railroad running east and west

Source: The Nation *no. 431 (October 2, 1873), 220–222.*

had, when it was first made, one end in the wilderness, and lay through a sparsely-settled and non-paying country; and indeed you know, too, that it is these railroads which have peopled the West and produced those enormous masses of products of which you boast so much in your speeches and articles; so that, if capitalists had always acted on the rules now laid down by you for the guidance of "railroad speculators," there would not be any West at all, and some of its finest cities would be collections of "three-quarter camps." Moreover; if half the stories you have been circulating during the last six months about the enormous profits of railroads and about their extortions be true, railroading is about the very best business in which unscrupulous and far-seeing capitalists could engage. There may be moral, but there are no financial objections to building or running them. If you had chosen to look at the figures, you could have satisfied yourselves then that what you are now shouting so loudly is strictly true—that they were not, except when well and honestly managed, by any means profitable, even in a very small number of cases; but instead of helping to improve their management, and have integrity and purity infused into it, you lifted up your voices in support of a scheme of virtual confiscation, which, if you were successful in carrying it out, would not only produce a financial convulsion, to which the one through which you are now passing would only bear the relation of a light breeze to a tornado, but would stop all railroad-building in the United States for twenty years to come, and make it a country which capitalists would avoid as they avoid Spain or Mexico.

But this is not all. The public cannot permit you in silence to hold, at one and the same time, two opposing theories of railroad property. You must not run with the hare and hold with the hounds. If you have no respect for your own intelligence, you must at least feign a little for ours. You were all maintaining one month ago that railroads were public highways, from which stockholders were only entitled to what the State chose to allow them, and on which, indeed, as some of you held, every citizen ought to have the right of running his own car. In that case, persons who spend money in making new ones are contributors to the public welfare on a great scale; and when they ruin themselves, it is our duty, not to abuse them as bad business men, but to honor and reward them as self-denying and unfortunate philanthropists. If, on the other hand, railroads are private property, to be managed, within certain wide limits, on business principles, for purposes of gain, the efforts you have been making during the last half-year to excite popular indignation against them, to cut down their earnings, and make the stockholders the objects of hostile legislation, have been, pardon us the expression, of a thoroughly nefarious character.

One thing more. We are all sickened, and fully as much as you appear to be, by the frauds and impurities of railroad management. We are generally agreed that these things have done much to bring about that distrust of railroad property which has worked the present panic. You have yourselves made a good deal of fuss about it. But up to this moment you have suggested no remedy. There is nothing that would do more for "the transportation problem," and other problems of even greater importance, than legislation that would bring railroads under the control of all the stockholders, and make directors feel their responsibility to the owner of *each share,* and smart for concealment and misrepresentation and malfeasance of all kinds. But so far as we have heard, you are not busying yourselves with this great reform at all. Your main object seems to be to plunder the unfortunate stockholder of the little the directors have left him, by making him carry goods at such rates as will relieve Western corn speculators from the consequences of their own folly and extravagance. While sympathizing with you on the dulness of "the off-year" in politics, and on the difficulty with which exciting and interesting topics have been discovered since the election, we submit to your judgment whether, even in ordinary times, our social and political condition is not too serious for such light and reckless handling of great interests as that in which you have been indulging, and whether the trepidation and anxiety which you see on every side of you at the present moment are not an illustration of the delicacy and complexity of the great machine which we have to manage, and by which we live, sufficient to convince you of the value of caution and sober-mindedness.

Paper Money as a Panacea.

A good many of the admirers of an irredeemable paper currency have begun to admit, sorrowfully but frankly, within the last few days, that whatever other virtues this currency may possess, it does not possess the power of preventing panics, for we are now passing through a well-developed panic in the midst of general soundness in trade. They are, however, a little hasty, it seems to us, in making this confession, because their experiment has not been tried under the necessary conditions. If they will recall their talk of a few years ago, they will find that the reason they gave for believing that inconvertible paper would protect us against crises was that, unlike gold, it could be increased indefinitely in quantity whenever the occasion called for it. Panics, they said, consist in the sudden withdrawal of money from circulation; if money can be supplied in sufficient quantity to fill up the vacuum, the panic passes away; when the money is gold coin this cannot be done, but if the money be paper it can be done. Therefore, in a country in which paper is the legal tender, all that is necessary to meet a panic is to issue more paper. This is in a measure true. If people are frightened, and hoard their legal tenders, the immediate inconvenience can be avoided by issuing more of them. But by each issue you stimulate the spirit of speculation out of which panics are bred, and you find not only that each successive panic has to be met by a larger issue, but that panics recur oftener, so that at last your remedy loses its power. It is, as has been often pointed out, the old story of "keeping up the strength" with brandy.

The friends of irredeemable paper have, however, no occasion to feel disheartened by what is now occurring. Their plan of restoring confidence cannot be tried, because nobody has been armed with power to try it. Nobody has any legal authority to stifle a panic by fresh issues. Our present currency is, therefore, even less capable of meeting a crisis like the present than gold, because it is more limited in quantity. Accordingly, we are witnessing the extraordinary spectacle of people hoarding paper money in a time of general distrust, and the banks, after thirteen years' suspension of specie payments, suspending paper payments also, and forcing the business world to use private checks and other "tokens." No higher compliment to the credit of the Government could well be paid than is paid by this spectacle; but, then, what a curious illustration it furnishes of the shiftlessness of our financial legislation!

The jubilation of the friends of specie payments is, however, almost as unjustifiable as the despair of the votaries of paper. There is no foundation that we know of for the notion, which many journals are preaching, that, if we had a redeemable currency, panics such as we are now witnessing would not occur. How anybody can propound such a doctrine in the teeth of the experience both of this country and of England, we do not understand. The greatest panics of the century have occurred on a "specie basis." The most radical and destructive panic of our history, that of 1857, occurred when all bank paper was as redeemable as bank paper is ever likely to be. Do not let us, therefore, while exposing the vices of our present currency, pretend, like quacks, that we know of a financial panacea which will make such crises as that through which we are now passing impossible. There is no such panacea in trade any more than in medicine. Panics have their origin in human nature, and will recur as long as man remains man; we may render them rarer or less destructive, but we cannot entirely prevent them, and this for reasons that may be easily stated. They admit of classification based on their extent, but they are in their origin and nature all the same. They all have their origin in a sudden fear that debtors will not pay what they owe, whether the debtors be banks or private individuals. Sometimes this fear arises out of the sudden discovery that production in some particular field has been overdone, or that undue expectations have been entertained as to the value of certain commodities, or out of the sudden discovery of weakness or dishonesty in some concern of unusually high character; but the fear in every case produces precisely the same effect: it leads men instantly to stop from entering into contracts and to take into their personal possession—or, in other words, to hoard—all the money they can command. The result is scarcity of money and paralysis of trade. In countries like England and America, in which nearly all business is done on credit and banks of issue supply a large proportion of the circulating medium, and in which the industrial activity is very great, of course the results of such occurrences are terribly disastrous.

Now, there is only one way of meeting such crises, and that is by pouring into the banks such an additional supply of money as will keep the wheels of business revolving and prevent any serious pinch being felt, until the country has got over its fright. This has been proved again and again, particularly in English experience, in which panics have been more common than in ours. It was peculiarly well illustrated by the panic of 1866 in London, which in many respects resembled that through which we are now passing, inasmuch as it was caused by the sudden failure of Overend, Gurney & Co., a house in whose wealth and honor the public had the utmost confidence. There was at once a wild rush of depositors to banks and trust companies, and people began shouting, "If the Gurneys are not sound, whom can we trust?" just as people here have been shouting, "If we cannot trust Jay Cooke & Co. and the Union Trust Company, and so on, whom can we trust?" The Government at once permitted the Bank of England to issue notes beyond the $70,000,000 limit, and the result was the panic ceased as if by magic, although in point of fact the Bank did not issue any new paper whatever. Now, what happened in this case was simply this: The Bank said to the public, that hoard as it might, or withdraw its deposits as it might, the vacuum would be filled by fresh funds, and the merchants would obtain their discounts all the same, until the fright was over. Everybody, therefore, feeling satisfied that he could have his money if he wanted it, ceased to want it. Of course a "credit panic," as it has been called — that is, a panic like that of 1846 in England, caused by a tremendous failure in the harvest, or like that of 1857 here, caused by general over-trading, and producing widespread insolvency — cannot be checked by a summary process of this kind, but it may be greatly mitigated. This amounts to saying that a panic is really a mental rather than an economical phenomenon, and has to be dealt with by remedies addressed to the imagination, which is the plain truth of the matter, although it is obscured by a good deal of financial cant.

No matter, therefore, what currency we may have, there must be lodged somewhere in our banking system the power to meet panics by temporary expansion, and it must be a power capable of being used promptly and with decision. In England, it is lodged in the Bank of England, which, under letters of license from the Government, either prevents panics or prevents their spread. Sometimes this is done, as in 1846 and 1857, by affording timely aid to houses such as Brown, Shipley & Co. and George Peabody, whose fall would spread universal terror and confusion. It is safe to say that, under such a system here, either Jay Cooke & Co. would have been helped through their difficulties, or the stoppage of Henry Clews & Co., which renewed the alarm on Tuesday, would have been prevented. Sometimes, of course, as in the case of Overend, Gurney & Co., the affairs of even a great house may get into such a condition that, however great the dismay its ruin may be likely to cause, it ought not to be prevented. When this occurs, the only thing to be done is to confine the panic within as narrow limits as possible.

Now, there is little chance, even if it were desirable, of the establishment of any great regulator, such as the Bank of England, in this country. It could not fix the rate of interest for the whole country, as the Bank of England does. But it seems very clear that the proportion of paper to coin in our circulating medium is to be increasingly large, and that, in other words, the welfare and prosperity of the country, and its immunity from great commercial disasters, will every year depend more and more on the condition of our banking system. If panics are to be repressed, and the legitimate business of the community to be carried through trying crises, it is the banks which must do it; and to do it, they must be armed with the power, under certain circumstances and conditions, to increase the volume of the currency. At present, our banking system, elaborate as it is, has not only no provision for one of the most dreaded contingencies of commercial civilization, but it is actually forced into restricting the supply of money when money is most needed. When the recent demand for a temporary supply of more money came upon us, it was found that nobody had authority to supply it; and, though the conduct of the banks has been admirable, they have shown that they are, under the present system, utterly unequal to the occasion, and Secretary Richardson's attempt to relieve them by the sale of bonds has simply resulted in adding $13,000,000 more greenbacks to the stock of the hoarders. It ought not to be necessary, at this time of day, to hold long consultations as to what ought to be done when the alarm caused by the failure of a great house threatens us with a commercial crisis. The machinery for dealing with such a contingency ought to exist, and be ready for instant use, as a fire-engine is. If it had been, the present panic would have ended on the second day. It is to be hoped that the supply of some such machinery will be one of the first pieces of work done by Congress next session, but it is as well to say that nothing of the kind can be devised in which the redeemability of paper does not play the leading part. No expansion on the part of banks can be permitted which is not checked and controlled by liability to have the paper returned for gold when the storm is passed; and it is a fair question whether some such restriction as the obligation to charge 10 per cent. discount, recently proposed by Mr. Lowe, on all unusual issues, ought not also to be added. The way in which the banks of this city have combined during the present crisis affords also a useful hint towards the construction of the *modus operandi*. The whole subject is one of vast importance, and strikingly resembles that on which a good deal of public attention has recently been bestowed — the best mode of saving cities from fire. It cannot be got rid of by abusing brokers and speculators. Brokers and speculators there will always be; and, when they fail or miscarry, they spread ruin among the innocent. The business of government is not to make the world perfect, but to make its imperfections as innocuous as possible.

103. The Destruction of the Plains Buffalo, 1870s

The Plains Indians depended on the buffalo for their survival. In the 1860s and 1870s, railroad construction and the expansion of white settlement into the plains threatened the buffalo with extinction. Men like Buffalo Bill Cody made the slaughter of buffalo into a form of entertainment, and white men began picking off buffalo by the tens of thousands, sometimes from the safety of a moving railroad car. Anglo-Americans knew full well that the elimination of the buffalo also meant the subjugation of the Plains Indians, with whom Anglos had been fighting for decades. In these pieces, Old Lady Horse and Pretty Shield reflect, from a later perspective, on the loss of the buffalo.

A. Old Lady Horse

Everything the Kiowas had came from the buffalo. Their tipis were made of buffalo hides, so were their clothes and moccasins. They ate buffalo meat. Their containers were made of hide, or of bladders or stomachs. The buffalo were the life of the Kiowas.

Most of all, the buffalo was part of the Kiowa religion. A white buffalo calf must be sacrificed in the Sun Dance. The priests used parts of the buffalo to make their prayers when they healed people or when they sang to the powers above.

So, when the white men wanted to build railroads, or when they wanted to farm or raise cattle, the buffalo still protected the Kiowas. They tore up the railroad tracks and the gardens. They chased the cattle off the ranges. The buffalo loved their people as much as the Kiowas loved them.

There was war between the buffalo and the white men. The white men built forts in the Kiowa country, and the woolly-headed buffalo soldiers [the Tenth Cavalry, made up of Negro troops] shot the buffalo as fast as they could, but the buffalo kept coming on, coming on, even into the post cemetery at Fort Sill. Soldiers were not enough to hold them back.

Then the white men hired hunters to do nothing but kill the buffalo. Up and down the plains those men ranged, shooting sometimes as many as a hundred buffalo a day. Behind them came the skinners with their wagons. They piled the hides and bones into the wagons until they were full, and then took their loads to the new railroad stations that were being built, to be shipped east to the market. Sometimes there would be a pile of bones as high as a man, stretching a mile along the railroad track.

The buffalo saw that their day was over. They could protect their people no longer. Sadly, the last remnant of the great herd gathered in council, and decided what they would do.

The Kiowas were camped on the north side of Mount Scott, those of them who were still free to camp. One young woman got up very early in the morning. The dawn mist was still rising from Medicine Creek, and as she looked across the water, peering through the haze, she saw the last buffalo herd appear like a spirit dream.

Straight to Mount Scott the leader of the herd walked. Behind him came the cows and their calves, and the few young males who had survived. As the woman watched, the face of the mountain opened.

Inside Mount Scott the world was green and fresh, as it had been when she was a small girl. The rivers ran clear, not red. The wild plums were in blossom, chasing the red buds up the inside slopes. Into this world of beauty the buffalo walked, never to be seen again.

Source: Alice Marriott and Carol K. Rachlin, *American Indian Mythology* (New York: Thomas Y. Crowell, 1968), 173–177. Reprinted in Colin Calloway, ed., *Our Hearts Fell to the Ground: Plains Indian Views of How the West Was Lost* (Boston: Bedford Book of St. Martin's Press, 1996), 129–130.

B. Pretty Shield

"Tst, tst, tst! I haven't seen a buffalo in more than forty years," she said slowly, as though she believed herself to be dreaming.

"The happiest days of my life were spent following the buffalo herds over our beautiful country. My mother and father and Goes-ahead, my man, were all kind, and we were so happy. Then, when my children came I believed I had everything that was good on this world. There were always so many, many buffalo, plenty of good fat meat for everybody.

"Since my man, Goes-ahead, went away twelve snows ago my heart has been falling down. I am old now, and alone, with so many grandchildren to watch," . . .

"Tell me what happened when the buffalo went away," I urged.

"Sickness came, strange sickness that nobody knew about, when there was no meat," she said, covering her face with both hands as though to shut out the sight of suffering. "My daughter stepped into a horse's track that was deep in the dried clay, and hurt her ankle. I could not heal her; nobody could. The white doctor told me that the same sickness that makes people cough themselves to death was in my daughter's ankle. I did not believe it, and yet she died, leaving six little children. Then my other daughter died, and left hers. These things would not have happened if we Crows had been living as we were intended to live. But how could we live in the old way when everything was gone?

"Ahh, my heart fell down when I began to see dead buffalo scattered all over our beautiful country, killed and skinned, and left to rot by white men, many, many hundreds of buffalo. The first I saw of this was in the Judith basin. The whole country there smelled of rotting meat. Even the flowers could not put down the bad smell. Our hearts were like stones. And yet nobody believed, even then, that the white man could kill *all* the buffalo. Since the beginning of things there had always been so many! Even the Lacota, bad as their hearts were for us, would not do such a thing as this; nor the Cheyenne, nor the Arapahoe, nor the Pecunnie; and yet the white man did this, even when he did not want the meat.

"We believed for a long time that the buffalo would again come to us; but they did not. We grew hungry and sick and afraid, all in one. Not believing their own eyes our hunters rode very far looking for buffalo, so far away that even if they had found a herd we could not have reached it in half a moon. 'Nothing; we found nothing,' they told us; and then, hungry, they stared at the empty plains, as though dreaming. After this their hearts were no good any more. If the Great White Chief in Washington had not given us food we should have been wiped out without even a chance to fight for ourselves.

"And then white men began to fence the plains so that we could not travel; and anyhow there was now little good in traveling, nothing to travel for. We began to stay in one place, and to grow lazy and sicker all the time. Our men had fought hard against our enemies, holding them back from our beautiful country by their bravery; but now, with everything else going wrong, we began to be whipped by weak foolishness. Our men, our leaders, began to drink the white man's whisky, letting it do their thinking. Because we were used to listening to our chiefs in the buffalo days, the days of war and excitement, we listened to them now; and we got whipped. Our wise-ones became fools, and drank the white man's whisky. But what else was there for us to do? We knew no other way than to listen to our chiefs and head men. Our old men used to be different; even our children were different when the buffalo were here."

Source: Frank B. Linderman, *Pretty-shield, Medicine Woman of the Crows* (Lincoln: University of Nebraska Press, 1972), 248–251. Reprinted in Colin Calloway, ed., *Our Hearts Fell to the Ground: Plains Indian Views of How the West Was Lost* (Boston: Bedford Book of St. Martin's Press, 1996), 130–132.

Chapter XVII

An Economy Transformed: The Rise of Big Business, 1877–1887

104. William Graham Sumner, "On a New Philosophy: That Poverty is the Best Policy"

William Graham Sumner was a famous professor of political and social science at Yale University. A vigorous believer in the theory of evolution and a militant advocate of laissez faire, he opposed all measures that threatened to interfere with competitive individualism.

It is commonly asserted that there are in the United States no classes, and any allusion to classes is resented. On the other hand, we constantly read and hear discussions of social topics in which the existence of social classes is assumed as a simple fact. "The poor," "the weak," "the laborers," are expressions which are used as if they had exact and well-understood definition. Discussions are made to bear upon the assumed rights, wrongs, and misfortunes of certain social classes; and all public speaking and writing consists, in a large measure, of the discussion of general plans for meeting the wishes of classes of people who have not been able to satisfy their own desires. These classes are sometimes discontented, and sometimes not. Sometimes they do not know that anything is amiss with them until the "friends of humanity" come to them with offers of aid. Sometimes they are discontented and envious. They do not take their achievements as a fair measure of their rights. They do not blame themselves or their parents for their lot, as compared with that of other people. Sometimes they claim that they have a right to everything of which they feel the need for their happiness on earth. To make such a claim against God and Nature would, of course, be only to say that we claim a right to live on earth if we can. But God and Nature have ordained the chances and conditions of life on earth once for all. The case cannot be reopened. We cannot get a revision of the laws of human life. We are absolutely shut up to the need and duty, if we would learn how to live happily, of investigating the laws of Nature, and deducing the rules of right living in the world as it is. These are very wearisome and commonplace tasks. They consist in labor and self-denial repeated over and over again in learning and doing. When the people whose claims we are considering are told to apply themselves to these tasks they become irritated and feel almost insulted. They formulate their claims as rights against society—that is, against some other men. In their view they have a right, not only to *pursue* happiness, but to get it; and if they fail to get it, they think they have a claim to the aid of other men—that is, to the labor and self-denial of other men—to get it for them. They find orators and poets who tell them that they have grievances, so long as they have unsatisfied desires.

Now, if there are groups of people who have a claim to other people's labor and self-denial, and if there are other people whose labor and self-denial are liable to be claimed by the first groups, then there certainly are "classes," and classes of the oldest and most vicious type. For a man who can command another man's labor and self-denial for the support of his own existence is a privileged person of the highest species conceivable on earth. Princes and paupers meet on this plane, and no other men are on it all. On the other hand, a man whose labor and self-denial may be diverted from his maintenance to

---

Source: William Graham Sumner, "On a New Philosophy: That Poverty is the Best Policy." *What Social Classes Owe to Each Other.* Public Domain Reprint.

that of some other man is not a free man, and approaches more or less toward the position of a slave. Therefore we shall find that, in all the notions which we are to discuss, this elementary contradiction, that there are classes and that there are not classes, will produce repeated confusion and absurdity. We shall find that, in our efforts to eliminate the old vices of class government, we are impeded and defeated by new products of the worst class theory. We shall find that all the schemes for producing equality and obliterating the organization of society produce a new differentiation based on the worst possible distinction—the right to claim and the duty to give one man's effort for another man's satisfaction. We shall find that every effort to realize equality necessitates a sacrifice of liberty.

It is very popular to pose as a "friend of humanity," or a "friend of the working classes." The character, however, is quite exotic in the United States. It is borrowed from England, where some men, otherwise of small account, have assumed it with great success and advantage. Anything which has a charitable sound and a kind-hearted tone generally passes without investigation, because it is disagreeable to assail it. Sermons, essays, and orations assume a conventional standpoint with regard to the poor, the weak, etc.; and it is allowed to pass as an unquestioned doctrine in regard to social classes that "the rich" ought to "care for the poor"; that Churches especially ought to collect capital from the rich and spend it for the poor; that parishes ought to be clusters of institutions by means of which one social class should perform its duties to another; and that clergymen, economists, and social philosophers have a technical and professional duty to devise schemes for "helping the poor." The preaching in England used all to be done to the poor—that they ought to be contented with their lot and respectful to their betters. Now, the greatest part of the preaching in America consists in injunctions to those who have taken care of themselves to perform their assumed duty to take care of others. Whatever may be one's private sentiments, the fear of appearing cold and hard-hearted causes these conventional theories of social duty and these assumptions of social fact to pass unchallenged.

Let us notice some distinctions which are of prime importance to a correct consideration of the subject which we intend to treat. Certain ills belong to the hardships of human life. They are natural. They are part of the struggle with Nature for existence. We cannot blame our fellow-men for our share of these. My neighbor and I are both struggling to free ourselves from these ills. The fact that my neighbor has succeeded in this struggle better than I constitutes no grievance for me. Certain other ills are due to the malice of men, and to the imperfections or errors of civil institutions. These ills are an object of agitation, and a subject for discussion. The former class of ills is to be met only by manly effort and energy; the latter may be corrected by associated effort. The former class of ills is constantly grouped and generalized, and made the object of social schemes. We shall see, as we go on, what that means. The second class of ills may fall on certain social classes, and reform will take the form of interference by other classes in favor of that one. The last fact is, no doubt, the reason why people have been led, not noticing distinctions, to believe that the same method was applicable to the other class of ills. The distinction here made between the ills which belong to the struggle for existence and those which are due to the faults of human institutions is of prime importance.

It will also be important, in order to clear up our ideas about the notions which are in fashion, to note the relation of the economic to the political significance of assumed duties of one class to another. That is to say, we may discuss the question whether one class owes duties to another by reference to the economic effects which will be produced on the classes and society; or we may discuss the political expediency of formulating and enforcing rights and duties respectively between the parties. In the former case we might assume that the givers of aid were willing to give it, and we might discuss the benefit or mischief of their activity. In the other case we must assume that some at least of those who were forced to give aid did so unwillingly. Here, then, there would be a question of rights. The question whether voluntary charity is mischievous or not is one thing; the question whether legislation which forces one man to aid another is right and wise, as well as economically beneficial, is quite another question. Great confusion and consequent error is produced by allowing these two questions to become entangled in the discussion. Especially we shall need to notice the attempts to apply legislative methods of reform to the ills which belong to the order of Nature.

There is no possible definition of "a poor man." A pauper is a person who cannot earn his living; whose producing powers have fallen positively below his necessary consumption; who cannot, therefore, pay his way. A human society needs the active co-operation and productive energy of every person in it. A man who is present as a consumer, yet who does not contribute either by land, labor, or capital to the work of society, is a burden. On no sound political theory ought such a person to share in the political power of the State. He drops out of the ranks of workers and producers. Society must support him. It accepts the burden, but he must be cancelled from the ranks of the rulers likewise. So much for the pauper. About him no more need be said. But he is not the "poor man." The "poor man" is an elastic term, under which any number of social fallacies may be hidden.

Neither is there any possible defamation of 'the' weak." Some are weak in one way, and some in another; and those who are weak in one sense are strong in another. In general, however, it may be said that those whom humanitarians and philanthropists call the weak are the ones through whom the productive and conservative forces of society are wasted. They constantly neutralize and destroy the finest efforts of the wise and industrious, and are a dead-weight on the society in all its struggles to realize any better things. Whether the people who mean no harm, but are weak in the essential powers necessary to the performance of one's duties in life, or those who are malicious and vicious, do the more mischief, is a question not easy to answer.

Under the names of the poor and the weak, the negligent, shiftless, inefficient, silly, and imprudent are fastened upon the industrious and prudent as a responsibility and a duty. On the one side, the terms are extended to cover the idle, intemperate, and vicious, who, by the combination, gain credit which they do not deserve, and which they could not get if they stood alone. On the other hand, the terms are extended to include wage-receivers of the humblest rank, who are degraded by the combination. The reader who desires to guard himself against fallacies should always scrutinize the terms "poor" and "weak" as used, so as to see which or how many of these classes they are made to cover.

The humanitarians, philanthropists, and reformers, looking at the facts of life as they present themselves, find enough which is sad and unpromising in the condition of many members of society. They see wealth and poverty side by side. They note great inequality of social position and social chances. They eagerly set about the attempt to account for what they see, and to devise schemes for remedying what they do not like. In their eagerness to recommend the less fortunate classes to pity and consideration they forget all about the rights of other classes; they gloss over all the faults of the classes in question, and they exaggerate their misfortunes and their virtues. They invent new theories of property, distorting rights and perpetuating injustice, as anyone is sure to do who sets about the readjustment of social relations with the interests of one group distinctly before his mind, and the interests of all other groups thrown into the background.

When I have read certain of these discussions I have thought that it must be quite disreputable to be respectable, quite dishonest to own property, quite unjust to go one's own way and earn one's own living, and that the only really admirable person was the good-for-nothing. The man who by his own effort raises himself above poverty appears, in these discussions, to be of no account. The man who has done nothing to raise himself above poverty finds that the social doctors flock about him, bringing the capital which they have collected from the other class, and promising him the aid of the State to give him what the other had to work for. In all these schemes and projects the organized intervention of society through the State is either planned or hoped for, and the State is thus made to become the protector and guardian of certain classes. The agents who are to direct the State action are, of course, the reformers and philanthropists. Their schemes, therefore, may always be reduced to this type—that A and B decide what C shall do for D. It will be interesting to inquire, at a later period of our discussion, who C is, and what the effect is upon him of all these arrangements. In all the discussions attention is concentrated on A and B, the noble social reformers, and on D, the "poor man." I call C the Forgotten Man, because I have never seen that any notice was taken of him in any of the discussions. When we have disposed of A, B, and D we can better appreciate the case of C, and I think that we shall find that he deserves our attention, for the worth of his character and the magnitude of his unmerited burdens. Here it may suffice to observe that, on the theories of the social philosophers to whom I have referred, we should get a new maxim of judicious living: Poverty is the best policy. If you get wealth, you will have to support other people; if you do not get wealth, it will be the duty of other people to support you.

No doubt one chief reason for the unclear and contradictory theories of class relations lies in the fact that our society, largely controlled in all its organization by one set of doctrines, still contains survivals of old social theories which are totally inconsistent with the former. In the Middle Ages men were united by custom and prescription into associations, ranks, guilds, and communities of various kinds. These ties endured as long as life lasted. Consequently society was dependent, throughout all its details, on status, and the tie, or bond, was sentimental. In our modern state, and in the United States more than anywhere else, the social structure is based on contract, and status is of the least importance. Contract, however, is rational—even rationalistic. It is also realistic, cold, and matter-of-fact. A contract relation is based on a sufficient reason, not on custom or prescription. It is not permanent. It endures only so long as the reason for it endures. In a state based on contract sentiment is out of place in any public or common affairs. It is relegated to the sphere of private and personal relations, where it depends not at all on class types, but on personal acquaintance and personal estimates. The sentimentalists among us always seize upon the survivals of the old order. They want to save them and restore them. Much of the loose chinking also which troubles us in our social discussions arises from the fact that men do not distinguish the elements of status and of contract which may be found in our society.

Whether social philosophers think it desirable or not, it is out of the question to go back to status or to the sentimental relations which once united baron and retainer, master and servant, teacher and pupil, comrade and comrade. That we have lost some grace and elegance is undeniable. That life once held more poetry and romance is true enough. But it seems impossible that any one who has studied the matter should doubt that we have gained immeasurably, and that our farther gains lie in going forward, not in going backward. The feudal ties can never be restored. If they could be restored they would bring back personal caprice, favoritism, sycophancy, and intrigue. A society based on contract, is a society of free and independent men, who form ties without favor or obligation, and cooperate without cringing or intrigue. A society based on contract, therefore, gives the utmost room and chance for *individual development, and for all the self-reliance and dignity of a free man.* That a society of free men, cooperating under contract, is by far the strongest society which has ever yet existed; that no such society has ever yet developed the full measure of strength of which it is capable; and that the only social improvements which are now conceivable lie in the direction of more complete realization of a society of free men united by contract, are points which cannot be controverted. It follows, however, that one man, in a free state, cannot claim help from, and cannot be charged to give help to, another. To understand the full meaning of this assertion it will be worthwhile to see what a free democracy is.

---

105. CHIEF JOSEPH, "AN INDIAN'S VIEWS OF INDIAN AFFAIRS," 1879

Chief Joseph was a leader of the Nez Pereés people, one of the greatest Indian strategists. Upon his father's death in 1873, Joseph became chief of the "non-reality" tribe who refused to cede their territories to the government. He died in 1904 on the Coville Reservation, far from the land he fought to keep for this people.

Introduction

I wish that I had words at command in which to express adequately the interest with which I have read the extraordinary narrative which follows, and which I have the privilege of introduction to the readers of this "Review." I feel, however, that this *apologia* is so boldly marked by the charming *naiveté* and tender pathos which characterize the red-man, that it needs no introduction, much less any authentication; while in its smothered fire, in its deep sense of eternal righteousness and of present evil, and in its hopeful longings for the coming of a better time, this Indian chief's appeal reminds us of one of the old Hebrew prophets of the days of the captivity.

I have no special knowledge of the history of the Nez Pereés, the Indian whose tale of sorrow Chief Joseph so pathetically tells—my Indian missions lying in a part at the West quite distant from their old home—and am not competent to judge their case upon its merits. The chief's narrative is, of course, *ex parte*, and many of his statements would no doubt be ardently disputed. General Howard, for instance, can hardly receive justice at his hands, so well known is he for his friendship to the Indian and for his distinguished success in pacifying some of the most desperate.

Source: Young, Joseph, "An Indian's View of Indian Affairs." *The North American Review,* 1879. Vol. XCCVIII, No. 269. Public Domain Reprint.

It should be remembered, too, in justice to the army, that it is rarely called upon to interfere in Indian affairs until the relations between the Indians and the whites have reached a desperate condition, and when the situation of affairs has become so involved and feeling on both sides runs so high that perhaps only more than human forbearance would attempt to solve the difficulty by disentangling the knot and not by cutting it.

Nevertheless, the chief's narrative is marked by so much candor, and so careful is he to quality his statements, when qualification seems necessary, that every reader will give him credit for speaking his honest, even should they be thought by some to be mistaken, convictions. The chief in his treatment of his defense, reminds one of those lawyers of whom we have heard that their splendid success was gained, not by disputation, but simply by their lucid and straightforward statement of their case. That he is something of a strategist as well as an advocate appears from this description of an event which occurred shortly after the breaking out of hostilities: "We crossed over Salmon River, hoping General Howard would follow. We were not disappointed. He did follow us, and we got between him and his supplies, and cut him off for three days." Occasionally the reader comes upon touches of those sentiments and feelings which at once establish a sense of kinship between all who possess them. Witness his description of his desperate attempts to rejoin his wife and children when a sudden dash of General Miles's soldiers had cut the Indian camp in two: "Almost seventy men, myself among them, were cut off. . . . I thought of my wife and children, who were now surrounded by soldiers, and I resolved to go to them. With a prayer in my mouth to the Great Spirit Chief who rules above, I dashed unarmed through the line of soldiers. . . . My clothes were cut to pieces, my horse was wounded, but I was not hurt." And again, when he speaks of his father's death: "I saw he was dying. I took his hand in mine. He said: 'My son, my body is returning to my mother Earth, and my spirit is going very soon to see the Great Spirit Chief. . . . A few more years and the white men will be all around you. They have their eyes on this land. My son, never forget my dying words. This country holds your father's body—never sell the bones of your father and your mother.' I pressed my father's hand and told him I would protect his grave with my life. My father smiled, and passed away to the spirit-land. I buried him in that beautiful valley of Winding Waters. I love that land more than all the rest of the world. A man who would not love his father's grave is worse than a wild animal."

His appeals to the natural rights of man are surprisingly fine, and, however some may despise them as the utterances of an Indian, they are just those which, in our Declaration of Independence, have been most admired. "We are all sprung from a woman," he says, "although we are unlike in many things. You are as you were made, and, as you were made, you can remain. We are just as we were made by the Great Spirit, and you can not change us: then why should children of one another quarrel? Why should one try to cheat another? I do not believe that the Great Spirit Chief gave one kind of men the right to tell another kind of men what they must do."

But I will not detain the readers of the "Review" from the pleasure of perusing for themselves Chief Joseph's statement longer than is necessary to express the hope that those who have time for no more will at least read its closing paragraph, and to remark that the narrative brings clearly out these facts which ought to be regarded as well-recognized principles in dealing with the red-man:

1. The folly of any mode of treatment of the Indian which is not based upon a cordial and operative acknowledgment of his rights as our *fellow man.*

2. The danger of riding rough-shod over a people who are capable of high enthusiasm, who know and value their national rights, and are brave enough to defend them.

3. The liability to want of harmony between different departments and different officials of our complex Government, from which it results that, while many promises are made to the Indians, few of them are kept. It is a home-thrust when Chief Joseph says: "The white people have too many chiefs. They do not understand each other. . . . I can not understand how the Government sends a man out to fight us, as it did General Miles, and then break his word. Such a Government has something wrong about it."

4. The unwisdom, in most cases in dealing with Indians, of which may be termed *military short-cuts,* instead of patient discussion, explanations, persuasion, and reasonable concessions.

5. The absence in an Indian tribe of any truly representative body competent to make a treaty which shall be binding upon all the bands. The failure to recognize this fact has been the source of endless difficulties. Chief Joseph, in this case, did not consider a treaty binding which his band had not agreed to, no matter how many other bands had signed it; and so it has been in many other cases.

6. Indian chiefs, however able and influential, are really without power, and for this reason, as well as others,

the Indians, when by the march of events they are brought into intimate relations with the whites, should at the earliest practicable moment be given the support and protection of our Government and of our law; not *local* law, however, which is apt to be the result of *special* legislative, adopted solely in the interest of the stronger race.

WILLIAM H. HARE, *Missionary Bishop of Niobrara.*

My friends, I have been asked to show you my heart. I am glad to have a chance to do so. I want the white people to understand my people. Some of you think an Indian is like a wild animal. This is a great mistake. I will tell you all about our people, and then you can judge whether an Indian is a man or not. I believe much trouble and blood would be saved if we opened our hearts more. I will tell you in my way how the Indian sees things. The white man has more words to tell you how they look to him, but it does not require many words to speak the truth. What I have to say will come from my heart, and I will speak with a straight tongue. Ah-cum-kin-i-ma-me-hut (the Great Spirit) is looking at me, and will hear me.

My name is In-mut-too-yah-lat-lat (Thunder traveling over the Mountains). I am chief of the Wallam-watkin band of Chute-pa-lu, or Nez Pereés (nose-pierced Indians). I was born in eastern Oregon, thirty-eight winters ago. My father was chief before me. When a young man, he was called Joseph by Mr. Spaulding, a missionary. He died a few years ago. There was no stain on his hands of the blood of a white man. He left a good name on the earth. He advised me well for my people.

Our fathers gave us many laws, which they had learned from their fathers. These laws were good. They told us to treat all men as they treated us; that we should never be the first to break a bargain; that it was a disgrace to tell a lie; that we should speak only the truth; that it was a shame for one man to take from another his wife, or his property without paying for it. We were taught to believe that the Great Spirit sees and hears everything, and that he never forgets; that hereafter he will give every man a spirit-home according to his deserts: if he has been a good man, he will have a good home; if he has been a bad man, he will have a bad home. This I believe, and all my people believe the same.

We did not know there were other people besides the Indian until about one hundred years ago, when some men with white faces came to our country. They brought many things with them to trade for furs and skins. They brought tobacco, which was new to us. They brought guns with flint stones on them, which frightened our women and children. Our people could not talk with these white-faced men, but they used signs which all people understand. These men were Frenchmen, and they called our people "Nez Pereés," because they wore rings in their noses for ornaments. Although very few of our people wear them now, we are still called by the same name. These French trappers said a great many things to our fathers, which have been planted in our hearts. Some were good for us, but some were bad. Our people were divided in opinion about these men. Some thought they taught more bad than good. An Indian respects a brave man, but he despises a coward. He loves a straight tongue, but he hates a forked tongue. The French trappers told us some truths and some lies.

The first white men of your people who came to our country were named Lewis and Clarke. They also brought many things that our people had never seen. They talked straight, and our people gave them a great feast, as a proof that their hearts were friendly. These men were very kind. They made presents to our chiefs and our people made presents to them. We had a great many horses, of which we gave them what they needed, and they gave us guns and tobacco in return. All the Nez Pereés made friends with Lewis and Clarke, and agreed to let them pass through their country, and never to make war on white men. This promise the Nez Pereés have never broken. No white man can accuse them of bad faith, and speak with a straight tongue. It has always been the pride of the Nez Pereés that they were the friends of the white men. When my father was a young man there came to our country a white man (Rev. Mr. Spaulding) who talked spirit law. He won the affections of our people because he spoke good things to them. At first he did not say anything about white men wanting to settle on our lands. Nothing was said about that until about twenty winters ago, when a number of white people came into our country and built houses and made farms. At first our people made no complaint. They thought there was room enough for all to live in peace, and said they were learning many things from the white men that seemed to be good. But we soon found that the white men were growing rich very fast, and were greedy to possess everything the Indian had. My father was the first to see through the schemes of the white men, and he warned his tribe to be careful about trading with them. He had suspicion of men who seemed so anxious to make money. I was a boy then, but I remember well my father's caution. He had sharper eyes than the rest of our people.

Next there came a white officer (Governor Stevens), who invited all the Nez Pereés to a treaty council. After the council was opened he made known his heart. He said there were a great many white people in the country, and many more would come; that he wanted the land marked out so that the Indians and white men could be separated. If they were to live in peace it was necessary, he said, that the Indians should have a country set apart for them, and in that country they must stay. My father, who represented his band, refused to have anything to do with the council, because he wished to be a free man. He claimed that no man owned any part of the earth, and a man could not sell what he did not own.

Mr. Spaulding took hold of my father's arm and said, "Come and sign the treaty." My father pushed him away, and said: "Why do you ask me to sign away my country? It is your business to talk to us about spirit matters, and not to talk to us about parting with our land." Governor Stevens urged my father to sign his treaty, but he refused. "I will not sign your paper," he said; "you go where you please, so do I; you are not a child, I am no child; I can think for myself. No man can think for me. I have no other home than this. I will not give it up to any man. My people would have no home. Take away your paper. I will not touch it with my hand."

My father left the council. Some of the chiefs at the other bands of the Nez Pereés signed the treaty, and then Governor Stevens gave them presents of blankets. My father cautioned his people to take no presents, for "after a while," he said, "they will claim that you have accepted pay for your country." Since that time four bands of the Nez Pereés have received annuities from the United States. My father was invited to many councils, and they tried hard to make him sign the treaty, but he was firm as the rock, and would not sign away his home. His refusal caused a difference among the Nez Pereés.

Eight years later (1863) was the next treaty council. A chief called Lawyer, because he was a great talker, took the lead in this council, and sold nearly all the Nez Pereés country. My father was not there. He said to me: "When you go into council with the white man, always remember your country. Do not give it away. The white man will cheat you out of your home. I have taken no pay from the United States. I have never sold our land." In this treaty Lawyer acted without authority from our band. He had no right to sell the Wallowa (*winding water*) country. That had always belonged to my father's own people, and the other bands had never disputed our right to it. No other Indians ever claimed Wallowa.

In order to have all people understand how much land we owned, my father planted poles around it and said:

"Inside is the home of my people—the white men may take the land outside. Inside this boundary all our people were born. It circles around the graves of our fathers, and we will never give up these graves to any man."

The United States claimed that they had bought all the Nez Pereés country outside of Lapwai Reservation from Lawyer and other chiefs, but we continued to live on this land in peace until eight years ago, when white men began to come inside the bounds my father had set. We warned them against this great wrong, but they would not leave our land, and some bad blood was raised. The white men represented that we were going upon the war-path. They reported many things that were false.

The United States Government again asked for a treaty council. My father had become blind and feeble. He could no longer speak for his people. It was then that I took my father's place as chief. In this council I made my first speech to white men. I said to the agent who held the council:

"I did not want to come to this council, but I came hoping that we could save blood. The white man has no right to come here and take our country. We have never accepted any presents from the Government. Neither Lawyer nor any other chief had authority to sell this land. It has always belonged to my people. It came unclouded to them from our fathers, and we will defend this land as long as a drop of Indian blood warms the hearts of our men."

The agent said he had orders, from the Great White Chief at Washington, for us to go upon the Lapwai Reservation, and that if we obeyed he would helps us in many ways. "You *must* move to the agency," he said. I answered him: "I will not. I do not need your help; we have plenty, and we are contented and happy if the white man will let us alone. The reservation is too small for so many people with all their stock. You can keep your presents; we can go to your towns and pay for all we need; we have plenty of horses and cattle to sell, and we won't have any help from you; we are free now; we can go where we please. Our fathers were born here. Here they lived, here they died, here are their graves. We will never leave them." The agent went away, and we had peace for a little while.

Soon after this my father sent for me. I saw he was dying. I took his hand in mine. He said: "My son, my body is returning to my mother earth, and my spirit is going very soon to see the Great Spirit Chief. When I am gone, think of your country. You are the chief of these people. They look to you to guide them. Always remember that your father never sold his country. You must stop your ears whenever you are asked to sign a treaty selling your home. A few years more, and white men will be all around you. They have their eyes on this land. My son, never forget my dying words. This country holds your father's body. Never sell the bones of your father and your mother." I pressed my father's hand and told him I would protect his grave with my life. My father smiled and passed away to the spirit-land.

I buried him in the beautiful valley of winding waters. I love that land more than all the rest of the world. A man who would not love his father's grave is worse than a wild animal.

For a short time we lived quietly. But this could not last. White men had found gold in the mountains around the land of winding water. They stole a great many horses from us, and we could not get them back because we were Indians. The white men told lies for each other. They drove off a great many of our cattle. Some white men branded our young cattle so they could claim them. We had no friend who would plead our cause before the law councils. It seemed to me that some of the white men in Wallowa were doing these things on purpose to get up a war. They knew that we were not strong enough to fight them. I labored hard to avoid trouble and bloodshed. We gave up some of our country to the white men, thinking that then we could have peace. We were mistaken. The white man would not let us alone. We could have avenged our wrongs many times, but we did not. Whenever the Government has asked us to help them against other Indians, we have never refused. When the white men were few and we were strong we could have killed them all off, but the Nez Pereés wished to live at peace.

If we have not done so, we have not been to blame. I believe that the old treaty has never been correctly reported. If we ever owned the land we own it still, for we never sold it. In the treaty councils the commissioners have claimed that our country had been sold to the Government. Suppose a white man should come to me and say, "Joseph, I like your horses, and I want to buy them." I say to him, "No, my horses suit me, I will not sell them." Then he goes to my neighbor, and say to him: "Joseph has some good horses. I want to buy them, but he refused to sell." My neighbor answers, "Pay me the money, and I will sell you Joseph's horses." The white man returns to me, and says, "Joseph, I have bought your horses, and you must let me have them." If we sold our lands to the Government, this is the way they were bought.

On account of the treaty made by the other bands of the Nez Pereés, the white men claimed my lands. We were troubled greatly by white men crowding over the line. Some of these were good men, and we lived on peaceful terms with them, but they were not all good.

Nearly every year the agent came over from Lapwai and ordered us on to the reservation. We always replied that we were satisfied to live in Wallowa. We were careful to refuse the presents or annuities which he offered.

Through all the years since the white men came to Wallowa we have been threatened and taunted by them and the treaty Nez Pereés. They have given us no rest. We have had a few good friends among white men, and they have always advised my people to bear these taunts without fighting. Our young men were quick-tempered, and I have had great trouble in keeping them from doing rash things. I have carried a heavy load on my back ever since I was a boy. I learned then that we were but few, while the white men were many, and that we could not hold our own with them. We were like deer. They were like grizzly bears. We had a small country. Their country was large. We were contented to let things remain as the Great Spirit made them. They were not; and would change the rivers and mountains if they did not suit them.

Year after year we have been threatened, but no war was made upon my people until General Howard came to our country two years ago and told us that he was the white war-chief of all that country. He said: "I have a great many soldiers at my back. I am going to bring them up here, and then I will talk to you again. I will not let white men laugh at me the next time I come. The country belongs to the Government, and I intend to make you go upon the reservation."

I remonstrated with him against bringing more soldiers to the Nez Pereés country. He had one house full of troops all the time at Fort Lapwai.

The next spring the agent at Umatilla agency sent an Indian runner to tell me to meet General Howard at Walla Walla. I could not go myself, but I sent my brother and five other head men to meet him, and they had a long talk.

General Howard said: "You have talked straight, and it is all right. You can stay in Wallowa." He insisted that my brother and his company should go with him to Fort Lapwai. When the party arrived there General Howard sent out runners and called all the Indians to a grand council. I was in that council. I said to General Howard,

"We are ready to listen." He answered that he would not talk then, but would hold a council next day, when he would talk plainly. I said to General Howard: "I am ready to talk today. I have been in a great many councils, but I am no wiser. We are all sprung from a woman, although we are unlike in many things. We can not be made over again. You are as you were made, and as you were made you can remain. We are just as we were made by the Great Spirit, and you can not change us; then why should children of one mother and one father quarrel—why should one try to cheat the other? I do not believe that the Great Spirit Chief gave one kind of men the right to tell another kind of men what they must do."

General Howard replied: "You deny my authority, do you? You want to dictate to me, do you?"

Then one of my chiefs—Too-hool-hool-suit—rose in the council and said to General Howard: "The Great Spirit Chief made the world as it is, and as he wanted it, and he made a part of it for us to live upon. I do not see where you get authority to say that we shall not live where he placed us."

General Howard lost his temper and said: "Shut up! I don't want to hear any more of such talk. The law says you shall go upon the reservation to live, and I want you to do so, but you persist in disobeying the law" (meaning the treaty). "If you do not move, I will take the matter into my own hands, and make you suffer for your disobedience."

Too-hool-hool-suit answered: "Who are you, that you ask us to talk, and then tell me I sha'n't talk? Are you the Great Spirit? Did you make the world? Did you make the sun? Did you make the rivers to run for us to drink? Did you make the grass to grow? Did you make all those things, that you talk to us as though we were boys? If you did, then you have the right to talk as you do."

General Howard replied, "You are an impudent fellow, and I will put you in the guard house," and then ordered a soldier to arrest him.

Too-hool-hool-suit made no resistance. He asked General Howard: "Is that your order? I don't care. I have expressed my heart to you. I have nothing to take back. I have spoken for my country. You can arrest me, but you can not change me or make me take back what I have said."

The soldiers came forward and seized my friend and took him to the guard-house. My men whispered among themselves whether they should let this thing be done. I counseled them to submit. I knew if we resisted that all the white men present, including General Howard would be killed in a moment, and we would be blamed. If I had said nothing, General Howard would never have given another unjust order against my men. I saw the danger, and, while they dragged Too-hool-hool-suit to prison, I arose and said: "*I am going to talk now.* I don't care whether you arrest me or not." I turned to my people and said: "The arrest of Too-hool-hool suit was wrong, but we will not resent the insult. We were invited to this council to express our hearts, and we have done so." Too-hool-hool suit was prisoner for five days before he was released.

The council broke up for that day. On the next morning General Howard came to my lodge, and invited me to go with him and White-Bird and Looking-Glass, to look for land for my people. As we rode along, we came to some good land that was already occupied by Indians and white people. General Howard, pointing to this land, said: "If you will come on to the reservation, I will give you these lands and move these people off."

I replied: "No. It would be wrong to disturb these people. I have no right to take their homes. I have never taken what did not belong to me. I will not now."

We rode all day upon the reservation, and found no good land unoccupied. I have been informed by men who do not lie that General Howard sent a letter that night, telling the soldier at Walla Walla to go to Wallowa Valley, and drive us out upon our return home.

In the council, next day, General Howard informed me, in a haughty spirit, that he would give my people *thirty days* to go back home, collect all their stock, and move on to the reservation, saying, "If you are not here in that time, I shall consider that you want to fight, and will send my soldiers to drive you on."

I said: "War can be avoided, and it ought to be avoided. I want no war. My people have always been the friends of the white man. Why are you in such a hurry? I can not get ready to move in thirty days. Our stock is scattered, and Snake River is very high. Let us wait until fall, then the river will be low. We want time to hunt up our stock and gather supplies for winter."

General Howard replied, "If you let the time run over one day, the soldiers will be there to drive you on to the reservation, and all your cattle and horses outside of the reservation at that time will fall into the hands of the white men."

I knew I had never sold my country, and that I had no land in Lapwai; but I did not want bloodshed. I did not want my people killed. I did not want anybody killed. Some of my people had been murdered by white men, and the white murderers were never punished for it. I told General Howard about this, and again said I wanted no war. I wanted the people who lived upon the lands I was to occupy at Lapwai to have time to gather their harvest.

I said in my heart that, rather than have war, I would give up my country. I would give up my father's grave. I would give up everything rather than have the blood of white men upon the hands of my people.

General Howard refused to allow me more than thirty days to move my people and their stock. I am sure that he began to prepare for war at once.

When I returned to Wallowa I found my people very much excited discovering that the soldiers were already in the Wallowa Valley. We held a council, and decided to move immediately, to avoid bloodshed.

Too-hool-hool suit, who felt outraged by his imprisonment, talked for war, and made many of my young men willing to fight rather than be driven like dogs from the land where they were born. He declared that blood alone would wash out the disgrace General Howard had put upon him. It required a strong heart to stand up against such talk, but I urged my people to be quiet, and not to begin a war.

We gathered all the stock we could find, and made an attempt to move. We left many of our horses and cattle in Wallowa, and we lost several hundred in crossing the river. All of my people succeeded in getting across in safety. Many of the Nez Pereés came together in Rocky Cañon to hold a grand council. I went with all my people. This council lasted ten days. There was a great deal of war-talk, and a great deal of excitement. There was one young brave present whose father had been killed by a white man five years before. This man's blood was bad against white men, and he left the council calling for revenge.

Again I counseled peace, and I thought the danger was past. We had not complied with General Howard's order because we could not, but we intended to do so as soon as possible. I was leaving the council to kill beef for my family, when news came that the young man whose father had been killed had gone out with several other hot blooded young braves and killed four white men. He rode up to the council and shouted: "Why do you sit here like women? The war has begun already." I was deeply grieved. All the lodges were moved except my brother's and my own. I saw clearly that the war was upon us when I learned that my young men had been secretly buying ammunition. I heard then that Too-hool-hool-suit, who had been imprisoned by General Howard, had succeeded in organizing a war-party. I knew that their acts would involve all my people. I saw that the war could not then be prevented. The time had passed. I counseled peace from the beginning. I knew that we were too weak to fight the United States. We had many grievances, but I knew that war would bring more. We had good white friends, who advised us against taking the war-path. My friend and brother, Mr. Chapman, who has been with us since the surrender, told us just how the war would end. Mr. Chapman took sides against us, and helped General Howard. I do not blame him for doing so. He tried hard to prevent bloodshed. We hoped the white settlers would not join the soldiers. Before the war commenced we had discussed this matter all over, and many of my people were in favor of warning them that if they took no part against us they should not be molested in the event of war being begun by General Howard. This plan was voted down in the war-council.

There were bad men among my people who had quarreled with white men, and they talked of their wrongs until they roused all the bad hearts in the council. Still I could not believe that they would begin the war. I know that my young men did a great wrong, but I ask, Who was first to blame? They had been insulted a thousand times; their fathers and brothers had been killed; their mothers and wives had been disgraced; they had been driven to madness by whisky sold to them by white men; they had been told by General Howard that all their horses and cattle which they had been unable to drive out of Wallowa were to fall into the hands of white men; and, added to all this, they were homeless and desperate.

I would have given my own life if I could have undone the killing of white men by my people. I blame my young men and I blame the white men. I blame General Howard for not giving my people time to get their stock away from Wallowa. I do not acknowledge that he had the right to order me to leave Wallowa at any time. I deny that either my father or myself ever sold that land. It is still our land. It may never again be our home, but my father sleeps there, and I love it as I love my mother. I left there, hoping to avoid bloodshed.

If General Howard had given me plenty of time to gather up my stock, and treated Too-hool-hool-suit as a man should be treated, there *would have been no war.*

My friends among white men have blamed me for the war. I am not to blame. When my young men began the killing, my heart was hurt. Although I did not justify them, I remembered all the insults I had endured, and my blood was on fire. Still I would have taken my people to the buffalo country without fighting, if possible.

I could see no other way to avoid a war. We moved over to White Bird Creek, sixteen miles away, and there encamped, intending to collect our stock before leaving; but the soldiers attacked us, and the first battle was fought. We numbered in that battle sixty men, and the soldiers a hundred. The fight lasted but a few minutes, when the soldiers retreated before us for twelve miles. They lost thirty-three killed, and had seven wounded. When an Indian fights, he only shoots to kill; but soldiers shoot at random. None of the soldiers were scalped. We do not believe in scalping, nor in killing wounded men. Soldiers do not kill many Indians unless they are wounded and left upon the battle-field. Then they kill Indians.

Seven days after the first battle, General Howard arrived in the Nez Pereés country, bringing seven hundred more soldiers. It was now war in earnest. We crossed over Salmon River, hoping General Howard would follow. We were not disappointed. He did follow us, and we got back between him and his supplies, and cut him off for three days. He sent out two companies to open the way. We attacked them, killing one officer, two guides, and ten men.

We withdrew, hoping the soldiers would follow, but they had got fighting enough for that day. They intrenched themselves, and next day we attacked them again. The battle lasted all day, and was renewed next morning. We killed four and wounded seven or eight.

About this time General Howard found out that we were in his rear. Five days later he attacked us with three hundred and fifty soldiers and settlers. We had two hundred and fifty warriors. The fight lasted twenty-seven hours. We lost four killed and several wounded. General Howard's loss was twenty-nine men killed and sixty wounded.

The following day the soldiers charged upon me, and we retreated with our families and stock a few miles away, leaving eighty lodges to fall into General Howard's hands.

Finding that we were outnumbered, we retreated to Bitter Root Valley. Here another body of soldiers came upon us and demanded our surrender. We refused. They said, "You can not get by us." We answered, "We are going by you without fighting if you will let us, but we are going by you anyhow." We then made a treaty with these soldiers. We agreed not to molest any one, and they agreed that we might pass through the Bitter Root country in peace. We bought provisions and traded stock with white men there.

We understood that there was to be no more war. We intended to go peaceably to the buffalo country, and leave the question of returning to our country to be settled afterward.

With this understanding we traveled on for four days, and, thinking that the trouble was all over, we stopped and prepared tent poles to take with us. We started again, and at the end of two days we saw three white men passing our camp. Thinking that peace had been made, we did not molest them. We could have killed or taken them prisoners, but we did not suspect them of being spies, which they were.

That night the soldiers surrounded our camp. About daybreak one of my men went out to look after his horses. The soldiers saw him and shot him like a coyote. I have since learned that these soldiers were not those we had left behind. They had come upon us from another direction. The new white war-chief's name was Gibbon. He charged upon us while some of my people were still asleep. We had a hard fight. Some of my men crept around and attacked the soldiers from the rear. In this battle we lost nearly all our lodges, but we finally drove General Gibbon back.

Finding that he was not able to capture us, he sent to his camp a few miles away for his big guns (cannons), but my men had captured them and all the ammunition. We damaged the big guns all we could, and carried away the powder and lead. In the fight with General Gibbon we lost fifty women and children and thirty fighting men. We remained long enough to bury our dead. The Nez Pereés never make war on women and children; we could have killed a great many women and children while the war lasted, but we would feel ashamed to do so cowardly an act.

We never scalp our enemies, but when General Howard came up and joined General Gibbon, their Indian scouts dug up our dead and scalped them. I have been told that General Howard did not order this great shame to be done.

We retreated as rapidly as we could toward the buffalo country. After six days General Howard came close to us, and we went out and attacked him, and captured nearly all his horses and mules (about two hundred and fifty head). We then marched on to the Yellowstone Basin.

On the way we captured one white man and two white women. We released them at the end of three days. They were treated kindly. The women were not insulted. Can the white soldiers tell me of one time when Indian women were taken prisoners, and held three days and then released without being insulted? Were the Nez Pereés women who fell into the hands of General

Howard's soldiers treated with as much respect? I deny that a Nez Pereé was ever guilty of such a crime.

A few days later we captured two more white men. One of them stole a horse and escaped. We gave the other a poor horse and told him he was free.

Nine days' march brought us to the mouth of Clarke's Fork of the Yellowstone. We did not know what had become of General Howard, but we supposed that he had sent for more horses and mules. He did not come up, but another new war-chief (General Sturgis) attacked us. We held him in check while we moved all our women and children and stock out of danger, leaving a few men to cover our retreat.

Several days passed, and we heard nothing of General Howard, or Gibbon, or Sturgis. We had repulsed each in turn, and began to feel secure, when another army, under General Miles, struck us. This was the fourth army, each of which outnumbered our fighting force, that we had encountered within sixty days.

We had no knowledge of General Miles's army until a short time before he made a charge upon us, cutting our camp in two, and capturing nearly all of our horses. About seventy men, myself among them, were cut off. My little daughter, twelve years of age, was with me. I gave her a rope, and told her to catch a horse and join the others who were cut off from the camp. I have not seen her since, but I have learned that she is alive and well.

I thought of my wife and children, who were now surrounded by soldier, and I resolved to go to them or die. With a prayer in my mouth to the Great Spirit Chief who rules above, I dashed unarmed through the line of solider. It seemed to me that there were guns on every side, before and behind me. My clothes were cut to pieces and my horse was wounded, but I was not hurt. As I reached the door of my lodge, my wife handed me my rifle, saying: "Here's your gun. Fight!"

The soldiers kept up a continuous fire. Six of my men were killed in one spot near me. Ten or twelve soldiers charged into our camp and got possession of two lodges, killing three Nez Pereés and losing three of their men, who fell inside our lines. I called my men to drive them back. We fought at close range, not more than twenty steps apart, and drove the soldiers back upon their main line, leaving their dead in our hands. We secured their arms and ammunition. We lost, the first day and night, eighteen men and three women. General Miles lost twenty-six killed and forty wounded. The following day General Miles sent a messenger into my camp under protection of a white flag. I sent my friend Yellow Bull to meet him.

Yellow Bull understood the messenger to say that General Miles wished me to consider the situation; that he did not want to kill my people unnecessarily. Yellow Bull understood this to be a demand for me to surrender and save blood. Upon reporting this message to me, Yellow Bull said he wondered whether General Miles was in earnest. I sent him back with my answer, that I had not made up my mind, but would think about it and send word soon. A little later he sent me some Cheyenne scouts with another message. I went out to meet them. They said they believed General Miles was sincere and really wanted peace. I walked on to General Miles's tent. He met me and we shook hands. He said, "Come, let us sit down by the fire and talk this matter over." I remained with him all night; next morning Yellow Bull came over to see if I was alive, and why I did not return.

General Miles would not let me leave the tent to see my friend alone.

Yellow Bull said to me: "They have got you in their power, and I am afraid they will never let you go again. I have an officer in our camp, and I will hold him until they let you go free."

I said: "I do not know what they mean to do with me, but if they kill me you must not kill the officer. It will do no good to avenge my death by killing him."

Yellow Bull returned to my camp. I did not make any agreement that day with General Miles. The battle was renewed while I was with him. I was very anxious about my people. I knew that we were near Sitting Bull's camp in King George's land, and I thought maybe the Nez Pereés who had escaped would return with assistance. No great damage was done to either party during the night.

On the following morning I returned to my camp by agreement, meeting the officer who had been a prisoner in my camp at the flag of truce. My people were divided about surrendering. We could have escaped from Bear Paw Mountain if we had left our wounded, old women, and children behind. We were unwilling to do this. We had never heard of a wounded Indian recovering while in the hands of white men.

On the evening of the fourth day General Howard came in with a small escort, together with my friend Chapman. We could now talk understandingly. General Miles said to me in plain words, "If you will come out and give up your arms, I will spare your lives and send you to your reservation." I do not know what passed between General Miles and General Howard.

I could not bear to see my wounded men and women suffer any longer; we had lost enough already. General Miles had promised that we might return to our own country with what stock we had left. I thought we could start again. I believe General Miles, or *I would never have surrendered*. I have heard that he has been censured for making the promise to return us to Lapwai. He could not have made any other terms with me at that time. I would have held him in check until my friends came to my assistance, and then neither of the generals nor their soldiers would have ever left Bear Paw Mountain alive.

On the fifth day I went to General Miles and gave up my gun, and said, "From where the sun now stands I will fight no more." My people needed rest—we wanted peace.

I was told we could go with General Miles to Tongue River and stay there until spring, when we would be sent back to our country. Finally it was decided that we were to be taken to Tongue River. We had nothing to say about it. After our arrival at Tongue River, General Miles received orders to take us to Bismarck. The reason given was, that subsistence would be cheaper there.

General Miles was opposed to this order. He said: "You must not blame me. I have endeavored to keep my word, but the chief who is over me has given the order, and I must obey it or resign. That would do you no good. Some other officer would carry out the order."

I believe General Miles would have kept his word if he could have done so. I do not blame him for what we have suffered since the surrender. I do not know who is to blame. We gave up all our horses—over eleven hundred—and all our saddles—over one hundred—and we have not heard from them since. Somebody has got our horses.

General Miles turned my people over to another soldier, and we were taken to Bismarck. Captain Johnson, who now had charge of us, received an order to take us to Fort Leavenworth. At Levenworth we were placed on a low river bottom, with no water except river-water to drink and cook with. We had always lived in a healthy country, where the mountains were high and the water was cold and clear. Many of my people sickened and died, and we buried them in this strange land. I can not tell how much my heart suffered for my people while at Leavenworth. The Great Spirit Chief who rules above seemed to be looking some other way, and did not see what was being done to my people.

During the hot days (July, 1878) we received noticed that we were to be moved farther away from our own country. We were not asked if we were willing to go. We were ordered to get into the railroad-cars. Three of my people died on the way to Baxter Springs. It was worse to die there than to die fighting in the mountains.

We were moved from Baxter Springs (Kansas) to the Indian Territory, and set down without our lodges. We had but little medicine, and we were nearly all sick. Seventy of my people have died since we moved there.

We have had a great many visitors who have talked many ways. Some of the chiefs (General Fish and Colonel Stickney) from Washington came to see us, and selected land for us to live upon. We have not moved to that land, for it is not a good place to live.

The Commissioner Chief (E. A. Hayt) came to see us. I told him, as I told every one, that I expected General Miles's word would be carried out. He said "it could not be done; that white men now lived in my country and all the land was taken up; that, if I returned to Wallowa, I could not live in peace; that law-papers were out against my young men who began the war, and that the Government could not protect my people." This talk fell like a heavy stone upon my heart. I saw that I could not gain anything by talking to him. Other law chiefs (Congressional Committee) came to see me and said they would help me to get a healthy country. I did not know who to believe. The white people have too many chiefs. They do not understand each other. They do not all talk alike.

The Commissioner Chief (Mr. Hayt) invited me to go with him and hunt for a better home than we have now. I like the land we found (west of the Osage reservation) better than any place I have seen in that country; but it is not a healthy land. There are no mountains and rivers. The water is warm. It is not a good country for stock. I do not believe my people can live there. I am afraid they will all die. The Indians who occupy that country are dying off. I promised Chief Hayt to go there, and do the best I could until the Government got ready to make good General Miles's word. I was not satisfied, but I could not help myself.

Then the Inspector Chief (General McNiel) came to my camp and we had a long talk. He said I ought to have a home in the mountain country north, and that he would write a letter to the Great Chief at Washington. Again the hope of seeing the mountains of Idaho and Oregon grew up in my heart.

At last I was granted permission to come to Washington and bring my friend Yellow Bull and our interpreter with me. I am glad we came. I have shaken hands with a great many friends, but there are some things I want to know which no one seems able to explain. I can not understand how the Government sends a man out to fight us, as it did General Miles, and then breaks his word. Such a Government has something wrong about it. I can not understand why so many chiefs are allowed to talk so many different ways, and promise so many different things. I have seen the Great Father Chief (the President), the next Great Chief (Secretary of the Interior), the Commissioner Chief (Hayt), the Law Chief (General Butler), and many other law chiefs (Congressmen), and they all say they are my friends, and that I shall have justice, but while their mouths all talk right I do not understand why nothing is done for my people. I have heard talk and talk, but nothing is done. Good words do not last long unless they amount to something. Words do not pay for my dead people. They do not pay for my country, now overrun by white men. They do not protect my father's grave. They do not pay for all my horses and cattle. Good words will not give me back my children. Good words will not make good the promise of your War Chief General Miles. Good words will not give my people good health and stop them from dying. Good words will not get my people a home where they can live in peace and take care of themselves. I am tired of talk that comes to nothing. It makes my heart sick when I remember all the good words and all the broken promises. There has been too much talking by men who had no right to talk. Too many misinterpretations have been made, too many misunderstandings have come up between the white men about the Indians. If the white man wants to live in peace with the Indian he can live in peace. There need be no trouble. Treat all man alike. Give them all the same law. Give them all an even chance to live and grow. All men were made by the same Great Spirit Chief. They are all brothers. The earth is the Miles of all people, and all people should have equal rights upon it. You might as well expect the rivers to run backward as that any man who was born a free man should be contented when penned up and denied liberty to go where he pleases. If you tie a horse to a stake, do you expect he will grow fat? If you pen an Indian up on a small spot of earth, and compel him to stay there, he will not be contented, nor will he grow and prosper. I have asked some of the great white chiefs where they get their authority to say to the Indian that he shall stay in one place, while he sees white men going where they please. They can not tell me.

I only ask of the Government to be treated as all other men are treated. If I can not go to my own home, let me have a home in some country where my people will not die so fast. I would like to go to Bitter Root Valley. There my people would be healthy; where they are now they are dying. Three have died since I left my camp to come to Washington.

When I think of our condition my heart is heavy. I see men of my race treated as outlaws and driven from country to country, or shot down like animals.

I know that my race must change. We can not hold our own with the white men as we are. We only ask an even chance to live as other men live. We ask to be recognized as men. We ask that the same law shall work alike on all men. If the Indian breaks the law, punish by the law. If the white man breaks the law, punish him also.

Let me be a free man—free to travel, free to stop, free to work, free to trade where I choose, free to choose my own teachers, free to follow the religion of my fathers, free to think and talk and act for myself—and I will obey every law, or submit to the penalty.

Whenever the white man treats the Indian as they treat each other, then we will have no more wars. We shall be all alike—brothers of one father and one mother, with one sky above us and one country around us, and one government for all. Then the Great Spirit Chief who rules above will smile upon this land, and send rain to wash out the bloody spots made by brothers' hands from the face of the earth. For this time the Indian race are waiting and praying. I hope that no more groans of wounded men and women will ever go to the ear of the Great Spirit Chief above, and that all people may be one people.

In mut-too-yah-lat-lat has spoken for his people.
YOUNG JOSEPH.
WASHINGTON CITY, D.C.

106. Looking Backward 2000–1887

Edward Bellamy became an overnight success in 1887 with his enormously influential "science fiction" novel, Looking Backward. *Clubs formed across the United States to discuss ways to bring his vision of a New America into being.*

Author's Preface

HISTORICAL SECTION SHAWMUT COLLEGE, BOSTON, DECEMBER 26, 2000.

Living as we do in the closing year of the twentieth century, enjoying the blessings of a social order at once so simple and logical that it seems but the triumph of common sense, it is no doubt difficult for those whose studies have not been largely historical to realize that the present organization of society is, in its completeness, less than a century old. No historical fact is, however, better established than that till nearly the end of the nineteenth century it was the general belief that the ancient industrial system, with all its shocking social consequences, was destined to last, with possibly a little patching, to the end of time. How strange and wellnigh incredible does it seem that so prodigious a moral and material transformation as has taken place since then could have been accomplished in so brief an interval. The readiness with which men accustom themselves, as matters of course, to improvements in their condition, which, when anticipated, seemed to leave nothing more to be desired, could not be more strikingly illustrated. What reflection could be better calculated to moderate the enthusiasm of reformers who count for their reward on the lively gratitude of future ages!

The object of this volume is to assist persons who, while desiring to gain a more definite idea of the social contrasts between the nineteenth and twentieth centuries, are daunted by the formal aspect of the histories which treat the subject. Warned by a teacher's experience that learning is accounted a weariness to the flesh, the author has sought to alleviate the instructive quality of the book by casting it in the form of a romantic narrative, which he would be glad to fancy not wholly devoid of interest in its own account.

The reader, to whom modern social institutions and their underlying principles are matters of course, may at times find Dr. Leete's explanations of them rather trite,—but it must be remembered that to Dr. Leete's guest they were not matters of course, and that this book is written for the express purpose of inducing the reader to forget for the nonce that they are so to him. One word more. The almost universal theme of the writers and orators who have celebrated this bimillennial epoch has been the future rather than the past, not the advance that has been made, but the progress that shall be made, ever onward and upward, till the race shall achieve its ineffable destiny. This is well, wholly well, but it seems to me that nowhere can we find more solid ground for daring anticipations of human development during the next one thousand years, than by "Looking Backward" upon the progress of the last one hundred.

That this volume may be so fortunate as to find readers whose interest in the subject shall incline them to overlook the deficiencies of the treatment is the hope in which the author steps aside and leaves Mr. Julian West to speak for himself.

Chapter V

When, in the course of the evening the ladies retired, leaving Dr. Leete and myself alone, he sounded me as to my disposition for sleep, saying that if I felt like it my bed was ready for me; but if I was inclined to wakefulness nothing would please him better than to bear me company. "I am a late bird, myself," he said, "and, without suspicion of flattery, I may say that a companion more interesting than yourself could scarcely be imagined. It is decidedly not often that one has a chance to converse with a man of the nineteenth century."

Source: Edward Bellamy, *Looking Backward,* preface and pp. 47–64. Originally published 1887, Houghton Mifflin Company. Public Domain Reprint.

Now I had been looking forward all the evening with some dread to the time when I should be alone, on retiring for the night. Surrounded by these most friendly strangers, stimulated and supported by their sympathetic interest, I had been able to keep my mental balance. Even then, however, in pauses of the conversation I had had glimpses, vivid as lightning flashes, of the horror of strangeness that was waiting to be faced when I could no longer command diversion. I knew I could not sleep that night, and as for lying awake and thinking, it argues no cowardice, I am sure, to confess that I was afraid of it. When, in reply to my host's question, I frankly told him this, he replied that it would be strange if I did not feel just so, but that I need have no anxiety about sleeping & whenever I wanted to go to bed, he would give me a dose which would insure me a sound night's sleep without fail. Next morning, no doubt I would awake with the feeling of an old citizen."

"Before I acquire that," I replied, "I must know a little more about the sort of Boston I have come back to. You told me when we were upon the house-top that though a century only had elapsed since I fell asleep, it had been marked by greater changes in the conditions of humanity than many a previous millennium. With the city before me I could well believe that, but I am very curious to know what some of the changes have been. To make a beginning somewhere, for the subject is doubtless a large one, what solution, if any, have you found for the labor question? It was the Sphinx's riddle of the nineteenth century, and when I dropped out the Sphinx was threatening to devour society, because the answer was not forthcoming. It is well worth sleeping a hundred years to learn what the right answer was, if, indeed, you have found it yet."

"As no such thing as the labor question is known nowadays," replied Dr. Leete, "and there is no way in which it could arise, I suppose we may claim to have solved it. Society would indeed have fully deserved being devoured if it had failed to answer a riddle so entirely simple. In fact, to speak by the book, it was not necessary for society to solve the riddle at all. It may be said to have solved itself. The solution came as the result of a process of industrial evolution which could not have terminated otherwise. All that society had to do was recognize and coöperate with that evolution, when its tendency had become unmistakable."

"I can only say," I answered, "that at the time I fell asleep no such evolution had been recognized."

"It was in 1887 that you fell into this sleep, I think you said."

"Yes, May 30th, 1887."

My companion regarded me musingly for some moments. Then he observed, "And you tell me that even then there was no general recognition of the nature of the crisis which society was nearing? Of course, I fully credit your statement. The singular blindness of your contemporaries to the signs of the times is a phenomenon commented on by many of our historians, but few facts of history are more difficult for us to realize, so obvious and unmistakable as we look back seem the indications, which must also have come under your eyes, of the transformation about to come to pass. I should be interested, Mr. West, if you would give me a little more definite idea of the view which you and men of your grade of intellect took of the state and prospects of society in 1887. You must, at least, have realized that the widespread industrial and social troubles, and the underlying dissatisfaction of all classes with the inequalities of society, and the general misery of mankind, were portents of great changes of some sort."

"We did, indeed, fully realize that," I replied. "We felt that society was dragging anchor and in danger of going drift. Whither it would drift nobody could say, but all feared the rocks."

"Nevertheless," said Dr. Leete, "the set of the current was perfectly perceptible if you had but taken pains to observe it, and it was not toward the rocks, but toward a deeper channel."

"We had a popular proverb," I replied, "that 'hindsight is better than foresight,' the force of which I shall now, no doubt, appreciate more fully than ever. All I can say is, that the prospect was such when I went into that long sleep that I should not have been surprised had I looked down from your house-top today on a heap of charred and moss-grown ruins instead of this glorious city."

Dr. Leete had listened to me with close attention and nodded thoughtfully as I finished speaking. "What you have said," he observed, "will be regarded as a most valuable vindication of Storiot, whose account of your era has been generally thought exaggerated in its picture of the gloom and confusion of men's minds. That a period of transition like that should be full of excitement and agitation was indeed to be looked for; but seeing how pain was the tendency of the forces in operation, it was natural to believe that hope rather than fear would have been the prevailing temper of the popular mind."

You have not yet told me what was the answer to the riddle which you found," I said. "I am impatient to know by what contradiction of natural sequence the peace and prosperity which you now seem to enjoy could have been the outcome of an era like my own."

"Excuse me," replied my host, "but do you smoke?" It was not till our cigars were lighted and drawing well that he resumed. "Since you are in the humor to talk rather than to sleep, as I certainly am, perhaps I cannot do better than to try to give you enough idea of our modern industrial system to dissipate at least the impression that there is any mystery about the process of its evolution. The Bostonians of your day had the reputation of being great askers of questions, and I am going to show my descent by asking you one to begin with. What should you name as the most prominent feature of the labor troubles of your day?"

"Why, the strikes, of course," I replied.

"Exactly; but what made the strikes so formidable?"

"The great labor organizations."

"And what was the motive of these great organizations?"

"The workmen claimed they had to organize to get their rights from the big corporations," I replied.

"That is just it," said Dr. Leete; "the organization of labor and the strikes were an effect, merely, of the concentration of capital in greater masses than had ever been known before. Before this concentration began, while as yet commerce and industry were conducted by innumerable petty concerns with small capital, instead of a small number of great concerns with vast capital, the individual workman was relatively important and independent in his relations to the employer. Moreover, when a little capital or a new idea was enough to start a man in business for himself, workingmen were constantly becoming employers and there was no hard and fast line between the two classes. Labor unions were needless then, and general strikes out of the question. But when the era of small concerns with small capital was succeeded by that of the great aggregations of capital, all this was changed. The individual laborer, who had been relatively important to the small employer, was reduced to insignificance and powerlessness over against the great corporation, while at the same time the way upward to the grade of employer was closed to him. Self-defense drove him to union with his fellows.

"The records of the period show that the outcry against the concentration of capital was furious. Men believed that it threatened society with a form of tyranny more abhorrent than it had ever endured. They believed that the great corporations were preparing for them the yoke of a baser servitude than had ever been imposed on the race, servitude not to men but to soulless machines incapable of any motive but insatiable greed. Looking back, we cannot wonder at their desperation, for certainly humanity was never confronted with a fate more sordid and hideous than would have been the era of corporate tyranny which they anticipated.

"Meanwhile, without being in the smallest degree checked by the clamor against it, the absorption of business by ever larger monopolies continued. In the United States there was not, after the beginning of the last quarter of the century, any opportunity whatever for individual enterprise in any important field of industry, unless backed by a great capital. During the last decade of the century, such small businesses as still remained were fast-failing survivals of a past epoch, or mere parasites on the great corporations or else existed in fields too small to attract the great capitalists. Small businesses, as far as they still remained, were reduced to the condition of rats and mice, living in holes and corners, and counting on evading notice for the enjoyment of existence. The railroads had gone on combining till a few great syndicates controlled every rail in the land. In manufactories, every important staple was controlled by a syndicate. These syndicates, pools, trusts, or whatever their name, fixed prices and crushed all competition except when combinations as vast as themselves arose. Then a struggle, resulting in a still greater consolidation, ensued. The great city bazar crushed its country rivals with branch stores, and in the city itself absorbed its smaller rivals till the business of a whole quarter was concentrated under one roof, with a hundred former proprietors of shops serving as clerks. Having no business of his own to put his money in, the small capitalist, at the same time that he took service under the corporation, found no other investment for his money but its stocks and bonds, thus becoming doubly dependent upon it.

"The fact that the desperate popular opposition to the consolidation of business in a few powerful hands had no effect to check it proves that there must have been a strong economical reason for it. The small capitalists with their innumerable petty concerns, had in fact yielded the field to the great aggregations of capital, because they belonged to a day of small things and were totally incompetent to the demands of an age of steam and telegraphs and the gigantic scale of its enterprises. To restore the former order of things, even if possible, would have involved returning to the day of stage-coaches. Oppressive and intolerable as was the régime of the great consolidations of capital, even its victims, while they cursed it, were forced to admit the prodigious increase of efficiency which had been imparted to the national industries, the vast economies effected by concentration of management and unity of organization, and to confess that since the new system had taken the place of the old the wealth of the world had increased at a rate before undreamed of. To be sure this vast increase had gone chiefly to make the rich richer, increasing the gap between them and the poor; but the fact remained that, as a means merely of producing wealth, capital had been proved efficient in proportion to its consolidation. The restoration of the old system with the subdivision of capital, if it were possible, might indeed bring back a greater equality of conditions, with more individual dignity and freedom, but it would be at the price of general poverty and the arrest of material progress.

"Was there, then, no way of commanding the services of the mighty wealth-producing principle of consolidated capital without bowing down to a plutocracy like that of Carthage? As soon as men began to ask themselves these questions, they found the answer ready for them. The movement toward the conduct of business by larger and larger aggregations of capital, the tendency toward monopolies, which had been so desperately and vainly resisted, was recognized at last, in its true significance, as a process which only needed to complete its logical evolution to open a golden future to humanity.

"Early in the last century the evolution was completed by the final consolidation of the entire capital of the nation. The industry and commerce of the country, ceasing to be conducted by a set of irresponsible corporations and syndicates of private persons at their caprice and for their profit, were intrusted to a single syndicate representing the people, to be conducted in the common interest for the common profit. The nation, that is to say, organized as the one great business corporation in which all other corporations were absorbed; it became the one capitalist in the place of all other capitalists, the sole employer, the final monopoly in which all previous and lesser monopolies were swallowed up, a monopoly in the profits and economies of which all citizens shared. The epoch of trusts had ended in The Great Trust. In a word, the people of the United States concluded to assume the conduct of their own business, just as one hundred odd years before they had assumed the conduct of their own government, organizing now for industrial purposes on precisely the same grounds that they had then organized for political purposes. At last strangely late in the world's history, the obvious fact was perceived that no business is so essentially the public business as the industry and commerce on which the people's livelihood depends, and that to entrust it to private persons to be managed for private profit is a folly similar in kind, though vastly greater in magnitude, to that of surrendering the functions of political government to kings and nobles to be conducted for their personal glorification."

"Such a stupendous change as you describe," said I, "did not, of course, take place without great bloodshed and terrible convulsions."

"On the contrary," replied Dr. Leete, "there was absolutely no violence. The change had been long foreseen. Public opinion had become fully ripe for it, and the whole mass of the people was behind it. There was no more possibility of opposing it by force than by argument. On the other hand the popular sentiment toward the great corporations and those identified with them had ceased to be one of bitterness, as they came to realize their necessity as a link, a transition phase, in the evolution of the true industrial system. The most violent foes of the great private monopolies were now forced to recognize how invaluable and indispensable had been their office in educating the people up to the point of assuming control of their own business. Fifty years before, the consolidation of the industries of the country under national control would have seemed a very daring experiment to the most sanguine. But by a series of object lessons, seen and studied by all men, the great corporations had taught the people an entirely new set of ideas on this subject. They had seen for many years syndicates handling revenues greater than those of states, and directing the labors of hundreds of thousands of men with an efficiency and economy unattainable in smaller operations. It had come to be recognized as an axiom that the larger the business the simpler the principles that can be applied to it; that, as the machine is truer than the hand, so the system, which in a great concern does the work of the master's eye in a small business, turns out more accurate results. Thus it came about that, thanks to the corporations themselves, when it was proposed that the nation should assume their functions, the suggestion implied nothing which seemed impracticable even to the timid. To be sure it was a step beyond any yet taken, a broader generalization, but the very fact that the nation would be the sole corporation in the field would, it was seen, relieve the undertaking of many difficulties with which the partial monopolies had contended."

Chapter VI

Dr. Leete ceased speaking, and I remained silent, endeavoring to form some general conception of the changes in the arrangements of society implied in the tremendous revolution which he had described.

Finally I said, "The idea of such an extension of the functions of government is, to say the least, rather overwhelming."

"Extension!" he repeated, "where is the extension?"

"In my day," I replied, "it was considered that the proper functions of government, strictly speaking, were limited to keeping the peace and defending the people against the public enemy, that is, to the military and police powers."

"And, in heaven's name, who are the public enemies?" examined Dr. Leete. "Are they France, England, Germany, or hunger, cold, and nakedness? In your day governments were accustomed, on the slightest international misunderstanding, to seize upon the bodies of citizens and deliver them over by hundreds of thousands to death and mutilation, wasting their treasures the while like water; and all this oftenest for no imaginable profit to the victims. We have no wars now, and our governments no war powers, but in order to protect every citizen against hunger, cold, and nakedness, and provide for all his physical and mental needs, the function is assumed of directing his industry for a term of years. No, Mr. West, I am sure on reflection you will perceive that it was in your age, not in ours, that the extension of the functions of governments were extraordinary. Not even for the best ends would men now allow their governments such powers as were then used for the more maleficent."

"Leaving comparisons aside," I said, "the demagoguery and corruption of our public men would have been considered, in my day, insuperable objections to any assumption by government of the charge of the national industries. We should have thought that no arrangement could be worse than to entrust the politicians with control of the wealth-producing machinery of the country. Its material interests were quite too much the football of parties as it was."

"No doubt you were right," rejoined Dr. Leete, "but all that is changed now. We have no parties or politicians, and as for demagoguery and corruption, they are words having only an historical significance."

"Human nature itself must have changed very much," I said.

"Not at all," was Dr. Leete's reply, "but the conditions of human life have changed, and with them the motives of human action. The organization of society with you was such that officials were under a constant temptation to misuse their power for the private profit of themselves or others. Under such circumstances it seems almost strange that you dared entrust them with any of your affairs. Nowadays, on the contrary, society is so constituted that there is absolutely no way in which an official, however ill-disposed, could possibly make any profit for himself or any one else by a misuse of his power. Let him be as bad an official as you please, he cannot be a corrupt one. There is no motive to be. The social system no longer offers a premium on dishonesty. But these are matters which you can only understand as you come, with time, to know us better."

"But you have not yet told me how you have settled the labor problem. It is the problem of capital which we have been discussing," I said. "After the nation had assumed conduct of the mills, machinery, railroads, farms, mines, and capital in general of the country, the labor question still remained. In assuming the responsibilities of capital the nation had assumed the difficulties of the capitalist's position."

"The moment the nation assumed the responsibilities of capital those difficulties vanished," replied Dr. Leete. "The national organization of labor under one direction was the complete solution of what was, in your day and under your system, justly regarded as the insoluble labor problems. When the nation became the sole employer, all the citizens, by virtue of their citizenship, became employees, to be distributed according to the needs of industry."

"That is," I suggested, "you have simply applied the principle of universal military service, as it was understood in our day, to the labor question."

"Yes," said Dr. Leete, "that was something which followed as a matter of course as soon as the nation had become the sole capitalist. The people were already accustomed to the idea that the obligation of every citizen, not physically disabled, to contribute his military services to the defense of the nation was equal and absolute. That it was equally the duty of every citizen to contribute his quota of industrial or intellectual services to the maintenance of the nation was equally evident, though it was not until the nation became the employer of labor that citizens were able to render this sort of service with any pretense either of universality or equity. No organization of labor was possible when the employing power was divided among hundreds or thousands of individuals and corporations, between which concert of any kind was neither desired, nor indeed feasible. It constantly happened then that vast numbers who desired to labor could find no opportunity, and on the other hand, those who desired to evade a part of all their debt and could easily do so."

"Service, now, I suppose, is compulsory upon all," I suggested.

"It is rather a matter of course than of compulsion," replied Dr. Leete. "It is regarded as so absolutely natural and reasonable that the idea of its being compulsory has ceased to be thought of. He would be thought to be an incredibly contemptible person who should need compulsion in such a case. Nevertheless, to speak of service being compulsory would be a weak way to state its absolute inevitableness. Our entire social order is so wholly based upon and deduced from it that if it were conceivable that a man could escape it, he would be left with no possible way to provide for his existence. He would have excluded himself from the world, cut himself off from his kind, in a word, committed suicide."

"Is the term of service in this industrial army for life?"

"On, no; it both begins later and ends earlier than the average working period in your day. Your workshops were filled with children and old men, but we hold the period of youth sacred to education, and the period of maturity, when the physical forces begin to flag, equally sacred to ease and agreeable relaxation. The period of industrial service is twenty-four years, beginning at the close of the course of education at twenty-one and terminating at forty-five. After forty-five, while discharged from labor, the citizen still remains liable to special calls, in cases of emergencies causing a sudden great increase in the demand for labor, till he reaches the age of fifty-five, but such calls are rarely, in fact almost never, made. The fifteenth day of October of every year is what we call Muster Day, because those who have reached the age of twenty-one are then mustered into the industrial service, and at the same time those who, after twenty-four years' service, have reached the age of forty-five, are honorably mustered out. It is the great day of the year with us, whence we reckon all other events, our Olympiad, save that it is annual."

Chapter XVIII

Urban Growth and Farm Protest, 1887–1893

107. Hon. William C. Oates, George Curtis, and T. V. Powderly, Chairman, The Homestead Strike, 1892

The Homestead Strike of 1892 focused the nation's attention on the problems of labor and management. The North American Review brought together three influential men to give their differing opinions on the strike and its meaning.

I. A Constitutional View
By Hon. William C. Oates

Homestead is a very comfortable-looking, neat little town of 10,000 to 12,000 inhabitants, situated on the left bank of the Monongahela River, seven miles east of the city of Pittsburg. Its inhabitants are chiefly laborers and mechanics of various degrees of skill, from the highest down to the ordinary laborer, with a competent number of small merchants and tradespeople. About one-half of the population are of foreign birth and represent various European nationalities.

About one mile up the river from the heart of the town are located the Homestead Works of Carnegie, Phipps & Co., the cost of which, exclusive of the ground, is near $6,000,000. At these works they manufacture structural materials used largely in fireproof buildings, such as beams, channels, etc. They also manufacture steel armor plates for use in the construction of war vessels. The 119-inch mill at which these plates are finished is one of the best of its kind in the world. The armor plate for the new Cruisers 9 and 10 now being constructed is manufactured here. The Navy Department has a contract with this company for 6,000 tons of armor plate to be used in the construction of our new war vessels. They also manufacture at Homestead all kinds of plate and do a general miscellaneous business.

Up to the last of June there were employed in these works about 3,800 men, including a number of boys. The pay-roll showed a disbursement for the month of May alone of something over $200,000. Wages have been from 14 cents per hour to the common laborer, that being the lowest, up to $280 per month (which was the highest paid in the month of May), a majority of the skilled laborers receiving $200 and less.

While the Carnegie company under its present management has been exacting, it has also performed many acts of liberality and kindness to its employees. It has at times loaned money to some of them to purchase lots and build their homes, for the use of which it has charged them but 6 per cent interest. It receives from them deposits upon which it pays them 6 per cent interest, the aggregate amount of which the last of June was $140,000.

On July 1, 1899, the company through its officers made a contract with a number of skilled workmen, through the Amalgamated Association of Iron and Steel Workers, to run for three years, or until the 30th of June, 1892.

The basis of that contract was a certain sum per ton of the products in different mills, and $25 per ton as the minimum price for 4 × 4 Bessemer steel billets, with a sliding scale so that if the market price of billets went above that figure the workmen would get the benefit of

Source: Views on the Homestead Strike. Reprinted from *North American Review,* 155 (September, 1892) 355–375. Public Domain Reprint.

the rise; if the market price fell below $25 per ton, the compensation of the workmen would not be less than the minimum. When this contract was about to expire, the company, through its President and chief manager, Mr. Frick, and its chief superintendent, Mr. Potter, submitted a proposition to the workmen, which proposed a reduction of the minimum of $22 per ton of steel billets; also a reduction in some of the departments of the amount of tonnage rate paid; also to change the time of the year when the contract should expire, from the 30th of June to the last day of December.

After considerable negotiation the company proposed to raise the minimum to $34 per ton, and the workmen offered to take $24—which was refused. The workmen also refused to accede to the proposed changes in the time of the expiration of the contract, on the ground that the company would have them at a disadvantage in any renewal of contract which would expire in mid-winter. The negotiations were broken off on the 24th of June.

Mr. Frick, who is a very intelligent and shrewd business man, gives as his chief reasons for the proposition to reduce the wages of his employees:

First, That the price of steel billets, blooms, slabs, etc., has fallen to such a figure in the market that, in justice to his company, the minimum should be reduced (or abolished, as there was no maximum); and,

Secondly, That the improved machinery put in some of the mills since the contract of 1889 doubles the output of the finished product with no increase in the number of laborers, which very greatly increases their tonnage compensation. This latter point is contested by the workmen and explained in several ways, so it would require an expert to pass a perfectly intelligent and just judgment upon the point. Mr. Frick testified before the Congressional Committee that his company has lost money this year, and he thinks the greater part of last year, on every ton of slabs, billets and blooms produced and sold by them. He claims that the McKinley law has nothing to do with this question; that it reduced the duties on all products, the like of which he manufactures, and still these are practically prohibitory, as the diminished amounts of importations clearly proves. He attributes the fall in price to increased domestic production.

In 1874 there were produced in the United States but 91,000 tons of steel ingots, whereas in 1890 the total production was 4,131,000 tons.

Our protective tariff laws, which destroy foreign competition, it is claimed, are enacted for the benefit of the skilled laborers employed by the manufacturers. The advocates of the McKinley tariff law during its consideration proclaimed its purpose to be to give the American market to the American manufacturer, and thereby to enable him pay his laborers higher wages. These promises have not been faithfully kept. Wages have in no case been increased, but in many instances they have been reduced. The promises made to the operatives have been disappointing. Mr. Frick claims that over-production has caused a most remarkable decline in prices within the last three years, and that this makes it necessary for the Carnegie company to reduce expenses.

The high protection extended by Congress to manufacturers, principally on such articles as this company has been manufacturing, has induced the investment of capital in the manufacture of iron and steel, until by this unnatural stimulus over-production has resulted. It disturbs the laws of trade—of supply and demand—and by thus producing more than there is a demand for, prices are driven down and a necessity is created for cutting down the expenses of the manufacturer, and it may be the wages of labor included. In this way the protective tariff disappoints the laboring man and becomes the parent of trusts, combines, strikes and lockouts. The manufacturer, no more than the laborer, can help it, though he is largely responsible for it. He asks Congress for the protection he receives and must bear the consequences. It disturbs and disappoints labor, while professing to protect and foster it. After the breaking off of negotiations on the 24th of June a feeling of estrangement rapidly developed between the employees at Homestead and the officers of the Carnegie company. Messrs. Frick and Potter were hanged in effigy within the works. On the 30th of June the works were closed. On July 1st the striking workmen congregated about the gates and stopped and persuaded the foremen and employees who came to enter to go away. An advisory committee of fifty was raised from the Amalgamated Association. The watchmen of the company were turned away from the works; guards were placed at all the entrances thereto, the river, streets and roads entering the town were patrolled by guards, and a rigid surveillance exercised over those who entered the town or apprehended the works.

When the sheriff came on the 4th of July and demanded to put deputies of his own selection in possession of the works, to guard them for the company, his request was declined, the striking workmen proposing to place guards of their own and give indemnity for the safety of the property, but this the sheriff declined because it would enable them to keep non-union men whom the company might employ from taking the places lately held by the strikers. On the 5th of July, when the sheriff sent twelve deputies to take possession of the works, they were not allowed to do so and were driven away.

As early as about the 20th of June Mr. Frick began negotiations with Robert A. Pinkerton of New York, for the employment of 300 watchmen to be placed in the works at Homestead. On the 25th he wrote a letter to Pinkerton giving instructions as to the movements of the guards, who were to rendezvous at Ashtabula, O., and from thence to be transported by rail to Youngstown, and from thence to be transported by boat up the river and landed in the works at Homestead.

Arms and ammunition for the men were sent in goods boxes from Chicago by William A. Pinkerton, according to the direction of Mr. Frick, and placed on Captain Rodgers's boats at Allegheny. On the evening of the 5th of July Captain Rodgers' boats, with Deputy Sheriff Gray, Superintendent Potter and some of his assistants on board, dropped down the river with two barges in tow, until they met the Pinkerton men, who were embarked on the barges. The boats took the barges in tow, and on the way up one of the steamers became disabled, while the other took both barges, endeavoring to land at Homestead before day, when the people would be asleep and the strikers would likely know nothing of it until after the Pinkerton men were safely within the picket fence surrounding the works. They did not violate any law of Pennsylvania; but they knew that the hostility to the Pinkerton men upon the part of all labor organizations was calculated to produce a breach of the peace.

The greatest mistake made by Mr. Frick was that he did not appeal to the State and county authorities for protection in the first instance. He began to negotiate for the employment of the Pinkerton forces before the negotiations for the re-employment of the workmen were broken off. His company had a legal right to put Pinkerton men or any other employees into the works at Homestead as guards or otherwise, provided in doing so it did not trespass upon the rights of person or property of others. It is but fair to say that this he tried to avoid. The Pinkertons are professional detectives, and guards or watchmen, and in the latter capacity may properly be characterized as a sort of private police or semi-military force.

Mr. Frick should have first appealed to the sheriff of his county for protection. He gave as a reason why he did not, his want of confidence in the efficiency of the sheriff and the deputies he would likely have employed. The sheriff may be a very inefficient officer and lacking in that pluck and energy that is so essential at times to be exercised by an executive officer, but had Mr. Frick and his learned attorneys urged the sheriff and aided him by their counsel, although his efforts in the discharge of his duty were but puerile and futile, if the officers of the Carnegie company had joined him in the appeal to the Governor, and Mr. Frick had gone to him in person and laid the facts before him, there is no doubt that Governor Pattison would, as he finally did do in obedience to a sense of official duty, have supplied a sufficient force to enable the sheriff to take possession and deliver the works to the officers of the company, to the end that they might operate them in whatever way they saw proper.

Men of wealth and capital, as well as the poor mechanics and laborers in this country, must learn to respect the law and the legally constituted authorities, and have recourse to these to redress their wrongs and obtain their rights in preference to undertaking to do these things by private or personal instrumentalities. If men of wealth and corporations may with impunity hire guards in great numbers to perform the functions of the county and State officials in protecting property and preserving the peace, its inevitable effect will be to bring local government and civil authority into contempt.

When Capt. Rodgers's boat with the barges in tow was approaching Homestead, just as day was breaking, a small steamer used by the strikers for patrol purposes set up a whistle, which was responded to by all the engines in town under their control. This caused a crowd to at once assemble along the bank of the river, where it kept pace with the boat, discharging firearms. When the crowd on shore reached the fence around the works they were temporarily halted, but tearing down a part of it they rushed through. A part of the crowd on the shore came down near to the boat when the gang-plank was pushed out. A short war of words was followed by firing on each side, which resulted ultimately in the death of three of the Pinkerton men and seven of the workmen, and the wounding of many on each side. After a brief fusillade those on shore fled in various directions, and the Pinkerton men retreated into their barges. An hour or two later, after having made the barges fast to the wharf, Capt. Rodgers took the wounded upon his boat, and with the Superintendent Potter and Deputy Sheriff Gray steamed up the river to take the wounded to a hospital. About 11 o'clock the boat returned, the deputy sheriff still on board. He said that it was his intention to tow the barges and the Pinkerton men away, but the boat received a heavy fire from the striking workmen with small arms and artillery from both sides of the river. One or two of her crew were either killed or severely wounded, and at one time the pilot for safety abandoned his post and let the steamer drift, so that it became impossible for her to take the barges in tow, and with great difficulty it ran the gauntlet of the fire and escaped to Pittsburg.

At this time the strikers on shore were endeavoring to use a piece of artillery upon the barges, but they could not depress it sufficiently and consequently fired over them. They also poured oil into the river above the barges and set it on fire, but this failed of its purpose, because the water in the river is slack at this point and the wind was blowing up instead of down the river. About five o'clock in the afternoon the Pinkertons displayed a white flag, and negotiated terms of surrender, by which they were allowed to take out their clothing, but their arms and everything else fell into the possession of the Homestead people. The barges were immediately set on fire and burned, and in their burning the pump-house belonging to the Carnegie company was also destroyed. The Pinkerton men now being practically prisoners of war, were marched up town to the skating rink for temporary imprisonment, and on their way, instead of receiving that protection with Mr. Hugh O'Donnell, the chairman of the Advisory Committee, in negotiating the terms of surrender had promised, they were brutally and outrageously maltreated. The injuries inflicted upon them, in some cases, were indecent as well as brutal. Whether these men were of good or bad character, the offence which they had committed against the feelings of the people of Homestead could in no degree justify the indignities with which they were treated.

The sheriff was notified and that night came down and took the prisoners away, informed Governor Pattison of what had transpired, and called upon him again for troops to enforce law and order, to which the Governor responded, as his duty under the law required.

I think that Mr. Frick, like many other manufacturers, is not infatuated with labor organizations, and hence is opposed to the Amalgamated Association and its methods, and had no very great desire to contract with his workmen through that organization. This was the true reason why he appeared to them as autocratic and uncompromising in his demands. They claim that he was too stern, brusque and autocratic to reason with them and hear their arguments. If the business of his company, on account of a fall in the market price of the products of the works, required a reduction of the wages of the employees, he should have appealed to their reason and shown them that the true state of the company's affairs. I am persuaded that if he had done so an agreement would have been reached and all the troubles which followed would thus have been avoided.

Secret political organizations are inconsistent with our American republican system of government, because the public at large has the right of participation in all matters pertaining to government. Laborers, farmers, and men engaged in any business, have the right to organize for their mutual benefit and protection, and even though their organization be secret that constitutes no objection if it is non-political. But no organization of laborers or others has the right of enforcing its wishes or the decrees of its councils by strong hand, setting at defiance the rights of others, or by violations of the law.

I have no doubt that the Amalgamated Association, which is, as I understand it, non-political, may be very useful to its members in many ways if properly limited and directed. While I do not assume it as to this association, there is such a thing as over-organization, to the extent of making the members thereof zealots, and then its unreasonable demands, like a boomerang in its rebound, injure its devotees more than the blow injures the supposed enemy at whom it is aimed, and in this way its usefulness is greatly impaired or destroyed.

The right of any man to labor, upon whatever terms he and his employer agree, whether he belong to a labor organization or not, and the right of a person or corporation (which in law is also a person) to employ any one to labor in a lawful business is secured by the laws of the land.

In this free country these rights must not be denied or abridged. To do so would destroy that personal freedom which has ever been the just pride and boast of American citizens. Even the "moral suasion" which the members of labor organizations may use to prevent non-union men from accepting employment must not be carried too far or it may become intimidation and coercion, and hence be unlawful. We must recognize the fact that in this country every man is the architect of his own fortune. A denial or obstruction of this right should not be tolerated, palliated, or excused. One entire system of government, State and Federal, is based upon the idea of the individual right of every citizen to life, liberty, and the pursuit of happiness. It is not the business of government to aid anyone in the acquisition of property, but it is the business of governments and their duty, each acting within its sphere, to protect the citizen, the humblest as well as the most autocratic, in the enjoyment of the right to his life, his liberty, and the pursuit of happiness. Not to make property for him, nor to furnish him the opportunity of making it, but to amply protect him in his lawful efforts to make it and to enjoy the fruits of his labor.

Congress has, from time to time, arrogated to itself the right to legislate in a manner and upon subjects of which it can properly have no jurisdiction, until the people have become educated to the idea that its powers to legislate are unlimited, and hence, whatever occurs that is deemed an evil, Congress is at once appealed to by thousands for a legislative remedy or relief. It is a familiar principle enunciated by every respectable commentator upon the constitution, and decided many times by the Supreme Court of the United States, that the powers of Congress must be sought alone in some express grant in the constitution, or be found necessary to carry into effect such powers as are therein granted; and that the states have exclusive jurisdiction of all local matters.

Congress, therefore, has no power to interfere by legislation in the labor troubles at Homestead, nor in any similar ones which may subsequently occur there or elsewhere. A voluntary arbitrary law was passed by Congress, applicable to railroad strikes, and there is also one in Pennsylvania applicable to her own affairs, but neither of them is of any practical utility. Parties will not have recourse to that method of settlement, and there is no way to enforce the award when rendered.

Nor is a compulsory arbitration law practicable. Such a law could only be enacted by the State, and compulsory arbitration would be no arbitration at all, since it would at once be the exercise of judicial power.

Courts can afford remedy for violated contracts, but in a case like that at Homestead, where the parties fail to agree,—where they fail to make a contract,—if the State could invest a tribunal with authority to step in and say that the proposition of the Carnegie Company was reasonable and that the striking workmen should accept it and go to work, thus making for them a contract which they refused to make, and the workmen did not choose to obey the award, how could it be enforced?

No legislative authority can deprive any man of the right to contract in respect to his own private property or labor and without his consent confer that power upon another person or tribunal. His discretion and personal right cannot be thus taken from him, for that would at once destroy his freedom.

The rights of property and personal liberty are secured by the fundamental laws of the state and nation, just as they were by the English common law and Magna Charta, which the old barons, sword in hand, wrested from King John, at Runnymede.

The legislature of every state should be diligent in enacting wise, conservative and just laws for the protection of both labor and capital, so that demagogues may have a narrower field for agitation. Unless something of this kind be done, within the next decade we may reasonably expect a revolution and bloodshed, which may work a change in the form of our government. Laboring men and poor people generally are much more interested in preventing this calamity than are the rich. The poor man derives but little benefit from a strong government, which would be the probable outcome of revolution.

Congress can contribute much towards allaying agitation by repealing all class legislation and greatly restricting foreign immigration.

WM. C. OATES

II. A Constitutional View
By George Ticknor Curtis

The editor of THE NORTH AMERICAN REVIEW has requested me to give my opinion on "the legality of the employment of Pinkerton detectives in such cases as the Homestead strike." The inquiry relates to other cases similar in all material respects to the recent occurrences at Homestead, in Pennsylvania. It also involves the relations of employers and employed in all similar branches of manufactures; the relations between the owners of mills, factories, etc., and the workmen whom they employ. A great deal has been written on the relations of capital and labor, and written to very little purpose. It is, however, not difficult to define the rights of property owners or capitalists on the one hand, and of workmen on the other; nor is it difficult to determine what society—by which I mean the legislative power—owes to each of them respectively.

The matter of the Homestead strike has been very much simplified by the statement made by the Messrs. Pinkerton on the 22d of July to the Judiciary Committee of the United States Senate. It appears that for the past twenty years what is called the Pinkerton agency has been a private concern, which has furnished detectives for the discovery of crime, and watchmen to guard the property of individuals and corporations during strikes. The men who have been so employed were not public officers or officers of the law, unless in a particular case they were made so by some public authority. They were not like any other private individual employed as watchmen to protect private property from the violence of a mob, from burglars, or any similar danger. They had the same rights of self-defence and the same right of defending the property of their employers.

Homestead is a borough on the Allegheny River, ten miles from Pittsburg. It contains about 10,000 inhabitants. Most of the male inhabitants are employed in one capacity or another, either as skilled or unskilled laborers, in the iron and steel manufacturing establishments. Their wages were exceptionally high. There exists among them, as there exists elsewhere, what is called a "trades-union." This is a body of workmen banded together for the purpose, among other things, of keeping up the price of labor, and, by means of a strike, of coercing their employers, when the latter do not accede to their terms. A strike is a concerted and sudden cessation of work at a given signal or order, issued by the authority of the union, in whom the power to issue it is vested by the members. Sometimes this authority is a single individual; sometimes it is an advisory committee. In all cases, when a strike is ordered, work ceases at once, to the great injury of employers and employed.

In the Homestead case, the existing agreement between the Carnegie Steel Company and their workmen about wages, had run out. Mr. Frick, the managing agent of the company, had an interview with the men, and offered a new scale of wages. This the men refused to accept. Mr. Frick then closed the mills. After this the workmen seized the mills, excluded the owners from the property by an overwhelming force, and prevented the employment of non-union men. Obviously, it was indispensable that something should be done to restore law and order, and to reinstate the owners of the mills in their property. The local officer of the law, whose duty it was to do this, was the sheriff of Allegheny County. His means consisted only of special deputy sheriffs appointed from the citizens at large, and sworn in as a temporary and extemporized force. In a population consisting largely of the striking workmen and their sympathizers, a force adequate to do what had to be done could not be obtained.

Thereupon the Carnegie Steel Company applied to the Pinkerton agency for a body of watchmen to protect their property. The agency refused to supply the men unless they should be sworn in as deputy sheriffs before going to Homestead. The account runs:

> "The agency was then assured that the sheriff of Allegheny County knew that the men were going to Homestead to act as watchmen to guard the property of the company, and that the sheriff had promised immediately upon any outbreak of disturbance to deputize all the Pinkerton watchmen as deputy sheriffs. On that condition only the agency consented to furnish about 300 watchmen. A large number of these were regular employees of the agency, who could be thoroughly trusted for integrity, prudence and sobriety. The sheriff's chief deputy, Gray, accompanied the men."

The men were sent down the Allegheny River on barges. It is immaterial whether there is or is not a law of Pennsylvania which prohibits the sending of a body of armed men into the State for any purpose. I understand that there is no such law in Pennsylvania, although there is such a law in some of the New England States. But the Pinkerton men were within the limits of the State before they were armed or needed to be. The boxes containing arms and ammunition were shipped from Chicago, *and were to be delivered at the Homestead yards.* These boxes, on board the barges, were not opened and the contents distributed until after the strikers had begun firing from the shore on the watchmen and it had become an evident matter of self-defence. Klein, one of the Pinkerton watchmen, had been killed by the strikers, and about five other men shot and wounded before the Pinkerton men began their fire in self-defence. Then it was impossible to shoot those firing from the shore at the barges, because the strikers had made a breastwork for themselves by placing women and children in front and firing from behind them.

The Pinkerton men were obliged to capitulate before they were allowed to land, and even then they were not permitted to go to the mills which they had been employed to protect. They were conducted by an overwhelming force of the strikers to Labor Hall, the place of meeting of the strikers. There they were made to promise to quit Homestead and never again to serve the mill owners. On their way from the hall they were insulted and brutally assailed by a mob, among whom the women were the most violent. They were withdrawn from the State by the agency, and thus the whole object for which they had been employed was prevented.

Under these circumstances, the sheriff of Allegheny County applied to the Governor of the State for a military force. The Governor declined to order out any of the troops of the State, until the sheriff had exhausted his means of restoring law and order by the appointment of special deputies. The sheriff made an ineffectual effort to do this, but the citizens responded in such few numbers that it would have been idle to rely on the civil arm alone. When the Governor was officially informed of this, he ordered out the entire division of the State militia, about 6,000 men, under General Snowden, a capable, prudent and experienced officer. The troops were marched to Homestead, and encamped on a hill that overlooks the town. It is only necessary to say, concerning this part of the history, that at the time at which I am writing there is every prospect that the strike will be completely put down, and thus the State of Pennsylvania will have rendered a great service to the whole country, employers and employed, capitalists and laborers.

On the indubitable facts of the Homestead case, which I have taken great pains to gather from authentic sources, I have no hesitation in expressing my opinion, as follows:

First, That the owners of the mills had a perfect legal right to employ any necessary number of men to defend their property.

Secondly, That all the acts of the Pinkerton men at Homestead were lawful; and that, as watchmen, they had a right to bear arms on the premises of the Carnegie company in order to protect life and property, whether they were or were not deputized by the sheriff of Allegheny County; and that the agency had the right to ship arms for such purposes from Chicago to the Carnegie yards at Homestead; and that, in view of the attack on the barges, the watchmen had the right to bear arms and defend themselves; and that all their acts in firing in self-defence from the barges after the attack on them were legally justifiable under the laws of the United States and the State of Pennsylvania.

Thirdly, That the killing of Klein by one or more of the riotous strikers was a murder.

Fourthly, That all who stood by, sympathizing with and encouraging the strikers, or not exerting themselves to prevent the strikers who were armed from firing on the barges, were accessories to the murder.

Having thus answered the question that was propounded to me, I shall devote the remainder of the space allotted for this article to the consideration of the duty of the legislative power in the States of this Union in reference to the whole subject of strikes. The stake that society has in all branches of manufacturing industries and in all the great lines of communication and travel is too vast to permit any body of men, large or small, on any pretext, to put a sudden stop to production, or to cause a sudden paralysis in the system of daily and hourly intercourse between different communities.

Unfortunately, there is one embarrassing difficulty. Whenever such a disturbance as that at Homestead occurs, politicians at once endeavor to turn it to the advantage of their political party; and men in high places, who ought to be ashamed of themselves, are often found encouraging the strikers, for the purpose of making what is called "political capital." Mr. Carnegie happens to be a Republican in politics, and his works at Homestead are an eminent instance of the beneficial effect of a protective tariff on the interests of American manufacturers and American laborers. For this reason, Democratic papers and politicians of free trade proclivities take the side of the strikers and endeavor to excite hatred of Mr. Carnegie and his business associates. On the other hand, some Republican papers and politicians are prone to charge the Democratic executive of Pennsylvania with pusillanimous hesitation because he did not at once respond to the call of the sheriff of Allegheny County. Whether we shall ever be entirely free from this disturbing element of politics in reference to this matter of strikes, is problematical. But it is certain that the duty of society remains the same.

The first duty of the legislative power is to emancipate the individual workmen from the tyranny of his class. Unless this be done, capitalists can afford no aid to the solution of any labor problem whatever. Of what avail is it that a mill owner or a railroad company is willing to make fair terms with workmen if the state of things is such that they cannot employ whom they please, on such terms as will be agreed to be the men who want employment? It is only by making the individual laborer a perfectly free man that society can do its duty to him and to those who wish to buy his labor for a price that he is willing to take, and which it is for the interest of those who are dependent upon him to have him take.

In opposition to this view, it will be said that the individual workman is a free agent now, and that if he chooses to join a trades-union and bind himself not to work for wages less than what the union permits him to take, it is his own affair; he is acting in his own right. There is a wide distinction between the physical power to do a thing and the moral and legal right to do it. Men have the physical power to commit suicide, but society does not allow that they have a moral or a legal right to do it. On the same principle, the individual workman should not be allowed to commit moral suicide by surrendering his liberty to the control of his fellow workmen. His labor is his capital, all that he has in the world, all that he and his family have to depend upon for subsistence from day to day. It is to him and them what money invested in real estate, machinery, etc., is to the capitalist. Deprive the capitalist of the power to determine what remuneration he shall derive from the employment of his invested money, and you do the same wrong as when you deprive the laborer of the free power to determine what remuneration he will be content to take for the employment of his capital, which consists of his muscular power and his acquired skill.

These doctrines may not be popular. They may not meet at once with universal acceptance. But until they are accepted and carried out in legislation, there can be no successful reconcilement between the interests of capital and the interests of labor; no adjustment of the rights of society and the rights of employers and employed.

In order that I may not be misunderstood, I will now draw the line between what it may and what it may not be permitted to workmen to do. Associations of workmen, formed for the purpose of discussing the subject of wages with their employers, of obtaining and diffusing information about the price of labor in different places, and of mutual assistance in time of sickness, are beneficial and should be encouraged. But the trades-unions do not confine themselves to these objects. They transcend the line which divides what they may from what they may not rightfully do. In this respect they do a double wrong:

First, They bind their members to strike when ordered to do so by the governing authority of the union. Now the right to renounce an employment is an individual and not a corporate right. The corporate body of a trades-union should not be permitted to bind their members to quit work, as a body, when ordered to do so by the governing authority of the association.

Secondly, The trades-union, as most of them are now organized, prevent non-union men from getting employment, by every species of intimidation, even by personal violence, and sometimes by murder.

This coercion of non-union men, however attempted and in whatever it ends, should be made a crime, and be punished with severity. It is contrary to the fundamental principles of our institutions. The Declaration of Independence says "we hold these truths to be self-evident, that all men are created equal; that they are endowed by their Creator with certain inalienable rights; that among these are life, liberty and the pursuit of happiness. That, to secure these rights, governments are instituted among men, deriving their just powers from the consent of the governed."

Be it observed that these are individual rights; that they are inalienable by the individual himself. We should not permit a man to sell himself into slavery or to sell his own life. He cannot alienate his right to life or his right to liberty. No more should he be permitted to alienate his right to the pursuit of happiness, by giving up his power to consult his own individual welfare, in obtaining the means of happiness; and by putting it in the power of those who are engaged in the same employment to take the bread out of his mouth. We have emancipated the colored race from slavery; certain portions of our own race need emancipation from a slavery that is just as bad.

GEORGE TICKNOR CURTIS.

III. A Knights of Labor's View. By T. V. Powderly, General Master Workman of the Knights of Labor.

The principle involved in the Homestead trouble is the same as that by which the founders of this republic were governed in rebelling against the British government. To have accepted decisions, decrees, and laws without question, and without a voice in their making, would have stamped the colonists as slaves. To accept, without inquiring the why or wherefore, such terms and wages as the Carnegie Steel Company saw fit to offer would stamp the brand of inferiority upon the workmen of Homestead. Independence is worth as much to the workingman as it can be to the employer. The right to sell his labor in the highest market is as dear to the workman as the right of the manufacturer to sell the product of that labor can possibly be to the latter. It is folly to assert that the workman has no right to a voice in determining what the minimum rate of compensation shall be. If the manufacturer is permitted to invade the market place and undersell competitors a reduction in the wages of his employees must inevitably follow. It was to protect the manufacturer as well as the workman that the Amalgamated Association insisted on a minimum rate of pay. The fixing of that rate imposed no hardship on the manufacturer; it gave no competitor the advantage over him, for the majority of mills were operated under the Amalgamated scale, and this of itself fixed a rate below which manufacturers would not sell. The minimum rate was therefore as advantageous to the manufacturer as to the workman in the steel trade. The question at issue between the Carnegie Steel Company and the steel workers does not so much concern the price as the right to a voice in fixing that price.

Individual employers no longer exist; the day no longer dawns on the employer taking his place in the shop among the men. When that condition of workshop life existed employer and employee experienced a feeling of lasting friendship for each other; the interests of each were faithfully guarded by the other. Now the employer of men may be three thousand miles away from the workshop; he may be a part of a syndicate or corporation which deals with the employees through a special agent or superintendent, whose desire to secure the confidence and good will of the corporation may cause him to create friction in order to demonstrate that he is vigilant in looking after the interests of those to whom he looks for favors. The corporation, composed of many men, is an association of capital which delegates its authority to an agent whose duty it is to deal with the workmen and make terms with them. The Amalgamated Association, and all other bodies of organized workmen, stand in the same relation to the men as the corporation does to the capitalists whose money is invested. One invests money, that is, his capital; the other invests his labor, which to him is not only his capital but his all. That the workman should have the same right to be heard through his legitimately appointed agent, the officer of the labor organization, that the corporation has to be heard through the superintendent of agent, is but equity. This is the bone of contention at Homestead, and in fact everywhere else where a labor organization attempts to guard the rights of its members.

Every law, every right, every concession which the workingmen now enjoy has come to them through the labor organization. Philanthropists have spoken honeyed words for the laboring man, but he has always been forced to knock, and knock hard, with his organization in order to take what equity would have accorded him without a struggle if greed had not entered its protest. Equality of rights is what the workmen are contesting for, and because of its immense wealth the Carnegie Steel Company denies that right. It is argued that this trouble is between the employer and the employed and that no other has the right to interfere. That is a doubtful position to take. In a store, in a small shop, or where but a few persons are interested, a strike or lockout may be said to affect only those directly engaged in it, but in the present instance the case presents a different aspect to the thoughtful person. If the great steel plant were not just where it is the town of Homestead would not be the flourishing place that it is. The establishment of that plant attracted workmen to the spot; they built homes, raised their families, and invested every dollar of their earnings there. Business men, professional men, and clergymen followed them, and a community of well-behaved, respectable citizens surrounds the steel works. The workmen by their labor made the steel works. The workmen by their labor made the steel works prosperous and great; on the other hand they made Homestead what it is. The men depend for their support on steady work, and the community back of them depends on their steady employment. Three parties are interested in this struggle, the Carnegie Steel Company, the employees of that concern, and the community. By community I mean the whole people. Other towns have grown up as Homestead grew, by the labor of workmen, and each one is to a certain extent interested in the welfare of the other. The articles manufactured in one place are sold in another, and a mutuality of interests exists to-day which did not, and could not, exist years ago when men required but few things to serve the every-day needs of life. The manager of the Carnegie Steel Company in asserting that he has the right to turn the makers of a prosperous town out of employment and out of the town,—for that naturally follows,—stands upon treacherous ground, for the makers of towns have equally as good a right to be heard as have the investors of money. If we go to a higher law than that of the land, the moral law, there will be no disputing the assertion that flesh and blood should receive more consideration than dollars and cents.

The Carnegie Steel Company and like concerns owe their prosperity to the protective laws of the United States. These laws were passed in the interest of labor. During discussion on the tariff laws it was never advanced as a reason why they should be passed, that capital would be protected,—the argument was always that labor would be protected. The workman has not been protected from foreign competition by the government. He has had to fight the battle for himself through the labor organization. Not only has he had to fight against foreign competition, largely attracted by our delusive tariff laws, but he has had to wage war with the employer for a share of that protection which his government decreed by law that he should have. Our government has enacted protective legislation in the interest of labor, if we read congressional speeches aright, but it quiescently allows the manufacturer to absorb the bulk of protection, and then throws its armies around the establishment at the slightest provocation when the workmen ask for what their government admitted that they had a right to enjoy.

What would have averted this trouble at Homestead, is asked? Industries which are protected by tariff laws should be open to inspection by government officials. When the managers of such concerns seek to absorb all of the protection the government should interfere on behalf of the workingmen. If we must have protection let us see to it that it protects the man who works.

At the hands of the law-making power of State and nation the Knights of Labor demand "the enactment of laws providing for arbitration between employers and employed, and to enforce the decision of the arbitrators." It should be a law in every State that in disputed case the employer should be obliged to select two arbitrators and the employees two, these four to select the fifth; this arbitration commission to have access to all books, papers, and facts bearing on the question at issue from both sides. It goes without saying that the commission should be made up of reasonable, well-disposed men, and that publicity would not be given to such information as they might become possessed of.

An established board of arbitration, appointed by a governor, or other authority, is simply no board of arbitration at all, for the reason that the workmen would have no voice in its selection, and the other side, having all the money and influence, would be tempted to "fix" such a board preparatory to engaging in a controversy with workingmen. For either side to refuse to appoint its arbitrators should be held to be cause for their appointment by the Governor of the State. No strike or lockout should be entered upon before the decision of the board of arbitrators. Provisions for appeal from the decision of the arbitrators should be made in order to prevent intimidation or money from influencing the board.

In no case should the introduction of an armed force, such as the Pinkerton detective agency arms and equips, be tolerated. The system which makes one man a millionaire makes tramps and paupers of thousands. The thousands go down to the brothels and slums, where they sprout the germs of anarchy and stand ready for any deed of desperation. The millionaire becomes more arrogant and unreasonable as his millions accumulate. Victimizing and blacklisting are the concomitants of the rule of industrial establishments by our millionaire "lords of industry," and these measures furnish recruits for the army of greed when organized labor enters its protest against such acts of injustice as has made tramps of other men under like circumstances. The employer who is satisfied with a reasonable profit will not fear to intrust his case to such a board of arbitrators as I have described. The employer who refuses arbitration fears for the justice of his cause. He who would acquire legitimately need not fear investigation; he who would steal must do it in the dark in order to be successful.

Those who harshly criticise the workmen of Homestead should put themselves in the place of these workmen for a few brief moments of thought. Picture the skill required to turn out faultless work, the loss of eyesight which follows a few years of toil before the seething furnace, the devotion to duty which must be shown in order to succeed. Then step outside of the mill and witness the erection of a high fence and its armament. Consider what it means and that it is being erected before a threat has been made or a disagreement considered among the possibilities. Think of the stigma which the erection of that fence casts on the man who works, the builder of the town; and then reflect that it is being built to serve as a prison-pen for those who must work so cheap that they will not be able to erect homes or maintain families in respectability. Ponder over the fact that when cheap men take the places of well-paid men, they do not buy carpets, organs, pianos, decent, respectable furniture or raiment, and that the makers of these articles elsewhere will be thrown out of employment, and that other manufacturers will be driven to bankruptcy because of a falling off in the demand for their product. Then read what Mr. Carnegie said six short years ago in speaking of the question of employing non-union, cheap men:

"To expect that one dependent upon his daily wage for the necessaries of life will stand by peaceably and see a new man employed in his stead is to expect much. This poor man may have a wife and children dependent upon his labor. Whether medicine for a sick child, or even nourishing food for a delicate wife, is procurable, depends upon his steady employment. In all but a very few departments of labor it is unnecessary, and, I think, improper, to subject men to such an ordeal. In the case of railways and a few other employments it is, of course, essential for the public wants that no interruption occur, and in such case substitutes must be employed; but the employer of labor will find it much more to his interest, wherever possible, to allow his works to remain idle and await the result of a dispute than to employ the class of men that can be induced to take the place of other men who have stopped work. Neither the best men as men, nor the best men as workers, are thus to be obtained. There is an unwritten law among the best workmen: 'Thou shalt not take thy neighbor's job.' No wise employer will lightly lose his old employees. Length of service counts for much in many ways. Calling upon strange men should be the last resort."

The introduction of an armed body of men at the outset was an indication that some man would be expected to "take his neighbor's job," and at once. The arbitrament of the sword was the first thought with the Carnegie Steel Company. The laws of Pennsylvania were disregarded in arming citizens of other States and assigning them to duty at Homestead. In that awful spectacle to which the eyes of humanity turned on the 6th of July could be seen the final abolition of brute force in the settlement of strikes and lockouts. What the law will not do for men they must do for themselves, and by the light of the blazing guns at Homestead it was written that arbitration must take the place of "Pinkertonism."

T. V. POWDERLY.

NOTE

*Statement of Mr. Robert Pinkerton to the Judiciary Committee of the United States Senate, July 22, 1892.

108. Michael Gold, *Jews Without Money*

Michael Gold offers a view of immigrant Jewish life before the turn of the century. His 1920 novel, Jews Without Money, *describes the same years around the turn of the century that Antin details.*

Jews and Christians

1

My mother never learned to like shoes. In Hungary, in her native village, she had rarely worn them, and she could see no reason for wearing them here.

"Does one wear shoes on one's hands?" she would ask. "How can one work in shoes? Shoes are only for people to show off in."

So she paddled about in bare feet whenever she could. This annoyed my father at those times when he was ambitious. To him not wearing shoes was like confessing to the world that one was poor. But my mother had no such false pride, and would even walk barefooted in the street.

Once my father bought her a diamond ring on the installment plan. It was during one of his periods of greatness, when he had earned a big week's pay, and the Boss had hinted at a foreman's job for him.

It was on a Saturday night, and he had been drinking beer with his fellow-workmen. He came home flushed and dramatic. With many flourishes and the hocus-pocus of a magician he extracted the ring from his vest pocket and placed it on my mother's finger.

"At last, Katie!" he said, kissing her with great ceremony, "at last you have a diamond ring! At last you can write home to Hungary that you too are wearing diamonds in America!"

"Pouf!" said my mother angrily, pushing him away. She snatched the ring from her finger as if it burned her. "What foolishness!"

"Foolishness!" my father exclaimed, indignantly. "What! it is foolish to wear diamonds?"

"Yes," said my stubborn mother.

"Every one wears diamonds!" said my father, "every one with a little pride."

"Let others be proud! I am a work horse," said my mother.

My father spat in disgust, and stalked off to find some intelligent males.

The ring remained in the family. It was our only negotiable capital. It was hidden among some towels and sheets in the bureau. In time of need it traveled to the pawnshop, to buy us food and rent. Many East Side families aspired to jewelry for this reason. Money vanished. Jewelry remained. This was the crude credit system of the East Side.

2

My mother was fond of calling herself a work horse. She was proud of the fact that she could work hard. She wanted no diamond rings, no fancy dresses, no decorations. She had a strong sense of reality, and felt that when one was poor, only strength could help one. But my father was a romantic, and dreamed of a bright easy future.

My humble funny little East Side mother! How can I ever forget this dark little woman with bright eyes, who hobbled about all day in bare feet, cursing in Elizabethan Yiddish, using the forbidden words "ladies" do not use, smacking us, beating us, fighting with her neighbors, helping her neighbors, busy from morn to midnight in the tenement struggle for life.

She would have stolen or killed for us. She would have let a railroad train run over her body if it could have helped us. She loved us with all the fierce painful love of a mother-wolf, and scolded us continually like a magpie.

Mother! Momma! I am still bound to you by the cords of birth. I cannot forget you. I must remain faithful to the poor because I cannot be faithless to you! I believe in the poor because I have known you. The world must be made gracious for the poor! Momma, you taught me that!

3

What a hard life she led. She had known nothing but work since her tenth year. Her father had died then, and

---

Source: Michael Gold, *Jews Without Money,* pp. 156–173. Copyright Liveright Publishing Corp. Reprinted by permission.

she was the oldest child of a large family. She went to work in a bakery, then did a man's labor on a farm.

When she was eighteen, relatives gathered seventy-five gulden, and sent her to America as the last hope for her family. She was to work here and send for her brothers and sisters.

The crossing made a deep mark on her mind. She spent seventeen agonized days in the filthy steerage, eating nothing but herrings and potatoes, because there was no *kosher* food.

Her first night in America was spent amid groans and confusion on the floor of a crowded cellar for immigrants. It was called the Nigger House.

A relative found her the next morning. He took her to a job. It was in an East Side restaurant where she was paid five dollars a month, with meals. She slept on a mattress in the evil, greasy kitchen. The working hours were from five to midnight.

In a year she saved enough money to send a ship ticket to her oldest brother.

"Yes, I have had all kinds of good times in America," she would chuckle grimly, when she told us of this time. "Yes, that first year in the restaurant I had lots of fun with the pots and pans.

"It's lucky I'm alive yet. It is a good land, but not for the poor. When the Messiah comes to America, he had better come in a fine automobile, with a dozen servants. If he comes here on a white horse, people will think he is just another poor immigrant. They may set him to work washing dishes in a restaurant."

4

She and my father had married in the old Jewish style; that is, they were brought together by a professional matrimonial broker. He charged them a commission for the service. It is as good a method as any. My parents came to love each other with an emotion deeper than romance; I am sure my father would have died for my mother. But she also made his head ache, and he told her so often.

She was a buttinsky. She tried to "reform" everybody, and fought people because they were "bad." She spoke her mind freely, and told every one exactly where the path of duty lay. She was always engaged in some complicated ethical brawl, and my father had to listen to all the details.

Or she was always finding people in trouble who needed her help. She helped them for days, weeks and months, with money, food, advice and the work of her hands.

She was a midwife in many hasty births, a nurse in sickness, a peacemaker in family battles.

She knew how to make a poultice for boils by chewing bread and mixing it with yellow soap; and how to cure colds with kerosene, and the use of herbs and other peasant remedies. She was a splendid cook and breadmaker, and shared all these secrets with the neighbors.

When a woman fell sick, the distracted husband appealed to my mother; and for weeks she'd drop in there twice a day, to cook the meals, and scrub the floors, and bathe the children, to joke, gossip, scold, love, to scatter her strength and goodness in the dark home.

It would have shocked her if any one had offered to pay for these services. It was simply something that had to be done for a neighbor.

Once there was a woman on our street who was going crazy. Her cigarmaker husband had deserted her and two children. The woman had spells, and could not sleep at night. She begged my mother to sleep with her. She was afraid she would kill her children during one of her spells.

So my mother slept there every night for more than a month.

How often have I seen my mother help families who were evicted because they could not pay rent. She wrapped herself in her old shawl, and went begging through the tenements for pennies. Puffing with bronchitis, she dragged herself up and down the steep landings of a hundred tenements, telling the sad tale with new emotion each time and begging for pennies.

But this is an old custom on the East Side; whenever a family is to be evicted, the neighboring mothers put on their shawls and beg from door to door.

5

My poor father, worrying over his own load of American troubles, had to listen to the tremendous details of all these tragedies. My mother could discover so many sick people! And so many bad people who needed to be fought! No wonder my father drank beer! No wonder he grabbed his head between his hands, and groaned:

"Stop! you give me a headache! I can't listen any more!"

"It is not your head, but your selfishness!" scoffed my mother.

"One has to be selfish in America," said my father. "It is dog eat dog over here. But you, you neglect your own family to help every passing stranger."

"*Pfui*, what a lie!" my mother spat. "When have my children been neglected?"

"But for God's sake," said my father, "haven't we enough troubles of our own? You're like a man with consumption. It is not enough for him to have this, he has to go skating so that he can break his leg, too."

"*Nu*, I can stand a broken leg," said my mother. "What is a leg when there is so much misery in the world?"

6

My mother was opposed to the Italians, Irish, Germans, and every other variety of Christian with whom we were surrounded.

"May eight and eighty black years fall on these *goys!*" she said, her black eyes flashing. "They live like pigs; they have ruined the world. And they hate and kill Jews. They may seem friendly to us to our faces, but behind our backs they laugh at us. I know them well. I have seen them in Hungary."

My father sat one evening at the supper table, drinking beer and reading a Yiddish newspaper. In the hot kitchen my mother was washing the dishes, and humming a Hungarian folk song.

"*Nu, nu!*" my father exclaimed, striking the table with his fist, "another railroad accident! Katie, I have always said it is dangerous to travel on these American railroads!"

"What has happened?" my mother gasped, appearing from the kitchen with steaming hands and face.

"What has happened, you ask?" my father repeated in the important tone of a pedant. "What has happened is that seventeen innocent people were killed in a railroad accident in New Jersey! And whose fault was it? The fault of the rich American railroads!"

My mother was horrified. She wiped her boiling face with her apron and muttered: "God help us and shield us! Were there any Jews among the dead?"

My father glanced rapidly through the list of names. "No," he said, "only Christians were killed."

My mother sighed with relief. She went back into her kitchen. She was no longer interested; Christians did not seem like people to her. They were abstractions. They were the great enemy, to be hated, feared and cursed. In Hungary three Christian peasant girls had once taunted her. Then they had gone in swimming, and had been drowned. This was God's punishment on them for persecuting a Jew. Another peasant had once plucked the beard of an old reverend Jew, and God struck him with lightning a week later. My mother was full of such anecdotes.

The East Side never forgot Europe. We children heard endless tales of the pogroms. Joey Cohen, who was born in Russia, could himself remember one. The Christians had hammered a nail into his uncle's head, and killed him. When we passed a Christian church we were careful to spit three times; otherwise bad luck was sure to befall us. We were obsessed by wild stories of how the Christians loved to kidnap Jewish children, to burn a cross on each cheek with a redhot poker. They also cut off children's ears, and made a kind of soup. Nigger had once seen Jewish ears for sale in the window of a Christian butcher shop.

"In the old days," my mother said, "the Christians hunted the Jews like rabbits. They would gather thousands in a big marketplace, and stuff pork down their throats with swords, and ask the Jews to be baptized. The Jews refused, of course. So they were burnt in great fires, and the Christians laughed, danced and made merry when they saw the poor Jews burning up like candles. Such are the Christians. May they burn some day, too."

These impressions sank into my heart, and in my bad dreams during the hot summer nights, dark Christian ogres the size of tenements moved all around me. They sat on my chest, and clutched my throat with slimy remorseless fingers, shrieking, "Jew, Jew! Jew!"

And I would spend long daylight hours wondering why the Christians hated us so, and form noble plans of how I would lead valiant Jewish armies when I grew up, in defense of the Jews.

7

But my mother was incapable of real hatred. Paradoxically she had many warm friends among the Italian and Irish neighbors. She was always apologetic about this. "These are not like other Christians," she would say, "these are good people." How could she resist another human being in trouble? How could she be indifferent when another was in pain? Her nature was made for universal sympathy, without thought of prejudice. Her hatred of Christians was really the outcry of a motherly soul against the boundless cruelty in life.

Betsy was an Italian woman who lived in the next tenement. She had a long, emaciated face covered with moles, engraved with suffering like an old yellow wood carving. Her coffee-colored eyes always seemed to have a veil over them, as if she were hiding a terrible secret. She avoided people; swathed in her long black scarf she stole down the street furtively, as if conscious of the eyes of the world.

Her husband was in jail for murder. One summer night (I shall never forget it), he burst from the tenement into the street, screaming like a madman. A revolver was in his hand. We were sitting on the stoop, calmly eating ice-cream cones. This spectacle of this wild swarthy Italian in his undershirt, shrieking, and waving a pistol, appalled us like a hallucination. He rushed by us, and dived into a cellar. A crowd gathered. A policeman ran up. He hadn't the nerve to follow the Italian into the cellar, but stood uncertainly on the sidewalk, growling: "Get up out of there, before I shoot yuh." At last the Italian stumbled out, sobbing like a child. His bronzed, rocky face was grotesquely twisted with grief. He wrung his hands, beat his chest, and clawed at his cheeks until the blood spurted. I have never heard such dreadful animal howls, the ferocious and dangerous agony of a dying wolf. He had just killed his brother in a quarrel over a card game.

This passion-blinded assassin was Betsy's husband. She was left with three children, and no friends. She could speak only Italian. My mother visited her, and through sheer sympathy, learned, in the course of several visits, a kind of pigeon-Italian. It was marvelous to hear my mother hold hour-long conversations with this woman, in a polyglot jargon that was a mixture of Italian, Yiddish, Hungarian and English. But the women understood each other.

My mother helped Betsy find a clothing shop that would give her basting work to do at home. My mother helped the Christian in many ways. And Betsy worshipped her. In the midst of her miseries she found time to knit a large wool shawl as a surprise for my mother. She brought it in one night, and cried and jabbered excitedly in Italian, and kissed my mother's hands. And my mother cried, and kissed her, too. We could not understand a word of what they were saying, but my mother kept repeating in Yiddish: "Ach, what a good woman this is! What a dear woman!" My mother treasured this shawl more than anything she owned. She liked to show it to every one, and tell the story of how Betsy had made it.

A shawl like that was worth over ten dollars, more than Betsy earned in a week. It must have taken weeks to knit, many overtime nights under the gaslight after a weary sixteen-hour day at basting clothing. Such gifts are worthy to be treasured; they are knitted in love.

8

There was an Irish family living on the top floor of our tenement. Mr. O'Brien was a truck-driver, a tall gloomy giant with a red face hard as shark-leather. He came home from work at nine and ten o'clock each night. Powerful and hairy in his blue overalls, he stamped ponderously up the stairs. If we children were playing in the halls, he brushed through our games, scowling at us as if he hated children.

"Get the hell out of my way; you're thick as bedbugs," he muttered, and we scattered from under the feet of the ferocious great Christian.

His wife was also large and red-faced, a soft, sad mountain of flesh waddling around under perpetual baskets of laundry. All Christian ladies did washing, all except the Italians. Mrs. O'Brien was kinder to children than her husband, but we feared her almost as much.

This couple was one of the scandals of the tenement. Night after night, in the restless sleep of our little commune, we heard as in a coöperative nightmare the anguished screams of the Irish mother down the airshaft. Her husband was drunk and was beating her.

"No, no, Jack, don't!" she screamed. "You'll frighten the boy."

This couple had a mysterious child whom nobody had ever seen, and the mother always mentioned him in these brutal midnight scenes.

"Tuh hell with the boy!" roared the man's voice, formidable and deep as a mad bull's. "Tuh hell with everything!"

Crash! he had knocked her down over a table. Windows flew open; heads popped into the airshaft from every side like a shower of curious balloons; the tenement was awake and fascinated. We could hear a child's frightened whimpering, then crash! another powerful blow stuck at a soft woman's body.

"Jack, don't! The neighbors will hear!"

"Tuh hell with the kikes! I'll set fire to the damn house and make the sheenies run like rats!"

Bang, crash, scream! The tenement listened with horror. These were the Christians again. No Jew was ever as violent as that. No Jew struck a woman. My mother, ever an agitator, led a campaign against the Irish couple, to force the landlord to put them out. "It is worse than the whores," said my mother, "having Christians in a tenement is worse."

9

But one quiet afternoon, who should burst into my mother's kitchen, pale and stammering with fright, but the Irish washerlady.

"Quick, my boy is choking to death! Help me! Get a doctor, for God's sake!"

My mother, without a superfluous word, sped like a fireman up the stairs, to help the child. It had swallowed a fishbone. My mother, expert and brave in such emergencies, put her finger down his throat and dislodged the bone. Then she had a long intimate talk with the Irish mother.

That night at the supper table, while my work-weary father was trying to eat hamburger steak, and read the Yiddish newspaper, and drink beer, and think about his troubles, and smoke and talk all at the same time, my mother irritated him by sighing profoundly.

"Ach, Herman," she said, "that Irish washerlady has so many misfortunes."

"*Pfui!*" my father spat impatiently, "so have I!"

"She is a good woman," said my mother, "even if she is a Christian. Her husband beats her, but she is sorry for him. He is not a bad man. He is only sad."

"*Gottenu!*" my father groaned in disgust with female logic. "I hope he beats you, too!"

"He was a farmer in Ireland," my mother went on dreamily. "He hates the city life here, but they are too poor to move to the country. And their boy has been sick for years. All their money goes for doctors. That's why he drinks and beats her, but her heart bleeds for him."

"Enough!" said my father, clutching his hair. "Enough, or I will go mad!"

My mother saw that he was really angry, so she took the empty soup plates into the kitchen. There she stirred something in a pot, and opened the stove to take out the noodle pudding. She brought this to the table.

"And, Herman," she said pensively, with the steaming pudding in her hands, "that woman used to gather mushrooms in the forest in Ireland. Just the way I gathered them in Hungary."

10

I was playing with the boys. We had been seized with the impulse to draw horses in chalk on the pavement. Then there was a fight, because Joey Cohen had written under his horse, "NIGGER LOVES LEAH." He also wrote this on an express wagon, on the stoop steps, and on the bock beer sign standing in front of the saloon. Nigger was about ready to punch Joey on the nose, when Mrs. O'Brien shambled up to us, slow, sad and huge, looming above us with the perpetual basket of laundry on her arm.

"Don't fight, boys," she said kindly in her clear Christian speech. "Will one of you do something for me? I will give any boy a nickel who will go up and play with my little boy. He is sick."

We were dumbfounded with fear. We stared at her and our mouths fell open. Even Nigger was scared.

Mrs. O'Brien looked right at me. "Will you do it?" she pleaded. I blushed, and suddenly ran off as if I had seen a devil. The other boys scattered. Mrs. O'Brien sighed, picked up her heavy basket, and hobbled on her way.

I told my mother that night. What did it mean? Was the Christian washerlady trying to snare me into her home, where she would burn a cross on my face with a hot poker?

"No," said my mother thoughtfully. "Go up there; it will be a good deed. The Christian child is lonely. Nothing can happen to you."

She took me there herself the next morning. And I found nothing to fear. It was a gray humid morning. In the yellow gloom of a bedroom narrow and damp like a coffin, a child with shrunken face lay in bed. His forehead was pale as marble. It was streaked with blue veins, and altogether too round and large for his head. His head was too large for his body. It dangled clumsily, though supported by a steel brace at the neck.

He looked at me with great mournful eyes. His nose wrinkled like a baby's, and he cried.

"Don't be frightened, Johnnie," said his mother, "this boy is a friend who has come to play with you."

I wound my top and spun it on the floor. He craned his stiff neck to watch. Then I put the top in his hand and tried to teach him to spin it, too. But he was too feeble for this sport. So he wept once more, and I was grieved for him. Was this one of the dreaded Christians?

109. THE POPULIST PARTY, THE OMAHA PLATFORM OF THE PEOPLE'S PARTY, 1892

The Omaha Platform was the clearest statement of the ideals of the Populist movement at the peak of its power and influence in 1892.

Populist Party Platform
July 4, 1892

The Preamble which appeared first in the St. Louis platform of March 1892, was written by Ignatius Donnelly of Minnesota. The most thorough history of the Populist movement is J.D. Hicks, *The Populist Revolt*, which contains an elaborate bibliography.

Assembled upon the 116th anniversary of the Declaration of Independence, the People's Party of America, in their first national convention, invoking upon their action the blessing of Almighty God, put forth in the name and on behalf of the people of this country, the following preamble and declaration of principles:

Preamble

The conditions which surround us best justify our co-operation; we meet in the midst of a nation brought to the verge of moral, political, and material ruin. Corruption dominates the ballot-box, the Legislatures, the Congress, and touches even the ermine of the bench. The people are demoralized; most of the States have been compelled to isolate the voters at the polling places to prevent universal intimidation and bribery. The newspapers are largely subsidized or muzzled, public opinion silenced, business prostrated, homes covered with mortgages, labor impoverished, and the land concentrating in the hands of capitalists. The urban workmen are denied the right to organize for self-protection, imported pauperized labor beats down their wages, a hireling standing army, unreorganized by our laws, is established to shoot them down, and they are rapidly degenerating into European conditions. The fruits of the toil of millions are boldly stolen to build up colossal fortunes for a few, unprecedented in the history of mankind; and the possessors of these, in turn, despise the Republic and endanger liberty. From the same prolific womb of governmental injustice we breed the two great classes—tramps and millionaires.

The national power to create money is appropriated to enrich bond-holders; a vast public debt payable in legal-tender currency has been funded into gold-bearing bonds, thereby adding millions to the burdens of the people.

Silver, which has been accepted as coin since the dawn of history, has been demonetized to add to the purchasing power of gold by decreasing the value of all forms of property as well as human labor, and the supply of currency is purposely abridged to fatten usurers, bankrupt enterprise, and enslave industry. A vast conspiracy against mankind has been organized on two continents, and it is rapidly taking possession of the world. If not met and overthrown at once it forebodes terrible social convulsions, the destruction of civilization, or the establishment of an absolute despotism.

We have witnessed for more than a quarter of a century the struggles of the two great political parties for power and plunder, while grievous wrongs have been inflicted upon the suffering people. We charge that the controlling influences dominating both these parties have permitted the existing dreadful conditions to develop without serious effort to prevent or restrain them. Neither do they now promise us any substantial reform. They have agreed together to ignore, in the coming campaign, every issue but one. They propose to drown the outcries of a plundered people with the uproar of a sham battle over the tariffs, so that capitalists, corporations, national banks, rings, trusts, watered stock, the demonetization of silver and the oppressions of the usurers may all be lost sight of. They propose to sacrifice our homes, lives, and children on the alter of mammon; to destroy the multitude in order to secure corruption funds from the millionaires.

Source: E. McPherson, "The Populist Party Platform." Originally from *A Handbook of Politics for 1892*, p. 269. Public Domain Reprint from *Documents of American History*, pp. 593–596.

109. The Populist Party, The Omaha Platform of the People's Party, 1892

Assembled on the anniversary of the birthday of the nation, and filled with the spirit of the grand general and chief who established our independence, we seek to restore the government of the Republic to the hands of the "plain immigrant." with which class it originated. We assert our purposes to be identical with the purposes of the National Constitution; to form a more perfect union and establish justice, insure domestic tranquility, provide for the common defence, promote the general welfare, and secure the blessings of liberty for ourselves and our posterity.

We declare that this Republic can only endure as a free government, while built upon the love of the people for each other and for the nation; that it cannot be pinned together by bayonets; that the Civil War is over, and that every passion and resentment which grew out of it must die with it, and that we must be in fact, as we are in name, one united brotherhood of free men.

Our country finds itself confronted by conditions for which there is no precedent in the history of the world; our annual agricultural productions amount to billions of dollars in value, which must, within a few weeks or months, be exchanged for billions of dollars' worth of commodities consumed in their production; the existing currency supply is wholly inadequate to make this exchange; the results are falling prices, the formation of combines and rings, the impoverishment of the producing class. We pledge ourselves that if given power we will labor to correct these evils by wise and reasonable legislation, in accordance with the terms of our platform.

We believe that the power of government—in other words, of the people—should be expanded (as in the case of postal service) as rapidly and as far as the good sense of an intelligent people and the teachings of experience shall justify, to the end that oppression, injustice, and poverty shall eventually cease in the land.

While our sympathies as a party of reform, are naturally upon the side of every proposition which will tend to make men intelligent, virtuous and temperate, we nevertheless regard these questions, important as they are, as secondary to the great issues now pressing for solution, and upon which not only our individual prosperity but the very existence of free institutions depend; and we ask all men to first help us to determine whether we are to have a republic to administer before we differ as to the conditions upon which it is to be administered, believing that the forces of reform this day organized will never cease to move forward until every wrong is righted and equal rights and equal privileges, securely established for all the men and women of this country.

Platform

We declare, therefore—

First.—That the union of the labor forces of the United States this day consummated shall be permanent and perpetual; may its spirit enter into all hearts for the salvation of the Republic and the uplifting of mankind.

Second.—Wealth belongs to him who creates it, and every dollar taken from industry without an equivalent is robbery. "If any will not work, neither shall he eat." The interests of rural and civil labor are the same; their enemies are identical.

Third.—We believe that the time has come when the railroad corporations will either own the people or the people must own the railroads; and should the government enter upon the work of owning and managing all railroads, we should favor an amendment to the constitution by which all persons engaged in the government service shall be placed under a civil-service regulation of the most rigid character, so as to prevent the increase of the power of the national administration by the use of such additional government employees.

FINANCE.—We demand a national currency, safe, sound, and flexible issued by the general government only, a full legal tender for all debts, public and private, and that without the use of banking corporations; a just, equitable, and efficient means of distribution direct to the people, at a tax not to exceed 2 per cent, per annum, to be provided as set forth in the sub-treasury plan of the Farmers' Alliance, or a better system; also by payments in discharge of its obligations for public improvements.

1. We demand free and unlimited coinage of silver and gold at the present legal ratio of 16 to 1.
2. We demand that the amount of circulating medium be speedily increased to not less than $50 per capita.
3. We demand a graduated income tax.
4. We believe that the money of the country should be kept as much as possible in the hands of the people, and hence we demand that all State and national revenues shall be limited to the necessary expenses of the government, economically and honestly administered.
5. We demand that postal savings banks be established by the government for the safe deposit of the earnings of the people and to facilitate exchange.

TRANSPORTATION.—Transportation being a means of exchange and a public necessity, the government should own and operate the railroads in the interest of the people. The telegraph and telephone, like the post-office system, being a necessity for the transmission of news, should be owned and operated by the government in the interest of the people.

LAND.—The land, including all the natural sources of wealth, is the heritage of the people, and should not be monopolized for speculative purposes, and alien ownership of land should be prohibited. All land now held by railroads and other corporations in excess of their actual needs, and all lands now owned by aliens should be reclaimed by the government and held for actual settlers only.

Expression of Sentiment

Your Committee on Platform and Resolutions beg leave unanimously to report the following:

Whereas, Other questions have been presented for our consideration, we hereby submit the following, not as a part of the Platform of the People's Party, but as resolutions expressive of the sentiment of this Convention.

1. RESOLVED, That we demand a free ballot and a fair count in all elections, and pledge ourselves to secure it to every legal voter without Federal intervention, through the adoption by the States of the unperverted Australian or secret ballot system.

2. RESOLVED, That the revenue derived from a graduated income tax should be applied to the reduction of the burden of taxation now levied upon the domestic industries of this country.

3. RESOLVED, That we pledge our support to fair and liberal pensions to ex-Union soldiers and sailors.

4. RESOLVED, That we condemn the fallacy of protecting American labor under the present system, which opens our ports to the pauper and criminal classes of the world and crowds out our wage-earners; and we denounce the present ineffective laws against contract labor, and demand the further restriction of undesirable emigration.

5. RESOLVED, That we cordially sympathize with the efforts of organized workingmen to shorten the hours of labor, and demand a rigid enforcement of the existing eight-hour law on Government work, and ask that a penalty clause be added to the said law.

6. RESOLVED, That we regard the maintenance of a large standing army of mercenaries, known as the Pinkerton system, as a menace to our liberties, and we demand its abolition; and we condemn the recent invasion of the Territory of Wyoming by the hired assassins of plutocracy, assisted by Federal officers.

7. RESOLVED, That we commend to the favorable consideration of the people and the reform press the legislative system known as the initiative and referendum.

8. RESOLVED, That we favor a constitutional provision limiting the office of President and Vice-President to one term, and providing for the election of Senators of the United States by a direct vote of the people.

9. RESOLVED, That we oppose any subsidy or national aid to any private corporation for any purpose.

10. RESOLVED, That this convention sympathizes with the Knights of Labor and their righteous contest with the tyrannical combine of clothing manufacturers of Rochester, and declare it to be a duty of all who hate tyranny and oppression to refuse to purchase the goods made by the said manufacturers, or to patronize any merchants who sell such goods.

110. Tom Watson and Anthony Wilson, The *People's Party Paper*, 1892

Tom Watson was the most flamboyant and popular candidate of the Southern Populists. He had been a young Democratic state legislator and United States Representative from Georgia in the 1880s and early 1890s before his conversion to the Populist cause. In the newspaper account of this speech, from Atlanta's People's Party Paper *from September of 1892, Watson tells his two thousand listeners in Sparta, Georgia, of the reasons for his policies. Watson steps aside for a while to give Anthony Wilson, a black Republican against whose seating in the Georgia legislature Watson had voted a few years earlier, a chance to speak. The relationship between blacks and whites was one of the most sensitive areas for white Populists, who wanted black votes but did not feel they could politically afford to be known as the "black man's party." Watson won overwhelmingly in all the rural districts a few weeks after this speech, but the heavy Democratic vote (much of which was fraudulent) in the city of Augusta defeated him. Watson later became a popular, overtly racist, Democratic United States Senator.*

Now, we said that there is another man, even worse than that. Who is that other man? The man who would grind the face of God's poor; the man who took the proceeds of your labor, when he sold the crop, and would not pay when Christmas came. (A voice: "God knows, we know them!")

Now, I say this, that there are dishonest employers, just as there are dishonest tenants, or dishonest laborers. Have there not been such? (Cries of "Yes! Yes"!) Such a man would work you all the year, whether you were black or white, and at the end of the year he would lock the corn in the crib, and put the money he received for it in his pocket; and when you come to ask him for a settlement, you had to whistle for your money. Ain't that so? (Cries of "Yes! Yes!") I say here now, that there are not many men who do that, but we said then and there, with reference to a man who would resort to such dishonest practices—no matter how white that land owner was, no matter how rich and powerful that land owner—if he resorted to such practices to defraud the white tenant or the black tenant, the white laborer or the black laborer, the white hireling or the black hireling, by keeping him working all the year round and then turning him and his wife and helpless children adrift, and not giving him his share of the labor, he was bigger rascal than the man that took the meat, the money, the credit and then failed to perform the stipulations of his contract. (Great applause and cries of: "That's the God's truth.") We said this: if you are going to punish the poor man for non-fulfillment of his contract, punish the rich man for the same offense, if you are going to punish the man who does not own the land, punish the man who does own the land—make no distinction on account of color, or property; feed them both out of the same spoon; accord "equal rights to all special privileges to none." (Clapping of hands and great cheering.)

Now let me go right on. I think we have about got rid of those fellows who were annoying us, and we are going to be happy to-day. I am going to tell you more of the truth directly, and will prove all I say, I do not ask you to take my word for anything. Now listen, and you will hear more about what was done than these Democrats will dare to tell you.

When I was a member of the legislature I drew up a bill and tried to have it enacted into law, which would directly help the laborer and the cropper all over the State of Georgia. How? You know that, as the law stands, you may rent a home for the year, and the land attached, and during the year I may take a portion of my rent from you or your wife [and] children, and forget to give you credit for it—I may take some in vegetables, and forget to give

Source: Tom Watson and Anthony Wilson, *People's Party Paper*, Atlanta, GA. Sept. 2, 1892. Public Domain Reprint.

you credit for it; I may take some in corn, and forget to give you credit for it; I may take some in poultry, and forget to give you credit for it; and at the end of the year you have two little bales of cotton, and in those little bales of cotton are locked up all your profits for the year's farming. You have watered your mouth thinking of the good things you were going to get when you had the money in your pocket. Perhaps you had promised the old lady a new dress, and your daughter a dress and a brand new red handkerchief each; perhaps you promised the boys new hats and boots, and yourself a new outfit, but in comes the sheriff and levies on these two bales of cotton. I tell you that it gives you a shrinkage about the vitals that will not be forgotten in many a day. You say "Boys, I paid nearly all the rent in such and such commodities; I owe only about ten or fifteen dollars." Well, the sheriff says: "Go and see your lawyer," and you go to long John Jordon (laughter), and say, "I paid all but ten or fifteen dollars on my rent, and here the sheriff has come and levied on the two bales of cotton that I depended upon to keep me in supplies and get myself and the old lady and children necessary clothing for the winter." And what does long John say? He tells you that you can go into the court house and fight the case if you give a bond for the costs of the suit, and the payment of the debt. Now, people do not like to go security for each other, and the poorer you are the less likely you are to find any one willing to go on your bond and save your tenement, and on account of your poverty, whether you be a poor white tenant or a poor black tenant, you have to go home with tears of disappointment in your eyes, and crushed hopes in your hearts because you could not go into the courthouse and defend your rights. (A brawny farmer: "I have seen that very thing done, that is the God's truth.")

Well, I introduced a bill into the legislature to open the court house door to the poorest tenant, whether black or a white, just as it was opened to the richest farmer. (Cries of "Thank you, thank you! God bless you.") I introduced a bill into the legislature to allow the tenant to swear that he could not pay that rent, that he could not give that bond, and then he could go into the Court House and appeal to a jury of his white neighbors who would not turn that cotton loose. Was not that a good and fair law? [Cries of "Yes! Yes"!] We proposed that should a jury of his neighbors decide in his favor, he should have his cotton, and not allow the landlord to pick it up and carry it away, and force him, whether white or black, to introduce a suit, and give a bond, in order to get the cotton back. Now, I introduced that in the legislature, and how many Democrats do you think voted for the bill? Only twenty-five. How many do you think voted against it, and said by their votes that because a man was poor and could not give a bone, the doors of the court house were closed against him—he could not contest with his landlord, and that is the law to-day? (Cries of "Shame Same!") Do you want to know the names of some of them that voted against that just law! L. L. Columbus, the leader of the House, of Wilkes county, who is a candidate for the Democratic party, and who pretends to be such a friend of the people in general, and the negroes in particular. Mr. Reese said, by his vote, that there ought to be discriminating conditions imposed on the tenant and not on the landlord. Who else voted against the bill so manifestly fair and equitable, down in Richmond county? Why in the name of God don't they mention Mr. Reese and Robey, if they want to show who have been hitting the poor negroes and the poor whites? (Several voices: "They know they are lying, and don't try to tell the truth.") Then when I was in the legislature you were taxed heavily to build bridges, and we did not see any reason why the great railroad corporations should not be taxed as well as the poorest man who had to come up and pay taxes on his wash pan; we did not see why your stump-tail cows, your hogs and your horses or mules should be taxed and the great mogul engine, that could haul thirty cars for these railroads, should be exempt. We thought that everyman should pay taxes according to his means. Who were some of the men who said by their votes that it was right for you to pay tax on your wagon, and wrong for the railroad to have to pay tax on the palace car; that it was right for you to be taxed to death to keep up roads and bridges, but it was wrong for the Central railroad to pay taxes? Who were some of the men who showed by their votes that they were in favor of that great wrong? Mr. Calvin, of Richmond county, and one of the men who is now running as elector at large on the Democratic ticket. Then there is another—long John Jordan (laughter), John T. Jordan. (Snickering), Go-ahead John Jordan. (A voice: "Ugly John Jordan." Great merriment.) He says, by his vote that it is all right for that farmer to pay tax, but it is all wrong for the railroads to do likewise. Who else? Mr. Hamilton Reese, of Wilkes county, voted the same way: Mr. Robey of Jefferson county, and several others, voted with them. All men who are high up in the councils of the Democratic party, and all men who are justly indignant at Col. Peek and myself for trying to enslave the poor negro. (Great laughter.) When the Hon. (?) John Jordan speaks to you again about my being the enemy of the poor colored man, or the poor white man, ask him why he thinks it is not right to tax the railroads on their mogul engine, their cars, their trucks, and their palace sleepers, and it is right to tax you on your horses, mules, wagons, household furniture, and garden implements.

Anthony Wilson's Speech

Fellow-citizens of Hancock county: It affords me much pleasure to be in your presence to-day, and especially on this occasion. Having heard my name ringing in the papers, and deeply conscious that I was becoming a campaign document, and hearing so much sympathy expressed for me in particular, and the colored people in general, it occurred to me that it was no more than right that I should appear before you for the purpose of setting this matter in its true light. [Applause.]

In the year 1862 I was elected to the Georgia Legislature as a member from the county of Camden. [A voice, "1882, not '62] Did I say '62? It was 1882—thank you. Well, Mr. Watson was there and Mr. McGregor was there, and many other gentlemen from all over the State. That contest came up in its form, but, as Mr. Watson told you a few moments ago, there were legal questions involved, and while I had the votes, my opponent had the law.

Mr. Roundtree, who held the minority at the time, told me that I had a good case, "but" says he, "you have left out the legal points in the case, and for that reason the committee is compelled to report against you, and we will make a minority report on the matter."

But the facts in the case were behind the returns; the committee went behind the returns and they disclosed certain facts, but certain legal technicalities had not been compelled with; then came the vote in the House, and when that vote came on, Mr. Watson, as well as many other gentlemen on the other side voted against me, voting the facts, as disclosed on the legal side of the question. They expressed themselves as being satisfied with the justice of my rights, and so they do now, but my case was not put in legal shape, and the law was against me. In view of all the fact, so far as I am concerned, I have only to say that, as far as the vote is concerned, there is nothing rankling in m[y] bosom; there is no hardness in my heart against Mr. Watson or the other sixty-one members who voted against me at that time.

These sixty-one who voted against me, and are now trying to create a prejudice against Mr. Watson, were probably honest in their votes then, and they may be honest in their course now. I will leave that to their own conscience and to you. (Great applause and laughter.)

I wish to relate an incident in connection with that contest. Two years later the chairman of the committee that made that report, Mr. Rountree, was an aspirant for the position of Solicitor-General in his District, and he said to me "I suppose that you are in a position to return the compliment now; I voted against you getting your seat in the legislature, and it is in your power to vote against me now." I said "No; I have no disposition to show any retaliation, I would cheerfully vote for you, but I have already promised to vote for another gentleman." (Long continued applause.)

There is another thing I want to call to your attention—you colored men, I mean. It is right, it is just that we colored men should stand by each other as the white men stand by each other, and I would not give the snap [of] my finger for the colored man that would sell his birth-right, or his State-right. Now, so far as you are concerned, when you come to cast your vote, exercise an intelligent discrimination in casting it for the cause of right and justice—I am not going to say how that should be. So far as I am concerned, I say to you [addressing his remarks to Mr. Watson,] as I said to Mr. Rountree, there is no feeling rankling in my bosom against you or any other gentleman who voted against me, and if these other honorable gentlemen were genuine in their sympathy my colored friend here would have heard of it two years ago. [Laughter.] They would not have waited until this late date. You never heard of Anthony Wilson until a few days ago. [Cries of "No! We did not."] Today you are called upon to sympathize with Anthony Wilson. You are called to cast your votes against the man who voted against Anthony Wilson, but I say, boys, examine the case well and go and cast your votes intelligently, and to please yourselves.

I am thankful, gentlemen, that you stopped long enough to hear the reasoning of the whole matter from the beginning, therefore, we ought to have patience to hear the conclusion of the whole matter.

There is another representative running for Congress in the adjoining District, and seven years ago what did he do? Why, he did the same thing, and nothing is mentioned about Anthony Wilson having received bad treatment at his hands, or why Anthony Wilson, or Anthony's colored friends ought to turn against him.

Another thing, I want to say a word in reference to the Eleventh District. Mr. Turner is running in the Eleventh District—In Anthony Wilson's District—and not a word is said about his vote, yet Anthony Wilson becomes a campaign Democrat two hundred miles from home.

Now gentlemen and fellow-citizens, this is a race for Congress. This is a movement called the People's party movement. There is a division between the people of the State of Georgia, and it behooves you, as colored people, to say which is the best course to pursue. Seventeen years ago you were told to get the scalawags and carpet-baggers from among you—to give them the cold shoulder. God be praised, the carpet-baggers and scalawags are gone, and you to-day say by your enthusiasm that you are willing to go with the Southern people; yet, there is another batch of Southern men who say that you are wrong yet. [Laughter and applause.] Well, according to that, I do not see that we are able to please anybody. If we go with the carpet-baggers and scalawags, we are wrong; if we go with the Southern people, we are wrong; if we go by ourselves, we are wrong. When will we do right? Where is the right place for the negro? [A voice, "In the third party."] Well, sir, decide for yourselves; that is what brought you out to-day; and I put this matter before you that you may decide for yourselves. You have been trying to have others decide for you, and you see that there is no chance for you to be set right by them, now decide for yourselves; and if you decide that the third party is the right thing, put your feet down and stay there. [Several voices, "We's already decided."]

Now, I want to say a few words on another question. [Voices: "Yes! we want to hear about that."] During the time that I was in the Georgia Legislature—I will say right here, before going any further, that there is no man in Georgia, white, black, green or blue, whose heart goes out more to the blessings of education of the people than mine, though totally uneducated, as the papers said yesterday. I say, too, that there is no man in the great State of Georgia, who leans more in that direction than I. I am in favor of educating the people, white and black, because the ignorant white man is as dangerous to the peace of the State as the ignorant black man; yet, if you look on the record you will find one of my votes recorded against the school bill—the same bill for which Mr. Watson is sought to be prejudiced for voting against as an enemy of the educating you colored people. A word of explanation. I did it in this wise: We were in that old capitol building on Marietta street, and we were told that it was unsafe—that it was very dangerous—and I well remember the great snow the last year I was in the Legislature, and upon entering the capital we were told that we had better get out as quick as we could. Seeing the great necessity of having a capitol that would be safe to meet in, and the pride of the city of Atlanta and the State of Georgia, we passed a bill appropriating $1,000,000 for that capitol, and immediately upon the heels of that came up a school bill to straddle a heavy tax upon you in addition to the million just appropriated. I thought, as one of you representatives, that would be too great a burden, and it would be the part of wisdom to let it rest for two years, and I therefore cast my vote against that measure. [Voice, "And you were right."] I thought we had better let the matter rest for two years, and when the capital was finished we could take a fresh start.

Now, then, my fellow-citizens, I did not come before you to make a speech; I simply came to set these matters right before you. I did not come to influence you in casting your ballots but to tell you the truth so that you could have an intelligent conception of the situation. [Cheers.] I have friends in all those parties, but I could not—would not—for one moment stifle my convictions to stifle the truth for the sake of my friendships, and no man is true to himself, to his country, or to his God, who would. [Great Cheering.] No man is a true citizen to his race or to his government who casts his vote against his conscience for a few dollars. [Many voices, "No! No! No" You're talking straight!"] Let us, my friends, rise above these things. Let us cease looking to others and look to ourselves—look upward—and cast our votes in the direction that we think will do the most good for the greatest number, and in doing that you will retain yourself-respect and the respect of the men who affect to look down upon you. [Great applause and shouts of approval.]

Now, then, I wish to say a few words in regard to my being here. I saw articles in the morning papers headed "Watson and Wilson," and then the writers went on to say that Watson had Wilson going around with him at a heavy expense. Well, sir if Mr. Watson has paid one cent for Anthony Wilson, Anthony Wilson does not know it. And I say it to Mr. Watson's face that he did not know that I was to be here until he saw me at Sandersville, to his great surprise. [Long continued cheering.] I will say further that from what Mr. Watson heard he expected to see me fighting him in this district for the vote he cast against me in the Georgia Legislature. But Anthony Wilson cherishes no resentments either against Mr. Watson on account of that vote, or against the other gentlemen who cast their votes against me, and are no so deeply sympathizing with Anthony Wilson for the great wrong done him by Mr. Watson. [Loud laughter and long continued applause.]

Now, let me give you an illustration of this case as it is presented to you: About two or three weeks ago, probably a month, a certain gentleman called upon me and asked me whether or not it would be possible for me to take the stump, and tell you, colored people of this district, the necessity of casting your votes against Mr. Watson on account of the manner in which he cast his vote against me. I told him then and there that our convention had not met; that I did not know when they would meet, or whether it would meet at all, but when it did meet, if it was decided to put a candidate in the field I could only champion that man in the field, and if they did not put a candidate in the field, then I would speak and vote as I saw fit. [Cheers.] Well, this day has rolled around, and I am here, my colored friends, to set this matter squarely before you that you may vote intelligently. I believe that every voter when he goes to the polls ought to know why he votes for the man of his choice. I am not here to tell you who that man is, but I am here to tell you the fats, and you can do the rest. [Cries of "You bet we'll do it for Watson!"]

I have been tossed from pillar to post by the newspapers, and I thought it was but right that I should come over here to-day and let you hear the truth. They say that Mr. Watson has paid me. [Shouts of "They have told a lie! They have told a lie!"] I will say, my friends, that Mr. Watson did not know about my coming here to-day until I appeared upon the scene. I came of my own free will and accord, in the interest, not of Mr. Watson, but of truth. [Cries of "Good! Good!"] I came because I believed that your votes would be diverted from the right to the wrong through misleading and untrue statements. Now, with the plain truth before you, vote for Mr. Black if you see fit, but do not do so, I beseech you, under the mistaken idea that you are righting Anthony Wilson's wrong. [Great cheering, and cries of "Hurrah for Watson! Goodbye, Jimme Black!"]

One word more and I have done. You have probably made your choice, I judge by you[r] enthusiasm, I have not made any choice for you. I am only one of the people, and whenever you make you choice I am with you. I am not the boss—I am one of the people—you are the bosses. If Watson is your choice, and you have said it on this and on other occasions by your enthusiasm, prove it on the day of election. [Cries of, "We will! We will! We will! Hurrah for Watson! Goodbye Jimmie Black!"]

[Some of the able correspondents, who spoke of Anthony God as an ignorant negro, may surpass him in concealing truth, but I doubt very much whether any of them can equal him in making a speech.—Reporter.]

Mr. Watson [in a mocking, laughing tone]: Now, fellow-citizens, ain't we in the soup? {Laughter.} Whose name is dennis now? [Renewed laughter, and a voice, "The're left."] Yes, they are over there in the grove without company, while we are here enjoying "a feast of reason and a flow of soul." [Great applause.]

They tried to make you believe that some great crime had been committed against Anthony Wilson; they tried to get Anthony Wilson to go everywhere and tell you so, and what does he tell you? [A voice, "He tells the truth."] Yes, my friend, he tells the truth; he tells you that I cast my vote just the same way that sixty other members did, believing that the vote was against him and that the law was against him; and he tells you furthermore that he has not been outraged at my hands; that I did not denounce him in the legislature; that I did not denounce his color in the legislature; that I acted as a sworn juror, doing what I believed to be right, and he says, further, that he believes I acted conscientiously. The democratic party, in spite of its barbecue, in spite of its brass bands, in spite of its Sidney Lewis lies, in spite of its false dodgers and artful dodgers, is staggering around over there in the grove, saying: "Mis'er Speaker, where was I at?" [A tremendous outburst of applause and laughter.] And when November comes and the votes are cast, and they repeat the question, "Mis'er Speaker, where was I at?" a disenthralled, long suffering deceived public will answer, "You are in the soup." [Increased laughter and applause.] I tell you we country boys can get ahead of these silk-hatted city politicians, and give them tow in the game. We understand this fight; we understand this sudden affection for the negro; we understand why the democrats have woke up to such a sudden affection for the colored people, and to Anthony Wilson in particular. Your votes have become very precious in their sight all at once. [Loud laughter, and a voice, "Ain't the tellin' de God's truf?"] They used to meet here in this court house, not more than half a dozen of the most properest men in the town. [Laughter.] Why, a big umbrella would keep the rain off the democratic party in Sparta. [Renewed laughter.] They would sit around a table, an it would not require a very large one either, and they would map out their policy and trot our and trim up the jade and tell you to mount, and if you did not like it you could lump it. [A voice, "That's right. Oh, how well we know it."] You had no voice in it. [A voice, "Right you are."] If you complained you were denounced as independents. [A burly voice, "The people's going to take a hand in denouncing."] If you refused to support the ticket, you were denounced as a radical; if you would not vote for the office holder, you could not vote for anybody. [An enthusiastic colored man at my elbow, "'Fore God, 'porter, he's knocking dem fellows silly."]

Gentlemen, this reform movement has knocked that higher than a kit. [A voice, "Oh, how glad I am of that."] Yes, and the people at large are glad of it; and the only men who are mad about it are the town ringsters who had you in their power, and made you walk the chalk line, whether you wanted to or not.

You men of Georgia, and of the other great State, know what was the matter. Hence, the farmer in the field, the skilled mechanic in the shop, the laborer in the factory, in the corn patch, in the cotton patch, rose in their majesty and said: "This is a government of the people, and by the people, and for the people," and that no little crowd of town politicians, that no little spindle shank editor should rule the people and make the laws. They said that the people should have a voice in the government; that the laborer should be heard; that the rights of the mechanic should be respected; that the farmer should get there; so they formed a great league in 1880. Col. Northen was down there. Col. Livingston was down there. Your great representatives of the Knights of Labor were down there. Your great representatives of the Farmer's Alliance were down there. And when they met they said this: "The more we work, the poorer we are; the more we toil, the more we suffer; but the men who do not toil are arrayed like Solomon in all his glory." [Great applause, laughter and cries of: "True, true, every word of it,"] they said that when the people are in rags, it must be from some other cause than that they produce too much clothing. If it was owing to the people producing too much cotton, they would have more clothing instead of less. [Cries of: "That's so."] They said that it was a very strange thing that the more corn the people made the less bread they had to eat. [A voice: "Skin 'em, Tom.' Another voice: "All the hide's done gone," and laughter.]

[Another plug-hatter rode up on horse-back, and trying to force his way into the crowd said: "A free dinner for everybody; you are all invited down to the barbecue—white and colored."]

Mr. Watson: "I hope the reporter will set that down, that while I was here speaking in defense of the people's cause, that while I was speaking in defense of the platform which Governor Northen helped to frame, that while I was speaking in defense of the platform which Col. Livingston aided in forming, that while I was speaking in defense of a platform which Col. W. L. Peek helped to formulate, that a plug-hatted freak rode up here on a horse and tried to bribe the people away from a discussion of these questions, of such vital interest to you all, by offering a free feast, and that the people arose in their majesty and might sand said "SKEDADDLE." [Wild applause.] There he goes! Well he may skedaddle. Oh, my friends, if there ever was a time when the people could not be bought, now is the time! If there ever was a time when the true, manly American people would not sell out their birthrights for a mess of democratic hog and hominy, now is the time! [Tumultuous applause.] They may spread their feasts; they may hire their brass bands; they may have their Governors; they may have their corporation lawyers; they may have the ringsters; but there is one thing they cannot have—that I have—and that is the great hearts of the common people. [The scene at this point was simply indescribable.]

[A voice: "Here he is, coming again. You men out there, tell him to get up and dust—run him off."]

[It turned out to be a fellow with a tin star and a club, the town being full of them that day, ostensibly hired to keep order.—Reporter.]

Mr. Watson: We are taking no man's orders to-day, whether that man be a Governor or a three-for-ten-cents bailiff. We are here in the majesty of the people, and here we are going to stay, no matter how the sun shines or the clouds lower. The sun's rays bear down upon me, as it does upon you, but let us show them that we are here, caring more for principle than for hog meat. We can eat to-night, and when we retire it will be with the proud consciousness of having discharged our duties as citizens first. Our first highest duty, as citizens, is to meet the issues presented to us, and thus get on higher planes of progress that will help the black, without injuring the white, and that will help the poor without injuring the rich. [Great applause.]

They say I am an advocate of social equality between the whites and the blacks. THAT IS AN ABSOLUTE FALSEHOOD, and the man who utter it, knows it. I have done no such thing, and you colored men know it as well as the men who formulated the slander. [Several colored men: "We know it to be lies."] It is best for your race and my race that we dwell apart in our private affairs. [Many voices among the colored: "That's so, boss."] It is best for you to your churches, and I will go to mine; it is best that you send your children to your colored school, and I'll send my children to mine; you invite your colored friends to your home, and I'll invite my friends to mine. (A voice from a colored man: "Now you's talking sense," and murmurs of approval all through the audience.) Now, here is the truth. (A voice: "That's where it hurts.") Yes, my friend, and here is where it hurts. I have said that there is no reason why the black man should not understand that the law that hurts me, as a farmer, hurts him, as farmer; that the same law that hurts me, as a cropper, hurts you, as a cropper; that the same law that hurts me, as a laborer, hurts you, as a laborer; that the same law that hurts me, as a mechanic, hurts you, as a mechanic. (A voice out in the audience: "Boys, ain't he getting there?" Another voice at my elbow: "He's been dar all the time.") Still others: "Yes, and he'll be dar in November, sho'."

I said that you ought not to take a certain position, just because you are black. In other words, you ought not to go one way just because the whites went the other, but that each race should study these questions and true to do the right thing by each other—should consider the interest of all—should vote for the enactment of just laws, and against unjust laws. [Great applause.] That the colored farmer and the white farmer, that the colored cropper, and the white cropper, that the white laborer and the colored laborer should stand shoulder to shoulder, and foot to foot, and win the victory that will bring blessings alike to all. That will benefit the black without injuring the white; that will give the poor, of whatever color, compensation for their honest labor, without injuring the rich. (Long continued applause.)

A voice: "Tell us some more about the dudes skedaddling."

Mr. Watson: "You just keep still, or the first thing you know, the Democrats will bring that barbecue up here; if they do not, it will b a lonesome barbecue, indeed. Lo! "They spread a feast, and no man come to partake thereof." (Laughter, loud and long.)

Now, let us go a little further. What is it Mr. Black promises to the people? What does he propose to advocate to help the people? We all say that we are too heavily in debt; that the price of cotton is too low; that the masse of the people are getting poorer from year to year; that the houses of the people are going into decay; that the taxes of the people cry out, more and more for relief. Now, what is it that the Democratic party promises to you in the way of relief? Do they propose to remove the source? (Voices: "No: they do not.")

Let us look at the way the Democrats propose to treat it, and the way we propose to treat it. We say that the government makes the money and allows the national banker to have it at one per cent; the national banker lets the New York banker have it at four per cent; the New York banker lets the Augusta banker have it as six per cent; the Augusta banker lets the merchant in the country have it at from thirty to fifty per cent, according to your necessities. How does it work with you men out in the country? Here is a colored man working for me; he turns into the field; he fellows the rows; he plows the corn; he chops the cotton, and at the end of the week he comes to me and says, "Mas Tom, I want to get something for the old lady and something for myself." Well, I take out a pencil and a piece of paper and write a few words and hand it to him, and you begin to well up right away. Why? You feel that you have not been fairly treated; you feel that I ought to pay you the cash; that when I gave you that order your merchant will make you dance juber [a voice, "Yes, and he does it every time:]; and you go home, having paid extortionate prices instead of paying cash and getting them as cheap as any other man. Why don't I pay you the money? I would rather pay the cash to the man I hire if I could pay cash, for there never was music like the clink of silver on Saturday night to the laboring man. [Voices: "Dat's so, boos."] Why do you have to pay that extortionate price if my credit is good and that merchant feels sure of getting his pay? Because he must have his profit for himself, and he must have something to make up for the profit that the banker in Augusta is going to make out of him, and also for the profit that the New York banker is making out of the Augusta banker. He would rather do business for cash. The profit would be smaller but more satisfactory. He would not have to sell our the poor man and see his wife and children in rags and tatter, and the whole trouble is that the government lets the national banker have monopoly of getting the money at one per cent; and putting you to the necessity of paying from thirty to fifty per cent; and it belongs to you as much as to him; it belongs to me as much as to the bond holder. The government lets the bond-holder have it on his bonds, but will not let you have it on your cotton; won't let the farmer have it on his wheat; nobody can have it except the bond-holder on his wealth. In other words, the money made for the benefit of all the people should not be kept in the hands of the few, but all the people should have a fair share of the money in circulation.

Now, what do we propose? The government issues money to the national banker on bonds of the government, running twenty or thirty years bearing 4, 5 or 6 per cent interest. Now, what makes those bonds good? Why the land that you till, the corn that you grow, the cotton that you raise, the wheat and other products of the farm. How is the bonded debt to be paid? By the taxes levied by the government on the horses, mules, corn, cotton, wheat, lands and every other sort of wealth which you produce. The national bankers get the right from the government to issue money for one per cent on bonds as security; and why, I ask you, should not your lands and cotton be as good as the bond which is secured by your lands and cotton? What keeps the trains running on your railroads? Corn and cotton. What keeps your stores open? Corn and cotton. What keeps the ships afloat? Corn and cotton. What keeps the laborer in the field? why, corn and cotton. Then why should not your corn and cotton get some of the benefit of the circulating medium, which belongs to you as much as to any man in America.

[Another rowdy contingent here attempted to create a disturbance, but the speaker kept the crowd in a good humor, and they enjoyed the bating which he so deftly applied.]

Let the bells ring, let the band play, let the democrat foam at the mouth, but I am going to make this speech or die trying.

I say that this system is a bad system. It hurts the farmer; it hurts the merchant; it hurts the country banker; in short, it hurts everybody except those near to the top, where monopoly is enthroned at the expense of all the people. (Great cheering.)

Now, how do we propose to remedy this? We say let the government issue the money direct to the people, and in sufficient quantities for the needs of the business of the country; let the people have loans on their lands, cotton and wheat, and a lower rate of interest. Why should the farmer not have it as well as the bond holder? Why abuse us because we want "equal rights for all and special privileges for none?" Here is a man who has more land than he knows what to do with; he stands in need of money to make that land yield him a profit; if he can get that money at 2 per cent, instead of taking a thousand pounds of cotton to pay that interest, he keeps those two bales of cotton and pays six or eight dollars in two shakes of a sheep's tail.

A voice out in the crowd: "Come down to the barbecue, boys; there is plenty of time yet." (Yells of derision.)

They say, "Come to the barbecue." I have got five to their one, and that is our usual majority. We will give you a barbecue that means a better understanding of these things that make you poorer from day to day in spite of your work; in spite of your efforts; in spite of your toil and sweat. I know that many of you have not understood it heretofore. You buy a piece of land; you pay from 8 to 20 per cent. interest on the money to enable you to build a home; you build a home to live in; you put a fence around the dwelling; your wife and children plant vines around the doors and windows; they climb and your are embowered in peace and contentment; when the storm comes you thank God that you and your wife and children are secured against its blasts, and your heart beats with gladness. But an evil day comes. The banker must get his pound of flesh. The sheriff makes his appearance, and you are turned out in the cold world because the government does not accord "equal rights to all, and special privileges to none." (Several voices: "We see the way it is going. Wait until election day.")

What else? You know that the tenants throughout this country are becoming more numerous from year to year, and the land owners less numerous. That is a bad sign. Farmers ought to own their farms. The farms of this country ought not to go into the hands of a few speculative land owners, but ought to be in the hands of the people who fought for it in times of war, and worked for it in time of peace. (Great applause.)

They say that we advocate the dividing of the land, and giving it away. That is all nonsense. (A voice: "That's one of the Ishmaelite's") Yes, that is one of the variegated show-my-light lies. (Laughter.) What we mean is that the laborer shall have the opportunity, by the proceeds of his labor, to buy from the landowner the little home that shall be a shelter for himself and his dear ones. Is that a good or a bad policy? Is that a just or an unjust policy? (Cries of "Good! Good! Just!")

111. Elizabeth Cady Stanton, "Solitude of Self," 1892

Elizabeth Cady Stanton was a leading proponent of woman suffrage throughout the second half of the nineteenth century. The brief statement in "Solitude of Self" encapsulates the philosophy behind her campaign for the vote. She was in her seventies when she delivered this address.

The point I wish plainly to bring before you on this occasion is the individuality of each human soul—our Protestant idea, the right of individual conscience and judgment—our republican idea, individual citizenship. In discussing the rights of woman, we are to consider, first, what belongs to her as an individual, in a world of her own, the arbiter of her own destiny, an imaginary Robinson Crusoe with her woman Friday on a solitary island. Her rights under such circumstances are to use all her faculties for her own safety and happiness.

Secondly, if we consider her as a citizen, as a member of a great nation, she must have the same rights as all other members, according to the fundamental principles of our Government.

Thirdly, viewed as a woman, an equal factor in civilization, her rights and duties are still the same—individual happiness and development.

Fourthly, it is only the incidental relations of life, such as mother, wife, sister, daughter, which may involve some special duties and training. In the usual discussion in regard to woman's sphere, such men as Herbert Spencer, Frederick Harrison and grant Allen uniformly subordinate her rights and duties as an individual, as a citizen, as a man, by his duties as a father, a husband, a brother or a son, some of which he may never undertake. Moreover he would be better fitted for these very relations, and whatever special work he might choose to do to earn his bread, by the complete development of all his faculties as an individual. Just so with woman. The education which will fit her to discharge the duties in the largest sphere of human usefulness, will best fit her for whatever special work she may be compelled to do.

The isolation of every human soul and the necessity of self-dependence must give each individual the right to choose his own surroundings. The strongest reason for giving woman all the opportunities for higher education, for the full development of her faculties, her forces of mind and body; for giving her the most enlarged freedom of thought and action; a complete emancipation from all forms of bondage, of custom, dependence, superstition; from all the crippling influences of fear—is the solitude and personal responsibility of her own individual life. The strongest reason why we ask for woman a voice in the government under which she lives; in the religion she is asked to believe; equality in social life, where she is the chief factor; a place in the trades and professions, where she may earn her bread, is because of her birthright to self-sovereignty; because, as an individual, she must rely on herself. . . .

To throw obstacles in the way of a complete education is like putting out the eyes; to deny the rights of property is like cutting off the hands. To refuse political equality is to rob the ostracized of all self-respect, of credit in the market place, of recompense in the world of work, of a voice in choosing those who make and administer the law, a choice in the jury before whom they are tried, and in the judge who decides their punishment. Shakespeare's play of Titus and Andronicus contains a terrible satire on woman's position in the nineteenth century—"Rude men seized the king's daughter, cut out her tongue, cut off her hands, and then bade her go call for water and wash her hands." What a picture of woman's position! Robbed of her natural rights, handicapped by law and custom at every turn, yet compelled to fight her own battles, and in the emergencies of life to fall back on herself for protection. . . .

How the little courtesies of life on the surface of society, deemed so important from man towards woman, fade into utter insignificance in view of the deeper tragedies in which she must play her part alone, where no human aid is possible!

Nothing strengthens the judgment and quickens the conscience like individual responsibility. Nothing adds

---

Source: Elizabeth Stanton, "Solitude of Self." Document 43 (IV:189–91), Feb. 20, 1892. Public Domain Reprint.

such dignity to character as the recognition of one's self-sovereignty; the right to an equal place, everywhere conceded—a place earned by personal merit, not an artificial attainment by inheritance, wealth, family and position. Conceding then that the responsibilities of life rest equally on man and woman, that their destiny is the same, they need the same preparation for time and eternity. The talk of sheltering woman from the fierce storms of life is the sheerest mockery, for they beat on her from every point of the compass, just as they do on man, and with more fatal results, for he has been trained to protect himself, to resist, to conquer. . . .

In music women speak again the language of Mendelssohn, Beethoven, Chopin, Schumann, and are worthy interpreters of their great thoughts. The poetry and novels of the century are theirs, and they have touched the keynote of reform in religion, politics and social life. They fill the editor's and professor's chair, plead at the bar of justice, walk the wards of the hospital, speak from the pulpit and the platform. Such is the type of womanhood that an enlightened public sentiment welcomes to-day, and such the triumph of the facts of life over the false theories of the past.

Is it, then, consistent to hold the developed woman of this day within the same narrow political limits as the dame with the spinning wheel and knitting needle occupied in the past? No, no! Machinery has taken the labors of woman as well as man on its tireless shoulders; the loom and the spinning wheel are but dreams of the past; the pen, the brush, the easel, the chisel, have taken their places, while the hopes and ambitions of women are essentially changed.

We see reason sufficient in the outer conditions of human beings for individual liberty and development, but when we consider the self-dependence of every human soul, we see the need of courage judgment and the exercise of every faculty of mind and body, strengthened and developed by use, in woman as well as man. . . .

CHAPTER XIX

A Troubled Nation Expands Outward, 1893–1901

112. WOMAN'S SUFFRAGE CONVENTION, "THE COLORADO CAMPAIGN," 1893

The account offered in "The Colorado Campaign" describes the techniques that advocates of female suffrage used to win the vote in the Western states.

The women realized the conflict before them in the near future, and Mrs. Ellis Meredith volunteered to visit the Woman's Congress, which was to meet at Chicago in May, during the World's Fair, and appeal for aid to the representatives of the National Association who would be there. Miss Susan B. Anthony, Mrs. Lucy Stone and other notables were present and appointed a meeting to listen to appeals. These asked help for the Constitutional Convention Campaign in New York and the Kansas Amendment Campaign, which were both considered very hopeful compared to what was thought in the East to be the almost hopeless campaign of Colorado. Mrs. Lillie Devereux Blake presented the claims of New York, Mrs. Laura M. Johns of Kansas, and Mrs. Meredith of Colorado. "Why was your campaign precipitated when our hands are so full?" was one of the discouraging questions. "Are all those Mexicans dead?" asked Miss Anthony, referring to the heavy vote against equal suffrage in the first Colorado campaign of 1877. "No," said Mrs. Meredith, "the Mexicans are all there yet;" but she explained that there were favorable influences now which did not then exist. In the labor unions women members voted, and this fact inclined the men belonging to them to grant the full franchise. The W.C.T.U., now organized throughout the State, had become a firm friend and advocate, and the ruling political party was favorable. Clearly this was the time to strike.

A promise of consideration and such aid as the National Association was able to furnish was given. Later they decided to send Mrs. Carrie Chapman Catt and guarantee her expenses in case she was not able to raise them in the State. From her past record, they thought it likely she would not only do that but put money in the treasury, and the result justified their expectations. She was a financial help, but, much as money was needed, her eloquence and judgment were worth more, and she always will have a warm place in the hearts of Colorado women who were active in the campaign of 1893.

When that campaign opened, there were just $25 in the treasury. Lucy Stone sent a donation of $100. Iowa and California gave aid, and there were small contributions in money from members of the E.S.A. and from auxiliary clubs formed by Mrs. Chapman Catt in different parts of the State.

Besides these, others already had been organized. In Longmont a club was formed in the spring of 1893 by Mesdames Mary L. Carr, Orpha Bacon, Rosetta Webb and Jane Lincoln. They took up the study of laws relating to the property rights of women and endeavored to awaken interest in the question to be settled the following November. The majority which Longmont gave for suffrage is a testimony to the value of their work. In Colorado Springs Mrs. Mary C. C. Bradford was president of a large local society which afterward became auxiliary to the State association, with Mrs. Ella L. C. Dwinnell as president, and did excellent work in El Paso

Source: The Woman's Suffrage Convention, "The Colorado Campaign, 1893," Document 46 (IIV:513–18). Public Domain Reprint.

County. In Greeley many of the workers of 1877 were still active. Mrs. Lillian Hartman Johnson organized a club in Durango and spoke for the cause. Mrs. A. Guthrie Brown formed one in Breckinridge of which Mesdames H. R. Steele, C. L. Westermann and E. G. Brown were active members.

All these clubs, large and small, scattered throughout the State, assisted in arousing public sentiment, but the situation in Denver was the one of most anxious interest. It is always in cities that reforms meet defeat, for there the opposing interests are better organized and more watchful. In no other State is the metropolis so much the center of its life as in Denver of Colorado. Through this modern Palmyra, which stands in the center of the continent and of the tide of commerce from East and West, flow all the veins and arteries of the State life. Arapahoe County, in which it is situated, contains more than one-fourth of the population of the entire State. Upon the women of Denver, therefore, was imposed a triple share of responsibility. Beside the importance of the large vote, there rested particularly upon the members of its suffrage club the burden of having invited this contest and made it a campaign issue.

In the early fall, the City League of Denver was organized with 100 members and Mrs. John L. Routt, wife of the ex-governor, as president. Mrs. Thomas M. Patterson and Mrs. N. P. Hill were prominent workers in this club. A Young Woman's League was formed by Misses Mary and Margaret Patterson and Miss Isabel Hill, and there were other leagues in various parts of the city. In all this work Mrs. Tyler was indefatigable.

Miss Minnie J. Reynolds, chairman of press work, enlisted the help of seventy-five per cent of the newspapers. In some cases editorial approval and assistance were given, in others space was allowed for suffrage matter. In August Mrs. Elizabeth Tabor donated the use of two rooms in the opera house block, one large enough to seat several hundred persons, the other a suitable office for the corresponding secretary. Dr. Minnie C. T. Love had acted gratuitously in that capacity and opened communication with suffragists throughout the State, but it was now deemed necessary to employ some one who could devote her entire time to the work. Miss Helen M. Reynolds was chosen and added to unusual capability the most earnest zeal. The rooms were furnished through loans of rugs, desks, chairs, etc.

Equal suffrage was indorsed by the county conventions of the Republican, Prohibition and Populist parties, and also at a called meeting of the Democratic State Central Committee. Many ministers and lawyers spoke in its favor. Among the latter were Charles S. Thomas, since governor of the State, J. Warner Mills, Judge L. C. Rockwell, Charles Hartzell, Eugene Engley and Attorney-General I. N. Stevens, who was one of the most trusted advisers.

There were also women speakers of experience: Mrs. Therese Jenkins of Wyoming, Mrs. Susan S. Fessenden of Massachusetts; Mrs. Dora Phelps Buell, Mrs. Mary Jewett Telford, president of the Woman's Relief Corps in the Department of Colorado and Wyoming and also president for several terms of the State W. C. T. U., who made a five-months' speaking tour; Mrs. Leonora Barry Lake of St. Louis, who spoke efficiently under the auspices of the Knights of Labor. Mrs. Laura Ormiston Chant of England delivered an address on her way westward.

Some women made speeches who never had been on the platform before but have since developed much oratorical ability. When needed, women who did not dare risk an unwritten address read papers. Meetings were held all over the city and State, "I should think," said a banker, "from the campaign the women are running that they had a barrel of money;" but he was a contributor to the fund and knew it was very limited. In all about $2,000 were raised, over $300 of which were spent for literature. Some of the most efficient leaflets were written by members of the association and printed in Denver. Nearly 150,000 of these were issued.

In the city press Mrs. Patience Mapleton represented the cause of the *Republican;* Mrs. Ellis Meredith in the *Rocky Mountain News.* There were house to house canvassers, distributors of literature and others who rendered most valuable assistance and yet whose names must necessarily remain unrecorded. The most of this service was given freely, but some of the women who devoted all their time received moderate salaries, for most of the workers belonged to the wage-earning class. The speakers asked no compensation but their expenses were frequently borne. Halls and churches had to be paid for and on several occasions opera houses were rented. When in the final report the expenses of election day were given as $17 a murmur of amusement ran through the audience.

The women who "had all the rights they wanted" appealed late in the campaign. Some of them sent communications to the papers, complaining of the effort to thrust the ballot upon them and add to the already onerous duties of life. When told that they would not be compelled to vote and that if silent influence was in their opinion more potent than the ballot, it would not be necessary to cast it aside for the weaker weapon, they responded indignantly that if they had the franchise of course it would be their duty to use it. Let it be noted that many of them have voted regularly ever since they were enfranchised, though some have reconsidered and returned to their silent influence.

The liquor element slept in fancied security until almost the eve of election, as they did not believe the amendment would receive popular sanction. When they awoke to the danger they immediately proceeded to assess all saloon keepers and as many as possible of their prominent patrons. They got out a large number of dodgers, which were put into the hands of passers by. These were an attack upon equal suffrage and the women who advocated it, and at the bottom of the first issue was a brewer's advertisement. This dodger stated that "only some old maids like Lucy Stone, Susan Anthony, Frances Willard, Elizabeth Stanton and Mary Livermore wanted to vote." They also employed an attorney to juggle the ballots so that they might be thrown out on a technicality. There was consternation among the suffragists when the ballot was finally produced bearing the words "For the Amendment." "Against the Amendment," for it was well known that the measure was not an "amendment." The best legal talent in Denver was consulted and an opinion rendered that the ruse would prove of no avail, as the intention was still clear. The women, however, issued a leaflet instructing the voters just where to put the cross on the ticket if they wished to vote for equal suffrage.

The suffragists were divided in opinion as to the presence of women at the polls on the election day which was to decide their fate. Some thought it might be prejudicial, but the friends among the men strongly approved their presence in order to influence voters. What future election could be of more importance to women than this, and why should they hesitate to show their interest? Under directions from suffrage headquarter workers at the polls distributed the leaflets, often supplementing them by their own eloquence. No woman received any discourtesy.

The night of November 7 was an anxious one. Women went home and lay awake wondering whether they had done everything possible to insure success, or whether failure might be the result of such omission. When the returns published the next morning, although incomplete, showed that success really had crowned their efforts it seemed almost too good to be true. All day long and in the evening people were coming and going at suffrage headquarters with greetings and congratulations. Women of all classes seemed drawn together by the new tie of citizenship.

The full returns gave the result as follows: For suffrage, 35,798; against, 29,451; an affirmative majority of 6,347.

113. Albert Beveridge, "The March of the Flag," 1898

Albert J. Beveridge was an American political orator and member of the United States Senate. The following speech, relating to the holding of the Philippine Islands by the United States, was delivered at Indianapolis in 1898. The passages are selected from the beginning, the middle and the close of the speech. His Introduction, "Public Speaking," is in Volume V, and another speech in Volume I. He died April 26, 1927.

Source: Albert Beveridge, "The March of the Flag," pp. 372–377. Speech delivered in 1898. Public Domain Reprint.

Fellow Citizens:—It is a noble land that God has given us; a land that can feed and clothe the world; a land whose coast lines would inclose have the country of Europe; a land set like a sentinel between the two imperial oceans of the globe, a greater England with a nobler destiny. It is a mighty people that He has planted on this soil; a people sprung from the most masterful blood of history; a people perpetually revitalized by the virile, man-producing working folk of all the earth; a people imperial by virtue of their power, by right of their institutions, by authority of their heaven-directed purposes—the propagandists and not the misers of liberty. It is a glorious history our God has bestowed upon His chosen people; a history whose keynote was struck by Liberty Bell; a history heroic with faith in our mission and our future; a history of statesmen who flung the boundaries of the republic out in unexplored lands and savage wildernesses; a history of soldiers who carried the flag across the blazing deserts and through the ranks of hostile mountains, even to the gates of sunset; a history of a multiplying people who overran a continent in half a century; a history of prophets who saw the consequences of evils inherited from the past, and of martyrs who died to save us from them; a history divinely logical, in the process of whose tremendous reasoning we find ourselves today.

Therefore, in this campaign, the question is larger than a party question. It is an American question. It is a world question. Shall the American people continue their resistless march toward the commercial supremacy of the world? Shall free institutions broaden their blessed reign as the children of liberty wax in strength, until the empire of our principles is established over the hearts of all mankind?

Have we no mission to perform, no duty to discharge to our fellow men? Has the Almighty Father endowed us with gifts beyond our deserts and marked us as the people of His peculiar favor, merely to rot in our own selfishness, as men and nations must who take cowardice for their companion and self for their deity—as China has, an India has, as Egypt has?

Shall we be as the man who had one talent and hid it, or as he who had ten talents and used them until they grew to riches? And shall we reap the reward that waits on our discharge of our high duty as the sovereign power of earth; shall we occupy new markets for what our farmers raise, new markets for what our factories make, new markets for what our merchants sell—aye, and, please God, new markets for what our ships shall carry?

Shall we avail ourselves of new sources of supply of what we do not raise or make, so that what are luxuries to-day will be necessities to-morrow? Shall our commerce be encouraged until, with Oceanica, the Orient, and the world. American trade shall be the imperial trade of the entire globe?

Shall we conduct the mightiest commerce of history with the best money known to man, or shall we use the pauper money of Mexico, of China, and of the Chicago platform?

What are the great acts of this administration? Not a failure of revenue; not a perpetual battle between the executive and legislative departments of government; not a rescue from dishonor by European syndicates at the price of tens of millions in cash and national humiliation unspeakable. These have not marked the past two years—the past two years, which have blossomed into four splendid months of glory.

But a war has marked it, the most holy ever waged by one nation against another—a war for civilization, a war for a permanent peace, a war which, under God, although we knew it not, swung open to the republic the portals of the commerce of the world. And the first question you must answer with your vote is whether you indorse that war. We are told that all citizens and every platform indorse the war, and I admit, with the joy of patriotism, that this is true. But that is only among ourselves, and we are of and to ourselves, and we are of and to ourselves no longer. This election takes place on the stage of the world, with all earth's nations for our auditors.

And the burning question of this campaign is, whether the American people will accept the gifts of events; whether they will as lifts their soaring destiny; whether they will proceed upon the lines of national development surveyed by the statesmen of our past; or whether, for the first time, the American people doubt their mission, question fate, prove apostate to the spirit of their race, and halt the ceaseless march of free institutions.

The opposition tells us that we ought not to govern a people without their consent. I answer: The rule of liberty, that all just government derives its authority from the consent of the governed, applies only to those who are capable of self-government. I answer: We govern the Indians without their consent, we govern our territories without their consent, we govern our children without their consent. I answer: How do you assume that our government would be without their consent? Would not the people of the Philippines prefer the just, humane, civilizing government of this republic to the savage, bloody rule of pillage and extortion from which we have rescued them?

Do not the blazing fires of joy and the ringing bells of gladness in Porto Rico prove the welcome of our flag?

And, regardless of this formula of words, made only for enlightened, self-governing peoples, do we owe no duty to the world? Shall we turn these people back to the reeking hands from which we have taken them? Shall we abandon them to their fate, with the wolves of conquest all about them—with Germany, Russia, France, even Japan, hungering for them? Shall we save them from those nations, to give them a self-rule of tragedy? It would be like giving a razor to a babe and telling it to shave itself. It would be like giving a typewriter to an Eskimo and telling him to publish one of the great dailies of the world. This proposition of the opposition makes the Declaration of Independence preposterous, as the reading of Job's lamentations would be at a wedding or an Altgeld speech on the Fourth of July.

They ask us how we will govern these new possessions. I answer: Out of local conditions and the necessities of the case methods of government will grow. If England can govern foreign lands, so can America. If Germany can govern foreign lands, so can America. If they can supervise protectorates, so can America. Why is it more difficult to administer Hawaii than New Mexico or California? Both had a savage and alien population; both were more remote from the seat of government when they came under our dominion than Hawaii is to-day.

Will you say that your vote that American ability to govern has decayed; that a century's experience in self-rule has failed of a result? Will you affirm by your vote that you are an infidel to American vigor and power and practical sense? Or, that we are of the ruling race of the world; that ours is the blood of government; ours the heart of dominion; ours the brain of genius of administration? Will you remember that we do but what our fathers did—we but pitch the tents of liberty farther westward, father southward—we only continue the march of the flag.

Why stand in the fatal stupor of financial fallacies muttering old sophistries that time has exploded, when opportunity beckons you all over the world—in Cuba, Hawaii, the Philippines, on the waters of commerce, in every market of the Occident and the Orient, and in your factories and stores and fields, here in our own beloved country, holy America, land of God's promise and home of God's providence?

There are so many real things to be done—canals to be dug, railways to be laid, forests to be felled, cities to be builded, unviolated fields to be tilled, priceless markets to be won, ships to be launched, peoples to be saved, civilization to be proclaimed, and the flag of liberty flung to the eager air of every sea. Is this an hour to waste upon triflers with nature's laws? Is this a season to give our destiny over to wordmongers and prosperity wreckers? Is this a day to think of office-seekers, to be cajoled by the politician's smile, or seduced by the handshake of hypocrisy? No! No! my fellow citizens!

It is an hour to remember your duty to the home. It is a moment to realize the opportunities fate has opened to this favored people and to you. It is a time to bethink you of the conquering march of the flag. It is a time to bethink you of your nation and its sovereignty of the seas. It is a time to remember that the God of our fathers is our God, and that the gifts and the duties He gave to them, enriched and multiplied, He renews to us, their children.

And so it is an hour for us to stand by the government at Washington, now confronting the enemy in diplomacy, as our loyal hearts on land and sea stood to their guns and stood by the flag when they faced the enemy in war. It is a time to strengthen and sustain that devoted man, servant of the people and of the most high God, who patiently, silently, safely is guiding the republic out into the ocean of world interests and possibilities infinite. It is a time to cheer the beloved President of God's chosen people, till the whole world is vocal with American loyalty to the American government.

Fellow Americans, we are God's chosen people. Younder at Bunker Hill and Yorktown His providence was above us. At New Orleans and on ensanguined seas His hand sustained us. Abraham Lincoln was His minister, and His was the Altar of Freedom the boys in blue set on a hundred battlefields. His power directed Dewey in the East, and delivered the Spanish fleet into our hands on the eve of Liberty's natal day, as He delivered the elder armada into the hands of our English sires two centuries ago. His great purposes are revealed in the progress of the flag, which surpasses the intention of congresses and cabinets, and leads us like a holier pillar of cloud by day and pillar of fire by night into situations unforeseen by finite wisdom, and duties unexpected by the unprophetic heart of selfishness. This American people cannot use a dishonest medium of exchange; it is ours to set the world its example of right and honor. We cannot fly from our world duties; it is ours to execute the purpose of a fate that has driven us to be greater than our small intentions. We cannot retreat from any soil where Providence has unfurled our banner; it is ours to save that soil for liberty and civilization. For liberty and civilization and God's promise fulfilled, the flag must henceforth be the symbol and the sign to all mankind—the flag!—

> Flag of the free heart's hope and home,
>   By angel hands to valor given,
> Thy stars have lit the welkin dome,
>   And all thy hues were born in heaven!
> Forever wave that standard sheet,
>   Where breathes the foe but falls before us.
> With freedom's soil beneath our feet,
>   And freedom's banner streaming o'er us!

114. Mark Twain, "To the Person Sitting in Darkness," 1901

Mark Twain, known to many for his humor, became deeply disenchanted with the course of American empire at the turn of the century. This account is a bitterly sarcastic attack on America's portrayal of its overseas expansion as a "Christianizing" crusade, as the spread of the nation's highest ideals abroad. Twain found hypocrisy and self-delusion where others thought they saw noble motives.

"Christmas will dawn in the United States over a people full of hope and aspiration and good cheer. Such a condition means contentment and happiness. The carping grumbler who may here and there go forth will find few to listen to him. The majority will wonder what is the matter with him and pass on."—*New York Tribune,* on Christmas Eve.

From *The Sun,* of New York:

"The purpose of this article is not to describe the terrible offences against humanity committed in the name of Politics in some of the most notorious East Side districts. *They could not be described, even verbally.* But it is the intention to let the great mass of more or less careless citizens of this beautiful metropolis of the New World get some conception of the havoc and ruin wrought to man, woman and child in the most densely populated and least known section of the city. Name, date and place can be supplied to those of little faith—or to any man who feels himself aggrieved. It is a plain statement of record and observation, written without license and without garnish.

"Imagine, if you can, a section of the city territory completely dominated by one man, without whose permission neither legitimate nor illegitimate business can be conducted; *where illegitimate business is encouraged and legitimate business discouraged;* where the respectable residents have to fasten their doors and windows summer nights and sit in their rooms with asphyxiating air and 100-degree temperature, rather than try to catch the faint whiff of breeze in their natural breathing places, the stoops of their homes; *where naked women dance by night in the streets, and unsexed men prowl like vultures through the darkness on 'business'* not only permitted but encouraged by the police; *where the education of infants begins with the knowledge of prostitution* and the training of little girls is training in the arts of Phryne; where *American girls brought up with the refinements of American homes* are imported from small towns up-State, Massachusetts, Connecticut and New Jersey, and kept as virtually prisoners as if they were locked up behind jail bars until they have lost all semblance of womanhood; *where small boys are taught to solicit for the women of disorderly houses;* where there is an organized society of young men *whose sole business in life is to corrupt young girls and turn them over to bawdy houses;* where men walking with their wives along the street are openly insulted; *where children that have adult diseases are the chief patrons of the hospitals and dispensaries;* where it is the rule, rather than the exception, that *murder, rape, robbery and theft go unpunished*—in short where the Premium of the most awful forms of Vice is the Profit of the politicians."

The following news from China appeared in *The Sun,* of New York, on Christmas Eve. The italics are mine:

"The Rev. Mr. Ament, of the American Board of Foreign Missions, has returned from a trip which he made for the purpose of collecting indemnities for damages done by Boxers. *Everywhere he went he compelled the Chinese to pay.* He says that all his native Christians are now provided for. He had 700 of them under his charge, and 300 were killed. He has *collected 300 taels for each* of these murders, and has *compelled full payment for all the property belonging to Christians* that was destroyed. He also assessed *fines* amounting to THIRTEEN TIMES the amount of the indemnity. *This money will be used for the propagation of the Gospel.*

"Mr. Ament declares that the compensation he has collected is *moderate,* when compared with the amount secured by the Catholics, who demand, in addition to money, *head for head.* They collect 500 taels for each murder of a Catholic. In the Wenchiu country, 680 Catholics were killed, and for this the European

---

Source: Mark Twain, "To the Person Sitting in Darkness." *North American Review,* NO. CLXXXI, February 1901. Public Domain Reprint.

Catholics here demand 750,000 strings of cash and 680 *heads*.

"In the course of a conversation, Mr. Ament referred to the attitude of the missionaries toward the Chinese. He said:

"'I deny emphatically that the missionaries are *vindictive,* that they *generally* looted, or that they have done anything *since* the siege that *the circumstances did not demand.* I criticise the Americans. *The soft hand of the Americans is not as good as the mailed fist of the Germans.* If you deal with the Chinese with a soft hand they will take advantage of it.'

"The statement that the French Government will return the loot taken by the French soldiers, is the source of the greatest amusement here. The French soldiers were more systematic looters than the Germans, and it is a fact that to-day *Catholic Christians,* carrying French flags and armed with modern guns, *are looting villages* in the Province of Chill."

By happy luck, we get all these glad tidings on Christmas Eve—just in time to enable us to celebrate the day with proper gaiety and enthusiasm. Our spirits soar, and we find we can even make jokes: Taels I win, Heads you lose.

Our Reverend Ament is the right man in the right place. What we want of our missionaries out there is, not that they shall merely represent in their acts and persons the grace and gentleness and charity and loving kindness of our religion, but that they shall also represent the American spirit. The oldest Americans are the Pawnees. Macallum's History says:

"When a white Boxer kills a Pawnee and destroys his property, the other Pawnees do not trouble to seek *him* out, they kill any white person that comes along; also, they make some white village pay deceased's heirs the full cash value of deceased, together with full cash value of the property destroyed; they also make the village pay, in addition, *thirteen times* the value of that property into a fund for the dissemination of the Pawnee religion, which they regard as the best of all religions for the softening and humanizing of the heart of man. It is their idea that it is only fair and right that the innocent should be made to suffer for the guilty, and that it is better that ninety and nine innocent should suffer than that one guilty person should escape."

Our Reverent Ament is justifiably jealous of those enterprising Catholics, who not only get big money for each lost convert, but get "head for head" besides. But he should soothe himself with the reflection that the entirety of their exactions are for their own pockets, whereas he, less selfishly, devotes only 300 taels per head to that service, and gives the whole vast thirteen repetitions of the property-indemnity to the service of propagating the Gospel. His magnanimity has won him the approval of his nation, and will get him a monument. Let him be content with these rewards. We all hold him dear for manfully defending his fellow missionaries from exaggerated charges which were beginning to distress us, but which his testimony has so considerably modified that we can now contemplate them without noticeable pain. For now we know that, even before the siege, the missionaries were not "generally" out looting, and that "since the siege," they have acted quite handsomely, except when "circumstances" crowded them. I am arranging for the monument. Subscriptions for it can be sent to the American Board; designs for it can be sent to me. Designs must allegorically set forth the Thirteen Reduplications of the Indemnity, and the Object for which they were exacted; as Ornaments, the designs must exhibit 680 Heads, so disposed as to give a pleasing and pretty effect; for the Catholics have done nicely, and are entitled to notice in the monument. Mottoes may be suggested, if any shall be discovered that will satisfactorily cover the ground.

Mr. Ament's financial feat of squeezing a thirteen-fold indemnity out of the pauper peasants to square other people's offenses, thus condemning them and their women and innocent little children to inevitable starvation and lingering death, in order that the blood-money so acquired might be *"used for propagation of the Gospel."* does not flutter my serenity; although the act and the words, taken together, concrete a blasphemy so hideous and so colossal that, without doubt, its mate is not findable in the history of this or of any other age. Yet, if a layman had done that thing and justified it with those words, I should have shuddered, I know. Or, if I had done the thing and said the words myself—however, the thought is unthinkable, irreverent as some imperfectly informed people think me. Sometimes an ordained minister sets out to be blasphemous. When this happens, the layman is out of the running; he stands no chance.

We have Mr. Ament's impassioned assurance that the missionaries are not "vindictive." Let us hope and pray that they will never become so, but will remain in the almost morbidly fair and just and gentle temper which is affording so much satisfaction to their brother and champion to-day.

The following is from the *New York Tribune* of Christmas Eve. It comes from that journal's Tokio correspondent. It has a strange and impudent sound, but the Japanese are but partially civilized as yet. When they become wholly civilized they will not talk so:

> "The missionary question, of course, occupies a foremost place in the discussion. It is now felt as essential that the Western Powers take cognizance of the sentiment here, that religious invasions of Oriental countries by powerful Western organizations are tantamount to filibustering expeditions, and should not only be discountenanced, but that stern measures should be adopted for their suppression. The feeling here is that the missionary organizations constitute a constant menace to peaceful international relations."

Shall we? That is, shall we go on conferring our Civilization upon the peoples that sit in darkness, or shall we give those poor things a rest? Shall we bang right ahead in our old-time, loud, pious way, and commit the new century to the game; or shall we sober up and sit down and think it over first? Would it not be prudent to get our Civilization-tools together, and see how much stock is left on hand in the way of Glass Beads and Theology, and Maxim Guns and Hymn Books, and Trade-Gin and Torches of Progress and Enlightenment (patent adjustable ones, good to fire villages with, upon occasion), and balance the books, and arrive at the profit and loss, so that we may intelligently decide whether to continue the business or set out the property and start a new Civilization Scheme on the proceeds?

Extending the Blessings of Civilization to our Brother who Sits in Darkness has been a good trade and has paid well, on the whole; and there is money in it yet, if carefully worked—but not enough, in my judgment, to make any considerable risk advisable. The People that Sit in Darkness are getting to be too scarce—too scarce and too shy. And such darkness as is now left is really of but an indifferent quality, and not dark enough for the game. The most of those People that Sit in Darkness have been furnished with more light than was good for them or profitable for us. We have been injudicious.

The Blessings-of-Civilization Trust, wisely and cautiously administered, is a Daisy. There is more money in it, more territory, more sovereignty, and other kinds of emolument, than there is to any other game that is played. But Christendom has been playing it badly of late years, and must certainly suffer by it, in my opinion. She has been so eager to get every stake that appeared on the green cloth, that the People who Sit in Darkness have noticed it—they have noticed it, and have begun to show alarm. They have become suspicious of the Blessings of Civilization. More—they have begun to examine them.

This is not well. The Blessings of Civilization are all right, and a good commercial property; there could not be a better, in a dim light. In the right kind of light, and at a proper distance, with the goods a little out of focus, they furnish this desirable exhibit to the Gentlemen who Sit in Darkness:

LOVE,	LAW AND ORDER,
JUSTICE,	LIBERTY,
GENTLENESS,	EQUALITY,
CHRISTIANITY,	HONORABLE DEALING,
PROTECTION TO	MERCY,
THE WEAK,	EDUCATION,
TEMPERANCE,	

—and so on.

There. Is it good? Sir, it is pie. It will bring into camp any idiot that sits in darkness anywhere. But not if we adulterate it. It is proper to be emphatic upon that point. This brand is strictly for Export—apparently. *Apparently.* Privately and confidentially, it is nothing of the kind. Privately and confidentially, it is merely an outside cover, gay and pretty and attractive, displaying the special patterns of our Civilization which we reserve for Home Consumption, while *inside* the bale is the Actual Thing that the Customer Sitting in Darkness buys with his blood and tears and land and liberty. That Actual Thing is, indeed, Civilization, but it is only for Export. Is there a difference between the two brands? In some of the details, yes.

We all know that the Business is being ruined. The reason is not far to seek. It is because our Mr. McKinley, and Mr. Chamberlain, and the Kaiser, and the Czar and the French have been exporting the Actual Thing *with the outside cover left off.* This is bad for the Game. It shows that these new players of it are not sufficiently acquainted with it.

It is a distress to look on and note the mismoves, they are so strange and so awkward. Mr. Chamberlain manufactures a war out of materials so inadequate and so fanciful that they make the boxes grieve and the gallery laugh, and he tries hard to persuade himself that it isn't purely a private raid for cash, but has sort of dim, vague respectability about it somewhere, if he could only find the spot; and that, by and by, he can scour the flag clean again after he has finished dragging it through the mud, and make it shine and flash in the vault of heaven once more as it had shone and flashed there a thousand years in the world's respect until he laid his unfaithful hand upon it. It is bad play—bad. For it exposes the Actual Thing to Them that Sit in Darkness, and they say:

"What! Christian against Christian? And only for money? Is *this* a case of magnanimity, forbearance, love, gentleness, mercy, protection of the weak—this strange and over-showy onslaught of an elephant upon a nest of field-mice, on the pretext that the mice had squeaked an insolence at him—conduct which 'no self-respecting government could allow to pass unavenged?' as Mr. Chamberlain said. Was that a good pretext in a small case, when it had not been a good pretext in a large one?—for only recently Russia had affronted the elephant three times and survived alive and unsmitten. Is this Civilization and Progress? Is it something better than we already possess? These harryings and burnings and desert-makings in the Transvaal—is this an improvement on our darkness? Is it, perhaps, possible that there are two kinds of Civilization—one for home consumption and one for the heathen market?"

Then They that Sit in Darkness are troubled, and shake their heads; and they read this extract from a letter of a British private, recounting his exploits in one of Methuen's victories, some days before the affair of Magersfontein, and they are troubled again:

> "We tore up the hill and into the intrenchments, and the Boers saw we had them; so they dropped their guns and went down on their knees and put up their hands clasped, and begged for mercy. And we gave it them— *with the long spoon.*"

The long spoon is the bayonet. See *Lloyd's Weekly,* London, of those days. The same number—and the same column—contained some quite unconscious satire in the form of shocked and bitter upbraidings of the Boers for their brutalities and inhumanities!

Next, to our heavy damage, the Kaiser went to playing the game without first mastering it. He lost a couple of missionaries in a riot in Shantung, and in his account he made an overcharge for them. China had to pay a hundred thousand dollars apiece for them, in money; twelve miles of territory, containing several millions of inhabitants and worth twenty million dollars; and to build a monument, and also a Christian church; whereas the people of China could have been depended upon to remember the missionaries without the help of these expensive memorials. This was all bad play. Bad, because it would not, and could not, and will not now or ever, deceive the Person Sitting in Darkness. He knows that it was an overcharge. He knows that a missionary is like any other man: he is worth merely what you can supply his place for, and no more. He is useful, but so is a doctor, so is a sheriff, so is an editor; but a just Emperor does not charge war-prices for such. A diligent, intelligent, but obscure missionary, and a diligent, intelligent country editor are worth much, and we know it; but they are not worth the earth. We esteem such an editor, and we are sorry to see him go; but, when he goes, we should consider twelve miles of territory, and a church, and a fortune, over-compensation for his loss. I mean, if he was a Chinese editor, and we had to settle for him. It is no proper figure for an editor or a missionary; one can get shop-worn kings for less. It was bad play on the Kaiser's part. It got this property, true; but it *produced the Chinese revolt,* the indignant uprising of China's traduced patriots, the Boxers. The results have been expensive to Germany, and to the other Disseminators of Progress and the Blessings of Civilization.

The Kaiser's claim was paid, yet it was bad play, for it could not fail to have an evil effect upon Persons Sitting in Darkness in China. They would muse upon the event, and be likely to say: "Civilization is gracious and beautiful, for such is its reputation; but can we afford it? There are rich Chinamen, perhaps they could afford it; but this tax is not laid upon them, it is laid upon the peasants of Shantung; it is they that must pay this mighty sum, and their wages are but four cents a day. Is this a better civilization than ours, and holier and higher and nobler? Is not this rapacity? Is not this extortion? Would Germany charge America two hundred thousand dollars for two missionaries, and shake the mailed fist in her face, and send warships, and send soldiers, and say: 'Seize twelve miles of territory, worth twenty millions of dollars, as additional pay for the missionaries; and make those peasants build a monument to the missionaries, and a costly Christian church to remember them by?' And later would Germany say to her soldiers: 'March through America and slay, *giving no quarter;* make the German face there, as has been our Hun-face here, a terror for a thousand years; march through the Great Republic and slay, slay, slay, carving a road for our offended religion through its heart and bowels?' Would Germany do like this to America, to England, to France, to Russia? Or only to China the helpless—imitating the elephant's assault upon the field-mice? Had we better invest in this Civilization—this Civilization which called Napoleon a buccaneer for carrying off Venice's bronze horses, but which steals our ancient astronomical instruments from our walls, and goes looting like common bandits-o-that is, all the alien soldiers except America's; and (Americans against excepted) storms frightened villages and cables the result to glad journals at home every day: "Chinese losses, 450 killed; ours, *one officer and two men wounded.*

Shall proceed against neighboring village tomorrow, where a *massacre* is reported.' Can we afford Civilization?"

And, next, Russia must go and play the game injudiciously. She affronts England once or twice—with the Person Sitting in Darkness observing and noting; by moral assistance of France and Germany, she robs Japan of her hard-earned spoil, all swimming in Chinese blood—Port Arthur—with the Person again observing and noting; then she seizes Manchuria, raids its villages, and chokes its great river with the swollen corpses of countless massacred peasants—that astonished Person still observing and nothing. And perhaps he is saying to himself: "It is yet *another* Civilized Power, with its banner of the Prince of Peace in one hand and its loot-basket and its butcher-knife in the other. Is there no salvation for us but to adopt Civilization and life ourselves down to its level?"

And by and by comes America, and our Master of the Game plays it badly—plays it as Mr. Chamberlain was playing it in South Africa. It was a mistake to do that; also, it was one which was quite unlooked for in a Master who was playing it so well in Cuba. In Cuba, he was playing the usual and regular *American* game, and it was winning, for there is no way to beat it. The Master, contemplating Cuba, said: "Here is an oppressed and friendless little nation which is willing to fight to be free; we go partners, and put up the strength of seventy million sympathizers and the resources of the United States: play!" Nothing but Europe combined could call that hand; and Europe cannot combine on anything. There, in Cuba, he was following our great traditions in a way which made us very proud of him, and proud of the deep dissatisfaction which his play was provoking in Continental Europe. Moved by a high inspiration, he threw out those stirring words which proclaimed that forcible annexation would be "criminal aggression;" and in that utterance fired another "shot heard round the world." The memory of that fine saying will be outlived by the remembrance of no act of his but one—that he forgot it within the twelvemonth, and its honorable gospel along with it.

For, presently, came the Philippine temptation. It was strong; it was too strong, and he made that bad mistake: he played the European game, the Chamberlain game. It was a pity; it was a great pity, that error; that one grievous error, that irrevocable error. For it was the very place and time to play the American game again. And at no cost. Rich winnings to be gathered in, too; rich and permanent; indestructible; a fortune transmissible forever to the children of the flag. Not land, not money, not dominion—no, something worth many times more than that dross: our share, the spectacle of a nation of long harassed and persecuted slaves set free through our influence; our posterity's share, the golden memory of that fair deed. The game was in our hands. If it had been played according to the American rules, Dewey would have sailed away from Manila as soon as he had destroyed the Spanish fleet—after putting up a sign on shore guaranteeing foreign property and life against damage by the Filipinos, and warning the Powers that interference with the emancipated patriots would be regarded as an act unfriendly to the United States. The Powers cannot combine, in even a bad cause, and the sign would not have been molested.

Dewey could have gone about his affairs elsewhere, and left the competent Filipino army to starve out the little Spanish garrison and send it home, and the Filipino citizens to set up the form of government they might prefer, and deal with the friars and their doubtful acquisitions according to Filipino ideas of fairness and justice—ideas which have since been tested and found to be of as high an order as any that prevail in Europe or America.

But we played the Chamberlain game, and lost the chance to add another Cuba and another honorable deed to our good record.

The more we examine the mistake, the more clearly we perceive that it is going to be bad for the Business. The Person Sitting in Darkness is almost sure to say: "There is something curious about this—curious and unaccountable. There must be two Americas: one that sets the captive free, and one that takes a once-captive's new freedom away from him, and picks a quarrel with him with nothing to found it on; then kills him to get his land."

The truth is, the Person Sitting in Darkness *is* saying things like that; and for the sake of the Business we must persuade him to look at the Philippine matter in another and healthier way. We must arrange his opinions for him. I believe it can be done; for Mr. Chamberlain has arranged England's opinion of the South African matter, and done it most cleverly and successfully. He presented the facts—some of the facts—and showed those confiding people what the facts meant. He did it statistically, which is a good way. He used the formula: "Twice 2 are 14, and 2 from 9 leaves 35." Figures are effective; figures will convince the elect.

Now, my plan is a still bolder one than Mr. Chamberlain's, though apparently a copy of it. Let us be franker than Mr. Chamberlain; let us audaciously present the whole of the facts, shirking none, then explain them according to Mr. Chamberlain's formula. This daring truthfulness will astonish and dazzle the Person Sitting in Darkness, and he will take the Explanation down before his mental vision has had time to get back into focus. Let us say to him:

"Our case is simple. On the 1st of May, Dewey destroyed the Spanish fleet. This left the Archipelago in the hands of its proper and rightful owners, the Filipino nation. Their army numbered 30,000 men, and they were competent to whip out or starve out the little Spanish garrison; then the people could set up a government of their own devising. Our traditions required that Dewey should now set up his warning sign, and go away. But the Master of the Game happened to think of another plan—the European plan. He acted upon it. This was, to send out an army—ostensibly to help the native patriots put the finishing touch upon their long and plucky struggle for independence, but really to take their land away from them and keep it. That is, in the interest of Progress and Civilization. The plan developed, stage by stage, and quite satisfactorily. We entered into a military alliance with the trusting Filipinos, and they hemmed in Manila on the land side, and by their valuable help the place, with its garrison of 8,000 or 10,000 Spaniards, was captured—a thing which we could not have accomplished unaided at that time. We got their help by—by ingenuity. We knew they were fighting for their independence, and that they had been at it for two years. We knew they supposed that we also were fighting in their worthy cause—just as we had helped the Cubans fight for Cuban independence—and we allowed them to go on thinking so. *Until Manila was ours and we could get along without them.* Then we showed our hand. Of course, they were surprised—that was natural; surprised and disappointed; disappointed and grieved. To them it looked un-American; uncharacteristic; foreign to our established traditions. And this was natural, too; for we were only playing the American Game in public—in private it was the European. It was neatly done, very neatly, and it bewildered them. They could not understand it; for we had been so friendly—so affectionate, even—with those simple-minded patriots! We, our own selves, had brought back out of exile their leader, their hero, their hope, their Washington—Aguinaldo; brought him in a warship, in high honor, under the sacred shelter and hospitality of the flag; brought him back and restored him to his people, and got their moving and eloquent gratitude for it. Yes, we had been so friendly to them, and had heartened them up in so many ways! We had lent them guns and ammunition; advised with them; exchanged pleasant courtesies with them; placed our sick and wounded in their kindly care; entrusted our Spanish prisoners to their humane and honest hands; fought shoulder to shoulder with them against "the common enemy" (our own phrase); praised their courage, praised their gallantry, praised their mercifulness, praised their fine and honorable conduct; borrowed their trenches, borrowed strong positions which they had previously captured from the Spaniard; petted them, lied to them—officially proclaiming that our land and naval forces came to give them their freedom and displace the bad Spanish government—fooled them, used them until we needed them no longer; then derided the sucked orange and threw it away. We kept the positions which we had beguiled them of; by and by, we moved a force forward and overlapped patriot ground—a clever thought, for we needed trouble, and this would produce it. A Filipino soldier, crossing the ground, where no one had a right to forbid him, was shot by our sentry. The badgered patriots resented this with arms, without waiting to know whether Aguinaldo, who was absent, would approve or not. Aguinaldo did not approve; but that availed nothing. What we wanted, in the interest of Progress and Civilization, was the Archipelago, unencumbered by patriots struggling for independence; and War was what we needed. We clinched our opportunity. It is Mr. Chamberlain's case over again—at least in its motive and intention; and we played the game as adroitly as he played it himself."

"We and the patriots having captured Manila, Spain's ownership of the Archipelago and her sovereignty over it were at an end—obliterated—annihilated—not a rag or shred of either remaining behind. It was then that we conceived the divinely humorous idea of *buying* both of these spectres from Spain! [It is quite safe to confess this to the Person Sitting in Darkness, since neither he nor any other sane person will believe it.] In buying those ghosts for twenty millions, we also contracted to take care of the friars and their accumulations. I think we agreed to propagate leprosy and smallpox, but as to this there is doubt. But it is not important, persons afflicted with friars do not mind other diseases.

"With our Treaty ratified, Manila subdued, and our Ghosts secured, we had no further use for Aguinaldo and the owners of the Archipelago. We forced a war, and we have been hunting America's guest and ally through the woods and swamps ever since."

At this point in the tale, it will be well to boast a little of our war-work and our heroisms in the field, so as to make our performance look as fine as England's in South

Africa; but I believe it will not be best to emphasize this too much. We must be cautious. Of course, we must read the war-telegrams to the Person, in order to keep up our frankness; but we can throw an air of humorousness over them, and that will modify their grim eloquence a little, and their rather indiscreet exhibitions of gory exultation. Before reading to him the following display heads of the dispatches of November 18, 1900, it will be well to practice on them in private first, so as to get the right tang of lightness and gaiety into them:

"ADMINISTRATION WEARY OF PROTRACTED HOSTILITIES!"
"REAL WAR AHEAD FOR FILIPINO REBELS!"[1]
"WILL SHOW NO MERCY!"
"KITCHENER'S PLAN ADOPTED!"

Kitchener knows how to handle disagreeable people who are fighting for their homes and liberties, and we must let on that we are merely imitating Kitchener, and have no national interest in the matter, further than to get ourselves admired by the Great Family of Nations, in which august company our Master of the Game has bought a place for us in the back row.

Of course, we must not venture to ignore our General MacArthur's reports—oh, why do they keep on printing those embarrassing things?—we must drop them trippingly from the tongue and take the chances:

"During the last ten months our losses have been 268 killed and 750 wounded; Filipino loss, *three thousand two hundred and twenty-seven killed,* and 694 wounded."

We must stand ready to grab the Person Sitting in Darkness, for he will swoon away at this confession, saying: "Good, God, those 'niggers' spare their wounded, and the Americans massacre theirs!"

We must bring him to, and coax him and coddle him, and assure him that the ways of Providence are best, and that it would not become us to find fault with them; and then, to show him that we are only imitators, not originators, we must read the following passage from the letter of an American soldier-lad in the Philippines to his mother, published in *Public Opinion,* of Decorah, Iowa, describing the finish of a victorious battle:

"WE NEVER LEFT ONE ALIVE. IF ONE WAS WOUNDED, WE WOULD RUN OUR BAYONETS THROUGH HIM."

Having now laid all the historical facts before the Person Sitting in Darkness, we should bring him to again, and explain them to him. We should say to him:

"They look doubtful, but in reality they are not. There have been lies; yes, but they were told in a good cause. We have been treacherous; but that was only in order that real good might come out of apparent evil. True, we have crushed a deceived and confiding people; we have stamped out a just and intelligent and well-ordered republic; we have stabbed an ally in the back and slapped the face of a guest; we have bought a Shadow from an enemy that hadn't it to sell; we have robbed a trusting friend of his land and his liberty; we have invited our clean young men to shoulder a discredited musket and do bandit's work under a flag which bandits have been accustomed to fear, not to follow; we have debauched America's honor and blackened her face before the world; but each detail was for the best. We know this. The Head of every State and Sovereignty in Christendom and ninety per cent. of every legislative body in Christendom, including our Congress and our fifty State Legislatures, are members not only of the church, but also of the Blessings-of-Civilization Trust. This world-girdling accumulation of trained morals, high principles, and justice, cannot do an unright thing, an unfair thing, an ungenerous thing, an unclean thing. It knows what it is about. Give yourself no uneasiness; it is all right."

Now then, that will convince the Person. You will see. It will restore the Business. Also, it will elect the Master of the Game to the vacant place in the Trinity of our national gods; and there on their high thrones the Three will sit, age after age, in the people's sight, each bearing the Emblem of his service: Washington, the Sword of the Liberator; Lincoln, the Slave's Broken Chains; the Master, the Chains Repaired.

It will give the business a splendid new start. You will see.

Everything is prosperous, now; everything is just as we should wish it. We have got the Archipelago, and we shall never give it up. Also, we have every reason to hope that we shall have an opportunity before very long to slip out of our Congressional contract with Cuba and give her something better in the place of it. It is a rich country, and many of us are already beginning to see that the contract was a sentimental mistake. But now—right now—is the best time to do some profitable rehabilitating work—work that will set us up and make us comfortable, and discourage gossip. We cannot conceal from ourselves that, privately, we are a little troubled about our uniform. It is one of our prides; it is acquainted with honor; it is familiar with great deeds and noble; we love it, we revere it; and so this errand it is on makes us uneasy. And our flag—another pride of ours, our chiefest!

We have worshipped it so; and when we have seen it in far lands—glimpsing it unexpectedly in that strange sky, waving its welcome and benediction to us—we have caught our breath, and uncovered our heads, and couldn't speak, for a moment, for the thought of what it was to us and the great ideals it stood for. Indeed, we *must* do something about these things; we must not have the flag out there, and the uniform. They are not needed there, we can manage in some other way. England manages, as regards the uniform, and so can we. We have to send soldiers—we can't get out of that—but we can disguise them. It is the way England does in South Africa. Even Mr. Chamberlain himself takes pride in England's honorable uniform, and makes the army down there wear an ugly and odious and appropriate disguise, of yellow stuff such as quarantine flags are made of, and which are hoisted to warn the healthy away from unclean disease and repulsive death. This cloth is called khaki. We could adopt it. It is light, comfortable, grotesque, and deceives the enemy, for he cannot conceive of a soldier being concealed in it.

And as for a flag for the Philippine Province, it is easily managed. We can have a special one—our States do it; we can have just our usual flag, with the white stripes painted black and the stars replaced by the skull and cross-bones.

And we do not need that Civil Commission out there. Having no powers, it has to invent them, and that kind of work cannot be effectively done by just anybody; an expert is required. Mr. Croker can be spared. We do not want the United States represented there, but only the Game.

By help of these suggested amendments, Progress and Civilization in that country can have a boom, and it will take in the Persons who are Sitting in Darkness, and we can resume Business at the old stand.

MARK TWAIN

On the Damned Race

I am the only man living who understand human nature; God has put me in charge of this branch office; when I retire there will be no one to take my place. I shall keep on doing my duty, for when I get over on the other side, I shall use my influence to have the human race drowned again; and this time drowned good, no omissions, no Ark.—JOHN MACY, *Mark Twain*

I have studied the human race with diligence and strong interest all these years in my own person; in myself I find in big or little proportion every quality and every defect that is findable in the mass of the race.—Mark Twain's Autobiography, published in *Mark Twain in Eruption*

To the Person Sitting in Darkness

I have always preached. . . . If the humor came of its own accord and uninvited, I have allowed it a place in my sermon, but I was not writing the sermon for the sake of the humor.—Mark Twain's Autobiography, published in *Mark Twain in Eruption*

"To the Person Sitting in Darkness" is Mark Twain's masterpiece of this kind of preaching. It is also the most timely of his short satires—strangely, perhaps, for it was certainly not written with an eye to posterity, and many of the events which inspired it are half forgotten. In fact, probably few periods in our history are at present so unfamiliar to the literate reader as the turn-of-the-century wars. Our ten weeks war with Spain, for example, is widely remembered now for the fact that the yellow press—Hearst and Pulitzer—supported it, and, of course, for the sinking of the *Maine* in Havana Harbor by persons still unidentified. More often forgotten is the fact that—according to historians who agree on little else—the basic cause of hostilities was American horror at Spanish colonial methods, and especially at the methods of General Weyler, who, in 1896, exterminated half of the population of Havana Province in *reconcentrado* camps; this was a year after the outbreak of the second Cuban revolution, led by José Martí, and two years before the United States intervened on Cuba's side. Intervention came after Congress guaranteed that the United States would not impose American sovereignty on Cuba. "The people of the island of Cuba," read the resolution, "are, and of right ought to be, free and independent."

The seeds of the Philippine War were sown in the peace treaty with Spain. For President McKinley's peace terms—for which neither this country nor Spain was prepared—were that Spain should not only free Cuba, but cede to us all her West Indian possessions, and sell us the Philippine Islands.

In the Philippines, as in Cuba, native armies were in revolt against Spain; their troops had recently cooperated with ours. The war which the United States fought to establish its sovereignty over the Filipinos, was far more bloody and expensive, and never so popular, as the war with Spain.

The Boer War, which Mark Twain so often likened to the Filipino affair, was also for empire. But a contributing cause was the discovery of gold and diamonds in the farmlands of South Africa. The numerous British settlers attracted by these discoveries were hated by the Boers (settlers of Dutch descent) and were heavily taxed, but denied citizenship. From 1899 to 1902 the British used against the Boers, and later against Boer guerrillas, the methods common to invading armies of the period; burnt countrysides, strings of blockhouses, and concentration camps in which masses of the civilian population perished.

When "To the Person Sitting in Darkness" appeared, it produced a cyclone; the sections on the missionaries in China produced savage public warfare between Mark Twain and the American Board of Foreign Missions—a warfare which continued until the Board fell silent.

The reparations extracted by the missionaries, which Mark Twain discusses below, followed upon the victory of an international army, including two thousand Americans, which, in August, 1900, took the city of Peking from Chinese armies led by the Boxers—who were "China's traduced patriots," according to Mark Twain. Supposedly, the international army was to punish antiforeign rioting by the Chinese, but, after China's defeat, the reparations extracted by the Great Powers—except the United States—were at least as rapacious as those extracted by the missionaries; the great difference was that they were not the work of professed men of God—and it was this work which Mark Twain ensured should live in infamy.

The germ of "To the Persons Sitting in Darkness" seems to have been this New Year's Greeting which Clemens published in the New York *Herald,* December 30, 1900:

A GREETING FROM THE NINETEENTH TO THE TWENTIETH CENTURY

> I bring you the stately nation named Christendom, returning, bedraggled, besmirched, and dishonored, from pirate raids in Kiao-Chou, Manchuria, South Africa, and the Philippines, with her soul full of meanness, her pocket full of boodle, and her mouth full of hypocrisies. Give her soap and towel, but hide the looking glass.

In January, 1901, Mark Twain wrote "To the Person Sitting in Darkness." He then sought advice on publishing it, for, as he said, he liked advice when it was his way. The wrong advice—from his friend, the Rev. Joseph Twichell—was received, and is now lost. Clemens' answer is not:

> *I* can't understand it! You are a public guide and teacher, Joe, and are under a heavy responsibility to men, young and old; if you teach your people—as you teach me—to hide their opinions when they believe the flag is being abused and dishonored, lest the utterance do them and a publisher a damage, how do you answer for it to your conscience? You are sorry for me; in the fair way of give and take, I am willing to be a little sorry for you.

In the same letter:

> . . . I'm not expecting anything but kicks for scoffing, and am expecting a diminution of my bread and butter by it, but if Livy [Mrs. Clemens] will let me I will have my say. This nation is like all the others that have been spewed upon the earth—ready to shout for any cause that will tickle its vanity or fill its pocket. What a hell of a heaven it will be, when they get all these hypocrites assembled there!

Livy "let" him. His old friend William Dean Howells also had no doubt that he should publish, although he did suggest that he hang himself afterwards.

Thanks partly to those two—the only two whose judgment Mark Twain entirely respected—"To the Person Sitting in Darkness" appeared in the February issue of the respectable and liberal *North American Review.* The effect, according to Clemens' biographer, Albert Bigelow Paine, was "as if he had thrown a great missile into the human hive. . . . Whatever other effect it may have had, it left no thinking person unawakened.

NOTES

[1] "Rebels!" Mumble that funny word—don't let the Person catch it distinctly.

115. Booker T. Washington, *Up From Slavery*, 1901

Booker T. Washington was the son of a female slave and a white man whose identity he never knew. He graduated from Hampton Institute in 1875 and taught there until he was chosen to organize the Tuskegee Institution in 1881. Although he privately used his resources and influence to fight segregation, in his famous Atlanta Exposition Speech of 1895 publicly urged black Southerners to focus their efforts on economic rather than political gains while he urged white Southerners to give their black neighbors a fair chance. Washington's policies won him extraordinary gifts from philanthropists, brought Southern legislative grants for black schools, and made him the "spokesman for his race." His autobiography, Up From Slavery *(1901), became a national bestseller.*

Source: Booker T. Washington, *Three Negro Classics,* "Up From Slavery," 1901. Public Domain Reprint.

Mr. President and Gentlemen of the Board of Directors and Citizens.

One-third of the population of the South is of the Negro race. No enterprise seeking the material, civil, or moral welfare of this section can disregard this element of our population and reach the highest success. I but convey to you, Mr. President and Directors, the sentiment of the masses of my race when I say that in no way have the value and manhood of the American Negro been more fittingly and generously recognized than by the managers of this magnificent Exposition at every stage of its progress. It is a recognition that will do more to cement the friendship of the two races than any occurrence since the dawn of our freedom.

Not only this, but the opportunity here afforded will awaken among us a new era of industrial progress. Ignorant and inexperienced, it is not strange that in the first years of our new life we began at the top instead of at the bottom; that a seat in Congress or the state legislature was more sought than real estate or industrial skill; that the political convention of stump speaking had more attractions than starting a dairy farm or truck garden.

A ship lost at sea for many days suddenly sighted a friendly vessel. From the mast of the unfortunate vessel was seen a signal, "Water, water; we die of thirst!" The answer from the friendly vessel at once came back. "Cast down your bucket where you are." A second time the signal, "Water, water; send us water!" ran up from the distressed vessel, and was answered, "Cast down your bucket where you are." And a third and fourth signal for water was answered, "Cast down your bucket where you are." The captain of the distressed vessel, at last heeding the injunction, cast down his bucket, and it came up full of fresh, sparkling water from the mouth of the Amazon River. To those of my race who depend on bettering their condition in a foreign land or who underestimate the importance of cultivating friendly relations with the Southern white man, who is their next-door neighbour, I would say: "Cast down your bucket where you are"—cast it down in making friends in every manly way of the people of all races by whom we are surrounded.

Cast it down in agriculture, mechanics, in commerce, in domestic service and in the professions. And in this connection it is well to bear in mind that whatever other sins the South may be called to bear, when it comes to business, pure and simple, it is in the South that the Negro is given a man's chance in the commercial world, and in nothing is this Exposition more eloquent than in emphasizing this chance. Our greatest danger is that in the great leap from slavery to freedom we may overlook the fact that the masses of us are to live by the productions of our hands, and fail to keep in mind that we shall prosper in proportion as we learn to dignify and glorify common labour and put brains and skill into the common occupations of life; shall prosper in proportion as we learn to draw the line between the superficial and the substantial, the ornamental gewgaws of life and the useful. No race can prosper till it learns that there is as much dignity in tilling a field as in writing a poem. It is at the bottom of life we must begin, and not at the top. Nor should we permit our grievances to overshadow our opportunities.

To those of the white race who look to the incoming of those of foreign birth and strange tongue and habits for the prosperity of the South, were I permitted I would repeat what I say to my own race, "Cast down your bucket where you are." Cast it down among the eight millions of Negroes whose habits you know, whose fidelity and love you have tested in days when to have proved treacherous meant the ruin of your firesides. Cast down your bucket among these people who have, without strikes and labour wars, tilled your fields, cleared your forests, built your railroads and cities, and brought forth treasures from the bowels of the earth, and helped make possible this magnificent representation of the progress of the South. Casting down your bucket among my people, helping and encouraging them as you are doing on these grounds, and to education of head, hand, and heart, you will find that they will buy your surplus land, make blossom the waste place in your fields, and run your factories. While doing this, you can be sure in the future, as in the past, that you and your families will be surrounded by the most patient, faithful, law-abiding, and unresentful people that the world has seen. As we have proved our loyalty to you in the past, in nursing your children, watching by the sickbed of your mothers and fathers, and often following them with tear-dimmed eyes to their graves, so in the future, in our humble way, we shall stand by you with a devotion that no foreigner can approach, ready to lay down our lives, if need be, in defence of yours, interlacing our industrial, commercial, civil, and religious life with yours in a way that shall make the interests of both races one. In all things that are purely social we can be as separate as the fingers, yet one as the hand in all things essential to mutual progress.

There is no defence or security for any of us except in the highest intelligence and development of all. If anywhere there are efforts tending to curtail the fullest growth of the Negro, let these efforts be turned into stimulating, encouraging, and making him the most useful and intelligent citizen. Effort or means so invested will pay a thousand per cent interest. These efforts will be twice blessed—"blessing him that gives and him that takes."

There is no escape through law of man or God from the inevitable:—

> The laws of changeless justice bind
>   Oppressor with oppressed;
> And close as sin and suffering joined
>   We march to fate abreast.

Nearly sixteen millions of hands will aid you in pulling the load upward, or they will pull against you the load downward. We shall constitute one-third and more of the ignorance and crime of the South, or one-third its intelligence and progress; we shall contribute one-third to the business and industrial prosperity of the South, or we shall prove a veritable body of death, stagnating, depressing, retarding every effort to advance the body politic.

Gentlemen of the Exposition, as we present to you our humble effort at an exhibition of our progress, you must not expect overmuch. Starting thirty years ago with ownership here and there in a few quilts and pumpkins and chickens (gathered from miscellaneous sources), remember the path that has led from these to the inventions and production of agricultural implements, buggies, steam engines, newspapers, books, statuary, carving, paintings, the management of drug-stores and banks, has not been trodden without contact with thorns and thistles. While we take pride in what we exhibit as a result of our independent efforts, we do not for a moment forget that our part in this exhibition would fall far short of your expectations but for the constant help that has come to our educational life, not only from the Southern states, but especially from Northern philanthropists, who have made their gifts a constant stream of blessing and encouragement.

The wisest among my race understand that the agitation of questions and social equality is the extremest folly, and that progress in the enjoyment of all the privileges that will come to us must be the result of severe and constant struggle rather than of artificial forcing. No race that has anything to contribute to the markets of the world is long in any degree ostracized. It is important and right that all privileges of the law be ours, but it is vastly more important that we be prepared for the exercises of these privileges. The opportunity to earn a dollar in a factory just now is worth infinitely more than the opportunity to spend a dollar in an opera-house.

In conclusion, may I repeat that nothing in thirty years has given us more hope and encouragement, and drawn us so near to you of the white race, as this opportunity offered by the Exposition; and here bending, as it were, over the altar that represents the results of the struggles of your race and mine, both starting practically emptyhanded three decades ago. I pledge that in your effort to work out the great and intricate problem which God has laid at the doors of the South, you shall have at all times the patient, sympathetic help of my race; only let this be constantly in mind, that, while from representations in these buildings of the product of field, of forest, of mine, of factory, letters, and art, much good will come, yet far above and beyond material benefits will be that higher good, that, let us pray God, will come, in a blotting out of sectional differences and racial animosities and suspicions, in a determination to administer absolute justice, in a willing obedience among all classes to the mandates of law. This, then, coupled with our material prosperity, will bring into our beloved South a new heaven and a new earth.

The first thing that I remember, after I had finished speaking, was the Governor Bullock rushed across the platform and took me by the hand, and that others did the same. I received so many and such hearty congratulations that I found it difficult to get out of the building. I did not appreciate to any degree, however, the impression which my address seemed to have made, until the next morning, when I went into the business part of the city. As soon as I was recognized, I was surprised to find myself pointed out and surrounded by a crowd of men who wished to shake hands with me. This was kept up on every street on to which I went, to an extent which embarrassed me so much that I went back to my boarding-place. The next morning I returned to Tuskegee. I found a crowd of people anxious to shake hands with me.

The papers in all parts of the United States published the address in full, and for months afterward there were complimentary editorial references to it. Mr. Clark Howell, the editor of the Atlanta *Constitution,* telegraphed to a New York paper, among other words, the following, "I do not exaggerate when I say that Professor Booker T. Washington's address yesterday was one of the most notable speeches, both as to character and as to the warmth of its reception, ever delivered to a Southern audience. The address was a revelation. The whole speech is a platform upon which blacks and whites can stand with full justice to each other."

The Boston *Transcript* said editorially: "The speech of Booker T. Washington at the Atlanta Exposition, this week, seems to have dwarfed all the other proceedings and the Exposition itself. The sensation that it has caused in the press has never been equalled."

I very soon began receiving all kinds of propositions from lecture bureaus, and editors of magazines and papers, to take the lecture platform, and to write articles. One lecture bureau offered me fifty thousand dollars, or two hundred dollars a night and expenses, if I would place my services at its disposal for a given period. To all these communications I replied that my life-work was at Tuskegee: and that whenever I spoke it must be in the interests of the Tuskegee school and my race, and that I would enter into no arrangements that seemed to place a mere commercial value upon my services.

Some days after its delivery I sent a copy of my address to the President of the United States, the Hon. Grover Cleveland. I received from him the following autographed reply:—

GRAY GABLES BUZZARD'S BAY, MASS., OCTOBER 6, 1895

BOOKER T. WASHINGTON, ESQ.:

MY DEAR SIR: I thank you for sending me a copy of your address delivered at the Atlanta Exposition.

I thank you with much enthusiasm for making the address. I have read it with intense interest, and I think the Exposition would be fully justified if it did not do more than furnish the opportunity for its delivery. Your words cannot fail to delight and encourage all who wish well for your race; and if our coloured fellow citizens do not from your utterances gather new hope and form new determinations to gain every valuable advantage offered them by their citizenship, it will be strange indeed.

Yours very truly,
GROVER CLEVELAND.

Later I met Mr. Cleveland, for the first time, when, as President, he visited the Atlanta Exposition. At the request of myself and others he consented to spend an hour in the Negro Building, for the purpose of inspecting the Negro exhibit and of giving the coloured people in attendance an opportunity to shake hands with him. As soon as I met Mr. Cleveland I became impressed with his simplicity, greatness, and rugged honesty. I have met him many times since then, both at public functions and at his private residence in Princeton, and the more I see of him the more I admire him. When he visited the Negro Building in Atlanta he seemed to give himself up wholly, for that hour, to the coloured people. He seemed to be as careful to shake hands with some old coloured "auntie" clad partially in rags, and to take as much pleasure in doing so, as if he were greeting some millionaire. Many of the coloured people took advantage of the occasion to get him to write his name in a book or on a slip of paper. He was as careful and patient in doing this as if he were putting his signature to some great state document.

Mr. Cleveland has not only shown his friendship for me in many personal ways, but has always consented to do anything I have asked of him for our school. This he has done, whether it was to make a personal donation or to use his influence in securing the donations of others. Judging from my personal acquaintance with Mr.

Cleveland, I do not believe that he is conscious of possessing any colour prejudice. He is too great for that. In my contact with people I find that, as a rule, it is only the little, narrow people who live for themselves, who never read good books, who do not travel, who never open up their souls in a way to permit them to come into contact with other souls—with the great outside world. No man whose vision is bounded by colour can come into contact with what is highest and best in the world. In meeting men, in many places, I have found that the happiest people are those who do the most for others; the most miserable are those who do the least. I have also found that few things, if any, are capable of making one so blind and narrow as race prejudice. I often say to our students, in the course of my talks to them on Sunday evenings in the chapel, that the longer I live and the more experience I have of the world, the more I am convinced that, after all, the one thing that is most worth living for—and dying for, if need be—is the opportunity of making some one else more happy and more useful.

The coloured people and the coloured newspapers at first seemed to be greatly pleased with the character of my Atlanta address, as well as with its reception. But after the first burst of enthusiasm began to die away, and the coloured people began reading the speech in cold type, some of them seemed to feel that I had been too liberal in my remarks toward the Southern whites, and that I had not spoken out strongly enough for what they termed the "rights" of the race. For a while there was a reaction, so far as a certain element of my own race was concerned, but later these reactionary ones seemed to have been won over to my way of believing and acting.

While speaking of changes in public sentiment, I recall that about ten years after the school at Tuskegee was established, I had an experience that I shall never forget. Dr. Lyman Abbott, then the pastor of Plymouth Church, and also editor of the *Outlook* (then the *Christian Union*), asked me to write a letter for his paper giving my opinion of the exact condition, mental and moral, of the coloured ministers in the South, as based upon my observations. I wrote the letter, giving the exact facts as I conceived them to be. The picture painted was a rather black one—or, since I am black, shall I say "white"? It could not be otherwise with a race but a few years out of slavery, a race which had not had time or opportunity to produce a competent ministry.

What I said soon reached every Negro minister in the country, I think, and the letters of condemnation which I received from them were not few. I think that for a year after the publication of this article every association and every conference or religious body of any kind, of my race, that met, did not fail before adjourning to pass a resolution condemning me, or calling upon me to retract or modify what I had said. Many of these organizations went so far in their resolutions as to advise parents to cease sending their children to Tuskegee. One association even appointed a "missionary" whose duty it was to warn the people against sending their children to Tuskegee. This missionary had a son in the school, and I noticed that, whatever the "missionary" might have said or done with regard to others, he was careful not to take his son away from the institution. Many of the coloured papers, especially those that were the organs of religious bodies, joined in the general chorus of condemnation or demands for retraction.

During the whole time of the excitement, and through all the criticism, I did not utter a word of explanation or retraction. I knew that I was right, and that time and the sober second thought of the people would vindicate me. It was not long before the bishops and other church leaders began to make a careful investigation of the conditions of the ministry, and they found out that I was right. In fact, the oldest and most influential bishop in one branch of the Methodist Church said that my words were far too mild. Very soon public sentiment began making itself felt, in demanding a purifying of the ministry. While this is not yet complete by any means, I think I may say, without egotism, and I have been told by many of our most influential ministers, that my words had much to do with starting a demand for the placing of a higher type of men in the pulpit. I have had the satisfaction of having many who once condemned me thank me heartily for my frank words.

The change of the attitude of the Negro ministry, so far as regards myself, is so complete that at the present time I have no warmer friends among any class than I have among the clergymen. The improvement in the character and life of the Negro ministers is one of the most gratifying evidences of the progress of the race. My experience with them, as well as other events in my life, convinced me that the thing to do, when one feels sure that he has said or done the right thing, and is condemned, is to stand still and keep quiet. If he is right, time will show it.

In the midst of the discussion which was going on concerning my Atlanta speech, I received the letter which I give below, from Dr. Gilman, the President of Johns Hopkins University, who had been made chairman of the judges of award in connection with the Atlanta

Exposition:—

> JOHNS HOPKINS UNIVERSITY, BALTIMORE,
> President's Office, September 30, 1895
>
> DEAR MR. WASHINGTON: Would it be agreeable to you to be one of the Judges of Award in the Department of Education at Atlanta? If so, I shall be glad to place your name upon the list. A line by telegraph will be welcomed.
>
> Yours very truly,
> D. C. GILMAN

I think I was even more surprised to receive this invitation than I had been to receive the invitation to speak at the opening of the Exposition. It was to be a part of my duty, as one of the jurors, to pass not only upon the exhibits of the coloured schools, but also upon those of the white schools. I accepted the position, and spent a month in Atlanta in performance of the duties which it entailed. The board of jurors was a large one, consisting in all of sixty members. It was about equally divided between Southern white people and Northern white people. Among them were college presidents, leading scientists and men of letters, and specialists in many subjects. When the group of jurors to which I was assigned met for organization, Mr. Thomas Nelson Page, who was one of the number, moved that I be made secretary of that division, and the motion was unanimously adopted. Nearly half of our division were Southern people. In performing my duties in the inspection of the exhibits of white schools I was in every case treated with respect, and at the close of our labours I parted from my associates with regret.

I am often asked to express myself more freely than I do upon the political condition and the political future of my race. These recollections of my experience in Atlanta give me the opportunity to do so briefly. My own belief is, although I have never before said so in so many words, that the time will come when the Negro in the South will be accorded all the political rights which his ability, character, and material possessions entitle him to. I think, though, that the opportunity to freely exercise such political rights will not come in any large degree through outside or artificial forcing, but will be accorded to the Negro by the Southern white people themselves, and that they will protect him in the exercise of those rights. Just as soon as the South gets over the old feeling that it is being forced by "foreigners," or "aliens," to do something which it does not want to do, I believe that the change in the direction that I have indicated is going to begin. In fact, there are indications that it is already beginning in a slight degree.

Let me illustrate my meaning. Suppose that some months before the opening of the Atlanta Exposition there had been a general demand from the press and public platform outside the South that a Negro be given a place on the opening programme, and that a Negro be placed upon the board of jurors of award. Would any such recognition of the race have taken place? I do not think so. The Atlanta officials went as far as they did because they felt it to be a pleasure, as well as a duty, to reward what they considered merit in the Negro race. Say what we will, there is something in human nature which we cannot blot out, which makes one man, in the end, recognize and reward merit in another, regardless of colour or race.

I believe it is the duty of the Negro—as the greater part of the race is already doing-to deport himself modestly in regard to political claims, depending upon the slow but sure influences that proceed from the possession of property, intelligence, and high character for the full recognition of his political rights. I think that the according of the full exercise of political rights is going to be a matter of natural, slow growth, not an over-night, gourd-vine affair. I do not believe that the Negro should cease voting, for a man cannot learn the exercise of self-government by ceasing to vote any more than a boy can learn to swim by keeping out of the water, but I do believe that in his voting he should more and more be influenced by those of intelligence and character who are his next-door neighbours.

I know coloured men who, through the encouragement, help, and advice of Southern white people, have accumulated thousands of dollars worth of property, but who, at the same time, would never think of going to those same persons for advice concerning the casting of their ballots. This, it seems to me, is unwise and unreasonable, and should cease. In saying this I do not mean that the Negro should truckle, or not vote from principle, for the instant he ceases to vote from principle he loses the confidence and respect for the Southern white man even.

I do not believe that any state should make a law that permits an ignorant and poverty-striken white man to vote, and prevents a black man in the same condition from voting. Such a law is not only unjust, but it will react, as all unjust laws do, in time; for the effect of such a law is to encourage the Negro to secure education and property, and at the same time it encourages the white man to remain in ignorance and poverty. I believe that in time, through the operation of intelligence and friendly race relations, all cheating at the ballot box in the South will cease. It will become apparent that the white man who begins by cheating a Negro out of his ballot soon learns to cheat a white man out of his, and that the man who does this ends his career of dishonesty by the theft of property or by some equally serious crime. In my opinion, the time will come when the South will encourage all of its citizens to vote. It will see that it pays better, from every standpoint, to have healthy, vigorous life than to have that political stagnation which always results when one-half of the population has no share and no interest in the Government.

As a rule, I believe in universal, free suffrage, but I believe that in the South we are confronted with peculiar conditions that justify the protection of the ballot in many of the states, for a while at least, either by an educational test, a property test, or by both combined; but whatever tests are required, they should be made to apply with equal and exact justice to both races.

116. W. E. B. DuBois, *The Souls of Black Folk*, 1901

W. E. B. DuBois took his Ph.D at Harvard in 1895. From 1897 to 1910 DuBois taught history at Atlanta University. At first an ally of Booker T. Washington, DuBois decided early in the twentieth century that black Americans needed to pursue the full range of rights accorded other Americans. He became a foe of Washington's brand of education and reform. His book The Souls of Black Folk *(1903) is one of the central documents of the African-American experience.*

Of Mr. Booker T. Washington And Others

From birth till death enslaved; in word, in deed,
   unmanned!
. . . .
Hereditary bondsmen! Know ye not
Who would be free themselves must strike the blow?
                                                    BYRON.

Easily the most striking thing in the history of the American Negro since 1876 is the ascendancy of Mr. Booker T. Washington. It began at the time when war memories and ideals were rapidly passing; a day of astonishing commercial development was drawing; a sense of doubt and hesitation overtook the freedmen's sons,—then it was that this leading began. Mr. Washington came, with a single definite programme, at the psychological moment when the nation was a little ashamed of having bestowed so much sentiment on Negroes, and was concentrating its energies on Dollars. His programme of industrial education, conciliation of the South, and submission and silence as to civil and political rights, was not wholly original; the Free Negroes from 1830 up to wartime had striven to build industrial schools, and the American Missionary Association had from the first taught various trades; and Price and others had sought a way of honorable alliance with the best of the Southerners. But Mr. Washington first indissolubly linked these things; he put enthusiasm, unlimited energy, and perfect faith into this programme, and changed it from a by-path into a veritable Way of Life. And the tale of the methods by which he did this is a fascinating study of human life.

It startled the nation to hear a Negro advocating such a programme after many decades of bitter complaint; it startled and won the applause of the Association, it interested and won the admiration of the North; and after a confused murmur of protest, it silenced if it did not convert the Negroes themselves.

To gain the sympathy and coöperation of the various elements comprising the white South was Mr. Washington's first task; and this, at the time Tuskegee was founded, seemed, for a black man, well-nigh impossible. And yet ten years later it was done in the words spoken at Atlanta: "In all things purely social we can be as separate as the five fingers, and yet one as the hand in all things essential to mutual progress." This "Atlanta Compro-

Source: Booker T. Washington, *Three Negro Classics.* "The Souls of Black Folks," 1901. Public Domain Reprint.

mise" is by all odds the most notable thing in Mr. Washington's career. The South interpreted it in different ways; the radicals received it as a complete surrender of the demand for civil and political equality; the conservatives, as a generously conceived working basis for mutual understanding. So both approved it, and to-day its author is certainly the most distinguished Southerner since Jefferson Davis, and the one with the largest personal following.

Next to this achievement comes Mr. Washington's work in gaining place and consideration in the North. Others less shrewd and tactful had formerly essayed to sit on these two stools and had fallen between them; but as Mr. Washington knew the heart of the South from birth and training, so by singular insight he intuitively grasped the spirit of the age which was dominating the North. And so thoroughly did he learn the speech and thought of triumphant commercialism, and the ideals of material prosperity, that the picture of a lone black boy poring over a French grammar amid the weeds and dirt of a neglected home soon seemed to him the acme of absurdities. One wonders what Socrates and St. Francis of Assisi would say to this.

And yet this very singleness of vision and thorough oneness with his age is a mark of the successful man. It is as though Nature must needs make men narrow in order to give them force. So Mr. Washington's cult has gained unquestioning followers, his work has wonderfully prospered, his friends are legion, and his enemies are confounded. To-day he stands as the one recognized spokesman of his ten million fellows, and one of the most notable figures in a nation of seventy millions. One hesitates, therefore, to criticize a life which, beginning with so little, has done so much. And yet the time is come when one may speak in all sincerity and utter courtesy of the mistakes and shortcomings of Mr. Washington's career, as well as of his triumphs, without being thought captious or envious, and without forgetting that it is easier to do ill than well in the world.

The criticism that has hitherto met Mr. Washington has not always been of this broad character. In the South especially has he had to walk warily to avoid the harshest judgments,—and naturally so, for he is dealing with the one subject of deepest sensitiveness to that section. Twice—once when at the Chicago celebration of the Spanish-American War he alluded to the color-prejudice that is "eating away the vitals of the South."—and once when he dined with President Roosevelt—has the resulting Southern criticism been violent enough to threaten seriously his popularity. In the North the feeling has several times forced itself into words, that Mr. Washington's counsels of submission overlooked certain elements of true manhood, and that his educational programme was unnecessarily narrow. Usually, however, such criticism has not found open expression, although, too, the spiritual sons of the Abolitionists have not been prepared to acknowledge that the schools founded before Tuskegee, by men of broad ideals and self-sacrificing spirit, were wholly failures or worthy of ridicule. While, then, criticism has not failed to follow Mr. Washington, yet the prevailing public opinion of the land has been but too willing to deliver the solution of a wearisome problem into his hands, and say, "If that is all you and your race ask, take it."

Among his own people, however, Mr. Washington has encountered the strongest and most lasting opposition, amounting at times to bitterness, and even to-day continuing strong and insistent even though largely silenced in outward expression by the public opinion of the nation. Some of this opposition is, of course, mere envy; the disappointment of displaced demagogues and the spite of narrow minds. But aside from this, there is among educated and thoughtful colored men in all parts of the land a feeling of deep regret, sorrow, and apprehension at the wide currency and ascendancy which some of Mr. Washington's theories have gained. These same men admire his sincerity of purpose, and are willing to forgive much to honest endeavor which is doing something worth the doing. They coöperate with Mr. Washington as far as they conscientiously can; and, indeed, it is no ordinary tribute to this man's tact and power that, steering as he must between so many diverse interests and opinions, he so largely retains the respect of all.

But the hushing of the criticism of honest opponents is a dangerous thing. It leads some of the best of the critics to unfortunate silence and paralysis of effort, and others to burst into speech so passionately and intemperately as to lose listeners. Honest and earnest criticism from those whose interests are most nearly touched,—criticism of writers by readers, of government by those governed, of leaders by those led,—this is the soul of democracy and the safeguard of modern society. If the best of the American Negroes receive by outer pressure a leader whom they had not recognized before, manifestly there is here a certain palpable gain. Yet there is also irreparable loss,—a loss of that peculiarly valuable education which a group receives when by search and criticism it finds and commissions its own leaders. The way in which this is done is at once the most elementary and the nicest problem of social growth. History is but the record of such group-leadership; and yet how definitely changeful is its type and character! And of all types and kinds, what can be more instructive than the leadership of a group within a group?—that curious double movement where real progress may be negative and actual advance be relative retrogression. All this is the social student's inspiration and despair.

Now in the past the American Negro has had instructive experience in the choosing of group leaders, founding thus a peculiar dynasty which in the light of present conditions is worth while studying. When sticks and stones and beasts form the sole environment of a people, their attitude is largely one of determined opposition to and conquest of natural forces. But when to earth and brute is added an environment of men and ideas, then the attitude of the imprisoned group may take three main forms,—a feeling of revolt and revenge; an attempt to adjust all thought and action to the will of the greater group; or, finally, a determined effort at self-realization and self-development despite environing opinion. The influence of all of these attitudes at various times can be traced in the history of the American Negro, and in the evolution of his successive leaders.

Before 1750, while the fire of African freedom still burned in the veins of the slaves, there was in all leadership or attempted leadership but the one motive of result and revenge,—typified in the terrible Maroons, the Danish blacks, and Cato of Stono, and veiling all the Americas in fear of insurrection. The liberalizing tendencies of the latter half of the eighteenth century brought, along with kindlier relations between black and white, thoughts of ultimate adjustment and assimilation. Such aspiration was especially voiced in the earnest songs of Phyllis, in the martyrdom of Attucks, the fighting of Salem and Poor, the intellectual accomplishments of Banneker and Derham, and the political demands of the Cuffes.

Stern financial and social stress after the war cooled much of the previous humanitarian ardor. The disappointment and impatience of the Negroes at the persistence of slavery and serfdom voiced itself in two movements. The slaves in the South, aroused undoubtedly by vague rumors of the Haitian revolt, made three fierce attempts at insurrection,—in 1800 under Gabriel in Virginia, in 1822 under Vesey in Carolina, and in 1831 again in Virginia under the terrible Nat Turner. In the Free States, on the other hand, a new and curious attempt at self-development was made. In Philadelphia and New York color-prescription led to a withdrawal of Negro communicants from white churches and the formation of a peculiar socio-religious institution among the Negroes known as the African Church,—an organization still living and controlling in its various branches over a million of men.

Walker's wild appeal against the trend of the times showed how the world was changing after the coming of the cotton-gin. By 1830 slavery seemed hopelessly fastened on the South, and the slaves thoroughly cowed into submission. The free Negroes of the North, inspired by the mulatto immigrants from the West Indies, began to change the basis of their demands; they recognized the slavery of slaves, but insisted that they themselves were freemen, and sought assimilation and amalgamation with the nation on the same terms with other men. Thus, Forten and Purvis of Philadelphia, Shad of Wilmington, Du Bois of New Haven, Barbadoes of Boston, and others, strove singly and together as men, they said, not as slaves; as "people of color," not as "Negroes." The trend of the times, however, refused them recognition save in individual and exceptional cases, considered them as one with all the despised blacks, and they soon found themselves striving to keep even the rights they formerly had of voting and working and moving as freemen. Schemers of migration and colonization arose among them; but these they refused to entertain, and they eventually turned to the Abolition movement as a final refuge.

Here, led by Remond, Nell, Wells-Brown, and Douglass, a new period of self-assertion and self-development dawned. To be sure, ultimate freedom and assimilation was the ideal before the leaders, but the assertion of the manhood rights of the Negro by himself was the main reliance, and John Brown's raid was the extreme of its logic. After the war and emancipation, the great form of Frederick Douglass, the greatest American Negro leader, still led the host. Self-assertion, especially in political lines, was the main programme, and behind Douglass came Elliot, Bruce, and Langston, and the Reconstruction politicians, and, less conspicuous but of greater social significance Alexander Crummell and Bishop Daniel Payne.

Then came the Revolution of 1876, the suppression of the Negro votes, the changing and shifting of ideals, and the seeking of new lights in the great night. Douglass, in his old age, still bravely stood for the ideals of his early manhood,—ultimate assimilation *through* self-assertion, and no other terms. For a time Price arose as a new leader, destined, it seemed, not to give up, but to re-state the old ideals in a form less repugnant to the white South. But he passed away in his prime. Then came the new leader. Nearly all the former one had become leaders by the silent suffrage of their fellows, had sought to lead their own people alone, and were usually, save Douglass, little known outside their race. But Booker T. Washington arose as essentially the leader not of one race but of two,—a compromiser between the South, the North, and the Negro. Naturally the Negroes resented, at first bitterly, signs of compromise which surrendered their civil and political rights, even though this was to be exchanged for larger chances of economic development. The rich and dominating North, however, was not only weary of the race problem, but was investing largely in Southern enterprises, and welcomed any method of peaceful coöperation. Thus, by national opinion, the Negroes began to recognize Mr. Washington's leadership; and the voice of criticism was hushed.

Mr. Washington represents in Negro thought the old attitude of adjustment and submission; but adjustment at such a peculiar time as to make his programme unique. This is an age of unusual economic development, and Mr. Washington's programme naturally takes an economic cast, becoming a gospel of Work and Money to such an extent as apparently almost completely to overshadow the higher aims of life. Moreover, this is an age when the more advanced races are coming in closer contact with the less developed races, and the race-feeling is therefore intensified; and Mr. Washington's programme practically accepts the alleged inferiority of the Negro races. Again, in our own land, the reaction from the sentiment of war time has given impetus to race-prejudice against Negroes, and Mr. Washington withdraws many of the high demands of Negroes as men and American citizens. In other periods of intensified prejudice all the Negro's tendency to self-assertion has been called forth; at this period a policy of submission is advocated. In the history of nearly all other races and peoples the doctrine preached at such crises has been that manly self-respect is worth more than lands and houses, and that a people who voluntarily surrender such respect, or cease striving for it, are not worth civilizing.

In answer to this, it has been claimed that the Negro can survive only through submission. Mr. Washington distinctly asks that black people give up, at least for the present, three things,—

First, political power,

Second, insistence on civil rights,

Third, higher education of Negro youth,—

and concentrate all their energies on industrial education, the accumulation of wealth, and the conciliation of the South. This policy has been courageously and insistently advocated for over fifteen years, and has been triumphant for perhaps ten years. As a result of this tender of the palm-branch, what has been the return? In these years there have occurred:

1. The disfranchisement of the Negro.

2. The legal creation of a distinct status of civil inferiority for the Negro.

3. The steady withdrawal of aid from institutions for the higher training of the Negro.

These movements are not, to be sure, direct results of Mr. Washington's teachings; but his propaganda has, without a shadow of doubt, helped their speedier accomplishment. The question then comes: Is it possible, and probable, that nine millions of men can make effective progress in economic lines if they are deprived of political rights, made a servile caste, and allowed only the most meagre chance for developing their exceptional men? If history and reason give any distinct answer to these questions, it is an emphatic *No*. And Mr. Washington thus faces the triple paradox of his career:

1. He is striving nobly to make Negro artisans businesses men and property-owners; but it is utterly impossible, under modern competitive methods, for workingmen and property-owners to defend their rights and exist without the right of suffrage.

2. He insists on thrift and self-respect, but at the same time counsels a silent submission to civic inferiority such as is bound to sap the manhood of any race in the long run.

3. He advocates common-school and industrial training, and depreciates institutions of higher learning; but neither the Negro common-schools, nor Tuskegee itself, could remain open a day were it not for teachers trained in Negro colleges, or trained by their graduates.

This triple paradox in Mr. Washington's position is the object of criticism by two classes of colored Americans. One class is spiritually descended from Toussaint the Savior, through Gabriel, Vesey, and Turner, and they represent the attitude of revolt and revenge; they hate the white South blindly and distrust the white race generally, and so far as they agree on definite action, think that the Negro's only hope lies in emigration beyond the borders of the United States. And yet, by the irony of fate, nothing has more effectually made this programme seem hopeless than the recent course of the United States toward weaker and darker peoples in the West Indies, Hawaii, and the Philippines,—for where in the world may we go and be safe from lying and brute force?

The other class of Negroes who cannot agree with Mr. Washington has hitherto said little aloud. They deprecate the sight of scattered counsels, of internal disagreement; and especially they dislike making their just criticism of a useful and earnest man an excuse for a general discharge of venom from small-minded opponents. Nevertheless, the questions involved are so fundamental and serious that it is difficult to see how men like the Grimkes, Kelly Miller, J. W. E. Bowen, and other representatives of this group, can much longer be silent. Such men feel in conscience bound to ask of this nation three things:

1. The right to vote.
2. Civic equality.
3. The education of youth according to ability.

They acknowledge Mr. Washington's invaluable service in counselling patience and courtesy in such demands; they do not ask that ignorant black men vote when ignorant whites are debarred, or that any reasonable restrictions in the suffrage should not be applied; they know that the low social level of the mass of the race is responsible for much discrimination against it, but they also know, and the nation knows, that relentless color-prejudice is more often a cause than a result of the Negro's degradation; they seek the abatement of this relic of barbarism, and not its systematic encouragement and pampering by all agencies of social power from the Associated Press to the Church of Christ. They advocate, with Mr. Washington, a broad system of Negro common schools supplemented by thorough industrial training; but they are surprised that a man of Mr. Washington's insight cannot see that no such educational system ever has rested or can rest on any other basis than that of the well-equipped college and university, and they insist that there is a demand for a few such institutions throughout the South to train the best of the Negro youth as teachers, professional men, and leaders.

This group of men honor Mr. Washington for his attitude of conciliation toward the white South; they accept the "Atlanta Compromise" in its broadest interpretation; they recognize, with him, many signs of promise, many men of high purpose and fair judgment, in this section; they know that no easy task has been laid upon a region already tottering under heavy burdens. But, nevertheless, they insist that the way to truth and right lies in straightforward honestly, not in indiscriminate flattery; in praising those of the South who do well and criticising uncompromisingly those who do ill; in taking advantage of the opportunities at hand and urging their fellows to do the same, but at the same time in remembering that only a firm adherence to their higher ideals and aspirations will ever keep those ideals with the realm of possibility.

They do not expect that the free right to vote, to enjoy civic rights, and to be educated, will come in a moment; they do not expect to see the bias and prejudices of years disappear at the blast of a trumpet; but they are absolutely certain that the way for a people to gain their reasonable rights is not by voluntarily throwing them away and insisting that they do not want them; that the way for a people to gain respect is not by continually belittling and ridiculing themselves; that, on the contrary, Negroes must insist continually, in season and out of season that voting is necessary to modern manhood, that color discrimination is barbarism, and that black boys need education as well as white boys.

In failing thus to state plainly and unequivocally the legitimate demands of their people, even at the cost of opposing an honored leader, the thinking classes of American Negroes would shirk a heavy responsibility,—a responsibility to themselves, a responsibility to the struggling masses, a responsibility to the darker races of men whose future depends so largely on this American experiment, but especially a responsibility to this nation,—this common Fatherland. It is wrong to encourage a man or a people in evil-doing; it is wrong to aid and abet a national crime simply because it is unpopular not to do so. The growing spirit of kindliness and reconciliation between the North and South after the frightful difference of a generation ago ought to be a source of deep congratulation to all, and especially to those whose mistreatment caused the war; but if that reconciliation is to be marked by the industrial slavery and civic-death of those same black men, with permanent legislation into a position of inferiority, then those black men, if they are really men, are called upon by every consideration of patriotism and loyalty to oppose such a course by all civilized methods, even though such opposition involves disagreement with Mr. Booker T. Washington. We have no right to sit silently by while the inevitable seeds are sown for a harvest of disaster to our children, black and white.

First, it is the duty of black men to judge the South discriminatingly. The present generation of Southerners are not responsible for the past, and they should not be blindly hated or blamed for it. Furthermore, to no class in the indiscriminate endorsement of the recent course of the South toward Negroes more nauseating than to the best thought of the South. The South is not "solid"; it is a land in the ferment of social change, wherein forces of all kinds are fighting for supremacy; and to praise the ill the South is to-day perpetrating is just as wrong as to condemn the good. Discriminating and broad-minded criticism is what the South needs,—

needs it for the sake of her own white sons and daughters, and for the insurance of robust, healthy mental and moral development.

To-day even the attitude of the Southern whites toward the blacks is not, as so many assume, in all cases the same; the ignorant Southerner hates the Negro, the workingmen fear his competition, the money-makers wish to use him as a laborer, some of the educated see a menace in his upward development; while others—usually the sons of the masters—wish to help him to rise. National opinion has enabled this last class to maintain the Negro common schools, and to protect the Negro partially in property, life, and limb. Through the pressure of the money-makers, the Negro is in danger of being reduced to semi-slavery, especially in the country districts; the workingmen, and those of the educated who fear the Negro, have united to disfranchise him, and some have urged his deportation; while the passions of the ignorant are easily aroused to lynch and abuse any black man. To praise this intricate whirl of thought and prejudice is nonsense; to inveigh indiscriminately against "the South" is unjust; but to use the same breath in praising Governor Aycock, exposing Senator Morgan, arguing with Mr. Thomas Nelson Page, and denouncing Senator Ben Tillman, is not only sane, but the imperative duty of thinking black men.

It would be unjust to Mr. Washington and not acknowledge that in several instances he has opposed movements in the South which were unjust to the Negro; he sent memorials to the Louisiana and Alabama constitutional conventions, he has spoken against lynching, and in other ways has openly or silently set his influence against sinister schemes and unfortunate happenings. Notwithstanding this, it is equally true to assert that on the whole the distinct impression left by Mr. Washington's propaganda is, first, that the South is justified in its present attitude toward the Negro because of the Negro's degradation; secondly, that the prime cause of the Negro's failure to rise more quickly is his wrong education in the past; and thirdly, that his future rise depends primarily on his own efforts. Each of these propositions is a dangerous half-truth. The supplementary truths must never be lost sight of: first, slavery and race-prejudice are potent if not sufficient causes of the Negro's position; second, industrial and common-school training were necessarily slow in planting because they had to await the black teachers trained by higher institutions,—it being extremely doubtful if any essentially different development was possible, and certainly in Tuskegee was unthinkable before 1880; and third, while it is a great truth to say that the Negro must strive and strive mightily to help himself, it is equally true that unless his striving be not simply seconded, but rather aroused and encouraged, by the initiative of the richer and wiser environing group, he cannot hope for great success.

In his failure to realize and impress this last point, Mr. Washington is especially to be criticised. His doctrine has tended to make the whites, North and South, shift the burden of the Negro problem to the Negro's shoulder and stand aside as critical and rather pessimistic spectators; when in fact the burden belongs to the nation, and the hands of none of us are clean if we bend not our energies to righting these great wrongs.

The South ought to be led, by candid and honest criticism, to assert her better self and do her full duty to the race she has cruelly wronged and is still wronging. The North—her co-partner in guilt—cannot salve her conscience by plastering it with gold. We cannot settle this problem by diplomacy and suaveness, by "policy" alone. If worse comes to worse, can the moral fibre of this country survive the slow throttling and murder of nine millions of men?

The black men of America have a duty to perform, a duty stern and delicate,—a forward movement to oppose a part of the work of their greatest leader. So far as Mr. Washington preaches Thrift, Patience, and Industrial Training for the masses, we must hold up his hands and strive with him, rejoicing in his honors and glorying in the strength of this Joshua called of God and of man to lead the headless host. But so far as Mr. Washington apologizes for injustice, North or South, does not rightly value the privilege and duty of voting, belittles the emasculating effects of caste distinctions, and opposes the higher training and ambition of our brighter minds,—so far as he, the South, or the Nation, does this,—we must unceasingly and firmly oppose them. By every civilized and peaceful method we must strive for the rights which the world accords to men, clinging unwaveringly to those great words which the sons of the Fathers would fain forget: "We hold these truths to be self-evident: That all men are created equal; that they are endowed by their Creator with certain unalienable rights; that among these are life, liberty, and the pursuit of happiness."

Chapter XX

Theodore Roosevelt and Progressive Reform, 1901–1909

117. ROOSEVELT, PANAMA AND COLUMBIA

The debate over the Panama Canal reignited long-festering distrust with the United States and the people of Latin America. In these three documents, Theodore Roosevelt explains his motives, the Colombian government expresses their anger, and Roosevelt expands his rationale throughout the hemisphere in the Roosevelt Corollary to the Monroe Doctrine.

Roosevelt's Case for Supporting the Panamanian Revolution, 1903

First, that the United States has for over half a century patiently and in good faith carried out its obligations under the treaty of 1846; second, that when for the first time it became possible for Colombia to do anything in requital of the services thus repeatedly rendered to it for fifty-seven years by the United States, the Columbian Government peremptorily and offensively refused thus to do its part, even though to do so would have been to its advantage and immeasurably to the advantage of the State of Panama, at that time under its jurisdiction; third, that throughout this period revolutions, riots, and factional disturbances of every kind have occurred one after the other in almost uninterrupted succession, some of them lasting for months and even for years, while the central government was unable to put them down or to

---

Source: Theodore Roosevelt on the Panamanian Revolution, 1903. Columbia's Grievances, 1904, and the Roosevelt Corollary to the Monroe Doctrine, 1904. Public Domain Reprint.

make peace with the rebels; fourth, that these disturbances instead of showing any sign of abating have tended to grow more numerous and more serious in the immediate past; fifth, that the control of Columbia over the Isthmus of Panama could not be maintained without the armed intervention and assistance of the United States. In other words, the Government of Columbia, though wholly unable to maintain order on the Isthmus, has nevertheless declined to ratify a treaty the conclusion of which opened the only chance to secure its own stability and to guarantee permanent peace on, and the construction of a canal across, the Isthmus.

Under such circumstances the Government of the United States would have been guilty of folly and weakness, amounting in their sum to a crime against the Nation; had it acted otherwise than it did when the revolution of November 3 last took place in Panama. This great enterprise of building the interoceanic canal can not be held up to gratify the whims, or out of respect to the governmental impotence, or to the even more sinister and evil political peculiarities, of people who, though they dwell afar off, yet against the wish of the actual dwellers on the Isthmus, assert an unreal supremacy over the territory. The possession of territory fraught with such peculiar capacities as the Isthmus in question carries with it obligations to mankind. The course of events has shown that this canal can not be built by private enterprise, or by any other nation than our own; therefore it must be built by the United States.

Every effort has been made by the Government of the United States to persuade Columbia to follow a course which was essentially not only to our interests and to the interests of the world, but to the interests of Columbia itself. These efforts have failed; and Columbia, by her persistence in repulsing the advances that have been made,

431

has forced us, for the sake of our own honor, and of the interest and well-being, not merely of our own people, but of the people of the Isthumus of Panama and the people of the civilized countries of the world, to take decisive steps to bring to an end a condition of affairs which has become intolerable.

Columbia's Grievances, 1904

First. That the said note of the 30th of December from your excellency is regarded by my Government as an intimation that the Columbian forces will be attacked by those of the United States on their entering the territory of Panama for the purpose of subduing the rebellion, and that for that reason, and owing to its inability to cope with the powerful American squadron that watches over the coasts of the Isthumus of Panama, it holds the Government of the United States responsible for all damages caused to it by the loss of that national territory.

Second. That since the 3d of November last the revolution of Panama would have yielded, or would not have taken place, if the American soldiers and the agents of the Panama Canal had not prevented the Columbian forces from proceeding on their march toward Panama, and that I, as commander in chief of the army of Columbia, would have succeeded in suppressing the revolution of Panama as early as the 20th of the same month if Admiral Coghlan had not notified me in an official note that he had orders from the Government to prevent the landing of Columbian forces throughout the territory of the Isthumus.

Third. That the charges officially made against the Government and Senate of Columbia that it was opposed to the work of the Panama Canal, and that its purpose was to obtain a greater amount of money from the American Government and to recover the concession of the French company are unfair and groundless, and the proof of this assertion is that the Columbian Senate refused to ratify the Hay-Herran treaty, not because a greater sum of money was demanded, but because the treaty was contrary to the constitution of the country, which prohibits the cession of sovereignty over national territory; but the necessity of the canal is so well recognized in Columbia that it was proposed, in the discussion of the Senate, to amend the constitution in order to remove the constitutional difficulty, and the minister of foreign relations, after the sessions of Congress were closed, directed the chargé d'affaires, Doctor Herran, to advise the Government of your excellency that that of Columbia was ready to enter into renewed negotiations for a canal convention, and that it purposed to remove the existing constitutional difficulties. The charge made against the Government of Columbia that it purposed to cancel the concession of the French company vanishes as soon as it be known that under the latest extension granted to it by Columbia the said concession would not lapse until the year 1910.

Fourth. That the failure of the Columbian Senate to ratify the Hay-Herran treaty, for the reasons above stated, can not be regarded as an act of discourtesy or unfriendliness, as the minister of foreign relations of Columbia, Señor Rico, told the minister of the United States, Mr. Beaupré, at Bogatá, because a treaty prior to its ratification is nothing but a project which, according to the laws of nations, neither confers rights nor imposes obligations, and therefore its rejection or delay in its ratification gives no ground for the adoption of measures tending to alter the relations of friendship between the two countries. If it were not so, the mere act of preparing a public treaty would be an occasion for serious danger instead of an element of peace and progress, which is the predicament in which Columbia finds itself at present, owing to her weakness.

Fifth. That while the treaty of 1846 gives to the Government of the United States the right to maintain and protect the free transit of the Isthumus at the request of Columbia and when the latter is unable to do so, it places it under the obligation of enforcing the respect of Columbia's sovereignty over the territory of the Isthumus, and that the American Government has now not only failed to discharge that duty, but has prevented the Columbian forces from recovering the national sovereignty on the Isthumus, and thus the said treaty of 1846 being in full force, Columbia holds that the Government of the United States has no other reason than that of its own strength and of Columbia's weakness for interpreting and applying it in the manner it has: that is to say, for availing itself of the advantages and rights conferred by the treaty, and refusing to fulfill the obligations imposed thereby.

Sixth. That it is known, from sworn statements, that the garrisons of Panama and Colon were bought with gold from the United States, toward the end of October, by the Panama revolutionists.

Seventh. That if these revolutionists had not relied, and did not now rely, on the armed protection of the United States, whose powerful squadrons on both the Pacific and Atlantic oceans have prevented, and are preventing since the 3d of November, the Columbian army from landing its forces, the Panama revolution would have been foiled by Columbia in a few hours.

Eighth. That the Government of Columbia, holding a perfect right that the cession of the compact with the French canal company be not effected without its express consent, has instituted an action against the said company before the French courts and asked that the contract made with the American Government be declared null and void.

Ninth. That on the grounds above stated, the Government of Columbia believes that it has been despoiled by that of the United States of its rights and sovereignty on the Isthumus of Panama, and not being possessed of the material strength to prevent this by the means of arms (although it does not forego this method, which it will use to the best of its ability), solemnly declares to the Government of the United States:

1. That the Government of the United States is responsible to that of Columbia for the dismemberment that has been made of its territory by the separation of Panama, by reason of the attitude that the said Government assumed there as soon as the revolution of the 3d of November broke out.

2. That this contract made between the United States and the French canal company is null, since it lacks the consent of Columbia, and the latter has already brought suit against the said canal company before the French courts in the defense of its interests.

3. That the Government of Columbia does not nor will it ever relinquish the rights it possesses over the territory of the Isthumus of which it is now despoiled by the American forces, and will at all times claim the said rights and try to vindicate them by every means within its reach, and that for that reason the title over the territory of the Isthumus that may be acquired by the United States for the opening of the canal is void, and Columbia reserves to herself the right to claim the said territory at any time.

4. That if the work of the Panama Canal is undertaken and carried to completion in disregard and trespass of the rights of Columbia, the latter puts it on record that she was denied justice by the United States; that she was forcibly despoiled of the territory of the Isthumus in clear violation of the treaty of 1846, and that she does not relinquish the rights she possesses over the said territory, and holds the United States responsible for the damages caused to her.

5. That Columbia, earnestly wishing that the work of the canal be carried into effect, not only because it suits her interests but also those of the commerce of the world, is disposed to enter into arrangements that would secure for the United States the execution and ownership of the said work and be based on respect for her honor and rights.

6. That the United States has never protected Columbia on the interest of Panama against foreign invasion, and that when it has intervened to prevent the interruption of the traffic it has been in help, or be it at the suggestion of the Government of Columbia. In this one instance it did not, on its own initiative, with the obvious purpose of protecting the secession of the interest. The guarantee of neutrality, if it were privileged, would estop the sovereign of the land from maintaining order, which is contrary to the fundamental principles of every government; and

7. That the course followed by the America Government at Panama at the time when Columbia enjoyed peace, after overcoming a revolution of three years' duration, which left her exhausted, is in favor of any rebellion, but not of the maintenance of order, which is contrary to the principles and antecedents of the policy of this great nation as established in the war of secession. . . .

The Roosevelt Corollary, 1904

It is not true that the United States feels any land hunger or entertains any projects as regards the other nations of the Western Hemisphere save such as are for their welfare. All that this country desires is to see the neighboring countries stable, orderly, and prosperous. Any country whose people conduct themselves well can count upon our hearty friendship. If a nation shows that it knows how to act with reasonable efficiency and decency in social and political matters, if it keeps order and pays its obligations, it need fear no interference from the United States. Chronic wrongdoing, or an impotence which results in a general loosening of the ties of civilized society, may in America, as elsewhere, ultimately require the intervention by some civilized nation, and in the Western Hemisphere the adherence of the United States to the Monroe Doctrine may force the United States, however reluctantly, in flagrant cases of such wrongdoing or impotence, to the exercise of an international police power. If every country washed by the Caribbean Sea would show the progress in stable and just civilization which the aid of the Platt amendment Cuba had shown since our troops left the island, and which so many of the republics in both Americas are constantly and brilliantly showing, all question of interference by this Nation with their affairs would be at an end. Our interests and those of our southern neighbors are in reality identical. They have great natural riches, and if within their borders the reign of law and justice obtains, prosperity is sure to come to them. While they thus obey the primary laws of civilized society they may rest assured that they will be treated by us in a spirit of cordial and helpful sympathy. We would interfere with them only in the last resort, and then only if it became evident that their inability or unwillingness to due justice at home and abroad had violated the rights of the United States or had invited foreign aggression to the detriment of the entire body of American nations. It is a mere truism to say that every nation, whether in America or anywhere else, which desires to maintain its freedom, its independence, must ultimately realize that the right of such independence can not be separated from the responsibility of making good use of it.

118. Mary Antin, *The Promised Land*, 1904

Mary Antin emigrated with her family from Poland in 1894 and attended Boston public schools. She later studied at Columbia and Barnard, but became a settlement worker at Hale House in Boston before receiving a degree. Her autobiography, The Promised Land, *reveals the hardships and aspirations of European Jews and extols America as a land of opportunity for the persecuted.*

Chapter IX

Having made such good time across the ocean, I ought to be able to proceed no less rapidly on *terra firma*, where, after all, I am more at home. And yet here is where I falter. Not that I hesitated, even for the space of a breath, in my first steps in America. There was no time to hesitate. The most ignorant immigrant, on landing, proceeds to give and receive greetings, to eat, sleep, and rise, after the manner of his own country; wherein he is corrected, admonished, and laughed at, whether by interested friend or the most indifferent strangers; and his American experience is thus begun. The process is spontaneous on all sides, like the education of the child by the family circle. But while the most stupid nursery maid is able to contribute her part toward the result, we do not expect an analysis of the process to be furnished by any member of the family, least of all by the engaging infant. The philosophical maiden aunt alone, or some other witness equally psychological and aloof, is able to trace the myriad efforts by which the little Johnnie or Nellie acquires a secure hold on the disjointed parts of the huge plaything, life.

Now I was not exactly an infant when I was set down, on a May day some fifteen years ago, in this pleasant nursery of America. I had long since acquired the use of my faculties, and had collected some bits of experience, practical and emotional, and had even learned to give an account of them. Still, I had very little perspective, and my observations and comparisons were superficial. I was too much carried away to analyze the forces that were moving me. My Polotzk I knew well before I began to judge it and experiment with it, America was bewilderingly strange, unimaginably complex, delightfully unexplored. I rushed impetuously out of the cage of my provincialism and looked eagerly about the brilliant universe. My question was, What have we here?—not, What does this mean? That query came much later. When I now become retrospectively introspective, I fall into the predicament of the centipede in the rhyme, who got along very smoothly until he was asked which leg came after which, whereupon he became so rattled that he couldn't take a step. I know I have come on a thousand feet, on wings, winds, and American machines,—I have leaped and run and climbed and crawled,—but to tell which step came after which I find a puzzling matter. Plenty of maiden aunts were present during my second infancy, in the guise of immigrant officials, school-teachers, settlement workers, and sundry other unprejudiced and critical observers. Their statistics I might properly

---

Source: Mary Antin. *The Promised Land,* 1904. Public Domain Reprint.

borrow to fill the gaps in my recollections, but I am prevented by my sense of harmony. The individual, we know, is a creature unknown to the statistician, whereas I undertook to give the personal view of everything. So I am bound to unravel, as well as I can, the tangle of events, outer and inner, which made up the first breathless years of my American life.

During his three years of probation, my father had made a number of false starts in business. His history for that period is the history of thousands who come to America, like him, with pockets empty, hands untrained to the use of tools, minds cramped by centuries of repression in their native land. Dozens of these men pass under your eyes every day, my American friend, too absorbed in their honest affairs to notice the looks of suspicion which you cast at them, the repugnance with which you shrink from their touch. You see them shuffle from door to door with a basket of spools and buttons, or bending over the sizzling irons in a basement tailor shop, or rummaging in your ash can, or moving a pushcart from curb to curb, at the command of the burly policeman. "The Jew peddler!" you say, and dismiss him from your premises and from your thoughts, never dreaming that the sordid drama of his days may have a moral that concerns you. What if the creature with the untidy beard carries in his bosom his citizenship papers? What if the cross-legged tailor is supporting a boy in college who is one day going to mend your state constitution for you? What if the ragpicker's daughters are hastening over the ocean to teach your children in the public schools? Think, every time you pass the greasy alien on the street, that he was born thousands of years before the oldest native American; and he may have something to communicate to you, when you two shall have learned a common language. Remember that his very physiognomy is a cipher the key to which it behooves you to search for most diligently.

By the time we joined my father, he had surveyed many avenues of approach toward the coveted citadel of fortune. One of these, heretofore untried, he now proposed to essay, armed with new courage, and cheered on by the presence of his family. In partnership with an energetic little man who had an English chapter in his history, he prepared to set up a refreshment booth on Crescent Beach. But while he was completing arrangements at the beach we remained in town, where we enjoyed the educational advantages of a thickly populated neighborhood; namely, Wall Street, in the West End of Boston.

Anybody who knows Boston knows that the West and North Ends are the wrong ends of that city. They form the tenement district, or, in the newer phrase, the slums of Boston. Anybody who is acquainted with the slums of any American metropolis knows that that is the quarter where poor immigrants foregather, to live, for the most part, as unkempt, half-washed, toiling, unaspiring foreigners; pitiful in the eyes of social missionaries, the despair of boards of health, the hope of ward politicians, the touchstone of American democracy. The well-versed metropolitan knows the slums as a sort of house of detention for poor aliens, where they live on probation till they can show a certificate of good citizenship.

He may know all this and yet not guess how Wall Street, in the West End, appears in the eyes of a little immigrant from Polotzk. What would the sophisticated sight-seer say about Union Place, off Wall Street, where my new home waited for me? He would say that it is no place at all, but a short box of an alley. Two rows of three-story tenements are its sides, a stingy strip of sky is its lid, a littered pavement is the floor, and a narrow mouth its exit.

But I saw a very different picture on my introduction to Union Place. I saw two imposing rows of brick buildings, loftier than any dwelling I had ever lived in. Brick was even on the ground for me to tread on, instead of common earth or boards. Many friendly windows stood open, filled with uncovered heads of women and children. I thought the people were interested in us, which was very neighborly. I looked up to the topmost row of windows, and my eyes were filled with the May blue of an American sky!

In our days of affluence in Russia we had been accustomed to upholstered parlors, embroidered linen, silver spoons and candlesticks, goblets of gold, kitchen shelves shinning with copper and brass. We had featherbeds heaped halfway to the ceiling; we had clothes presses dusky with velvet and silk and fine woollen. The three small rooms into which my father now ushered us, up one flight of stairs, contained only the necessary beds, with lean mattresses; a few wooden chairs; a table or two; a mysterious iron structure, which later turned out to be a stove; a couple of unornamental kerosene lamps; and a scanty array of cooking-utensils and crockery. And yet we were all impressed with our new home and its furniture. It was not only because we had just passed through our seven lean years, cooking in earthen vessels, eating black bread on holidays and wearing cotton; it was chiefly because these wooden chairs and tin pans were American chairs and pans that they shone glorious in our eyes. And if there was anything lacking for comfort or decoration we expected it to be presently supplied—at least, we children did. Perhaps my mother alone, of us newcomers, appreciated the shabbiness of the little apartment, and realized that for her there was as yet no laying down of the burden of poverty.

Our initiation into American ways began with the first step on the new soil. My father found occasion to instruct or correct us even on the way from the pier to Wall Street, which journey we made crowded together in a rickety cab. He told us not to lean out of the windows, not to point, and explained the word "greenhorn." We did not want to be "greenhorns," and gave the strictest attention to my father's instructions. I do not know when my parents found opportunity to review together the history of Polotzk in the three years past, for we children had no patience with the subject; my mother's narrative was constantly interrupted by irrelevant questions, interjections, and explanations.

The first meal was an object lesson of much variety. My father produced several kinds of food, ready to eat, without any cooking, from little tin cans that had printing all over them. He attempted to introduce us to a queer, slippery kind of fruit, which he called "banana," but had to give it up for the time being. After the meal, he had better luck with a curious piece of furniture on runners, which he called "rocking-chair." There were five of us newcomers, and we found five different ways of getting into the American machine of perpetual motion, and as many ways of getting out of it. One born and bred to use of a rocking-chair cannot imagine how ludicrous people can make themselves when attempting to use it for the first time. We laughed immoderately over our various experiments with the novelty, which was a wholesome way of letting off steam after the usual excitement of the day.

In our flat we did not think of such a thing as storing the coal in the bathtub. There was no bathtub. So in the evening of the first day my father conducted us to the public baths. As we moved along in a little procession, I was delighted with the illumination of the streets. So many lamps, and they burned until morning, my father said, and so people did not need to carry lanterns. In America, then, everything was free, as we had heard in Russia. Light was free; the streets were as bright as a synagogue on a holy day. Music was free; we had been serenaded, to our gaping delight, by a brass band of many pieces, soon after our installation on Union Place.

Education was free. That subject my father had written about repeatedly, as comprising his chief hope for us children, the essence of American opportunity, the treasure that no thief could touch, not even misfortune or poverty. It was the one thing that he was able to promise us when he sent for us; surer, safer than bread or shelter. On our second day I was thrilled with the realization of what this freedom of education meant. A little girl from across the alley came and offered to conduct us to school. My father was out, but we five between us had a few words of English by this time. We knew the word school. We understood. This child, who had never seen us till yesterday, who could not pronounce our names, who was not much better dressed than we, was able to offer us the freedom of the schools of Boston! No application made, no question asked, no examinations, rulings, exclusions; no machinations, no fees. The doors stood open for every one of us. The smallest child could show us the way.

This incident impressed me more than anything I had heard in advance of the freedom of education in America. It was a concrete proof—almost the thing itself. One had to experience it to understand it.

It was a great disappointment to be told by my father that we were not to enter upon our school career at once. It was too near the end of the term, he said, and we were going to move to Crescent Beach in a week or so. We had to wait until the opening of the schools in September. What a loss of precious time—from May till September!

Not that the time was really lost. Even the interval on Union Place was crowded with lessons and experience. We had to visit the stores and be dressed from head to foot in American clothing; we had to learn the mysteries of the iron stove, the washboard, and the speaking-tube; we had to learn to trade with the fruit peddler through the window, and not to be afraid of the policeman; and, above all, we had to learn English.

The kind people who assisted us in these important matters form a group by themselves in the gallery of my friends. If I had never seen them from those early days till now, I should still have remembered them with gratitude. When I enumerate the long list of my American teachers, I must begin with those who came to us on Wall Street and taught us our first steps. To my mother, in her perplexity over the cookstove, the woman who showed her how to make the fire was an angel of deliverance. A fairy godmother to us children was she who led us to a wonderful country called "uptown," where, in a dazzlingly beautiful palace called a "department store," we exchanged our hateful homemade European costumes, which pointed us out as "greenhorns" to the children on the street, for real American machine-made garments, and issued forth glorified in each other's eyes.

With our despised immigrant clothing we shed also our impossible Hebrew names. A committee of our friends, several years ahead of us in American experience, but their heads together and concocted America names for us all. Those of our real names that had no pleasing American equivalents they ruthlessly discarded, content if they retained the initials. My mother, possessing a name that was not easily translatable, was punished with the undignified nickname of Annie. Fetchke, Joseph, and Deborah issued as Frieda, Joseph and Dora, respectively. As for poor me, I was simply cheated. The name they gave me was hardly new. My Hebrew name being Maryashe in full, Mashke for short, Russianized into Marya (*Mar-ya*), my friends said that it would hold good in English as *Mary;* which was very disappointing, as I longed to possess a strange-sounding American name like the others.

I am forgetting the consolation I had, in this matter of names, from the use of my surname, which I have had no occasion to mention until now. I found on my arrival that my father was "Mr. Antin" on the slightest provocation, and not, as in Polotzk, on state occasions alone. And so I was "Mary Antin," and I felt very important to answer to such a dignified title. It was just like America that even plain people should wear their surnames on week days.

As a family we were so diligent under instruction, so adaptable, and so clever in hiding our deficiencies, that when we made the journey to Crescent Beach, in the wake of our small wagon-load of household goods, my father had very little occasion to admonish us on the way, and I am sure he was not ashamed of us. So much we had achieved toward our Americanization during the two weeks since our landing.

Crescent Beach is a name that is printed in very small type on the maps of the environs of Boston, but a life-size strip of sand curves from Winthrop to Lynn; and that is historic ground in the annals of my family. The place is now a popular resort for holiday crowds, and is famous under the name of Revere Beach. When the reunited Antins made their stand there, however, there were no boulevards, no stately bath-houses, no hotels, no gaudy amusement places, no illumination, no showmen, no tawdry rabble. There was only the bright clean sweep of sand, the summer sea, and the summer sky. At high tide the whole Atlantic rushed in, tossing the seaweeds in his mane; at low tide he rushed out, growling and gnashing his granite teeth. Between tides a baby might play on the beach, digging with pebbles and shells, till it lay asleep on the sand. The whole sun shone by day, troops of stars by night, and the great moon in its season.

Into this grand cycle of the seaside day I came to live and learn and play. A few people came with me, as I have already intimated; but the main thing was that *I* came to live on the edge of the sea — I, who had spent my life inland, believing that the great waters of the world were spread out before me in the Dvina. My idea of the human world has grown enormously during the long journey; my idea of the earth had expanded with every day at sea; my idea of the world outside the earth now budded and swelled during my prolonged experience of the wide and unobstructed heavens.

Not that I got any inkling of the conception of a multiple world. I had had no lessons in cosmogony, and had no spontaneous revelation of the true position of the earth in the universe. For me, as for my fathers, the sun set and rose, and I did not feel the earth rushing through space. But I lay stretched out in the sun, my eyes level with the sea, till I seemed to be absorbed bodily by the very materials of the world around me; till I could not feel my hand as separate from the warm sand in which it was buried. Or I crouched on the beach at full moon, wondering, wondering, between the two splendors of the sky and the sea. Or I ran out to meet the incoming storm, my face full in the wind, my being a-tingle with an awesome delight to the tips of my fog-matted locks flying behind; and stood clinging to some stake or upturned boat, shaken by the roar and rumble of the waves. So clinging, I pretended that I was in danger, and was deliciously frightened; I held on with both hands, and shook my head, exulting in the tumult around me, equally ready to laugh or sob. Or else I sat, on the stillest days, with my back to the sea, not looking at all, but just listening to the rustle of the waves on the sand; not thinking at all, but just breathing with the sea.

Thus courting the influence of sea and sky and variable weather, I was bound to have dreams, hints, imaginings. It was no more than this, perhaps: that the world as I knew it was not large enough to contain all that I saw and felt; that the thoughts that flashed through my mind, not half understood, unrelated to my utterable thoughts, concerned something for which I had as yet no name. Every imaginative growing child has these flashes of intuition, especially one that became intimate with some one aspect of nature. With me it was the growing time, that idle summer by the sea, and I grew all the faster because I had been so cramped before. My mind, too, had so recently been worked upon by the impressive experience of a change of country that I was more than commonly alive to impressions, which are the seeds of ideas.

Let no one suppose that I spent my time entirely, or even chiefly, in inspired solitude. By far the best part of my day was spent in play — frank, hearty, boisterous play, such as comes natural to American children. In Polotzk I had already begun to be considered too old for play, excepting set games or organized frolics. Here I found myself included with children who still played, and I willingly returned to childhood. There were plenty of playfellows. My father's energetic little partner had a little wife and a large family. He kept them in the little cottage next to ours; and that the shanty survived the tumultuous presence of that brood is a wonder to me today. The young Wilners included an assortment of boys, girls, and twins, of every possible variety of age, size, disposition, and sex. They swarmed in and out of the cottage all day long, wearing the door-sill hollow, and trampling the ground to powder. They swung out of windows like monkeys, slid up the roof like flies, and shot out of trees like fowls. Even a small person like me couldn't go anywhere without being run over by a Wilner; and I could never tell which Wilner it was because none of them ever stood still long enough to be identified; and also because I suspected that they were in the habit of interchanging conspicuous articles of clothing, which was very confusing.

You would suppose that the little mother must have been utterly lost, bewildered, trodden down in this horde of urchins; but you are mistaken. Mrs. Wilner was a positively majestic little person. She ruled her brood with the utmost coolness and strictness. She had even the biggest boy under her thumb, frequently under her palm. If they enjoyed the wildest freedom outdoors, indoors the young Wilners lived by the clock. And so at five o'clock in the evening, on even days in the week, my father's partner's children could be seen in two long rows around the supper table. You could tell them apart on this occasion, because they all had their faces washed. And this is the time to count them: there are twelve little Wilners at table.

I managed to retain my identity in this multitude somehow, and while I was very much impressed with their numbers, I even dared to pick and choose my friends among the Wilners. One or two of the smaller boys I liked best of all, for a game of hide-and-seek or a frolic on the beach. We played in the water like ducks, never taking the trouble to get dry. One day I waded out with one of the boys, to see which of us dared go farthest. The tide was extremely low, and we had not wet our knees when we began to look back to see if familiar objects were still in sight. I thought we had been wading for hours, and still the water was so shallow and quiet. My companion was marching straight ahead, so I did the same. Suddenly a swell lifted us almost off our feet, and we clutched at each other simultaneously. There was a lesser swell, and little waves began to run, and a sigh went up from the sea. The tide was turning—perhaps a storm was on the way—and we were miles, dreadful miles from dry land.

Boy and girl turned without a word, four determined bare legs ploughing through the water, four scared eyes straining toward the land. Through an eternity of toil and far they kept dumbly on, death at their heels, pride still in their hearts. At last they reach high-water mark—six hours before full tide.

Each has seen the other afraid, and each rejoices in the knowledge. But only the boy is sure of his tongue.

"You was scared, warn't you?" he taunts.

The girl understand so much, and is able to reply:—

"You can schwimmen, I not."

"Betcher life I can schwimmen," the other mocks.

And the girl walks off, angry and hurt.

"An' I can walk on my hands," the tormentor calls after her. "Say, you greenhorn, why don'tcher look?"

The girl keeps straight on, vowing that she would never walk with that rude boy again, neither by land nor sea, not even though the waters should part at his bidding.

I am forgetting the more serious business which had brought us to Crescent Beach. While we children disported ourselves like mermaids and mermen in the surf, our respective fathers dispensed cold lemonade, hot peanuts, and pink popcorn, and piled up our respective fortunes, nickel by nickel, penny by penny. I was very proud of my connection with the public life of the beach. I admired greatly our shining soda fountain, the rows of sparking glasses, the pyramids of oranges, the sausage chains, the next white counter, and the bright array of tin spoons. It seemed to me that none of the other refreshment stands on the beach—there were a few—were half so attractive as ours. I thought my father looked very well in a long white apron and shirt sleeves. He dished out ice cream with enthusiasm, so I supposed he was getting rich. It never occurred to me to compare his present occupation with the position for which he had been originally destined; or if I thought about it, I was just as well content, for by this time I had by heart my father's saying, "America is not Polotzk." All occupations were respectable, all men were equal, in America.

If I admired the soda fountain and the sausage chains, I almost worshipped the partner, Mr. Wilner. I was content to stand for an hour at a time watching him make potato chips. In his cook's cap and apron, with a ladle in his hand and a smile on his face, he moved about with the greatest agility, whisking his raw materials out of nowhere, dipping into his bubbling kettle with a flourish, and bringing forth the finished product with a caper. Such potato chips were not to be had anywhere else on Crescent Beach. Thin as tissue paper, crisp as dry snow, and salt as the sea—such thirst-producing, lemonade-selling, nickel-bringing potato chips only Mr. Wilner could make. On holidays, when dozens of family parties came out by every train from town, he could hardly keep up with the demand for his potato chips. And with a waiting crowd around him our partner was at his best. He was as voluble as he was skillful, and as witty as he was voluble; at least so I guessed from the laughter that frequently drowned his voice. I could not understand his jokes, but if I could get near enough to watch his lips and his smile and his merry eyes, I was happy. That any one could talk so fast, and in English, was marvel enough, but that this prodigy should belong to *our* establishment was a fact to thrill me. I had never seen anything like Mr. Wilner, except a wedding jester; but then he spoke common Yiddish. So proud was I of the talent and good taste displayed at our stand that if my father beckoned to me in the crowd and sent me on an errand, I hoped the people noticed that I, too, was connected with the establishment.

And all this splendor and glory and distinction came to a sudden end. There was some trouble about a license—some fee or fine—there was a storm in the night that damaged the soda fountain and other fixtures—there was talk and consultation between the houses of Antin and Wilner—and the promising partnership was dissolved. No more would the merry partner gather the crowd on the beach; no more would the twelve young Wilner gambol like mermen and mermaids in the surf. And the less numerous tribe of Antin must also say farewell to the jolly seaside life; for men in such humble business as my father's carry their families, along with their other earthly goods, wherever they go, after the manner of the gypsies. The jealous Atlantic, in conspiracy with the Sunday law, had torn it out. We must seek our luck elsewhere.

In Polotzk we had supposed that "America" was practically synonymous with "Boston." When we landed in Boston, the horizon was pushed back, and we annexed Crescent Beach. And now, espying other lands of promise, we took possession of the province of Chelsea, in the name of our necessity.

In Chelsea, as in Boston, we made our stand in the wrong end of the town. Arlington Street was inhabited by poor Jews, poor Negroes, and a sprinkling of poor Irish. The side streets leading from it were occupied by more poor Jews and Negroes. It was a proper locality for a man without capital to do business. My father rented a tenement with a store in the basement. He put in a few barrels of flour and of sugar, a few boxes of crackers, a few gallons of kerosene, an assortment of soap of "save the coupon" brands; in the cellar, a few barrels of potatoes, and a pyramid of kindling-wood; in the showcase, an alluring display of penny candy. He put out his sign, with a gilt-lettered warning of "Strictly Cash," and proceeded to give credit indiscriminately. That was the regular way to do business on Arlington Street. My father, in his three years' apprenticeship, had learned the tricks of many trades. He knew when and how to "bluff." The legend of "Strictly Cash" was a protection against notoriously irresponsible customers; while none of the "good" customers, who had a record for paying regularly on Saturday, hesitated to enter the store with empty purses.

If my father knew the tricks of the trade, my mother could be counted on to throw all her talent and tact into the business. Of course she had no English yet, but as she could perform the acts of weighing, measuring, and mental computation of fractions mechanically, she was able to give her whole attention to the dark mysteries of the language, as intercourse with her customers gave her opportunity. In this she made such rapid progress that she soon lost all sense of disadvantage, and conducted herself behind the counter very much as if she were back in her old store in Polotzk. It was far more cosey than Polotzk—at least, so it seemed to me; for behind the store was the kitchen, where, in the intervals of slack trade, she did her cooking and washing. Arlington Street customers were used to waiting while the storekeeper salted the coup or rescued a loaf from the oven.

Once more Fortune favored my family with a thin little smile, and my father, in reply to a friendly inquiry, would say, "One makes a living," with a shrug of the shoulders that added "but nothing to boast of." It was characteristic of my attitude toward bread-and-butter matters that this contented me, and I felt free to devote myself to the conquest of my new world. Looking back to those critical years, I see myself always behaving like a child let loose in a garden to play and dig and chase the butterflies. Occasionally, indeed, I was stung by the wasp of family trouble; but I knew a healing ointment—my faith in America. My father had come to America to make a living. America, which was free and fair and kind, must presently yield him what he sought. I had come to America to see a new world, and I followed my own ends with the utmost assiduity; only, as I ran out to explore, I would look back to see if my house were in order behind me—if my family still kept its head above water.

In after years, when I passed as an American among Americans, if I was suddenly made aware of the past that lay forgotten,—if a letter from Russia, or a paragraph in the newspaper, or a conversation overheard in the streetcar, suddenly reminded me of what I might have been,— I thought it miracle enough that I, Mashke, the granddaughter of Raphael the Russian, born to a humble destiny, should be at home in an American metropolis, be free to fashion my own life, and should dream my dreams in English phrases. But in the beginning my admiration was spent on more concrete embodiments of the splendors of America; such as fine houses, gay shops, electric engines and apparatus, public buildings, illuminations, and parades. My early letters to my Russian friends were filled with boastful descriptions of these glories of my new country. No native citizen of Chelsea took such pride and delight in its institutions as I did. It required no fife and drum corps, no Fourth of July procession, to set me tingling with patriotism. Even the common agents and instruments of municipal life, such as the letter carrier and the fire engine, I regarded with a measure of respect. I know what I thought of people who said that Chelsea was a very small, dull, unaspiring town, with no discernible excuse for a separate name or existence.

The apex of my civic pride and personal contentment was reached on the bright September morning when I entered the public school. That day I must always remember, even if I life to be so old that I cannot tell my name. To most people their first day at school is a memorable occasion. In my case the importance of the day was a hundred times magnified, on account of the years I had waited, the road I had come, and the conscious ambitions I entertained.

I am wearily aware that I am speaking in extreme figures, in superlatives. I wish I knew some other way to render the mental life of the immigrant child of reasoning age. I may have been ever so much an exception in acuteness of observation, powers of comparison, and abnormal self-consciousness; none the less were my thoughts and conduct typical of the attitude of the intelligent immigrant child toward American institutions. And what the child thinks and feels is a reflection of the hopes, desires, and purposes of the parents who brought him overseas, no matter how precocious and independent the child may be. Your immigrant inspectors will tell you what poverty the foreigner brings in his baggage, what want in his pockets. Let the overgrown boy of twelve, reverently drawing his letters in the baby class, testify to the noble dreams and high ideals that may be hidden beneath the greasy caftan of the immigrant. Speaking for the Jews, at least, I know I am safe in inviting such an investigation.

Who were my companions on my first day at school? Whose hand was in mine, as I stood, overcome with awe, by the teacher's desk, and whispered my name as my father prompted? Was it Frieda's steady, capable hand? Was it her loyal heart that throbbed, beat for beat with mine, as it had done through all our childish adventures? Frieda's heart did throb that day, but not with my emotions. My heart pulsed with joy and pride and ambition; in her heart longing fought with abnegation. For I was led to the schoolroom, with its sunshine and its singing and the teacher's cheery smile; while she was led to the workshop, with its foul air, care-lined faces, and the foreman's stern command. Our going to school was the fulfillment of my father's best promises to us, and Frieda's share in it was to fashion and fit the calico frocks in which the baby sister and I made our first appearance in a public schoolroom.

I remember to this day the gray pattern of the calico, so affectionately did I regard it as it hung upon the wall—my consecration robe awaiting the beatific day. And Frieda, I am sure, remembers it, too, so longingly did she regard it as the crisp, starchy breadths of it slid between her fingers. But whatever were her longings, she said nothing of them; she bent over the sewing-machine humming an Old-World melody. In every straight, smooth seam, perhaps, she tucked away some lingering impulse of childhood; but she matched the scrolls and flowers with the utmost care. If a sudden shock of rebellion made her straighten up for an instant, the next instant she was bending to adjust a ruffle to the best advantage. And when the momentous day arrived, and the little sister and I stood up to be arrayed, it was Frieda herself who patted and smoothed my stiff new calico; who made me turn round and round, to see that I was perfect; who stooped to pull out a disfiguring basting-thread. If there was anything in her heart besides sisterly love and pride and good-will, as we parted that morning, it was a sense of loss and a woman's acquiescence in her fate; for we had been close friends, and now our ways would lie apart. Longing she felt, but no envy. She did not grudge me what she was denied. Until that morning we had been children together, but now, at the fiat of her destiny, she became a woman, with all a woman's cares; whilst I, so little younger than she, was bidden to dance at the May festival of untroubled childhood.

I wish, for my comfort, that I could say that I had some notion of the difference in our lots, some sense of the injustice to her, of the indulgence to me. I wish I could even say that I gave serious thought to the matter. There had always been a distinction between us rather out of proportion to the difference in our years. Her good health and domestic instincts had made is natural for her to become my mother's right hand, in the years preceeding the emigration, when there were no more servants or dependents. Then there was the family tradition that Mary was the quicker, the brighter of the two, and that hers could be no common lot. Frieda was relied upon for help, and her sister for glory. And when I failed as a milliner's apprentice, while Frieda made excellent progress at the dressmaker's our fates, indeed, were sealed. It was understood, even before we reached Boston, that she would go to work and I to school. In view of the family prejudices, it was the inevitable course. No injustice was intended. My father sent us hand in hand to school, before he had ever thought of America. If, in America, he had been able to support his family unaided, it would have been the culmination of his best hopes to see all his children at school, with equal advantages at home. But when he had done his best, and was still unable to provide even bread and shelter for us all, he was compelled to make us children self-supporting as fast as it was practicable. There was no choosing possible; Frieda was the oldest, the strongest, the best prepared, and the only one who was of legal age to be put to work.

My father has nothing to answer for. He divided the world between his children in accordance with the laws of the country and the compulsion of his circumstances. I have no need of defending him. It is myself that I would like to defend, and I cannot. I remember that I accepted the arrangements made for my sister and me without much reflection, and everything that was planned for my advantage I took as a matter of course. I was no heartless monster, but a decidedly self-centered child. If my sister had seemed unhappy it would have troubled me; but I am ashamed to recall that I did not consider how little it was that contented her. I was so preoccupied with my own happiness that I did not half perceive the splendid devotion of her attitude towards me, the sweetness of her joy in my good luck. She not only stood by approvingly when I was helped to everything; she cheerfully waited on my herself. And I took everything from her hand as if it were my due.

The two of us stood a moment in the doorway of the tenement house on Arlington Street, that wonderful September morning when I first went to school. It was I that ran away, on winged feet of joy and expectation; it was she whose feet were bound in the treadmill of daily toil. And I was so blind that I did not see that the glory lay on her, and not on me.

Father himself conducted us to school. He would not have delegated that mission to the President of the United States. He had awaited the day with impatience equal to mine, and the visions he saw as he hurried us over the sun-flecked pavements transcended all my dreams. Almost his first act on landing on American soil, three years before, had been his application for naturalization. He had taken the remaining steps in the process with eager promptness, and at the earliest moment allowed by the law, he became a citizen of the United States. It is true that he had left home in search of bread for his hungry family, but he went blessing the necessity that drove him to America. The boasted freedom of the New World meant to him far more than the right to reside, travel, and work wherever he pleased; it meant the freedom to speak his thoughts, to throw off the shackles of superstition, to test his own fate, unhindered by political or religious tyranny. He was only a young man when he landed—thirty-two; and most of his life he had been held in leading-strings. He was hungry for his untasted manhood.

Three years passed in sordid struggle and disappointment. He was not prepared to make a living even in America, where the day laborer eats wheat instead of rye. Apparently the American flag could not protect him against the pursuing Nemesis of his limitations; he must expiate the sins of his fathers who slept across the seas. He had been endowed at birth with a poor constitution, a nervous, restless temperament, and an abundance of hindering prejudices. In his boyhood his body was starved, that his mind might be stuffed with useless learning. In his youth this dearly gotten learning was sold, and the price was the bread and salt which he had not been trained to earn for himself. Under the wedding canopy he was bound for life to a girl whose features were still strange to him; and he was bidden to multiply himself, that scared learning might be perpetuated in his sons, to the glory of the God of his fathers. All this while he had been led about as a creature without a will, a chattel, an instrument. In his maturity he awoke, and found himself poor in health, poor in purse, poor in useful knowledge, and hampered on all sides. At the first nod of opportunity he broke away from his prison, and strove to atone for his wasted youth by a life of useful labor; while at the same time he sought to lighten the gloom of his narrow scholarship by freely partaking of modern ideas. But his utmost endeavor still left him far from his goal.

In business, nothing prospered with him. Some fault of hand or mind or temperament led him to failure where other men found success. Wherever the blame for his disabilities be placed, he reaped the bitter fruit. "Give me bread!" he cried to America. "What will you do to earn it?" the challenge came back. And he found that he was master of no art, of no trade; that even his precious learning was of no avail, because he had only the most antiquated methods of communicating it.

So in his primary quest he had failed. There was left him the compensation of intellectual freedom. That he sought to realize in every possible way. He had very little opportunity to prosecute his education, which, in truth, had never been begun. His struggle for a bare living left him no time to take advantage of the public evening school; but he lost nothing of what was to be learned through reading, through attendance at public meetings, through exercising the rights of citizenship. Even here he was hindered by a natural inability to acquire the English language. In time, indeed, he learned to read, to follow a conversation or lecture; but he never learned to write correctly, and his pronunciation remains extremely foreign to this day.

If education, culture, the higher life were shining things to be worshipped from afar, he had still a means left whereby he could draw one step nearer to them. He could send his children to school, to learn all those things that he knew by fame to be desirable. The common school, at least, perhaps high school; for one or two, perhaps even college! His children should be students, should fill his house with books and intellectual company; and thus he would walk by proxy in the Elysian Fields of liberal learning. As for the children themselves, he knew no surer way to their advancement and happiness.

So it was with a heart full of longing and hope that my father led us to school on that first day. He took long strides in his eagerness, the rest of us running and hopping to keep up.

At last the four of us stood around the teacher's desk; and my father, in his impossible English, gave us over in her charge, with some broken word of his hopes for us that his swelling heart could no longer contain. I venture to say that Miss Nixon was struck by something uncommon in the group we made, something outside of Semitic features and the abashed manner of the alien. My little sister was as pretty as a doll, with her clear pink-and-white face, short golden curls, and eyes like blue violets when you caught them looking up. My brother might have been a girl, too, with his cherubic contours of face, rich red color, glossy black hair, and fine eyebrows. Whatever secret fears were in his heart, remembering his former teachers, who had taught us with the rod, he stood up straight and uncringing before the American teacher, his cap respectfully doffed. Next to him stood a starved-looking girl with eyes ready to pop out, and short dark curls that would not have made much of a wig for a Jewish bride.

All three children carried themselves rather better than the common run of "green" pupils that were brought to Miss Nixon. But the figure that challenged attention to the group was the tall, straight father, with his earnest face and fine forehead, nervous hands eloquent in gesture, and a voice full of feeling. This foreigner, who brought his children to school as if it were an act of consecration, who regarded the teacher of the primer class with reverence, who spoke of visions, like a man inspired, in a common schoolroom, was not like other aliens, who brought their children in dull obedience to the law; was not the native fathers, who brought their unmanageable boys, glad to be relieved of their care. I think Miss Nixon guessed what my father's best English could not convey. I think she divined that by the simple act of delivering our school certificates to her he took possession of America.

119. Upton Sinclair, *The Jungle*, 1906

Upton Sinclair put muckraking in fictional form in his immensely successful novel, **The Jungle.**

One of the first consequences of the discovery of the union was that Jurgis became desirous of learning English. He wanted to know what was going on at the meetings and to be able to take part in them; and so he began to look about him, and to try to pick up words. The children, who were at school, and learning fast, would teach him a few, and a friend loaned him a little book that had some in it, and Ona would read them to him. Then Jurgis became sorry that he could not read himself; and later on in the winter, when some one told him that there was a night school that was free, he went and enrolled. After that, every evening that he got home from the yards in time, he would go to the school; he would go even if he were in time for only half an hour. They were teaching him both to read and to speak English—and they would have taught him other things, if only he had had a little time.

Also the union made another great difference with him—it made him begin to pay attention to the country. It was the beginning of democracy with him. It was a little state, the union, a miniature republic; its affairs were every man's affairs, and every man had a real say about them. In other words, in the union Jurgis learned to talk politics. In the place where he had come from there had not been any politics—in Russia one thought of the government as an affliction like the lightning and the hail. "Duck, little brother, duck," the wise old peasants would whisper; "everything passes away." And when Jurgis had first come to America he had supposed that it was the same. He had heard people say that it was a free country—but what did that mean? He found that here, precisely as in Russia, there were rich men who owned everything; and if one could not find any work, was not the hunger he began to feel the same sort of hunger?

When Jurgis had been working about three weeks at Brown's, there had come to him one noontime a man who was employed as a night watchman, and who asked him if he would not like to take out naturalization papers and become a citizen. Jurgis did not know what that meant, but the man explained the advantages. In the first place, it would not cost him anything, and it would get him half a day off, with his pay just the same; and then when election time came he would be able to vote—and there was something in that. Jurgis was naturally glad to accept, and so the night watchman said a few words to the boss, and he was excused for the rest of the day. When, later on, he wanted a holiday to get married he could not get it; and as for a holiday with pay just the same—what power had wrought that miracle heaven only knew! However, he went with the man, who picked up several other newly landed immigrants, Poles, Lithuanians, and Slovaks, and took them all outside, where stood a great four-horse tally-ho coach, with fifteen or twenty men already in it. It was a fine chance to see the sights of the city, and the party had a merry time, with plenty of beer handed up from inside. So they drove downtown and stopped before an imposing granite building, in which they interviewed an official, who had the papers all ready, with only the names to be filled in. So each man in turn took an oath of which he did not understand a word, and then was presented with a handsome ornamented document with a big red seal and the shield of the United States upon it, and was told that he had become a citizen of the Republic and the equal of the President himself.

A month or two later Jurgis had another interview with this same man, who told him where to go to "register." And then finally, when election day came, the packing houses posted a notice that men who desired to vote might remain away until nine that morning, and the same night watchman took Jurgis and the rest of his flock into the back room of a saloon, and showed each of them where and how to mark a ballot, and then gave each two dollars, and took them to the polling place, where there was a policeman on duty especially to see that they got through all right. Jurgis felt quite proud of this good luck till he got home and met Jonas, who had taken the leader aside and whispered to him, offering to vote three times for four dollars, which offer had been accepted.

Source: Upton Sinclair. *The Jungle.* Chapter 9, 1906. Public Domain Reprint.

And now in the union Jurgis met men who explained all this mystery to him; and he learned that American differed from Russia in that its government existed under the form of a democracy. The officials who ruled it, and got all the graft, had to be elected first; and so there were two rival sets of grafters, known as political parties, and the one got the office which bought the most votes. Now and then the election was very close, and that was the time the poor man came in. In the stockyards this was only in national and state elections, for in local elections the Democratic party always carried everything. The ruler of the district was therefore the Democratic boss, a little Irishman named Mike Scully. Scully held an important party office in the state, and bossed even the mayor of the city, it was said; it was his boast that he carried the stockyards in his pocket. He was an enormously rich man—he had a hand in all the big graft in the neighborhood. It was Scully, for instance, who owned that dump which Jurgis and Ona had seen the first day of their arrival. Not only did he own the dump, but he owned the brick factory as well; and first he took out the clay and made it into bricks, and then he had the city bring garbage to fill up the hole, so that he could build houses to sell to the people. Then, too, he sold the bricks to the city, at his own price, and the city came and got them in its own wagons. And also he owned the other hole nearby, where the stagnant water was; and it was he who cut the ice and sold it; and what was more, if the men told truth, he had not had to pay any taxes for the water, and he had built the ice house out of city lumber, and had not had to pay anything for that. The newspapers had got hold of that story, and there had been a scandal, but Scully had hired somebody to confess and take all the blame, and then skip the country. It was said, too, that he had built his brick kiln in the same way, and that the workmen were on the city payroll while they did it; however, one had to press closely to get these things out of the men, for it was not their business, and Mike Scully was a good man to stand in with. A note signed by him was equal to a job any time at the packing houses; and also he employed a good many men himself, and worked them only eight hours a day, and paid them the highest wages. This give him many friends—all of whom he had gotten together into the "War-Whoop League," whose clubhouse you might see just outside of the yards. It was the biggest clubhouse, and the biggest club, in all Chicago; and they had prize fights every now and then, and cock fights and even dog fights. The policemen in the district all belonged to the league, and instead of suppressing the fights, they sold tickets for them. The man that had taken Jurgis to be naturalized was one of these "Indians," as they were called, and on election day there would be hundreds of them out, and all with big wads of money in their pockets and free drinks at every saloon in the district. That was another thing, the men said—all the saloon keepers had to be "Indians," and to put up on demand, otherwise they could not do business on Sundays, nor have any gambling at all. In the same way Scully had all the jobs in the fire department at his disposal, and all the rest of the city graft in the stockyards district; he was building a block of flats somewhere up on Ashland Avenue, and the man who was overseeing it for him was drawing pay as a city inspector of sewers. The city inspector of water pipes had been dead and buried for over a year, but somebody was still drawing his pay. The city inspector of sidewalks was bar keeper at the War-Whoop Café—and maybe he could not make it uncomfortable for any tradesman who did not stand in with Scully!

Even the packers were in awe of him, so the men said. It gave them pleasure to believe this, for Scully stood as the people's man, and boasted of it boldly when election day came. The packers had wanted a bridge at Ashland Avenue, but they had not been able to get it till they had seen Scully; and it was the same with "Bubbly Creek," which the city had threatened to make the packers cover over, till Scully had come to their aid. "Bubbly Creek," is an arm of the Chicago River, and forms the southern boundary of the yards; all the drainage of the square mile of packing houses empties into it, so that it is really a great open sewer a hundred or two feet wide. One long arm of it is blind, and the filth stays there forever and a day. The grease and chemicals that are poured into it undergo all sorts of strange transformations, which are the cause of its name; it is constantly in motion, as if huge fish were feeding in it, or great leviathans were disporting themselves in its depths. Bubbles of carbonic acid gas will rise to the surface and burst, and make rings two or three feet wide. Here and there the grease and filth have caked solid, and the creek looks like a bed of lava; chickens walk about on it, feeding, and many times an unwary stranger has started to stroll across, and vanished temporarily. The packers used to leave the creek that way, till every now and then the surface would catch on fire and burn furiously, and the fire department would have to come and put it out. Once, however, an ingenious stranger came and started to gather this filth in scows, to make lard out of; then the packers took the cue, and got out an injunction to stop him, and afterwards gathered it themselves. The banks of "Bubbly Creek" are plastered thick with hairs, and this also the packers gather and clean.

And there were things even stranger than this, according to the gossip of the men. The packers had secret mains through which they stole billions of gallons of the city's water. The newspapers had been full of this scandal—once there had even been an investigation, and an actual uncovering of the pipes; but nobody had been punished, and the thing went right on. And then there was the condemned meat industry, with its endless horrors. The people of Chicago saw the government inspectors in Packingtown, and they all took that to mean that they were protected from diseased meat; they did not understand that these hundred and sixty-three inspectors had been appointed at the request of the packers, and that they were paid by the United States government to certify that all the diseased meat was kept in the state. They had no authority beyond that; for the inspection of meat to be sold in the city and state the whole force in Packingtown consisted of three henchmen of the local political machine!* And shortly afterward one of these, a physician, made the discovery that the carcasses of steers which had been condemned as tubercular by the government inspectors, and which therefore contained ptomaines, which are deadly poisons, were left upon an open platform and carted away to be sold in the city; and so he insisted that these carcasses be treated with an injection of kerosene—and was ordered to resign the same week! So indignant were the packers that they went farther, and compelled the mayor to abolish the whole bureau of inspection; so that since then there has not been even a pretence of any interference with the graft. There was said to be two thousand dollars a week hush money from the tubercular steers alone, and as much again from the hogs which had died of cholera on the trains, and which you might see any day being loaded into box cars and hauled away to a place called Globe, in Indiana, where they made a fancy grade of lard.

Jurgis heard of these things little by little, in the gossip of those who were obliged to perpetrate them. It seemed as if every time you met a person from a new department, you heard of new swindles and new crimes. There was, for instance, a Lithuanian who was a cattle butcher for the plant where Marija had worked, which killed meat for canning only; and to hear this man describe the animals which came to his place would have been worthwhile for a Dante or a Zola. It seemed that they must have agencies all over the country, to hunt out old and crippled and diseased cattle to be canned. There were cattle which had been fed on "whiskey malt," the refuse of the breweries, and had become what the men called "steerly"—which means covered with boils. It was a nasty job killing these, for when you plunged your knife into them they would burst and splash foulsmelling stuff into your face; and when a man's sleeves were smeared with blood, and his hands steeped in it, how was he ever to wipe his face, or to clear his eyes so that he could see? It was stuff such as this that made the "embalmed beef" that had killed several times as many United States soldiers as all the bullets of the Spaniards; only the army beef, besides, was not fresh canned, it was old stuff that had been lying for years in the cellars.

Then one Sunday evening, Jurgis sat puffing his pipe by the kitchen stove, and talking with an old fellow whom Jonas had introduced, and who worked in the canningrooms at Durham's; and so Jurgis learned a few things about the great and only Durham canned goods, which had become a national institution. They were regular alchemists at Durham's; they advertised a mushroom-catsup, and the men who made it did not know what a mushroom looked like. They advertised "potted chicken"—and it was like the boarding-house soup of the comic papers, through which a chicken had walked with rubbers on. Perhaps they had a secret process for making chickens chemically—who knows? said Jurgis's friend; the things that went into the mixture were tripe, and the fat of pork, and beef suet, and hearts of beef, and finally the waste ends of veal, when they had any. They put these up in several grades, and sold them at several prices; but the contents of the cans all came out of the same hopper. And then there was "potted game" and "potted grouse," "potted ham," and "deviled ham"—devyled, as the men called it. "De-vyled" ham was made out of the waste ends of smoked beef that were too small to be sliced by the machines; and also tripe, dyed with chemicals so that it would not show white, and trimmings of hams and corned beef, and potatoes, skins and all, and finally the hard cartilaginous gullets of beef, after the tongues had been cut out. All this ingenious mixture was ground up and flavored with spices to make it taste like something. Anybody who could invent a new imitation had been sure of a fortune from old Durham, said Jurgis's informant, but it was hard to think of anything new in a place where so many sharp wits had been at work for so long; where men welcomed tuberculosis in the cattle they were feeding, because it made them fatten more quickly; and where they bought up all the old rancid butter left over in the grocery stores of a continent, and "oxidized" it by a forced-air process, to take away the odor, rechurned it with skim milk and sold it in bricks in the cities! Up to a year or two ago it had been the custom to kill horses in the yards—ostensibly for fertilizer; but after long agitation the newspapers had been able to make the public realize that the horses were being canned. Now it was against the law to kill horses in Packingtown, and the law was really complied with—for the present, at any rate. Any day, however, one might see sharp-horned and shaggy-haired creatures running with the sheep—and yet what a job you would have to get the public to believe that a good part of what it buys for lamb and mutton is really goat's flesh!

There was another interesting set of statistics that a person might have gathered in Packingtown—those of the various afflictions of the workers. When Jurgis had first inspected the packing plants with Szedvilas, he had marveled while he listened to the tale of all the things that were made out of the carcasses of animals, and of all the lesser industries that were maintained there; now he found that each one of these lesser industries was a separate little inferno, in its way as horrible as the killing-beds, the source and fountain of them all. The workers in each of them had their own peculiar diseases. And the wandering visitor might be sceptical about all the swindles, but he could not be sceptical about these, for the worker bore the evidence of them about on his own person—generally he had only to hold out his hand.

There were the men in the pickle rooms, for instance, where old Antanas had gotten his death; scarce a one of these that had not some spot of horror on his person. Let a man so much as scrape his finger pushing a truck in the pickle rooms, and he might have a sore that would put him out of the world; all the joints in his fingers might be eaten by the acid, one by one. Of the butchers and floorsmen, the beef boners and trimmers, and all those who used knives, you could scarcely find a person who had the use of his thumb; time and time again the base of it had been slashed, till it was a mere lump of flesh against which the man pressed the knife to hold it. The hands of these men would be criss-crossed with cuts, until you could no longer pretend to count them or to trace them. They would have no nails,—they had worn them off pulling hides; their knuckles were swollen so that their fingers spread out like a fan. There were men who worked in the cooking rooms, in the midst of steam and sickening odors, by artificial light; in these rooms the germs of tuberculosis might live for two years, but the supply was renewed every hour. There were the beef luggers, who carried two-hundred-pound quarters into the refrigerator cars, a fearful kind of work, that began at four o'clock in the morning, and that wore out the most powerful men in a few years. There were those who worked in the chilling rooms, and whose special disease was rheumatism; the time limit that a man could work in the chilling rooms was said to be five years. There were the wool pluckers, whose hands went to pieces even sooner than the hands of the pickle men; for the pelts of the sheep had to be painted with acid to loosen the wool, and then the pluckers had to pull out this wool with their bare hands, till the acid had eaten their fingers off. There were those who made the tins for the canned meat, and their hands, too, were a maze of cuts, and each cut represented a chance for blood poisoning. Some worked at the stamping machines, and it was very seldom that one could work long there at the pace that was set, and not give out and forget himself, and have a part of his hand chopped off. There were the "hoisters," as they were called, whose task it was to press the lever which lifted the dead cattle off the floor. They ran along upon a rafter, peering down through the damp and the steam, and as old Durham's architects had not built the killing room for the convenience of the hoisters, at every few feet they would have to stoop under a beam, say four feet above the one they ran on, which got them into the habit of stooping, so that in a few years they would be walking like chimpanzees. Worst of any, however, were the fertilizer men, and those who served in the cooking rooms. These people could not be shown to the visitor—for the odor of a fertilizer man would scare any ordinary visitor at a hundred yards, and as for the other men, who worked in tank rooms full of steam, and in some of which there were open vats near the level of the floor, their peculiar trouble was that they fell into the vats; and when they were fished out, there was never enough of them left to be worth exhibiting—sometimes they would be overlooked for days, till all but the bones of them had gone out to the world as Durham's Pure Leaf Lard!

Notes

*"Rules and Regulations for the Inspection of Live Stock and their Products." United States Department of Agriculture, Bureau of Animal Industries, Order No. 125:—

SECTION 1. Proprietors of slaughterhouse, canning, salting, packing, or rendering establishments engaged in the slaughtering of cattle, sheep, or swine, or the packing of any of their products, *the carcasses or products of which are to become subjects of interstate or foreign com-*

merce, shall make application to the Secretary of Agriculture for inspection of said animals and their products...

SECTION 15. Such rejected or condemned animals shall at once be removed by the owners from the pens containing animals which have been inspected and found to be free from disease and fit for human food, and *shall be disposed of in accordance with the laws, ordinances, and regulations of the state and municipality in which said rejected or condemned animals are located*. . . .

SECTION 25. A microscopic examination for trichinae shall be made of all swine products exported to countries requiring such examination. *No microscopic examination will be made of hogs slaughtered for interstate trade, but this examination shall be confined to those intended for the export trade.*

Chapter XXI

Progressivism at High Tide, 1909–1914

120. Gifford Pinchot, *The Fight for Conservation*, 1910

In the title of his autobiography, Breaking New Ground *(1947), Gifford Pinchot (1865–1946) gave his own succinct evaluation of his importance to American conservation. Despite this self-inflation and easy dismissal of his predecessors' achievements, Pinchot was in fact the popular symbol of resource conservation for perhaps a decade or more.*

The principles which the word conservation has come to embody are not many, and they are exceedingly simple. I have had occasion to say a good many times that no other great movement has ever achieved such progress in so short a time, or made itself felt in so many directions with such vigor and effectiveness, as the movement for the conservation of natural resources.

Forestry made good its position in the United States before the conservation movement was born. As a forester I am glad to believe that conservation began with forestry, and that the principles which govern the Forest Service in particular and forestry in general are also the ideas that control conservation.

The first idea of real foresight in connection with natural resources arose in connection with the forest. From it sprang the movement which gathered impetus until it culminated in the great convention of governors at Washington in May, 1908. Then came the second official meeting of the National Conservation movement, December 1908, in convention, come together to express their judgment on what ought to be done, and to contribute, as only such meetings can, to the formation of effective public opinion.

The movement so begun and so prosecuted has gathered immense swing and impetus. In 1907 few knew what conservation meant. Now it has become a household word. While at first conservation was supposed to apply only to forests, we see now that its sweep extends even beyond the natural resources.

The principles which govern the conservation movement, like all great and effective things, are simple and easily understood. Yet it is often hard to make the simple, easy, and direct facts about a movement of this kind known to the people generally.

The first great fact about conservation is that it stands for development. There has been a fundamental misconception that conservation means nothing but the husbanding of resources for future generations. There could be no more serious mistake. Conservation does mean provision for the future, but it means also and first of all the recognition of the right of the present generation to the fullest necessary use of all the resources with which this country is so abundantly blessed. Conservation demands the welfare of this generation first, and afterward the welfare of the generations to follow.

The first principle of conservation is development, the use of the natural resources now existing on this continent for the benefit of the people who live here now. There may be just as much waste in neglecting the development and use of certain natural resources as there is in their destruction. We have a limited supply of coal, and only a limited supply. Whether it is to last for a hundred or a hundred and fifty or a thousand years, the coal is limited in amount, unless through geological changes

---

Source: Gifford Pinchot. *The Fight for Conservation,* 1910. pp. 40–52, 71–78, 109–119. Public Domain Reprint.

449

which we shall not live to see, there will never be any more of it than there is now. But coal is in a sense the vital essence of our civilization. If it can be preserved, if the life of the mines can be extended, if by preventing waste there can be more coal left in this country after we of this generation have made every needed use of this source of power, then we shall have deserved well of our descendants.

Conservation stands emphatically for the development and use of water-power now, without delay. It stands for the immediate construction of navigable waterways under a broad and comprehensive plan as assistants to the railroads. More coal and more iron are required to move a ton of freight by rail than by water, three to one. In every case and in every direction the conservation movement has development for its first principle, and at the very beginning of its work. The development of our natural resources and the fullest use of them for the present generation is the first duty of this generation. So much for development.

In the second place conservation stands for the prevention of waste. There has come gradually in this country an understanding that waste is not a good thing and that the attack on waste is an industrial necessity. I recall very well indeed how, in the early days of forest fires, they were considered simply and solely as acts of God, against which any opposition was hopeless and any attempt to control them not merely hopeless but childish. It was assumed that they came in the natural order of things, as inevitably as the seasons or the rising and setting of the sun. Today we understand that forest fires are wholly within the control of men. So we are coming in like manner to understand that the prevention of waste in all other directions is a simple matter of good business. The first duty of the human race is to control the earth it lives upon.

We are in a position more and more completely to say how far the waste and destruction of natural resources are to be allowed to go on and where they are to stop. It is curious that the effort to stop waste, like the effort to stop forest fires, has often been considered as a matter controlled wholly by economic law. I think there could be no greater mistake. Forest fires were allowed to burn long after the people had means to stop them. The idea that men were helpless in the face of them held long after the time had passed when the means of control were fully within our reach. It was the old story that "as a man thinketh, so is he," we came to see that we could stop forest fires, and we found that the means had long been at hand. When at length we came to see that the control of logging in certain directions was profitable, we found it had long been possible. In all these matters of waste of natural resources, the education of the people to understand that they can stop the leakage comes before the actual stopping and after the means of stopping it have long been ready at our hands.

In addition to the principles of development and preservation of our resources there is a third principle. It is this: The natural resources must be developed and preserved for the benefit of the many, and not merely for the profit of a few. We are coming to understand in this country that public action for public benefit has a very much wider field to cover and a much larger part to play than was the case when there were resources enough for every one, and before certain constitutional provisions had given so tremendously strong a position to vested rights and property in general.

A few years ago President Hadley, of Yale, wrote an article which has not attracted the attention it should. The point of it was that by reason of the XIVth amendment to the Constitution, property rights in the United States occupy a stronger position than in any other country in the civilized world. It becomes then a matter of multiplied importance, since property rights once granted are so strongly entrenched, to see that they shall be so granted that the people shall get their fair share of the benefit which comes from the development of the resources which belong to us all. The time to do that is now. By so doing we shall avoid the difficulties and conflicts which will surely arise if we allow vested rights to accrue outside the possibility of governmental and popular control.

The conservation idea covers a wider range than the field of natural resources alone. Conservation means the greatest good to the greatest number for the longest time. One of its great contributions is just this, that it had added to the worn and well-known phrase, "the greatest good to the greatest number," the additional words "for the longest time," thus recognizing that this nation of ours must be made to endure as the best possible home for all its people.

Conservation advocates the use of foresight, prudence, thrift, and intelligence in dealing with public matters, for the same reasons, and in the same way that we each use foresight, prudence, thrift, and intelligence in dealing with our own private affairs. It proclaims the right and duty of the people to act for the benefit of the people. Conservation demands the application of common-sense to the common problems for the common good.

The principles of conservation thus described—development, preservation, the common good—have a general application which is growing rapidly wider. The development of resources and the prevention of waste and loss, the protection the public interests, by foresight, prudence, and the ordinary business and home-making virtues, all these apply to other things as well as to the natural resources. There is, in fact, no interest of the people to which the principles of conservation do not apply.

The conservation point of view is valuable in the education of our people as well as in forestry; it applies to the body politic as well as to the earth and its minerals. A municipal franchise is as properly within its sphere as a franchise for water-power. The same point of view governs in both. It applies as much to the subject of good roads as to waterways, and the training of our people in citizenship is as germane to it as the productiveness of the earth. The application of common-sense to any problem for the nation's good will lead directly to national efficiency wherever applied. In other words, and that is the burden of the message, we are coming to see the logical and inevitable outcome that these principles, which arose in forestry and have their bloom in the conservation of natural resources, will have their fruit in the increase and promotion of national efficiency along other lines of national life.

The outgrowth of conservation, the inevitable result, is national efficiency. In the great commercial struggle between nations which is eventually to determine the welfare of all, national efficiency will be the deciding factor. So from every point of view conservation is a good thing for the American people.

The National Forest Service, one of the chief agencies of the conservation movement, is trying to be useful to the people of this nation. The service recognizes, and recognizes it more and more strongly all the time, that whatever it has done or is doing has just one object, and that object is the welfare of the plain American citizen. Unless the Forest Service has served the people, and is able to contribute to their welfare it has failed in its work and should be abolished. But just so far as by cooperation, by intelligence, by attention to the work laid upon it, it contributes to the welfare of our citizens, it is a good thing and should be allowed to go on with its work.

The Natural Forests are in the west. Headquarters of the service have been established throughout the western country, because its work cannot be done effectively and properly without the closest contact and the most hearty cooperation with the western people. It is the duty of the Forest Service to see to it that the timber, water-powers, mines, and every other resource of the forests is used for the benefit of the people who live in the neighborhood or who may have a share in the welfare of each locality. It is equally its duty to cooperate with all our people in every section of our land to conserve a fundamental resource, without which this nation cannot prosper.

The business of the people of the United States, performed by the government of the United States, is a vast and a most important one; it is the housekeeping of the American nation. As a business proposition it does not attract anything like the attention that it ought. Unfortunately we have come into the habit of considering the government of the United States as a political organization rather than as a business organization.

Now this question, which the governors of the states and the representatives of great interests were called to Washington to consider in 1908, is fundamentally a business question, and it is along business lines that it must be considered and solved, if the problem is to be solved at all. Manufacturers are dealing with the necessity for producing a definite output as a result of definite expenditure and definite effort. The government of the United States is doing exactly the same thing. The manufacturer's product can be measured in dollars and cents. The product of the government of the United States can be measured partly in dollars and cents, but far more importantly in the welfare and contentment and happiness of the people over which it is called upon to preside.

The keynote of that conservation conference in Washington was forethought and foresight. The keynote of success in any line of life, or one of the great keynotes, must be forethought and foresight. If we, as a nation, are to continue the wonderful growth we have had, it is forethought and foresight which must give us the capacity to go on as we have been going. I dwell on this because it seems to me to be one of the most curious of all things in the history of the United States today that we should have grasped this principle so tremendously and so vigorously in our daily lives, in the conduct of our own business, and yet have failed so completely to make the obvious application in the things which concern the nation.

It is curiously true that great aggregations of individuals and organized bodies are apt to be less farsighted, less moral, less intelligent along certain lines than the individual citizen; or at least that their standards are lower; a principle which is illustrated by the fact that we have got over settling disputes between individuals by the strong hand, but not yet between nations.

So we have allowed ourselves as a nation, in the flush of the tremendous progress that we have made, to fail to look at the end from the beginning and to put ourselves in a position where the normal operation of natural laws threatens to bring us to a halt in a way which will make every man, woman, and child in the nation feel the pinch when it comes.

No man may rightly fail to take a great pride in what has been accomplished by means of the destruction of our natural resources so far as it has gone. It is a paradoxical statement, perhaps, but nevertheless true, because out of this attack on what nature has given we have won a kind of prosperity and a kind of civilization and a kind of man that are new in the world. For example, nothing like the rapidity of the destruction of American forests has ever been known in forest history, and nothing like the efficiency and vigor and inventiveness of the American lumberman has ever been developed by any attack on any forests elsewhere. Probably the most effective tool that the human mind and hand have ever made is the American axe. So the American business man has grasped his opportunities and used them and developed them and invented about them, thought them into lines of success, and thus has developed into a new business man, with a vigor and effectiveness and a cutting-edge that has never been equalled anywhere else. We have gained out of the vast destruction of our natural resources a degree of vigor and power and efficiency of which every man of us ought to be proud.

Now that is done. We have accomplished these big things. What is the next step? Shall we go on in the same lines to the certain destruction of the prosperity which we have created, or shall we take the obvious lesson of all human history, turn our backs on the uncivilized point of view, and adopt toward our natural resources the average prudence and average foresight and average care that we long ago adopted as a rule of our daily life?

The conservation movement is calling the attention of the American people to the fact that they are trustees. The fact seems to me so plain as to require only a statement of it, to carry conviction. Can we reasonably fail to recognize the obligation which rests upon us in this matter? And, if we do fail to recognize it, can we reasonably expect even a fairly good reputation at the hands of our descendants?

Business prudence and business common-sense indicate as strongly as anything can the absolute necessity of a change in point of view on the part of the people of the United States regarding their natural resources. The way we have been handling them is not good business. Purely on the side of dollars and cents, it is not good business to kill the goose that lays the golden egg, to burn up half our forests, to waste our coal, and to remove from under the feet of those who are coming after us the opportunity for equal happiness with ourselves. The thing we ought to leave to them is not merely an opportunity for equal happiness and equal prosperity, but for a vastly increased fund of both.

Conservation is not merely a question of business, but a question of a vastly higher duty. In dealing with our natural resources we have come to a place at last where every consideration of patriotism, every consideration of love of country, of gratitude for things that the land and the institutions of this nation have given us, call upon us for a return. If we owe anything to the United States, if this country has been good to us, if it has given us our prosperity, our education, and our chance of happiness, then there is a duty resting upon us. That duty is to see, so far as in us lies, that those who are coming after us shall have the same opportunity for happiness we have had ourselves. Apart from any business consideration, apart from the question of immediate dollar, this problem of the future wealth and happiness and prosperity of the people of the United States has a right to our attention. It rises far above all matters of temporary individual business advantage, and becomes a great question of national preservation. We all have the unquestionable right to a reasonable use of natural resources during our lifetime, we all may use, and should use, the good things that were put here for our use, for in the last analysis this question of conservation is the question of national preservation and national efficiency.

The American people have evidently made up their minds that our natural resources must be conserved. That is good. But it settles only half the question. For whose benefit shall they be conserved—for the benefit of the many, or for the use of profit of the few? The great conflict now being fought will decide. There is no other question before us that begins to be so important, or that will be so difficult to straddle, as the great question between special interest and equal opportunity, between the privileges of the few and the rights of the many, between government by men for human welfare and government by money for profit, between the men who stand for the Roosevelt policies and the men who stand against them. This is the heart of the conservation problem today.

The conservation issue is a moral issue. When a few men get possession of one of the necessaries of life, either through ownership of a natural resource or through unfair business methods, and use that control to extort undue profits, as in the recent cases of the sugar trust and the beef-packers, they injure the average man without good reason, and they are guilty of a moral wrong. It does not matter whether the undue profit comes through stifling competition by rebates or other crooked devices, through corruption of public officials, or through seizing and monopolizing resources which belong to the people. The result is always the same—a toll levied on the cost of living through special privilege.

The income of the average family in the United States is less than $600 a year. To increase the cost of living to such a family beyond the reasonable profits of legitimate business is wrong. It is not merely a question of a few cents more a day for the necessaries of life, or of a few cents less a day for wages. Far more is at stake—the health or sickness of little babies, the education or ignorance of children, virtue or vice in young daughters, honesty or criminality in young sons, the working power of bread-winners, the integrity of families, the provision for old age—in a word, the welfare and happiness or the misery and degradation of the plain people are involved in the costs of living.

To the special interest an unjust rise in the cost of living means simply higher profit, but to those who pay it, that profit is measured in schooling, warm clothing, a reserve to meet emergencies, a fair chance to make the fight for comfort, decency, and right living.

I believe in our form of government and I believe in the golden rule. But we must face the truth that monopoly of the sources of production makes it impossible for vast numbers of men and women to earn a fair living. Right here the conservation question touches the daily life of the great body of our people, who pay the cost of special privilege. And the price is heavy. That price may be the chance to save the boys from the saloons and the corner gang, and the girls from worse, and to make good citizens of them instead of bad, for an appalling proportion of the tragedies of life spring directly from the lack of a little money. Thousands of daughters of the poor fall into the hands of the white-slave traders because their poverty leaves them without protection. Thousands of families, as the Pittsburgh survey has shown us, lead lives of brutalizing overwork in return for the barest living. Is it fair that these thousands of families should have less than they need in order that a few families should have swollen fortunes at their expense? Let him who dares deny that there is wickedness in grinding the faces of the poor, or assert that these are not moral questions which strike the very homes of our people. If these are not moral questions, there are no moral questions.

The people of this country have lost vastly more than they can ever regain by gifts of public property, forever and without charge, to men who gave nothing in return. It is true that we have made superb material progress under this system, but it is not well for us to rejoice too freely in the slices the special interests have given us from the great loaf of the property of all the people.

The people of the United States have been the complacent victims of a system of grab, often perpetrated by men who would have been surprised beyond measure to be accused of wrong-doing, and many of whom in their private lives were model citizens. But they have suffered from a curious moral perversion by which it becomes praiseworthy to do for a corporation things which they would refuse with the loftiest scorn to do for themselves. Fortunately for us all that delusion is passing rapidly away.

President Hadley well said that "the fundamental division of powers in the Constitution of the United States is between voters on the one hand and property-owners on the other." When property gets possession of the voting power also, little is left for the people. That is why the unholy alliance between business and politics is the most dangerous fact in our political life. I believe the American people are tired of that alliance. They are weary of politics for revenue only. It is time to take business out of politics, and keep it out—time for the political activity of this nation to be aimed squarely at the welfare of all of us, and squarely away from the excessive profits of a few of us.

A man is not bad because he is rich, nor good because he is poor. There is no monopoly of virtue. I hold no brief for the poor against the rich nor for the wage-earner against the capitalist. Exceptional capacity in business, as in any other line of life, should meet with exceptional reward. Rich men have served this country greatly. Washington was a rich man. But it is very clear that excessive profits from the control of natural resources, monopolized by a few, are not worth to this nation the tremendous price they cost us.

We have allowed the great corporations to occupy with their own men the strategic points in business, in social, and in political life. It is our fault more than theirs. We have allowed it when we could have stopped it. Too often we have seemed to forget that a man in public life can no more serve both the special interests and the people than he can serve God and mammon. There is no reason why the American people should not take into their hands again the full political power which is theirs by right, and which they exercised before the special interests began to nullify the will of the majority. There are many men who believe, and who will always believe, in the divine right of money to rule. With such men argument, compromise, or conciliation is useless or worse. The only thing to do with them is to fight them and beat them. It has been done, and it can be done again.

It is the honorable distinction of the Forest Service that it has been more constantly, more violently and more bitterly attacked by the representatives of the special interests in recent years than any other government bureau. These attacks have increased in violence and bitterness just in proportion as the service has offered effective opposition to predatory wealth. The more successful the Forest Service has been in preventing land-grabbing and the absorption of water power by the special interests, the more ingenious, the more devious, and the more dangerous these attacks have become. A favorite one is to assert that the Forest Service, in its zeal for the public welfare, has played ducks and drakes with the acts of Congress. The fact is, on the contrary, that the Service has had warrant of law for everything it has done. Not once since it was created has any charge of illegality, despite the most searching investigation and the bitterest attack, ever led to reversal of reproof by either house of Congress or by any congressional committee. Not once has the Forest Service been defeated or reversed as to any vital legal principle underlying its work in any court of administrative tribunal of last resort. It is the first duty of a public officer to obey the law. But it is his second duty, and a close second, to do everything the law will let him do for the public good, and not merely what the law directs or compels him to do. Unless the public service is alive enough to serve the people with enthusiasm, there is very little to be said for it.

Another, and unusually plausible, form of attack, is to demand that all land not now bearing trees shall be thrown out of the National Forests. For centuries forest fires have burned through the western mountains, and much land thus deforested is scattered throughout the National Forests awaiting reforestation. This land is not valuable for agriculture, and will contribute more to the general welfare under forest than in any other way. To exclude it from the National Forests would be no more reasonable than it would be in a city to remove from taxation and municipal control every building lot not now covered by a house. It would be no more reasonable than to condemn and take away from our farmers every acre of land that did not bear a crop last year, or to confiscate a man's winter overcoat because he was not wearing it in July. A generation in the life of a nation is no longer than a season in the life of a man. With a fair chance we can and will reclothe these denuded mountains with forests, and we ask for that chance.

Still another attack, nearly successful two years ago, was an attempt to prevent the Forest Service from telling the people, through the press, what it is accomplishing for them, and how much this nation needs the forest. If the Forest Service cannot tell what it is doing the time will come when there will be nothing to tell. It is just as necessary for the people to know what is being done to help them as to know what is being done to hurt them. Publicity is the essential and indispensable condition of clean and effective public service.

Since the Forest Service called public attention to the rapid absorption of the water-power sites and the threatening growth of a great water-power monopoly, the attacks upon it have increased with marked rapidity. I anticipate that they will continue to do so. Still greater opposition is promised in the near future. There is but one protection—an awakened and determined public opinion. That is why I tell the facts.

121. John Muir, *The Yosemite*, 1912

The first national park in America was Yellowstone, established by Congress in 1872. Eighteen years later, due in great measure to John Muir's advocacy, Yosemite Valley was given the same security. Then in 1908 Secretary of the Interior James Garfield approved a long-standing application from the city of San Francisco to build a water reservoir right in the middle of Yosemite Park. The approval ignited a fire that for five years burned straight through the ranks of environmentalists. For Pinchot and the regular conservative technocrats the decision was eminently sound; the benefits of clean water, electric power, and fire protection for the city easily outweighed the loss of what Pinchot called the "swampy floor" of the valley. But by this time another band had formed, bent on preserving the wilderness from the resource experts. Muir had organized the Sierra Club in 1892 to keep Yosemite chaste and unimpaired. Now around this nucleus the preservationists across the nation coalesced to delay the project as long as they could. Although Woodrow Wilson finally decided against them, Muir and his activists won a larger victory when the National Park Service was created in 1916, providing new official sanction for the picturesque as well as the productive in nature.

Source: John Muir. *The Yosemite*, 1912, pp. 249–262. Public Domain Reprint.

Yosemite is so wonderful that we are apt to regard it as an exceptional creation, the only valley of its kind in the world; but nature is not so poor as to have only one of anything. Several other Yosemites have been discovered in the Sierra that occupy the same relative positions on the Range and were formed by the same sources in the same kind of granite. One of these, the Hetch Hetchy Valley, is in the Yosemite National Park about twenty miles from Yosemite and is easily accessible to all sorts of travelers by a road and trail that leaves the Big Oak Flat road at Bronson Meadows a few miles below Crane Flat, and to mountaineers by way of Yosemite Creek basin and the head of the middle fork of the Tuolumne.

It is said to have been discovered by Joseph Screech, a hunter, in 1850, a year before the discovery of the great Yosemite. After my first visit to it in the autumn of 1871, I have always called it the "Toulumne Yosemite," for it is a wonderfully exact counterpart of the Merced Yosemite, not only in its sublime rocks and waterfalls but in the gardens, groves and meadows of its flowery parklike floor. The floor of Yosemite is about 4000 feet above the sea, the Hetch Hetchy floor about 3700 feet. And as the Merced River flows through Yosemite, so does the Tuolumne through Hetch Hetchy. The walls of both are of gray granite, rise abruptly from the floor, are sculptured in the same style and in both every rock is a glacier monument.

Standing boldly out from the south wall is a strikingly picturesque rock called by the Indians, Kolana, the outermost of a group 2300 feet high, corresponding with the Cathedral Rocks of Yosemite both in relative position and form. On the opposite side of the valley, facing Kolana, there is a counterpart of the El Capitan that rises sheer and plain to a height of 1800 feet, and over its massive brow flows a stream which makes the most graceful fall I have ever seen. From the edge of the cliff to the top of an earthquake talus it is perfectly free in the air for a thousand feet before it is broken into cascades among talus boulders. It is in all its glory in June, when the snow is melting fast, but fades and vanishes toward the end of summer. The only fall I know with which it may fairly be compared is the Yosemite Bridal Veil; but it excels even that favorite fall both in height and airy-fairy beauty and behavior. Lowlanders are apt to suppose that mountain streams in their wild career over cliffs lose control of themselves and tumble in a noisy chaos of mist and spray. On the contrary, on no part of their travels are they more harmonious and self-controlled. Imagine yourself in Hetch Hetchy on a sunny day in June, standing waist-deep in grass and flowers [as I have often stood], while the great pines sway dreamily with scarcely perceptible motion. Looking northward across the valley you see a plain, gray granite cliff rising abruptly out of the gardens and groves to a height of 1800 feet, and in front of it Tueeulala's silvery scarf burning with irised sun-fire. In the first white outburst at the head there is abundance of visible energy, but it is speedily hushed and concealed in divine repose, and its tranquil progress to the base of the cliff is like that of a downy feather in a still room. Now observe the fineness and marvelous distinctness of the various sun-illumined fabrics into which the water is woven; they sift and float from form to form down the face of the grand gray rock in so leisurely and unconfused a manner that you can examine their texture, and patterns and tones of color as you would a piece of embroidery held in the hand. Toward the top of the fall you see groups of booming, cometlike masses, their solid, white heads separate, their tails like combed silk interlacing among delicate gray and purple shadows, ever forming and dissolving, worn out by friction in their rush through the air. Most of these vanish a few hundred feet below the summit, changing to varied forms of cloudlike drapery. Near the bottom the width of the fall has increased from about twenty-five feet to a hundred feet. Here it is composed of yet finer tissues, and is still without a trace of disorder—air, water, and sunlight woven into stuff that spirits might wear.

So fine a fall might well seem sufficient to glorify any valley, but here, as in Yosemite, nature seems in nowise moderate, for a short distance to the eastward of Tueeulala booms and thunders the great Hetch Hetchy Fall, Wapama, so near that you have both of them in full view from the same standpoint. It is the counterpart of the Yosemite Fall, but has a much greater volume of water, is about 1700 feet in height, and appears to be nearly vertical, though considerably inclined, and is dashed into huge outbounding bosses of foam on projecting shelves and knobs. No two falls could be more unlike—Tueeulala out in the open sunshine descending like thistledown; Wapama in a jagged, shadowy gorge roaring and thundering, pounding its way like an earthquake avalanche.

Besides this glorious pair there is a broad, massive fall on the main river a short distance above the head of the valley. Its position is something like that of the Vernal in Yosemite, and its roar as it plunges into a surging trout-pool may be heard a long way, though it is only about twenty feet high. On Rancheria Creek, a large stream, corresponding in position with the Yosemite Tenaya Creek, there is a chain of cascades joined here and there with swift flashing plumes like the one between the Vernal and Nevada Falls, making magnificent shows as they go their glacier-sculptured way, sliding, leaping, hurrahing, covered with crisp clashing spray made glorious with sifting sunshine. And besides all these a few small streams come over the walls at wide intervals, leaping from ledge to ledge with birdlike song and watering many a hidden cliff-garden and fernery, but they are too unshowy to be noticed in so grand a place.

The correspondence between the Hetch Hetchy walls in their trends, sculpture, physical structure, and general arrangement of the main rock masses and those of the Yosemite Valley has excited the wondering admiration of every observer. We have seen that the El Capitan and Cathedral rocks occupy the same relative positions in both valleys; so also do their Yosemite points and North Domes. Again, that part of the Yosemite north wall immediately to the east of the Yosemite Falls has two horizontal benches, about 500 and 1500 feet above the floor, timbered with golden-cup oak. Two benches similarly situated and timbered occur on the same relative portion of the Hetch Hetchy north wall, to the east of Wapama Fall, and on no other. The Yosemite is bounded at the head by the great Half Dome. Hetch Hetchy is bounded in the same way, though its head rock is incomparably less wonderful and sublime in form.

The floor of the valley is about three and a half miles long, and from a fourth to half a mile wide. The lower portion is mostly a level meadow about a mile long, with the trees restricted to the sides and the river banks, and partially separated from the main, upper, forested portion by a low bar of glacier-polished granite across which the river breaks in rapid.

The principal trees are the yellow and sugar pines, digger pine, incense cedar, Douglas spruce, silver fit, the California and golden-cup oaks, balsam cottonwood, Nuttall's flowering dogwood, alder, maple, laurel, tumion, etc. The most abundant and influential are the great yellow or silver pines like those of Yosemite, the tallest over two hundred feet in height, and the oaks assembled in magnificent groves with massive rugged trunks four to six feet in diameter, and broad, shady, wide-spreading heads. The shrubs forming a conspicuous flowery clumps and tangles are manzanita, azalea, spirea, brier-rose, several species of ceanothus, calycanthus, philadelphus, wild cherry, etc.; with abundance of showy and fragrant herbaceous plants growing about them or out in the open in beds by themselves—lilies, Mariposa tulips, brodiaeas, orchids, iris, spraguea, draperia, collomia, collinsia, castillja, nemophila, larkspur, columbine, goldenrods, sunflowers, mints of many species, honeysuckle, etc. Many fine ferns dwell here also, especially the beautiful and interesting rockferns—pellaea, and cheilanthes of several species—fringing and rosetting dry rock-piles and ledges, woodwardia and asplenium on damp spots with fronds six or seven feet high, the delicate maidenhair in mossy nooks by the falls, and the sturdy, broad-shouldered pteris covering nearly all the dry ground beneath the oaks and pines.

It appears, therefore, that Hetch Hetchy Valley, far from being a plain, common, rock-bound meadow, as many who have not seen it seem to suppose, is a grand landscape garden, one of nature's rarest and most precious mountain temples. As in Yosemite, the sublime rocks of its walls seem to glow with life, whether leaning back in repose or standing erect in thoughtful attitudes, giving welcome to storms and calms alike, their brows in the sky, their feet set in the groves and gay flowery meadows, while birds, bees, and butterflies help the river and waterfalls to stir all the air into music—things frail and fleeting and types of permanence meeting here and blending, just as they do in Yosemite, to draw her lovers into close and confiding communion with her.

Sad to say, this most precious and sublime feature of the Yosemite National Park, one of the greatest of all our natural resources for the uplifting joy and peace and health of the people, is in danger of being dammed and made into a reservoir to help supply San Francisco with water and light, thus flooding it from wall to wall and burying its gardens and groves one or two hundred feet deep. This grossly destructive commercial scheme has long been planned and urged (though water as pure and abundant can be got from sources outside of the people's park, in a dozen different places), because of the comparative cheapness of the dam and of the territory which it is sought to divert from the great uses to which it was dedicated in the act of 1890 establishing the Yosemite National Park.

The making of gardens and parks goes on with civilization all over the world, and they increase both in size and number as their value is recognized. Everybody needs beauty as well as bread, places to play in and pray in, where nature may heal and cheer and give strength to body and soul alike. This natural beauty-hunger is made manifest in the little windowsill gardens of the poor, though perhaps only a geranium slip in a broken cup, as well as in the carefully tended rose and lily gardens of the rich, the thousands of spacious city parks and botanical gardens, and in our magnificent national parks—the Yellowstone, Yosemite, Sequoia, etc.—nature's sublime wonderlands, the admiration and joy of the world. Nevertheless, like anything else worth while, from the very beginning, however well guarded, they have always been subject to attack by despoiling gainseekers and mischief-makers of every degree from Satan to Senators, eagerly trying to make everything immediately and selfishly commercial, with schemes disguised in smug-smiling philanthropy, industriously, sham-piously crying, "Conservation, conservation, panutilization," that man and beast may be fed and the dear nation made great. Thus long ago a few enterprising merchants utilized the Jerusalem temple as a place of business instead of a place of prayer, changing money, buying and selling cattle and sheep and doves; and earlier still, the first forest reservation, including only one tree, was likewise despoiled. Ever since the establishment of the Yosemite National Park, strife has been going on around its borders and I suppose this will go on as part of the universal battle between right and wrong, however much its boundaries may be shorn, or its wild beauty destroyed.

The most delightful and wonderful camp grounds in the park are its three great valleys—Yosemite, Hetch Hetchy, and Upper Tuolumne; and they are also the most important places with reference to their positions relative to the other great features—the Merced and Tuolumne Cañons, and the High Sierra peaks need glaciers, etc., at the head of the rivers. The main part of the Tuolumne Valley is a spacious flowery lawn four or five miles long, surrounded by magnificent snowy mountains, slightly separated from other beautiful meadows, which together make a series about twelve miles in length, the highest reaching to the feet of Mount Dana, Mount Gibbs, Mount Lyell and Mount McClure. It is about 8500 feet above the sea, and forms the grand central High Sierra camp ground from which excursions are made to the noble mountains, domes, glaciers, etc.; across the range to the Mono Lake and volcanoes and down the Tuolumne Cañon to Hetch Hetchy. Should Hetch Hetchy be submerged for a reservoir, as proposed, not only would it be utterly destroyed, but the sublime cañon way to the heart of the High Sierra would be hopelessly blocked and the great camping ground, as the watershed of a city drinking system, virtually would be closed to the public. So far as I have learned, few of all the thousands who have seen the park and seek rest and peace in it are in favor of this outrageous scheme.

One of my later visits to the valley was made in the autumn of 1907 with the late William Keith, the artist.

The leaf colors were then ripe, and the great godlike rocks in repose seemed to glow with life. The artist, under their spell, wandered day after day along the river and through the groves and gardens, studying the wonderful scenery; and, after making about forty sketches, declared with enthusiasm that although its walls were less sublime in height, picturesque beauty and charm Hetch Hetchy surpassed even Yosemite.

That any one would try to destroy such a place seems incredible; but sad experience shows that there are people good enough and bad enough for anything. The proponents of the dam scheme bring forward a lot of bad arguments to prove that the only righteous thing to do with the people's parks is to destroy them bit by bit as they are able. Their arguments are curiously like those of the devil, devised for the destruction of the first garden — so much of the very best Eden fruit going to waste; so much of the best Tuolumne water and Tuolumne scenery going to waste. Few of their statements are even partly true, and all are misleading.

Thus, Hetch Hetchy, they say, is a "low-lying meadow." On the contrary, it is a high-lying natural landscape garden. . . .

"It is a common minor feature, like thousands of others." On the contrary is a very uncommon feature, after Yosemite, the rarest and in many ways the most important in the National Park.

"Damning and submerging it 175 feet deep would enhance its beauty by forming a crystal-clear lake." Landscape gardens, places of recreation and worship, are never made beautiful by destroying and burying them.

The beautiful sham lake, forsooth, would be only an eyesore, a dismal blot on the landscape, like many others to be seen in the Sierra. For, instead of keeping it at the same level all the year, allowing nature centuries of time to make new shores, it would, of course, be full only a month or two in the spring, when the snow is melting fast; then it would be gradually drained, exposing the slimy sides of the basin and shallower parts of the bottom, with the gathered drift and waste, death and decay of the upper basins, caught here instead of being swept on to decent natural burial along the banks of the river or in the sea. Thus the Hetch Hetchy dam-lake would be only a rough imitation of a natural lake for a few of the spring months, an open sepulcher for the others.

"Hetch Hetchy water is the purest of all to be found in the Sierra, unpolluted, and forever unpollutable." On the contrary, excepting that of the Merced below Yosemite, it is less pure than that of most of the other Sierra streams, because of the sewerage of camp grounds draining into it, especially of the Big Tuolumne Meadows camp ground, occupied by hundreds of tourists and mountaineers, with their animals, for months every summer, soon to be followed by thousands from all the world.

These temple destroyers, devotees of ravaging commercialism, seem to have a perfect contempt for nature, and, instead of lifting their eyes to the God of the mountains, lift them to the Almighty Dollar.

Dam Hetch Hetchy! As well dam for water-tanks the people's cathedrals and churches, for no holier temple has ever been consecrated by the heart of man.

122. Edward A. Ross, "American and Immigrant Blood," December 1913

Edward A. Ross was one of the most influential psychologists in the United States; he invented the concept of "adolescence." As this excerpt reveals, he also subscribed to notions of heredity and racial "purity" popular in the early twentieth century.

> In these pages Professor Ross carries his study of our present immigration into the very throbbing heart of this nation. He shows how the sturdy blood of northern Europe once poured its red riches into American arteries to strengthen and to quicken, and he exhibits by contrast the vitiated and diseased and enfeebling mixtures making in recent years. The near, inevitable future is apparent. This paper constitutes one of the gravest and most important considerations ever laid before the American people.
>
> —The Editor

There is a certain anthracite town of 26,000 inhabitants in which are writ the large moral and social consequences of injecting 10,000 sixteenth-century people into a twentieth-century community. By their presence the foreigners necessarily lower the general plane of intelligence, self-restraint, refinement, orderliness, and efficiency. With them, of course, comes an increase of drink and of the crimes from drink. The great excess of men among them leads to sexual immorality and the diffusion of private diseases. A primitive midwifery is practised, and the ignorance of the poor mothers fills the cemetery with tiny graves. The women go about their homes barefoot, and their rooms and clothing reek of the odors of cooking and uncleanliness. The standards of modesty are Elizabethan. The miners bathe in the kitchen before the females and children of the household, and women soon to become mothers appear in public unconcerned. The foreigners attend church regularly, but their noisy amusements banish the quiet Sunday. The foreign men, three eighths of whom are illiterate, pride themselves on their physical strength rather than on their skill, and are willing to take jobs requiring nothing but brawn.

Barriers of speech, education, and religious faith split the people into unsympathetic, even hostile camps. The worst element in the community makes use of the ignorance and venality of the foreign-born voters to exclude the better citizens from any share in the control of local affairs. In this babel no newspaper becomes strong enough to mold and lead public opinion. On account of the smallness of the English-reading public, the English daily has so few subscribers that it cannot afford to offend any of them by exposing municipal rottenness. The chance to prey on the ignorant foreign tempts the cupidity and corrupts the ethics of local business and professional men. The Slavic thirst, multiplying saloons up to one for every twenty-six families, is communicated to Americans, and results in an increase of liquor crimes among all classes. In like manner familiarity with the immodesties of the foreigners coarsens the native-born.

With the basest Americans and the lowest foreigners united by thirst and greed, while the decent Americans and the decent foreigners understand one another too little for team-work, it is not surprising that the municipal government is poor and that the taxpayers are robbed. Only a few of the main streets are paved; the rest are muddy and poorly guttered. Outside the central portion of the city one meets with open sewage, garbage, dungheaps, and foul odors. Sidewalks are lacking or in bad repair. The police force, composed of four Lithuanians, two Poles, one German, and one Irishman, is so inefficient that "pistol-toting" after nightfall is common among all classes. At times hold-ups have been so frequent that it was not considered safe for a well-dressed person to show himself in the foreign sections after dark. In the words of a prominent local criminal lawyer:

> We have a police force that can't speak English. Within the last few years there have been six unavenged murders in this town. Why, if there were anybody I wanted to get rid of, I'd entice him here, shoot him down in the street, and then go around and say good-by to the police.

Source: Edward Alsworth Ross. "American and Immigrant Blood," pp. 225–232. *Century Magazine,* Dec. 1913. Public Domain Reprint.

Here in a nutshell are presented the social effects that naturally follow the introduction into an advanced people of great numbers of backward immigrants. One need not question the fundamental worth of the immigrants or their possibilities in order to argue that they must act as a drag on the social progress of the nation that incorporates them.

Illiteracy

Among us there are not two million foreign-born illiterates, while the number of foreign-born men of voting age unable to read and write has passed the million mark. The confessed literacy of the multitudes coming from southern and eastern Europe is 35.8 per cent, as against 2.7 per cent for the dwindling streams from the North and West. We know that the actual state is somewhat worse than these figures indicate. As the lands of ignorance discharge their surplus into our country, we must expect to meet fellow-citizens who, in the words of the Commissioner of Immigration at New York, "do not know the days of the week, the months of the year, their own ages, or the name of any country in Europe outside their own." Or, as another official puts it:

> In our daily official duties we come to know as belonging to a normal human adult type the individual who cannot count to twenty every time correctly; who can tell the sum of two and two, but not of nine and six; name the days of the week, but not the months of the year; who knows that he has arrived at New York or Boston, as the case may be, but does not know the route he followed from his home or how long it took to reach here; who says he is destined to America, but has to rely on showing a written address for further particulars; who swears he paid his own passage, but is unable to tell what it cost, and at the same time shows an order for railroad transportation to destination prepaid in this country.

While sister countries are fast nearing the goal of complete adult literacy, deteriorating immigration makes it very hard to lift the plane of popular intelligence in the United States. The foreign-born between twenty and thirty-four years of age, late-comers of course, show five times the illiteracy of native whites of the same age. But those above forty-five years of age, mostly earlier immigrants, have scarcely twice and illiteracy of native whites above forty-five. This shows how much wider is the gulf between the Americans of to-day and the new immigrants than that between the Americans of a generation ago and the old immigrants.

Thanks to extraordinary educational efforts, the illiteracy of native white voters dropped a third during the last decade; that is, from 4.9 per cent to 3.5 per cent. But the illiteracy of the foreign-born men rose to 12 per cent; so that the proportion of white men in this country unable to read and write any language declined only 9 per cent when, but for the influx of illiterates, it would have fallen 30 per cent.

In the despatches of August 16, 1912, is an account of a gathering of ten thousand afflicted people at a shrine at Carey, Ohio, reputed to possess a miraculous healing virtue. Special trains brought together multitudes of credulous, and at least one "miracle" was reported. As this country fills up with the densely ignorant, there will be more of this sort of thing. The characteristic features of the Middle Ages may be expected to appear among us to the degree that our population comes to be composed of persons at the medieval level of culture.

Yellow Journalism

In accounting for yellow journalism, no one seems to have noticed that the saffron newspapers are aimed at a sub-American mind groping its way out of a fog. The scare-heads, red and green ink, pictures, words of one syllable, gong effects, and appeal to the primitive emotions, are apt to jar upon the home-bred farmer or mechanic. "After all," he reflects, "I am not a child." Since its success in the great cities, this style of newspaper has been tried everywhere; but it appears there are soils in which the "yellows" will not thrive. When a population is sixty per cent. American stock, the editor who takes for granted some intelligence in his reader outlasts the howling dervish. But when the native stock falls below thirty per cent and the foreign element exceeds it, yellowness tends to become endemic. False simplicity, distortion, and crude emotionalism are the resources of newspapers striving to reach and interest undeveloped minds. But the arts that win the immigrant deprave the taste of native readers and lower the intelligence of the community.

Peonage

The friendless, exploitable alien by his presence tends to corrupt our laws and practices respecting labor. In 1908 the House of Representatives directed the Immigration Commission to report on the treatment and conditions of work of immigrants in certain Southern States "and other States." The last phrase was introduced merely to avoid the appearance of sectionalism, for no congressman dreamed that peonage existed anywhere save in the South. The investigation disclosed, however, the startling fact that immigrant peonage exists in every State but Oklahoma and Connecticut. In the West the commission found "many cases of involuntary servitude," but no prosecutions. It was in the lumber-camps of Maine that the commission found "the most complete system of peonage in the country."

Caste Spirit

The desire to cure certain ills has been slow to develop among us because the victims are aliens who, we imagine, don't mind it very much. On learning that the low pay of the Italian navvy forbids meat, we recall that all Italians prefer macaroni, anyhow. With downtrodden immigrants we do not sympathize as we would with downtrodden Americans. The foreign-born laborers are "wops" and don't count; the others are "white men." After a great mine disaster a Pittsburgh newspaper posted the bulletin: "Four hundred miners killed. Fifteen Americans." Of late a great split has opened between the American and Americanized working-men and the foreigners, with their new sense of being exploited and despised. The break shows itself sensationally in the bitter fight between the American Federation of Labor and the Industrial Workers of the World. The former denounces the red-flat methods of the latter, ignores I.W.W. strikes, and allows its members to become strike-breakers. When the latter precipitates a strike in some industry in which the Federationists are numerous, we shall see an unprecedented warfare between native and foreign groups of working-men. It is significant of the coming cleavage that the mother of the I.W.W., the Western Federation of Miners, at once the most American and the most radical of the great labor-unions, has disowned the daughter organization since its leaders sought to rally inflammable and irresponsible immigrants with the fierce cry, "Sabotage. No Truce."

The Position of Women

Perhaps the most sensitive index of moral advancement is the position assigned to woman. Never is there a genuine advance that does not leave her more planet and less satellite. Until recently nowhere else in the world did women enjoy the freedom and encouragement they received in America. It is folly, however, to suppose that their lot will not be affected by the presence of six millions from belated Europe and from Asia, where consideration for the weaker sex is certainly not greater than that of the English before the Puritan Reformation.

With most of our Slavic nationalities, it is said, the boy may strike his sister with impunity, but the girl who strikes her brother is likely to be chastised. Few of the latter immigrants think of giving the daughter as good a chance as the son. Among the American students in our colleges there are three young men to one young woman. For the native students of foreign fathers the ratio is four to one, and for the foreign-born eight to one. The Italians keep their daughters close, and marry them off very early.

In the 1909 strike of the New York shirt-waist makers, all the nationalities responded to the union ideal save the Italian girls. More than that, hundreds of them slipped into the strikers' jobs. Mystified by the strange, stolid resistance of the brown-eyed girls to all entreaties, the strike-leaders visited their homes. There they found that the Italian woman, instead of being a free moral agent, is absolutely subject to the will of her nearest male relative, and the man would not take the wife, sister, or daughter out of the shop unless he was well paid for it.

Eastern European peasants are brutal in the assertion of marital rights, so when the poor immigrant woman, noticing the lot of the American wife, comes to the point of rebelling against the animal family, she runs the risk of rough treatment. Some nationalities are almost Oriental in the way they seclude their women. It is significant that the Ruthenian, Polish, Portuguese, southern Italian, and Greek female employees who have lived here from five to ten years are further behind their men-folk in speaking English than the women from northern and western Europe.

That the woman's movement in America is to meet with hard sledding cannot be doubted. The conservatism of our East has been buttressed by millions of immigrants bred in the coarse peasant philosophy of sex. It may be long before women win in the East the recognition they have won in the more American parts of the country. Recently the school board of New York, on motion of Commissioner Abraham Stern, refused even to allow discussion of a woman teacher's petition for a year's leave of absence without pay in order to have a baby. This moved "The Independent," which has been a Mark Tapley on the immigration question, to remark: "The wave of recent immigration has brought with it the Oriental conception of woman's status. . . . We must not shut our eyes to the fact that in the future the Christian conception of womanhood is not to be maintained in this country without a struggle."

It might here be added that the teacher has now been dismissed.

Vice

From a half to three fifths of the immigration between 1868–88 was male, but the new immigration shows a male preponderance of about three to one. Among those from Austria there are 155 males to 100 females. Among those from Hungary the proportion is 161 to 100; from Italy, 191; from Asiatic Turkey 210; from European Turkey, 769; from the Balkan States, 1107; from Greece, 1192. A quarter of the Polish husbands in industry, a third of the married Slovak and Italian men, nearly half of the Magyars and Russians, three fifths of the Croatians, three fourths of the Greeks and Rumanians, and nine tenths of the Bulgarians, have left their wives in the old country.

Two million more immigrant men than immigrant women! Can any one ask what this leads to? In colonial times the consequences of split-family immigration were so bad that Massachusetts and Connecticut passed laws requiring spouses to return to their mates in England unless they were "come over to make way for their families." We are broader-minded, and will interfere with nothing that does not wound prosperity. The testimony of foreign consuls and leaders among foreign-born leaves no doubt that in some instances the woman cook of the immigrant boarding-house is common to the inmates.

Housing

In the South Side of Pittsburgh there are streets lined with the decent homes of German steel-workers. A glance down the paved passage leading to the rear of the house reveals absolute cleanliness, and four times out of five one glimpses a tree, a flower garden, an arbor, or a mass of vines. In Wood's Run, a few miles away, one finds the Slavic laborers of the Pressed Steel Car Company huddled in dilapidated rented dwellings so noisome and repulsive that one must visit the lower quarters of Canton to meet their like. One cause of the difference is that the Slavs are largely transients, who do nothing to house themselves because they are saving in order to return to their native village.

The fact that a growing proportion of our immigrant, having left families behind them, form no strong local attachments and have no desire to build homes here is one reason why of late the housing problem has become acute in American industrial centers.

Overgrowth of Cities

Not least among the multiplying symptoms of social ill health in this country is the undue growth of cities. A million city-dwellers create ten times the amount of "problem" presented by a million on the farms. Now, as one traverses the gamut that leads from farms to towns, from towns to cities, and from little cities to big, the proportion of American stock steadily diminishes while the foreign stock increases its representation until in the great cities it constitutes three fourths or even four fifths of the population.

It is not that the immigrants love streets and crowds. Two thirds of them are farm bred, but they dropped down in cities, and they find it easier to herd there with their fellows than to make their way into the open country. Our cities would be fewer and smaller had they fed on nothing but country-bred Americans. The later alien influx has rushed us into the thick of urban problems, and these are gravest where Americans are fewest. Congestion, misliving, segregation, corruption, and confusion are seen in motley groups like New York, Jersey City, Paterson, and Fall River rather than in native centers like Indianapolis, Columbus, Nashville, and Los Angeles.

Pauperism

Ten years ago two fifths of the paupers in our almshouses were foreign-born, but most of them had come over in the old careless days when we allowed European poorhouses to send us their inmates. Now that our authorities turn back such as appear likely to become a public charge, the obvious pauper is not entering this country. We know that virtually every Greek in America is self-supporting. The Syrians are said to be singularly independent. The Slavs and the Magyars are sturdy in spirit, and the numerous indigent. Hebrews are for the most part cared for by their own race.

Nevertheless, dispensers of charity agree that many southern Italians are landing with the most extravagant ideas of what is coming to them. They apply at once for relief with the air: "Here we are. Now, what are you going to do for us?" They even *insist* on relief as a right. At home it had been noised about that in foolish America baskets of food are actually sent in to the needy, and some are coming over expressly to obtain such largess. Probably none are so infected with spiritual hookworm as the immigrants from Naples. It will be recalled that when Garibaldi and his thousand were fighting to break the Bourbon tyranny in the South, the Neapolitans, would hurrah for them, but would not even care for the wounded.

Says the Forty-seventh Annual Report of the New York Juvenile Asylum:

> It is remarkable that recently arrived immigrants who display small adaptability in American standards are by no means slow in learning about this and other institutions where they may safely leave their children to be fed, clothed, and cared for at the public expense. This is one of the inducements which led them to leave their native land.

Charity experts are very pessimistic as to what we shall see when those who come in their youth have passed their prime and met the cumulative effects of overwork, city life, drink, and vice. Still darker are their forebodings for a second generation, reared too often by ignorant, avaricious rustics lodging in damp cellars, sleeping with their windows shut, and living on the bad, cheap food of cities. Of the Italians in Boston, Dr. Bushee writes:

> They show the beginnings of a degenerate class, such as has been fully developed among the Irish. . . . If allowed to continue in unwholesome conditions, we may be sure that the next generation will bring forth a large crop of dependents, delinquents and defectives to fill up our public institutions.

Says a charity superintendent working in a huge Polish quarter:

> It is the second generation that will give us trouble. The parents come with rugged peasant health, and may of them keep their strength even in the slum. But their children often start life weakened physically and mentally by the conditions under which they were reared. They have been raised in close, unsanitary quarters, in overlarge families, by parents who drunk up or saved too much, spent too little on the children, or worked them too soon. Their sole salvation is the open country, and they can't be pushed into the country. All of us are aghast at the weak fiber of the second generation. Every year I see the morass of helpless poverty getting bigger. The evil harvest of past mistakes is ripening, but it will take twenty years before we see the worst of it. If immigration were cut off short to-day, the burden from past neglect and exploitation would go on increasing for years.

The Wayward Child of the Immigrant

In 1908 nine tenths of the 2600 complaints of children going wrong made to the Juvenile Protective Association of Chicago related to the children of immigrants. It is said that four fifths of the youths brought before the Juvenile Court of Chicago come from the homes of the foreign-born. In Pittsburgh the proportion is at least two thirds. However startling these signs of moral breakdown in the families of the new immigrants, there is nothing mysterious about it. The lower the state from which the alien comes, the more of a grotesque he will appear in the shrewd eyes of his partly Americanized children. "Obedience to parents seems to by dying out among the Jews," says a Boston charity visitor. "The children feel it is n't necessary to obey a mother who wears a shawl or a father who wears a full beard." "Sometimes it is the young daughter who rules a Jewish family," observes a Pittsburgh settlement head, "because she alone knows what is 'American.' But see how this results in a great number of Jewish girls going astray. Since the mother continues to shave her head and wear a wig as she did in Poland, the daughter assumes that mother is equally old-fogyish when she insists that a nice girl does n't paint her face or run with boys in the evening."

Through their knowledge of our speech and ways, the children have a great advantage in their efforts to slip the parental leash. The bad boy tells his father that whipping "does n't go" in this country. Reversing the natural order, the child becomes the fount of knowledge, and the parents hang on the lips of their precocious offspring. If the policeman inquires about some escapade or the truant officer gives warning, it is the scamp himself who must interpret between parent and officer. The immigrant is braced by certain Old World loyalties, but his child may grow up loyal to nothing whatever, a rank egoist and an incorrigible who will give us vast trouble before we are done with him.

Still, the child is not always to blame. "Often the homes are so crowded and dirty," says a probation officer, "that no boy can go right. The Slavs save so greedily that their children become disgusted with the wretched home conditions and sleep out." One hears of foreign-born with several boarders sending their children out to beg or to steal coal. In one city investigation showed that only a third of the Italian children taken from school on their fourteenth birthday were needed as bread-winners. Their parents thought only of the sixty cents a week. In another only one fourteenth of the Italian school children are above the primary grades, and one eleventh of the Slavic, as against two fifths of the American school children in grammar grades or high school. Miss Addams tells of a young man from the south of Italy who was mourning the death of his little girl of twelve. In his grief he said quite simply: "She was my oldest kid. In two years she would have supported me, and now I shall have to work five or six years longer until the next one can do it." He expected to retire permanently at thirty-four.

Insanity About the Foreign-born

Not only do the foreign-born appear to be more subject to insanity than the native-born, but when insane they are more likely to become a public charge. Of the asylum population they appear to constitute about a third. In New York during the year ending September 30, 1911, 4218 patients who were immigrants or of immigrant parents were admitted to the insane hospitals of the State. This is three quarters of the melancholy intake for that year. Only one out of nine of the first admissions from New York City was of native stock. The New York State Hospital Commission declares that "the frequency of insanity in our foreign production is 2.19 times greater than those of native birth." In New York City is "is 2.48 times that of the native-born."

Excessive insanity is probably a part of the price of foreign-born pay for the opportunities of a strange and stimulating environment, with greater strains than some of them are able to bear. America calls forth powerful reactions in these people. Here they feel themselves in the grasp of giant forces they can neither withstand nor comprehend. The passions and the exertions, the hopes and the fears, the exultations and the despairs, America excites in the immigrant are likely to be intenser than anything he would have experienced in his natal village.

In view of the fact that every year New York cares for 15,000 foreign-born insane at a cost of $3,500,000 and that the State's sad harvest of demented immigrants during the single year 1911 will cost about $8,000,000 before they die or are discharged, there is some offset to be made to the profits drawn from the immigrants by the transporting companies, landlords, real-estate men, employers, contractors, brewers, and liquor-dealers of the State. Besides, there is the cost of the paupers and the law-breaks of foreign origin. All such burdens, however, since they fall upon the public at large, do not detract from or qualify that private or business man's prosperity which it is the office of the true modern statesmen to promote.

Immigration and the Separate School

In a polyglot mining town of Minnesota is a superintendent who has made the public school a bigger factor in Americanization than I have found it anywhere else. The law gives him the children until they are sixteen, and he hold them all. His school buildings are civic and social centers. Through the winter, in his high school auditorium, which seats 1200 persons, he gives a course of entertainment which is self-supporting, although his "talent" for a single evening will cost as much as $200. By means of the 400 foreigners in his night schools he has a grip on the voters which his foes have learned to dread. Under his lead the community has broken the mine-boss cellar and won real self-government. The people trust him and bring him their troubles. He has jurisdiction over everything that can affect the children of the town, and his conception is wide. Wielding both legal and moral authority, he is, as it were, a corporation president and a medieval bishop rolled into one.

This man sets no limit to the transforming power of the public school. He insists that the right sort of schooling will not only alter the expression, but will even change the shape of the skull and the bony formation of the face. In his office is a beautiful tabouret made by a "wild boy" within a year after he had been brought in kicking and screaming. He scoffs at the fear of a lack of patriotism in the foreign-born or their children. He knows just how to create the sentiment. He has flag drills and special programs, and in the Fourth of July parade and the Decoration day procession the schools have always a fine float. He declares he can build human beings to order, and will not worry about immigrant so long as the public school is given a chance at the second generation.

But is the public school to have this chance?

Multitudes of the new immigrants adhere to churches which do not believe in the public schools. "Their pupils," observed a priest to me, "are like wild children." Said a bishop: "No branches can be safely taught divorced from religion. We believe that geography, history, and even language ought to be presented from our point of view." Hence with great rapidity the children of

Roman Catholics are being drawn apart into parochial schools. In Cleveland one third of the population is supposed to be Catholic, and the 27,500 pupils in the parochial schools are nearly one third of all school children. In Chicago there are 112,000 in the parish schools to 300,000 in the public schools. In New York the proportion is about one sixth. In twenty-eight leading American cities the attendance of parish schools increased sixty per cent between 1897 and 1910, as against an increase of from forty-five to fifty per cent in the attendance of the public schools. The total number of children in the parochial schools is about 1,400,000. Separate education is a settled Catholic policy, and the bishops say they expect to enroll finally the children of all their people.

To bring this about, the public schools are denounced from the pulpit as "Godless" and "immoral," their product as mannerless and disobedient. "We think," says a Slovak leader, "that the parochial school pupils are more pious, more respectful toward parents and toward all persons in authority." The Polish, Lithuanian, or Slovak priest, less often the German or Bohemian, says bluntly: "If you send your children to the public school, they will go to hell." Sometimes the priest threatens to exclude from the confessional parents who send their children to the public school. An archbishop recently decreed that parents who without permission send their children to the public school after they have made their first communion "commit a grievous sin and cannot receive the sacraments of the church." Within the immigrant groups there is active opposition, but it appears to be futile. In a certain district in Chicago where the public-school teachers had felt they could hold their own, the foreign mothers came at last to take away their children's schoolbooks, weeping because they were forced to transfer their children to the parish school.

Now, the parish school tends to segregate the children of the foreign-born. Parents are forme for groups of the same speech, so a parish school will embrace children of only one nationality—German, Polish, Bohemian, Lithuanian, Croatian, Slovak, Magyar, Portuguese, or French Canadian, as the case may be. Often priest and teachers have been imported, and only the mother-tongue is used. "English," says a school superintendent, "comes to be taught as a purely ornamental language like French in the public high school." Hence American-born are leaving school not only unable to read and write English, but scarcely able to speak it. The foreign-speech school, while it binds the young to their parents, to their people, and to the old country, cuts them off from America. Says a Chicago Lithuanian leader: "There are 3000 of our children in the parochial schools here. The teachers are ignorant, illiterate spinsters from Lithuania who have studied here two or three years. When at fourteen the pupils quit school, they are no more advanced, than the public-school pupils of ten. This is why 50,000 Lithuanians here have only twenty children in the high school."

When, now, to the removal of the second generation from the public school there is added, as is often the case, the endeavor to keep them away from the social center, the small park field-house, the public playground, the social settlement, the secular American press and welfare work in the factories, it is plain that those optimists who imagine that assimilation of the immigrant is proceeding unhindered are living in a fool's paradise.

Social Decline

"Our descendants," a social worker remarked to me, "will look back on the nineteenth century as our Golden Age, just as we look back on Greece." Thoughtful people whose work takes them into the slime at the bottom of our foreignized cities and industrial centers find decline actually upon us. A visiting nurse who has worked for seven years in the stockyards district of Chicago reports that of late the drinking habit is taking hold of foreign women at an alarming rate. In the saloons there the dignified stein has given way to the beer pail. In the Range towns of Minnesota there are 356 saloons, of which eighty-one are run by native-born, the rest chiefly by recent immigrants. Into a Pennsylvania coal town of 1800 people, mostly foreign-born, are shipped each week a carload of beer and a barrel of whisky. Where the new foreign-born are numerous, women and children frequent the saloon as freely as the men. In the cities family desertion is growing at a great rate among foreign-born husbands. Facts are justifying the forecast made ten years ago by H.G. Wells: "If things go on as they are going, the great mass of them will remain a very low lower class—will remain largely illiterate, industrialized peasants."

Chapter XXII

Over There and Over Here: The Impact of World War I, 1914–1921

123. Margaret Sanger, *My Fight for Birth Control*, 1915

Margaret Sanger coined the term "birth control" and throughout her life worked to make contraception and information about it available to Americans. The sixth of eleven children, she studied nursing. She was working as an obstetrical nurse to support her family in 1912 when she discovered the conditions she describes here. She studied contraception in Europe and returned to the United States in 1914 to establish the first birth control clinic in the country, for which she was repeatedly jailed.

Early in the year 1912 I came to a sudden realization that my work as a nurse and my activities in social service were entirely palliative and consequently futile and useless to relieve the misery I saw all about me.

For several years I had had the good fortune to have the children's paternal grandmother living with us and sharing in their care, thereby releasing more of my time and renewed energy for the many activities and professional work of the nursing field. I had longed for this opportunity, and it now enabled me to share in the financial responsibility of the home, which, owing to the heavy expenditures caused by my illness, I felt was the only self-respecting thing to do. I eventually took special obstetrical and surgical cases assigned to me from time to time, and had glimpses into the lives of rich and poor alike.

When I look back upon that period it seems only a short time ago; yet in the brief interval conditions have changed enormously. At that time it was not the usual thing for a poor woman to go to a hospital to give birth to her baby. She preferred to stay at home. She was afraid of hospitals when any serious ailment was involved. That is not the case today. Women of all classes are more likely to have their babies in lying-in hospitals or in private sanatoriums than at home; but in those days a woman's own bedroom, no matter how inconveniently arranged, was the usual place for confinement. That was the day of home nursing, and it gave a trained nurse splendid opportunities to learn social conditions through actual contact with them.

Were it possible for me to depict the revolting conditions existing in the homes of some of the women I attended in that one year, one would find it hard to believe. There was at that time, and doubtless is still today, a sub-stratum of men and women whose lives are absolutely untouched by social agencies.

The way they live is almost beyond belief. They hate and fear any prying into their homes or into their lives. They resent being talked to. The women slink in and out of their homes on their way to market like rats from their holes. The men beat their wives sometimes black and blue, but no one interferes. The children are cuffed, kicked and chased about, but woe to the child who dares to tell tales out of the home! Crime or drink is often the source of this secret aloofness; usually there is something to hide, a skeleton in the closet somewhere. The men are sullen, unskilled workers, picking up odd jobs now and

Source: Margaret Sanger. *My Fight for Birth Control,* 1915. Public Domain Reprint.

then, unemployed usually, sauntering in and out of the house at all hours of the day and night.

The women keep apart from other women in the neighborhood. Often they are suspected of picking a pocket or "lifting" an article when occasion arises. Pregnancy is an almost chronic condition amongst them. I knew of one woman who had given birth to eight children with no professional care whatever. The last one was born in the kitchen, witnessed by a son of ten years who, under his mother's direction, cleaned the bed, wrapped the placenta and soiled articles in paper, and threw them out of the window into the court below.

They reject help of any kind and want you to "mind your own business." Birth and death they consider their own affairs. They survive as best they can, suspicious of everyone, deathly afraid of police and officials of every kind.

They are the submerged, untouched classes which no labor union, no church nor organization of a highly expensive, organized city ever reaches and rarely tries to reach. They are beyond the scope of organized charity or religion; not even the Salvation Army touches them. It was a sad consolation to hear other women in the stratum just slightly above breathe contented sighs and thank God that they had not sunk so low as that.

It is among the mothers here that the most difficult problems arise—the outcasts of society with theft, filth, perjury, cruelty, brutality, oozing from beneath.

Ignorance and neglect go on day by day; children born to breathe but a few hours and pass out of life; pregnant women toiling early and late to give food to four or five children, always hungry; boarders taken into homes where there is not sufficient room for the family; little girls eight and ten years of age sleeping in the same room with dirty, foul smelling, loathsome men; women whose weary, pregnant, shapeless bodies refused to accommodate themselves to the husbands' desires find husbands looked with lustful eyes upon other women, sometimes upon their own little daughters, six and seven years of age.

In this atmosphere abortions and birth become the main theme of conversation. On Saturday nights I have seen groups of fifty to one hundred women going into questionable offices well known in the community for cheap abortions. I asked several women what took place there, and they all gave the same reply; a quick examination, a probe inserted into the uterus and turned a few times to disturb the fertilized ovum, and then the woman was sent home. Usually the flow began the next day and often continued for four or five weeks. Sometimes an ambulance carried the victim to the hospital for a curetage; and if she returned home at all she was looked upon as a lucky woman.

This state of things became a nightmare with me. There seemed no sense to it at all, no reason for such a waste of mother life, no right to exhaust women's vitality and to throw them on the scrap-heap before the age of thirty-five.

Everywhere I looked, misery and fear stalked—men fearful of losing their jobs, women fearful that even worse conditions might come upon them. The menace of another pregnancy hung like a word over the head of every poor woman came in contact with that year. The question which met me was always the same: What can I do to keep from it? or, What can I do to get out of this? Sometimes they talked among themselves bitterly.

"It's the rich that know the tricks," they'd say, "while we have all the kids." Then, if the women were Roman Catholics, they talked about "Yankee tricks," and asked me if I knew what the Protestants did to keep their families down. When I said that I didn't believe that the rich knew much more than they did I was laughed at and suspected of holding back information for money. They would nudge each other and say something about paying me before I left the case if I would reveal the "secret."

It all sickened me. It was heartbreaking to witness the rapt, anxious, eager expression on their pale, worried faces as I told them necessary details concerning cleanliness and hygiene of their sex organs. It was appalling how little they knew of the terms I was using, yet how familiar they were with those organs and their functions and how unafraid to try anything, no matter what the results.

I heard over and over again of their desperate efforts at bringing themselves "around"—drinking various herb-teas, taking drops of turpentine on sugar, steaming over a chamber of boiling coffee or of turpentine water, rolling down stairs, and finally inserting slipper-elm sticks, or knitting needles, or shoe hooks into the uterus. I used to shudder with horror as I heard the details and, worse yet, learned of the conditions *behind the reason* for such desperate actions. Day after day these stories were poured into my ears. I knew hundreds of these women personally, and knew much of their hopeless, barren, dreary lives.

What relief I had came when I shifted my work for a few weeks to the then fashionable Riverside Drive or to the upper western section of New York City, but inevitably I was called back into the lower East or West Side as if magnetically attracted by its misery.

The contrast in conditions seems only to intensify the horrors of those poverty-stricken homes, and each time I returned it was to hear that Mrs. Cohen had been carried to a hospital but had never come back, that Mrs. Kelly had sent the children to a neighbor's and had put her head into the gas oven to end her misery. Many of the women had consulted midwives, social workers and doctors at the dispensary and asked a way to limit their families, but they were denied this help, sometimes indignantly or gruffly, sometimes jokingly; but always knowledge was denied them. Life for them had but one choice: either to abandon themselves to incessant childbearing, or to terminate their pregnancies through abortions. Is it any wonder they resigned themselves hopelessly, as the Jewish and Italian mothers, or fell into drunkenness, as the Irish and Scotch? The latter were often beaten by husbands, as well as by their sons and daughters. They were driven and cowed, and only as beasts of burden were allowed to exist. Life for them was full of fear.

Words fail to express the impressions these lives made on my sensitive nature. My own happy love life became a reproach. These other lives began to clutch at all I held dear. The intimate knowledge of these misshapen, hapless, desperate women seemed to separate me from the right of happiness.

They claimed my thoughts night and day. One by one these women, with their worried, sad, pensive and aging faces would marshal themselves before me in my dreams, sometimes appealingly, sometimes accusingly. I could not escape from the facts of their misery, either was I able to see the way out of their problems and their troubles. Like one walking in a sleep, I kept on.

Finally the thing began to shape itself, to become accumulative during the three weeks I spent in the home of a desperately sick woman living on Grand Street, a lower section of New York's East Side.

Mrs. Sacks was only twenty-eight years old; her husband, an unskilled worker, thirty-two. Three children, aged five, three and one, were none too strong nor sturdy, and it took all the earnings of the father and the ingenuity of the mother to keep them clean, provide them with air and proper food, and give them a chance to grow into decent manhood and womanhood.

Both parents were devoted to these children and to each other. The woman had become pregnant and had taken various drugs and purgatives, as advised by her neighbors. Then, in desperation, she had used some instrument lent to her by a friend. She was found prostrate on the floor amidst the crying children when her husband returned from work. Neighbors advised against the ambulance, and a friendly doctor was called. The husband would not hear of her going to a hospital, and as a little money had been saved in the bank, a nurse was called and the battle for that precious life began.

It was in the middle of July. The three-room apartment was turned into a hospital for the dying patient. Never had I worked so fast, never so concentratedly as I did to keep alive that little mother. Neighbor women came and went during the day doing the odds and ends necessary for our comfort. The children were sent to friends and relatives and the doctor and I settled ourselves to outdo the force and power of an outraged nature.

Never had I known such conditions could exist. July's sultry days and nights were melted into a torpid inferno. Day after day, night after night, I slept only in brief snatches, ever too anxious about the condition of that feeble heart bravely carrying on, to stay long from the bedside of the patient. With but one toilet for the building and that on the floor below, everything had to be carried down for disposal, while ice, food and other necessities had to be carried three flights up. It was one of those old airshaft buildings of which there were several thousand then standing in New York City.

At the end of two weeks recovery was in sight, and at the end of three weeks I was preparing to leave the fragile patient to take up the ordinary duties of her life, including those of wifehood and motherhood. Everyone was congratulating her on her recovery. All the kindness of sympathetic and understanding neighbors poured in upon her in the shape of convalescent dishes, soups, custards, and drinks. Still she appeared to be despondent and worried. She seemed to sit apart in her thoughts as if she had no part in these congratulatory messages and endearing welcomes. I thought at first that she still retained some of her unconscious memories and dwelt upon them in her silences.

But as the hour for my departure came nearer, her anxiety increased, and finally with trembling voice she said: "Another baby will finish me, I suppose."

"It's too early to talk about that," I said, and resolved that I would turn the question over to the doctor for his advice. When he came I said: "Mrs. Sacks is worried about having another baby."

"She well might be," replied the doctor, and then he stood before and said: "Any more such capers, young woman, and there will be no need to call me."

"Yes, yes—I know, Doctor," said the patient with trembling voice, "but," and she hesitated as if it took all of her courage to say it, "*what* can I do to prevent getting that way again?"

"Oh ho!" laughed the doctor good naturedly. "You want your cake while you eat it to, do you? Well, it can't be done." Then, familiarly slapping her on the back and picking up his hat and bag to depart, he said, "I'll tell you the only sure thing to do. Tell Jake to sleep on the roof."

With those words he closed the door and went down the stairs, leaving us both petrified and stunned.

Tears sprang to my eyes, and a lump came in my throat as I looked at that face before me. It was stamped with sheer horror. I thought for a moment she might have gone insane, but she conquered her feelings, whatever they may have been, and turning to me in desperation said: "He can't understand, can he?—he's a man after all—but you do, don't you?" You're a woman and you'll tell me the secret and I'll never tell it to a soul."

She clasped her hands as if in prayer, she leaned over and looked straight into my eyes and beseechingly implored me to tell her something—something *I really did not know*. It was like being on a rack and tortured for a crime one had not committed. To plead guilty would stop the agony; otherwise the rack kept turning.

I had to turn away from that imploring face. I could not answer her then. I quieted her as best I could. She saw that I was moved by the tears in my eyes. I promised that I would come back in a few days and tell her what she wanted to know. The few simple means of limiting the family like *coitus interruptus* or the condom were laughed at by the neighboring women when told these were the means used by men in the well-to-do families. That was not believed, and I knew such an answer would be swept aside as useless were I to tell her this at such a time.

A little later when she slept I left the house, and made up my mind that I'd keep away from those cases in the future. I felt helpless to do anything at all. I seemed chained hand and foot, and longed for an earthquake or a volcano to shake the world out of its lethargy into facing these monstrous atrocities.

The intelligent reasoning of the young mother—how to *prevent* getting that way again—how sensible, how just she had been—yes, I promised myself I'd go back and have a long talk with her and tell her more, and perhaps she would not laugh but would believe that those methods were all that were really known.

But time flew past, and weeks rolled into months. That wistful, appealing face haunted me day and night. I could not banish from my mind memories of that trembling voice begging so humbly for knowledge she had a right to have. I was about to retire one night three months later when the telephone rang and an agitated man's voice begged me to come at once to help his wife who was sick again. It was the hospital of Mrs. Sacks, and I intuitively knew before I left the telephone that it was almost useless to go.

I dreaded to face that woman. I was tempted to send someone else in my place. I longed for an accident on the subway, or on the street—anything to prevent my going into that home. But on I went just the same. I arrived a few minutes after the doctor, the same one who had given her such noble advice. The woman was dying. She was unconscious. She died within ten minutes after my arrival. It was the same result, the same story told a thousand times before—death from abortion. She had become pregnant, had used drugs, had then consulted a five-dollar professional abortionist, and death followed.

The doctor shook his head as he rose from listening for the heart beat. I knew she had already passed on; without a groan, a sign or recognition of our belated presence she had gone into the Great Beyond as thousands of mothers go every year. I looked at that drawn face now stilled in death. I placed her thin hands across her breast and recalled how hard they had pleaded with me on that last memorable occasion of parting. The gentle woman, the devoted mother, the loving wife had passed on leaving behind her a frantic husband, helpless in his loneliness, bewildered in his helplessness as he paced up and down the room, hands clenching his head, moaning "My God! My God! My God!"

The Revolution came—but not as it has been pictured nor as history relates that revolutions have come. It came in my own life. It began in my very being as I walked home that night after I had closed the eyes and covered with a sheet the body of that little helpless mother whose life had been sacrificed to ignorance.

After I left that desolate house I walked and walked and walked; for hours and hours I kept on, bag in hand, thinking, regretting, dreading to stop; fearful of my conscience, dreading to face my own accusing soul. At three in the morning I arrived home still clutching a heavy load the weight of which I was quite unconscious.

I entered the house quietly, as was my custom, and looked out of the window down upon the dimly lighted, sleeping city. As I stood at the window and looked out, the miseries and problems of that sleeping city arose before me in a clear vision like a panorama; crowded homes, too many children; babies dying in infancy; mothers overworked; baby nurseries; children neglected and hungry—mothers so nervously wrought they could not give the little things the comfort nor care they needed; mothers half sick most of their lives—"always ailing, never failing"; women made into drudges; children working in cellars; children aged six and seven pushed into the labor market to help earn a living; another baby on the way; still another; yet another; a baby born dead—great relief, an older child dies—sorrow; but nevertheless relief—insurance helps; a mother's death—children scattered into institutions; the father, desperate, drunken; he slinks way to become an outcast in a society which has trapped him.

Another picture of the young couple full of hope with faith in themselves. They start life fresh. They are brave and courageous. The first baby is welcome; parents and relatives come from near and far to witness this mystery. The next year the second baby arrives; all agree it's a little early, but husband receives congratulations. The third child arrives, and yet a fourth. Within five years four children are born. The mother, racked and worn, decides this can't go on, and attempts to interrupt the next pregnancy. The siren of the ambulance—death of the mother—orphan children—poverty, misery, slums, child labor, unhappiness, ignorance, destitution!

One after another these pictures unreeled themselves before me. For hours I stood, motionless and tense, expecting something to happen. I watched the lights go out, I saw the darkness gradually give way to the first shimmer of dawn, and then a colorful sky heralded the rise of the sun. I knew a new day had come for me and a new world as well.

It was like an illumination. I could now see clearly the various social strata of our life; all its mass problems seemed to be centered around uncontrolled breeding. There was only one thing to be done: call out, start the alarm, set the heather on fire! Awaken the womanhood of America to free the motherhood of the world! I released from my almost paralyzed hand the nursing bag which unconsciously I had clutched, threw it across the room, tore the uniform from my body, flung it into a corner, and renounced all palliative work forever.

I would never go back again to nurse women's ailing bodies while their miseries were as vast as the stars. I was now finished with superficial cures, with doctors and nurses and social workers who were brought face to face with this overwhelming truth of women's needs and yet turned to pass on the other side. They must be made to see these facts. I resolved that women should have knowledge of contraception. They have every right to know about their own bodies. I would strike out—I would scream from the housetops. I would tell the world what was going on in the lives of these poor women. I *would* be heard. No matter what it should cost. *I would be heard.*

I went to bed and slept.

That decision gave me the first undisturbed sleep I had had in over a year. I slept soundly and free from dreams, free from haunting faces.

I announced to my family the following day that I had finished nursing, that I would never go on another case—and I never have.

I asked doctors what one could do and was told I'd better kept off that subject or Anthony Comstock would get me. I was told that there were laws against that sort of thing. This was the reply from every medical man and woman I approached.

Then I consulted the "up and doing" progressive women who then called themselves Feminists. Most of them were shocked at the mention of abortion, while others were scarcely able to keep from laughing at the idea of my making a public campaign around the idea of too many children. "It can't be done," they said. "You are too sympathetic. You can't do a thing about it until we get the vote. Go home to your children and let things alone."

When I review the situation and see myself in the eyes of those who gave me such circumspect advice, I can see what they felt. I was considered a conservative person, bourgeoise from the radical point of view. I was not trained in the arts of the propagandist, I had no money with which to start a rousing campaign. I was not a trained writer nor speaker, never having lifted my voice in public above the throng. I had no social position. I had no influential friends. I was digging deep into an illegal subject, alone and unaided. It seemed to them that I was scheduled from Blackwell's Island or the penitentiary, and it looked as if I was determined to get there.

I spent my time reading in the vain hope that I would get the "secret" women were asking for. I read Havelock Ellis' then forbidden volumes of *Psychology of Sex* in one gulp, and had psychic indigestion for several months afterwards.

The following spring found me still seeking and more determined than ever to find out something about contraception and its mysteries. Why was it so difficult to obtain information on this subject? Where was it hidden? Why would no one discuss it? It was like the missing link in the evolution of medical science. It was like the lost trail in the journey toward freedom. Seek it I would. If it was in existence it should be found. I would never give up until I had obtained it, nor stop until the working women of my generation in the country of my birth were acquainted with its substance. I was so settled in this determination that I ceased to worry further about the details of how this should be brought about. I approached this problem in a manner characteristic of my makeup. I settled the principle first and left the details to work themselves out. In other words, I put some of the burden of this great task into the hands of the gods.

The effect of this conviction, however, began to have a tremendous bearing upon my personal life. My three lovely, healthy children were full of life, vigor and happiness. They were glorious examples of wanted children, mentally and physically. Gradually, however, there came over me the feeling and dread that the road to my goal was to separate me from their lives, from their development, growth and happiness. The feeling grew stronger and stronger within me, and this, together with my temporary psychic indigestion, led me to gather the three of them onto a Fall River boat one late afternoon in June and sail off to Provincetown, Massachusetts.

I tried to run away from life, from its turmoil and perplexities. I wanted the quiet of the sea, the loneliness of the dunes, to be alone with myself forever. I wanted to have the children solely to myself, too. I wanted to drive away that descending, foreboding barrier of separation by closer contact with them. I wanted to feed, to bathe, to clothe them myself. I wanted to bind them to me and allow nothing to force us apart. I clutched at them like a drowning woman in a raging current, as if to save myself from its swiftness.

In Provincetown I rented a small cottage on the beach far on the outskirts of the picturesque Cape Cod village, toward Truro. In 1913 Provincetown was not the busy resort of artists and art students it has become these summers, now that policemen are needed to control the incessant motor traffic.

We found ourselves among a congenial group of social rebels and writers: Mary Heaton Vorse, the social leader of this group, and her husband, Joseph O'Brien; Hutchins Hapgood and his charming wife, the novelist Neith Boyce; Charles Hawthorne, who had discovered Provincetown for his fellow artists and conducted a summer school there. It was not until 1914 that the hegira to Provincetown began; now until 1916 that the Provincetown Players were organized and gave the first production of a play of Eugene O'Neill on a dilapidated wharf belonging to Mary Heaton Vorse.

Our own cottage verandah faced the day, and when the tide was high the children would sit on the steps and dip their toes into the water. When the tide was out we had two miles of beach for our front yard on which they skipped and ran. These days were filled with the joy of playing and romping with the children, away from the turmoil and from the ever pulling desire to be into the fight and battle of life. It was a wonderful place in which to forget the woes of the world.

The late William D. Haywood—"Big Bill," as he was affectionately called—was in Provincetown that summer. He had been East advising the workers in Patterson who had been on strike in the silk mills. His health was failing, and the strain of work had put him on the verge of a nervous breakdown. Jessie Ashley, that aristocratic rebel gentlewoman, had carried "Bill" off for a much needed rest by the sea.

This picturesque hero of the Western Federation of Miners reminded me of the giant Polyphemus I had read about in the Odyssey as a child. One of his eyes had been destroyed in some violent mine explosion. This gave him the habit of turning his head slightly when he looked at you. He gave the impression of a bull ready to attack an adversary. In reality "Big Bill" was as gentle as a child. His frame was enormous; he was like a giant in stature. He had emerged from the celebrated Haywood-Moyer-Pettibone case in Butte, Montana, an intransigent rebel against the then existing conditions of the workers. Like his young friend, John Reed, poor Bill was destined years later to die the death of an exile in Soviet Russia.

But that summers in Provincetown our outlook was sanguine, and there was no shadow of disillusion on the horizon of our sky-blue hopes.

Bill came to see me often. We talked and read together day after day. He was a keen student of human nature, though like many American men he knew nothing of the finer sensibilities of woman's being. Still, I remember a remark of his one day as we walked along the beach. "Say girl," he said, "you're getting ready to kick over the traces!"

Then, taking my hand and pointing to the children, he added: "Don't do anything to spoil their happiness—will you?"

Despite the joy of those days I knew that I was only delaying the inevitable. It was no use. I could not forget the mothers bringing to birth children in poverty and misery. Even the fishermen's wives in Provincetown had the same dread, the same problems and fear of pregnancy as the workingmen's wives in the slums of New York. They were like a great army of untouchables. Their voices were never raised, their agonies were unrevealed, their hopelessness ignored by church and society. This, the greatest of problem, as untouched as if it did not exist.

I went back and forth to Boston during these months to study in the medical library, ever seeking the information which was to relieve women of the burden of unlimited childbearing.

At the end of six months I was convinced that there was no practical medical information on contraception available in America. I had visited the Library of Congress in Washington, I had pored over books in the library of the New York Academy of Medicine and in the Boston Public Library, to find only the information no more reliable than that already obtainable from "back fence gossip" in any small town. It was discouraging to contemplate, but I refused to accept defeat.

Since childhood I had always been interested in social and political questions and had looked thoroughly into Free Trade, Socialism of its various kinds and schools, Syndicalism, as well as the theories of the Industrial Workers of the World. While I had heard of Malthus and knew there was a Malthusian doctrine, I had associated it in my mind with overpopulation and economic pressure, and not with knowledge of contraception or any artificial means of family limitation.

I had previously cast my lot with the women of the Socialist movement. I listened intently to all debates, arguments and theories of this great school of liberal thought. Their ardent and passionate faith in legislation, however, I could never share. Their answer to the misery of women and the ignorance of contraceptive knowledge was like that of the Feminists: "Wait until we get the vote to put *us* in power!"

Wherever I turned, from every one I approached I met the same answer: "Wait!" "Wait until women get the vote." "Wait until the Socialists are in power." "Wait for the Social Revolution." "Wait for the Industrial Revolution." Thus I lost my faith in the social schemes and organization of that day.

Only the boys of the I.W.W. seemed to grasp the economic significance of this great social question. At once they visualized its importance, and instead of saying "Wait" they gave me names of organizers in the silk, woolen and copper industries, and offered their assistance to get any facts on family limitation I secured direct to the workingmen and their wives.

Again "Big Bill" Haywood came to my aid with that cheering encouragement of which I was so sorely in need. He never wasted words in advising me to "wait." I owe him a debt of gratitude which I am proud to acknowledge. It was he who suggested that I go to France and see for myself the conditions resulting from generations of family limitation. This idea, together with my interest in the social experiment then going on in Glasgow, convinced me that I was to find new ways to solve old problems in Europe. I decided to go and see.

124. WOODROW WILSON, AN ADDRESS TO THE JOINT SESSION OF CONGRESS, 1917

Woodrow Wilson's rationale for going to war with Germany is forcefully articulated in his speech before Congress in 1917.

2 April, 1917   8:30 P.M.

Gentlemen of the Congress: I have called the Congress into extraordinary session because there are serious, very serious, choices of policy to be made, and made immediately, which it was neither right nor constitutionally permissible that I should assume the responsibility of making.

On the third of February last I officially laid before you the extraordinary announcement of the Imperial German Government that on and after the first day of February it was its purpose to put aside all restraints of law or of humanity and use its submarines to sink every vessel that sought to approach either the ports of Great Britain and Ireland or the western coasts of Europe or any of the ports controlled by the enemies of Germany within the Mediterranean. That had seemed to be the object of the German submarine warfare earlier in the

Source: Woodrow Wilson. "Address to a Joint Session of Congress." April 2, 1917. Public Domain Reprint.

war, but since April of last year the Imperial Government had somewhat restrained the commanders of its undersea craft in conformity with its promise then given to us that passenger boats should not be sunk and that due warning would be given to all other vessels which its submarines might seek to destroy, when no resistance was offered or escape attempted, and care taken that their crews were given at least a fair chance to save their lives in their open boats. The precautions taken were meagre and haphazard enough, as was proved in distressing instance after instance in the progress of the cruel and unmanly business, but a certain degree of restraint was observed. The new policy has swept every restriction aside. Vessels of every kind, whatever their flag, their character, their cargo, their destination, their errand, have been ruthlessly sent to the bottom without warning and without thought of help or mercy for those on board, the vessels of friendly neutrals along with those of belligerents. Even hospital ships and ships carrying relief to the sorely bereaved and stricken people of Belgium, though the latter were provided with safe conduct through the proscribed areas by the German Government itself and were distinguished by unmistakable marks of identity, have been sunk with the same reckless lack of compassion or of principle.

I was for a little while unable to believe that such things would in fact be done by any government that had hitherto subscribed to the humane practices of civilized nations. International law had its origin in the attempt to set up some law which would be respected and observed upon the seas, where no nation had right of dominion and where lay the free highways of the world. By painful stage after stage has that law been built up, with meagre enough results, indeed, after all was accomplished that could be accomplished, but always with a clear view, at least, of what the heart and conscience of mankind demanded. This minimum of right the German Government has swept aside under the plea of retaliation and necessity and because it had no weapons which it could use at sea except these which it is impossible to employ as it is employing them without throwing to the winds all scruples of humanity or of respect for the understandings that were supposed to underlie the intercourse of the world. I am not now thinking of the loss of property involved, immense and serious as that is, but only of the wanton and wholesale destruction of the lives of non-combatants, men, women, and children, engaged in pursuits which have always, even in the darkest periods of modern history, been deemed innocent and legitimate. Property can be paid for; the lives of peaceful and innocent people cannot be. The present German submarine warfare against commerce is a warfare against mankind.

It is a war against all nations. American ships have been sunk, American lives taken, in ways which it has stirred us very deeply to learn of, but the ships and people of other neutral and friendly nations have been sunk and overwhelmed in the waters in the same way. There has been no discrimination. The challenge is to all mankind. Each nation must decide for itself how it will meet it. The choice we make for ourselves must be made with a moderation of counsel and a temperateness of judgment befitting our character and our motives as a nation. We must put excited feeling away. Our motive will not be revenge or the victorious assertion of the physical might of the nation, but only the vindication of the right, of human right, of which we are only a single champion.

When I addressed the Congress on the twenty-sixth of February last, I thought that it would suffice to assert our neutral rights with arms, our right to use the seas against unlawful interference, our right to keep our people save against unlawful violence. But armed neutrality, it now appears, is impracticable. Because submarines are in effect outlaws when used as the German submarines have been used against merchant shipping, it is impossible to defend ships against their attacks as the law of nations has assumed that merchantmen would defend themselves against privateers or cruisers, visible craft giving chase upon the open sea. It is common prudence in such circumstances, grim necessity, indeed, to endeavour to destroy them before they have shown their own intention. They must be dealt with upon sight, if dealt with at all. The German Government denies the right of neutrals to use arms at all within the areas of the sea which it has proscribed, even in the defense of rights which no modern publicist has ever before questioned their right to defend. The intimation is conveyed that the armed guards which we have placed on our merchant ships will be treated as beyond the pale of law and subject to be dealt with as pirates would be. Armed neutrality is ineffectual enough at best; in such circumstances and in the face of such pretensions it is worse than ineffectual: it is likely only to produce what it was meant to prevent; it is practically certain to draw us into the war without either the rights or the effectiveness of belligerents. There is one choice we cannot make, we are incapable of making: we will not choose the path of submission and suffer the most sacred rights of our nation and our people to be ignored or violated. The wrongs against which we now array ourselves are no common wrongs; they cut to the very roots of human life.

With a profound sense of the solemn and even tragical character of the step I am taking and of the grave responsibilities which it involves, but in unhesitating obedience to what I deem my constitutional duty, I advise that the Congress declare the recent course of the Imperial German Government to be in fact nothing less than war against the government and people of the United States; that it formally accept the status of belligerent which has thus been thrust upon it; and that it take immediate steps not only to put the country in a more thorough state of defense but also to exert all its power and employ all its resources to bring the Government of the German Empire to terms and end the war.

What this will involve is clear. It will involve the utmost practicable cooperation in counsel and action with the governments now at war with Germany, and, as incident to that, the extension to those governments of the most liberal financial credits, in order that our resources may so far as possible be added to theirs. It will involve the organization and mobilization of all the material resources of the country to supply the materials of war and serve the incidental needs of the nation in the most abundant and yet the most economical and efficient way possible. It will involve the immediate full equipment of the navy in all respects but particularly in supplying it with the best means of dealing with the enemy's submarines. It will involve the immediate addition to the armed forces of the United States already provided for by law in case of war at least five hundred thousand men, who should, in my opinion, be chosen upon the principle of universal liability to service, and also the authorization of subsequent additional increments of equal force so soon as they may be needed and can be handled in training. It will involve also, of course, the granting of adequate credits to the Government, sustained, I hope, so far as they can equitably be sustained by the present generation, by well conceived taxation.

I say sustained so far as may be equitable by taxation because it seems to me that it would be most unwise to base the credits which will now be necessary entirely on money borrowed. It is our duty, I most respectfully urge, to protect our people so far as we may against the very serious hardships and evils which would be likely to arise out of the inflation which would be produced by vast loans.

In carrying out the measures by which these things are to be accomplished we should keep constantly in mind the wisdom of interfering as little as possible in our own preparation and in the equipment of our own military forces with the duty,—for it will be a very practical duty,—of supplying the nations already at war with Germany with the materials which they can obtain only from us or by our assistance. They are in the field and we should help them in every way to be effective there.

I shall take the liberty of suggesting, through the several executive departments of the Government, for the consideration of your committees, measures for the accomplishment of the several objects I have mentioned. I hope that it will be your pleasure to deal with them as having been framed after very careful thought by the branch of the Government upon which the responsibility of conducting the war and safeguarding the nation will most directly fall.

While we do these things, these deeply momentous things, let us be very clear, and make very clear to all the world what our motives and our objects are. My own thought has not been driven from its habitual and normal course by the unhappy events of the last two months, and I do not believe that the thought of the nation has been altered or clouded by them. I have exactly the same things in mind now that I had in mind when I addressed the Senate on the twenty-second of January last; the same that I had in mind when I addressed the Congress on the third of February and on the twenty-sixth of February. Our object now, as then, is to vindicate the principles of peace and justice in the life of the world as against selfish and autocratic power and to setup amongst the really free and self-governed peoples of the world such a concert of purpose and of action as will henceforth ensure the observance of those principles. Neutrality is no longer feasible or desirable where the peace of the world is involved and the freedom of its peoples, and the menace to that peace and freedom lies in the existence of autocratic governments backed by organized force which is controlled wholly by their will, not by the will of their people. We have seen the last of neutrality in such circumstances. We are at the beginning of an age in which it will be insisted that the same standards of conduct and of responsibility for wrong done shall be observed among nations and their governments that are observed among the individual citizens of civilized states.

We have no quarrel with the German people. We have no feeling towards them but one of sympathy and friendship. It was not upon their impulse that their government acted in entering this war. It was not with their previous knowledge or approval. It was a war determined upon as wars used to be determined upon in the old, unhappy days when peoples were nowhere consulted by their rulers and wars were provoked and waged in the interest of dynasties or of little groups of ambitious men who were accustomed to use their fellow men as pawns and tools. Self-governed nations do not fill their neighbour states with spies or set the course of intrigue to bring about some critical posture of affairs which will give them an opportunity to strike and make conquest. Such designs can be successfully worked out only under cover and where no one has the right to ask questions. Cunningly contrived plans of deception or aggression, carried, it may be, from generation to generation, can be worked out and kept from the light only within the privacy of courts or behind the carefully guarded confidences of a narrow and privileged class. They are happily impossible where public opinion commands and insists upon full information concerning all the nation's affairs.

A steadfast concert for peace can never be maintained except by a partnership of democratic nations. No autocratic government could be trusted to keep faith within it or observe its covenants. It must be a league of honour, a partnership of opinion. Intrigue would eat its vitals away; the plottings of inner circles who could plan what they would and render account to no one would be a corruption seated at its very heart. Only free peoples can hold their purpose and their honour steady to a common end and prefer the interests of mankind to any narrow interest of their own.

Does not every American feel that assurance has been added to our hope for the future peace of the world by the wonderful and heartening things that have been happening within the last few weeks in Russia? Russia was known by those who knew it best to have been always in fact democratic at heart, in all the vital habits of her thought, in all the intimate relationships of her people that spoke their natural instinct, their habitual attitude towards life. The autocracy that crowned the summit of her political structure, long as it had stood and terrible as was the reality of its power, was not in fact Russian in origin, character, or purpose; and now it has been shaken off and the great, generous Russian people have been added in all their naive majesty and might to the forces that are fighting for freedom in the world, for justice, and for peace. Here is a fit partner for a League of Honour.

One of the things that has served to convince us that the Prussian autocracy was not and could never be our friend is that from the very outset of the present war it has filled our unsuspecting communities and even our offices of government with spies and set criminal intrigues everywhere afoot against our national unity of counsel, our peace within and without, our industries and our commerce. Indeed it is now evident that its spies were here even before the war began; and it is unhappily not a matter of conjecture but a fact proved in our courts of justice that the intrigues which have more than once come perilously near to disturbing the peace and dislocating the industries of the country have been carried on at the instigation, with the support, and even under the personal direction of official agents of the Imperial Government accredited to the Government of the United States. Even in checking these things and trying to extirpate them we have sought to put the most generous interpretation possible upon them because we knew that their source lay, not in any hostile feeling or purpose of the German people toward us (who were, no doubt as ignorant of them as we ourselves were), but only in the selfish designs of a Government that did what it pleased and told its people nothing. But they have played their part in serving to convince us at last that that Government entertains no real friendship for us and means to act against our peace and security at its convenience. That it means to stir up enemies against us at our very doors is the intercepted note to the German Minister at Mexico City is eloquent evidence.

We are accepting this challenge of hostile purpose because we know that in such a government, following such methods, we can never have a friend; and that in the presence of its organized power, always lying in wait to accomplish we know not what purpose, there can be no assured security for the democratic governments of the world. We are now about to accept gauge of battle with this natural foe to liberty and shall, if necessary, spend the whole force of the nation to check and nullify its pretensions and its power. We are glad, now that we see the facts with no veil of false pretence about them, to fight thus for the ultimate peace of the world and for the liberation of its peoples, the German peoples included: for the rights of nations great and small and the privilege of men everywhere to choose their way of life and of obedience. The world must be made safe for democracy. Its peace must be planted upon the tested foundations of political liberty. We have no selfish ends to serve. We desire no conquest, no dominion. We seek no indemnities for ourselves, no material compensation for the sacrifices we shall freely make. We are but one of the champions of the rights of mankind. We shall be satisfied when those rights have been made as secure as the faith and freedom of nations can make them.

Just because we fight without rancour and without selfish object, seeking nothing for ourselves but what we shall wish to share with all free peoples, we shall, I feel confident, conduct our operations as belligerents without passion and ourselves observe with proud punctilio the principles of right and of fair play we profess to be fighting for.

I have said nothing of the governments allied with the Imperial Government of Germany because they have not made war upon us or challenged us to defend our right and our honour. The Austro-Hungarian Government has, indeed, avowed its unqualified endorsement and acceptance of the reckless and lawless submarine warfare adopted now without disguise by the Imperial German Government, and it has therefore not been possible for this Government to receive Count Tarnowski, the Ambassador recently accredited to this Government by the Imperial and Royal Government of Austria-Hungary; but that Government has not actually engaged in warfare against citizens of the United States on the seas, and I take the liberty, for the present at least, of postponing a discussion of our relations with the authorities at Vienna. We enter this war only where we are clearly forced into it because there are no other means of defending our rights.

It will be all the easier for us to conduct ourselves as belligerents in a high spirit of right and fairness because we act without animus, not in enmity towards a people or with the desire to bring any injury of disadvantage upon them, but only in armed opposition to an irresponsible government which has thrown aside all considerations of humanity and of right and is running amuck. We are, let me say again, the sincere friends of the German people, and shall desire nothing so much as the early re-establishment of intimate relations of mutual advantage between us,—however hard it may be for them, for the time being, to believe that this is spoken from our hearts. We have borne with their present government through all these bitter months because of that friendship,—exercising a patience and forbearance which would otherwise have been impossible. We shall, happily, still have an opportunity to prove that friendship in our daily attitude and actions towards the millions of men and women of German birth and native sympathy who live amongst us and share our life, and we shall be proud to prove it towards all who are in fact loyal to their neighbours and to the Government in the hour of test. They are, most of them, as true and loyal Americans as if they had never known any other fealty or allegiance. They will be prompt to stand with us in rebuking and restraining the few who may be of a different mind and purpose. If there should be disloyalty, it will be dealt with with a firm hand of stern repression; but, if it lifts its head at all, it will lift it only here and there and without countenance except from a lawless and malignant few.

It is a distressing and oppressive duty, Gentlemen of the Congress, which I have performed in thus addressing you. There are, it may be, many months of fiery trial and sacrifice ahead of us. It is a fearful thing to lead this great peaceful people into war, into the most terrible and disastrous of all wars, civilization itself seeming to be in the balance. But the right is more precious than peace, and we shall fight for the things which we have always carried nearest our hearts,—for democracy, for the right of those who submit to authority to have a voice in their own governments, for the rights and liberties of small nations, for a universal dominion of right by such a concert of free peoples as shall bring peace and safety to all nations and make the world itself at last free. To such a task we can dedicate our lives and our fortunes, everything that we are and everything that we have, with the pride of those who know that the day has come when America is privileged to spend her blood and her might for the principles that gave her birth and happiness and the peace which she has treasured. God helping her, she can do no other.

Printed reading copy (WP, DLC)

125. George Norris, "A Speech in the Senate," 1917

Senator George Norris of Nebraska, a U.S. Senator and prominent Progressive in 1917, expresses the doubts and fears that many reformers felt about the war declared by the most "Progressive" of our Presidents.

... I am bitterly opposed to my country entering the war, but if, not withstanding my opposition, we do enter it, all of my energy and all of my power will be behind our flag in carrying it on to victory.

The resolution now before the Senate is a declaration of war. Before taking this momentous step, and while standing on the brink of this terrible vortex, we ought to pause and calmly and judiciously consider the terrible consequences of the step we are about to take. We ought to consider likewise the route we have recently traveled and ascertain whether we have reached our present position in a way that is compatible with the neutral position which we claimed to occupy at the beginning and through the various stages of this unholy and unrighteous war.

No close student of recent history will deny that both Great Britain and Germany have, on numerous occasions since the beginning of the war, flagrantly violated in the most serious manner the rights of neutral vessels and neutral nations under existing international law as recognized up to the beginning of this war by the civilized world.

The reason given by the President in asking Congress to declare war against Germany is that the German Government has declared certain war zones, within which, by the use of submarines, she sinks, without notice, American ships and destroys American lives. . . .

It will be seen that the British Government declared the north of Scotland route into the Baltic Sea as dangerous and the English Channel route into the Baltic Sea as safe.

The German Government in its order did exactly the reverse. It declared the north of Scotland route into the Baltic Sea as safe and the English Channel route into the Baltic Sea as dangerous. . . .

Thus we have the two declarations of the two Governments, each declaring a military zone and warning neutral shipping from going into the prohibited area. England sought to make her order effective by the use of submerged mines. Germany sought to make her order effective by the use of submarines. Both of these orders were illegal and contrary to all international law as well as the principles of humanity. Under international law no belligerent Government has the right to place submerged mines in the high seas. Neither has it any right to take human life without notice by the use of submarines. If there is any difference in the ground of humanity between these two instrumentalities, it is certainly in favor of the submarines. The submarine can exercise some degree of discretion and judgement. The submerged mine always destroys without notice, friend and foe alike, guilty and innocent the same. In carrying out these two policies both Great Britain and Germany have sunk American ships and destroyed American lives without provocation and without notice. There have been more ships sunk and more American lives lost from the action of submarines than from English mines in the North Sea; for the simple reason that we finally acquiesced in the British war zone and kept our ships out of it, while in the German war zone we have refused to recognize its legality and have not kept either our ships or our citizens out of its area. If American ships had gone into the British war zone in defiance of Great Britain's order, as they have gone into the German war zone in defiance of the German Government's order, there would have been many more American lives lost and many more American ships sunk by the instrumentality of the mines than the instrumentality of the submarines. . . .

The only difference is that in the case of Germany we have persisted in our protest, while in the case of England we have submitted.

There are a great many American citizens who feel that we owe it as a duty to humanity to take part in this war. Many instances of cruelty and inhumanity can be found on both sides. Men are often biased in their judgement on account of their sympathy and their interests. To my mind, what we ought to have maintained from

---

Source: George Norris. "A Speech in the Senate," April 4, 1917. Public Domain Reprint.

the beginning was the strictest neutrality. If we had done this I do not believe we would have been on the verge of war at the present time. We had a right as a nation, if we desired, to cease at any time to be neutral. While many such people are moved by selfish motives and hopes of gain, I have no doubt but that in a great many instances, through what I believe to be a misunderstanding of the real condition, there are many honest, patriotic citizens who think we ought to engage in this war and who are behind the President in his demand that we should declare war against Germany. I think such people err in judgement and to a great extent have been misled as to the real history and the true facts by the almost unanimous demand of the great combination of wealth that has a direct financial interest in our participation in the war. We have loaned many hundreds of millions of dollars to the allies in this controversy. While such action was legal and countenanced by international law, there is no doubt in my mind but the enormous amount of money loaned to the allies in this country has been instrumental in bringing about a public sentiment in favor of our country taking a course that would make every bond worth a hundred cents on the dollar and making the payment of every debt certain and sure. Through this instrumentality and also through the instrumentality of others who have not only made millions out of the war in the manufacture of munitions, etc., and who would expect to make millions more if our country can be drawn into the catastrophe, a large number of the great newspapers and news agencies of the country have been controlled and enlisted in the greatest propaganda that the world has ever known, to manufacture sentiment in favor of war. It is not demanded that the American citizens shall be used as insurance policies to guarantee the safe delivery of munitions of war to belligerent nations. The enormous profits of munition manufacturers, stockbrokers, and bond dealers must be still further increased by our entrance into the war. This has brought us to the present moment, when Congress, urged by the President and backed by the artificial sentiment, is about to declare war and engulf our country in the greatest holocaust that the world has ever known. . . .

I know that I am powerless to stop it. I know that this war madness has taken possession of the financial and political powers of our country. I know that nothing I can say will stay the blow that is soon to fall. I feel that we are committing a sin against humanity and against our countrymen. I would like to say to this war god, You shall not coin into gold the lifeblood of my brethren. I would like to prevent this terrible catastrophe from falling upon my people. I would be willing to surrender my own life if I could cause this awful cup to pass. I charge no man here with a wrong motive, but it seems to me that this war craze has robbed us of our judgement. I wish we might delay our action until reason could again be enthroned in the brain of man. I feel that we are about to put the dollar sign upon the American flag.

I have no sympathy with the military spirit that dominates the Kaiser and his advisers. I do not believe that they represent the heart of the great German people. I have no more sympathy with the submarine policy of Germany than I have with the mine-laying policy of England. I have heard with rejoicing of the overthrow of the Czar of Russia and the movement in that great country toward the establishment of a government where the common people will have their rights, liberty, and freedom respected. I hope and pray that a similar revolution may take place in Germany, that the Kaiser may be overthrown, and that on the ruins of his military despotism may be established a German republic, where the great German people may work out their worldly destiny. The working out of that problem is not an American burden. We ought to remember the advice of the Father of our Country and keep out of entangling alliances. Let Europe solve her problems as we have solved ours. Let Europe bear her burdens as we have borne ours. In the greatest war of our history and at the time it occurred, we were engaged in solving an American problem. We settled the question of human slavery and washed our flag clean by the sacrifice of human blood. It was a great problem and a great burden, but we solved it ourselves. Never once did we think of asking Europe to take part in its solution. Never once did any European nation undertake to settle the great question. We solved it, and history has rendered a unanimous verdict that we solved it right. The troubles of Europe ought to be settled by Europe, and wherever our sympathies may lie, disagreeing as we do, we ought to remain absolutely neutral and permit them to settle their questions without our interference. We are now the greatest neutral nation. Upon the passage of this resolution we will have joined Europe in the great catastrophe and taken America into entanglements that will not end with this war, but will live and bring their evil influences upon many generations yet unborn.

126. Mother Jones, "The Steel Strike of 1919"

Mary Harris "Mother" Jones was a well-known labor advocate, active throughout the United States, called "mother" because she was in her sixties when she became most famous. She had been a dressmaker, a Populist, a member of the Knights of Labor, and had marched with miners' wives in the coal fields. In this piece, she contrasts the ideals of the United States in the Great War and back home.

During the war the working people were made to believe they amounted to something. Gompers, the President of the American Federation of labor, conferred with copper kings and lumber kings and coal kings, speaking for the organized workers. Up and down the land the workers heard the word, "democracy." They were asked to work for it. To give their wages to it. To give their lives for it. They were told that their labor, their money, their flesh were the bulwarks against tyranny and autocracy.

So believing, the steel workers, 300,000 of them, rose en masse against Kaiser Gary, the President of the American Steel Corporation. The slaves asked their czar for the abolition of the twelve-hour day, for a crumb from the huge loaf of profits made in the great war, and for the right to organize.

Czar Gary met his workers as is the customary way with tyrants. He could not shoot them down as did Czar Nicholas when petitioned by his peasants. But he ordered the constabulary out. He ordered forth his two faithful generals: fear and starvation, one to clutch at the worker's throat and the other at his stomach and the stomachs of his little children.

When the steel strike was being organized, I was in Seattle with Jay G. Brown, President of the Shingle Workers of America.

"We ought to go east and help organize those slaves," I said to Brown.

"They'll throw us in jail, Mother!" he said.

"Well, they're our own jails, aren't they? Our class builds them."

I came East. So did Jay G. Brown—a devoted worker for the cause of the steel slaves.

The strike in the steel industry was called in September, 1919. Gary as spokesman for the industry refused to consider any sort of appointment with his workers. What did it matter to him that thousands of workers in Bethlehem, Pennsylvania, worked in front of scorching furnaces twelve long hours, through the day, through the night, while he visited the Holy Land where Our Lord was born in a manger!

I traveled up and down the Monongahela River. Most of the places where the steel workers were on strike meetings were forbidden. If I were to stop to talk to a woman on the street about her child, a cossack would come charging down upon us and we would have to run for our lives. If I were to talk to a man in the streets of Braddock, we would be arrested for unlawful assembly.

In the towns of Sharon and Farrell, Pennsylvania, the lick-spittle authorities forbade all assembly. The workers by the thousands marched into Ohio where the Constitution of the United States instead of the Steel Corporation's constitution was law.

I asked a Pole where he was going. I was visiting his sick wife; taking a bit of milk to her new baby. Her husband was washing his best shirt in the sink.

"Where I go? Tomorrow I go to America," he said, meaning he was going on the march to Ohio.

I spoke often to the strikers. Many of them were foreigners but they knew what I said. I told them, "We are going to see whether Pennsylvania belongs to Kaiser Gary or to Uncle Sam. If Gary's got it, we are going to take it away from him and give it back to Uncle Sam. When we are ready we can scare and starve and lick the whole gang. Your boys went over to Europe. They were told to clean up the Kaiser. Well, they did it. And now you and your boys are going to clean up the kaisers at home. Even if they have to do it with a leg off and an arm gone, and eyes out.

Source: Mother Jones. *The Autobiography of Mother Jones.* pp. 209–226. Charles H. Kerr Publishing Copyright 1976. Reprinted by permission.

"Our Kaisers sit up and smoke seventy-five cent cigars and have lackeys with knee pants bring them champagne while you starve, while you grow old at forty, stoking their furnaces. You pull in your belts while they banquet. They have stomachs two miles long and two miles wide and you fill them. Our Kaisers have stomachs of steel and hearts of steel and tears of steel for the 'poor Belgians.'

"If Gary wants to work twelve hours a day let him go in the blooming mills and work. What we want is a little leisure, time for music, playgrounds, a decent home, books, and the things that make life worth while."

I was speaking in Homestead. A group of organizers were with me in an automobile. As soon as a word was said, the speaker was immediately arrested by the steel bosses' sheriffs. I rose to speak. An officer grabbed me.

"Under arrest!" he said.

We were taken to jail. A great mob of people collected outside the prison. There was angry talk. The jailer got scared. He thought there might be lynching and he guessed who would be lynched. The mayor was in the jail, too, confering with the jailer. He was scared. He looked out of the office windows and he saw hundreds of workers milling around and heard them muttering.

The jailer came to Mr. Brown and asked him what he had better do.

"Why don't you let Mother Jones go out and speak to them," he said. "They'll do anything she says."

So the jailer came to me and asked me to speak to the boys outside and ask them to go home.

I went outside the jail and told the boys I was going to be released shortly on bond, and that they should go home now and not give any trouble. I got them in a good humor and pretty soon they went away. Meanwhile while I was speaking, the mayor sneaked out the back way.

We were ordered to appear in the Pittsburgh court the next morning. A cranky old judge asked me if I had had a permit to speak on the streets.

"Yes, sir," said I. "I had a permit."

"Who issued it?" he growled.

"Patrick Henry; Thomas Jefferson; John Adams!" said I.

The mention of those patriots who gave us our charter of liberties made the old steel judge sore. He fined us all heavily.

During the strike I was frequently arrested. So were all the leaders. We expected that. I never knew whether I would find John Fitzpatrick and William Foster at headquarters when I went up to Pittsburgh. Hundreds of threatening letters came to them. Gunmen followed them. Their lives were in constant danger. Citizens Alliances—the little shopkeepers dependent upon the smile of the steel companies—threatened to drive them out. Never had a strike been led by more devoted, able, unselfish men. Never a thought for themselves. Only for the men on strike, men striking to bring back America to America.

In Foster's office no chairs were permitted by the authorities. That would have been construed as "a meeting." Here men gathered in silent groups, to get what word they could of the strike.

How was it going in Ohio?

How was it going in Pennsylvania?

How in the Mesaba country?

The workers were divided from one another. Spies working among the Ohio workers told of the break in the strike in Pennsylvania. In Pennsylvania, they told of the break in Ohio. With meetings forbidden, with mails censored, with no means of communication allowed, the strikers could not know of the progress of their strike. Then fear would clutch their throats.

One day two men came into Headquarters. One of them showed his wrists. They told in broken English of being seized by officers, taken to a hotel room. One of them was handcuffed for a day to a bed. His wrists swelled. He begged the officers to release him. He writhed in pain. They laughed and asked him if he would go to work. Though mad with pain he said no. At night they let him go . . . without a word, without redress.

Organizers would come in with bandages on their heads. They had been beaten. They would stop a second before the picture of Fanny Sellins, the young girl whom the constabulary had shot as she bent protectingly over some children. She had died. They had only been beaten.

Foreigners were forever rushing in with tales of violence. They did not understand. Wasn't this America? Hadn't they come to America to be free?

We could not get the story of the struggle of these slaves over to the public. The press groveled at the feet of the steel Gods. The local pulpits dared not speak. Intimidation stalked the churches, the schools, the theaters. The rule of steel was absolute.

Although the strike was sponsored by the American Federation of Labor, under instructions from the Steel Trust, the public were fed daily stories of revolution and Bolshevism and Russian gold supporting the strike.

I saw the parade in Gary. Parades were forbidden in the Steel King's own town. Some two hundred soldiers who had come back from Europe where they had fought to make America safe from tyrants, marched. They were steel workers. They had on their faded uniforms and the steel hats which protected them from German bombs. In the line of march I saw young fellows with arms gone, with crutches, with deep scars across the face—heroes they were! Workers in the cheap cotton clothes of the working class fell in behind them. Silently the thousands walked through the streets and alleys of Gary. Saying no word. With no martial music such as sent the boys into the fight with the Kaiser across the water. Marching in silence. Disbanding in silence.

The next day the newspapers carried across the country a story of "mob violence" in Gary. Then I saw another parade. Into Gary marched United States soldiers under General Wood. They brought their bayonets, their long range guns, trucks with mounted machine guns, field artillery. Then came violence. The soldiers broke up the picket line. Worse than that, they broke the ideal in the hearts of thousands of foreigners, their ideal of America. Into the blast furnace along with steel went their dream that America was a government for the people—the poor, the oppressed.

I sat in the kitchen with the wife of a steel worker. It was a tiny kitchen. Three men sat at the table playing cards on the oil cloth table cover. They sat in their under shirts and trousers. Babies crawled on the floor. Above our heads hung wet clothes.

"The worse thing about this strike, Mother, is having the men folks all home all the time. There's no place for them to go. If they walk out they get chased by the mounted police. If they visit another house, the house gets raided and the men get arrested for 'holding a meeting.' They daren't even sit on the steps. Officers chase them in. It's fierce, Mother, with the boarders all home. When the men are working, half of them are sleeping, and the other half are in the mills. And I can hang my clothes out in the yard. Now I daren't. The guards make us stay in. They chase us out of our own yards. It's hell, Mother, with the men home all day and the clothes hanging around too. And the kids are frightened. The guards chase them in the house. That makes it worse. The kids, and the men all home and the clothes hanging around."

That was another way the steel tyrants fought their slaves. They crowded them into their wretched kennels, piling them on top of one another until their nerves were on edge. Men and women and babies and children and cooking and washing and dressing and undressing. This condition wore terribly on the women.

"Mother, seems like I'm going crazy!" women would say to me. "I'm scared to go out and I go crazy if I stay in with everything lumped on top of me!"

"The men are not going back?"

When I asked the women that question they would stop their complaints. "My man go back, I kill him!" You should see their eyes!

I went to Duquesne. Mayor Crawford, the brother of the President of the McKeesport Tin Plate Company, naturally saw the strike through steel-rimmed glasses. Jay Brown and I asked him for a permit to address the strikers.

"So you want a permit to speak in Duquesne, do you?" he grinned.

"We do that," said I, "as American citizens demanding our constitutional rights."

He laughed aloud. "Jesus Christ himself could not hold a meeting in Duquesne!" said he.

"I have no doubt of that," said I, "not while you are mayor. "You may remember, however, that He drove such men as you out of the temple!"

He laughed again. Steel makes one feel secure.

We spoke. We were arrested and taken to jail. While in my cell, a group of worthy citizens, including some town officials and some preachers came to see me.

"Mother Jones," they said, "why don't you use your great gifts and your knowledge of men for something better and higher than agitating?"

"There was a man once," said I, "who had great gifts and a knowledge of men and he agitated against a powerful government that sought to make men serfs, to grind them down. He founded this nation that men might be free. He was a gentleman agitator!"

"Are you referring to George Washington?" said one of the group.

"I am so," said I. "And there was a man once who had the gift of a tender heart and he agitated against powerful men, against invested wealth, for the freedom of black men. He agitated against slavery!"

"Are you speaking of Abraham Lincoln?" said a little man who was peeking at me over another fellow's shoulder.

"I am that," said I.

"And there was a man once who walked among men, among the poor and the despised and the lowly, and he agitated against the powers of Rome, against the lickspittle Jews of the local pie counter; he agitated for the Kingdom of God!"

"Are you speaking of Jesus Christ?" said a preacher.

"I am," said I. "The agitator you nailed to a cross some centuries ago. I did not know that his name was known in the region of steel!"

They all said nothing and left.

I went in a house in Monessen where I heard a woman sobbing. "They have taken my man away and I do not know where they have taken him!" Two little sobbing children clung to her gingham apron. Her tears fell on their little heads.

"I will find out for you. Tell me what happened."

"Yesterday two men come. They open door; not knock. They come bust in. They say 'You husband go back to Russia. He big Bolshevik!' I say, 'Who you?' They say, 'We big government United States. Big detect!'"

"They open everything. They open trunks. They throw everything on floor. They take everything from old country. They say my husband never came back. They say my husband go to Russia. Perhaps they hang him up, they say."

"They will not hang him. Is your husband Bolshevik?"

"No. He what you call Hunkie in America. He got friend. Friend very good. Friend come see him many times. Play cards. Talk 'bout damn boss. Talk 'bout damn job. Talk just 'bout all damn things. This friend say, 'You like better Russia? Work people now got country.'

"My husband say, 'Sure I like Russia. Russia all right. Maybe workmans got chance there.'

"This friend say, 'You like tea?'

"My man say, 'Sure I like!'

"Pretty soon they go walk together. My man not come home. All night gone. Next day come high detect. They say my man Bolshevik. His friend say so.'"

"Have you been to the jail?"

"Yes, they say he not there. They say he been gone to Russia."

"Here's five dollars," I said. "Now you take care of those little ones and I'll get your man for you."

He was in prison. I found him. Arrested by the United States Secret Service men who worked in connection with the Steel Company's private spies. Scores of workers were in jail, arrested on charges of holding radical thoughts. Holding radical thoughts and even the conservative demand for a shorter day, a better wage, the right to organize was punished with guns and prisons and torture!

He with dozens of others were later freed. With nothing against them. Five hundred "under cover" men worked in Monessen, sneaking into men's houses, into their unions, into their hearts, into their casual thoughts, sneaking and betraying. Five hundred Judas Iscariots betraying the workers for a handful of silver dollars.

With vermin like these must the worker struggle. Rather would the Steel Kings pay hundreds of thousands of dollars to these parasites than give the workers a living wage, a wage which would enable them to live as free men.

I was speaking in Mingo. There was a big crowd there. Most of them were foreigners but they would stand for hours listening to the speakers, trying to fit the English words to the feelings in their hearts. Their patient faces looked up into mine. Slag, the finely powdered dust of the steel mills, was ground into the furrows of their foreheads, into the lines about their mouths. The mark of steel was indelibly stamped upon them. They belonged to steel, branded as are cattle on the plains by their owners.

I said to them, "Steel stock has gone up. Steel profits are enormous. Steel dividends are making men rich over night. The war—your war—has made the steel lords richer than the emperors of old Rome. And their profits are not from steel alone but from your bodies with their innumerable burns; their profits are your early old age, your swollen feet, your wearied muscles. You go without warm winter clothes that Gary and his gang may go to Florida to warm their blood. You puddle steel twelve hours a day! Your children play in the muck of mud puddles while the children of the Forty Thieves take their French and dancing lessons, and have their fingernails manicured!"

As I was about to step down from the little platform I saw the crowd in one part of the hall milling around. Some one was trying to pass out leaflets and an organizer was trying to stop him. I heard the organizer say, "No sir, that's all right but you can't do it here! What do you want to get us in for!"

The fellow who had the leaflets insisted on distributing them. I pushed my way over to where the disturbance was.

"Lad," said I, "let me see one of those leaflets."

"It's about Russia, Mother," said the organizer, and you know we can't have that!"

I took a leaflet. It asked the assistance of everyone in getting the government to lift the blockade against Russia, as hundreds of thousands of women and little children were starving for food, and thousands were dying for want of medicine and hospital necessities.

"What is the matter with these leaflets?" I asked the organizer.

"Nothing, Mother, only if we allow them to be distributed the story will go out that the strike is engineered from Moscow. We can't mix issues. I'm afraid to let these dodgers circulate."

"Women and children blockaded and starving! Men, women and children dying for lack of hospital necessities. This strike will not be won by turning a deaf ear to suffering where-ever it occurs. There's only one thing to be afraid of . . . of not being a man!"

The struggle for freedom went on. Went on against colossal odds. Steel was against them. And the government was against them, from the remote government at Washington down to the tiny official of the steel village. There was dissension in the ranks of labor. Ambition and prejudice played their part.

Human flesh, warm and soft and capable of being wounded, went naked up against steel; steel that is cold as old stars, and harder than death and incapable of pain. Bayonets and guns and steel rails and battle ships, bombs and bullets are made of steel. And only babies are made of flesh. More babies to grow up and work in steel, to hurl themselves against the bayonets, to know the tempered resistance of steel.

The strike was broken. Broken by the scabs brought in under the protection of the troops. Broken by breaking men's belief in the outcome of their struggle. Broken by breaking men's hearts. Broken by the press, by the government. In a little over a hundred days, the strike shivered to pieces.

The slaves went back to the furnaces, to the mills, to the heat and the roar, to the long hours — to slavery.

At headquarters men wept. I wept with them. A young man put his hands on my shoulders.

"Mother," he sobbed. "It's over."

A red glare from the mills lighted the sky. It made me think of Hell.

"Lad," said I, "It is not over. There's a fiercer light than those hell fires over yonder! It is the white light of freedom burning in men's hearts!"

Back to the mills trudged the men, accepting the terms of the despot, Gary; accepting hours that made them old, old men at forty; that threw them on the scrap heap, along with the slag from the mills, at early middle age; that made of them nothing but brutes that slept and worked, that worked and slept. The sound of their feet marching back into the mills was the sound of a funeral procession, and the corpse they followed was part of their selves. It was their hope.

Gary and his gang celebrated the victory with banquets and rejoicing. Three hundred thousand workers, living below the living wage, ate the bread of bitterness.

I say, as I said in the town of Gary, it is the damn gang of robbers and their band of political thieves who will start the next American Revolution; just as it was they who started this strike. Fifty thousand American lads died on the battle fields of Europe that the world might be more democratic. Their buddies came home and fought the American workingman when he protested an autocracy beyond the dream of the Kaiser. Had these same soldiers helped the steel workers, we could have given Gary Morgan and his gang a free pass to hell. All the world's history has produced no more brutal and savage times than these, and this nation will perish if we do not change these conditions.

Christ himself would agitate against them. He would agitate against the plutocrats and hypocrites who tell the workers to go down on their knees and get right with God. Christ, the carpenter's son, would tell them to stand up on their feet and fight for righteousness and justice on the earth.

127. John Dos Passos, "The Scene of Battle," 1919

Disillusioned with war, with Woodrow Wilson's failures to honor his own pledges about the peace, and with civilization itself, many of the writers of the decade between the Armistice and the Crash were sickened by their memories of the horrors civilized society had perpetrated on itself. John Dos Passos (1896–), in the last few pages of 1919, *the second volume of the trilogy* U.S.A., *shows the new barbarism of war. Although this selection was written shortly after the Crash, Dos Passos had seen the war as a volunteer in an ambulance corps. His recoil from the mass butchery was a typical reaction, but the intensity and the swirling, cinematic promise are peculiarly his own.*

The Body of an American

Whereas the Congress of the United States by a concurrent resolution adopted on the 14th day of March last authorized the Secretary of War to cause to brought to the United States to body of an American who was a member of the American expeditionary forces in Europe who lost his life during the world war and whose identity has not been established for burial in the Memorial Amphitheater of the National Cemetery at Arlington, Virginia.

In the tarpaper morque at Chalons-sur-Marne in the reek of chloride of lime and the dead, they picked out the pine box that held all that was left of

enie menie minie moe plenty other pine boxes stacked up their containing what they'd scraped up of Richard Roe

and other persons or persons unknown. Only one can go. How did they pick John Doe?

Make sure he aint a dinge, boys,

make sure he ain't a guinea or a kike,

how can you tell a guy's hundred percent when all you're got's a gunnysack full of bones, bronze buttons stamped with the screaming eagle and a pair of roll puttees?

. . . and the gagging chloride and the puky dirt-stench of the yearold dead . . .

The day withal was too meaningful and tragic for applause. Silence, tears, songs and prayer, muffled drums and soft music were the instrumentalities today of national approbation.

John Doe was born (thudding din of blood in love into the shuddering soar of a man and a woman alone indeed together lurching into

and ninemonths sick drowse waking into scared agony and the pain and blood and mess of birth). John Doe was born

and raised in Brooklyn, in Memphis, near the lakefront in Cleveland, Ohio, in the stench in the stockyards in Chi, on Beacon Hill, in an old brick house in Alexandria, Virginia, on Telegraph Hill, in a halftimbered Tudor cottage in Portland the city of roses.

in the Lying-In Hospital old Morgan endowed on Stuyvesant Square,

across the railroad tracks, out near the country club, in a shack cabin tenement apartmenthouse exclusive residential suburb;

scion of one of the best families in the social register, won first prize in the baby parade at Coronado Beach, was marbles champion of the Little Rock grammarschools, crack basketball player at the Bonneville High, quarterback at the State Reformatory, having saved the sheriff's kid from drowning in the Little Missouri River was invited to Washington to be photographed shaking hands with the President on the White House steps;—

though this was a time of mourning, such as assemblage necessarily has about a touch of color. In the boxes are seen the court uniforms of foreign diplomats, the

---

Source: John Dos Passos, "The Body of an American" from *1919*, pp. 467–473. Copyright John Dos Passos, 1960. Published by Houghton Mifflin Co. Reprinted by permission. [Reprinted with permission of MacMillan College Publishing Company from THE CULTURE OF THE TWENTIES, edited by Loren Baritz. Copyright 1970 by MacMillan College Publishing Company.]

gold braid of our own and foreign fleets and armies, the black of the conventional morning dress of American statesmen, the varicolored furs and outdoor wrapping garments of mothers and sisters come to mourn, the drab and blue of soldiers and sailors, the glitter of musical instruments and the white and black of a vested choir

—busboy harvestiff hogcaller boyscout champeen cornshucker of Western Kansas bellhop at the United States Hotel at Saratoga Springs office boy callboy fruiter telephone lineman longshoreman lumberjack plumber's helper,

worked for an exterminating company in Union City, filled pipes in an opium joint in Trenton N.J.

Y.M.C.A. secretary, express agent, truckdriver, fordemachanic, sold books in Denver, Colorado; Madams would you be willing to help a young man work his way through college?

President Harding, with a reverence seemingly more significant because of his high temporal station, concluded his speech:

> We are met today to pay the impersonal tribute; the name of him whose body lies before us took flight with his imperishable soul . . .
>
> as a typical soldier of this representative democracy he fought and died believing in the indisputable justice of his country's cause . . .

by rising his right hand and asking the thousands within the sound of his voice to join in the prayer:

> Our Father which art in heaven hallowed be thy name . . .

Naked he went into the army;

they weighed you, measured you, looked for flat feet, squeezed your penis to see if you had clap, looked up your anus to see if you had piles, counted your teeth, made you cough, listened to your heart and lungs, made you read the letters on the card, charted your urine and your intelligence,

gave you a service record for a future (imperishable soul)

and an identification tag stamped with your serial number to hang around your neck, issued O D regulation equipment, a condiment can and a copy of the articles of war.

Attn'SHUN suck in your cut you c———r wipe that mile off your face eyes right wattja think dis is a choirchsocial? For-war-D'ARCH.

John Doe
and Richard Roe and other person or persons unknown

drilled hiked, manual of arms, ate slum, learned to salute, to soldier, to loaf in the latrines, forbidden to smoke on deck, overseas guard duty, forty men and eight horses, shortarm inspection and the ping of shrapnel and the shrill bullets combing the air and the sorehead woodpeckers the machineguns mud cooties gasmasks and the itch.

Say feller tell me how I can get back to my outfit.

John Doe had a head

for twentyodd years intensely the nerves of the eyes the ears the palate the tongue the fingers the toes the armpits, the nerves warmfeeling under the skin charged the coiled brain with hurt sweet warm cold mind must dont sayings print headlines:

Though shant not the multiplication table long division, Now is the time for all good men knocks but once at a young man's door, It's a great life if Ish gebibbel, The first five years'll be the Safety First, Suppose a hun tried to rape your my country right or wrong, Catch 'em young, What he dont know wont treat 'em rough, Tell 'em nothing, He got what was coming to him he got his, This is a white man's country, Kick the bucket, Gone west, If you dont like it you can croaked him

Say buddy cant you tell me how I can get back to my outfit?

Cant help jumpin when them things go off, give me the trots them things do. I lost my identification tag swimmin in the Marne, roughhousin with a guy while we was waiting to be deloused, in bed with a girl named Jeanne (Love moving picture wet French postcard dream began with saltpeter in the coffee and ended at the propho station);—

Say soldier for chrissake cant you tell me how I can get back to my outfit?

John Doe's
heart pumped blood:

alive thudding silence of blood in your ears down in the clearing in the Oregon forest where the punkins were punkin-color pouring into the blood through the eyes and the fall-colored trees and the bronze hoppers were hopping through the dry grass, where tiny striped snails hung on the underside of the blades and the flies hummed, wasps droned, bumblebees buzzed, and the woods smelt of wine and mushrooms and apples, homey smell of fall pouring into the blood,

and I dropped the tin hat and the sweaty pack and lay flat with the dogday sun licking my throat and adamssapple and the tight skin over the breastbone.

The shell had his number on it.
The blood ran into the ground.

The service record dropped out of the filing cabinet when the quartermaster sergeant got blotto that time they had to pack up and leave the billets in a hurry.

The identification tag was in the bottom of the Marne.

The blood ran into the ground, the brains oozed out of the cracked skull and were licked up by the trenchrats, the belly swelled and raised a generation of bluebottle flies,

and the incorruptible skeleton,

and the scraps of dried viscera and skin bundled in khaki

> they took to Chalons-sur-Marne
> and laid it out neat in a pine coffin
> and took it home to God's Country on a battleship
> and buried it in a sarcopaghus in the Memorial Amphitheater in the Arlington National Cemetery
> and draped the Old Glory over it
> and the bugler played taps
> and Mr. Harding prayed to God and the diplomats and the generals and the admirals and the brasshats and the politicians and the handsomely dressed ladies out of the society column of the *Washington Post* stood up solemn
> and thought how beautiful sad Old Glory God's Country it was to have the bugler play taps and the three volleys made their ears ring.

Where his chest ought to have been they pinned the Congressional Medal, the D.S.C., the Medaille Militaire, the Belgian Croix de Guerre, the Italian gold medal, the Vitutea Militara sent by Queen Marie of Rumania, the Czechoslovak war cross, the Virtuiti Militari of the Poles, a wreath sent by Hamilton Fish, Jr., of New York, and a little wampum presented by a deputation of Arizona redskins in warpaint and feathers. All the Washingtonians brought flowers.

Woodrow Wilson brought a bouquet of poppies.

Chapter XXIII

The Age of Jazz and Mass Culture, 1921–1927

128. Sinclair Lewis, "Boosters — Pep!," 1922

Sinclair Lewis (1885–1951) mastered the style, rhythm, and feel of provincial America. Beginning with Main Street *(1920), he continued to cover this terrain in a series of novels:* Babbitt *(1922),* Arrowsmith *(1925),* Elmer Gantry *(1927), and* Dodsworth *(1929). Awarded the Nobel Prize for literature in 1930, Lewis in his acceptance speech admitted what only a few critics had already seen: his own attitude toward the provincial American was not unmixed scorn. The dull country doctors, hicks who could easily be taken in, pathetic, and earnest do-gooders, frenetic boosters, and the rest, were, for Lewis, the kind of folks he had known in his home town, Sauk Center, Minnesota. There was at least some affection softening his disdain. In* Babbitt, *however, Lewis introduced word into our language, and George F. Babbitt has become the almost universal symbol of the provincial mentality. With his carefully standardized facade as the Solid Citizen, with his lapel pin proclaiming "Boosters — Pep!" and with his cliché-filled life as a real-estate salesman, Babbitt was the citadel the advocates of change during the Twenties would have to conquer. The following passages should show how difficult such a victory would be.*

Chapter 1

I

The towers of Zenith aspired above the morning, mist; austere towers of steel and cement and limestone, sturdy as cliffs and delicate as silver rods. They were neither citadels nor churches, but frankly and beautifully office-buildings.

The mist took pity on the fretted structures of earlier generations: the Post Office with its shingle-tortured mansard, the red brick minarets of hulking old houses, factories with stingy and sooted windows, wooden tenements colored like mud. The city was full of such grotesqueries, but the clean towers were thrusting them from the business center, and on the farther hills were shining new houses, homes — they seemed — for laughter and tranquility.

Over a concrete bridge fled a limousine of long sleek hood and noiseless engine. These people in evening clothes were returning from an all-night rehearsal of a Little Theater play, an artistic adventure considerably illuminated by champagne. Below the bridge curved a railroad, a maze of green and crimson lights. The New York Flyer boomed past, and twenty lines of polished steel leaped into the glare.

In one of the skyscrapers the wires of the Associated Press were closing down. The telegraph operators wearily

---

Source: Sinclair Lewis, *Babbitt,* Chap. 1, pp. 1–13, Chap. V, pp. 52–58, Copyright 1922 by Harcourt, Brace & World, Inc., renewed by Sinclair Lewis. Reprinted by permission.
[Reprinted with permission of Macmillan College Publishing Company from THE CULTURE OF THE TWENTIES, edited by Loren Baritz. Copyright 1970 by MacMillan College Publishing Company.]

489

raised their celluloid eye-shades after a night of talking with Paris and Peking. Through the building crawled the scrubwomen, yawning, their old shoes slapping. The dawn mist spun away. Cues of men with lunch-boxes clumped toward the immensity of new factories, sheets of glass and hollow tile, glittering shops where five thousand men worked beneath one roof, pouring out the honest wares that would be sold up the Euphrates and across the veldt. The whistles rolled out in greeting a chorus cheerful as the April dawn; the song of labor in a city built—it seemed—for giants.

II

There was nothing of the giant in the aspect of the man who was beginning to awaken on the sleeping porch of a Dutch Colonial house in that residential district of Zenith known as Floral Heights.

His name was George F. Babbitt. He was forty-six years old now, in April, 1920, and he made nothing in particular, neither butter nor shoes nor poetry, but he was nimble in the calling of selling houses for more than people could afford to pay.

His large head was pink, his brown hair thin and dry. His face was babyish in slumber, despite his wrinkles and the red spectacle-dents on the slopes of his nose. He was not fat but he was exceedingly well fed; his cheeks were pads, and the unroughened hand which lay helpless upon the khaki-colored blanket was slightly puffy. He seemed prosperous, extremely married and unromantic; and although unromantic, appeared this sleeping-porch, which looked on one sizeable elm, two respectable glass-plots, a cement driveway, and a corrugated iron garage. Yet Babbitt was again dreaming of the fairy child, a dream more romantic than scarlet padogas by a silver sea.

For years the fairy child had come to him. Where others saw but George Babbitt, she discerned gallant youth. She waited for him, in the darkness beyond mysterious groves. When at last he could slip away from the crowded house he darted to her. His wife, his clamoring friends, sought to follow, but he escaped, the girl fleet beside him, and they crouched together on a shadowy hillside. She was so slim, so white, so eager! She cried that he was gay and valiant, that she would wait for him, that they would sail—

Rumble and bang of the milk-truck.

Babbitt moaned, turned over, struggled back toward his dream. He could see only her face now, beyond misty waters. The furnace-man slammed the basement door. A dog barked in the next year. As Babbitt sank blissfully into a dim warm tide, the paper-carrier went by whistling, and the rolled-up *Advocate* thumped the front door. Babbitt roused, his stomach constricted with alarm. As he relaxed, he was pierced by the familiar and irritating rattle of some one cranking a Ford: snap-ah-ah, snap-ah-ah, snap-ah-ah. Himself a pious motorist, Babbitt cranked with the unseen driver, with him waited through taut hours for the roar of the starting engine, with him agonized as the roar ceased and again began the infernal patient snap-ah-ah—a round, flat sound, a shivering cold-morning sound, a sound infuriating and inescapable. Not till he rising voice of the motor told him that the Ford was moving was he released from the panting tension. He glanced once at his favorite tree, elm twigs against the gold patina of sky, and fumbled for sleep as for a drug. He who had been a boy very credulous of life was no longer greatly interested in the possible and improbable adventures of each new day.

He escaped from reality till the alarm-clock rang, at seven-twenty.

III

It was the best of nationally advertised and quantitatively produced alarm-clocks, with all modern attachments, including cathedral chime, intermittent alarm, and a phosphorescent dial. Babbitt was proud of being awakened by such a rich device. Socially it was almost as creditable as buying expensive cord tires.

He sulkily admitted now that there was no more escape, but he lay and detested the grind of the real-estate business, and disliked his family, and disliked himself for disliking them. The evening before, he had played poker at Vergil Gunch's till midnight, and after such holidays he was irritable before breakfast. It may have been the tremendous home-brewed beer of the prohibition-era and the cigars to which that beer enticed him; it may have been resentment of return from this fine, bold man-world to a restricted region of wives and stenographers, and of suggestions not to smoke so much.

From the bedroom bedside the sleeping-porch, his wife's detestably cheerful "Time to get up, Georgie-boy," and the itchy sound, the brisk and scratch sound, of combing hairs out of a stiff brush.

He grunted; he dragged his thick legs, in faded baby-blue pajamas, from under the khaki blanket; he sat on the edge of the cot, running his fingers through his wild hair, while his plump feet mechanically felt for his slippers. He looked regretfully at the blanket—forever a suggestion to him of freedom and heroism. He had bought it for a camping trip which had never come off. It symbolized gorgeous loafing, gorgeous cursing, virile flannel shirts.

He creaked to his feet, groaning at the waves of pain which passed behind his eyeballs. Though he waited for their scorching recurrence, he looked blurrily out at the yard. It delighted him, as always; it was the neat yard of a successful business man of Zenith; that is, it was perfection, and made him also perfect. He regarded the corrugated iron garage. For the three-hundred-and-sixty-fifth time in a year he reflected, "No class to that tin shack. Have to build me a frame garage. But by golly it's the only thing on the place that isn't up-to-date!" While he stared he thought of a community garage for his acreage development, Glen Oriole. He stopped puffing and jiggling. His arms were akimbo. His petulant, sleep-swollen face was set in hard lines. He suddenly seemed capable, an official, a man to contrive, to direct, to get things done.

On the vigor of his idea he was carried down the hard, clean, unused-looking hall into the bathroom.

Though the house was not large it had, like all houses on Floral Heights, an altogether royal bathroom of porcelain and glazed tile and metal sleek as silver. The towel-rack was a rod of clear glass set in nickel. The tub was long enough for a Prussian Guard, and above the set bowl was a sensational exhibit of toothbrush holder, shaving-brush holder, soap-dish, sponge-dish, and medicine-cabinet, so glittering and so ingenious that they resembled an electrical instrument-board. But the Babbitt whose god was Modern Appliances was not pleased. The air of the bathroom. "Verona has been at it again! 'Stead of sticking to Lilidol, like I've re-peat-ed-ly asked her, she's gone and gotten some confounded stinkum stuff that makes you sick!"

The bath-math was wrinkled and the floor was wet. (His daughter Verona eccentrically took baths in the morning, now and then.) He slipped on the mat, and slid against the tub. He said "Damn!" Furiously he snatched up his tube of shaving-cream, furiously he lathered, with a belligerent slapping of the unctuous brush, furiously he raked his plump cheeks with a safety-razor. It pulled. The blade was dull. He said, "Damn—oh-oh-damn it."

He hunted through the medicine-cabinet for a packet of new razor-blades (reflecting, as invariably, "Be cheaper to buy one of those dinguses and strop your own blades") and when he discovered the packet, behind the round box of bicarbonate of soda, he thought ill of his wife for putting it there and very well of himself for not saying "Damn." But he did say it, immediately afterward, when with wet and soap-slippery fingers he tried to remove the horrible little envelope and crisp clinging oiled paper from the new blade.

Then there was the problem, oft-pondered, never solved, of what to do with the old blade, which might imperil the fingers of his young. As usually, he tossed it on top of the medicine-cabinet, with a mental note that some day he must remove the fifty or sixty other blades that were also temporarily piled up there. He finished his shaving in a growing testiness increased by his spinning headache and by the emptiness in his stomach. When he was done, his round face smooth and streamy and his eyes stinging from soapy water, he reached for a towel. The family towels were wet, wet and clammy and vile, all of them, wet, he found, as he blindly snatched them— his own face-towel, his wife's, Verona, Ted's, Tinka's, and the lone bath-towel with the huge welt of initial. Then George F. Babbitt did a dismaying thing. He wiped his face on the guest-towel! It was a pansy-embroidered trifle which always hung there to indicate that the Babbitts were in the best Floral Heights society. No one had ever used it. No guest had ever dared to. Guests secretively took a corner of the nearest regular towel.

He was raging, "By golly, here they go and use up all the towels, every doggone one of 'em, and they use 'em and get 'em all wet and sopping, and never put out a dry one for me—of course, I'm the goat!—and then I want one and—I'm the only person in the doggone house that's got the slightest doggone bit of consideration for other people and thoughtfulness and consider that there may be others that may want to use the doggone bathroom after me and consider—"

He was pitching the chill abominations into the bathtub, pleased by the vindictiveness of that desolate flapping sound; and in the midst of his wife serenely trotted it, observing serenely, "Why Georgie dear, what are you doing? Are you going to wash out the towels? Why, you needn't wash out the towels. Oh, Georgie, you didn't go and use the guest-towel, did you?"

It is not recorded that he was able to answer.

For the first time in weeks he was sufficiently roused by his wife to look at her.

IV

Myra Babbitt—Mrs. George F. Babbitt—was definitely mature. She had creases from the corner of her mouth to the bottom of her chin, and her plump neck bagged. But the thing that marked her as having passed the line was that she no longer had reticences before her husband,

and no longer worried about not having reticences. She was in a petticoat now, and corsets which bulged, and unaware of being seen in bulgy corset. She had become so dully habituated to married life than in her full matronliness she was as sexless as an anemic nun. She was a good woman, a kind woman, a diligent woman, but no one, save perhaps Tinka, her ten-year-old, was at all interested in her, or entirely aware that she was alive.

After a rather thorough discussion of all the domestic and social aspects of towels she apologized to Babbitt for his having an alcoholic headache; had he recovered enough to endure the search for a B.V.D. undershirt which had, he pointed out, malevolently been concealed among his clean pajamas.

He was fairly amiable in the conference on the brown suit.

"What do you think, Myra?" He pawed at the clothes hunched on a chair in their bedroom, while she moved about mysteriously adjusting and patting her petticoat and, to his jaundiced eye, never seemed to get on with her dressing. "How about it? Shall I wear the brown suit another day?"

"Well, it looks awfully nice on you."

"I know, but gosh, it needs pressing."

"That's so. Perhaps it does."

"It certainly could stand being pressed, all right."

"Yes, perhaps it wouldn't hurt to be pressed."

"But gee, the coat doesn't need pressing. No sense in having the whole darn suit pressed, when the coat doesn't need it."

"That's so."

"But the pants certainly need it, all right. Look at them — look at those wrinkles — the pants certainly do need pressing."

"That's so. Oh, Georgie, why couldn't you wear the brown coat with the blue trousers we were wondering what we'd do with them?"

"Good Lord! Did you ever in all my life know me to wear the coat of one suit and the pants of another? What do you think I am? A busted bookkeeper?"

"Well, why don't you put on the dark suit to-day, and stop in at the tailor and leave the brown trousers?"

"Well, they certainly need — Now where the devil is that gray suit? Oh, yes, here we are."

He was able to get through the other cries of dressing with comparative resoluteness and calm.

His first adornment was the sleeveless dimity B.V.D. undershirt, in which he resembled a small boy humorlessly wearing a cheesecloth tabard at a civic pageant. He never put on B.V.D.'s without thanking the God of Progress that he didn't wear tight, long, old-fashioned undergarments, like his father-in-law and partner, Henry Thompson. His second embellishment was combing and slicking back his hair. It gave him a tremendous forehead, arching up two inches beyond the former hair-line. But most wonder-working of all was the donning of his spectacles.

There is character in spectacles — the pretentious, tortoiseshell, the meek pince-nez of the school teacher, the twisted silver-framed glasses of the old villager. Babbitt's spectacles had huge, circular, frameless lenses of the very best glass; the ear-pieces were thin bars of gold. In them he was the modern business man; one who gave orders to clerks and drove a car and played occasional golf and was scholarly in regard to Salesmanship. His head suddenly appeared not babyish but weighty, and you noted his heavy, blunt nose, his straight mouth and thick, long upper lip, his chin overfleshy but strong; with respect you beheld him on the rest of his uniform as a Solid Citizen.

The gray suit was well cut, well made, and completely undistinguished. It was a standard suit. White piping on the V of the vest added a flavor of law and learning. His shoes were black laced boots, good boots, honest boots, standard boots, extraordinarily uninteresting boots. The only frivolity was in his purple knitted scarf. With considerable comment on the matter to Mrs. B (who, acrobatically fastening the back of her blouse to her skirt with a safety-pin, did not hear a word he said), he chose between the purple scarf and a tapestry effect with stringless brown harps among blown palms, and into it he thrust a snake-head pin with opal eyes.

A sensational event was changing from the brown suit to the gray the contents of his pockets. He was earnest about these objects. They were of eternal importance, like baseball or the Republican Party. They included a fountain pen and a silver pencil (always lacking a supply of new leads) which belonged in the righthand upper vest pocket. Without them he would have felt naked. On his watch-chain were a gold penknife, silver cigar-cutter, seven keys (the use of two which he had forgotten), and incidentally a good watch. Depending from the chain was a large, yellowish elk's-tooth — proclamation of his membership in the Benevolent and Protective Order of Elks. Most significant of all was his loose-leaf pocket note-book, that modern and efficient note-book which contained the addresses of people whom he had forgotten, prudent memoranda of postal money-orders which had reached their destinations months ago, stamps which had lost their mucilage, clippings of verses by T. Cholmondeley Frink and of the newspaper editorials from which Babbitt got his opinions and his polysyllable, notes to be sure and do things which he did not intend to do, and one curious inscription—D.S.S.D.M.Y.P.D.F.

But he had no cigarette-case. No one had ever happened to give him one, so he hadn't the habit, and people who carried cigarette-cases he regarded as effeminate.

Last, he stuck in his lapel the Boosters' Club button. With the conciseness of great art the button displayed two words: "Boosters—Pep!" It made Babbitt feel loyal and important. It associated him with Good Fellows, with men who were nice and human, and important in business circles. It was his V.C., his Legion of Honor ribbon, his Phi Beta Kappa key.

With the subtleties of dressing ran other complex worries. "I feel kind of punk this morning," he said. "I think I had too much dinner last evening. You oughtn't to serve those heavy banana fritters."

"But you asked me to have some."

"I know, but—I tell you, when a fellow gets past forty he has to look after his digestion. There's a lot of fellow that don't take proper care of themselves. I tell you at forty a man's a fool or his doctor—I mean, his own doctor. Folks don't give enough attention to this matter of dieting. Now I think—course a man ought to have a good meal after the day's work, but it would be a good thing for both of us if we took lighter hunches."

"But Georgie, here at home I always do have a light lunch."

"Mean to imply I make a hog of myself, eating downtown? Yes, sure! You'd have a swell time if you had to eat the truck that new steward hands out to as at the Athletic Club! But I certainly do feel out of sorts, this morning. Funny, got a pain down here on the left side—but no, that wouldn't be appendicitis, would it? Last night, when I was driving over to Verg Gunch's. I felt a pain in my stomach, too. Right here it was—kind of a sharp shooting pain. I—Where'd that dime go to? Why don't you serve more prunes at breakfast? Of course I eat an apple every evening—an apple a day keeps the doctor away—but still, you ought to have more prunes, and not all these fancy doodads."

"The last time I had prunes you didn't eat them."

"Well, I didn't feel like eating 'em, I suppose. Matter of fact, I think I did eat some of 'em. Anyway—I tell you it's mighty important to—I was saying to Verg Gunch, just last evening, most people don't take sufficient care of their diges—"

"Shall we have the Gunches for our dinner, next week?"

"Why sure; you bet."

"Now see here, George: I want you to put on your nice dinner-jacket that evening."

"Rats! The rest of 'em won't want to dress."

"Of course they will. You remember when you didn't dress for the Littlefields' supper-party, and all the rest did, and how embarrassed you were."

"Embarrassed, hell! I wasn't embarrassed. Everybody knows I can put on as expensive a Tux, as anybody else, and I should worry if I don't happen to have it on sometimes. All darn nuisance, anyway. All right for a woman, that stays around the house all the time, but when a fellow's worked like the dickens all day, he doesn't want to go and hustle his head off getting into the soup-and-fish for a lot of folks that he's seen in just reg'lar ordinary clothes that same day."

You know you enjoy being seen in one. The other evening you admitted you were glad I'd insisted on your dressing. You said you felt a lot better for it. And oh, Georgie, I do wish you wouldn't say 'Tux.' It's 'dinner-jacket.'"

"Rats, what's the odds?"

"Well, it's what all the nice folks say. Suppose Lucile McKelvey heard you calling it a 'Tux.'"

"Well, that's all right now! Lucile McKelvey can't pull anything on me! Her folks are common as mud, even if her husband and her dad are millionaires! I suppose you're trying to rub in *your* exalted social position! Well, let me tell you that your revered paternal ancestor, Henry T., doesn't even call it a 'Tux.'! He calls it a 'bobtail jacket for a ringtail monkey,' and you couldn't get him into one unless you chloroformed him!"

"Now don't be horrid, George."

"Well, I don't want to be horrid, but Lord! you're getting as fussy as Verona. Ever since she got out of college she's been too rambunctious to live with—doesn't know what she wants—well, I know what she wants!—all she wants is to marry a millionaire, and live in Europe, and hold some preacher's hand, and simultaneously at the same time stay right here in Zenith and be some blooming kind of socialist agitator or boss charity-worker or some damn thing! Lord, and Ted is just as bad! He wants to go to college, and he doesn't want to go to college. Only one of three that knows her own mind is Tinka. Simply can't understand how I ever came to have a pair of shilly-shallying children like Rone and Ted. I may not be any Rockefeller or James J. Shakespeare, but I certainly do know my own mind, and I do keep right on plugging along in the office and—Do you know the latest? Far as I can figure out, Ted's new bee is he'd like to be a movie actor and—And here I've told him a hundred times, if he'll go to college and law-school and make good, I'll set him up in business—Verona just exactly as bad. Doesn't know what she wants. Well, well, come on! Aren't you ready yet? The girl rang the bell three minutes ago."

V

Before he followed his wife, Babbitt stood at the westernmost window of their room. This residential settlement, Floral Heights, was on a rise; and though the center of the city was there miles away—Zenith had between three and four hundred thousand inhabitants now—he could see the top of the Second National Tower, an Indiana limestone building of thirty-five stories.

Its shining walls rose against April sky to a simple cornice like a streak of white fire. Integrity was in the tower, and decision. It bore its strength lightly as a tall soldier. As Babbitt stared, the nervousness was soothed from his face, his slack chin lifted in reverence. All he articulated was, "That's one lovely sight!" but he was inspired by the rhythm of the city; his love of it renewed. He beheld the tower as a temple-spire of the religion of business, a faith passionate, exalted, surpassing common men; and he clumped down to breakfast he whistled the ballad, "Oh, by gee, by gosh, by jingo" as though it were a hymn melancholy and noble. . . .

[Chapter V]

II

As he drove he glanced with the fondness of familiarity at the buildings.

A stranger suddenly dropped into the business-center of Zenith could not have told whether he was in a city of Oregon or Georgia, Ohio or Maine, Oklahoma or Manitoba. But to Babbitt every inch was individual and stirring. As always he noted that the California Building across the way was three stories lower, therefore three stories less beautiful, than his own Reeves Building. As always when he passed the Parthenon Shoe Shine Parlor, a one-story hut which beside the granite and red-brick ponderousness of the old California Building resembled a bath-house under a cliff, he commented, "Gosh, ought to get my shoes shined this afternoon. Keep forgetting it." At the Simplex Office Furniture Shop, the National Cash Register Agency, he yearned for a dictaphone, for a typewriter which would add and multiply, as a poet yearns for quartos or a physician for radium.

At the Nobby Men's Wear Shop he took his left hand off the steering-wheel to touch his scarf, and thought well of himself as one who bought expensive ties "and could pay cash for 'em, by golly"; and at the United Cigar Store, with its crimson and gold alertness, he reflected, "Wonder if I need some cigars—idiot—plumb forgot—t' cut down my fool smoking." He looked at his bank, the Miners' and Drovers' National, and considered how clever and solid he was to bank with so marbled an establishment. His high moment came in the clash of traffic when he was halted at the corner beneath the lofty Second National Tower. His car was banked with four others in a line of steel restless as cavalry, while the crosstown traffic, limousines and enormous moving-vans and insistent motor-cycles, poured by; on the farther corner, pneumatic riveters rang on the sun-plated skeleton of a new building; and out of this tornado flashed the inspiration of a familiar face, and a fellow Booster shouted, "H' are you, George!" Babbitt waved in neighborly fashion, and slid on with the traffic as the policeman lifted his hand. He noted how quickly his car picked up. He felt superior and powerful, like a shuttle of polished steel darting in a vast machine.

As always he ignored the next two blocks, decayed blocks not yet reclaimed from the grime and shabbiness of the Zenith of 1885. While he was passing the five-and-ten-cent store, the Dakota Lodging House, Corcordia Hall with its lodge-rooms and the offices of fortune-tellers and chiropractors, he thought of how much money he made, and he boasted a little and worried a little and did old familiar sums:

"Four hundred and fifty plunks this morning from the Lyte deal. But taxes due. Let's see; I ought to pull out eight thousand net this year, and save fifteen hundred of that—no, not if I put up garage and—Let's see: six hundred and forty clear last month, and twelve times six-forty makes—makes—let see: six times twelve is seventy-two hundred and— Oh rats, anyway, I'll make eight thousand—gee now, that's not bad; mighty few fellows pulling down eight thousand dollars a year—eight thousand good hard iron dollars—but there isn't more than five per cent of the people in the whole United States that makes more than Uncle George does, by golly! Right up at the top of the heap! But—Way expenses are—Family wasting gasoline, and always dressed like millionaires, and sending that eighty a month to Mother—And all these stenographers and salesmen gouging me for every cent they can get—"

The effect of his scientific budget-planning was that he felt at once triumphantly wealthy and perilously poor, and in the midst of these dissertations he stopped his car, rushed into a small news-and-miscellany shop, and bought the electric cigar-lighter which he had coveted for a week. He dodged his conscience by being jerky and noisy, and by shouting at the clerk, "Guess this will prett' near pay for itself in matches, eh?"

It was a pretty thing, a nickeled cylinder with an almost silvery socket, to be attached to the dashboard of his car. It was not only, as the placard on the counter observed, "a dandy little refinement, lending the last touch of class to a gentleman's auto," but a priceless time-saver. By freeing him from halting the car to light a match, it would in a month or two easily save ten minutes.

As he drove on he glanced at it. "Pretty nice. Always wanted one," he said wistfully. "The one thing a smoker needs, too."

Then he remembered that he had given up smoking.

"Darn it!" he mourned. "Oh well, I suppose I'll hit a cigar once in a while. And—Be a great convenience for other folks. Might make just the difference in getting chummy with some fellow that would put over a sale. And—Certainly looks nice there. Certainly is a might clever little jigger. Gives the last touch of refinement and class. I—By golly, I guess I can afford it if I want to! Not going to be the only member of this family that never has a single doggone luxury!"

Thus, laden with treasure, after three and a half blocks of romantic adventure, he drove up to the club.

III

The Zenith Athletic Club is not athletic and it isn't exactly a club, but it is Zenith in perfection. It has an active and smoke-misted billiard room, it is represented by baseball and football teams, and in the pool and the gymnasium a tenth of the members sporadically try to reduce. But most of its three thousand members use it as a café in which to lunch, play cards, tell stories, meet customers, and entertain out-of-town uncles at dinner. It is the largest club in the city, and its chief hatred is the conservative Union Club, which all sound members of the Athletic call "a rotten, snobbish, dull, expensive old hole—not one Good Mixer in the place—you couldn't hire me to join." Statistics show that no member of the Athletic has ever refused election to the Union, and of those who are elected, sixty-seven per cent, resign from the Athletic and are thereafter hard to say, in the drowsy sanctity of the Union lounge, "The Athletic would be a pretty good hotel, if it were more exclusive."

The Athletic Club building is nine stories high, yellow brick with glassy roof-garden above and portico of huge limestone columns below. The lobby, with its thick pillars of porous Caen stone, its pointed vaulting, and a brown glazed-tile floor like well-baked breadcrust, is a combination of cathedral-crypt and rathskellar. The members rush into the lobby as though they were shopping and hadn't much time for it. Thus did Babbitt enter, and to the group standing by the cigar-counter he whooped, "How's the boys? How's the boys? Well, well, fine day!"

Jovially they whooped back—Vergil Gunch, the coal-dealer, Sidney Finkelstein, the ladies'-ready-to-wear buyer for Parcher & Stein's department store, and Professor John K. Pumphrey, owner of the Riteway Business College and instructor in Public Speaking, Business English, Scenario Writing, and Commercial Law. Though Babbitt admired this savant and appreciated Sidney Finkelstein as "a mighty smart buyer and a good liberal spender" it was to Vergil Gunch that he turned with enthusiasm. Mr. Gunch was president of the Boosters' Club, a weekly lunch-club, local chapter of a national organization which promoted sound business and friendliness among Regular Fellows. He was also no less an official than Esteemed Leading Knight in the Benevolent and Protective Order of Elks, and it was rumored that at the next election he would be a candidate for Exalted Ruler. He was a jolly man, given to oratory and to chumminess with the arts. He called on the famous actors and vaudeville artists when they came to town, gave them cigars, addressed them by their first names, and—sometimes—succeeded in bringing them to the Boosters' lunches to give The Boys a Free Entertainment. He was a large man with hair *en brosse*, and he knew the latest jokes, but he played poker close to the chest. It was at his party that Babbitt had sucked in the virus of to-day's restlessness.

Gunch shouted, "How's the old Bolsheviki?" How do you feel, the morning after the night before?"

"Oh, boy! Some head! That was a regular party you threw, Verg! Hope you haven't forgotten I took that last cute little jack-pot!" Babbitt bellowed. (He was three feet from Gunch.)

"That's all right now! What I'll hand you next time, Georgie! Say, juh notice in the paper the way the New York Assembly stood up to the Reds?"

"You bit I did. That was fine, eh? Nice day to-day."

"Yes, it's one might fine spring day, but nights still cold."

"Yeh, you're right they are! Had to have coupla blankets last night, out on the sleeping-porch. Say, Sid,"

Babbitt turned to Finkelstein, the buyer, "got something wanta ask you about. I went out and bought me an electric cigar-lighter for the car, this noon, and—"

"Good hunch!" said Finkelstein, while even the learned Professor Pumphrey, a bulbous man with a pepper-and-salt cutaway and a pipe-organ voice, commented, "That makes a dandy accessory. Cigar-lighter gives tone to the dashboard."

"Yep, finally decided I'd buy me one. Got the best on the market, the clerk said it was. Paid five bucks for it. Just wondered if I got stuck. What do they charge for 'em at the store, Sid?"

Finkelstein asserted that five dollars was not too great a sum, not for a really high-class lighter which was suitably nickeled and provided with connections of the very best quality. "I always say—and believe me, I base it on a pretty fairly extensive mercantile experience—the best is the cheapest in the long run. Of course if a fellow wants to be a Jew about it, he can get cheap junk, but in the long *run*, the cheapest thing is—the best you can get! Now you take here just th' other day: I got a new top for my old boat and some upholstery, and I paid out a hundred and twenty-six fifty, and of course a lot of fellows would say that was too much—Lord, if the Old Folks—they live in one of those hick towns up-date and they simply can't get onto the way a city fellow's mind works, and then, of course, they're Jews, and they'd lie right down and die if they knew Sid had anted up a hundred and twenty-six bones. But I don't figure I was stuck, George, not a bit. Machine looks brand new now—not that it's so darned old, of course; had it less 'n three years, but I give it hard service; never drive less 'n a hundred miles on Sunday and, uh—Oh, I don't really think you got stuck, George. In the *long* run, the best is, you might say, it's unquestionably the cheapest."

"That's right," said Vergil Gunch. "That's the way I look at it. If a fellow is keyed up to what you might call intensive living, the way you get it here in Zenith—all the hustle and mental activity that's going on with a bunch of live-wires like the Boosters and here in the Z.A.C., why, he's got to save his nerves by having the best."

Babbitt nodded his head at every fifth word in the roaring rhythm; and by the conclusion, in Gunch's renowned humorous vein, he was enchanted.

"Still, at that, Joseph, don't know's you can afford it. I've heard your business has been kind of under the eye of the gov'ment since you stole the tail of Eathorne Park and sold it!"

"Oh, you're a great little josher, Verg. But when it comes to kidding, how about this report that you stole the black marble steps off the post-office, and sold 'em for high-grade coal!" In delight Babbitt patted Gunch's back, stroked his arm.

"That's all right, but what I wanted to know is: who's the real-estate shark that bought that coal for his apartment-houses?"

"I guess that'll hold you for a while, George?" said Finkelstein. "I'll tell you, though, boys, what I did hear: George's missus went into the gents' wear department at Parcher's to buy him some collars, and before she could give his neck-size the clerk slips her some thirteens. 'How juh know the size?' says Mrs. Babbitt, and the clerk says, 'Men that let their wives buy collars for 'em always wear thirteen, madam.' How's that! That's pretty good, eh? How's that, eh? I guess that'll about fix you, George!"

129. Ernest Hemingway, "Soldier's Home," 1925

The toughness, economy, and control of the literary style of Ernest Hemingway (1898–1961) made it one of the major literary forces during and since the 1920s. Searching for personal authenticity in a world gone mad with comfort and anonymity, Hemingway always remained the tough guy from Oak Park, Illinois. In the revealing story, "Soldier's Home," Hemingway says much of what he was to repeat in longer works. The central figure of the story, Harold Krebs, is forced to distort and exaggerate his war experiences in order to retain attention; these lies lead to nausea and turn him against his own experience.

Krebs went to the war from a Methodist college in Kansas. There is a picture which shows him among his fraternity brothers, all of them wearing exactly the same height and style collar. He enlisted in the Marines in 1917 and did not return to the United States until the second division returned from the Rhine in the summer of 1919.

There is a picture which shows him on the Rhine with two German girls and another corporal. Krebs and the corporal look too big for their uniforms. The German girls are not beautiful. The Rhine does not show in the picture.

By the time Krebs returned to his home town in Oklahoma the greeting of heroes was over. He came back much too late. The men from the town who had been drafted had all been welcomed elaborately on their return. There had been a great deal of hysteria. Now the reaction had set in. People seemed to think it was rather ridiculous for Krebs to be getting back so late, years after the war was over.

At first Krebs, who had been at Belleau Wood, Soissons, the Champagne, St. Mihiel and in the Argonne did not want to talk about the war at all. Later he felt the need to talk but no one wanted to hear about it. His town had heard too many atrocity stories to be thrilled by actualities. Krebs found that to be listened to at all he had to lie, and after he had done this twice he, too, had a reaction against the war and against talking about it. A distaste for everything that had happened to him in the war set in because of the lies he had told. All of the times that had been able to make him feel cool and clear inside himself when he thought of them; the times so long back when he had done the one thing, the only thing for a man to do, easily and naturally, when he might have done something else, now lost their cool, valuable quality and then were lost themselves.

His lies were quite unimportant lies and consisted in attributing to himself things other men has seen, done or heard of, and stating as facts certain apocryphal incidents familiar to all soldiers. Even his lies were not sensational at the pool room. His acquaintances, who had heard detailed accounts of German women found chained to machine guns in the Argonne forest and who could not comprehend, or were barred by their patriotism from interest in, any German machine gunners who were not chained, were not thrilled by his stories.

Krebs acquired the nausea in regard to experience that is the result of untruth or exaggeration, and when he occasionally met another man who had really been a soldier and they talked a few minutes in the dressing room at a dance he fell into the easy pose of the old soldier among other soldiers: that he had been badly, sickeningly frightened all the time. In this way he lost everything.

During this time, it was late summer, he was sleeping late in bed, getting up to walk down town to the library to get a book, eating lunch at home, reading on the front porch until he became bored and then walking down through the town to spend the hottest hours of the day in the cool dark of the pool room. He loved to play pool.

In the evening he practiced on his clarinet, strolled down town, read and went to bed. He was still a hero of

---

Source: Ernest Hemingway, "Soldier's Home," in *In Our Time.* Reprinted with permission of Charles Scribner's Sons, an Imprint of MacMillan Publishing Company. Copyright 1925 by Charles Scribner's Sons; renewal copyright 1953 by Ernest Hemingway.

his two young sisters. His mother would have given him breakfast in bed if he had wanted it. She often came in when he was in bed and asked him to tell her about the war, but her attention always wandered. His father was non-committal.

Before Krebs went away to the war he had never been allowed to drive the family motor car. His father was in the real estate business and always wanted the car to be at his command when he required it to take clients out into the country to show them a piece of farm property. The car always stood outside the First National Bank building where his father had an office on the second floor. Now, after the war, it was still the same car.

Nothing was changed in the town except that the young girls had grown up. But they lived in such a complicated world of already defined alliances and shifting feuds that Krebs did not feel the energy or the courage to break into. He liked to look at them, though. There were so many good-looking young girls. Most of them had their hair cut short. When he went away only little girls wore their hair like that or girls that were fast. They all wore sweaters and shirt waists with round Dutch collars. It was a pattern. He liked to look at them from the front porch as they walked on the other side of the street. He liked to watch them walking under the shade of the trees. He liked the round Dutch collars above their sweaters. He liked their silk stockings and flat shoes. He liked their bobbed hair and the way they walked.

When he was in town their appeal to him was not very strong. He did not like them when he saw them in the Greek's ice cream parlor. He did not want them themselves really. They were too complicated. There was something else. Vaguely he wanted a girl but he did not want to have to work to get her. He would have liked to have a girl but he did not want to have to spend a long time getting her. He did not want to get into the intrigue and the politics. He did not want to have to do any courting. He did not want to tell any more lies. It wasn't worth it.

He did not want any consequences. He did not want any consequences ever again. He wanted to live along without consequences. Besides he did not really need a girl. The army had taught him that. It was all right to pose as though you had to have a girl. Nearly everybody did that. But it wasn't true. You did not need a girl. That was the funny thing. First a fellow boasted how girls mean nothing to him, that he never thought of them, that they could not touch him. Then a fellow boasted that he could not get along without girls, that he had to have them all the time, that he could not go to sleep without them.

That was all a lie. It was a lie both ways. You did not need a girl unless you thought about them. He learned that in the army. Then sooner or later you always got one. When you were really ripe for a girl you always got one. You did not have to think about it. Sooner or later it would come. He had learned that in the army.

Now he would have liked a girl if she had come to him and not wanted to talk. But here at home it was all too complicated. He knew he could never get through it all again. It was not worth the trouble. That was the thing about French girls and German girls. There was not all this talking. You couldn't talk much and you did not need to talk. It was simple and you were friends. He thought about France and then he began to think about Germany. On the whole he had liked Germany better. He did not want to leave Germany. He did not want to come home. Still, he had come home. He sat on the front porch.

He liked the girls that were walking along the other side of the street. He liked the look of them much better than the French girls or the German girls. But the world they were in was not the world he was in. He would like to have one of them. But it was not worth it. They were such a nice pattern. He liked the pattern. It was exciting. But he would not go through all the talking. He did not want one badly enough. He liked to look at them all, though. It was not worth it. Not now when things were getting good again.

He sat there on the porch reading a book on the war. It was a history and he was reading about all the engagements he had been in. It was the most interesting reading he had ever done. He wished there were more maps. He looked forward with a good feeling to reading all the really good histories when they would come out with good detail maps. Now he was really learning about the war. He had been a good soldier. That made a difference.

One morning after he had been home about a month his mother came into his bedroom and sat on the bed. She smoothed her apron.

"I had a talk with your father last night, Harold," she said, "and he is willing for you to take the car out in the evenings."

"Yeah?" said Krebs, who was not fully awake. "Take the car out? Yeah?"

"Yes. Your father has felt for some time that you should be able to take the car out in the evenings whenever you wished but we only talked it over last night."

"I'll bet you made him," Krebs said.

"No. It was your father's suggestion that we talk the matter over."

"Yeah. I'll bet you made him." Krebs sat up in bed.

"Will you come down to breakfast, Harold? his mother said.

"As soon as I get my clothes on," Krebs said.

His mother went out of the room and he could hear her frying something downstairs while he washed, shaved and dressed to go down to the dining-room for breakfast. While he was eating breakfast his sister brought in the mail.

"Well, Hare," she said. "You old sleepyhead. What do you ever get up for?"

Krebs looked at her. He liked her. She was his best sister.

"Have you got the paper?" he asked.

She handed him the Kansas City *Star* and he shucked off its brown wrapper and opened it to the sporting page. He folded the *Star* open and propped it against the water pitcher with his cereal dish to steady it, so he could read while he ate.

"Harold," his mother stood in the kitchen doorway, "Harold, please don't muss up the paper. Your father can't read his *Star* if it's been mused."

"I won't muss it," Krebs said.

His sister sat down at the table and watched him while he read.

"We're playing indoor over at school this afternoon," she said. "I'm going to pitch."

"Good," said Krebs. "How the old wing?"

"I can pitch better than lots of the boys. I tell them all you taught me. The other girls aren't much good."

"Yeah?" said Krebs.

"I tell them all you're my beau. Aren't you my beau, Hare?"

"You bet."

"Couldn't your brother really be your beau just because he's your brother?"

"I don't know."

"Sure you know. Couldn't you be my beau, Hare, if I was old enough and if you wanted to."

"Sure. You're my girl now."

"Am I really your girl?"

"Sure."

"Do you love me?"

"Uh, huh."

"Will you love me always?"

"Sure."

"Will you come over and watch me play indoor?"

"Maybe."

"Aw, Hare, you don't love me. If you loved me, you'd want to come over and watch me play indoor."

Kreb's mother came into the dining-room from the kitchen. She carried a plate with two fried eggs and some crisp bacon on it and a plate of buckwheat cakes.

"You run along, Helen," she said. "I want to talk to Harold."

She put the eggs and bacon down in front of him and brought in a jug of maple syrup for the buckwheat cakes. Then she sat down across the table from Krebs.

"I wish you'd put down the paper a minute, Harold," she said.

Krebs took down the paper and folded it.

"Have you decided what you are going to do yet, Harold?" his mother said, taking off her glasses.

"No," said Krebs.

"Don't you think it's about time?" His mother did not say this in a mean way. She seemed worried.

"I hadn't thought about it," Krebs said.

"God has some work for everyone to do," his mother said. "There can be no idle hands in His Kingdom."

"I'm not in His Kingdom," Krebs said.

"We are all of us in His Kingdom."

Krebs felt embarrassed and resentful, as always.

"I've worried about you so much, Harold," his mother went on. "I know the temptations you must have been exposed to. I know how weak men are. I know what your own dear grandfather, my own father, told us about the Civil War and I have prayed for you. I pray for you all day long, Harold."

Krebs looked at the bacon fat hardening on his plate.

"Your father is worried too," his mother went on. "HE thinks you have lost your ambition, that you haven't got a definite aim in life. Charley Simmons, who is just your age, has a good job and is going to be married. The boys are all settling down; they're all determined to get somewhere; you can see that boys like Charley Simmons are on their way to being really a credit to the community."

Krebs said nothing.

"Don't look that way, Harold," his mother said. "You know we love you and I want to tell you for your own good how matters stand. Your father does not want to hamper your freedom. He thinks you should be allowed to drive the car. If you want to take some of the nice girls out riding with you, we are only too pleased. We want you to enjoy yourself. But you are going to have to settle down to work, Harold. Your father doesn't care what you start in at. All work is honorable as he says. But you've got to make a start at something. He asked me to speak to you this morning and then you can stop in and see him at his office."

"Is that all?" Krebs said.

"Yes. Don't you love your mother, dear boy?"

"No," Krebs said.

His mother looked at him across the table. Her eyes were shiny. She started crying.

"I don't love anybody," Krebs said.

It wasn't any good. He couldn't tell her, he couldn't make her see it. It was silly to have said it. HE had only hurt her. He went over and took hold of her arm. She was crying with her head in her hands.

"I didn't mean it," he said. "I was just angry at something. I didn't mean I didn't love you."

His mother went on crying. Krebs put his arms on her shoulder.

"Can't you believe me, mother?"

His mother shook her head.

"Please, please, mother. Please believe me."

"All right," his mother said chokily. She looked up at him. "I believe you, Harold."

Krebs kissed her hair. She put her face up to him.

"I'm your mother," she said. "I held you next to my heart when you were a tiny baby."

Krebs felt sick and vaguely nauseated.

"I know, Mummy," he said. "I'll try and be a good boy for you."

"Would you kneel and pray with me, Harold," his mother asked.

They knelt down beside the dining-room table and Krebs' mother prayed.

"Now, you pray, Harold," she said.

"I can't," Krebs said.

"Try, Harold."

"I can't."

"Do you want me to pray for you?"

"Yes."

So his mother prayed for him and then they stood up and Krebs kissed his mother and went out of the house. He had tried so to keep his life from being complicated. Still, none of it had touched him. He had felt sorry for his mother and she had made him lie. He would go to Kansas City and get a job and she would feel all right about it. There would be one more scene before he got away. He would not go down to his father's office. He would miss that one. He wanted his life to go smoothly. It had just gotten going that way. Well, that was all over now, anyway. He would go over to the schoolyard and watch Helen play indoor baseball.

130. H. L. Mencken, "Was Bryan Sincere?," 1925

William Jennings Bryan died a few days after the close of the Scopes trial, and H. L. Mencken (1880–1956) noted the fact in a three-page editorial in The American Mercury. *Mencken's reputation in the Twenties was enormous, based in part on his literary felicity, searing wit, and absolutely complete disdain for the country yokels, their spokesmen, their politics, and their way of life. He tried to represent the urbane, civilized men beset by all the crudeness and crassness of provincial America. Understanding the tension between urban and village America, Mencken found his perfect but dangerous fool in Bryan, as the following characterization of "The Great Commoner" will show.*

Source: H. L. Mencken, "Editorial." *The American Mercury*, VI, 22 (October 1925), pp. 158–160. From "Obituary of William Jennings Bryan" by H.L. Mencken. Reprinted by permission of *The American Mercury*. [Reprinted with permission of MacMillan College Publishing Company from THE CULTURE OF THE TWENTIES, edited by Loren Baritz, Copyright 1970 by MacMillan College Publishing Company.]

Had it been marked by historians that the late William Jennings Bryan's last secular act on this earth was to catch flies? A curious detail, and not without its sardonic overtones. He was the most sedulous fly-catcher in American history, and by long odds the most successful. His quarry, of course, was not *Musca domesica* but *Homo neandertalensis*. For forty years he tracked it with snare and blunderbuss, up and down the backways of the Republic. Wherever the flambeaux of Chautauqua smoked and guttered, and the bilge of Idealism ran in the veins, and Baptist pastors dammed the brooks with the saved, and men gathered who were weary and heavy laden, and their wives who were unyielding multiparous and full of Peruna—there the indefatigable Jennings set up his traps and spread his bait. He knew every forlorn country town in the South and West, and he could crowd the most remote of them to suffocation by simply winding his horn. The city proletariat, transiently flustered by him in 1896, quickly penetrated his buncombe and would have no more of him; the gallery jeered him at every Democratic national convention for twenty-five years. But out where the grass grows high, and the horned cattle dream away the lazy days, and men still fear the powers and principalities of the air—out there between the corn-rows he held his old puissance to the end. There was no need of beaters to drive in his game. The news that he was coming was enough. For miles the flivver dust would choke the roads. And when he rose at the end of the day to discharge his Message there would be such breathless attention, such a rapt and enchanted ecstasy, such a sweet rustle of amens as the world had not known since Jonathan fell to Herod's headsman.

There was something peculiarly fitting in the fact that his last days were spent in a one-horse Tennessee village, and that death found him there. The man felt at home in such scenes. He liked people who sweated freely, and were not debauched by the refinements of the toilet. Making his progress up and down the Main street of little Dayton, surrounded by gaping primates from the upland valleys of the Cumberland Range, his coat laid aside, his bare arms and hairy chest shining damply, his bald head sprinkled with dust—so accoutred and on display he was obviously happy. He liked getting up early in the morning, to the tune of cocks crowing on the dunghill. He liked the heavy, greasy victuals of the farm house kitchen. He liked country lawyers, country pastors, all country people. I believe that this liking was sincere—perhaps the only sincere thing in the man. His nose showed no uneasiness when a hill-man in faded overalls and hickory shirt accosted him on the street, and besought him for light upon some mystery of Holy Writ. The simian gabble of a country town was not gabble to him, but wisdom of an occult and superior sort. In the presence of city folks he was palpably uneasy. Their clothes, I suspect, annoyed him, and he was suspicious of their too delicate manners. He knew all the while that they were laughing at him—if not at his baroque theology, then at least at his alpaca pantaloons. But the yokels never laughed at him. To them he was not the huntsman but the prophet, and toward the end, as he gradually forsook mundane politics for purely ghostly concerns, they began to elevate him in their hierarchy. When he died he was the peer of Abraham. Another curious detail: his old enemy, Wilson, aspiring to the same white and shining robe, came down with a thump. But Bryan made the grade. His place in the Tennessee hagiocracy is secure. If the village barber saved any of his hair, then it is curing gall-stones down there today.

II

But what label will he bear in more urbane regions? One, I fear, of a far less flattering kind. Bryan lived too long, and descended too deeply into the mud, to be taken seriously hereafter by fully literate men, even of the kind who write schoolbooks. There was a scattering of sweet words in his funeral notices, but it was no more than a response to conventional sentimentality. The best verdict the most romantic editorial writer could dredge up, save in the eloquent South, was to the general effect that his imbecilities were excused by his earnestness—that under his clowning, as under that of the juggler of Notre Dame, there was the zeal of a steadfast soul. But this was apology, not praise; precisely the same thing might be said of Mary Baker G. Eddy, the late Czar Nicholas, or Czolgosz. The truth is that even Bryan's sincerity will probably yield to what is called, in other fields, definitive criticism. Was he sincere when he opposed imperialism in the Philippines, or when he fed it with deserving Democrats in Santo Domingo? Was he sincere when he tried to shove the Prohibitionists under the table, or when he seized their banner and began to lead them with loud whoops? Was he sincere when he bellowed against war, or when he dreamed of himself as a tin-solder in uniform, with a grave reserved among the generals? Was he sincere when he denounced the late John W. Davis, or when he swallowed Davis? Was he sincere when he fawned over Champ Clark, or when he betrayed Clark? Was he sincere when he pleaded for tolerance in New York, or when he bawled for the fagot and the stake in Tennessee?

This talk of sincerity, I confess, fatigues me. If the fellow was sincere, then so was P.T. Barnum. The word is disgraced and degraded by such uses. He was, in fact, a charlatan, a mountebank, a zany without shame or dignity. What animated him from end to end of his grotesque career was simply ambition—the ambition of a common man to get his hand upon the collar of his superiors, or, failing that, to get his thumb into their eyes. He was born with a roaring voice, and it had the trick of inflaming half-wits. His whole career was devoted to raising these half-wits against their betters, that he himself might shine. His last battle will be grossly misunderstood if it is thought of as a mere exercise in fanaticism—that is, if Bryan the Fundamentalist Pope is mistaken for one of the bucolic Fundamentalists. There was much more in it than that, as everyone knows who saw him on the field. What moved him, at bottom, was simply hatred of the city men who had laughed at him so long, and brought him at last to so tatterdemalion an estate. He lusted for revenge upon them. He yearned to lead the anthropoid rabble against them, to set *Homo neandertalensis* upon them, to punish them for the execution they had done upon him by attacking the very vitals of their civilization. He went far beyond the bounds of any merely religious frenzy, however inordinate. When he began denouncing the notion that man is a mammal even some of the hinds at Dayton were agape. And when, brought upon Darrow's cruel hook, he writhed and tossed in a very fury of malignancy, bawling against the baldest elements of sense and decency like a man frantic—when he came to that tragic climax there were snickers among the hinds as well as hosannas.

Upon that hook, in truth, Bryan committed suicide, as a legend as well as in the body. He staggered from the rustic court ready to die, and he staggered from it ready to be forgotten, save as a character in a third-rate farce, witless and in execrable taste. The chances are that history will put the peak of democracy in his time; it has been on the downward curve among us since the campaign of 1896. He will be remembered, perhaps, as its supreme impostor, the *reductio ad absurdum* of its pretension. Bryan came very near being President of the United States. In 1896, it is possible, he was actually elected. He lived long enough to make patriots thank the inscrutable gods for Harding, even for Coolidge. Dulness has got into the White House, and the smell of cabbage boiling, but there is at least nothing to compare to the intolerable buffoonery that went on in Tennessee. The President of the United States doesn't believe that the earth is square, and that witches should be put to death, and that Jonah swallowed the whale. The Golden Text is not painted weekly on the White House wall, and there is no need to keep ambassadors waiting while Pastor Simpson, of Smithsville, prays for rain in the Blue Room. We have escaped something—by a narrow margin, but still safely.

III

That is, so far. The Fundamentalists continue at the wake, and sense gets a sort of reprieve. The legislature of Georgia, so the news comes, has shelved the anti-evolution bill, and turns its back upon the legislature of Tennessee. Elsewhere minorities prepare for battle—here and there with some assurance of success. But it is too early, it seems to me, to send the firemen home; the fire is still burning on many a far-flung hill, and it may begin to roar again at any moment. The evil that men do lives after them. Bryan, in his malice, started something that it will not be easy to stop. In ten thousand country towns his old heelers, the evangelical pastors, are propagating his gospel, and everywhere the yokels are ready for it. When he disappeared from the big cities, the big cities made the capital error of assuming that he was done for. If they heard of him at all, it was only as a crimp for real-estate speculators—the heroic foe of the unearned increment hauling it in with both hands. He seemed preposterous, and hence harmless. But all the while he was busy among his old lieges, preparing for a *jacquerie* that should floor all his enemies at one blow. He did the job completely. He has vast skill at such enterprises. Heave an egg out of a Pullman window, and you will hit a Fundamentalist almost anywhere in the United States today. They swarm in the country towns, inflamed by their pastors, and with a saint, now, to venerate. They are thick in the mean streets behind the gasworks. They are everywhere that learning is too heavy a burden for mortal minds, even the vague, pathetic learning on tap in little red schoolhouses. They march with the Klan, with the Christian Endeavor Society, with the Junior Order of United American Mechanics, with the Epworth League, with all the rococo bands that poor and unhappy folk organize to bring some light of purpose into their lives. They have had a thrill, and they are ready for more.

Such is Bryan's legacy to his country. He couldn't be President, but he could at least help magnificently in the solemn business of shutting off the presidency from every intelligent and self-respecting man. The storm, perhaps won't last long, as time goes in history. It may help, indeed, to break up the democratic delusion, now already showing weakness, and so hasten its own end. But while it lasts it will blow off some roofs and flood some sanctuaries.

131. W. B. Riley, "The Fundamentalists' Point of View," 1927

Religious Fundamentalism was provincial America's most characteristic attribute during the Twenties. It was, as both its advocates and critics agreed, a folk movement, of the countryside and small towns. The sensational Scopes trial had emphasized some of the bitterness elicited by the confrontation of Fundamentalism and liberalism, but that trial was merely a dramatic moment in a continuing battle. The following selection by W. B. Riley, a pastor of the First Baptist Church of Minneapolis, a founder of the Anti-Evolution League, and president of the World's Christian Fundamentals Association, reveals the doctrinal and emotional pitch of this essentially provincial mentality. Riley wrote many books defending Fundamentalism, along with the following article, an unusually lucid and articulate assertion of this position. It was the position that Sinclair Lewis explored in **Elmer Gantry,** *and the one that drove H. L. Mencken to his most devastating prose. It was also the one that typified many millions of Americans in virtually every non-urban area of the nation.*

What is Fundamentalism? It would be quite impossible, within the limits of a single article, so to treat the subject as to satisfy all interested parties. There are too many features of this Christian faith for one to attempt a delineation. But there are at least three major propositions that must appear in any adequate reply and they are these: It is the Christian Creed; it is the Christian Character; it is the Christian Commission.

Source: Reprinted with permission from *Current History* magazine, p. 434–440. June 1927. Copyright 1927, Current History, Inc.

The Greater Christian Doctrines

Fundamentalism undertakes to reaffirm the greater Christian doctrines. Mark this phrase, "the greater Christian doctrines." It does not attempt to set forth every Christian doctrine. It has never known the elaboration that characterizes the great denominational confessions. But it did lay them side by side, and, out of their extensive statements, elect nine points upon which to rest its claims to Christian attention. They were and are as follows:

1. We believe in the Scriptures of the Old and New Testament as verbally inspired by God and inerrant in the original writings, and that they are of supreme and final authority in faith and life.
2. We believe in one God, eternally existing in three persons, Father, Son and Holy Spirit.
3. We believe Jesus Christ was begotten by the Holy Spirit, and born of the Virgin Mary, and is true God and true man.
4. We believe that man was created in the image of God, that he sinned and thereby incurred not only physical death, but also that spiritual death which is separation from God; and that all human beings are born with a sinful nature, and, in the case of those who reach moral responsibility, become sinners in thought, word and deed.
5. We believe that the Lord Jesus Christ died for our sins according to the Scriptures as a representative and substitutionary sacrifice; and that all that believe in Him are justified on the ground of His shed blood.
6. We believe in the resurrection of the crucified body of our Lord, in His ascension into Heaven, and in His present life there for us, as High Priest and Advocate.
7. We believe in "that blessed hope," the personal, premillennial and imminent return of our Lord and Saviour, Jesus Christ.
8. We believe that all who receive by faith that Lord Jesus Christ are born again of the Holy Spirit and thereby become children of God.

9. We believe in the bodily resurrection of the just and the unjust, the everlasting felicity of the saved and the everlasting conscious suffering of the lost.

It would seem absolutely clear, therefore, that many of the liberal writers of recent years have never taken the pains to ask for the basis of our belief. . . .

Modernism when it comes to deal with the Fundamentals movement is suddenly possessed with a strange imagination. If you want to know what the movement is *not* and who is leaders are *not*, read their descriptions of both. Certainly as to what we believe, the above declaration leaves no doubt, and only the man ignorant of the Bible or utterly indifferent to its teachings, could ever call into question that these nine points constitute the greater essentials in the New Testament doctrinal system.

Fundamentalism insists upon the plain intent of Scripture-speech. The members of this movement have no sympathy whatever for that weasel method of sucking the meaning out of words and then presenting the empty shells in an attempt to palm them off as giving the Christian faith a new and another interpretation. The absurdities to which such a spiritualizing method may lead are fully revealed in the writings of Mary Baker Eddy and modernists in general. When one is permitted to discard established and scientific definitions and to create, at will, his own glossary, language fails to be longer a vehicle of thought, and inspiration itself may mean anything or nothing, according to the preference of its employer. . . .

"Forever Settled in Heaven"

There are men who would join us tomorrow if we omitted the seventh point from our doctrinal statement, and they marvel that we permit it to remain in our declaration, knowing its divisive effect. Our answer is: Fundamentalism insists upon the plain intent of Scripture-speech and knows no method by which it can logically receive the multiplied and harmonious teachings of the Book concerning one doctrine and reject them concerning another. The greater doctrines are not individual opinions that can be handled about at pleasure. In the judgment of the Fundamentalists they are "forever settled in heaven." "Holy men of God, who spake as if they were borne along by the Holy Ghost," have told us the truth—God's truth—and truth is as unchangeable as imperishable. "Scripture cannot be broke." The "truth of the Lord endureth forever." . . . And it not only endures forever, but it remains forever the same—the same in words, the same in meaning, the same in spiritual intent. God's work is incapable of improvement. The sun is old, but the world needs no new or improved one!

Fundamentalism is forever the antithesis of modernist critical theology. It is made up of another and an opposing school. Modernism submits all Scripture to the judgment of man. According to its method he may reject any portion of the Book as uninspired, unprofitable, and even undesirable, and accept another portion as from God because its sentences suit him, or its teachings inspire him. Fundamentalism, on the contrary, makes the Bible "the supreme and final authority in faith and life." Its teachings determine every question upon which they have spoken with some degree of fullness, and its mandates are only disregarded by the unbelieving, the materialistic and the immoral. Fundamentalists hold that the world is illumined and the Church is instructed and even science itself is confirmed, when true, and condemned when false, by the clear teachings of the open Book, while Liberalism, as *The Nation* once said, "pretends to preach the higher criticism by interpreting the sacred writings as esoteric fables." In other words, the two have nothing in common save church membership, and all the world wonders that they do or can remain together; and the thinking world knows that but one tie holds them, and that is the billions of dollars invested.

Nine out of ten of those dollars, if not ninety-nine out of every hundred of them, spent to construct the great denominational universities, colleges, schools of second grade, theological seminaries, great denominational mission stations, the multiplied hospitals that bear denominational names, the immense publication societies and the expensive magazines, were given by Fundamentalists and filched by modernists. It took hundreds of years to collect this money and construct these institutions. It has taken only a quarter of a century for the liberal bandits to capture them, and the only fellowship that remains to bind modernists and Fundamentalists in one body, or a score of bodies, is the Irish fellowship of a free fight—Fundamentalists fighting to retain what they have founded, and modernists fighting to keep their hold on what they have filched. It is a spectacle to grieve angels and amuse devils; but we doubt not that even the devils know where justice lies, and the angels from heaven sympathize with the fight and trust that faithful men will carry on.

Creed alone is neither competent nor convincing. Creed, in the abstract, is cold and dead, but creed incarnate constitutes Christianity as positively as the word incarnate constituted the Christ. Christianity roots in a creed and fruits in character. . . .

Creed and Conduct

The man who combines an unshaken faith in the authority and integrity of the Bible with an aggressive uprightness in conduct, is the man who approaches, in some human measure, the perfect copy in the Christ life, for in His words the most watchful enemies were unable to catch Him and against His works no worthy objection was ever urged. . . .

The proofs of Fundamentalism, then, are not in words, but in deeds. This has been the conception of Fundamentalists from the first, for while the World's Christian Fundamentals Association, as an organization, is but nine years old, the Christian Fundamentalism has back of it two thousand years of glorious history. It was Fundamentalism that produced the Book of Acts. You will find every essential feature of our creed in Peter's sermon at Pentecost, even to the Second Coming. It was Fundamentalism that conquered the Roman Empire, and in one hundred years revised the conduct of men and brought in and established laws of righteousness, including regard for the Sabbath, the rights of the Church in the State, and the recognition of law versus anarchy. It was Fundamentalism that challenged corrupt Rome in Martin Luther's time and called out a people whose clean and wholesome conduct became the condemnation of foul papal practices, and turned the thought of the general public from the coercive measures of a corrupt Church to the intelligent and voluntary service of the King of Glory. It was Fundamentalism that faced the heresy of Deism one hundred and forty years ago, and in an open and fair field fought the battle to the finish, and slew that infidel monster as effectually as Saint George was ever imagined to have trampled the dragon. And it was Fundamentalist evangelists who so uniformly led the common people back to the "faith once delivered" as to bury atheism practically out of sight for one hundred years.

But to battling Fundamentalism has forever added building. Of all the colleges that Congregationalism, of nearly one hundred years ago, contributed to America, commencing with Harvard in the East, dotting practically every State in the Union with at least one. Fundamentalism built the entire line. The same remark applies to the Baptist, Presbyterian and Methodist institutions known to the whole American continent. . . .

Of what value is our boasted accomplishment of mechanical and electrical and chemical discoveries, if, while they are contributing to our material prosperity, they are more rapidly still undermining our morals? The whole doctrine of evolution is not only lacking a single illustration in the processes of nature, but it is being disproven by the program of man, for mechanical invention resulting in moral decay, is not even progress, but degeneration instead. Babylon, Persia, Greece and Rome—each of them reached a climax of material development and then deliberately committed suicide by moral degeneracy. . . .

Future of Fundamentalism

The future of Fundamentalism is not with claims, but with conquests. Glorious as is our past, history provides only an adequate base upon which to build. Fundamentalists will never need to apologize for the part they have played in education; they have produced it; or for their relationship to colleges and universities and theological seminaries, and all forms of social service; they have created them! . . . Now that modernism has come in to filch from us these creations of our creed, we must either wrest them from bandit hands or begin and build again. In the last few years, in fact, since the modernist-highwaymen rose up to trouble the Church and snatch its dearest treasures, it has shown itself as virile as the promise of Christ, "The gates of hell shall not prevail against it," ever indicated. Today there are one hundred schools and colleges connected with our Fundamentalist Association, some of which have escaped the covetous clutches of modernism, but most of which have been brought into being as a protest against modernism itself. Their growth has been so phenomenal as to prove that the old tree is fruitful still, and that the finest fruit is to be found upon its newest branches, orthodox churches, Fundamentalist colleges, sound Bible training schools, evangelical publication societies, multiplied Bible conferences and stanch defenders of the faith in ever increasing numbers in each denomination. . . .

Plight of Modernism

The greatest menace to Fundamentalism today is not the outright modernist. It is that middle-of-the-roader who is milking his denomination with one hand and every wealthy Fundamentalist approachable with the other, in behalf of what he maintains will be "a new

Fundamentalist theological seminary," but who, when once the bucket is filled, will walk away with it to turn it over, again, as has been so often done, to the enemies of Christ. It is this course, employed by not a few in the last five years, that makes it difficult for the sound Fundamentalist institutions to secure help from those who believe with them. . . .

Imagine a mission board willing to send out upon the foreign fields, and fight for their retention and maintenance there, men who deny that declaration in its entirety, disputing alike the atonement made by Christ and His victory over the grave. There is not a week but brings us some report from foreign fields of division on the field itself over the promulgation of "another gospel," "which is no gospel"; of foreign mission schools that scoff at Moses and exalt Darwin; that reduce Christ to the level of a man and degrade Him to the descendant of a monkey, and of mission secretaries that hold to scorn the precious blood He shed, and denominate the declaration of it, "the gospel of shambles."

"Epilepsy of Darwinism"

The tragedy of it all! However, it takes hold of the . . . believers as they think of "the cup of salvation" sent to the Japanese and learn that some man or woman has, while wearing the name of missionary, put into that cup the deadly poison of modernism and made it to effect for those who drink of it, no redemption, but an epilepsy of Darwinism. . . . Think of theological seminaries, endowed to the extent of millions, and still pleading with Fundamentalists to give them more, training the children of Trinitarian believers in the Unitarian philosophy, and sending them forth to pulpits at home and abroad! It is to this non-spiritual, anti-Christian and insane procedure that Fundamentalism objects. Holding absolutely to the authority and integrity of God's Word, it believe itself commissioned by the risen Christ to "teach all nations, baptizing them in the name of the Father and of the Son and of the Holy Ghost." . . .

The Christian commission is to make disciples and not denominationalists. A disciple is a man taught, an instructed believer. We properly translate our commission, "Go ye, therefore, and disciple all nations." The history of the rights of denominationalism might be an interesting study, but it would clearly demonstrate no divinity. There is nothing in the New Testament to advocate or even justify its existence. The Bible is not a book so difficult of understanding as to separate men into factions. The trouble is they have come to it with their prejudiced opinions, with their fixed philosophies and have tried to find in its sacred pages the differences of inherited heresies, and denominationalism has been the result. . . .

Strangest of all things, the very men who are now seeking to save denominationalism do not seem to realize that they have taken the very steps that lead the way to her destruction. The explosion of the Interchurch Movement was a blast that loosened every denominational foundation. By the wild attempt to combine in *one* people whose creeds were utterly antagonistic; to unite together those who held the Church authoritative, and those who held the Bible authoritative; and those who held their own inner conscience authoritative, they produced the elements that effected explosion. Just as chlorine and hydrogen exposed to light produce an instant and destructive blast, so this Darwin-conceived attempt to ignore the great fundamentals of the Christian faith, bind in one body Unitarian, Trinitarian and atheist, when the light of God's truth was turned upon it, exploded the whole machine erected for the production of this combination. While certain high officials have found soft ecclesiastical positions upon which to land, millions of dollars went up in that smoke and not one fragment has ever since been found. It is practically the same men, ecclesiastical potentates, who have put their heads together and have agreed upon the division of fields at home and abroad, the cooperation of laborers irrespective of what views they might hold or what gospel they might preach, reducing even the gospel itself to a negligible quantity and asking nothing other than a cooperative endeavor in drawing salaries, enjoying offices, thinking out programs, pulling off feasts, and fleecing the uninformed in behalf of a world-scheme that gave no promise to the world itself. In nature and character such a scheme is a thinly disguised enemy of the Gospel of God's grace and the true Church of Christ.

Some of us have seen enough! Our hearts are sick with the sight! We know that our denominationalism means nothing to us but a deception. It seems to bind into a brotherhood men that have nothing in common, but branding with the same name, when the great truth is that in every evangelical denomination, certainly, and as we profoundly believe, even in Rome herself, there are thousands, hundreds of thousands, and millions upon millions of men who are practically in faith and heart *one,* and who ought to, perhaps without longer delay, surrender up to the modernist-marauders these institutions, now so uniformly manned by unbelievers, as a liability and not an asset. As a new organization we could then go forth as brethren in the Lord, as poor, perhaps, as were the original disciples, but believing His Word and trusting His blood, declare afresh the mission of the Church of Christ and continue the task, undertaken by the apostles, twenty centuries ago, of preaching the gospel to every creature and hastening the day of the coming King.

Who are my brethren? Baptists? Not necessarily, and, in thousands of instances, no! My brethren are those who believe in a personal God, in an inspired Book, and in a redeeming Christ.

CHAPTER XXIV

The Great Depression, 1927–1933

132. BEATRICE M. HINKLE, "AGAINST THE DOUBLE STANDARD," 1930

A growing awareness of the changing roles of women during the 1920s was evident almost everywhere. It was not merely that now women could vote, or that they dared to bare their knees, although both facts were important. The change seemed to involve something basic; some writers suggested that an assault was being mounted against the very principle of masculine supremacy. The world of the Gibson girl was clearly a man's world, and many modern and emancipated women would have none of it. In the following article, Dr. Beatrice M. Hinkle (1872–1953), a psychoanalyst, argues that growing economic independence meant that women were newly free to reject the old double standard. Women who had broken away from economic servitude were evidently no longer willing to personify the morality which men had never lived up to. The freedom from men meant a freedom to discover what it meant to be an individual human being, one with a mind, an earning capacity, and a desire to repudiate not merely

the faith of the fathers but the fathers themselves.

In the general discussions of morality which are the fashion just now, sex morality seems to occupy the chief place. Indeed, judging from the amount of talk on this subject one would be inclined to think it the outstanding problem of our time. Certain the whole of humanity is concerned in and vitally affected by the sexual aspect of life. Sexuality in its capacity as an agent of transformation is the source of power underlying the creativeness of man. In its direct expression, including its influence upon human relationships in general, it is a woman's particular concern. The position of importance it is assuming seems, therefore, to be justified, regardless of the protests of the intellect and the wish of the ego to minimize its significance.

A general weakening of traditional standards of ethics and morals and their gradual loss of control over the conduct of individuals have long been observed in other activities—in business affairs and in the world of men's relations with each other. This has taken place so quietly and with so much specious rationalizing that sharp practices and shady conduct which formerly would have produced scandals, shame, and social taboos now scarcely cause a protest from society. These aspects of morality belong to the masculine world in particular and produce little agitation, while the upheaval in sex morals particularly affects the feminine world and by many people can scarcely be considered calmly enough for an examination. The changes in this field are the most recent and are being produced by women; they are taking place in full view of all with no apologies and with little hesitation. They appear, therefore, most striking and disturbing. It

---

Source: Beatrice M. Hinkle, "Women and the New Morality," *Our Changing Morality,* ed. Fred Kirchway (New York: Albert and Charles Boni, 1930), pp. 235–249. [Reprinted with permission of MacMillan College Publishing Company from THE CULTURE OF THE TWENTIES, edited by Loren Baritz, Copyright 1970 by MacMillan College Publishing Company.]

can be said that in the general disintegration of old standards, women are the active agents in the field of sexual morality and men the passive, almost bewildered accessories to the overthrow of their long and firmly organized control of women's sexual conduct.

The old sex morality, with its double standard, has for years been criticized and attacked by fair-minded persons of both sexes. It has been recognized that this unequal condition produced effects as unfortunate for the favored sex as for the restricted one, and that because of this it could not be maintained indefinitely by a psychologically developing people. As a matter of course, whenever the single standard was mentioned, the standard governing women was invariably meant, and the fact was ignored that it is easier to break down restrictions than to force them upon those who have hitherto enjoyed comparative freedom. Furthermore, it was not realized that a sex morality imposed by repression and the power of custom creates artificial conceptions and will eventually break down.

This forced morality is in fact at the present time quite obviously disintegrating. We see women assuming the right to act as their impulses dictate with much the same freedom that men have enjoyed for so long. The single standard is rapidly becoming a *fait accompli*, but instead of the standard identified with women it is nearer the standard associated with men. According to a universal psychological law, actual reality eventually overtakes and replaces the cultural ideal.

Although this overthrow of old customs and sex ideals must be chiefly attributed to the economic independence of women brought about through the industrialism of our age, it is safe to say that no man thought ahead far enough or understood the psychology of women sufficiently to anticipate the fruit of this economic emancipation. As long as women were dependent upon men for the support of themselves and their children there could be no development of a real morality, for the love and feelings of the woman were so intermingled with her economic necessities that the higher love impulses was largely undifferentiated from the impulse of self-preservation. True morality can only develop when the object or situation is considered for itself, not when it is bound up with ulterior and extraneous elements which vitiate the whole. The old morality has failed and is disintegrating fast, because it was imposed from without instead of evolving from within.

A morality which has value for all time and is not dependent upon custom or external cultural fashions can arise only from a high development of the psychological functions of thinking and feeling, with the developed individual as the determiner of values instead of general custom or some one else's opinion. The function of feeling and the realm of the emotions have been universally regarded as women's special province; therefore it is women who are specially concerned with testing out moral values involving sexual behavior. Women have been reproached by men again and again as being only sexual creatures, and they have meekly accepted the reproach. Now, instead of examining the statement, they have accepted the sexual problem of man as though it were their own, and with it the weight of man's conflict and his articulateness. For sexuality as a problem and a conflict definitely belongs to man's psychology; it is he primarily who has been ashamed of his domination by this power and has struggled valiantly to free himself; his egoistic and sexual impulses have always been at war with each other. But whoever heard of women being ashamed of yielding to the power of love? Instead they gloried in the surrender of themselves and counted themselves blessed when love ruled. It is this need of man to escape from the power of the sensual appeal that has made his scorn sex and look upon the great creative power of life as something shameful and inferior, and in modern days treat it as a joke or with the indifferent superficiality which betrays emasculation and inadequacy.

One has only to "listen in" where any large groups of men, young or old, are gathered together in easy familiarity (the army camps were recent examples on a large scale) to discover the degree to which sexuality still dominates the minds of men, even though its expression is confined so largely to the jocose and the obscene. Many men can corroborate this report from a military camp—"we have sexuality in all its dirty and infantile forms served daily for breakfast, lunch, and dinner." It is the inferior and inadequate aspect of masculine sexuality that has made it necessary for man to conceive it as something shameful and unclean, and to insist that woman must carry his purity for him and live the restrictions and suppression that rightly belonged to him. Woman on her part became an easy victim of his ideas and convictions, because of the very fact that the function of feeling and the emotions so largely dominate her psychology. The translation of feeling into thought-forms has been slow and difficult. About herself woman has been quite inarticulate and largely unconscious. This inarticulateness inevitably made her accept man's standards and values for her, for little directed thinking is achieved without form and words. Because of her sexual fertility and fruitfulness woman has no sexual conflict; therefore, man easily unloaded his psychological burden upon her, and claimed freedom for the satisfaction of his own desires.

Thus, woman was made a symbol or personification of man's morality. She had to live for him that which he was unable to live for himself. This was the reason for his indignation at moral transgressions on her part. She had injured the symbol and revealed his weakness to him. However, with the discovery by women that they could be economically independent of men, they commenced to find themselves interesting. As they have gradually come to think for themselves about fundamental questions, there has been a tremendous activity and busyness in regard to the very subject which was previously taboo.

A recent writer boasts that men have changed their attitude regarding sexual problems very little and are not much concerned in the new interest of women. This is probably true, for man has contributed all he has to give to the subject. He has laid down his taboos and externalized his restrictions, chiefly applicable to the other sex, and he is finished with the subject—bored by having it thrust forward as an unfinished problem needing reconsideration. All of his knowledge or understanding of the sexual aspect of life—the aspect underlying human creativeness, the faulty development of which is responsible for a large part of his woes, "can be told in two hours to any intelligent sixteen year old boy," another writer recently stated. It is this youthful ignorance and assurance that the last word has been spoken on this subject that has awakened women, no longer dependent economically, to the fact that they must also become independent of men intellectually if they wish to gain expression for their knowledge or to form their own rules of conduct based on their psychology. In the true scientific spirit of the age they are now experimenting, and using nature's method of trial and error to find out for themselves by conscious living experience what feeling has vaguely told them. This is the first step towards objectifying and clarifying woman's intuitive knowledge.

With the revolt of women against the old restrictions and the demand for freedom to experience for themselves, there has appeared a most significant phase of the changed morality—the new relation of women toward each other. The significance of this enormous change which has been taking place very quietly and yet very rapidly is scarcely appreciated. However, when one realizes that only a generation ago the newspapers were still publishing their funny paragraphs at the expense of women ("The dear creatures; how they love one another"), the great difference in their relations today becomes evident. The generally accepted distinction between the personal loyalties of the sexes can be summed up in the statement that women are loyal in love and disloyal in friendship, while men are loyal in friendship and disloyal in love. It is this attitude of women that is gradually disappearing with the awakening of a new sense of themselves as individuals. Their changed attitude towards each other—the recognition of their own values, and the growing realization that only in solidarity can any permanent impression be made on the old conception of woman as a inferior, dependent creature, useful for one purpose only—constitutes the most marked difference between their present social condition and that of the past.

As long as women remained psychologically unawakened, their individual values were swallowed up in their biological value for the race. They were under the unconscious domination of their sexual fruitfulness and an enemy of themselves as individuals. Weininger gives as the chief difference between the masculine and feminine creeds that "Man's religion consists in a supreme belief in himself—woman's in a supreme belief in other people." These other people being men, the sex rivalry among women that has so long stood in the way of their further development is easily understood. It has been a vicious circle which could only be broken by women's gaining another significance in the eyes of the world and in their own eyes. This other significance is the economic importance which they have acquired in the world of men.

It makes little difference within the social structure how many individual women exist who have forged a position for themselves and have won a freedom and independence equal to that possessed by the ordinary man, so long as they are isolated phenomena having little understanding of the peculiar difficulties and problems of women as a whole, and no relation with each other. These women have always existed in all culture periods, but they have produced little effect upon the social condition or psychology of women in general. There was no group action because the majority of women were inarticulate. The woman who was different became abnormal in the eyes of the world.

This lack of an adequate self-consciousness among women, their general inability to translate feeling into form capable of being understood by the masculine mind, accounts for their acceptance of the statements made about them by men in an effort to understand creatures apparently so different from themselves. There is no doubt that woman's inarticulateness about herself, even when her feelings were very different from those she was told were normal, has been responsible for a vast amount of the nonsense written about her.

This passive acceptance of the opinions of others has been most disastrous for woman's development. Her superior psychological processes consist of feelings and intuitions, and when these are stultified or violated by being forced into a false relation, or are inhibited from development, the entire personality is crippled. The inadequate development of the function of thought and the dominating role played by the function of feeling in the psychology of woman have produced an obviously one-sided effect and have caused men to postulate theories about her, which are given forth as though they were the last word to be said—fixed and unchangeable. Indeed the statement that women are incapable of change and that no growth is possible for them is one of the favorite assertions of the masculine writers upon the subject of women's psychology. As the present is the first time in our historical period in which there has been any general opportunity for women as a whole to think for themselves and to develop in new ways, the basis for this assertion does not exist, and it obviously conceals an unconscious wish that women should not change.

The effect of collective ideas and cultural traditions upon the personality is immeasurable. The greatest general change that is taking place today is the weakening of these ideas and the refusal of women to be bound by them. Women are for the first time demanding to live the forbidden experiences directly and draw conclusions on this basis. I do not mean to imply that traditional moral standards controlling woman's sexual conduct have never been transgressed in the past. They have very frequently been transgressed, but secretly and without inner justification. The great difference today lies in the open defiance of these customs with feelings of entire justification, or even a non-recognition of a necessity for justification. In other words, there has arisen a feeling of moral rightness in the present conduct, and wrongness in the former morality. Actually the condition is one in which natural, long-restrained desire is being substituted for collective moral rules, and individuals are largely becoming a law unto themselves. It is difficult to predict what will be the result of the revolt, but it is certain that this is the preceding condition which renders it possible for a new morality in the real sense to be born within the individual. It has already produced the first condition of all conscious psychic development—a moral conflict—and woman has gained a problem.

In the general chaos of conflicting feelings she is losing her instinctive adaptation to her biological role as race bearer, and is attempting adaptation to man's reality. She is making the effort to win for herself some differentiation and development, of the ego function apart from her instinctive processes. This is the great problem confronting woman today; how can she gain a relation to both racial and individual obligations, instead of possessing one to the exclusion of the other? Must she lose that which has been and still is her greatest strength and value? I for one do not think so, although I am fully conscious of the tremendous psychic effort and responsibility involved in the changing standards. It is necessary that women learn to accept themselves and to value themselves as beings possessing a worth at least equal to that of the other sex, instead of unthinkingly accepting standard based on masculine psychology. Then women will recognize the necessity of developing their total psychic capacities just as it is necessary for men to do, but they will see that this does not involve imitation of men or repudiation of their most valuable psychic functioning. The real truth is that it has at last become apparent to many women that men cannot redeem them.

It is not the purpose of this article to deal with the practical issues involved in the new moral freedom. One thing however is clearly evident: Women are demanding a reality in their relations with men that heretofore has been lacking, and they refuse longer to cater to the traditional notions of them created by men, in which their true feelings and personalities were disregarded and denied. This is the first result of the new morality.

133. Woody Guthrie, "Hard Hitting Songs for Hard-Hit People"

Woody Guthrie became famous for his songs of protest in the 1930s. His song, "This Land is Your Land," was banned for its socialist undertones.

Howdy Friend:

Here's a book of songs that's going to last a mighty long time, because these are the kind of songs that folks make up when they're a-singing about their hard luck, and hard luck is one thing that you sing louder about than you do about boots and saddles, or moons on the river, or cigarettes a shining in the dark.

There's a heap of people in the country that's a having the hardest time of their life right this minute; and songs are just like having babies. You can take either, but can't fake it, and if you try to fake it, you don't fool anybody except yourself.

For the last eight years I've been a rambling man, from Oklahoma to California and back three times by freight train, highway, and thumb, and I've been stranded, and disbanded, busted, disgusted with people of all sorts, sizes, shapes and calibres—folks that wandered around over the country looking for work, down and out, and hungry half of the time. I've slept on and with them, with their feet in my face and my feet in theirs—in bed rolls with Canadian Lumberjacks, in greasy rotten shacks and tents with the Okies and Arkies that are grazing today over the state of California and Arizona like a herd of lost buffalo with the hot hoof and empty mouth disease.

Then to New York in the month of February, the thumb route, in the snow that blanketed from Big Springs, Texas, north to New York, and south again into even Florida . . . Walking down the big road, no job, no money, no home . . . no nothing. Nights I slept in jails, and the cells were piled high with young boys, strong men, and old men; and they talked and they sung, and they told you the story of their life, how it used to be, how it got to be, how the home went to pieces, how the young wife died or left, how the mother died in the insane asylum, how Dad tried twice to kill himself, and lay flat on his back for 18 months—and then crops got to where they wouldn't bring nothing, work in the factories would kill a dog, work on the belt line killed your soul, work in the cement and limestone quarries withered your lungs, work in the cotton mills shot your feet and legs all to hell, work in the steel mills burned your system up like a gnat that lit in the melting pot, and—always, always had to fight and argue and cuss and swear, and shoot and slaughter and wade mud and sling blood—to try to get a nickel more out of the rich bosses. But out of all of this mixing bowl of hell and high waters by George, the hard working folks have done something that the bosses, his sons, his wives, his whores, and his daughters have failed to do—the working folks have walked bare handed against clubs, gas bombs, billys, blackjacks, saps, knucks, machine guns, and log chains—and they sang their way through the whole dirty mess. And that's why I say the songs in this book will be sung coast to coast acrost the country a hundred years after all nickel phonographs have turned back into dust.

I ain't a writer, I want that understood, I'm just a little one-cylinder guitar picker. But I don't get no kick out of these here songs that are imitation and made up by guys that's paid by the week to write 'em up—that reminds me of a crow a settin on a fence post a singing when some guy is a sawing his leg off at the same time. I like the song the old hen sings just before she flogs hell out of you for pestering her young chicks.

This book is a song book of that kind. It's a song book that come from the lungs of the workin' folks—and every little song was easy and simple, but mighty pretty, and it caught on like a whirlwind—it didn't need sheet music, it didn't need nickel phonographs, and it didn't take nothing but a little fanning from the bosses, the landlords, the deputies, and the cops, and the big shots, and the bankers, and the business men to flare up like an oil field on fire, and the big cloud of black smoke turn into a cyclone—and cut a swath straight to the door of the man that started the whole thing, the greedy rich people.

Source: Woody Guthrie. "Hard Hitting Songs for Hard Hit People." Oak Publications, 1967. Reprinted by permission.

You'll find the songs the hungry farmers sing as they bend their backs and drag their sacks, and split their fingers to pieces grabbing your shirts and dresses out of the thorns on a cotton boll. You'll find the blues. The blues are my favorite, because the blues are the saddest and lonesomest, and say the right thing in a way that most preachers ought to pattern after. All honky tonk and dance hall blues had parents, and those parents was the blues that come from the workers in the factories, mills, mines, crops, orchards, and oil fields — but by the time a blues reaches a honky tonk music box, it is changed from chains to kisses, and from a cold prison cell to a warm bed with a hot mama, and from a sunstroke on a chain gang, to a chock house song, or a brand new baby and a bottle of gin.

You'll find a bunch of songs made up by folks back in the hills of old Kentucky. The hills was full of coal. The men was full of pep and wanted to work. But houses wasn't no good, and wages was next to nothing. Kids died like flies. The mothers couldn't pay the doctor, so the doctor didn't come. It was the midwives, the women like old Aunt Molly Jackson, that rolled up her sleeves, spit out the window, grabbed a wash pan in one hand and a armful of old pads and rags, and old newspapers, and dived under the covers and old rotten blankets — to come up with a brand new human being in one hand and a hungry mother in the other. Aunt Molly was just a coal miner's wife, and a coal miner's daughter, but she took the place of the doctor in 850 cases, because the coal miners didn't have the money.

You'll find the songs that were scribbled down on the margins of almanacs with a penny pencil, and sung to the rhythms of splinters and rocks that the Winchester rifles kicked up in your face as you sang them. I still wonder who was on the tail end of the rifles. Also in the Kentucky Coal Miner Songs, you'll sing the two wrote by Jim Garland, "Greenback Dollar" and "Harry Simms" — a couple of ringtail tooters you're bound to like.

Sarah Ogan, she's the half sister of Aunt Molly, about half as old, and a mighty good worker and singer — she keeps up the spirit of the men that dig for a hamburger in a big black hole in the ground, and are promised pie in the sky when they die and get to heaven, provided they go deep enough in the hole, and stay down there long enough.

Then the next batch of wrong colored eggs to hatch — out pops the New Deal songs — the songs that the people sung when they heard the mighty good sounding promises of a re-shuffle, a honest deck, and a brand new deal from the big shots. A Straight flush, the Ace for One Big Union, the King for One Happy Family, the Queen for a happy mother with a full cupboard, the Jack for a hard working young man with money enough in his pockets to show his gal a good time, and the ten spot for the ten commandments that are overlooked too damn much by the big boys.

Next you'll run across some songs called "Songs of the One Big Union" — which is the same Big Union that Abe Lincoln lived for and fought for and died for. Something has happened to that Big Union since Abe Lincoln was here. It has been raped. The Banking men has got their Big Union, and the Land Lords has got their Big Union, and the Merchants has got their Kiwanis and Lions Club, and the Finance Men has got their Big Union, and the Associated Farmers has got their Big Union, but down south and out west, on the cotton farms, and working in the orchards and fruit crops it is a jail house offence for a few common everyday workers to form them a Union, and get together for higher wages and honest pay and fair treatment. It's damn funny how all of the big boys are in Big Unions, but they cuss and raise old billy hell when us poor damn working guys try to get together and make us a Working Man's Union. This Book is full of songs that the working folks made up about the beatings and the sluggings and the cheatings and the killings that they got when they said they was a going to form them a Working Man's Union. It is a jail house crime for a poor damn working man to even hold a meeting with other working men. They call you a red or a radical or something, and throw you and your family off of the farm and let you starve to death . . . These songs will echo that song of starvation till the world looks level — till the world is level — and there ain't no rich men, and there ain't no poor men, and every man on earth is at work and his family is living as human beings instead of like a nest of rats.

A last section of this book is called Mulligan Stew which are songs that you make up when you're a trying to speak something that's on your mind . . . telling your troubles to the blue sky, or a walkin' down the road with your 2 little kids by the hand, thinking of your wife that's just died with her third one — and you get to speaking your mind — maybe to yourself the first time, then when you get it a little better fixed in your head, and you squeeze out all the words you don't need, and you boil it down to just a few that tell the whole story of your hard luck. Then you talk it or sing it to somebody you meet in the hobo jungle or stranded high and dry in the skid row section of a big town, or just fresh kicked off a Georgia farm, and a going nowhere, just a walkin' along, and a draggin' your feet along in the deep sand, and — then you hear him sing you his song or tell you his tale, and you think, That's a mighty funny thing. His song is just like mine. And my tale is just like his. And everywhere you ramble, under California R.R. bridges, or the mosquito swamps of Louisiana, or the dustbowl deserts of the Texas plains — it's a different man, a different woman, a different kid a speaking his mind, but it's the same old tale, and the same old song. Maybe different words. Maybe different tune. But it's hard times, and the same hard times. The same big song. This book is that song.

You'll find a section in this book about Prison & Outlaw songs. I know how it is in the states I've rambled through. In the prisons the boys sing about the long, lonesome days in the cold old cell, and the dark nights in the old steeltank and a lot of the best songs you ever heard come from these boys and women that sweat all day in the pea patch, chain gang, a makin' big ones out of little ones, and new roads out of cow trails — new paved roads for a big black limousine to roll over with a lady in a fur coat and a screwball poodle dog a sniffing at her mouth. Prisoners ain't shooting the bull when they sing a mournful song, it's the real stuff. And they sing about the "man that took them by the arm," and about the "man with the law in his hand" and about the "man a settin' up in the jury box," and the "man on th' judges bench," and the "guard come a walkin' down that graveyard hall," and about the "man with th' jail house key," — and the "guard a walkin' by my door" — and about the "sweethearts that walk past the window," and the old mother that wept and tore her hair, and the father that pleaded at the bar, and the little girl that sets in the moonlight alone, and waits for the sentence to roll by. These outlaws may be using the wrong system when they rob banks and hijack the rich traveler, and shoot their way out of a gamblin' game, and shoot down a man in a jewelry store, or blow down the pawn shop owner, but I think I know what's on these old boys minds. Something like this: "Two little children a layin' in the bed, both of them so hungry that they cain't lift up their head . . ."

I know how it was with me, there's been a many a time that I set around with my head hanging down, broke, clothes no good, old slouchy shoes, and no place to go to have a good time, and no money to spend on the women, and a sleeping in cattle cars like a whiteface steer, and a starving for days at a time up and down the railroad tracks and then a seeing other people all fixed up with a good high rolling car, and good suits of clothes, and high priced whiskey, and more pretty gals than one. Even had money to blow on damn fool rings and necklaces and bracelets around their necks and arms — and I would just set there by the side of the road and think . . . Just one of them diamonds would buy a little farm with a nice little house and a water well and a gourd dipper, and forty acres of good bottom land to raise a crop on, and a good rich garden spot up next to the house, and a couple of jersey cows with nice big tits, and some chickens to wake me up of a morning, and . . . the whole picture of the little house and piece of land would go through my head every time I seen a drunk man with three drunk women a driving a big Lincoln Zephyr down the road — with money to burn, and they didn't even know where the money was coming from . . . yes, siree, it's a mighty tempting thing, mighty tempting.

Now, I might be a little haywired, but I ain't no big hand to like a song because it's pretty, or because it's fancy, or done up with a big smile and a pink ribbon, I'm a man to like songs that ain't sung too good. Big hand to sing songs that ain't really much account. I mean, you know, talking about good music, and fancy runs, and expert music, I like songs, by george, that's sung by folks that ain't musicians, and ain't able to read music, don't know one note from another'n, and — say something that amounts to something. That a way you can say what you got to say just singing it and if you use the same dern tune, or change it around twice, and turn it upside down, why that still don't amount to a dern, you have spoke what you had to speak, and if folks don't like the music, well, you can still pass better than some political speakers.

But it just so happens that these songs here, they're pretty, they're easy, they got something to say, and they say it in a way you can understand, and if you go off somewhere and change 'em around a little bit, well, that don't hurt nothin'. Maybe you got a new song. You have, if you said what you really had to say — about how the old world looks to you, or how it ought to be fixed.

Hells bells, I'm a going to fool around here and make a song writer out of you. — No, I couldn't do that — wouldn't do it if I could. I ruther have you just like you are. You are a songbird right this minute. Today you're a better songbird than you was yesterday, 'cause you know a little bit more, you seen a little bit more, and all you got to do is just park yourself under a shade tree, or maybe at a desk, if you still got a desk, and haul off and write down some way you think this old world could be fixed so's it would be twice as level and half as steep, and take the knocks out of it, and grind the valves, and tighten the rods, and take up the bearings, and put a boot in the casing, and make the whole trip a little bit smoother, and a little bit more like a trip instead of a trap.

It wouldn't have to be fancy words. It wouldn't have to be a fancy tune. The fancier it is the worse it is. The plainer it is the easier it is, and the easier it is, the better it is—and the words don't even have to be spelt right.

You can write it down with the stub of a burnt match, or with an old chewed up penny pencil, on the back of a sack, or on the edge of a almanac, or you could pitch in and write your walls full of your own songs. They don't even have to rhyme to suit me. If they don't rhyme a tall, well, then it's prose, and all of the college boys will study on it for a couple of hundred years, and because they cain't make heads nor tails of it, they'll swear you're a natural born song writer, maybe call you a natural born genius.

This book is songs like that. If you're too highbrow for that, you can take your pants and go home right now, but please leave the book—some people might want to look through it.

If you're so rich that you look down on these kind of songs, that's a dam good sign you're a standing on your head, and I would suggest that you leave your pocketbook and wife and ice box and dog and catch out east on a west bound freight, and rattle around over this United States for a year or so, and meet and see and get to knowing the people, and if you will drop me a postal card, and enclose a 3¢ Uncle Sam Postage Stamp—strawberry or grape, either one, both flavors are good—why, I'll send you back a full and complete list of the addresses of the railroad bridges that 500,000 of my relatives are stranded under right this minute. (From east coast to west coast, and I ain't a coastin', I mean, I ain't a boasting.) It's the—it's you wax dummies in the glass cases I'm a roasting. If you are one, you know it already, I don't have to sing it to you, and I don't have to preach it to you, your own song is in your own heart, and the reason you're so damn mixed up and sad, and high tempered and high strung, it's because that song is always a ringing in you own ears—and it's your own song, you made it up, you added a verse here, and verse yonder, and a word now, and a word then—till—you don't need a book a tellin' about songs, yours is already ringing and singing in your ears.

The only trouble is with you, you hold it back, you hide it, you keep it down, you kick it down, you sing over it, and under it, and off to all four sides, and you get out on limbs and you sing it, and you get lost in so called arts and sciences and all sorts of high fangled stuff like "intellect" and "inspiration" and "religion" and "business" and "reputation" and "pride" and "me"—and you say, talk, live, breathe, and exercise everything in the world, except that real old song that's in your heart.

Thank heaven, one day we'll all find out that all of our songs was just little notes in a great big song, and when we do, the rich will disappear like the morning fog, and the poor will vanish like a drunkard's dream—and we'll all be one big happy family, waking up with the chickens, chickens we don't owe nothing on, and a skipping through the morning dew, just as far as you want to skip.

I've got off of the subject 719 times in less than 15 pages. I told you I ain't no good as a writer, but—well, looks like you're already this far along, and I feel so sorry for you a having to try to wade through my writing like a barefooted kid through a sand-burr patch—think I'll just thank you for your visit, borrow fifty cents if you got it to spare, and try to throw some sort of trash or weeds or rags or something on this infernal typewriter—and maybe it'll sort of quit.

True as the average,

WOODROW WILSON GUTHRIE, or just plain old Woody

Jesus Christ Was a Man

I wrote this song looking out of a rooming house window in New York City in the winter of 1940. I saw how the poor folks lived, and then I saw how the rich folks lived, and the poor folks down and out and cold and hungry, and the rich ones out drinking good whiskey and celebrating and wasting handfulls of money at gambling and women, and I got to thinking about what Jesus said, and what if He was to walk into New York City and preach like He used to. They'd lock Him back in jail as sure as you're reading this. "Even as you've done it unto the least of these little ones, you have done it unto me."

> Jesus Christ was a man that
>   traveled through the land,
> A Carpenter true and brave;
> He said to the rich, "Give your
>   goods to the poor",
> So they laid Jesus Christ in his
>   grave.
>
> <u>Chorus</u>
>
> Yes, Jesus was a man, a
>   Carpenter by Hand,
> A Carpenter true and brave.

And a dirty little coward called
  Judas Iscariot,
He laid Jesus Christ in His grave.

The people of the land took Jesus
  by the Hand,
They followed him far and wide;
"I come not to bring you Peace, but
  a Sword."
So they killed Jesus Christ on the
  sly.

He went to the sick and He went to
  the poor,
He went to the hungry and the lame;
He said that the poor would win this
  world,
So they laid Jesus Christ in His
  grave.

One day Jesus stopped at a rich
  man's door,
"What must I do to be saved?"
"You must sell your goods and
  give it to the poor",
So they laid Jesus Christ in His
  grave.

They nailed Him there to die on a
  cross in the sky,
In lightning and thunder and
  rain;
And Judas Iscariot he committed
  suicide,
When they laid poor Jesus in his
  grave.

This wide wicked world of soldiers
  and slaves,
Rich man, poor man and thief;
If Jesus was to preach what He
  preached in Galilee,
They would lay Jesus Christ in His
  grave.

When the love of the poor shall
  turn into hate,
When the patience of the workers
  gives away;
"Twould be better for you rich if
  you'd never been born"
For you laid Jesus Christ in His
  grave.

134. NATE SHAW, *ALL GOD'S DANGERS*, CA. 1933

Nate Shaw's oral autobiography, the story of the life of a black sharecropper in Alabama in the first half of the twentieth century, won the National Book Award in 1974. This episode tells of the violent opposition he met when he attempted to join the Sharecropper's Union in the 1930s.

I was livin on Mr. Watson's place, buyin from him since he took full control from the Federal Land Bank, and Mr. Grace just went ahead and drifted my business over to Mr. Watson's hands. And in that, I learnt that the banker had a disposition to help this man Watson dig at me. That was in '31. And when Mr. Watson got a little toehold, he told me, "Bring me the cotton this fall, bring me the cotton."

When he told me that I got disheartened. I didn't want him messin with me—still, I didn't let him take a mortgage on anything I owned. I was my own man, had been for many years, and God knows I weren't goin to turn the calendar back on myself.

I always sold all of my cotton myself but one year, 1907, the first year I worked for Mr. Curtis; brought him my cotton to sell by his orders. I seen my daddy sell his own cotton; and sometimes the white man would sell it. And if my daddy owed him any money, he had no choice but to let him sell it. Mighty seldom my daddy ever got anything out of a cotton crop. Many times the white man wouldn't tell my daddy nothin bout the price he got for that cotton; weren't no use for him to tell him nothin, weren't no way to dispute him.

Source: Nate Shaw. *All God's Dangers,* pp. 300–333. Copyright Random House, 1984. Reprinted by permission.

I was shy of Mr. Watson, I didn't want no business with him at all. But eventually, he pulled at me so hard decided to buy twenty bushels of corn from him. How come did I get that corn? Well, my plow horses would eat it, bit my mules wouldn't eat no corn at that time; they didn't eat nothin but sweet feed. But my plow stock, regular plow stock, would eat corn. And I fell a little shy of corn that year; didn't need much and I went to Mr. Watson to get it—just givin him enough of my business, I hoped, to keep him off of me. But it didn't do no good. And that corn he let me have, he took it away from somebody else, I knowed that, but I couldn't do nothin about it.

That's all I traded in Mr. Watson's store except for a few, things, spring of the year. Startin late up toward July or August I quit goin in there at all; wouldn't go in there for a pinch of salt. I didn't owe him for forty or fifty dollars and I had plenty of cotton to pay all of my debts—and cotton was bringin a low price, too. He had done taken my business over with the Federal Land Bank and I just thought: weren't no use of me cryin, I had enough cotton to pay him what I would have paid the Federal Land Bank and all I owed him at the store, too.

He wanted more than that. Kept trying every year, practically, to get a mortgage on my stuff, but he didn't get it. That poisoned him. Sure as you born, he picked at me all the time. But he couldn't move me. We was on a seesaw and a zigzag, but I just shed him off as best I could by not goin his way. Along them times I wasn't botherin with any of the white people too much because I was making it on my own. I was buyin guano from whoever I wanted and I wasn't buyin it from him.

So carried him three good bales of cotton. He was out of his store and gone when I got there. His clerks was in there but the couldn't tell me nothin, and I didn't particularly ask them. Carried the cotton to the warehouse, had it weighed, left it there in Mr. Watson's name, by Nate Shaw. A few days after that I went back to town to see him about it, see about a settlement for what little I owed him and get my business reconciled. Jumped up and told me—I asked him for a settlement—"Aw, there aint no use of that, Nate, there aint no use of that." Walked away from me.

I seed if he couldn't do me one way he was goin to do me another. He wouldn't give me no settlement, wouldn't his big talk. He read just exactly his pedigrees that I knew and felt in my heart and had heard a whole lot about. Denied me altogether. And that three bales of cotton would have overpaid him, I know; it wouldn't a stopped at no forty- or fifty-dollar debt. It was bringin a price enough, even at five cents—that would have brought over seventy-five dollars. Don't you see? Don't you see? Five hundredpound-weight bales—I weren't a straight fool, I knowed I paid him more in the cotton than I owed him. Wouldn't go to his book here he had me charged, tell me what the cotton brought definitely, just took the cotton and went on.

But in '32 I wound up with all of em. I went on to the government and the government furnished me. The news was out through the settlement—the federal people was in Beaufort puttin out for the farmers.

I told my wife one mornin—I'd made up my mind that I was through with Watson, I was burnt up. And I said, "Darlin, I'm going to Apafalya this mornin to take care of some business at the depot. And after that, I don't know if it will be today or tomorrow, I fully intend to go to Beaufort to see the federal people."

I drove my car to town and parked it. He had done meddled me there before about havin a closed Chevrolet car, '28 Chevrolet; done walked up to my car and looked it over, had the assurance to tell me, "I see how come you can't pay your debts—" just doggin at me—"I see how come you can't pay your debts, sittin in a closed model car?"

I said, "Mr. Watson, what have I ever owed you and didn't pay you?"

He said, "You just a fool Negro," and he walked on off. He had it in for me. He knew I had good stock and I was a good worker and all like that. He just aimed to use his power and break me down; he'd been doin to people that way before then.

All right. That day I drove into town on my Chevrolet and parked it as soon as I got there. I walked on down the street and looked ahead of me and there was Watson standin there with his foot propped against the bank—bank was just below his store and the drugstore was between his store and the bank. Fellow by the name of Mose Todd, was supposed to be a little relation to me—I seed it was him Mr. Watson was standin there talkin to. I walked on by and got a little below em, just in hearin distance, and I stopped to hear their conversation. Mr. Watson considered me to be one of his Negroes too, and that gave me good encouragement to stop and sidle around and listen at him. I aint said a word that mornin to nobody. Just held my breath and looked at him and listened. Mose was standin there on the walkway with his head down and it looked like he was tryin to beg Watson to do somethin. I heard Mr. Watson tell Mose Todd, "No, I aint puttin out a dollar this year. I aint puttin out a thing. All of my men has got their own stock, they got

134. NATE SHAW, ALL GOD'S DANGERS, CA. 1933

their land to work, they got corn enough to feed their stock, and I aint puttin out a dollar. They all in shape to make a crop. And I'm going to let em go and go ahead; I aint puttin out nothin."

I thought to myself right quick, 'You aint goin to put out nothin, how do you expect for em to make it? I know them people needs fertilize if nothin else, and you not puttin out a dollar. That's mighty bad—farmers can't get no furnishin at all out of you. They come to depend on you and now you leavin em to theirselves. I know what you goin to do; you goin to look for what they make this fall. You goin to do it, I know, you goin to look to take it and aint furnished em nothin.'

And just as sure as you born, if he had a claim against em they couldn't transact with nobody else. They was his niggers and he could do with em like he wanted to and nobody else wouldn't fool with em. I figured this, and I might have been a fool to think it, me being a colored fellow and knowin the rules of the state of Alabama, partly, if I didn't know em all: if you furnishes nothin, right and justice should say it's nothin you get. If you don't carry me on and help me, the law ought to take care of me and give me how much time I need to pay you whatever I owe you. Cotton was down then, too, wavin about at the bottom, five and six cents.

I standin there catchin it, wouldn't say a word. I hadn't even whispered to Mr. Watson, and wouldn't do it, just stood there until I caught all I could catch. And I understood, reasonably, that they was talking bout Mose's business, and those had been one of Watson's customers for years. Now Watson was turnin him away. He just definitely told Mose to his head, right before me—I didn't question him because I had my route picked out. I was aimin to go to Beaufort to see if I could get furnished by the federal government, branch line. I just set out to move my little concerns out of his reach. O, he went down on Mose that morning; told him what he were goin to do and what he weren't.

I just eventually walked on off and went on to the depot where I'd started to go. Seed after my little matters down there and I turned around and went straight back up through town. Watson and Mose Todd both, when I looked up the street, was gone. Well, it didn't matter a continental with me where they was gone, I weren't takin hold with him no more for nothin. I had a right to get loose from him and he didn't have no sort of papers against me that's what I was dotin on. His first step in business with me, he proved he just wanted to wind me up and get a mortgage on every bit of my personal property and take it over with the land, and if I crooked my little finger or wanted to leave, I'd lose everything I had, leave it right there. He woulda had a mortgage on it and I couldn't a moved it. Do you reckon I was going to be fool enough to stand around and let him do that? I did have a little goatsense and I was goin to stick him up right when I left him and wind up with him.

So, I kept movin till I got on my car and I come on home. Next day, with the full consent of my mind what to do, I crawled on my car—there was Leroy Roberts, Virgil Jones, and Sam MacFarland wanted to go to Beaufort with me on the same occasion to get in with the federal loan deal. Virgil and Leroy was Watson's niggers too, I know they was. So, me and them three fellows went on to Beaufort that mornin and when we got to Pottstown on route—it was cold that mornin and the boys took a notion they wanted to stop for some smokin tobacco. We stopped there and they disappeared into one of the stores and I walked on in to Mr. Billy Thompson's store—he sold dry goods there and run a little druggist business too—and I went on around to the back room where the heater was. And Mr. V. Basil, white gentleman, was sittin by the stove cross-legged. The whole community knowed Mr. Basil, coloreds and whites.

I said, "Good mornin, Mr. Basil."

"Hello, Nate."

We talked and from one thing to another he put in talkin bout how the times was for furnishin people the pressure was on. I stood there and warmed, talked with Mr. Basil. He was a man that wore a mustache so long you could almost tie it around the back of his neck, Mr. V. Basil. Stood there and talked with him awhile bout the hard times, men puttin out money on farmers and couldn't get it back, farmers weren't able to pay their debts and he, too, he was goin to quit, he weren't goin to let his farmers have nothin, wouldn't put out nothin. He talked Mr. Watson's talk that mornin—I listened at him.

I said, "Well, Mr. Basil"—in a friendly way—"you a moneyed man, why don't you help the boys this time around? All of em has stuck by their word in the past"—I weren't talkin at him for nothin for myself, I wouldn't fool with him. I said, "Why don't you help the boys? You got plenty of money—" with a smile on my face.

He said, "Hell, yes, Nate. I got plenty damn money. And I got plenty damn sense with it."

I laughed.

He said, "What kind of fool would a man be— No, I aint goin to keep puttin out my money until they drain me and get the last dollar I have, foolin around here farmin, and I can't get it back. No, I aint goin to do it."

He went rock bottom against puttin out his money. I said to myself, 'I don't want your money. I'm just feelin out your mind on the subject.'

The boys got ready to go. I got on my car, cranked it up, and we pulled out. When we got to Beaufort, all we boys, they took us in the office there one by one—didn't meet us all there standin at once—and one by one let us put in our complaints and what we wanted and all. All of em went in before me and when they come out they told me they went through all right, got agreement to be helped. I was the last man in before the federal people to talk to em—all white people businessmen, no colored folks in it; only way a colored person was in there, he went in there to be furnished. So I told em my circumstances: didn't owe anybody, anything. I was clear and I knowed it, told em straight. Well, I had done paid what I owed the devil—Watson—and got wound up with him, unbeknownst to him so he made out. I thought I had the privilege then to do business with anybody I wanted to because I had done cleared myself up and I knew Watson didn't have no mortgage on nothin I had. And I knowed I stood a better chance with the government than I did with any of these folks here, absolutely. I wouldn't turn around to look at one of em if the government was beckonin me to come in with them. They knowed it too, and they didn't like for the government to come into this country and meddle with their hands.

Well, they just gladly fixed me up. The federal government took me over and furnished me that year, 1932. Less interest, less interest on the loan money with them than with anybody I ever knowed. Altogether a different proposition.

They told me, "Look out in your mailbox on such-and-such a day and you'll find a check there for you to buy your fertilize. And after that, you can draw your other checks, all that you need to make your crop."

That certain date I went out to my mailbox and the check was there. I took that check and I come over here to Calusa with my wife to have it cashed. And when they cashed it for me they asked me if I wanted to leave it there in the bank I said, "No, sir, I don't want to leave nary a penny. That's my fertilize money and I need it."

Went right on back home and in a day or two I got Mr. Horace Tucker to take his truck with a long trailer to it and when he stopped drivin we was in Union Springs. Drove right up to the guano factory in that little old city and bought all the guano I needed and loaded it on Mr. Horace's truck—the company did, the hands there workin—and carried it on home. Couldn't get me no soda there, soda was scarce, and the next day Mr. Horace carried me to Opelika on that truck—same man, same truck. He weren't gettin nothing for himself he went for me. Of course, I paid him, didn't expect but to pay him for them trips, drivin that trailer truck and haulin my fertilize. Well, couldn't get no soda at Opelika but I got some ammonia chemical to answer in place of it. Mr. Horace Tucker wasn't a nicer white man for accommodation you in the whole settlement.

The second government check was my supply check; it come several weeks later and I used the money strictly for groceries—and that was flour, sugar, and coffee, but for no meat and lard, I didn't need that, raised my meat and lard at home.

I went on and made my crop that year, '32. Didn't go to Apafalya nary a tune for nothin. And after crops was laid by I hauled a little lumber, spot haulin, no regular operation. I got home one evenin-night—I was workin right close to my home then, and my wife told me, "Darlin, Mr. Watson come through here today."

I said, "He did?"

She said, "Yes."

I said, "Did he stop?"

She said, "No, he never did quit drivin, just drivin along slow and lookin every whichway."

All right. That was on a Thursday. He went right on back to Apafalya after he drove around the men what had been dealin with him and he printed up some cards and sent em around, one to me, one to Leroy Roberts, one to Virgil Jones—we was *his* men. Said on the card, "Those who consider that they are my customers, come out to Apafalya Saturday evenin and get em some beef."

My wife asked me, "Darlin, is you goin to go to Apafalya like the note say?"

I said, "If I do, I'll walk on my hands."

Weren't nothin to that note but a sham. He just wanted us to come out there so he could question us about how we was doin our business. The other boys done as they pleased along them lines, they was all grown. I never did ask Virgil Jones did he go get that beef, and I never did ask Leroy Roberts; it weren't none of my concern. But I know what Nate Shaw done. I weren't hungry for none of his beef, and I never would get so hungry that I couldn't get somethin to eat other ways. I wouldn't be fool enough to go out there huntin no beef if I were down to my last piece of bread. My children will tell you, any of em, they never knowed what it was to get hungry and couldn't get somethin to eat.

The panic was on that year—cotton was cheap, had done hit the bottom. And when the wind-up come, the government gave me a date to comply and bring my cotton to the warehouse that the government rented here in Calusa. You could sell your cotton yourself and pay the government cash or pool your cotton in the government's name at the warehouse, just so much cotton as they told you, accordin to the price they figured. The order come to me to pool so many hundred pounds of lint cotton.

As the panic was on, the government was lenient and kind to their customers. And that poolin, that would give the cotton a chance to go up—but I'm satisfied that I paid to store that cotton out of the amount of cotton they called for. I didn't worry bout the cotton goin up or down no more that year once I turned my cotton loose. The government was just takin a chance of gettin what I owed out of it.

That fall, I come up to the requirement. The bales of cotton that I pooled weighed a little over what they asked for. I went on, after I put the cotton in the warehouse in the name of the government—so much lint, so many bales weighin so-and-so—went back home and I finished gatherin my crop. My wife got a bale of cotton weighed five hundred and sixty-five pounds. Me and my children worked to make it on my wife's mother's and father's place. Gathered that cotton, ginned it, had that big bale belonged to my wife and three bales I had for myself that I held back after carryin the government three bales. I took up one of them bales one mornin, the lightest bale I had, me and my boys put it on the wagon and I told em to carry it to the market and sell it and bring back the money—they done it, just like Papa said do. I gived every nickel of that money to my wife to use to buy the children and herself some shoes and clothes as far as it would go. It weren't no great sum of money—cotton only brought five cents that year, as little as it ever brought in my lifetime.

All right. I took them other two bales of mine and headed em up to the door of my cotton house, weatherboarded cotton house I'd built when I moved on the place, rolled that cotton in there and stood it up. Took my wife's bale and stood it up beside my two bales—they was lighter bales than her'n. I locked the door. Left em there and that's where they was standin when I was put in the penitentiary.

From the first bale of cotton to the last one, that Vernon said, "Vernon, come on and go to the gin with me; me and you will go to the gin today."

Went on down there to Tucker's crossroads to the gin, walked in there and made arrangements about ginnin my cotton, had that bale of cotton ginned, went on back home, and I never did haul another bale of cotton to the gin that fall myself. Next bale of cotton, Vernon hauled it to the gin—first time I'd ever trusted him complete, he was grown then. "Vernon, time to go to the gin now, we got a bale of cotton. Take it to the gin." He hitched them mules to that wagon and pulled off. Them mules was game as the devil, but he managed it and he done it gladly.

My mules at that time was named Mary and Dela; Mary was a black mule and Dela was what you might call a bay-colored mule. Both of em was heavy mules, big enough for farm use, road use, anywhere you put em. That Mary mule was the devil on hinges, no doubt. I didn't dread sending Vernon off with her and Dela though, because I knowed if there was any chance in the world they could be handled, Vernon would handle em. Sometimes he'd go to the gin and be late comin back. I'd walk out the house, go out to the road and look up the road see if I could see him. And when that boy come in sight with them mules and that bale of cotton sittin up in the wagon behind him, that Mary mule would have her head in the air, her heels up in the corner next to the double-tree. I could see the devil was in her. I'd stand there, heap of times, Vernon'd hit the yard, I'd say, "Old Mary is good and hot, aint she, son?" "Yes, Papa, she's been cuttin a fool ever since we left for the gin?" She didn't stand a automobile anyway, she heard one coming behind her, she'd stampede like the devil, dodge from it and lean off and then, after it passed, she'd break to ran. She was the most devilish mule ever I had but she was as good a workin mule as ever was hitched up. But that way she had, you had to watch chances to live behind Mary. She'd spill you, tear up the wagon, and do everything else if that bay mule, old Dela, would second her; that's all it took. But Vernon was able to hold her and talk to her—it took a heap of talk, holdin didn't do no good a heap of times. Come along in front of the house with her head throwed out in the air and go through to the back yard between the car shed and the house—goin to the barn. O, she was a pissripper. Vernon held her in though—he went with me the first bale I hauled to the gin in '32, made my arrangements bout ginnin not only the bale I brought that day, but for up until my last bale that year, whether I was to be there or not. Vernon was on the wagon haulin it himself when the last bale was hauled. And that Mary mule would come in there every time just like a tiger. I hated her ways but I had faith enough in Vernon to believe he'd stay with her.

There was a white gentleman by the name of Leonard Wilcox—his sister lives right up there at Pottstown today, she married Mr. Grady Rudd for her second husband; and that was her brother runnin all over the country, singin, "Watson say he goin to take all Nate Shaw got this fall and all Virgil Jones—he goin to take everything they got."

Well, he was tellin it around for several weeks and at that time he never did tell me directly about it. And I wondered how come he went tellin it to other colored fellows. I reckon he was tellin whites too. "Watson say he goin to take all old Nate Shaw got this fall and old Virgil Jones."

Well, one day this white man come by my house, right after gatherin time, and he hadn't never told me nothin about it, skippin me, tellin it to everybody in the whole settlement around, just singin it. I was out there by my well and my well was close to the road and I looked down the road and here he come, Mr. Leonard Wilcox. Come on up to me and stopped. Here's his song with me: "Watson say he goin to take all you got this fall, and all old Virgil Jones got."

I looked at him and I said, "He did?"

Said, "Yeah. Take all you and old Virgil Jones got this fall."

I said, "Well, there's a law for that and the law obliges the likes of him as well as me. I aint goin to hide. When he starts, it's goin to be trouble."

A heap of families, while I was living on the Tucker place down on Sitimachas, was leavin goin north. Some of my neighbors even picked up and left. The boll weevil was sendin a lot of em out, no doubt. I knowed several men went north, some with their families and some without; they sent for their families when they got to where they was goin. More went besides what I knowed of, from all parts of this southern country. They was dissatisfied with the way of life here in the south—and when I was livin on the Pollard place it come pretty wide open to me and touched the hem of my garment. But my family was prosperin right here, I didn't pay no attention to leavin. I wanted to stay and work for better conditions. I knowed I was in a bad way of life here but I didn't intend to get out—*that* never come in my mind. I thought somehow, some way, I'd overcome it. I was a farmin man at that time and I knowed more about this country than I knowed about the northern states. I've always been man enough to sick up for my family, and love them, and try to support em, and I just thought definitely I could keep it up. In other words, I was determined to try.

And durin the pressure years, a union begin to operate in this country, called it the Sharecroppers Union—that was a nice name, I thought—organization, that riot come off at Crane's Ford in '31. I looked deep in that thing, tool heard more than I seed and I taken that in consideration. And I knowed what was goin on was a turnabout on the southern man, white and colored; it was somethin unusual. And I heard about it bein a organization for the poor class of people—that's just what I wanted to get into, too; I wanted to know the secrets of it enough that I could become in the knowledge of it. Now I heard talk about trucks comin into this country deliverin guns to the colored people but I decided all that was talk, tryin to accuse the niggers of gettin into somethin here that maybe they weren't—and maybe they were. But didn't no trucks haul no guns to nobody. Colored people hadn't been armed up for nothin; it was told like that just to agitate the thing further. Of course, some of these colored folks in here had some good guns—you know a Winchester rifle is a pretty good gun itself. But they didn't have nothin above that. It weren't nothin that nobody sent in here for em to use, just their own stuff.

Well they killed a man up there, colored fellow; his name was Adam Cole. And they tell me—I didn't see it but I heard lots about it and I never did hear nothin about it that backed me off—Kurt Beall, the High Sheriff for Tukabahchee County, got shot in the stomach. He run up there to break up this meeting business amongst the colored people and someone in that crowd shot him. That kind of broke him up from runnin in places like that.

And these white folks woke up and stretched themselves and commenced a runnin around meddlin with niggers about this organization. And it's a close thing today. One old man—and he was as big a skunk as ever sneaked in the woods—old man Mac Sloane, come up to me one day—he didn't come to my home, he met me on the outside—old man Mac Sloane come to me hot as a stove iron, "Nate, do you belong to that mess they carryin on in this country?"

I just cut him off short. I didn't belong to it at that time, but I was eager to join and I was aimin to join, just hadn't got the right opportunity.

"No, I don't belong to nothin."

Mac Sloane, white man, said, "You stay out of it. That damn thing will get you killed. You stay out of it. These niggers runnin around here carryin on some kind of meetin—you better stay out of it."

I said to myself, 'You a fool if you think you can keep me from joinin.' I went right on and joined it, just as quick as the next meeting come. Running around and givin me orders—he suspected I might be the kind of man to belong to such an organization; put the finger on me before I ever joined. And he done just the thing to push me into it—gived me orders not to join.

The teachers of this organization begin to drive through this country—they couldn't let what they was doin be known. One of em was a colored fella; I disremember his name but he did tell us his name. He wanted us to organize and he was—with us a whole lot of time, holdin meetins with us—that was part of his job. We colored farmers would meet and the first thing we had to do was join the organization. And it was said, we didn't want no bad men in it at all, no weak-hearted fellows that would be liable to give the thing away. It was secret with them all that joined it; they knowed to keep their mouths shut and meet the meetins. And this teacher said—don't know where his home was; he had a different way of talkin than we did—"I call em stool pigeons if they broadcast the news about what's happenin." And said, if a nigger, like myself, went and let out any secrets to the white folks about the organization, the word was, "Do away with him."

Had the meetins at our houses or anywhere we could have em where, we could keep a look and a watch-out that nobody was comin in on us. Small meetins, sometimes there'd be a dozen, sometimes there'd be more, sometimes there's be less—niggers was scared, niggers was scared, that's tellin the truth. White folks in this country didn't allow niggers to have no organization no secret meetings. They kept up with you and watched you, didn't allow you to associate in a crowd, unless it was your family or your church. It just worked in a way that the nigger wasn't allowed to have nothin but church services and, O, they liked to see you goin to church, too. Sometimes white people would come into the Negro church and set there and listen at the meetin. Of course, it weren't nothin but a church service goin on. But if a nigger walked into a white church, he'd just be driven out, if they didn't kill him. But if a Negro was a servant for white people, then they'd carry him to church with em, accept him to come in and take a seat on the back seat and listen at the white people. But if you was an independent Negro you better stay away from there. But if you was a white man's dear flunky, doin what he said do, or even on the woman's side, if they was maids for the white people, well thought of, they'd take em out to their home churches, dupe em up in a way. They knowed they weren't goin to cause no trouble and if they did, they'd just been knocked out of the box and called in close question. But they never did act disorderly; just set there and listened at the white folks' meetin quiet as a lamb. And when the white folks would come in the colored churches, good God, the niggers would get busy givin em first class seats—if there was any in that buildin the white folks got em. They was white people; they classed theirselves over the colored and the colored people never did do nothin but dance to what the white people said and thought. White people was their bosses and their controllers and the colored people went along with it. White men, white women—I been there—go in colored churches and be seated. Nigger aint got nothin to do but run around there and give em the nicest seats.

First thing the organization wanted for the colored people was the privilege to have a organization. That's one of the best things they ever could fight for and get on foot. From my boy days comin along, ever since I been in God's world, I've never had no rights, no voice in nothin that the white man didn't want me to have—even been cut out of education, book learnin, been deprived of that. How could I favor such rulins as have been the past?

The teacher would send out literatures and these literatures would get around in colored folks' boxes and they got so bold they went to puttin em in white folks' boxes. I couldn't definitely say what them literatures said—I aint a readin man—but they said enough that the big white men didn't like it at all. Malcolm Todd, who married my wife's oldest sister, he heard a white man say, "The Lord is bringin down the world, the Lord is bringin down the world."

Well, it was many conditions that called for such a organization as that niggers had to get back and get back quick when the white man spoke. Had to be humble and submissive under em. My color needed a protection so long, so long. You couldn't get a nigger to poke his head out in them days for nothin—scared, and I looked at it from another angle and that was the worst thing that could ever hit my attention. We had too many colored people that if they knowed anything was goin on amongst their own color, any sort of plot at all, they'd turn it in to the white people. No use to try gettin together to do somethin bout the conditions we was livin under because somebody would run and stick his head under the white man's shirttail, and that was that. I call em Uncle Toms. They'll prowl into the niggers' business to get the dope and carry it to the white folks. Uncle Tom's a devil of a man; he's a enemy to his race.

Niggers was scared to run their business together, buy their fertilize together, sell their cotton together, because the white man—the average colored man was workin on the white man's place, and if he weren't on the white man's race he had to cooperate with the white man to get furnished and so on. And the white man held the final rule over the Negro—"Bring the cotton to me." I heard it; it was told to others and it was told to me.

Conditions has been outrageous every way that you can think against the colored race of people. Didn't allow em to do this, didn't allow em to do that, didn't allow em to do the other. Knowin and comin into the knowledge of what was goin on and how it was goin on in the United States as far as I knowed, which was the state of Alabama as far as I knowed, Tukabachee County—I knew that it was a weak time amongst the colored people. They couldn't demand nothin; they was subject to lose what they had if they demanded any more.

Good God, there wasn't but few privileges that we was allowed. If you was flesh and blood and human and you tended to want to help and support your friends in the community and make something of yourself—white folks didn't allow you that privilege. But we had the privilege of workin for the white man—he who had the chance had better do it; get yourself together and get over yonder in Mr. So-and-so's field or anywhere else he told you and do what he tell you to do. And when pay time come he'd pay you what he wanted to, and in many cases it'd be less than what he'd pay a white man. And some work, like pickin cotton in the fields, white folks didn't fill a basket—most of em. That was niggers' work. And if a poor white man got out there and picked cotton, he was pickin cotton like a nigger. Colored man just been a dog for this country for years and years. White man didn't ask you how you felt about what he wanted to do; he'd just go ahead and do it and you had to fall under his rulins. And bein in his home country, he been allowed to do as he please by the capital of the United States.

I heard talk when I was a boy of how the colored people come to America. Now the talk that I heard might not be exactly how it was but I have no reason to argue with the words. It all comes down to this: the colored people was transferred here from Africa just like you transfer a drove of stock. White man gathered em up in the distant countries; they didn't have no knowledge of where they was goin, they had to move by orders, had no idea of where they was goin. Passed em across the water in some form or fashion and they was put over in this country and sold just like you'd go out here and sell a hog, a horse, a cow, just so. They was black people—all of em was dark at that time—but they wasn't recognized as people. They had no say-so, they had no choice noway. Well, after they got over here—I has a hard tune keepin myself together when I thinks about it—they was put under the possession of marsters and mistresses, just like your beast comes under the possession of you when you buy it. Had no voice, no privilege, only had to go by orders every way.

And whoever come to be bought by such-and-such a one, why, they was his. And when he wanted he'd sell em and swap em. And I was told that in the time the colored was under bondage—niggers as they called em, right quick—they was divided out like this: one white man that bought a drove would give his children so many colored folks apiece, just like he'd give em a hog, make his children a present of em just like that.

And the nigger was handicapped to death. He had to go by orders, he had to come by orders; when he knocked off he knocked off by orders. And the only way the nigger come out from under that marster, he was sold to some other man. That big fellow out yonder with so many colored people, he noticed this man's crowd, he knowed what he had, and all of em knowed what they had—it was a business proposition. So some of em would take a fancy to some of that man's slaves over yonder; look around, walk around, and take a fancy to em. More than likely, if I wanted, I'd buy that woman or that man from that marster over yonder. And if that marster had a nice lookin, healthy colored man, I'd give him a pile of money for that big Negro, carry him home and put him with my crowd and produce a mess of younguns like himself. They didn't like so much the little scrawny colored people, weren't able to work much. If the marster caught a little, bitty, scrawny nigger foolin round amongst his women, there'd be no holdin up on the whippin he'd get. They wanted these big healthy fellows, big healthy women; they wanted to create a race of people to suit em.

If there was any way in the world that I could buy the one I wanted, well, I wouldn't have to ask the nigger nothin, I'd talk—this marster over here would talk to that marster over yonder about you. And if he could buy you he'd buy you, if the man would sell. Just like you was a cow or a mule, he'd buy you out the drove. You had no choice. I realize what that meant. I might belong to you and you might have a woman over here too that was my wife. Or I stayed with her if it was your request for me to stay with that woman; but if it wasn't, I couldn't—for breedin purposes. And you got the privilege of sellin me away from my wife, if the boss man over yonder wanted me or if you just needed the money; it was in your power to sell me. I had no choice, weren't allowed no choice. I'd have to get gone from that woman, made no difference if I loved her or not. You know it's nature for men to love women, and for women to love men; they loved each other in them days, too. And they just abused nature by selling me. "You got to do what I say, you aint no more than the mule you plow, in my sight. You belong to me, you aint nothin but my property." It just points right to that, you look at it. I'm just your property. I got a wife here, I love her. You see fit to move me, that marster man over yonder wants to buy me—that runs deep with me, I can't forget it. It was like that too, or maybe worser. A heap of things you hear and you aint experienced it, you can't feel it like you experienced it.

I belong to you. You got me livin here. Got plenty of others livin here too, them's your servants. That boss man over yonder, marster of his crowd over yonder somewhere, he look over the situation and see me; maybe he like my looks, he like my ways, regardless to what I think, you can do with me as you please. He come to you and make you an offer to buy me. Well, you realize that I'm your mainline servant, you'll price me high to him and he gets me, he got to pay a price just like he was payin for a mule or a horse or a hog—I has no choice, I has no voice or nothin, I'm just handicapped to death and I got to go where old marster puts me. Marster sees fit to sell me, he going to sell me and pocket up a pile of money off me.

They told me that good able-bodied Negroes and Negroes with good health sold for a pretty penny. I might be a carpenter I might be a blacksmith, or I might just work in the field. You'd sell me accordin to what I was worth to you. That man over yonder buys me, I'd cost him somethin.

And the owners of these colored people would fall out with one another about em. That was their livin: they had it all figured out how much a certain colored man or colored woman cost em to buy and raise and how much they would make off of that nigger as long as they owned him. It run that way for years, they tell me, it run that way for years. A time of brutish acts, brutish acts.

The old boss man, the old marster, disregarded the nigger, disregarded him in everything, but he slipped under the covers at the colored woman, and here's how that was done: poor colored women, slaves in them days, didn't know nothin but to do what they was told to do, bow for the marster. Old marster, he'd wait his chance and when his wife would leave home for pleasure or enjoyment or anything he might cause her to be away from home—and they had housemaids and they was always the best lookin colored women, the most obedient colored women— they run for that today. Old marster, old missus, maybe both of em would pick out one of the nigger women that looked like she'd suit em. They'd put her in the house as a maid to cook, iron, wash, take care of the house, keep it decent and clean—just pick out the nicest one and give her a job in the house to keep that house cleaned up and cook food for their table; in other words, a housewoman. Old missus would go anywhere she wanted to go and leave that colored woman there. Old master would slip around, he wanted to get to that colored woman. And he'd wait till it was quiet and all, until his wife left home—she gone, he'd sneak around there, make that colored woman lay down on the bed for him, pop it to her as much as he wanted to. She had to lay down for him, poor woman; didn't, no tellin what would happen. She belonged to him but he wanted to keep his doins outside of his wife, wouldn't fool with that woman long as his wife was there; he knowed that would cause trouble.

That's the way it was cut out and that's the way it was done and I've lived amongst the very people it was done to, enough to tell it close. I've dug up the root and branch of it. And I can say they wanted to be free, have their rights as they was created by God above. God gived the colored man and gived the colored woman some knowledge and it was knowledge enough to know they wasn't free. I have lived in bondage myself, just like bondage, and I can say they wanted to be free.

I was able when I was just ten or twelve years old to understand how they was treatin the colored folks in this country. I used to say—I criticized it and had every thought as I could have against such as that when I was a boy. I used to say, "I won't stand to rest the way they treatin colored folks in this country, I won't stand it." And I showed it to em. I give em what they wanted when I was a boy, but somehow or other I got to where I couldn't keep that spirit in me, I had to do somethin.

I wasn't over ten or twelve years old until I begin to come into the knowledge of more different things wrong than I can really tell. They'd overpower you every way— meet colored folks in the road, young colored boys when I was a boy, beat em up, whip em up, make em get in the field and go to work. I knowed too darn well they weren't payin em nothin hardly. These people in this country, that was right down their alley. Done that—called it vagrancy. It was just like slavery, God knows it weren't a bit of difference. In place of ever changin and gettin better, it was gettin worser and worser as I come up in this world.

The way I caught it and the way I can explain it accordin to my best ideas, this here organization was workin to bring us out bad places where we stood at that time and been standin since the colored people has remembrance. They didn't say to us how this was goin to happen—we didn't have time to work up a plan; only I felt it, I could feel it was somethin good. It was goin to rise us out—of these old slum conditions which that we had been undergoin since slavery times, bring a clearer life to live, push the white man back.

I heard this spoke by the officials, the people that was advertisin this union: they was tired of the rich man gettin richer and the poor man gettin poorer. They seed it was a freeze-out. Tired, tired of that way of life. That's the way I looked into it, and the rest of em, some of em looked at it that way too. And we put these thoughts in our literatures. I didn't never put out none myself; if I'd a done put em out I couldn't a read em. But we had some in our home when I was arrested—they never was sharp enough to get em, but they got so many others. And it's all got lost today. My people was treated in such a way that they done good to save their lives by the help that helped em. Couldn't save no literatures.

The first teacher attracted the attention of several of us by his talkin about the future comin. He told us, and we agreed, the future days follows the present And if we didn't do something for ourselves today, tomorrow wouldn't be no different. But you know, people is people in this world. You can show em a thing that means a benefit to em and they'll run off; can't see where today might end and tomorrow begin. They held the meetins all right, but they was shy like rats. And what was they lookin for? They was keepin their eyes open for stool pigeons and give aways; that throwed a check in the business. It showed that they—we—didn't have no confidence in each other.

Well, we was taught at our meetins that when trouble comes, stand up for one another. Whatever we was goin to do, whatever that was, we was goin to do it together. And by colored people in this country havin any kind of sense that was profitable at all, they joined this organization. I was eager for it, eager.

I paid a small dues when I joined, nothin to hurt me, not more than a few cents. Somebody had to take care of the teacher. He was helpin us, that was his job, and we had to look out for him. I don't know whether he had a wife and children or where they was if he did have, but *he* had to live. He was comin regular and holdin meetins—he had more knowledge and authority, than we had and from his words I went out and talked it over with folks. I went to several places, even out the other side of Apafalya, and informed some people I knew about the organization. Some of em went in, too, by my descriptions. I told em it was a good thing in favor of the colored race and it was so far a over-average help—as far as I was taught I told em what the organization was goin to do. The organization would back you up and fight your battles with you, do this and do that and do the other, as far as I was taught by the travelin man.

I recommended it thoroughly to particular ones I knowed—some of em was too scared to join and some of em was too scared not to join; they didn't want to be left alone when push come to shove. I recommended it to my brother Peter, but he never did join it. He was livin on Mr. Watson's individual place at that time, about a mile and a half from me on the Crane's Ford road toward Apafalya. He got along with Mr. Watson by givin him what he made—Mr. Watson got it all, that's the truth of it. My brother Peter was easy and high-mouthed and he just settled down to that. He made up his mind that he weren't goin to have anything, and after that, why, nothin could hurt him. He's my own dear brother—he said he was discouraged of this organization but I knowed he was afraid.

Here's the rule of our colored people in this country, that I growed up in the knowledge of: they'll dote on a thing, they'll like it, still a heap stays shy of it. They knowed that their heads was liable to be cracked, if nothin else, about belongin to somethin that the white man didn't allow em to belong to. All of em was willing to it in their minds, but they was shy in their acts. It's just like the old man and the bear. When the bear was comin in the house, he warned his wife about it—we colored people, some of us is like that today—the old man jumped up and run up in the loft where the bear couldn't get him. The old woman, when the bear walked in, she grabbed the fire iron and she labored with the bear until she killed him. And when she killed him, then the old man come down from the loft, sayin, "Old lady, aint we brave, aint we brave. We killed that bear. We killed that bear." And hadn't done nothin but killed himself runnin. He'll talk a whole lot but he's too scared to talk a hold.

In a few weeks' time it come off, it come off. Mr. Watson sent the deputy sheriff to Virgil Jones' to attach his stock and bring it away from there. Virgil had got word of the plot and he come to warn me and several other men of the organization. I knowed I was goin to be next because my name was ringing in it as loud as Virgil Jones' was. Virgil come and told me about it on a Saturday evenin. That next Monday mornin I fixed myself up and walked over there, bout a mile from where I was livin. My wife's baby sister was livin on a little plantation right near there, her and her husband. I went over by their house that mornin and went on out across the road to Virgil Jones'. Got there and good God I run into a crowd, and Virgil Logan, deputy sheriff, was there fixin to attach up everything. I just walked up like somebody walkin about, that's the way I played it.

Several of us met there too, but we had no plan strictly about what we was goin to do. Leroy Roberts and two or three more of em come there early and left before I got there. Well, the devil started his work that mornin. I asked Mr. Logan, the deputy sheriff, I knowed him; he lived right over here at Pottstown at that time and he was a Tukabahchee deputy for the state of Alabama—I asked Mr. Logan kindly, talkin to all of em, "What's the matter here? What's this all about?"

The deputy said, "I'm goin to take all old Virgil Jones got this mornin."

Well, I knowed doggone well accordin to the quotation I was goin to be next. He just starting on Virgil Jones first. I stretched my eyes and said, "Mr. Logan, please sir, don't take what he's got. He's got a wife and children and if you take all his stuff you'll leave his folks hungry. He aint got a dime left to support em if you take what he's got."

I begged him not to do it, begged him. "You'll dispossess him of bein able to feed his family."

Our teacher, the man that put out this organization in this part of the country, he told us to act humble, be straight; his teachin, to not go at a thing too rapid and forcible. Be quiet, whatever we do, let it work in a way of virtue. They got a song to this effect, did have years ago: "Low is the way to the bright new world, let the heaven light shine on me." Low is the way, humble and low is the way for me. That's what I tried to give Logan, too. I tried to go by the union's orders.

"Please, sir, don't take it. Go to the ones that authorized you to take his stuff, if you please, sir, and tell em to give him a chance. He'll work to pay what he owes em."

I knowed it was Watson gived him orders what to do, or Beall, the High Sheriff Kurt Beall, he was backin it up.

The deputy said, "I got orders to take it and I'll be damned—"

I asked him humble and begged him not to do it. "Go back to the ones that gived you orders to do this and tell em the circumstances. He aint able to support his family. Aint got a dime to support his family."

He said, "I got orders to take it and I'll be damned if I aint goin to take it."

Well, that brought up a whole lot of hard words then. I just politely told him he weren't goin to do it, he were not going to do it. "Well, if you take it, I'll be damned if you don't take it over my dead body. Go ahead and take it."

He got hot. After a while I seed Cecil Pickett go in the lot with bridles in his hands to catch Virgil Jones' mules. That was a colored fellow had no sense; white folks could get to do anything they wanted him to do. He come over there that mornin on the deputy sheriff's car. He was one of Logan's superintendin Negroes and he didn't know no better than to come over with Logan and help take what Virgil Jones had—that was the white folks' rule: when they got ready to anything, didn't matter what it was, they'd carry a nigger with em. O, they could get some nigger to follow em to hell and back. I feel angry over that today—

I told Cece Pickett that morning, goin to the gate with bridles in his hands—I don't know where he got them bridles but he had em, goin in that lot to catch them mules. Lookin right at him. He walked up to the lot gate, unlatched it, and walked in. I didn't see the mules but I reckoned they was in the stable. I said, "What are you goin in there for?"

Mr. Logan said, "He's goin in there to catch them mules. That's what he's goin for."

I said, "You just as well to come out. Catch no mules there this mornin, till a further investigation."

Kept a walkin—I said, "Well, you can go ahead and catch em but you won't get em out of that lot; go catch em, go on."

When I told Cece Pickett that he stopped. Looked at me and he looked at Logan, looked at me and looked at Logan.

I said, "Go ahead and catch em, if you that game. I'll be damned if you won't ever bring em out of that gate?"

Somebody, got to stand up. If we don't we niggers in this country are easy prey. Nigger had anything a white man wanted, the white man took it; made no difference how the cut might have come, he took it.

Mr. Logan seed I meant it—I was crowin so strong and I was fixin to start a shootin frolic then.

"Come out, Cece," Logan said, "Come on back, Cece. Let em alone. Come out."

Then the deputy walked up to me and said, "You done said enough already, for me to be done killed you."

I said, "Well, if you want to kill me, I'm right before you. Kill me, kill me. Aint nothin between us but the air. Kill me."

I didn't change my disposition at all; if my orders hadn't a been listened to, the devil woulda took place sooner than it did.

A nigger by the name of Eph Todd seed me lowerin the scrape on Logan and he runned up on me from behind and grabbed a hold of me. Good God, I throwed a fit because it popped in my mind that quick—I heard many a time in my life that a man will meddle you when another man is fixin to kill you; he'll come up and grab you, maybe hold you for the other to kill you. I looked around and cussed him out and he left there. The deputy sheriff looked at me—I kept my eyes on him—and he walked away, just saunterin along.

One come and round the water was hot—Virgil Logan. He told the crowd that mornin, shyin away from em, "I'll just go and get Kurt Beall! he'll come down there and kill the last damn one of you. You know how he is"—well, all the niggers knowed that Mr. Kurt Beall was a bad fellow—"When he comes in he comes in shootin."

I told him, "Go ahead and get him—" every man there heard it—"go ahead and get Mr. Beall, I'll be here when he comes."

He left then. Drove away in his automobile and took Cece Pickett with him. Went to Beaufort and delivered the message to the High Sheriff, Kurt Beall.

After he left, I went to Virgil Jones' house one time to see who was in there, and there was four, five, or six settin in there and they was so quiet. Virgil Jones was there, but his wife and children was long gone, I don't know where they was. Sam MacFarland was there. Boss Hatch was there—they never did catch Boss Hatch neither. And there was some more of em. I stood there and looked at em and I could see they was scared. I went right back out the door where I could keep my eyes open, just keep a watchin for them officers to drive in. After a while, about twelve thirty or one o'clock—I know it was early after dinner—I looked down the road and I seed that car comin. Well, I knowed that was the same car that left there that mornin. And I called the boys, "Hey, fellas, come on out, come on out"—I know they heard me—"Yonder they come, yonder come the officers."

Good God almighty, when I told em that next thing I heard em runnin out of that house, hittin it to the swamps, just cleanin up from there. I reckon some of em peeped out the door or a window and seed them officers. So, stampedin, stampedin, stampedin out of there and they was still runnin scared when I come out of prison.

I just stood right on and I was standin alone. I seed there was weak spots in them men and there was bad acts comin up, but I didn't run a step. I stood there and they all runned out of there like rats runnin out of a woodpile, and all of em that run, run out the back. I didn't let that worry me; I just taken it for granted and let em go. I didn't think about gettin shot and I didn't think about not gettin shot. I thought this: a organization is a organization and if I don't mean nothin by joinin I ought to keep my ass out of it. But if I'm sworn to stand up for all the poor colored farmers—and poor white farmers if they'd taken a notion to join—I've got to do it. Weren't no use under God's sun to treat colored people like we'd been treated here in the state of Alabama. Work hard and look how they do you. Look how they done my daddy in his time and look how Mr. Watson tried to do me. Dug at me and dug at me, couldn't handle me, then he made me bring him the cotton. I carried it to him—I was workin for a easy way out—didn't carry him all of it but I carried him more than enough to pay him what I owed him. Still he dug at me and he dug at his other niggers too. Virgil Jones—he was in the organization, he was solid in bein with us, but when the showdown come he run like the rest of em. Some of em is yet standin with a watery mouth, ready when times are made better by those that's men enough and women enough to stand up, when the thing ever comes into effect; they goin to run up then and accept the good of it and they won't give you a bit more credit for riskin your life than they would a rabbit.

Virgil Jones was a friend to me. He was rentin his farm—he weren't buyin it and he weren't rentin it from Mr. Watson; Mr. Watson didn't own that place. But Mr. Watson was dealin with him furnishin him—had been—that's what I understood. And he claimed that Virgil owed him money. I don't know how much Virgil owed him or if he owed him at all, but that weren't the issue with me. I was forced that year to face what was happenin—

So, them officers runned that car up out there to the road comin to that house, and that house stood a good little piece off the public road. Four of em come back there that evenin. I was outdoors, walkin around, watchin for em to come. Virgil Logan done dashed off and went and got what he could but he didn't get Kurt

Beall. He wouldn't come there; he'd done got shot at that rip-it at Crane's Ford and he was shy, he wouldn't come down there. And after all this trouble was over, blessed God if a white man didn't shoot Sheriff Beall down and kill him. Since then, since then. There was a ruckus up there above Beaufort between a man and his wife and he sent his deputies to cool the water and they couldn't do nothin. He decided he'd go up there and do it and they tell it—and there good evidence to back it—soon as he got there the white man killed him.

Well, I didn't care if Kurt Beall come back and I didn't care if he didn't. Who came back with Logan? Lew Badger from Hamilton, just up above Beaufort Byron Ward, Kurt Beall's deputy from Beaufort; and a old fellow by the name of Platt I never did see him before but I knowed of him. And of course, Virgil Logan come back with em. They stopped that car and jumped out of it and come right straight toward the front of the house in a fast walk—they weren't trottin but they was walkin as fast as they could walk. I stood there and looked at em till they got up to me. And when they hit the edge of the yard, Virgil Logan pointed his finger and said, "There stands Nate Shaw. That's him right there."

He just kept a walkin; him and Lew Badger went on around the house. Platt and Ward come straight to me. I noticed that Platt had a automatic shotgun—I could see about four inches of the barrel; he'd pulled the stock of it under a big brown weather coat. Platt walked right up to me. Ward went to the doorsteps and just laid down nearly, peepin in the house to see who was in there, me watchin Platt and watchin Ward too. They surrounded that house then and Platt walked up just above, five paces from me and stopped; that's as close as he come. And he stood there, flashin his eyes over me, keepin his gun pointed on me. Right at that present time I was the only fellow out there. All the rest of em done run away and gone to the swamps and woods where the sheriffs couldn't see em.

Everything was so quiet there—Mr. Platt stood and looked at me, looked at me; wouldn't say a word, wouldn't say "umph," wouldn't even grunt. Looked at me from my head to my foot. Stood there for the longest and kept that gun presented right to me. Well, I was just as impudent as I could be—he didn't know it though. He'd run up against somebody that weren't scared. If they didn't want me to do nothin to em they oughta just stayed away from there or killed me at the start, on first sight, because I was goin to try em, sure as I was alive.

I reckon Platt was lookin for a crooked move someway. I was standin there with my hands in my pockets, just so. Only my finger was on the trigger of my pistol and the pistol was in my hand. I'd carried that .32 Smith and Wesson there with me that mornin and concealed it from view. I had on a pair of Big-8 overalls, brand new, and the pockets was deep. And I had on a white cowboy hat and my jumper—that's the way I was dressed. And a pair of Red Wing boots about knee high. I was beginnin to get prepared for winter it was already December, before Christmas, December of '32. I don't know what date it was but I know it was on a Monday.

Well, everything got quiet and Mr. Logan and Mr. Badger was around there lookin in the back of the house. And Mr. Ward was busy at the doorstep there, just a few steps from where me and Mr. Platt was—Mr. Platt weren't sayin a word, he just lookin me over.

After awhile—I stood there just as long as I wanted to and I decided I'd go back in the house and get out from amongst em, and if nothing else, see if the house was clean—which it was, clean out, didn't a man show up in my sight but Mr. Platt. I weren't goin to stand right up there and look at him shoot me so I turned and walked off from him, started on into the house. And Mr. Ward was there at the doorstep. He just raised up and fastened his hand to my arm. I was a pretty good man then, I was young—I aint dead yet, thank the Lord—soon as he grabbed that arm, I just loosed up what I was holdin in my pocket and come out with a naked hand. Then I snapped him up to me and gave him a jolt and a fling—off he went like a leech. I never offered to hit him, I just flung him loose from my arm. Nobody hadn't said nothin to me, not a word.

All right. I started on again into the house, right on. Took one or to steps—BOOM—Mr. Platt throwed his gun on me. I didn't stop, the game didn't fall for him. BOOM BOOM—shot me two more times before I could get in the door. Blood commenced a flyin—I never did quit walkin. He filled my hind end up from the bend of my legs to my hips with shot. I walked on in the door, stopped right in the hallway and looked back. He was standin right close to a big old oak tree right in line with the door. Run my hand in my pocket, snatched out my .32 Smith and Wesson and I commenced a shootin at Platt. Good God he jumped behind that tree soon as that pistol fired; he jumped like lightnin. My mind told me: just keep shootin the tree, just keep shootin and maybe he'll get scared and run; you'll have a chance at him then. But as the devil would have it the more I shot the tighter he drawed up behind that tree until I quit shootin. I seed his head poke around the tree—that tree saved him—and he seed what I was doin: good God almighty, I was reloadin and before I could reload my gun, them two sheriffs round the house, Mr. Logan and Mr. Badger pulled out across the corn field headin to the road. Them two that had come to me, Mr. Platt and Mr. Ward, all I seed was their backs runnin. Every one of them officers outrun the devil away from there. I don't know how many people they might have, thought was in that house, but that .32 Smith and Wesson was barkin too much for em to stand. They didn't see where the shots was comin from nobody but Mr. Platt knowed that.

They hitched up to their ass-wagon and took off. And five minutes after that man shot me three times—I was standin in the door lookin out—my feet was just sloshin in blood. Now if that aint the truth the truth aint never been told. I was just burnt up with shot. Wonder they had't shot my secrets out.

I come out the door with my pistol shot clean out and I seed Sam MacFarland layin to the left there, bleedin at the mouth. I couldn't say to save my life where Sam come from. I walked up to him, looked at him—I was sorry, I hated that. He went for a little kin to me, Sam MacFarland did. And they tell me that Mr. Mac Sloane come there—grand rascal, he didn't live long hisself—and stomped Sam MacFarland's head. I done gone home then and gone to the doctor. And some of em told it that that nigger Cece Pickett shot Sam, but I never seed Cece come back there with them white men that evenin.

I walked on away from the house and went down to the south side of the barn where there was four or five fellows standin; had done runned up out of the swamps and they was armed. And the officers' car was out there side of the road and them officers had done runned to it. And when they seed that crowd of niggers at the barn throw up their guns they jumped in the car. Boss Hatch, chunky-built, dark complexioned fellow, he had a Winchester and he couldn't operate it. Little Waldo Ramsey—he was there he told him, "Give it to me." Boss Hatch handed it to him. Little Waldo took that rifle and he shook it up, juiced it, changed the sight, dropped on his knees and throwed that rifle up on that car. I was standin there, just as bloody as a hog, lookin right at him. He cut down on that car, knocked the glass out and injured the stock of one of them deputies' rifles—so they said in court.

I walked on home after I was shot, and time I walked in the yard I seed my wife run out of the house. Vernon had done reported conditions to her and stirred her all up. I didn't know Vernon had been nowhere about. Virgil Jones' house set way back off the road but there was another house, Sam MacFarland's house, settin right beside the road. Well, Vernon was up there by that house lookin down on that shootin business. He didn't come down there though.

I walked on in home just shot all to pieces in my seat. Vernon and Hannah taken me on my Chevrolet car, and a fellow by the name of Ambrose Butler, one of the Butler boys, got on that car with us as a friend and a protection, and when Vernon stopped drivin, the casins on them car wheels was touchin the hospital steps, Tuskegee hospital. It was called to be sixteen miles from my house to Tuskegee. Hannah went in there and got a entrance for me and they sent stretched out—two men with a stretcher come out to the car. I asked em, "What you all doin bringing that out here for?"

Said, "Brought it to get you."

I said, "If you just sort of help me out of this car I can walk in there myself. You don't have to tote me."

They helped me out—my wife and son helped me out and I walked in there. Doctors put me on the table and commenced a pickin shot out of me, and some more come in the room there and asked me how come I got shot and so on. But you got to keep some things to yourself, my judgment told me. Be careful, not tell everything. I didn't tell em it was the organization act because I couldn't afford to tell that to people I didn't know. I told em it was a riot, just a riot between the blacks and the whites.

So they treated me—they had to treat me—but they wouldn't keep me that night, a man of their own color. Scared the white folks would come after me and find me there and maybe tear the place up or accuse em of helpin me. It was their duty to doctor me and they did, they did, but they wouldn't keep me. They didn't tell me where to go, they didn't tell me where not to go, just leave that hospital that night. So I left. I couldn't stay there without authority.

My wife carried me away from there and on down deeper in Macon County, anglin southwest out of Tuskegee over in Quitman's Flats, to her cousin's, and I stayed there that night. Her and Vernon went on back home and run into a shootin frolic and a whole lot of devilment when they got there that night. A riot crowd come to my home and shot all over my people and around em, shot with shotguns and rifles. One shot hit one of my little girls in the jaw—Leah Ann; it weren't no bad wound, it didn't leave a mark. But it scared her and scared em all to death.

Tuesday evenin that mob crowd caught Vernon and told him if he didn't tell em where I was they'd kill him. Some of em wanted to carry him off from the house—

and there was a old well out there, I spect that well was forty foot deep. Of course, I had throwed many a old dead chicken in it—that well'd be dry as long as I knowed about it. No doubt, if he hadn't told em just where I was, why they'd a got him out there and seed that old well and throwed him in there. They'd a done it. I ain't got no confidence in these folks.

They had heard that my wife and Vernon had gone to carry me somewhere but they didn't know where. Somebody told that secret. And when they got back home—that night, the night before they caught Vernon and forced him to tell em where I was my wife runned into her brother somewhere or other and she told *him* where I was. And he come tearin down to me—I hated it—he come in there a late hour of the night. I asked him, "Where'd you come from?"

He said, "I come from up there at home."

I said, "You have no business comin down here. They goin to catch you too in it. They goin to come here at me. They goin to rally and raise the devil and shoot folks and kill em till they find me. Now you here too."

He had a breech-loader in his hands and I said, "What you goin to do with that gun? They goin to hurt you if they find you here with that."

I couldn't move him. He wouldn't leave his brother-in-law and he wouldn't get shed of that gun.

So, Tuesday evenin, bout two o'clock, the white men come runnin there to my wife's cousin huntin me up where Vernon said they left me, him and my wife, his mother, left me. Folks' house I was hidin at—this woman was a cousin to my wife and also to little Waldo; she was a married woman but her husband weren't at home.

And so, when I heard the cars rollin up to the house that boy coulda got away if he'd a done it. They didn't know definitely he'd been at Virgil Jones' house that mornin because he was off in the swamps and he could have stayed out of it after that. Now them Tukabahchee deputies *might* have knowed he was there, but them men that come after me from Tuskegee that evenin didn't know it.

I said, "Here they come." I knowed it was them. "They rollin in here after me."

Little Waldo jumped up and runned out the house on the far side—he was too game, he didn't use his sense. I begged him not to go, I begged him to leave his gun in the house but he ran out and they killed him, good as killed him. I told him to stash hisself off in the woods and get away. He oughta knowed with them officers runnin down on him he'd be just like a rabbit, but he wouldn't consider that. And they weren't after him; they didn't know he was down there with me. And blessed God, when he went out of that house, he went out shootin and took off on a run. They just throwed their rifles on him—old Bert Calhoun, he'd been sheriff at Tuskegee for years. He was in there helpin shoot him down. And Cliff Soule, he was head man, at that time; he done defeated Bert Calhoun for sheriff and I couldn't swear that he done the shootin—but Bert Calhoun and some other Tuskegee white men, they shot at little Waldo until—I heard the shots, I was in the house. Soon as the bullets ceased, the guns ceased shootin, here come Mr. Soule in the house to get me. Found me there sittin up in a chair. Mr. Cliff Soule—I had been a friend to him when he lived out here close to me in the country. He had his boy haulin lumber for the Graham-Pike Lumber Company and many a day I helped his daddy's mules. Harvey Soule was the boy and when I got into trouble his father wanted to kill me, Cliff Soule. Many a time I took my mules loose from my wagon—and it was known, good God, my mules never did fall back from a load—and I had Harvey Soule to take his mules loose and get em out the way and I'd bring my mules to his wagon and pull it out from where his mules done backed up and run it into a ditch with a load of lumber on it. Tell him, "Move your mules—" He had a nice lookin black-colored mule, she was blocky-built, heavy; and a old longlegged sorrel mule, good lookin mule, between a sorrel and a red. If he took a notion he wouldn't pull—he'd get out there in the road, stop and stall and lie wouldn't pull the hat off your head. And I'd hitch my mules to Mr. Soule's wagon and call em. Doggone it, that mule would come out of that ditch. Done it every time. Now his daddy come to kill me. I knowed that regardless to what you done, some of these white folks would just receive your labor and your kind favors and soon as you stepped aside and done somethin they didn't like, they'd be ready to destroy you. Cliff Soule was one of them kind. Come in there, "Uh-huh, here he is. Get up and get out of here."

I got up and walked out. And I had to pick up little Waldo and lay him in the back of the sheriff's car on the floor. Carried him on to Tuskegee and put him in jail, and he shot up like he was. And where they shot him, I looked at it: one bullet hit the side of his head and just split the skin. Next place they shot a hole in him, just between the top of his shoulder and his heart. And the next place he was shot was through the wrist. They shot at him with rifles just like they was takin a walk, shot at him till they shot him down. I was listenin at the rifles cryin behind that boy.

When they come there to arrest me, they made Vernon get on the car with em and bring em directly to me. He was sittin in the sheriff's car when they loaded me and little Waldo in there. Vernon waited for his chance to talk with me and he said, "Papa, if I hadn't told you where you was they would have killed me. They said they would."

I said, "You done right, son, you done right. Tell em where I'm at every time and save yourself. I'd rather go down than for them to harm any of my boys."

We left out from Quitman's Flats goin to Tuskegee; got up the road a good ways, Cliff Soule looked around and said, "Nate, I wouldn't a thought that of you. We didn't know that there was such tricks in you. We always' taken you to be the leadin darky for Tukabahchee County."

Yeah, I was leadin. I preached many and many a time to my color: don't mess with these white folks in a way to keep trouble built up on your back.

I just listened at him. I knowed it wouldn't do me no good to call up any of my goodness and kindness. I asked him, then, "Mr. Soule, what have I done wrong? If it's wrong, worse things than that have happened."

"Well, just shut up; don't tell me nothin."

That put my boots on still tighter and laced em up. I didn't have no voice—and soon as they heard of me bein in a thing like that, why, they was surprised; they thought I'd be a check to hold the other niggers out. But when I wouldn't stand under their whip they arrested me for *bad* crimes—that's the way they termed it, *bad*—fightin a crowd of sheriffs over what was mine and what was my friend's. O, that was terrible. Weren't it terrible?

Wednesday morning they called up Beaufort to come down there and get me. Old man Kurt Beall and Ward, his deputy, dropped down there quick and took me and Vernon both. But they didn't take little Waldo—Ooooooo, that boy was crazy about me as if I had been his own dear brother. When the sheriff come around and got me out of Tuskegee jail that boy let into hollerin, "Nate, Nate"

---

135. Studs Terkel, "Campus Life in the Depression"

Young people were among those most affected by the Great Depression. The brief accounts offered here in Studs Terkel's **Hard Times** *give an idea of the decisions students faced.*

Pauline Kael

When I attended Berkeley in 1936, so many of the kids had actually lost their fathers. They had wandered off in disgrace because they couldn't support their families. Other fathers had killed themselves, so the family could have the insurance. Families had totally broken down.

Source: From *Hard Times* by Studs Terkel. Copyright 1970 by Studs Terkel. Reprinted by permission of Pantheon Books, a division of Random House, Inc.

Each father took it as his personal failure. These middle-class men apparently had no social sense of what was going on, so they killed themselves.

It was still the Depression. There were kids who didn't have a place to sleep, huddling under bridges on the campus. I had a scholarship, but there were times when I didn't have food. The meals were often three candy bars. We lived communally and I remember feeding other kids by cooking up more spaghetti than I can ever consider again.

There was an embarrassment at college where a lot of the kids were well-heeled. I still have a resentment against the fraternity boys and the sorority girls with their cashmere sweaters and the pearls. Even now, when I lecture at colleges, I have this feeling about those terribly overdressed kids. It wasn't a hatred because I wanted these things, but because they didn't understand what was going on.

I was a reader for seven courses a semester, and I made $50 a month. I think I was the only girl on the labor board at Berkeley. We were trying to get the minimum wage on the campus raised to forty cents an hour. These well-dressed kids couldn't understand our interest. There was a real division between the poor who were trying to improve things on the campus and the rich kids who didn't give a damn.

Berkeley was a cauldron in the late Thirties. You no sooner enrolled than you got an invitation from the Trotskyites and the Stalinists. Both were wooing you. I enrolled at sixteen, so it was a little overpowering at the time. I remember joining the Teachers Assistants Union. We had our own version of Mario Savio. He's now a lawyer specializing in bankruptcies. We did elect a liberal as president of the student body. It was a miracle in those days.

The fraternity boys, often acted as strikebreakers in San Francisco—the athletes and the engineering students. And the poor boys were trying to get their forty cents an hour. The college administration could always count on the frat boys to put down any student movement.

It's different today, the fraternities and sororities having so much less power. . . .

Robert Gard

PROFESSOR OF DRAMA, UNIVERSITY OF WISCONSIN.

I set out for the University of Kansas on a September morning with $30 that I'd borrowed from my local bank. I had one suit and one necktie and one pair of shoes. My mother had spent several days putting together a couple of wooden cases of canned fruits and vegetables. My father, a country lawyer, had taken as a legal fee a 1915 Buick touring car. It was not in particularly good condition, but it was good enough to get me there. It fell to pieces and it never got back home anymore.

I had no idea how long the $30 would last, but it sure would have to go a long way because I had nothing else. The semester fee was $22, so that left me $8 to go. Fortunately, I got a job driving a car for the dean of the law school. That's how I got through the first year.

What a pleasure it was to get a pound of hamburger, which you could buy for about five cents, take it up to the Union Pacific Railroad tracks and have a cookout. And some excellent conversation. And maybe swim in the Kaw River.

One friend of mine came to college equipped. He had an old Model T Ford Sedan, about a 1919 model. He had this thing fitted up as a house. He lived in it all year long. He cooked and slept and studied inside that Model T Ford Sedan. How he managed I will never know. I once went there for dinner. He cooked a pretty good one on a little stove he had in this thing. He was a brilliant student. I don't know where he is now, but I shouldn't be surprised if he's the head of some big corporation. (Laughs.) Survival. . . .

The weak ones, I don't suppose, really survived. There were many breakdowns. From malnutrition very likely. I know there were students actually starving.

Some of them engaged in strange occupations. There was a biological company that would pay a penny apiece for cockroaches. They needed these in research, I guess. Some students went cockroach hunting every night. They'd box 'em and sell them to this firm.

I remember the feverish intellectual discussion we had. There were many new movements. On the literary scene, there was something called the Proletarian Novel. There was the Federal Theater and the Living Newspaper. For the first time, we began to get socially conscious. We began to wonder about ourselves and our society.

We were mostly farm boys and, to some extent, these ideas were alien to us. We had never really thought about them before. But it was a period of necessity. It brought us face to face with these economic problems and the rest. . . . All in all, a painful time, but a glorious time.

Chance Stoner

A financial consultant on Wall Street.

"I actually in my own life did not see any difference between the Twenties and the Thirties. I was living in a small Virginia town, and it was poverty-stricken. You had five thousand rural bank failures in the Twenties. . . . My father was a typewriter salesman who did the best he could . . ."

They gave me a $100 scholarship to the University of Virginia. That's in 1931, which was damn good. And my mother gave me $100. I had a pair of khaki pants, a pair of sneakers and a khaki shirt. That was it.

The first year on the campus, I organized a Marxist study class. The students fell into two groups. About nine hundred of them had automobiles. About nine hundred had jobs or scholarships. The other nine hundred fell in between. We had real class warfare. The automobile boys and the fraternities—we had thirty-three little Greek palaces on fraternity row—they had charge of the student government. So I organized the other nine hundred, and we took the student government away from them and rewrote the constitution.

I spent half my time on radical activities. I was trying to organize a union in Charlottesville—and bringing Negroes to speak on the campus. We had the first black man to speak there since Reconstruction. He was an old Socialist.

This threw the dean into a fit. He still believed in slavery. He forbade the use of any university building. I was then writing a weekly column for the campus paper. So I attacked the dean: "What manner of small-minded men have inherited Mr. Jefferson's university?" (Laughs.) It was reprinted all over the Eastern seaboard. On the front pages of newspapers, including *The New York Times*. (Laughs.)

The president sent for me. He had a stack five inches high of clippings. He said, "Now look what you've done." (Laughs.) I said, "It's not my fault. The man's been properly invited, he's qualified and he's going to speak at the Episcopal Church chapel." The dean was one of the deacons of the church. So we had quite a time of it.

There were writings on the sidewalk of the university: "Down With Imperialistic War. Scholarships Not Battleships." Again I was invited to the president's office. He asked me if I couldn't stop people from writing all over the sidewalk. I said to him: We're perfectly willing to abide by a general rule. If the secret societies and fraternities aren't permitted to write on the steps or sidewalks, we won't either. So he walked me to the window and outside in great purple letters was the slogan: "Down With Imperialist War." He said, "Couldn't you *please* at least get the spelling right?" (Laughs.)

In 1935, we had the first official shutdown of all university classes for a peace demonstration. Guess who the featured speaker was? J. B. Matthews. He later ran the Un-American Activities Committee, as staff director for Martin Dies. He was the man who invented the complete file and cross-reference system, and the theory of associations and fronts and all the rest of it. A very remarkable fella. He started out as a Protestant minister, came to socialism and wound up with Martin Dies. Joe McCarthy was impossible without J. B. Matthews. And we shut down the university for him. . . . Oh, well. . . .

I was a troublemaker then. (Laughs.) I wish I still were.

Chapter XXV

The New Deal, 1933–1939

136. Ralph Shaw, "The New Deal: Its Unsound Theories and Irreconcilable Policies," 1935

Franklin D. Roosevelt was widely attacked and hated by those who felt he was destroying American institutions. The critique offered by Ralph Shaw was typical of persons posed on the farthest right.

"What experience and history teach is this: That peoples and governments never have learned anything from history, nor acted on principles deduced from it." (Hegel)

The accuracy of the statement contained in the foregoing quotation from Hegel could never be more fittingly illustrated than by the conditions which obtain in this country at the present time.

We Americans, and especially the members of our profession, are confused, bewildered and dismayed, but not because of a mere economic depression. Like depressions have existed since authentic history began and will doubtless continue for countless years to come until, if ever, millennium arrives. But millennium is not yet here, and in the meantime we are confused, bewildered and dismayed by reason of novel, weird, fantastic and vague legislation in contravention of all past experience and quite beyond the comprehension of a normal mind.

We listen to legislators, executives, and demagogues who talk in terms of billions of dollars, of millions of families on relief, and we are told of hitherto unknown principles, rights, duties, obligations and regulations.

These laws and regulations are so complex that they stupefy reason. The figures are so stupendous that no one can understand them or apply them, just as years ago when, as children in school, we were told that the sun was so many millions of miles away from the earth, we said, "Oh," but it didn't mean anything concrete or tangible to our childish minds.

Accordingly, this morning I propose, if I can, to reduce all these grandiose figures and strange and weird concepts of right, duties, obligations and regulations to first principles, and to illustrate them in such simple terms and phraseology that he who runs can read and understand.

Two Postulates

Without fear of successful contradiction, I submit to this convention of able lawyers, that a nation is nothing more or less than an accumulation of families; that the family is the basic unit of government and that families are composed of individuals with interests in common because of long, intimate and familiar relationship. Further, that what is true, of "the family" is equally true of a group of families, and is also equally true of the grand accumulation of families which constitute the nation.

If a family continues to overspend, it goes broke and it necessarily follows that if a nation continues to overspend, it must also become bankrupt, its credit destroyed and the standard of living of the individuals who compose it be reduced to the want level.

This is such a self-evident proposition that I almost crave your indulgence for making it.

Source: Ralph Shaw, "The New Deal: Its Unsound Theories and Irreconcilable Policies," American Liberty League Address, 1935, Public Domain Reprint.

In connection with the foregoing proposition, and as a part of it (for the two should be considered jointly), I submit for your consideration a postulate or aphorism, the accuracy of which is also not open to debate. It is as follows:

> "Justice to one is injustice to no one, But mercy to some may be injustice to many."

I urge your earnest consideration of these postulates. If they are constantly borne in mind, then irrespective of how the New Deal is defined—whether it is merely aimed towards recovery, as some of its adherents claim; or whether it is merely pointed towards reform, as some of its adherents claim; or whether it has a more sinister objective (reference to which will be made hereinafter)—the fact remains that, bearing these postulates in mind, there will be no difficulty in analyzing, dissecting and thoroughly appreciating the unsound principles and irreconcilable policies of the so-called "New Deal."

Some of the empirical idealists who are sponsoring it predicate their support upon what they call the desirability or necessity of "social" justice. Of course, we lawyers know that "justice" is "justice" whether it be in the courtroom or in the ballroom or in the market place, and that the preface of the word "social" to the word "justice" adds nothing to its meaning or luster. But because these empirical idealists seem to attach some importance to the word "social" as a prefix to the word "justice," suppose we consider the phrase in its entirety.

The New Deal's Conception of "Social Injustice" and "Social Justice"

Just what is "social justice" or "social injustice?"

Suppose we apply the phrase to what is ordinarily called the social side of life.

Here we have on the one hand a beautiful, charming, comely woman, or a brilliant, intelligent man, and on the other hand an unintelligent, unattractive, dowdy woman, or a shiftless, unkempt, unattractive man. Certainly, the former have a great advantage over the latter in all of the social activities and competitions of life. Is that a social injustice? Under the theories of the New Deal, it surely must be. Therefore, according to New Deal theories, society should proceed to remedy the injustice by law.

Obviously, however, since society can not possibly enforce a law which would vest in the homely and the unintelligent the qualities of comeliness and intelligence, in order to remedy the injustice, the law must find some way to mar or destroy the charm and intelligence of those who have the advantage. Thus, we obtain so-called "social justice." Obviously, however, such an inhuman process is gross injustice to those who are maimed.

Nevertheless, that's the logic of the New Deal.

Transfer the consideration of the phrase "social justice" to the realm of athletics. Here we have a ten second man on the university track team; your Bobby Jones at golf (I would like to call him our Bobby Jones because, after all, he is a national figure); Ty Cobb, of baseball fame, or Dixie Howell as a fullback. Their competitors are unable to successfully compete with them. Is that a social injustice? Is it fair that one man should run in ten seconds, while his competitor can't run in better than twenty? Is it fair that Mr. Jones should have an advantage over his competitors at golf, or Mr. Cobb at baseball, or Mr. Howell in football?

Obviously, if logic means anything these gentlemen have an advantage in competition with their competitors to which they are not entitled.

Accordingly, society passes a law to remove the injustice. However, since society can not enforce a law which would increase the speed of the twenty second man to ten seconds, or make a golfer out of a dub, or a brilliant baseball player or fullback out of a third-rate substitute, society, by law, hamstrings the ten second man, maims Mr. Jones, Mr. Cobb and Mr. Howell to the end that their excellence is impaired and their superiority is destroyed. Thus, irrespective of the injustice to the gentlemen we have hamstrung and maimed, "social justice" has been accomplished.

That is the logic of the New Deal.

Still again—apply the phrase "social justice" to the industrial side of life. On the one hand you have a thrifty, ambitious or lucky (if you please) group of men, in whatever line of endeavor they may be engaged, and on the other a group who are thriftless and indolent and unlucky. The former succeed. They attain an enviable status in society, a competency, nay, even a vast fortune for themselves and their descendants. Is that a social injustice? If the tenets of the New Deal are to be accurately applied, it surely is. So the Legislature passes a law to remedy it.

Obviously, however, since society, by law, can not energize the thriftless and the incompetent and place them on a parity with the thrifty and the competent, society, by law, proceeds to destroy the capacity of the thrifty, or their incentive to exercise it. Thus New Dealers claim society has destroyed "social injustice" and weeded out the "privileged." But—is that justice to those whose capacity and incentive have been weeded out? The New Dealers say that it is.

That is the logic of the New Deal.

To reverse the situation, here's an evangelical broadcaster of national reputation with a voice, a command of rhetoric and an extraordinary capacity for influencing people who can't think for themselves. Others who desire to influence the same class of people may not compete successfully with him. Isn't that a social injustice? Oughtn't it be remedied by law?

According to the tenets of the New Deal it is, and it should. But, since society knows of no law which will vest in the unskillful the capacity to influence and move the unthinking, society proceeds by law to emasculate the voice of the evangelical broadcaster of national reputation.

Isn't that an "injustice" to the broadcaster? Personally, I think it is. Nevertheless, that's the logic of the New Deal.

I illustrate further. Here are five gentlemen in the front row. They are starting out in life in the same city block or on adjacent farms or plantations. Each has the right to plan for himself as he wishes for the future. They each establish, or ought to establish each for himself, the standard of life which they wish. Certainly, even New Dealers would concede that.

Number one is frugal, thrifty and continent—if you please, lucky. Over the years he accumulates sufficient to take care of himself and his family in his declining years. The next three are not so farsighted and lucky (if you please), but they do fairly well. The fifth has no vision, or if he has, refuses to exercise it; no energy, or if he has, prefers to spend it in riotous living. He brings a family into the world of such size and number that there is not the remotest chance of his ever being able to provide for them, either in good-times or bad. Then comes depression.

Number one, because of his foresight and vision and luck (if you please) is able to get through with comparative comfort. Number two, three and four, by exercising then the virtues which number one has exercised always, are able to pull through, but number five is starving.

Now, this discussion has nothing whatever to do with what any one or all of the four may voluntarily do for number five. This discussion is centered only upon what society ought to compel number one to do for number five. If the New Dealers are running society, by law and against his will, they take away from number one the results of his foresight and thrift and give it to number five.

Is that justice to number one? Is that not punishing number one for his virtue and rewarding number five for his vice?

That, however, is the logic and avowed purpose of the New Deal.

Just one further illustration before I leave this branch of this address.

Last September in California I was arguing with a New Dealer about the virtues of Sinclair's EPIC, sometimes called "Ending Poverty in California," and sometimes paraphrased as "Everybody Poor in California." We were making no headway. Finally the New Dealer, who thoroughly believed in what he was defending said, "We are not getting anywhere. Suppose we begin again. Suppose we start from something about which we both agree. Of course (he said), you believe in the 'more abundant life' for the 'underprivileged.'"

"Well (I said), not so fast. Suppose you define the phrase 'the more abundant life' and suppose you define the word 'underprivileged.'"

Of course, he couldn't do it in any satisfactory phraseology and neither can any one else, be he ever so blest with a honied vocabulary. The phrase "the more abundant life for the underprivileged" is just a glamorous combination of words to lull the thoughtless and the indigent into beautiful daydreams of accomplishment and happiness without effort on their part.

Then I said to the New Dealer:

"If you mean by the more abundant life that one would like to see every man who does not have what he wants get it, if he can, then every one believes in the 'more abundant life.' But if you mean by the more abundant life that every man who does not have what he wants, has the right to demand and take it, or under the guise of law, either through taxes or by force, have it taken for him from somebody else, I don't believe in the so-called 'more abundant life' and no nation could survive under such a regime. But what is far more important, suppose we discuss the meaning of the word 'underprivileged.'"

It couldn't be done, and since the abstract was getting no results, I suggested a switch to the concrete and asked him where he would place a certain individual whom we both knew, was he privileged or underprivileged? The New Dealer said with a sneer, "Oh, he is one of the privileged."

"Well (I said), where would you have placed him forty years ago, when (as I knew the fact to be) like millions of other citizens, he walked the streets of a large city looking for a job, with few acquaintances and no friends, without a dime in his pockets except the money that he had borrowed—where would you have placed him then?"

Both logic and honesty required him to say, "At that time he was one of the underprivileged."

"Well," I asked (and I now ask every individual in this audience and in this country who is sufficiently interested in the subject to consider the question), "what was it that took the one time 'underprivileged' into the ranks of the 'privileged'? The State gave him no bounty; no privileges, no exclusive grant, to magnificent largess. It was work, character, natural ability and good luck, if you please."

Another question necessarily follows: Is it "social justice" to deprive such a man of what he has accomplished and to destroy his incentive to accomplish more, and give it to somebody else? The New Dealer is forced to answer this inquiry "Yes."

That is the logic of the New Deal.

LaFollette's Representative

Some months ago an attractive young man came into my office in Chicago and presented his card. In the lower left-hand corner there appeared the words, "Special Representative of the Honorable Robert M. LaFollette, Senator from Wisconsin." I don't know whether Senator LaFollette sent him or not, but the gentleman said he did.

After the amenities of the occasion were over, he said he had called to enlist me as one of a group in Illinois to sponsor Senator LaFollette's social propaganda in my State.

Upon inquiry as to the nature of his program, he said:

"Senator LaFollette has a number of planks in his program, to the first of which, I am sure, you will agree. The first is: Every man has a right to a job."

I asked, "Are you using the terms advisedly?"

He repeated, "Certainly. Every man has a right to a job."

"Well," I said, "to me rights connote 'duties.' It is inconceivable to think of a right without a correlative duty. If every man has a right to a job, then it is somebody's duty to give him a job, because 'rights' are enforceable against those who owe 'duties.'"

Continuing, I said, "Here is a supposed stranger at the door. He wants a job. Is it your duty to give him a job?"

"Certainly not," was the answer.

"Well," I asked, "is it my duty to give him a job?"

"Certainly not," was the answer.

"Well," I said, "don't we (you and I) fairly represent a cross-section of society? Whose duty is it to give the stranger a job?"

"No," I said, "a man, by his own energy, intelligence, thrift, tenacity of purpose, enterprise and all of the other virtues which go to make men efficient, must get a job for himself, if he can. A decent and desirable society can never survive by imposing duties where there are not correlative rights or *vice versa*."

The logic of the New Deal is that "duties" may be imposed by law upon some and vested as "rights" in others, but the recipients of the "rights" under New Deal law have no obligations of any kind to those upon whom the duties are imposed.

A New Slavery

Ladies and gentlemen, prior to the year 1860 there existed in our country a social status recognized by law. Under that status, some groups in the society had the right, by law, to expropriate the time and labor of other groups. The exploiters were under no legal obligation to the exploited, except as enlightened self-love imposed it. The status was called slavery.

On the one hand stood the masters, among whom were my ancestors. On the other were the slaves.

Seventy years have since elapsed and according to the New Dealers a new status in society is now being created.

Under this new status, it is proposed by taxation to confiscate the property of some citizens; expropriate the time and labor of those who work and are still willing to work and to give the proceeds thereof to those who don't work, many of whom are unwilling to work. The latter have a legal right to enjoy the property, the time and the service of the former. The former have merely a duty which they may be compelled to perform. Those who receive the benefits of the property taken and the time and labor expropriated are under no obligation whatever to those from whom it is taken.

I don't know what you call it, but I call such a status slavery. The only difference between this present status and the slavery that obtained prior to 1860 is this: That in the present status the inefficient become the masters and the efficient and the thrifty are the slaves.

That is the logic of the New Deal.

But, says some one who is troubled by the logic of this analysis and desires to divert the mind from reason to sentiment, you are placing too much emphasis on "property rights" and not enough on "human rights."

The answer is simple and convincing. In the first place, property has no rights. The correct phrase is "rights in property." If there is such a thing as a human right, I know of no human right which is dearer to civilized man than the right to work for, acquire and keep for his own, property.

Property is substantially synonymous with capital. Capital means safety. Nations with capital have high standards of living. Families with capital have certain freedom from want. Capital has never been acquired by any one except through thrift, frugality, saving, foresight and vision (with sometimes a little luck), either by the person who acquired it or by some ancestor who acquired it for him.

The Unsoundness of "Sharing the Wealth" Theory

But, says some one gifted with more demagogic vision than with keen power of logical analysis, some people have taken more than their fair share of the capital.

Never was there a more malicious misrepresentation of an economic fact made by an ambitious demagogue to thoughtless people incapable of thinking for themselves.

Such an assertion connotes the concept that in some way, somehow, there has been created a pile of wealth, loaded upon a table, from which some people have seized more than their fair share. Such a suggestion indicates a total want on the part of the individual making it, whenever it is made, wherever it is made, or by whomsoever it is made, of the true concept of how capital or wealth is created.

One illustration will suffice. I suppose that if the slogan "Share the Wealth" should ever be translated into an actual effort to do so, the fortune which Mr. Ford is credited with having amassed would be taken from him. But the fact is that that wealth would never have existed if it had not been for Mr. Ford or some other genius equally as capable. It was not created by some one else and piled upon the table and then seized by him. On the contrary, he created the wealth himself, and by his genius and ability, management and vision, he put into operation the activities which created it.

He produced a car by the production of which he brought luxury to millions of homes otherwise unobtainable. He gave employment to millions of employees in his own factories and in the factories and mines and railroads which produce and transport the raw material. He made it himself. In so doing, he added materially to the wealth and happiness of millions. To take away from him by law the results of his achievement and give it to somebody else who has accomplished nothing but failure would be a crime not only against him but a crime against society.

Yet in its ultimate analysis that's what the New Deal advocates. That is the logic of the New Deal.

Summary of New Deal Theories

Ladies and gentlemen, I have been attempting during this portion of my address, by illustration or otherwise, to put the logic or lack of logic of the New Deal in such plain phrases that a high school student could thoroughly understand and grasp. However, the whole theory of the New Deal may be summed up in a few sentences.

The New Deal is nothing more or less than an effort sponsored by inexperienced sentimentalists and demagogues to take away from the thrifty what the thrifty or their ancestors have accumulated, or may accumulate, and to give it to others who have not earned it, or whose ancestors haven't earned it for them, and who never would have earned it and never will earn it, and thus indirectly to destroy the incentive for all future accumulation. Such a purpose is in defiance of everything that history teaches and of the tenets upon which our civilization has been founded.

The Declaration of Independence recites, and our whole theory of society is predicated upon the concept:

> "That men are endowed by their Creator with certain inalienable rights; that among these rights are life, liberty and the pursuit of happiness."

As children we were taught that it was the right and duty of each man to pursue and acquire happiness for himself. But the New Deal says that this is not so; that it is not the duty of each one to acquire happiness and contentment for himself, if he can, but that the duty is imposed upon somebody else to make other people happy and furnish them contentment, even if in so doing he makes himself unhappy and is destroyed.

Thank God, since the decision of the Supreme Court in *Railroad Retirement Board v. Alton Railroad* on May

6th, there is grave doubt as to whether such a duty exists or may be imposed by one group upon another under the Constitution of the United States.

Present Legal Status

I pass to the second branch of this address to-wit, the legal status and the irreconcilability of New Deal legislation.

As to its constitutionality: In my judgment, it is not fitting at this time for me to indulge in prophecies as to what the Supreme Court of the United States will hold in certain cases involving this identical question which have already been, or so will be, argued before it.

Suffice it to say that as early as 1866, in *Ex parte Milligan,* in the 4th of Wallace, on page 212, referring to the Constitution of the United States, the Supreme Court of the United States used the following language:

> "No doctrine, involving more pernicious conclusions, was ever invented by the wit of man than that of its (the Constitution's) provisions can be suspended during the exigencies of government."

Still again in 1907, in *Kansas v. Colorado,* when the government was claiming the right to exercise a power not granted to it by the Constitution, the Supreme Court, referring to the Tenth Amendment, said on page 90:

> "this amendment, which was seemingly adopted with prescience of just such contention as the present, disclosed the widespread fear that the National Government might, under the pressure of a supposed general welfare, attempt to exercise powers which had not been granted. . . . The people who adopted the Constitution knew that in the nature of things they could not foresee all the questions which might arise in the future, all the circumstances which might call for the exercise of further national powers than those granted to the United States, and after making provision for an amendment to the Constitution by which any needed additional powers would be granted, they reserved to themselves all powers not so delegated."

Within the recent past in the lower courts, that distinguished counselor and citizen, the Honorable Forney Johnson, has been successful in applying the constitutional principles in which I believe to the Tennessee Valley Authority. I express the hope that he will be equally as successful in the Supreme Court.

In *Panama Refining Company v. Ryan,* 293 U.S. 388, the Oil Code and the legislation purporting to authorize it have been held unconstitutional.

In the case of *Railroad Retirement Board, et al. v. The Alton Railroad Co.* (already referred to), the Railroad Pension Bill has been declared unconstitutional.

On Monday, the 27th instant, the Supreme Court handed down its now two famous decisions in the *Frazier-Lemke* and *Schechter Cases.* In one it held the Frazier-Lemke Act unconstitutional. In the other, to-wit, the *Schechter Case,* broadly speaking, it held the N. I. R. A. Act unconstitutional. Both decisions were unanimous, though in the *Schechter Case* two Justices, in an opinion especially concurring, expressed the thought that the Court had gone too far.

It is much too soon for a careful lawyer to attempt to analyze and dissect the far-reaching effect of these two decisions, but it may be safely said that in them the Court has measured up to the high ideals of its past.

To the end that you may thoroughly understand the all-important questions involved in the *Schechter Case,* the following is quoted from the argument of Mr. Frederick H. Wood, one of the Schechter Company's counsel:

> "The Congress, therefore, affirmatively undertook by this act to authorize the President to regulate the wages and hours of persons employed under the codes established under the act. Some 540 codes have been adopted under the act. Every one of these codes contains a regulation of hours and wages required to be observed by all the members of the industry to which it applies, to be enforced by criminal prosecution.
>
> "The codes so approved range from the regulation of the children's garment industry, to the regulation of persons 'engaged in the preparation of dead human bodies, for burial' and the erection of monuments over such bodies after they have been buried—thus literally undertaking to regulate how man activity from the cradle to the grave, and beyond."

The concluding sentence of Mr. Wood's brilliant argument is as follows:

> "If, as many may believe, the Federal Government should be converted into some form of national socialistic state—whether Soviet, Fascist or Nazi—it may be accomplished only by the sole missions of a Constitutional amendment, upon which submission the people of the United States will have a right to determine whether or not they desire such change to be made. It may not be accomplished by an Act of Congress."

The Court in its decision in the *Schechter Case* has apparently adopted the views so eloquently stated by Mr. Wood, to-wit, that a change may not be made in the Constitution of the United States by a mere wish of a New Dealer enacted into law by complacent Congress.

These two cases were pet cases of the New Dealers. By its decisions in these cases, the Court has delivered another stinging rebuke.

I express the ardent hope that when decisions in other cases yet to come are handed down, involving other fantastic theories of New Dealers, the Court will see no reason for modifying the decisions in the *Oil Case,* the *Pension Case,* the *Frazier-Lemke Case* and the *Schechter Case.*

But suppose we indulge in the assumption that the Court, in some other case, for some reason which seems logical to it, gives some constitutional encouragement to the New Dealers; or suppose we should indulge in the unthinkable assumption that the Court may be packed for the express purpose of forcing a constitutional decision, irrespective of reason, logic and ethics. What then may be said?

I submit for your consideration that the conglomeration of heterogeneous laws enacted by the Congress at the request of the New Dealers and the regulations issued under the pretended authority thereof are so full of unsound, absurd, uneconomic, irreconcilable and contradictory policies as to justify the suspicion, even though it may not prove the fact, that they were not passed for the pretended purpose of reform or the stimulated purpose of recovery, but, on the contrary, as many believe, were and are deliberately calculated and designed to destroy liberty and the civilization which we inherited from our ancestors or, stated in other words, were and are deliberately designed to Sovietize or Nazi-ize the Republic; but in any event to destroy it.

Conclusion

But why go further? I submit to your intelligence that:

You can't recover prosperity by producing less and less and dividing more and more.

You can't recover prosperity by making security insecure.

You can't recover prosperity by seizing the accumulation of the thrifty and distributing it to the thriftless and the unlucky.

You can't recover prosperity by confiscating property and giving away other people's money.

You can't recover prosperity by dishonoring governmental pledges, by teaching citizens to dishonor their own pledges and to attribute their misfortunes to the failure of some one else to perform a duty which some one else never owed them at any time under any circumstances.

If you could do this, to use the language of your own distinguished Governor, "You can make water run uphill. You can spend yourself out of debt. You can drink yourself sober."

Ladies and gentlemen of the Georgia Bar Association, though almost done, this address would be far from complete if I did not make one final indictment.

The New Deal is the enemy of and the destroyer of the most precious heritage of the English speaking race—the heritage of liberty.

Since King John was compelled to grant Magna Carta on the field of Runnymede, the English speaking race has fought, bled and died for liberty. They have never knowingly surrendered it.

Private enterprise under the protection of liberty, has created a standard of living in America today, enjoyed by rich and poor alike, beyond and above that enjoyed by any other nation since authentic history began.

All agree that this could not possibly have been attained except by free men acting under the aegis of liberty.

But the New Deal is the deadly enemy of liberty. It seeks by indirect methods and miasmic influence to destroy indirectly what it would never dare to challenge the American people to surrender.

Through the control of credit; the control of business; the control of agriculture; the control of transportation; the control of the supposed freedom of the air; and the control liberty, the New Dealers have attempted to seize complete governmental authority over the entire economic life of the nation. The attempted subordination of the press, directly or indirectly, has not yet been abandoned.

The fact is, though it is called the New Deal, it is not a new deal. It is the same weapon of despotism which monarchs and dictators have used since history began. There is no escape from its malignity.

It fiddles while Rome burns.

It discourages incentive.

It retards recovery and may wholly prevent it.

Its arguments are threats and bulldozing and grand juries.

Its profligate wastage surpasses the imagination.

It paralyzes hope and creates fear.

It is saturated with pretense and insincerity.

It corrupts morality and breaks faith with its own nationals.

Its bureaucracy is as offensive as the army of a Stalin.

It creates more debts in time of peace than in time of war.

It flagrantly violates the great political platform upon which it was swept into power by a hopeful nation.

It destroys, or attempts to destroy, the Constitution—the bulwark of our liberties.

Because of it, our children and our children's children will arise to call us "Cursed."

In short, unless annihilated, it will annihilate the Republic.

Instead of free men, we shall be slaves.

That, ladies and gentlemen, is my opinion of and my indictment of the New Deal.

I thank you.

137. C.P.U.S.A., Central Committee Statement, The Communist Party on the Results of Elections, 1936

Socialism and Communism won many adherents in the 1930s among those who saw in the Great Depression the beginning of the collapse of capitalist society under the weight of its own failures.

The American people gave a hard blow to the reactionary forces in last Tuesday's election. Despite the return to power of Roosevelt and his middle-of-the-way policy, and the presence within the Democratic Party of powerful reactionary groups, the forces advocating democracy scored a victory which is a setback to the Hearst-Liberty League-Wall Street drive toward fascism and to all extreme reactionaries. The main task confronting the toiling masses of the country is to take advantage of the favorable outcome of the elections by pressing forward aggressively for the satisfaction of their immediate economic and political demands.

The campaign and the election results clearly show the sharpening of class lines in the United States. On the one side stood the great mass of the voting population. On the other stood an unprecedented concentration of organized wealth and reaction. Never before was the political struggle so much a question of the poor and downtrodden against the rich and the oppressors. The election struggles sharpened class alignments, and the check to reaction administered by the forces of democracy will speed up the differentiation of the population along class lines.

The masses of the people still expressed their discontent and their fear of fascism, their demands for constructive social legislative measures, and for a higher standard of living within the framework of the two-party system. The results reflected a determination on the part of the people to defeat the Landon-Knox forces at all costs. They reflected a preference for the Roosevelt ticket with the belief that through its victory the people could secure those essential things which they today desire.

The overwhelming vote for Roosevelt was primarily due to extraordinary activities of new forces, of new movements, representing the broad masses of the people—workers, farmers, middle class groups. On a national scale this was expressed by the increased activities of the trade unions, particularly of the C.I.O. and Labor's Non-Partisan League, by the farm organizations and by the bolt of progressives from the Republican Party. On a state scale it was expressed by such movements as the Minnesota Farmer-Labor Party, the Wisconsin Farmer-Labor Progressive Federation, the American Labor Party in New York, the Commonwealth Federation in Washington, the California EPIC movement, and many others—movements that in no sense were identical with the Democratic machine, but which set as their objective the defeat of the Hearst-Liberty League combination backing Landon and Knox.

The defeat of Landon was due to a growing political and class awareness on the part of the workers and farm-

Source: Statement of the Central Committee issued November 7, 1936. *The Communist* 15 (Dec. 1936), 1104–1111.

ers and large sections of the middle class. They saw through and rejected the Red-baiting campaign of Hearst and the Republican Party. They did not succumb to the unbridled demagogy of the Republicans and their stooges, Coughlin, Townsend and Lemke. They saw that the issue was progress or reaction, and they voted in overwhelming numbers against reaction, against Wall Street, for progress and for a better life for the people.

The awakening of the masses of the people, the role they are playing in the destiny of the nation, their fight for better economic conditions and more democratic rights, show that the tradition of Farmer-Labor democracy in the United States is being reborn. This people's democracy which backed Jefferson, Jackson and the Populist movements of the 90's is being revived. It is coming to life in a different setting and in a more advanced form to protect the American people, their liberties and their standard of living from the rule of decaying, reactionary capitalism and its worst products—fascism and war. The union of farmers and workers is coming to life today not as a silent partner of the capitalist politicians, which was its role in the past. It is emerging now as an independent force, led by labor and increasingly conscious of its role as a barrier to reaction, fascism and war.

The people expressed in their vote last Tuesday not primarily their satisfaction with the things Roosevelt had accomplished, but a fear of the consequences of a reactionary victory and a determination to realize their aims in a very real sense. They gave Roosevelt a people's mandate to achieve very definite objectives in the course of the next four years.

In striving for the defeat of the Landon-Knox ticket, huge masses accepted at face value those promises, both direct and implied, made by Roosevelt. They took the words of Roosevelt, in his last Madison Square Garden meeting, as a pledge. In that speech he said:

> Of course we will continue to seek to improve working conditions for the workers of America—to reduce hours over-long, to increase wages that spell starvation, to end the labor of children, to wipe out sweat shops. Of course we will continue every effort to end monopoly of business, to support collective bargaining. . . . For all these we have only just begun to fight."

From this and other declarations made by President Roosevelt during his campaign, the people will expect to realize the following main aims:

Higher wages, shorter hours, the right to organize and real collective bargaining.

Real social security with full protection, or jobs for the unemployed.

Protection for the farmers from evictions and foreclosures, with prices for farm products sufficient to meet the cost of production, with a satisfactory margin of profit for the farmers.

Complete equality for the Negro people, with the elimination of persecution, segregation, jim-crowism and lynching—the enforcement of the Thirteenth, Fourteenth and Fifteenth Amendments of the United States Constitution.

A system of taxation which will take the burdens off the mass of the people, particularly the elimination of sales taxes and the like, and place the tax burden on those able to pay—the rich.

Protection from the people from the assault of the monopolies on their living standards.

Legislation beneficial to the women and youth of the country, giving them those guarantees of economic security and equality which for them are burning issues.

The adoption by the United States government of such policies in the international arena as will make it an active, aggressive force for peace, cooperating with the Soviet Union and other nations striving for the maintenance of peace, against the war moves of the aggressor nations—Germany, Italy and Japan.

Definite measures to curb the powers of the Supreme Court, once and for all preventing it from nullifying or hampering the execution of social legislation beneficial to the people.

These are the needs and hopes that the people voted for. But these hopes cannot be realized without mass demands upon the government and independent struggles for these demands.

This must now be done without delay. Now is the time for the people to press forward and strike decisive blows at the forces of reaction. But although the reactionaries are checked, they are by no means decisively defeated. They will exert tremendous pressure on Roosevelt and on Congress to block measures beneficial to the people. They will use every means of terror and repression to prevent the forward movement of the masses. The Liberty Leaguers, the Hearsts, the big bankers and industrialists will do everything within their power to realize, *through the Roosevelt regime,* those policies which they sought to realize through a Landon-Knox victory. Within the Democratic Party itself, through the reactionary forces constituting its basis in the South, through the corrupt reactionary Democratic machine in the industrial centers (Tammany in New York, the Hague machine in

New Jersey, the Kelly-Nash machine in Chicago, etc.) they will strive to defeat the people's will.

The only guarantee that the mandate of the people will be realized in life is through the independent organization of the people; through the building of more powerful trade unions, particularly in the mass production industries; and through the organization of labor's forces politically in an all-inclusive Farmer-Labor Party. Only thus will the people be able to carry forward the struggle for their aims.

In fact, unless the greatest haste is shown in building the Farmer-Labor movement, uniting all progressive forces, the way will be left open for the building of a reactionary, a fascist movement of the type of the Coughlin-Lemke Union Party movement which served as a cloak for Landon in the last campaign.

The organization of the people independently is the thing that at the moment will alone assure the realization of those demands expressed in the people's mandate last Tuesday. The workers must carry forward the most intensive organizing drive to build the trade unions, to establish them in the mass production industries, to carry forward the fight for their economic demand. The workers, the farmers, and progressive middle class groups must clearly formulate their legislative proposals to be submitted to the new Congress in January, to be fought for there, as well as in the various state legislatures. The fight for the needs and desires of the people must go forward through the trade unions, through the political struggle for legislative demand.

The election results are a mandate by the working class and the people as a whole to the American Federation of Labor meeting in national convention at Tampa, to the C.I.O., to Labor's Non-Partisan League, to the Farmer-Labor Party on Minnesota, to the Wisconsin Farmer-Labor Progressive Federation, to the California EPIC movement, to the Washington Commonwealth Federation, to the American Labor Party, to all farm, unemployed and progressive organizations, to the Socialist and Communist Parties.

The mandate is to build the independent power of the people, to take advantage of the opportunity which lies ahead to consolidate the progressive forces and to move forward decisively to a People's Front, to the national Farmer-Labor Party. Reaction has been checked but the people now must take advantage of the setback they have given to Wall Street to build their forces, to consolidate their ranks and to organize the Farmer-Labor Party.

In the elections, labor was in the main united against the menace of reaction. The unity and strength of labor are necessary for the future progress of the American people.

The workers must use their election unity to press forward on all fronts and, in the first place, to organize the unorganized in the mass production industries. They must rally to the support of the steel drive, whose success will strengthen the entire American people and the Farmer-Labor movement. They must take advantage of the decisive defeat of Hutcheson and the other Liberty League agents in the ranks of labor to work for a united and powerful American Federation of Labor, based on industrial unionism and the widest trade union democracy.

In the elections, the movement for a Farmer-Labor Party, as distinct from the Left forces within the Democratic Party, became more clear. On a national scale, Labor's Non-Partisan League already gave a certain independent character to the political activities of the labor movement. In New York this expressed itself through the American Labor Party as a movement separate from that of the old parties. In other states (California, Washington, etc.), though working through the old parties, the progressive forces, labor, farmers and middle class groups already gave to their movement an independent character.

In several states (Minnesota, Wisconsin) the forces of the people already organized themselves into completely independent political movements. Farmer-Labor in character, and more clearly expressing the people's demand. These movements already represent the unity of the trade unions farmers' organizations and middle class groups in a federation of Farmer-Labor political forces. In these cases the Communist Party gave its support to the building of these movements and to the Farmer-Labor candidates.

The overwhelming and unprecedented victory of the movements in Minnesota and Wisconsin are living proof of the value of the People's Front. They show that an all-inclusive Farmer-Labor movement is the road to victory. These movements were subjected to the most vicious attacks from the Right. The reactionaries tried to frighten the masses with their Red-baiting, pointing to the support given by the Communist Party to these movements. The victories won in Wisconsin and Minnesota are proof that large sections of the American people favor a united, all-inclusive people's movement of trade unionists, of farmers, of middle class progressive, of Communists and Socialists, in the fight against reaction and for the needs of the people.

The overwhelming sweep against reaction creates favorable conditions for the advance of the forces of progress and peace, against the forces of fascism and war. Now is the time to build a genuine people's movement for peace. Now is the time to build a broad, American national Peace Congress, of all genuine peace forces. Now is the time to work for collaboration with the peace policies of the Soviet Union and the forces of peace throughout the world.

The defeat of Landon and Hearst showed that the American people are uncompromisingly opposed to the forces of reaction and fascism both here and abroad. They hate the Hitlers and Mussolinis as much as they hate the Hearsts and the Coughlins. That is why it was necessary for the Republicans to cloak their reactionary plans with the wildest demagogy. That is why the forces of reaction in the election campaign fought under the banner of "democracy" in a battle in which the democratic forces were all in the other camp. But the American people saw through these fascist tactics. They defeated the Red-baiters. They administered a defeat to those who would take American on the Bloody road of fascism. The overwhelming vote against reaction was a rebuke to Hearst, Coughlin, and the other reactionaries who support the Spanish fascists. It showed that large sections of the American people are in sympathy with the struggle of the Spanish people to maintain their democracy. It showed that the American people will respond to a positive approach on the part of the administration to cooperate with the forces of democracy throughout the world, and assist the friendly democratic Spanish government. The international significance of the election lies in the rebuke given by the American people to Hearst and the other reactionaries who try to throw the United States on the side of fascism and the war-makers. This beginning of the crystallization towards the People's Front is an expression of the world-wide movement against reaction and fascism, and will strengthen the progressive and peace forces of the world.

The Communist Party gave all its energy to the defeat of the forces of reaction, to the building of the Farmer-Labor Party, toward the strengthening of its own position as the revolutionary vanguard of the working class movement. In each state and locality it concretely faced the problem of the unity of the progressive forces against reaction. In those states where the movement was already taking on a definitely Farmer-Labor character, it gave support to these movements. In other states it gave support, with various qualifications, to the crystallization of progressive forces within the old parties, placing always in the forefront the central objective of defeating reaction and the building of the Farmer-Labor Party.

It realized that in the present situation, the possibilities existed for the crystallization of a new anti-fascist people's movement that would soon find its expression in a national Farmer-Labor Party. Everywhere we furthered those measures and those movements that would help in the formation of such a Farmer-Labor Party. Therefore, the increasing influence and strength of the Communist Party cannot primarily be measured by the vote for its presidential candidates, in view of the determination of the masses to defeat Hearst-Landon reaction by concentrating upon President Roosevelt's re-election. The growing influence of the Party was unmistakably seen during the campaign in the increased vote for local candidates in a number of states, in the support and successes for local Farmer-Labor Party candidates, by the many huge election meetings and in the response of large sections of the population to the appeal of the Party, after Tampa and Terre Haute, in defense of civil liberties.

In this respect the position of the Communist Party is to be sharply contrasted with that of the Socialist Party.

In contrast to the Communist Party, which recognized that the fight for socialism was inseparably connected with the fight against reaction in the 1936 elections and therefore concentrated on the defeat of the Hearst-Landon reactionaries, the Socialist Party incorrectly declared that the immediate issue in the campaign was that of socialism versus capitalism, thereby playing directly into the hands of the Hearst-Liberty League-Landon forces. Norman Thomas said that "the immediate demand of the Socialists is socialism". The Socialist Party enthroned within its own party the counter-revolutionary Trotskyites and in its policies accepted to an increasing degree those disruptive, wrecking policies which are harmful to the whole labor movement, as well as to the Socialist Party itself.

The Socialist Party, by adopting a reformist and sectarian policy, failed to contribute toward the realignment of progressive forces and suffered disastrously as a result, as seen in the catastrophic drop in its vote. The Socialist Party weakened its relationship with the labor movement and with all of the progressive forces of the country.

The crisis now existing in the Socialist Party following the elections can only be ended when the Socialist Party rids itself of the Trotskyite disrupters, makes a united front with the Communist Party, and aids in the furthering of the people's movement against reaction, fascism, and war, and in the movement for an all-inclusive Farmer-Labor Party.

As a result of its election policies, the influence of the Communist Party in the trade unions, in the ranks of the progressives, among the Farmer-Laborites is greater than ever before. We have been and will continue to be an active and growing force furthering the differentiation among the masses, advancing the movement toward a Farmer-Labor Party!

Large sections of the people realize that we have contributed in the way of unity of the broad masses of the workers, farmers and progressive groups.

After the elections the Communist Party, all its members, all its sympathizers have the task of pushing forward on every front with the objective of realizing those aims listed above. It is our task to promote the organization of all progressive forces independently, the building of the Farmer-Labor Party as a coalition of the trade unions, the farmers, the Negro people, the Communists, the Socialists and all progressive groups.

On the trade union front it is the task of our Party to help in the organization of the unorganized, to win their demands for higher wages, for shorter hours, for the recognition of their unions, for the right of collective bargaining, and to work for a united powerful American Federation of Labor.

It is our task to aid in the unification of all the best forces of the country, including the trade unions, the religious and pacifist groups, of opponents of war, in a mighty movement that will cooperate on a world scale with all of the forces of peace. A movement that will press the government toward a course of cooperation with the Soviet Union and those other nations advocating and working for peace, to pursue such policies in the creation of this peace movement as will make realizable the correct slogan of our Party: "Keep America out of war by keeping war out of the world."

Our influence has been increased, our membership has grown. It is our task to build our Party, to draw into its ranks all of those honest, working class and revolutionary forces who see in our Party the most powerful force in rallying the people for their immediate needs, and in carrying them forward in the struggle for socialism. The present economic upturn cannot and will not do away with the general crisis of capitalism. More and more the masses will come to realize that only a new social order—socialism—can bring a full and lasting solution of their problem.

The Communist Party fully recognizes its obligations to the American working class and to the people as a whole. It will continue to fight with all its power for the progress, happiness, freedom and prosperity of the American people. It will continue with redoubled energy and strength, derived from the increased confidence of the masses, directed for the People's Front, for the Farmer-Labor Party, for progress and peace, for the speeding up of the day when the American People will abolish capitalism and take the road to socialism.

The ranks of our Party are growing. Greater numbers will now be recruited. We will carry forward the banner of Communism, the banner of Marx, Engels, Lenin and Stalin with increased strength, with the knowledge that we have the growing confidence of the masses.

Forward under the banner of the Communist Party! Into the Farmer-Labor Party, the consolidated forces of progress against reaction! Forward under the banner of Communism—the Americanism of the twentieth century!

Communist Party, U.S.A.
William Z. Foster, Chairman
Earl Browder, General Secretary

138. JOHN STEINBECK, *THE GRAPES OF WRATH*, 1939

John Steinbeck captured the mood of the nation after nearly a decade of depression in his enormously successful novel, The Grapes of Wrath.

The owners of the land came onto the land, or more often a spokesman for the owners came. They came in closed cars, and they felt the dry earth with their fingers, and sometimes they drove bit earth augers into the ground for soil tests. The tenants, from their sun-beaten dooryards, watched uneasily when the closed cars drove along the fields. And at last the owner men drove into the dooryards and sat in their cars to talk out of the windows. The tenant men stood beside the cars for a while, and then squatted on their hams and found sticks with which to mark the dust.

In the open doors the women stood looking out, and behind them the children—corn-headed children, with wide eyes, one bare foot on top of the other bare foot, and the toes working. The women and the children watched their men talking to the owner men. They were silent.

Some of the owner men were kind because they hated what they had to do, and some of them were angry because they hated to be cruel, and some of them were cold because they had long ago found out that one could not be an owner unless one were cold. And all of them were caught in something larger than themselves. Some of them hated the mathematics that drove them, and some were afraid, and some worshiped the mathematics because it provided a refuge from thought and from feeling. If a bank of finance company owned the land, the owner man said, The Bank—or the Company—needs—wants—insists—must have—as though the Bank or the Company were a monster, with thought and feeling, which had ensnared them. These last would take no responsibility for the banks or the companies because they were men and slaves, while the banks were machines and masters all at the same time. Some of the owner men were a little proud to be slaves to such cold and powerful masters. The owner men sat in the cars and explained. You know the land is poor. You've scrabbled at it long enough, God knows.

The squatting tenant men nodded and wondered and drew figures in the dust, and yes, they knew, God knows. If the dust only wouldn't fly. If the top would only stay on the soil, it might not be so bad.

The owner men went on leading to their point: You know the land's getting poorer. You know what cotton does to the land; robs it, sucks all the blood out of it.

The squatters nodded—they knew, God knew. If they could only rotate the crops they might pump blood back into the land.

Well, it's too late. And the owner men explained the workings and the thinkings of the monster that was stronger than they were. A man can hold land if he can just eat and pay taxes; he can do that.

Yes, he can do that until his crops fail one day and he has to borrow money from a bank.

But—you see, a bank or a company can't do that, because those creatures don't breathe air, don't eat sidemeat. They breathe profits; they eat the interest on money. If they don't get it, they die the way you die without air, without side-meat. It is a sad thing, but it is so. It is just so.

The squatting men raised their eyes to understand. Can't we just hang on? Maybe the next year will be a good year. God knows how much cotton next year. And with all the wars—God knows what price cotton will bring. Don't they make explosives out of cotton? And uniforms? Get enough wars and cotton'll hit the ceiling. Next year, maybe. They looked up questioningly.

We can't depend on it. The bank—the monster has to have profits all the time. It can't wait. It'll die. No, taxes go on. When the monster stops growing, it dies. It can't stay one size.

Soft fingers began to tap the sill of the car window, and hard fingers tightened on the restless drawing sticks. In the doorways of the sun-beaten tenant houses, women sighed and then shifted feet so that the one that had been down was now on top, and the toes working. Dogs came sniffing near the owner cars and wetted on all four tires one after another. And chickens lay in the sunny dust

---

Source: John Steinbeck, *The Grapes of Wrath.* Chapter Five. Copyright Penguin USA 1939, Reprinted by permission.

and fluffed their feathers to get the cleansing dust down to the skin. In the little sties the pigs grunted inquiringly over the muddy remnants of the slops.

The squatting men looked down again. What do you want us to do? We can't take less share of the crop—we're half starved now. The kids are hungry all the time. We got no clothes, torn an' ragged. If all the neighbors weren't the same, we'd be ashamed to go to meeting.

And at last the owner men came to the point. The tenant system won't work any more. One man on a tractor can take the place of twelve or fourteen families. Pay him a wage and take all the crop. We have to do it. We don't like to do it. But the monster's sick. Something's happened to the monster.

But you'll kill the land with cotton.

We know. We've got to take cotton quick before the land dies. Then we'll sell the land. Lots of families in the East would like to own a piece of land.

The tenant men looked up alarmed. But what'll happen to us? How'll we eat?

You'll have to get off the land. The plow'll go through the dooryard.

And now the squatting men stood up angrily. Grampa took up the land, and he had to kill the Indians and drive them away. And Pa was born here, and he killed weeds and snakes. Then a bad year came and he had to borrow a little money. An' we was born here. There in the door—our children born here. And Pa had to borrow money. The bank owned the land then, but we stayed and we got a little bit of what we raised.

We know that—all that. It's not us, it's the bank. A bank isn't like a man. Or an owner with fifty thousand acres, he isn't like a man either. That's the monster.

Sure, cried the tenant men, but it's our land. We measured it and broke it up. We were born on it, and we got killed on it, died on it. Even if it's no good, it's still ours. That's what makes it ours—being born on it, working it, dying on it. That makes ownership, not a paper with numbers on it.

We're sorry. It's not us. It's the monster. The bank isn't like a man.

Yes, but the bank is only made of men.

No, you're wrong there—quite wrong there. The bank is something else than men. It happens that every man in a bank hates what the bank does, and yet the bank does it. The bank is something more than men, I tell you. It's the monster. Men made it, but they can't control it.

The tenant cried, Grampa killed Indians, Pa killed snakes for the land. Maybe we can kill banks—they're worse than Indians and snakes. Maybe we got to fight to keep our land, like Pa and Grampa did.

And now the owner men grew angry. You'll have to go.

But it's ours, the tenant men cried. We—

No. The bank, the monster owns it. You'll have to go.

We'll get our guns, like Grampa when the Indians came. What then?

Well—first the sheriff, and then the troops. You'll be stealing if you try to stay, you'll be murderers if you kill to stay. The monster isn't men, but it can make men do what it wants.

But if we go, where'll we go? How'll we go? We got no money.

We're sorry, said the owner men. The bank, the fifty-thousand-acre owner can't be responsible. You're on land that isn't yours. Once over the line maybe you can pick cotton in the fall. Maybe you can go on relief. Why don't you go on west to California? There's work there, and it never gets cold. Why, you can reach out anywhere and pick an orange. Why, there's always some kind of crop to work in. Why don't you go there? And the owner men started their cars and rolled away.

The tenant men squatted down on their hams again to mark the dust with a stick, to figure, to wonder. Their sun-burned faces were dark, and their sun-whipped eyes were light. The women moved cautiously out of the doorways toward their men, and the children crept behind the women, cautiously, ready to run. The bigger boys squatted beside their fathers, because that made them men. After a time the women asked, "What did he want?"

And the men looked up for a second, and the smolder of pain was in their eyes. We got to get off. America tractor and a superintendent. Like factories.

Where'll we go? the women asked.

We don't know. We don't know.

And the women were quickly, quietly back into the houses and herded the children ahead of them. They knew that a man so hurt and so perplexed may turn in anger, even on people he loves. They left the men alone to figure and to wonder in the dust.

After a time perhaps the tenant man looked about—at the pump put in ten years ago, with a goose-neck handle and iron flowers on the spout, at the chopping block where a thousand chickens had been killed, at the hand plow lying in the shed, and the patent crib hanging in the rafters over it.

The children crowded about the women in the houses. What we going to do, Ma? Where we going to go?

The women said, We don't know, yet. Go out and play. But don't go near your father. He might whale you if you go near him. And the women went on with the work, but all the time they watched the men squatting in the dust—perplexed and figuring.

The tractors came over the roads and into the fields, great crawlers moving like insects, having the incredible strength of insects. They crawled over the ground, laying the track and rolling on it and picking it up. Diesel tractors, puttering while they stood idle; they thundered when they moved, and then settled down to a droning roar. Snub-nosed monsters, raising the dust and sticking their snouts into it, straight down the country, across the country, through fences, through dooryards, in and out of gullies in straight lines. They did not run on the ground, but on their own roadbeds. They ignored hills and gulches, water courses, fences, houses.

The man sitting in the iron seat did not look like a man; gloved, goggled, rubber dust mask over nose and mouth, he was a part of the monster, a robot in the seat. The thunder of the cylinders sounded through the country, became one with the air and the earth, so that earth and air muttered in sympathetic vibration. The driver could not control it—straight across country it went, cutting through a dozen farms and straight back. A twitch at the controls could swerve the cat', but the driver's hands could not twitch because the monster that built the tractor, the monster that sent the tractor out, had somehow got into the driver's hands, into his brain and muscle, had goggled him and muzzled him—goggled his mind, muzzled his speech, goggled his perception, muzzled his protest. He could not see the land as it was, he could not smell the land as it smelled; his feet did not stamp the clods or feel the warmth and power of the earth. He sat in an iron seat, and stepped on iron pedals. He could not cheer or beat or curse or encourage the extension of his power, and because of this he could not cheer or whip or curse or encourage himself. He did not know or own or trust or beseech the land. If a seed dropped did not germinate, it was nothing. If the young thrusting plant withered in drought or drowned in a flood of rain, it was no more to the driver than to the tractor.

He loved the land no more than the bank loved the land. He could admire the tractor—its machined surfaces, its surge of power, the roar of its detonating cylinders; but it was not his tractor. Behind the tractor rolled the shining disks, cutting the earth with blades—not plowing but surgery, pushing the cut earth to the right where the second row of disks cut it and pushed it to the left; slicing blades shining, polished by the cut earth. And pulled behind the disks, the harrows combing with iron teeth so that the little clods broke up and the earth lay smooth. Behind the harrows, the long seeders—twelve curved iron penes erected in the foundry, orgasms set by gears, raping methodically, raping without passion. The driver sat in his iron seat and he was proud of the straight lines he did not will, proud of the tractor he did not own or love, proud of the power he could not control. And when that crop grew, and was harvested, no man had crumbled a hot clod in his fingers and let the earth sift past his fingertips. No man had touched the seed, or lusted for the growth. Men ate what they had not raised, had no connection with the bread. The land bore under iron, and under iron gradually died; for it was not loved or hated, it had no prayers or curses.

At noon the tractor driver stopped sometimes near a tenant house and opened his lunch: sandwiches wrapped in waxed paper, white bread, pickle, cheese, Spam, a piece of pie branded like an engine part. He ate without relish. And tenants not yet moved away came out to see him, looked curiously while the goggles were taken off, and the rubber dust mask, leaving white circles around the eyes and a large white circle around nose and mouth. The exhaust of the tractor puttered on, for fuel is so cheap it is more efficient to leave the engine running than to heat the Diesel nose for a new start. Curious children crowded close, ragged children who ate their fried dough as they watched. They watched hungrily the unwrapping of the sandwiches, and their hunger-sharpened noses smelled the pickle, cheese, and Spam. They didn't speak to the driver. They watched his hand as it carried food to his mouth. They did not watch him chewing; their eyes followed the hand that held the sandwich. After a while the tenant who could not leave the place came out and squatted in the shade beside the tractor.

"Why, you're Joe Davis's boy!"

"Sure," the driver said.

"Well, what you doing this kind of work for—against your own people?"

"Three dollars a day. I got damn sick of creeping for my dinner—and not getting it. I got a wife and kids. We got to eat. Three dollars a day, and it comes every day."

"That's right," the tenant said. "But for your three dollars a day fifteen or twenty families can't eat at all. Nearly a hundred people have to go out and wander on the roads for your three dollars a day. Is that right?"

And the driver said, "Can't think of that. Got to think of my own kids. Three dollars a day, and it comes every day. Times are changing, mister, don't you know? Can't make a living on the land unless you've got two, five, ten thousand acres and a tractor. Crop land isn't for little guys like us any more. You don't kick up a howl because you can't make Fords, or because you're not the telephone company. Well, crops are like that now. Nothing to do about it. You try to get three dollars a day someplace. That's the only way."

The tenant pondered. "Funny thing how it is. If a man owns a little property, that property is him, it's part of him, and it's like him. If he owns property only so he can walk on it and handle it and be sad when it isn't doing well, and feel fine when the rain falls on it, the property is him, and some way he's bigger because he owns it. Even if he isn't successful he's big with his property. That is so."

And the tenant pondered more. "But let a man get property he doesn't see, or can't take time to get his fingers in, or can't be there to walk on it—why, then the property is the man. He can't do what he wants, he can't think what he wants. The property is the man, stronger than he is. And he is small, not big. Only his possessions are big—and he's the servant of his property. That is so, too."

The driver munched the branded pie and threw the crust away. "Times are changed, don't you know? Thinking about stuff like that don't feed the kids. Get your three dollars a day, feed your kids. You got no call to worry about anybody's kids but your own. You get a reputation for talking like that, and you'll never get three dollars a day. Big shots won't give you three dollars a day if you worry about anything but your three dollars a day."

"Nearly a hundred people on the road for your three dollars. Where will we go?"

"And that reminds me," the driver said, "you better get out soon. I'm going through the dooryard after dinner."

"You filled in the well this morning."

"I know. Had to keep the line straight. But I'm going through the dooryard after dinner. Got to keep the lines straight. And—well, you know Joe Davis, my old man, so I'll tell you this. I got orders wherever there's a family not moved out—if I have an accident—you know, get too close and cave the house in a little—well, I might get a couple of dollars. And my youngest kid never had no shoes yet."

"I built it with my hands. Straightened old nails to put the sheathing on. Rafters are wired to the stringers with baling wire. It's mine. I built it. You bump it down—I'll be in the window with a rifle. You even come too close and I'll pot you like a rabbit."

"It's not me. There's nothing I can do. I'll lose my job if I don't do it. And look—suppose you kill me? They'll just hang you, but long before you're hung there'll be another guy on the tractor, and he'll bump the house down. You're not killing the right guy."

"That's so," the tenant said. "You gave you orders? I'll go after him. He's the one to kill."

"You're wrong. He got his orders from the bank. The bank told him, 'Clear those people out or it's your job.'"

"Well, there's a president of the bank. There's a board of directors. I'll fill up the magazine of the rifle and go into the bank."

The driver said, "Fellow was telling me the bank gets orders from the East. The orders were, 'Make the land show profit or we'll close you up.'"

"But where does it stop? Who can we shoot? I don't aim to starve to death before I kill the man that's starving me."

"I don't know. Maybe there's nobody to shoot. Maybe the thing isn't men at all. Maybe, like you said, the property's doing it. Anyway I told you my orders."

"I got to figure," the tenant said. "We all got to figure. There's some way to stop this. It's not like lightning or earthquakes. We've got a bad thing made by men, and by God that's something we can change." The tenant sat in his doorway, and the driver thundered his engine and started off, tracks falling and curving, harrows combing, and the phalli of the seeder slipping into the ground. Across the dooryard the tractor cut, and the hard, foot-beaten ground was seeded field, and the tractor cut through again; the uncut space was ten feet wide. And back he came. The iron guard bit into the house-corner, crumbled the wall, and wrenched the little house from its foundation, so that it fell sideways, crushed like a bug. And the driver was goggled and a rubber mask covered his nose and mouth. The tractor cut a straight line on, and the air and the ground vibrated with its thunder. The tenant man stared after it, his rifle in his hand. His wife was beside him, and the quiet children behind. And all of them stared after the tractor.

Chapter XXVI

The Second World War, 1940–1945

139. Steve Weisman, "Pearl Harbor in the Mind of Japan"

The fiftieth anniversary of the bombing of Pearl Harbor unleashed a barrage of commentary on the meaning of that event. In this article from the New York Times Magazine, *a reporter finds the Japanese ideas disquieting.*

The sky was cloudy before dawn on Dec. 7, 1941, as Lieut. Zenji Abe awoke in his cabin on the Akagi, one of a half-dozen Japanese aircraft carriers waiting in heavy seas a few hundred miles north of Hawaii. Having trained for months for this day, Abe felt little anxiety. He washed, shaved, dressed and tucked a picture of his wife and son in his pocket. Then he offered prayers at a Shinto shrine below deck.

In the night air, the carrier's colored lights reminded the young lieutenant of fireflies. Soon the first wave of what would become an onslaught of 350 planes took off and streaked south. Leader of a squadron of dive bombers in the second wave, Abe was halfway to the same target when his radio crackled with *"Tora! Tora! Tora!"* ("Tiger! Tiger! Tiger!"), the code indicating that the attack has been a complete surprise to the United States Pacific force stationed at Pearl Harbor.

"After we bombed our targets, the only thing on my mind was getting out of there," recalls Abe, an unassuming, retired plastics company executive living in a tiny apartment in the Tokyo suburbs. "It wasn't until later that I realized I had participated in a historic moment."

Members of Abe's generation all have searing firsthand memories of what is called in Japan "the Pacific war." Some remember coming home to houses burned to the ground. People in their 50's and 60's remember blacking out militarist passages in their textbooks at the behest of Gen. Douglas A. MacArthur during the American occupation. All look back on the war with a mixture of horror and sadness.

Next month, from a completely different perspective, the United States will be remembering the 50th anniversary of the most devastating military attack in its history—2,403 Americans killed and 21 ships and 328 aircraft damaged or destroyed. The crucial turning point of World War II, Pearl Harbor galvanized Americans into a single-minded determination to win. For the United States, Pearl Harbor will forever symbolize the disastrous consequences of complacency and evoke the moment the nation awoke from isolationism to global responsibilities that continue to this day.

For the United States, the war tends to be seen as a long-ago event with little relevance today. But for Japan, what strikes any foreign resident is how World War II daily asserts its contemporary claims. It is a remarkable presence, not so much in the lives of ordinary Japanese, but as a subtext to the way the nation talks about itself, sees itself and debates policy issues of all kinds. The more Japan pushes to the future, it seems, the more it is borne back to the past.

When Japan was pressured to become involved in the Persian Gulf war, many Japanese were reminded of the events that led to the tragedy of 50 years ago, even though the circumstances prior to the Gulf conflict were very different from those preceding the Pearl Harbor attack. They spoke with such anguish about the dangers of militarism that it often seemed as if World War II had

Source: Steven R. Weisman, "Pearl Harbor in the Mind of Japan." Copyright *The New York Times Magazine,* November 3, 1991. Reprinted by permission.

happened yesterday. Japan was exposed as a pacifist country, but it was a pacifism that also saw a war *against* aggression as unjustifiable.

Although Tokyo contributed $13 billion to the military efforts against Iraq, that campaign was disliked in Japan. A cover story in a popular weekly magazine noted that many Japanese, remembering what had been done to them in World War II, sympathized with Iraq as a victim of American bombing. These Japanese, it said, felt "it would have been extremely delightful if Saddam Hussein had staged a sneak attack on the United States."

The gulf war was also described by many Japanese critics as another instance of American treachery. In a newspaper column, Hiroshi Yamada, executive director of the Osaka Stock Exchange, charged that Washington had lured Iraq into the gulf war the same way, he said, that it had tricked Japan. This is only an elaboration of a popular notion: Washington knew about Pearl Harbor but let it happen anyway so that Americans would be more willing to go to war. (American historians long ago rejected this contention. There *were* serious reports of possible Japanese designs on Pearl Harbor, but they were lost in a flood of contradictory signals. Gordon W. Prange, the late University of Maryland professor who studied the matter over nearly four decades, wrote that the signs were dismissed because of "the roof disbelief that the Japanese would undertake the risky venture.")

For Japanese, the Pacific war casts a deep and complex shadow, creating a peculiar mixture of the desire to remember and the desire to forget. Most vaguely think of the war as an awful experience that must never be repeated. At the same time, as Japan assumes greater power in the world, its citizens—two-thirds of whom were born after the war had ended—are increasingly irritated by demands that Tokyo continue to express remorse. "How long must we apologize for the mistakes we have made?" asks Noboru Kojima, a popular 64-year-old military historian.

Members of Japan's conservative establishment also speak of the attack on Pearl Harbor as a mistake, not a crime. The "date which will live in infamy," in President Roosevelt's words, is seen in Japan as a relatively unimportant event. There will be no Pearl Harbor ceremonies in Japan this year. There are none any year. Indeed, only a tiny percentage of the 1.4 million Japanese tourists visiting Hawaii each year bother to go the Pearl Harbor Memorial.

Today, histories, movies, comic books and textbooks in Japan all emphasize how the Japanese suffered as much as anyone—from starvation, American incendiary bombs and finally the atomic blasts in Hiroshima and Nagasaki in August 1945.

Japanese say that they have learned the lessons of war, but for most they are the lessons of innocent passengers, hijacked by ultranationalist militarists whose fanaticism brought Japan to disaster. To most people, such a view means eternal vigilance against a resurgent military today. A growing rightist minority, however, has transformed the sense of victimization into a call for Japan to assert its interests more aggressively, even if they are antithetical to those of the United States.

The dangerous paradox of the war for Japanese is that while emotions remain high, so does ignorance. A restless new generation is waiting to assume leadership of the most powerful nation in Asia. Yet in contrast to Germany textbooks, Japanese textbooks whitewash the war. Some 20 million people died in the Pacific war, and Japan itself lost 2.5 million lives, had 10 million men under arms and forced millions of prisoners into hard labor. But after Emperor Hirohito died in 1989, grainy footage of the Japanese occupation of much of China amazed young television viewers, who had not known about it.

As the anniversary of Pearl Harbor approaches, many Japanese fear that the commemoration ceremonies in Hawaii and elsewhere will aggravate resentments over their nation's peacetime transformation into the economic powerhouse of Asia—the very status it once sought by military means. A flood of articles warns Americans against using the anniversary to bash Japan. Among the recent titles in magazines are "The Occupation of Japan Has Not Ended" and "Why Hate the United States Now."

To live in Japan is to experience constant reminders of the Pacific war. Every week brings some new revelation or disclosure: a diary, a memoir, some testimony that receives attention in the news media.

Last year, an oral history recorded by an aide to Emperor Hirohito revealed that the late emperor said that if he had tried to stop the attack on Pearl Harbor, "it would have led to a coup d'état" and possibly his own assassination. The revelation offered powerful new evidence that Hirohito gave some thought to trying to stop the war, only to resign himself to it.

This summer saw the startling publication of notes written by Gen. Hideko Tojo, Japan's war-time Prime Minister, while he was held prisoner after the war. Defiantly defending the attack on Pearl Harbor as forced by "inhuman" economic sanctions imposed by Washington, Tojo, who was hanged in 1948 as a war criminal, wrote: "For Japan, doing nothing would have meant the destruction of the nation."

Tojo's notes, scribbled in the margin of poetry books kept by his family, held the familiar argument that Pearl Harbor was not a sneak attack, as most Americans remember it, because Tokyo notified Washington of its hostile intentions the day of the raid. What Tojo omitted was that, because of a mix-up in communication, including a delay in translating the message, the warning was not delivered to Secretary of State Cordell Hull until nearly an hour after the attack had begun. (Washington had cracked Japanese military codes and learned that some sort of attack on Allied forces in the Pacific was imminent.)

Tojo's prison notes raised the question often asked in Japan: Who actually was responsible for the war? A Government spokesman recently turned down a suggestion that Japan apologize for Pearl Harbor, saying that blame for the war must be shared by all the combatants, including the United States. "It will take decades or even centuries before the correct judgment is delivered on who is responsible for the war," said Nobuo Ishihara, deputy chief cabinet secretary, echoing a view widely shared in Japan.

Of course, most American historians would have little trouble rendering a judgment on Japan's singular responsibility, if not guilt. Japan annexed Manchuria in 1931, made a bloody sweep through China in 1937 and in 1941—after Japan became an ally of Germany and Paris fell to the Nazis—it drove into French Indochina. (Korea had been forcibly annexed prior to World War I, in 1910.)

Beginning with the decision to move naval vessels from Southern California to Pearl Harbor in 1940, the United States responded to Japanese military aggression with warnings and protests. In a series of ever tighter economic sanctions, Washington banned sales to Japan of high-octane aviation gasoline and then iron and steel scrap. Finally, Washington froze all Japanese assets in the United States, making it impossible for Japan to pay for American oil imports and resulting in a cutoff of 80 percent of Japan's oil supplies. These steps, intended as protests short of war, were seen in Tokyo as provocations; Tokyo policy makers felt they had to disable the American Navy at Pearl Harbor while Japanese forces tried to capture new oil reserves in the Dutch East Indies, which the Japanese occupied in 1942.

Japan's culpability before and during the war remains a raw issue among those who had suffered from its militarism. Millions of Asians were brought to Japan to do forced labor at armaments, factories and elsewhere, often under appalling conditions. A newly published diary offers rare details of the harsh life of a Korean laborer at a Nagasaki shipyard. And an association of Koreans in Japan made public what they said were records from steel factories and other industries frantically pushing Korean laborers, many of whom were seriously ill, to work harder as Japan began losing the war.

Koreans still demand compensation for these hardships, even though their requests are invariably rejected by the Government. A women's group from South Korea arrived in Tokyo earlier this year to present what it said were records that tens of thousands of women brought from Korea were forced to work as prostitutes for Japanese soldiers during the war. Again, Japan rejected their pleas for compensation.

Small groups of antiwar activities have long been publicizing their efforts to confront the Government with evidence of wartime atrocities. This summer, the Japan China Friendship Association in Tokyo sponsored an exhibition on the "war of aggression" in China, featuring pictures, war memorabilia and a videotape. In the videotape, three military officers confessed to beheading or torturing unspecified numbers of Chinese civilians—by drowning or burning them with hot irons—over a period of several months in Nanjing.

Two years ago, construction workers unearthed a few dozen human skulls at the site of an old building that several historians said was a headquarters of the infamous military medical groups that did gruesome experiments on Chinese prisoners of war. Doctors and others who were present at those experiments have said there were human vivisections, but the Government declined to look into how the skulls got there. Japanese historians doing research on the wartime biological warfare program recently accused authorities of blocking disclosures of the experiments.

In Asia, Japan pays a continuous price for not negotiating a formal set of reparations with China or Korea. There were reparations in the 1950s with South Vietnam, Burma, the Philippines and Indonesia. But that $1.15 billion package was widely seen as a kind of investment insuring access to raw materials and overseas markets for its businesses—an access Japan had gone to war to get.

Tokyo negotiated a post-war package of $500 million in loans and grants for South Korea in 1965 but avoided the word "reparations." China abandoned its claim to reparations when it gained Japanese diplomatic recognition in 1972. But because the reparations issue has been shunted aside, China and Korea made it a point to bring up the war—infuriating Japanese diplomatics—in virtually all negotiations.

Japanese officials routinely apologize for the war during trips abroad or visits by foreign leaders at home, but their statements always seem unsatisfying. Not surprisingly, the former victims of Japanese aggression take a particular interest in the way the war is discussed in Japan. While debating whether to send minesweepers to the Persian Gulf or noncombat troops on United Nations peacekeeping missions, Japan must constantly reassure Asian countries of its peaceful intentions. And Beijing and Seoul still protest the annual visit by Japanese cabinet members to the Yasukuni shrine in Tokyo, where military heroes are enshrined and where videotapes offer a thoroughly unrepentant version of the war.

This year, China protested a renewed debate in Japan over war atrocities. Its focus was a magazine article by Shintaro Ishihara, a popular rightist novelist and leading light of the ruling Liberal Democratic Party in Parliament. Ishihara declared that accounts of the 1937 "rape of Nanjing"—where the Chinese say that hundreds of thousands of civilians were killed—were "a fabrication." In a new book, "A Japan That Can Firmly Say No," he also proclaimed that it was time for Tokyo to reestablish its wartime goal of a Greater East Asia Co-Prosperity Sphere.

The root causes of all these diplomatic steps and missteps date from the early postwar years. After the war, Germany made an attempt to "cleanse" itself of its Nazi past; nothing comparable took place in Japan. Also, although a few former Nazis serves in the postwar Governments, some postwar leaders had been prominent in wartime resistance: Konrad Adenauer had been in jail during the Nazi period and Willy Brandt had gone into exile. But no comparable guardians of moral conscience assumed positions of leadership as Japan struggled—at the behest of the American occupying forces—to create a democracy, having had almost no experience with democratic institutions.

The problem was compounded by American zigs and zags. Early in the occupation, the United States sought to purge Japan's leadership and bureaucracy of people involved in the war. But after China fell to the Communists in 1949 and the Korean War broke out a year later, Washington changed its mind, deciding to foster a stable conservative in Japan to challenge Communism in Asia. In some cases, admitted war criminals were encouraged to resume Government duties.

Furthermore, unlike Germany, Japan has never come forward with a definitive statement of wartime responsibility. No senior Japanese leader has made anything like the electrifying speech of President Richard von Weizsacker of Germany, who declared in 1985 that "all of us, whether guilty or not, whether old or young, must accept the past" and "keep alive the memories" of the war.

The tendency of Japanese to see themselves as the victims, rather than the perpetrators, of war is especially apparent in popular culture. In a well-known children's tale, "The Pitiful Elephants," zoo keepers worry about the animals during the American bombing raids of Tokyo. Nearly every Japanese child learns the story of the decision to kill the zoo animals: how the elephants being wise, refuse to eat the toxic food they are given, how they cannot be injected with poison because their skin is too tough.

In one children's book version, the anguished moment comes when the zoo keepers decide to starve the elephants. The final page shows the dying beasts with tearful zoo keepers shaking their fists at the sky, shouting "Stop the war! Stop the war!" as American B-29s fly overhead.

Self-pity is also evident in one of the most popular movies this year in Japan, "Rhapsody in August," directed by the patriarch of Japanese cinema, Akira Kurosawa. At the film's dramatic turning point, a Japanese-American played by Richard Gere apologized to his Japanese cousins for the dropping of the atom bomb on Nagasaki. But there are no references to anything Japan did that might have provoked the American attack. At a news conference earlier this year, Kurosawa was asked if Japan might also have something to apologize for. With a shrug, he said Japanese find it hard to be remorseful because they were "never aware of what was going on."

To understand Japan as a victim, one has to visit the memorials at Hiroshima and Nagasaki. Some 200,000 people died in the atomic blasts there that ended the war. (Today, some Japanese historians acknowledge that, judging from the more than 200,000 who died in the Allied attack on Okinawa, more Japanese would have perished if an all-out assault on the main islands had been launched by the United States.

It is virtually impossible for anyone to see the skeletal shell of the old five-story doomed exhibition hall by a river bank in downtown Hiroshima and not be deeply moved. Akihiro Takahashi, a director of the Hiroshima Peace Culture Foundation, knows every exhibit by heart: maps of the hypocenter; a burned-out clock frozen at 8:15 A.M.; row after row of display cases of charred clothing, melted glass and photographs of mutilated victims.

Takahashi says he was in fourth grade when he heard about Pearl Harbor, and he admits feeling elated that Japan had been successful. But he is haunted more by memories of Aug. 6, 1945, when he, then a teenager, was standing in a schoolyard just as the sky roared with a blinding flash and turned pitch black. Blown more than 30 feet away, he could see that the entire city was on fire. Today, Takahashi's right hand is shriveled and his legs and arms are covered with scars.

"When Americans say Pearl Harbor, Pearl Harbor, Pearl Harbor, I am obliged to point something out." Takahashi says. "Look at the order to drop the atomic bomb, and you see the American military intentionally targeted innocent citizens. That was not the case with Pearl Harbor."

This year, the Mayor of Hiroshima apologized for Japanese wartime aggression, referring to Pearl Harbor as an example—the first time such a sentiment had been expressed at the annual commemoration of the dropping of the atom bomb on that city. But last year when the city was expanding its museum on the bombing, some antiwar groups demanded that there be an exhibition to remind visitors that Japan had been the aggressor in the war. The demand was rejected.

For Japanese, the Pacific war has been largely bled of its significance by a "history of the passive voice, or 'victims' history," noted Carol Gluck, professor of history at Columbia University. Writing last year in the journal *Daedalus*, she pointed out that in Japanese textbooks "the war appears as a natural catastrophe which 'happened' to Japan, as if without the intervention of human agency."

Many Japanese legitimately point out that the idea of exonerating the Japanese people was established by the United States itself. According to the Allied-sponsored Tokyo War Crimes Tribunal, a handful of leaders conspired to make war, ignoring the wishes of the people. Thus the trials and convictions of 28 leaders (7 of whom were hanged in December 1948) served American interests in isolating the main culprits and placing the Japanese people in order to enlist them as an ally against Communism.

Nonetheless, Japan's inclination to see itself as a victim comes more deeply from within than without. Part of it is human nature—the desire of any defeated people to see the past in the most favorable light. Then, too, in Japan history tends not to be taught in terms of justice or right and wrong; instead, it embodies the Confucian idea of the statesman adjusting to great historical forces rather than the Western notion that great leaders can change the course of history. From this follows the country's fatalistic approach to the war.

"Japanese people are very literate and they like the subject of history," says Fusako Tsunoda, author of popular historical novels. "But people don't like to dwell on what they did wrong. They'd rather wash out the past and say: it ended and we lost it, so let's think about rebuilding the country now."

In trying to play down Japanese aggression, the Ministry of Education has made some clumsy attempts to sanitize the past. Its move in 1982 to substitute the word "advance" for Japan's "invasion" of China was blocked only because Japan became embarrassed by Chinese protests. Generally, Japanese courts have upheld whitewashing references to war aggression, rejecting lawsuits brought by teachers and textbook writers.

Japanese textbooks fail to satisfy anyone. Conservatives complain that the books underplay patriotic themes and deal with the unpleasant past by trying to erase it. They complain that wartime leaders like General Tojo and Adm. Isoroku Yamamoto (the brilliant strategist who planned the Pearl Harbor attack in spite of deep misgivings) have become virtual nonpersons. "Without teaching about military power, how can you judge or assess the results of war?" asks Hiroyuki Agawa, a biographer of Admiral Yamamoto.

A recent newspaper article quoted a high-school teacher complaining that his students were surprised to learn that there had been a war with the United States. The first thing they wanted to know, he said, was who won.

Even a group of college students belonging to a Japanese-American friendship organization who were interviewed for this article showed a one-sided knowledge of the war. Yes, they said, not only do textbooks give the war short shrift, but the topic always comes up at the end of the year—when everyone is too preoccupied by exams and vacation to pay attention.

Asked about the underlying causes of war, they listed the collapse of the world economy, the rise of Japanese fascism and Japanese feelings of economic vulnerability. "Basically," said Hajime Etoh, a law student, "I believe the war occurred for economic reasons. Earlier this century, Japan didn't have enough land or financial resources or colonies to compete with the United States and the United Kingdom. Japan thought that taking over China was the only way to survive."

If the war were basically a clash of economic interests, why should Japan feel guilty about it? "instinctively I reject the idea that Japan must be seen as a criminal," said Yoko Ooshima, a student of international law, as the others nodded in agreement.

In Japan, there are historians who do see the nation's wartime behavior as criminal, but they are generally leftists. The 1968 classic history, "The Pacific War," by Saburo Ienaga, is a reminder of the self-delusion and cruelty of the ultranationalist Japanese leaders throughout the 1930s, when the country was rocked by assassinations, a military takeover, and a growing conviction that it had to rid Asia of white-skinned devils. But the book also seems to exonerate the Japanese people of responsibility since they had been hoodwinked by their leaders.

The group to grapple most successfully with the complex issues of the war are historians with a centrist approach. Their outstanding achievement is the eight-volume history "The Road to the Pacific War" (1962-63). This comprehensive history debunks the popular belief that the Japanese public were passive bystanders. Instead, many admired the militarists and their early victories—the popular trust in the army a result of the migration of rural people to the cities, their feeling of displacement, powerlessness and resentment toward politicians who appeared incapable of action.

One question still nags at Japanese historians: Could the war have been avoided? Many contend that their American counterparts have not adequately explored the opportunities presented to President Roosevelt to arrive at a common ground with Japan and avert a conflict. And many who say Japan was essentially at fault also feel that Roosevelt's demands—that Japan relinquish Manchuria, China and Southeast Asia before negotiations could commence—only made Tokyo more intransigent and dangerous.

Japanese and American historians still disagree on a number of major issues about the war. In fact, on the issue of American responsibility they may be moving further apart. In the late 60's, American historians were more willing to question American motives in Asia. Today, their tone is much less apologetic.

Participants of a conference in 1969—the first time Japanese and American historians pooled their resources to study World War II—recall how the Americans were so guilt-ridden over the Vietnam conflict they even criticized Roosevelt for his intransigence.

The conclusion of the participants, published in "Pearl Harbor as History" (1973), was a model of even-handedness. Its introduction noted the amazing scholarly consensus that "blame for the war could not be attributed primarily to either the United States or Japan."

Times have changed. Particularly after the Persian Gulf war and the collapse of Communism in the Soviet Union, Roosevelt's drawing a line in the sand is no longer seen as improper.

Anyone following Japanese-American frictions cannot help but note the parallels between the early 1940s and now. Fifty years after the attack on Pearl Harbor, Washington is still debating the wisdom of economic pressure on Tokyo. Will American trade sanctions provoke Japan into greater intransigence or retaliation?

Then and now, the vocabulary of Japanese-American relations is often framed in bellicose terms. Japanese speak of their "second strike": if Washington cuts off Japanese imports, Tokyo can strangle the American economy by cutting off investments or purchases of Treasury bonds.

Tension between Japan and the United States today has many causes, but much of it is rooted in the growing perception in both countries that Japan has become an economic juggernaut in spite of—and perhaps even because of—the war.

For one thing, it is no longer widely accepted that Japan was little more than a warmongering country before the war and that a "new Japan" rose out of the ashes of defeat to achieve a modern economic miracle. Most analysts, especially those in the United States, now that the "miracle" was partly a result of the close cooperation between big industrial cartels and the Government. That partnership, established in the 1920's and 1930s, was forged in the fires of war.

Tokyo went to war to expel rival colonial empires from Asia, but its goal was to assure access to natural resources, markets and freedom of the seas. Japan had prospered because it obtained all these things, not only by dint of its own hard work, but also because of the generosity (and self-interest) of the United States.

Today Japan's nearly $50 billion in Asian holdings makes it the largest single source of investment and growth, dwarfing American resources in the same region. Asians are increasingly looking to Japan for leadership. The British, the French, the Dutch are all going or gone. American troops are also pulling out.

Although Japan has been America's biggest ally in Asia in recent decades, another hostile element of Pearl Harbor days lingers. During the war, both the Japanese and Americans indulged in an orgy of racial hatred. As John W. Dower, professor of history at the Massachusetts Institute of Technology, noted in "War Without Mercy" (1986), the Japanese stereotype was that Americans were white imperialists, bent on subjugating Asia, whereas in American eyes the Japanese were subhuman, or superhuman, in their fanaticism.

"That vicious racial stereotypes were transformed does not mean that they were dispelled," wrote Dower. "They remain latent, capable of being revived by both sides in times of crisis and tension. Indeed, many Japanese still see themselves as victims of racism—tortured, for example, by the question of why they, alone, suffered atom-bomb attacks.

The Pearl Harbor anniversary could provide an occasion for more recriminations or an opportunity for more understanding. Akira Iriye, a 57-year-old American-trained history professor at Harvard University who has retained his Japanese citizenship, is an apt symbol of the synthesis that Japan may need to achieve.

"I remember being in grade school when, as the war grew worse, our teachers became more and more fanatical over the spiritual superiority of Japan," Iriye says. "Then once the war ended, they completely reversed themselves, talking about democracy and peace. It was very disillusioning, even to a 10-year-old.

"Today, the Japanese are clearly not teaching the war very well. It's very disturbing to me. I don't see anything sinister about the Americans' remembering Pearl Harbor. The Japanese may be nervous, but we should all use it as an opportunity for both sides to get to know each other better."

140. Studs Terkel, *The Good War*

Studs Terkel, a well-known radio talk-show host and author from Chicago, reached the best-seller list in 1984 with this oral history of what most Americans remember as the last indisputably "good war": World War II.

Hajimi Kito and Hideko Tamura (Tammy) Friedman

They are *hibakusha*,[1] survivors of Hiroshima. He lives in Japan. She, married to an American, lives in a suburb of Chicago. On this occasion, they have met for the first time in a Chicago radio study.

They are listening to the words of a young Japanese woman who is also a *hibakusha*. It is a tape recording of 1960. She recalls August 6, 1945.

WOMAN'S VOICE: I was looking up in the sky, trying to spot the airplane. Then I saw a big flash in the sky, so I hid my face on the ground. I remember that I must have been blown away by the impact. When I regained my consciousness, I couldn't find any of my friends. They were either blown to bits or burned. All my clothes were torn away, except my very undergarment. My skin just peeled off and was hanging from my body. I had that over my arms, legs, and face.

The heat was so intense that I jumped into the nearby river, the small river that was running through the city. All my friends were in the river—(She cries. The interpreter stops in mid-sentence and stifles a sob: "I don't think I can say it—")

KITO: (After a long pause) When I hear that young woman's voice, I immediately recall the moment thirty-seven years ago. I was there in the army at the time the bomb was dropped. I was a nineteen-year-old soldier. Young children were running toward me. I remember hearing lots of voices, elementary-school children were coming to us for rescue. What I remember most are the screams for water. There were so many people, you couldn't possibly provide water for a fraction of them. It was just an impossibility. And they did die. We had to carry these bodies and burn, cremate them in some way. Because they were corpses now. I can still hear those voices very clearly.

FRIEDMAN: I was in my home, which happened to be a very protected kind of shelter. My grandfather was an industrialist, and we lived on a huge estate with very thick walls and beams. The house did not collapse to the ground. The thick walls protected me against the effects of radiation. Although I was affected, it was not as

---

Source: Studs Terkel, *The Good War*, pp. 538–542. Copyright 1984 by Terkel. Reprinted by permission of Pantheon Books, a division of Random House, Inc.

intensely as it might have been had I lived in a smaller house.

I was eleven years old. A few days after the bomb fell, I was looking for my mother. I was going through places, amongst the people who were not getting aid. We had very, very little help. It was completely overwhelming to all the communities around. We had depleted resources to begin with.

People were barely having food to eat for themselves, and clothing. All I had were five grains of dried beans in my hand that I clutched all that day. I was well enough to be on my feet, but almost all the others I saw were laying in the spaces, in schoolyards and other public places.

I was going around from place to place, calling for my mother: "If you are here, if you are there, please answer me." I would have been devastated if someone answered, because I wouldn't have known what to do, to help. Yet, a child is desperately looking for her mother. Because I felt so helpless, I devised something in my head. A sort of magic.

I thought I would sing some lullabies that she loved singing, that she used to sing to me. I said in my head, God, I ask you now, would you sort of, like the wind, carry the tune and comfort her as if she could hear it? I remember crying and sobbing as I was singing.

There's a beach near Tokyo, Kamakura. Although we happened to be in Hiroshima at the time, we were from Tokyo. We used to walk along this beach and collect sea shells. She would sing this song. (She sings it. Mr. Kito softly joins her.)

Did you find your mother?

No, she is still listed among the missing, although my father ran into a woman who thought she knew where my mother might have fallen. My mother had to be with a group of people of the block. Neighborhood block groups were organized because there was a mass evacuation. My mother was the one of our family who had to go.

She left about seven-thirty in the morning. Where she went was very close to the center of the explosion. When the bomb exploded, this woman was not too far from her. The woman had small children, and she just bent over to protect her children. My mother, with the flash, put her hands over her ears and ran inside. Then she saw the concrete fall on my mother. This tale was told to my father about a month after the explosion. It's most likely that she died.

My father went to the place where this woman took him. He said there were a number of remains. They were so burned that it was difficult to tell which one might have been my mother. So he collected little bones from each remains and brought them home and we kind of buried them as my mother.

KITO: All my family were in the city of Nagoya, so none of them were injured by the bomb. But my friends in the army with me, there's no trace of what happened to them. I would say, from about the seventh of August, thousands of maggots would infest the wounds of the thousands of injured that I came upon. As the maggots would squirm on the surface of these injuries, it was very painful for these survivors. They would scream to us, plead with us, "Please take these maggots off our bodies." Where there are maggots from head to toe on all these bodies, it was impossible for me, one soldier, to try to help so many people.

We consulted a military doctor nearby. All the medications had been used up, there was no supply left. What should we do?

The doctor said, "This is impossible. We can't do anything." He said, "Sterilize their wounds with salt water." So we boiled water in a large pot and put in a whole jug of salt. Since the entire bodies were infected, we just used a broom. We couldn't possibly do each part of the body with our fingers. We took a broom, dipped it into the salt water, and painted over the bodies.

The children, who were lying down, unable to move, leaped up. In the local dialect, they would say, "I'm gonna run, I must run." I remember this scene very clearly.

A woman in the studio interjects: "The word Mr. Kito used in hashira. *It means 'it hurts.'" The interpreter corrects her: in the local dialect it means "thank you."*

Since I was from Nagoya, I didn't understand that dialect. I thought they were saying they had to run. So I was trying to hold them in place, to keep them still. Shortly after, they died.

Of course there were no family members of these children to take back their dead. What we did was to take the timber from the buildings nearby. We built up a funeral pyre to burn these corpses.

FRIEDMAN: I was going through these very places looking for my mother.

Something devastating happens to your system. It lasts for a prolonged period of time. You are in shock. In order for you to function, you must desensitize yourself.

You may be moving automatically, with the simple instinct to survive. You do not feel as if you were in a real situation. You feel as if—I can't believe this is happening to me. As if you are looking at television, something detached, outside your feelings.

KITO: I don't think of myself as transporting corpses when I was going through the task of cremating them. I was just carrying an object. I was thinking. Okay, today, I carried x number of corpses, that is what I did today. This is how objective I felt about it. Any sense of sympathy or pathos about what happened to these human being was just blown away somewhere. I was just doing the tasks. I needed a very long time in order to return to some sort of normal state.

Did survivors—yourselves, perhaps—ever experience guilt at having survived?

FRIEDMAN: Oh yes. I had a deep feeling of guilt, depression about that day for a long, long time. I worked it out through hypnosis. I hypnotized myself and relived the time, the event of the Hiroshima explosion. Rather than remembering it as if I'm seeing it on the stage and hearing only loud sounds like exploding ammunition, I began to hear smaller voices and smaller sounds in the background, calling for help. That I hadn't really heard. I saw more things coming back more vividly than my actual recollection of the time. Then I was able to say that this was why I truly felt guilty. That I wasn't able to help them.

KITO: I have come to think that the people who died are calling upon us survivors not to make a meaningless waste out of their deaths. That is how I have been able to change the guilt into activity.

POSTSCRIPT: *There is considerable discrimination in Japan against* hibakusha. *It is frequently extended toward their children as well: socially as well as economically. "Not only* hibakusha, *but their children, are refused employment," said Mrs. Kito. "There are many among them who do not want it known that they are* hibakusha."

NOTE

[1] *Hibakusha* is the name given by the Japanese to the survivors of the atom bomb. There are four groups of *hibakusha:* (1) people who were directly affected; (2) those who, afterwards, entered the city limits; (3) those, outside the area, who take care of those who were bombed; (4) those who were in their mother's womb.

---

141. Leo Szilard, "Chicago Scientists' Petition to the President," July 17, 1945

(Drafted by Leo Szilard and signed by 68 members of the Metallurgical Laboratory in Chicago)

Discoveries of which the people of the United States are not aware may affect the welfare of this nation in the near future. The liberation of atomic power which has been achieved places atomic bombs in the hands of the Army. It places in your hands, as Commander-in-Chief, the fateful decision whether or not to sanction the use of such bombs in the present phase of the war against Japan.

We, the undersigned scientists, have been working in the field of atomic power. Until recently we have had to fear that the United States might be attacked by atomic bombs during this war and that her only defense might lie in a counterattack by the same means. Today, with the defeat of Germany, this danger is averted and we feel impelled to say what follows:

The war has to be brought speedily to a successful conclusion and attacks by atomic bombs may very well be an effective method of warfare. We feel, however, that such attacks on Japan could not be justified, at least not until the terms which will be imposed after the war on

Source: S. R. Weart and Gertrude Weiss, "Chicago Scientists' Petition to the President," July 17, 1945, Leo Szilard: His Version of the Facts, Vol. 2, Copyright MIT Press, 1978, pp. 211–12. Reprinted by permission.

Japan were made public in detail and Japan were given an opportunity to surrender.

If such, public announcement gave assurance to the Japanese that they could look forward to a life devoted to peaceful pursuits in their homeland and if Japan still refused to surrender, our action might then, in certain circumstances, find itself forced to resort to the use of atomic bombs. Such a step, however, ought not to be at any time without seriously considering the moral responsibilities which are involved.

The development of atomic power will provide the nation with new means of destruction. The atomic bombs at our disposal represent only the first step in this direction, and there is almost no limit to the destructive power which will become available in the course of their future development. Thus a nation which sets the precedent of using these newly liberated forces of nature for purposes of destruction may have to bear the responsibility of opening the door to an era of devastation on an unimaginable scale.

If after the war a situation is allowed to develop in the world which permits rival powers to be in uncontrolled possession of these new means of destruction, the cities of the United States as well as the cities of other nations will be in continuous danger of sudden annihilation. All the resources of the United States, moral and material, may have to be mobilized to prevent the advent of such a world situation. Its prevention is at present the solemn responsibility of the United States—singled out by virtue of her lead in the field of atomic power.

The added material strength which this lead gives to the United States brings with it the obligation of restraint and if we were to violate this obligation our moral position would be weakened in the eyes of the world and in our own eyes. It would then be more difficult for us to live up to our responsibility of bringing the unloosened forces of destruction under control.

In view of the foregoing, we, the undersigned, respectfully petition: first, that you exercise your power as Commander-in-Chief to rule that the United States will not resort to the use of atomic bombs in this war unless the terms which will be imposed upon Japan have been made public in detail and Japan knowing these terms has refused to surrender; second, that in such an event the question whether or not to use atomic bombs be decided by you in the light of the consideration presented in this petition as well as all the other moral responsibilities which are involved.

142. President Truman, White House Press Release on Hiroshima, August 6, 1945

Statement by the President of the United States

Sixteen hours ago an American airplane dropped one bomb on Hiroshima, an important Japanese Army base. That bomb had more power than 20,000 tons of T.N.T. It had more than two thousand times the blast power of the British "Grand Slam" which is the largest bomb ever yet used in the history of warfare.

The Japanese began the war from the air at Pearl Harbor. They have been repaid many fold. And the end is not yet. With this bomb we have now added a new and revolutionary increase in destruction to supplement the growing power of our armed forces. In their present form these bombs are now in production and even more powerful forms are in development.

It is an atomic bomb. It is a harnessing of the basic power of the universe. The force from which the sun draws its power has been loosed against those who brought war to the Far East.

Before 1939, it was the accepted belief of scientists that it was theoretically possible to release atomic energy. But no one knew any practical method of doing it. By 1942, however, we knew that the Germans were working feverishly to find a way to add atomic energy to the other engines of war with which they hoped to enslave the world. But they failed. We may be grateful to Providence

Source: White House Release on Hiroshima, August 6, 1945, from Foreign Relations of the United States, *Potsdam,* Vol. 2. Washington, DC, 1960, pp. 1380–81. Public Domain Reprint.

that the Germans got the V-1's and the V-2's late and in limited quantities and even more grateful that they did not get the atomic bomb at all.

The battle of the laboratories held fateful risks for us as well as the battles of the air, land and sea, and we have now won the battle of the laboratories as we have won the other battles.

Beginning in 1940, before Pearl Harbor, scientific knowledge useful in war was pooled between the United States and Great Britain, and many priceless helps to our victories have come from that arrangement. Under that general policy the research on the atomic bomb was begun. With American and British scientists working together we entered the race of discovery against the Germans.

The United States had available the large numbers of scientists of distinction in the many needed areas of knowledge. It had the tremendous industrial and financial resources necessary for the project and they could be devoted to it without undue impairment of other vital war work. In the United States the laboratory work and the production plants, on which a substantial start had already been made, would be out of reach of enemy bombing, while at that time Britain was exposed to constant air attack and was still threatened with the possibility of invasion. For these reasons Prime Minister Churchill and President Roosevelt agreed that it was wise to carry on the project here. We now have two great plants and many lesser works devoted to the production of atomic power. Employment during peak construction numbered 125,000 and over 65,000 individuals are even now engaged in operating the plants. Many have worked there for two and a half years. Few know what they have been producing. They see great quantities of material going in and they see nothing coming out of these plants, for the physical size of the explosive charge is exceedingly small. We have spent two billion dollars on the greasiest scientific gamble in history—we won.

But the greatest marvel is not the size of the enterprise, its secrecy, nor its cost, but the achievement of scientific brains in putting together infinitely complex pieces of knowledge held by many men in different fields of science into a workable plan. And hardly less marvelous has been the capacity of industry to design, and of labor to operate, the machines and methods to do things never done before so that the brain child of many minds came forth in physical shape and performed as it was supposed to do. Both science and industry worked under the direction of the United States Army, which achieved a unique success in managing so diverse a problem in the advancement of knowledge in an amazingly short time. It is doubtful if such another combination could be got together in the world. What has been done is the greatest achievement of organized science in history. It was done under high pressure and without failure.

We are now prepared to obliterate more rapidly and completely every productive enterprise the Japanese has above ground in any city. We shall destroy their docks, their factories, and their communications. Let there be no mistake; we shall completely destroy Japan's power to make war.

It was to save the Japanese people from utter destruction that the ultimatum of July 26 was issued at Potsdam. Their leaders promptly rejected that ultimatum. If they do not now accept our terms they may expect a rain of ruin from the air, the like of which has never been seen on this earth. Behind this air attack will follow sea and land forces in such numbers and power as they have not yet seen and with the fighting skill of which they are already well aware.

The Secretary of War, who has kept in personal touch with all phases of this project, will immediately make public a statement giving further details.

His statement will give facts concerning the sites of Oak Ridge near Knoxville, Tennessee, and at Richland near Pasco, Washington, and an installation near Santa Fe, New Mexico. Although the workers at the sites have been making materials to be used in producing the greatest destructive forces in history they have not themselves been in danger beyond that of many other occupations, for the utmost care has been taken of their safety.

The fact that we can release atomic energy ushers in a new era in man's understanding of nature's forces. Atomic energy may in the future supplement the power that now comes from coal, oil, and falling water, but at present it cannot be produced on a basis to compete with them commercially. Before that comes there must be a long period of intensive research.

It has never been the habit of the scientists of this country of the policy of this Government to withhold from the world scientific knowledge. Normally, therefore, everything about the work with atomic energy would be made public.

But under present circumstances it is not intended to divulge the technical processes of production or all the military applications, pending further examination of possible methods of protecting us and the rest of the world from the danger of sudden destruction.

I shall recommend that the Congress of the United States consider promptly the establishment of an appropriate commission to control the production and use of atomic power within the United States. I shall give further consideration and make further recommendations to the Congress as to how atomic power can become a powerful and forceful influence towards the maintenance of world peace.

143. Paul Fussell, "Hiroshima: A Soldier's View"

Many years ago in New York I saw on the side of a bus a whiskey ad which I've remembered all this time, for it's been for me a model of the brief poem. Indeed, I've come upon a few short poems subsequently that evinced more genuine poetic talent. The ad consists of two lines of "free verse," thus:

> In life, experience is the great teacher.
> In Scotch, Teacher's is the great experience.

For present purposes we can jettison the second line (licking our lips ruefully as it disappears), leaving the first to encapsulate a principle whose banality suggests that it enshrines a most useful truth. I bring up the matter this August, the 36th anniversary of the A-bombing of Hiroshima and Nagasaki, to focus on something suggested by the long debate about the ethics, if any, of that affair: namely, the importance of experience, sheer vulgar experience, in influencing, if not determining, one's views about the first use of the bomb. And the experience I'm talking about is that of having come to grips, face to face, with an enemy who designs your death. The experience is common to those in the infantry and the Marines and even the line Navy, to those, in short, who fought the Second World War mindful always that their mission was, as they were repeatedly told, "to close with the enemy and destroy him." I think there's something to be learned about that war, as well as about the tendency of historical memory unwittingly to resolve ambiguity, by considering some of the ways testimonies emanating from experience complicate attitudes about the cruel ending of that cruel war.

"What did you do in the Great War, Daddy?" The recruiting poster deserves ridicule and contempt, of course, but its question is embarrassingly relevant here. The problem is one that touches on the matter of social class in America. Most of those with firsthand experience of the war at its worst were relatively inarticulate and have remained silent. Few of those destined to be destroyed if the main islands had had to be invaded went on to become our most eloquent men of letters or our most impressive ethical theorists of professors of history or international jurists. The testimony of experience has come largely from rough diamonds like James Jones and William Manchester, who experienced the war in the infantry and the Marine Corps. Both would agree with the point, if not perhaps the tone, of a remark about Hiroshima made by a naval officer menaced by the kamikazes off Okinawa: "Those were the best burned women and children I ever saw." Anticipating objection from the inexperienced, Jones, in his book *WWII*, is careful to precede his chapter on Hiroshima with one detailing the plans already in motion for the infantry assaults on the home islands of Kyushu, scheduled for November 1945, and ultimately Honshu. The forthcoming invasion of Kyushu, he notes, "was well into its collecting and stockpiling stages before the war ended." (The island of Saipan was designated a main ammunition and supply base for the invasion, and if you visit it today you can see some of the assembled stuff still sitting there.) "The assault troops were chosen and already in training," Jones reminds us, and he illuminates the situation by the light of experience:

> What it must have been like to some old-timer buck sergeant or staff sergeant who had been through Guadalcanal or Bouganville or the Philippines, to stand on some beach and watch this huge war machine beginning to stir and move all round him and know that he very likely had survived this far only to fall dead on the dirt of Japan's home islands, hardly bears thinking about.

On the other hand, John Kenneth Galbriath is persuaded that the Japanese would have surrendered by November without an invasion. He thinks the atom bombs were not

---

Source: Paul Fussell, "Hiroshima: A Soldier's View," by Paul Fussell. Reprinted by permission of *The New Republic*, August 22 & 29, 1981, The New Republic, Inc.

decisive in bringing about the surrender and he implies that their use was unjustified. What did he do in the war? He was in the Office of Price Administration in Washington, and then he was director of the United States Bombing Survey. He was 37 in 1945, and I don't demand that he experience having his ass shot off. I just note that he didn't. In saying this I'm aware of its offensive implications *ad hominem*. But here I think that approach justified. What's at stake in an infantry assault is so entirely unthinkable to those without experience of one, even if they possess very wide-ranging imaginations and sympathies, that experience is crucial in this case.

A similar remoteness from experience, as well as a similar rationalistic abstraction, seems to lie behind the reaction of an anonymous reviewer of William Manchester's *Goodbye Darkness: A Memoir of the Pacific War* for the *New York Review of Books*. First of all the reviewer dislikes Manchester's calling the enemy Nips and Japs, but what really shakes him (her?) is this passage:

> After Biak the enemy withdrew to deep caverns. Rooting them out became a bloody business which reached its ultimate horrors in the last month of the war. You think of the lives which would have been lost in an invasion of Japan's home islands—a staggering number of Americans but millions more of Japanese—and you thank God for the atomic bomb.

Thank God for the atomic bomb. From this, "one recoils," says the reviewer. One does, doesn't one?

In an interesting exchange last year in the *New York Review of Books,* Joseph Alsop and David Joravsky set forth the by now familiar arguments on both sides of the debate. You'll be able to guess which sides they chose once you know that Alsop experienced capture by the Japanese at Hong Kong in 1942 and that Joravsky made no mortal contact with the Japan: a young soldier, he was on his way to the Pacific when the war ended. The editors of the *New York Review* have given their debate the tendentious title "Was the Hiroshima Bomb Necessary?"—surely an unanswerable question (unlike "Was It Effective?") and one suggesting the intellectual difficulties involved in imposing *ex post facto* a rational ethics on this event. Alsop focuses on the power and fanaticism of War Minister Anami, who insisted that Japan fight to the bitter end, defending the main islands with the same means and tenacity with which it had defended Iwo and Okinawa. He concludes: "Japanese surrender could never have been obtained, at any rate without the honor-satisfying bloodbath envisioned by . . . Anami, if the hideous destruction of Hiroshima and Nagasaki had not finally galvanized the peace advocates into tearing up the entire Japanese book of rules. "The Japanese planned to deploy the undefeated bulk of their ground forces, over two million men, plus 12,000 kamikaze planes, in a suicidal defense. That fact, says Alsop, makes it absurd to "hold the common view, by now hardly challenged by anyone, that the decision to drop the two bombs on Japan was wicked in itself, and that President Truman and all others who joined in making or who [like Oppenheimer] assented to this decision shared in the wickedness." And in explanation of "the two bombs." Alsop adds: "The true, climatic, and successful effort of the Japanese peace advocates . . . did not begin in deadly earnest until *after* the second bomb had destroyed Nagasaki. The Nagasaki bomb was thus the trigger to all the developments that led to peace."

Joravsky, now a professor of history at Northwestern, argues on the other hand that those who decided to use the bomb on cities betray defects of "reason and self-restraint." It all needn't have happened," He asserted, "if the US government had been willing to take a few more days and to be a bit more thoughtful in opening the age of nuclear warfare." But of course in its view it wasn't doing that: that's a historian's tidy hindsight. The government was ending the war conclusively, as well as irrationally remembering Pearl Harbor with a vengeance. It didn't know then what everyone now knows about leukemia and carcinoma and birth defects. History, as Eliot's "Gerontion" notes,

> . . . has many cunning passages, contrived
>   corridors
> And issues, deceives with whispering ambitions,
> Guides us by vanities . . .
>   Think
> Neither fear nor courage save us.
> Unnatural vices
> Are fathered by our heroism. Virtues
> Are forced upon us by our impudent crimes.

Understanding the past means feeling its pressure on your pulses and that's harder than Joravsky thinks.

The Alsop-Joravsky debate, which can be seen as reducing finally to a collision between experience and theory, was conducted with a certain civilized respect for evidence. Not so the way the new scurrilous agitprop *New Statesman* conceives those favoring the bomb and those opposing. They are, on the one hand, says Bruce Page, "the imperialist class-forces acting through Harry Truman," and, on the other hand, those representing "the humane, democratic virtues"—in short, "fascists" opposed to "populists." But ironically the bomb saved the lives not of any imperialists but only of the low and humble, the quintessentially democratic huddled masses—the conscripted enlisted men manning the fated invasion divisions. Bruce Page was nine years old when the war ended. For a man of that experience, phrases like "imperialist class-forces" come easily, and the issues look perfectly clear.

He's not the only one to have forgotten, if he ever knew, the savagery of the Pacific war. The dramatic postwar Japanese success at hustling and merchandising and tourism has (happily, in many ways) effaced for most people important elements of the assault context in which Hiroshima should be viewed. It is easy to forget what Japan was like before it was first destroyed and then humiliated, tamed, and constitutionalized by the West. "Implacable, treacherous, barbaric"—those were Admiral Halsey's characterizations of the enemy, and at the time few facing the Japanese would deny that they fit to a T. One remembers the captured American airmen locked for years in packing-crates, the prisoners decapitated, the gleeful use of bayonets on civilians. The degree which Americans register shock and extraordinary shame about the Hiroshima bomb correlates closely with lack of information about the war.

And the savagery was not just on one side. There was much sadism and brutality—undeniably racist—on ours. No Marine was fully persuaded of his manly adequacy who didn't have a well-washed Japanese skull to caress and who didn't have a go at treating surrendering Japs as rifle targets. Herman Wouk remembers it correctly while analyzing Ensign Keith in *The Caine Mutiny:* "Like most of the naval executions of Kwajalein, he seemed to regard the enemy as a species of animal pest." And the enemy felt the same way about us: "From the grim and desperate taciturnity with which the Japanese died, they seemed on their side to believe they were contending with an invasion of large armed ants." Hiroshima seems to follow in natural sequence: "This obliviousness on both sides to the fact that the opponents were human beings may perhaps be cited as the key to the many massacres of the Pacific war." Since the Japanese resisted so madly, let's pour gasoline into their emplacements and light it and shoot the people afire who try to get out. Why not? Why not blow them all up? Why not, indeed, drop a new kind of big bomb on them? Why allow one more American high school kid to see his intestines blown out of his body and spread before him in the dirt while he screams when we can end the whole thing just like that?

On Okinawa, only weeks before Hiroshima, 123,000 Japanese and Americans *killed* each other. "Just awful" was the comment not of some pacifist but of MacArthur. One million American casualties was his estimate of the cost of the forthcoming invasion. And that invasion was not just a hypothetical threat, as some theorists have argued. It was genuinely in train, as I know because I was to be in it. When the bomb ended the war I was in the 45th Infantry Division, which had been through the European war to the degree that it had needed to be reconstituted two or three times. We were in a staging area near Reims, ready to be shipped across the United States for final preparation in the Philippines. My division was to take part in the invasion of Honshu in March 1946. (The earlier invasion of Kyushu was to be carried out by 700,000 infantry already in the Pacific.) I was a 21-year-old second lieutenant leading a rifle platoon. Although still officially in one piece, in the German war I had already been wounded in the leg and back severely enough to be adjudged, after the war, 40 percent disabled. But even if my legs buckled whenever I jumped out of the back of the truck, my condition was held to be satisfactory for whatever lay ahead. When the bombs dropped and news began to circulate that "Operation Olympic" would not, after all, take place, that we would not be obliged to run up the beaches near Tokyo assault-firing while being mortared and shelled, for all the fake manliness of our facades we cried with relief and joy. We were going to live. We were going to grow up to adulthood after all. When the *Enola Gay* dropped the package, "There were cheers," says John Toland, "over the intercom; it meant the end of the war."

Those who cried and cheered are very different from high-minded, guilt-ridden GIs we're told about by the late. J. Glenn Gray in *The Warriors* (1959). During the war in Europe Gray was an interrogator in the Counter Intelligence Corps, and in that capacity he underwent the war at division level. After the war he became a professor of philosophy at Colorado College (never, I've thought, the venue of very much reality) and a distinguished editor of Heidegger. There's no doubt that Gray's outlook on everything was noble and elevated. But *The Warriors,* his meditation on modern soldiering, gives every sign of remoteness from experience. Division headquarters is miles behind the places where the soldiers experience terror and madness and relieve these pressures by sadism. "Where the news of the atomic bombing of Hiroshima and Nagasaki came," Gray asks us to believe, "many an American soldier felt shocked and ashamed." But why, we ask? Because we'd bombed civilians? We'd been doing that for years and, besides the two bombs, wiped out 10,000 Japanese troops, not now mentioned, John Hersey's kindly physicians and Jesuit priests being more touching. Were Gray's soldiers shocked and ashamed because we'd obliterated whole towns? We'd done that plenty of times. If at division headquarters felt shocked and ashamed, down in the rifle companies none did, although Gray says they did:

> The combat soldier knew better than did Americans at home what those bombs meant in suffering and injustice. The man of conscience realized intuitively that the vast majority of Japanese in both cities were no more, if no less, guilty of the war than were his own parents, sisters, or brothers.

I find this canting nonsense: the purpose of dropping the bombs was not to "punish" people but to stop the war. To intensify the shame he insists we feel, Gray seems willing to fiddle the facts. The Hiroshima bomb, he says, was dropped "without any warning." But actually, two days before, 720,000 leaflets were dropped on the city urging everyone to get out and indicating that the place was going to be obliterated. Of course few left.

Experience whispers that the pity is not that we used the bomb to end the Japanese war but that it wasn't really earlier to end the German one. If only it could have been rushed into production faster and dropped at the right moment on the Reich chancellery or Berchtesgaden or Hitler's military headquarters in East Prussia or—Wagnerian *coupe de théâtre*—at Rommel's phony state funeral, most of the Nazi hierarchy could have been pulverized immediately, saving not just the embarrassment of the Nuremburg trials but the lives of about four million Jews, Poles, Slavs, gypsies, and other "subhumans," not to mention the lives and limbs of millions of Allied and Axis soldiers. If the bomb could have been ready even as late as July 1944, it could have reinforced the Von Stauffenberg plot and ended the war then and there. If the bomb had only been ready in time, the men of my infantry platoon would not have been killed and maimed.

All this is not to deny that like the Russian revolution, the atomic bombing of Japan was a vast historical tragedy, and every passing year magnifies the dilemma into which it has thrown the contemporary world. As with the Russian revolution there are two sides—that's why it's a tragedy rather than a disaster—and unless we are simple-mindedly cruel, like Bruce Page, we need to be painfully aware of both at once. To observe that from the viewpoint of the war's victims-to-be the bomb was precisely the right thing to drop is to purchase no immunity from horror. See, for example, the new book *Unforgettable Fire: Pictures Drawn by Atomic Bomb Survivors,* issued by the Japan Broadcasting Corporation and distributed here by Pantheon Books. It presents a number of amateur colored-pencil, pastel, and watercolor depictions of the scene of the Hiroshima bombing made by the middle-aged and elderly survivors for a peace exhibition in 1975. In addition to the heartrending pictures the book offers brief moments of memoir, not for the weak-stomached:

> While taking my severely wounded wife out to the riverbank. . . , I was horrified indeed at the sight of a stark naked man standing in the rain with his eyeball in his palm. He looked to be in great pain but there was nothing that I could do for him. I wonder what became of him. Even today, I vividly remember the sight. It was simply miserable.

The drawings and paintings, whose often childish style makes them doubly touching, are of skin hanging down, breasts torn off, people bleeding and burning, dying mothers nursing dead babies. A bloody woman holds a bloody child in the ruins of a house, and the artist remembering her calling, "Please help this child! Someone, please help this child. Please help! Someone, please." As Samuel Johnson said of the smothering of the innocent Desdemona in another tragedy, "It is not to be endured." Nor, we should notice, is an infantryman's account of having his arm blown off in the Arno Valley in Italy in 1944:

> I wanted to die and die fast. I wanted to forget this miserable world. I cursed the war, I cursed the people who were responsible for it, I cursed God for putting me here . . . to suffer for something I never did or knew anything about. For this was hell, and I never imagined anything or anyone could suffer so bitterly. I screamed and cursed. Why? Why? What had I done to deserve this? But no answer came. I yelled for medics, because subconsciously I wanted to live. I tried to apply my right hand over my bleeding stump, but I didn't have the strength to hold it. I looked to the left of me and saw the bloody mess that was once my left arm; its fingers and palm were turned upward, like a flower looking to the sun for its strength.

The future scholar-critic of rhetoric who writes *The History of Canting in the Twentieth Century* will find much to study in the utterances of those who dilate on the wickedness of the bomb-droppers. He will realize that such utterance can perform for the speaker a valuable double function. First, it can display the fineness of his moral weave. And second, by implication it can also inform the audience that during the war he was no socially so unfortunate as to find himself at the cutting edge of the ground forces, where he might have had to compromise the pure clarity of his moral vision by the experience of weighing his own life against other people's. Down there, which is where the other people were in the war, is the place where coarse self-interest is the rule. When the young soldier with the wild eyes comes at you firing, do you shoot him in the foot, hoping he'll be hurt badly enough to drop or mis-aim the gun with which he is going to kill you, or do you shoot him in the chest and make certain he stops being your mortal enemy? It would be stupid to expect soldier to be very sensitive humanitarians ("Moderation in war is imbecility"—Admiral of the Fleet Lord Fisher); actually, only the barest decencies can be expected of them. They didn't star the war, except in the terrible sense hinted in Frederic Manning's observation based on his experience in the Great War: "War is waged by men; not by beasts, or by gods. It is a peculiarly human activity. To call it a crime against mankind is to miss at least half its significance; it is also the punishment of a crime." Knowing that fact by experience, soldiers have every motive for wanting a war stopped, by any means.

The predictable stupidity, parochialism, and greed in the postwar international mismanagement of the whole nuclear problem should not tempt us to mis-imagine the circumstances of the bomb's first "use." Nor should our well-justified fears and suspicions occasioned by the capture of the nuclear business by the mendacious classes (cf. Three Mile Island) tempt us to infer retrospectively extraordinary corruption, cruelty, and swinishness in those who decided to drop the bomb. Times change. Harry Truman was not a fascist, but a democrat. He was as close to a real egalitarian as we've seen in high office for a very long time. He is the only president in my lifetime who ever had the experience of commanding a small unit of ground troops obliged to kill people. He knew better than his subsequent critics what he was doing. The past, which as always did not know the future, acted in ways that ask to be imagined before they are condemned. Or even before they are simplified.

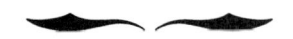

144. Robert S. Abbott, "Splitting the Atom of Race Hate," August 18, 1945

When the frightful horror and devastating of the new atomic bomb was unleashed on Japan, the shock was not only felt in Hiroshima but in every city and hamlet throughout the world. A tremor of foreboding fear must have shaken the spirits of men everywhere—an awesome dread lest this most formidable weapon of destruction turns out to be a Frankenstein to be turned against its democratic creators at some future date.

Out of this haunting peril, out of this night of terror, there must be a dawn somewhere.

To thinking people the earth over, it is hard to dodge this inescapable conclusion: if the foremost world scientists and two billion dollars can be harnessed during war to impose sudden death on millions, to destroy entire cities, why not do as much to create and prolong life, to construct vast, livable dwellings for the ill-housed, ill-clad, and ill-fed?

If science and dollars can be mobilized for war, why not for peace? If in an era of war lust millions of man hours and billions of dollars are spent on hate, why not as much to promote liberty, equality and fraternity in an era of peace?

In these trying war days, America has again discovered that science advances at a phenomenal rate to bring sacrifices to the God of Mars. Is peace so undesirable that science will not do as much to keep men from shouldering arms?

Truly in all the world today, man has no more dangerous enemy than hate—hate of other men, whether it be for their race, their religion, or their nationality.

Source: Robert Abbott, "Splitting the Atom of Race Hate." *The Chicago Defender,* Editorial Page, August 18, 1945. Reprinted by permission.

It should not stagger the imagination to picture thousands of social scientists and other experts ??? by the same two billion dollars that went into the atomic bomb at work in America to isolate and destroy the venom of racial hate.

And why not?

If an ounce of prevention is worth a pound of cure, certainly there is no better American investment today than the prevention of race hate that have innate in them the seeds of tomorrow's wars.

Chapter XXVII

Postwar America, 1946–1952

145. George Kennan, "The Sources of Soviet Conduct," July 1947

George Kennan was a minor official at the U.S. Embassy in Moscow when he cabled an 8,000-word memorandum, "The Sources of Soviet Conduct," and captured the attention of his superiors at the State Department. He was brought back to Washington and named head of the department's branch for long-term planning.

I

The political personality of Soviet power as we know it today is the product of ideology and circumstances: ideology inherited by the present Soviet leaders from the movement in which they had their political origin, and circumstances of the power which they now have exercised for nearly three decades in Russia. There can be few tasks of psychological analysis more difficult than to try to trace the interaction of these two forces and the relative role of each of the determination of official Soviet conduct. Yet the attempt must be made if that conduct is to be understood and effectively countered.

It is difficult to summarize the set of ideological concepts with which the Soviet leaders came into power. Marxian ideology, in its Russian-Communist projection, has always been in process of subtle evolution. The materials on which it bases itself are extensive and complex.

But the outstanding features of Communist thought as it existed in 1916 may perhaps be summarized as follows: (a) that the central factor in the life of man, the fact which determines the character of public life and the "physiognomy of society," is the system by which material goods are produced and exchanged; (b) that the capitalist system of production is a nefarious one which inevitably leads of the exploitation of the working class by the capital-owning class and is incapable of developing adequately the economic resources of society or of distributing fairly the material goods produced by human labor; (c) that capitalism contains the seeds of its own destruction and must, in view of the inability of the capital-owning class to adjust itself to economic change, result eventually and inescapably in a revolutionary transfer of power to the working class; and (d) that imperialism, the final phase of capitalism, leads directly to war and revolution.

The rest may be outlined in Lenin's own words: "Unevenness of economic and political development is the inflexible law of capitalism. It follows from this that the victory of Socialism may come originally in a few capitalist countries or even in a single capitalist country. The victorious proletariat of that country, having expropriated the capitalists and having organized Socialist production at home, would rise against the remaining capitalist world, drawing to itself in the process the oppressed classes of other countries." It must be noted that there was no assumption that capitalism would perish without proletarian revolution. A final push was needed from a revolutionary proletariat movement in order to tip over the tottering structure. But it was regarded as inevitable that sooner or later that push be given.

For fifty years prior to the outbreak of the Revolution, this pattern of thought had exercised great fascination for

Source: George Kennan, "The Sources of Soviet Conduct." *Foreign Affairs,* XXV, No. 4, July 1947, pp. 566–82. Copyright 1947 by Council on Foreign Relations, Inc. Reprinted by permission.

the members of the Russian revolutionary movement. Frustrated, discontented, hopeless of finding self-expression—or too impatient to seek it—in the confining limits of the Tsarist political system, yet lacking wide popular support for their choice of bloody revolution as a means of social betterment, these revolutionists found in Marxist theory a highly convenient rationalization for their own instinctive desires. It afforded pseudo-scientific justification for their impatience, for their categoric denial of all values in the Tsarist system, for their yearning for power and revenge and for their inclination to cut corners in the pursuit of it. It is therefor no wonder that they had come to believe implicitly in the truth and soundness of the Marxian-Leninist teachings, so congenial to their own impulses and emotions. Their sincerity need not be impugned. This is a phenomenon as old as human nature itself. It has never been more aptly described than by Edward Gibbon, who wrote in *The Decline and Fall of the Roman Empire:* "From enthusiasm to imposture the step is perilous and slippery, the demon of Socrates affords a memorable instance how a wise man may deceive himself; how a good man may deceive others, how the conscience may slumber in a mixed and middle state between self-illusion and voluntary fraud." And it was with this set of conceptions that the members of the Bolshevik Party entered into power.

Now it must be noted that through all the years of preparation for revolution, the attention of these men, as indeed of Marx himself, had been centered less on the future form which Socialism would take than on the necessary overthrow of rival power which, in their view, had to precede the introduction of Socialism. Their views, therefore, on the positive program to be put into effect, once power was attained, were for the most part nebulous, visionary and impractical. Beyond the nationalization of industry and the expropriation of large private capital holdings there was no agreed program. The treatment of the peasantry, which according to the Marxist formulation was not of the proletariat, had always been a vague spot in the pattern of Communist thought; and it remained an object of controversy and vacillation for the first ten years of Communist power.

The circumstances of the immediate post-Revolution period—the existence of Russia of civil war and foreign intervention, together with the obvious fact that the Communists represented only a tiny minority of the Russian people—made the establishment of dictatorial power a necessity. The experience with "war Communism" and the abrupt attempt to eliminate private production and trade had unfortunate economic consequences and caused further bitterness against the new revolutionary regime. While the temporary relaxation of the effort to communize Russia, represented by the New Economic Policy, alleviated some of this economic distress and thereby served its purpose, it also made it evident that the "capitalistic sector of society" was still prepared to profit at once from any relaxation of governmental pressure, and would, if permitted to continue to exist, always constitute a powerful opposing element to the Soviet regime and a serious rival for influence in the country. Somewhat the same situation prevailed with respect to the individual peasant who, in his own small way, was also a private producer.

Lenin, had he lived, might have proved a great enough man to reconcile these conflicting forces to the ultimate benefit of Russian society, though this is questionable. But be that as it may, Stalin, and those whom he led in the struggle for succession to Lenin's position of leadership, were not the men to tolerate rival political forces in the sphere of power which they coveted. Their sense of insecurity was too great. Their particular brand of fanaticism, unmodified by any of the Anglo-Saxon traditions of compromise, was too fierce and too jealous to envisage any permanent sharing of power. From the Russian-Asiatic world out of which they had emerged they carried with them a skepticism as to the possibilities of permanent and peaceful coexistence of rival forces. Easily persuaded of their own doctrinaire "rightness," they insisted on the submission or destruction of all competing power. Outside of the Communist Party, Russian society was to have no rigidity. There were to be no forms of collective human activity or association which would not be dominated by the Party. No other force in Russian society was to be permitted to share vitality or integrity. Only the Party was to have structure. All else was to be an amorphous mass.

And within the Party the same principle was to apply. The mass of Party members might go through the motions of election, deliberation, decision and action; but in these motions they were to be animated not by their own individual wills but by the awesome breath of the Party leadership and the overbrooding presence of "the world."

Let it be stressed again that subjectively these men probably did not seek absolutism for its own sake. They doubtless believed—and found it easy to believe—that they alone knew what was good for society and that they would accomplish that good once their power was secure and unchallengeable. But in seeking that security of their own rule they were prepared to recognize no restrictions, either of God or man, on the character of their methods.

And until such time as that security might be achieved, they placed far down on their scale of operational priorities the comforts and happiness of the peoples entrusted to their care.

Now the outstanding circumstance concerning the Soviet regime is that down to the present day this process of political consolidation has never been completed and the men in the Kremlin have continued to be predominantly absorbed with the struggle to secure and make absolute the power which they seized in November 1917. They have endeavored to secure it primarily against forces at home, within Soviet society itself. But they have also endeavored to secure it against the outside world. For ideology, as we have seen, taught them that the outside world was hostile and that it was their duty eventually to overthrow the political forces beyond their borders. The powerful hands of Russian history and tradition reached up to sustain them in this feeling. Finally, their own aggressive intransigence with respect to the outside world began to find its own reaction; and they were soon forced, to use another Gibbonesque phrase, "to chastise the contumacy" which they themselves had provoked. It is an undeniable privilege of every man to prove himself right in the thesis that the world is his enemy; for if he reiterates it frequently enough and makes it the background of his conduct he is bound eventually to be right.

Now it lies in the nature of the mental world of the Soviet leaders, as well as in the character of their ideology, that no opposition to them can be officially recognized as having any merit or justification whatsoever. Such opposition can flow, in theory, only from the hostile and incorrigible forces of dying capitalism. As long as remnants of capitalism were officially recognized as existing in Russia, it was possible to place on them, as an internal element, part of the blame for the maintenance of a dictatorial form of society. But as these remnants were liquidated, little by little, this justification fell away; and when it was indicated officially that they had been finally destroyed, it disappeared altogether. And this fact created one of the most basic of the compulsions which came to act upon the Soviet regime: since capitalism no longer existed in Russia and since it could not be admitted that there could be serious or widespread opposition to the Kremlin springing spontaneously from the liberated masses under its authority, it became necessary to justify the retention of the dictatorship by stressing the menace of capitalism abroad.

This began at an early date. In 1924, Stalin specifically defended the retention of the "organs of suppression," meaning, among others, the army and the secret police, on the ground that "as long as there is a capitalist encirclement there will be danger of intervention with all the consequences that flow from that danger." In accordance with that theory, and from that time on, all internal opposition forces in Russia have consistently been portrayed as the agents of foreign forces of reaction antagonistic to Soviet power.

By the same token, tremendous emphasis has been placed on the original Communist thesis of a basic antagonism between the capitalist and Socialist worlds. It is clear, from many indications, that this emphasis is not founded in reality. The real facts concerning it have been confused by the existence abroad of genuine resentment provoked by Soviet philosophy and tactics and occasionally by the existence of great centers of military power, notably the Nazi regime in Germany and the Japanese Government of the late 1930s, which did indeed have aggressive designs against the Soviet Union. But there is ample evidence that the stress laid in Moscow on the menace confronting Soviet society from the world outside its borders is founded not in the realities of foreign antagonism but in the necessity of explaining away the maintenance of dictatorial authority at home.

Now the maintenance of this pattern of Soviet power, namely, the pursuit of unlimited authority domestically, accompanied by the cultivation of the semi-myth of implacable foreign hostility, has gone far to shape the actual machinery of Soviet power as we know it today. Internal organs of administration which did not serve this purpose withered on the vine. Organs which did serve this purpose became vastly swollen. The security of Soviet power came to rest on the iron discipline of the Party, on the severity and ubiquity of the secret police, and on the uncompromising economic monopolism of the state. The "organs of suppression," in which the Soviet leaders had sought security from rival forces, became in large measure the masters of those whom they were designed to serve. Today the major part of the structure of Soviet power is committed to the perfection of the dictatorship and to the maintenance of the concept of Russia as in a state of siege, with the enemy lowering beyond the walls. And the millions of human beings who form that part of the structure of power must defend at all costs this concept of Russia's position, for without it they are themselves superfluous.

As things stand today, the rulers can no longer dream of parting with these organs of suppression. The quest for absolute power, pursued now for nearly three decades with a ruthlessness unparalleled (in scope at least) in modern times, has again produced internally, as it did externally, its own reaction. The excesses of the police apparatus have fanned the potential opposition to the regime into something far greater and more dangerous than it could have been before those excesses began.

But least of all can the rulers dispense with the fiction by which the maintenance of dictatorial power has been defended. For this fiction has been canonized in Soviet philosophy by the excesses already committed in its name; and it is now anchored in the Soviet structure of thought by bonds far greater than those of mere ideology.

II

So much for the historical background. What does it spell in terms of the political personality of Soviet power as we know it today?

Of the original ideology, nothing has been officially junked. Belief is maintained in the basic badness of capitalism, in the inevitability of its destruction, in the obligation of the proletariat to assist in that destruction and to take power into its own hands. But stress has come to be laid primarily on those concepts which relate most specifically to the Soviet regime itself: to its position as the sole truly Socialist regime in a dark and misguided world, and to the relationships of power within it.

The first of these concepts is that of the innate antagonism between capitalism and Socialism. We have seen how deeply that concept has become imbedded in foundations of Soviet power. It has profound implications for Russia's conduct as a member of international society. It means that there can never be on Moscow's side any sincere assumption of a community of aims between the Soviet Union and powers which are regarded as capitalism. It must invariably be assumed in Moscow that the aims of the capitalist world are antagonistic to the Soviet regime and, therefore, to the interests of the peoples it controls. If the Soviet Government occasionally sets its signature to documents which would indicate the contrary, this is to be regarded as a tactical maneuver permissible in dealing with the enemy (who is without honor) and should be taken in the spirit of *caveat emptor*. Basically, the antagonism remains. It is postulated. And from it flow many of the phenomena which we find disturbing in the Kremlin's conduct of foreign policy: the secretiveness, the lack of frankness, the duplicity, the war suspiciousness, and the basic unfriendliness of purpose. These phenomena are there to stay, for the foreseeable future. There can be variations of degree and of emphasis.

When there is something the Russians want from us, one or the other of these features of their policy must be thrust temporarily into the background; and when that happens there will always be Americans who will leap forward with gleeful announcements that "the Russians have changed," and some who will even try to take credit for having brought about such "changes." But we should not be misled by tactical maneuvers. These characteristics of Soviet policy, like the postulate from which they flow, are basic to the internal nature of Soviet power, and will be with us, whether in the foreground or the background, until the internal nature of Soviet power is changed.

This means that we are going to continue for a long time to find the Russians difficult to deal with. It does not mean that they should be considered as embarked upon a do-or-die program to overthrow our society by a given date. The theory of the inevitability of the eventual fall of capitalism has the fortunate connotation that there is no hurry about it. The forces of progress can take their time in preparing the final *coup de grâce*. Meanwhile, what is vital is that the "Socialist fatherland"—that oasis of power which has been already won for Socialism in the person of the Soviet Union—should be cherished and defended by all good Communists at home and abroad, its fortunes promoted, its enemies badgered and confounded. The promotion of premature, "adventuristic" revolutionary projects abroad which might embarrass Soviet power in any way would be an inexcusable, even a counter-revolutionary act. The cause of Socialism is the support and promotion of Soviet power, as defined in Moscow.

This brings us to the second of the concepts important to contemporary Soviet outlook. That is the infallibility of the Kremlin. The Soviet concept of power, which permits no focal points of organization outside the Party itself, requires that the Party leadership remain in theory the sole repository of truth. For if truth were to be found elsewhere, there would be justification for its expression in organized activity. But it is precisely that which the Kremlin cannot and will not permit.

The leadership of the Communist Party is therefore always right, and has been always right ever since in 1929. Stalin formalized his personal power by announcing that decision of the Politburo were being taken unanimously.

On the principle of infallibility there rests the iron discipline of the Communist Party. In fact, the two concepts are mutually self-supporting. Perfect discipline requires recognition of infallibility. Infallibility requires the observance of discipline. And the two together go far to determine the behaviorism of the entire Soviet apparatus of power. But their effect cannot be understood unless a third factor be taken into account: namely, the fact that the leadership is at liberty to put forward for tactical purposes any particular thesis which it finds useful to the cause at any particular moment and to require the faithful and unquestioning acceptance of that thesis by the members of the movement as a whole. This means that truth is not a constant but is actually created, for all intents and purposes, by the Soviet leaders themselves. It may vary from week to week, from month to month. It is nothing absolute and immutable—nothing which flows from objective reality. It is only the most recent manifestation of the wisdom of those in whom the ultimate wisdom is supposed to reside, because they represent the logic of history. The accumulative effect of these factors is to give to the whole subordinate apparatus of Soviet power an unshakable stubbornness and steadfastness in its orientation. This orientation can be changed at will by the Kremlin but by no other power. Once a given party line has been laid down on a given issue of current policy, the whole Soviet governmental machine, including the mechanism of diplomacy, moves inexorably along the prescribed path, like a persistent toy automobile wound up and headed in a given direction, stopping only when it meets with some unanswerable force. The individuals who are the components of this machine are unamenable to argument or reason which comes to them from outside sources. Their whole training has taught them to mistrust and discount the glib persuasiveness of the outside world. Like the white dog before the phonograph, they hear only the "master's voice." And if they are to be called off from the purposes last dictated to them, it is the master who must call them off. Thus the foreign representative cannot hope that his words will make any impression on them. The most that he can hope is that they will be transmitted to those at the top, who are capable of changing the party line. But even those are not likely to be swayed by any normal logic in the words of the bourgeois representatives. Since there can be no appeal to common purposes, there can be no appeal to common mental approaches. For this reason, facts speak louder than words to the ears of the Kremlin; and words carry the greatest weight when they have the right of reflecting, or being backed up by, facts of unchallengeable validity.

But we have seen that the Kremlin is under no ideological compulsion to accomplish its purposes in a hurry. Like the Church, it is dealing in ideological concepts which are of long-term validity, and it can afford to be patient. It has no right to risk the existing achievements of the revolution for the sake of vain baubles of the future. The very teachings of Lenin himself require great caution and flexibility in the pursuit of Communist purposes. Again, these precepts are fortified by the lessons of Russian history: of centuries of obscure battles between nomadic forces over the stretches of a vast unfortified plain. Here caution, circumspection, flexibility and deception are the valuable qualities; and their value finds natural appreciation in the Russian or the oriental mind. Thus the Kremlin has no compunction about retreating in the face of superior force. And being under the compulsion of no timetable, it does not get panicky under the necessity for such retreats. Its political action is a fluid stream which moves constantly, wherever it is permitted to move, toward a given goal. Its main concern is to make sure that it has filled every nook and cranny available to it in the basis of world power. But if it finds unassailable barriers in its path, it accepts these philosophically and accommodates itself to them. The main thing is that there should always be pressure, increasing constant pressure, toward the desired goal. There is no trace of any feeling in Soviet psychology that that goal must be reached at any given time.

These considerations make Soviet diplomacy at once easier and more difficult to deal with than the diplomacy of individual aggressive leaders like Napoleon and Hitler. On the one hand it is more sensitive to contrary force, more ready to yield on individual sectors of the diplomatic front when that force is felt to be too strong, and thus more rational in the logic and rhetoric of power. On the other hand it cannot be easily defeated or discouraged by a single victory on the part of its opponents. And the patient persistence by which it is animated means that it can be effectively countered not by sporadic acts which represent the momentary whims of democratic opinion but only by intelligent long-range policies on the part of Russia's adversaries—policies no less steady in their purpose, and no less variegated and resourceful in their application, than those of the Soviet Union itself.

In these circumstances it is clear that the main element of any United States policy toward the Soviet Union must be that of a long-term, patient but firm and vigilant containment of Russian expansive tendencies. It is important to note, however, that such a policy has nothing to do with outward histrionics: with threats or blustering or superfluous gestures of outward "toughness." While the Kremlin is basically flexible in its reaction to political realities, it is by no means unamenable to considerations of prestige. Like almost any other government, it can be placed by tactless and threatening gestures in a position where it cannot afford to yield even though this might be dictated by its sense of realism. The Russian leaders are keen judges of human psychology, and as such they are highly conscious that loss of temper and of self-control is never a source of strength in political affairs. They are quick to exploit such evidences of weakness. For these reasons, it is a *sine qua non* of successful dealing with Russia that the foreign government in question should remain at all times cool and collected and that its demands on Russian policy should be put forward in such a manner as to leave the way open for a compliance not too detrimental to Russian prestige.

III

In light of the above, it will be clearly seen that the Soviet pressure against the free institutions of the Western world is something that can be contained by the adroit and vigilant application of counter-force at a series of constantly shifting geographical and political points, corresponding to the shifts and maneuvers of Soviet policy, but which cannot be charmed or talked out of existence. The Russians look forward to a duel of infinite duration, and they see that already they have scored great successes. It must be borne in mind that there was a time when the Communist Party represented far more of a minority in the sphere of Russian national life than Soviet power today represents in the world community.

But if ideology convinces the rulers of Russia that truth is on their side and that they can therefore afford to wait, those of us on whom that ideology has no claim are free to examine objectively the validity of that premise. The Soviet thesis not only implies complete lack of control by the West over its own economic destiny, it likewise assumes a Russian unity, discipline and patience over an infinite period. Let us bring this apocalyptic vision down to earth, and suppose that the Western world finds the strength and resourcefulness to contain Soviet power over a period of ten to fifteen years. What does that spell for Russia itself?

The Soviet leaders, taking advantage of the contributions of modern technique to the arts of despotism, have solved the question of obedience within the confines of their power. Few challenge their authority; and even those who do are unable to make that challenge valid as against the organs of suppression of the state.

The Kremlin has also proved able to accomplish its purpose of building up in Russia, regardless of the interests of the inhabitants, an industrial foundation of heavy metallurgy, which is, to be sure, not yet complete but which is nevertheless continuing to grow and is approaching those of the other major industrial countries. All of this, however, both the maintenance of internal political security and the building of heavy industry, has been carried out at a terrible cost in human life and in human hopes and energies. It has necessitated the use of forced labor on a scale unprecedented in modern times under conditions of peace. It has involved the neglect or abuse of other phases of Soviet economic life, particularly agriculture, consumers' goods production, housing, and transportation.

To all that, the war has added its tremendous toll of destruction, death and human exhaustion. In consequence of this, we have in Russia today a population which is physically and spiritually tired. The mass of the people are disillusioned, skeptical and no longer as accessible as they once were to the magical attraction which Soviet power still radiates to its followers abroad. The avidity with which people seized upon the slight respite accorded to the Church for tactical reasons during the war was eloquent testimony to the fact that their capacity for faith and devotion found little expression in the purposes of the regime.

In these circumstances, there are limits to the physical and nervous strength of people themselves. These limits are absolute ones, and are binding even for the cruelest dictatorship, because beyond them people cannot be driven. The forced labor camps and the other agencies of constraint provide temporary means of compelling people to work longer hours than their own volition or mere economic pressure would dictate; but if people survive them at all they become old before their time and must be considered as human casualties to the demands of dictatorship. In either case their best powers are no longer available to Soviet and can no longer be enlisted in the service of the state.

Here only the younger generation can help. The younger generation, despite all vicissitudes and sufferings, is numerous and vigorous; and the Russians are a talented people. But it still remains to be seen what will be the effects on mature performance of the abnormal emotional strains of childhood which power dictatorship created and which were enormously increased by the war. Such things as normal security and placidity of home environment have practically ceased to exist in the Soviet Union outside of the most remote farms and villages. And observers are not yet sure whether that it is not going to leave its mark on the over-all capacity of the generation now coming into maturity.

In addition to this, we have the fact that Soviet economic development, while it can list certain formidable achievements, has been precariously spotty and uneven. Russian Communists who speak of the "uneven development of capitalism" should blush at the contemplation of their own national economy. Here certain branches of economic life, such as the metallurgical and machine industries, have been pushed out of all proportion to other sectors of the economy. Here is a nation striving to become in a short period one of the great industrial nations of the world while it still has no highway network worthy of the name and only a relatively primitive network of railways. Much has been done to increase efficiency of labor and to teach primitive peasants something about the operation of machines. But maintenance is still a crying deficiency of all Soviet economy. Construction is hasty and poor in quality. Depreciation must be enormous. And in vast sectors of economic life it has not yet been possible to instill into labor anything like that general culture of production and technical self-respect which characterizes the skilled worker of the West.

It is difficult to see how these deficiencies can be corrected at an early date by a tired and dispirited population working largely under the shadow of fear and compulsion. And as long as they are not overcome, Russia will remain economically a vulnerable, and in a certain sense an impotent, nation, capable of exporting its enthusiasms and of radiating the strange charm of its primitive political vitality but unable to back up those articles of export by the real evidences of material power and prosperity.

Meanwhile, a great uncertainty hangs over the political life of the Soviet Union. That is the uncertainty involved in the transfer of power from one individual or group of individuals to others.

This is, of course, outstandingly the problem of the personal position of Stalin. We must remember that his succession to Lenin's pinnacle of preeminence in the Communist movement was the only such transfer of individual authority which the Soviet Union has experienced. That transfer took twelve years to consolidate. It cost the lives of millions of people and shook the state to its foundations, the attendant tremors were felt all through the international revolutionary movement, to the disadvantage of the Kremlin itself.

It is always possible that another transfer of preeminent power may take place quietly and inconspicuously, with no repercussions anywhere. But again, it is possible that the questions involved may unleash, to use some of Lenin's words, one of those "incredibly swift transitions" from "delicate deceit" to "wild violence" which characterize Russian history, and may shake Soviet power to its foundations.

But this is not only a question of Stalin himself. There has been, since 1938, a dangerous congealment of political life in the higher circles of Soviet power. The All-Union Party Congress, in theory the supreme body of the Party, is supposed to meet not less often than once in three years. It will soon be eight full years since its last meeting. During this period membership in the Party has numerically doubled. Party mortality during the war was enormous, and today well over half of the Party members are persons who have entered since the last Party congress was held. Meanwhile, the same small group of men has carried on at the top through an amazing series of national vicissitudes. Surely there is some reason why the experiences of the war brought basic political changes to every one of the great governments of the West. Surely the causes of that phenomenon are basic enough to be present somewhere in the obscurity of Soviet political life, as well. And yet no recognition has been given to these cause in Russia.

It must be surmised from this that even within so highly disciplined an organization as the Communist Party there must be a growing divergence in age, outlook and interest between the great mass of Party members, only so recently recruited into the movement, and the little self-perpetuating clique of men at the top, whom most of these Party members have never met, with whom they have never conversed, and with whom they can have no political intimacy.

Who can say whether, in these circumstances, the eventual rejuvenation of the higher spheres of authority (which can only be a matter of time) can take place smoothly and peacefully, or whether rivals in the quest for higher power will not eventually reach down into these politically immature and inexperienced masses in order to find support for their respective claims. If this were ever to happen, strange consequences could flow for the Communist Party: for the membership at large has been exercised only in the practices of iron discipline and obedience and not in the arts of compromise and accommodation. And if disunity were ever to seize and paralyze the Party, the chaos and weakness of Russian society would be revealed in forms beyond description. For we have seen that Soviet power is only a crust concealing an amorphous mass of human beings among whom no independent organizational structure is tolerated. In Russia there is not even such a thing as local government. The present generation of Russians have never known spontaneity of collective action. If, consequently, anything were ever to occur to disrupt the unity and efficacy of the Party as a political instrument, Soviet Russia might be changed overnight from one of the strongest to one of the weakest and most pitiable of national societies.

Thus the future of Soviet power may not be by any means as secure as Russian capacity for self-delusion would make it appear to the men in the Kremlin. That they can keep power themselves, they have demonstrated. That they can quietly and easily turn it over to other remains to be proved. Meanwhile, the hardships of their rule and the vicissitudes of international life have taken a heavy toll of the strength and hopes of the great people on whom their power rests. It is curious to note that the ideological power of Soviet authority is strongest today in areas beyond the frontiers of Russia, beyond the reach of its police power. This phenomenon brings to mind a comparison used by Thomas Mann in his great novel *Buddenbrooks*. Observing that human institutions often show the greatest outward brilliance at a moment when inner decay is in reality farthest advanced, he compared the Buddenbrook family, in the days of its greatest glamour to one of those stars whose light shines most brightly on this world when in reality it has long since ceased to exist. And who can say with assurance that the strong light still cast by the Kremlin on the dissatisfied peoples of the Western world is not the powerful afterglow of a constellation which is in actuality on the wane? This cannot be proved. And it cannot be disproved. But the possibility remains (and in the opinion of this writer it is a strong one) that Soviet power, like the capitalist world of its conception, bears within it the seeds of its own decay, and that the sprouting of these seeds is well advanced.

IV

It is clear that the United States cannot expect in the foreseeable future to enjoy political intimacy with the Soviet regime. It must continue to regard the Soviet Union as a rival, not a partner, in the political arena. It must continue to expect that Soviet politics will reflect no abstract love of peace and stability, no real faith in the possibility of a permanent happy coexistence of the Socialist and capitalist worlds, but rather a cautious, persistent pressure toward the disruption and weakening of all rival influence and rival power.

Balanced against this are the facts that Russia, as opposed to the Western world in general, is still by far the weaker party, that Soviet policy is highly flexible, and that Soviet society may well contain deficiencies which will eventually weaken its own total potential. This would of itself warrant the United States entering with reasonable confidence upon a policy of firm containment, designed to confront the Russians with unalterable counter-force at every point where they show signs of encroaching upon the interests of a peaceful and stable world.

But in actuality the possibilities for American policy are by no means limited to holding the line and hoping for the best. It is entirely possible for the United States to influence by its actions the internal developments, both within Russia and throughout the international Communist movement, by which Russian policy is largely determined. This is not only a question of the modest measure of informational activity which this government can conduct in the Soviet Union and elsewhere, although that, too, is important. It is rather a question of the degree to which the United States can create among the peoples of the world generally the impression of a country which knows what it wants, which is coping successfully with the problems of its internal life and with the responsibilities of a World Power, and which has a spiritual vitality capable of holding its own among the major ideological currents of the time. To the extent that such an impression can be created and maintained, the aims of Russian Communism must appear sterile and quixotic, the hopes and enthusiasm of Moscow's supporters must wane, and added strain must be imposed on the Kremlin's foreign policies. For the palsied decrepitude of the capitalist world is the keystone of Communist philosophy. Even the failure of the United States to experience the early economic depression which the ravens of the Red Square have been predicting with such complacent confidence since hostilities ceased would have deep and important repercussions throughout the Communist world.

By the same token, exhibitions of indecision, disunity and internal disintegration within this country have an exhilarating effect on the whole Communist movement. At each evidence of these tendencies, a thrill of hope and excitement goes through the Communist world; a new jauntiness can be noted in the Moscow tread; new groups of foreign supporters climb on to what they can only view as the band wagon of international politics; and Russian pressure increases all along the line in international affairs.

It would be an exaggeration to say that American behavior unassisted and alone could exercise a power of life and death over the Communist movement and bring about the early fall of Soviet power in Russia. But the

United States has it in its power to increase enormously the strains under which Soviet policy must operate, to force upon the Kremlin a far greater degree of moderation and circumspection than it has had to observe in recent years, and in this way to promote tendencies which must eventually find their outlet in either the break-up or the gradual mellowing of Soviet power. For no mystical, Messianic movement—and particularly not that of the Kremlin—can face frustration indefinitely without eventually adjusting itself in one way or another to the logic of that state of affairs.

Thus the decision will really fall in large measure in this country itself. The issue of Soviet-American relations is in essence a test of the over-all worth of the United States as a nation among nations. To avoid destruction the United States need only measure up to its own best traditions and prove itself worthy of preservations as a great nation.

Surely, there was never a fairer case of national quality than this. In the light of these circumstances, the thoughtful observer of Russian-American relations will find no cause for complaint in the Kremlin's challenge to American society. He will rather experience a certain gratitude to Providence which, by providing the American people with this implacable challenge, has made their entire security as a nation dependent on their pulling themselves together and accepting the responsibilities of moral and political leadership that history plainly intended them to bear.

146. THE CHARLOTTESVILLE TRIBUNE, "ARE WE READY FOR TOTAL ABOLITION OF RACIAL SEGREGATION?," JANUARY 6, 1951

As we write this editorial, we do so fully cognizant of the unpopular note it will have for some of our readers. Facts are usually popular. The real purpose of this article is to provoke some serious thinking on the all important subject of racial segregation.

As our nation stands at the crossroads in her young but illustrious history, so stands our race as the major minority group in the United States of America.

We have made and are still making great progress toward achieving first-class citizenship for all our people. So rapidly have the lines of segregation between the races been lowered that from some camps of our group now comes the cry for "total abolition of racial segregation."

As a warning to my people may I remind you of the late Mussolini, who, with his legion of "Black Shirts" over-ran weak and defenseless Ethiopia even in defiance of Italy's World War I allies.

May I remind you of Hitler's German Army marching into several small European countries, with them capitulating without the firing of a single shot.

Had it not been for the fighting sons of America and our allies who collaborated in World War II, in stopping the ruthless German march toward world conquest Russia, today would not be ??

Neither group is prepared for instant and total abolition of racial segregation. Whether they agree or not, one group possesses a superiority complex and the other the inferiority complex and to some extent they are both right.

We know that every normal human being, regardless of color, place of birth or servitude possesses the same innate potentialities. But when those potentialities are developed in one and not the other, in that respect one becomes superior to the other.

With one racial group exposed to all the contact and culture of modern civilization and the other group (with rare exceptions) denied those opportunities, how can they be equal, at least in that respect?

In a recent meeting the speaker of the evening said, "I am for immediate abolition of every form of racial segregation." The speaker continued by saying, "start today that the infants may not know the curse of racial segregation." To some that may have been good oratory. But to others it was very poor logic.

Source: "Are We Ready for Total Abolition of Racial Segregation?" *The Charlottesville Tribune,* Jan. 6, 1951. Editorial. Copyright 1951. Charlottesville Tribune. Reprinted by permission.

578 — Chapter XXVII POSTWAR AMERICA, 1946–1952

If the speaker could reduce all the American peoples to the stage of infants, his theory might work. But how would he change overnight the opinions of all who have passed the infancy age? Certainly he would find it far more difficult than talking ? progress toward achieving ? citizenship for all our people. So rapidly have the lines of segregation between the races been lowered that from some camps of our group now comes the fry for "total abolition of racial segregation."

As a warning to my people may I remind you of the late Mussolini, who, with his legion of "Black Shirts" over-ran weak and defenseless Ethiopia even in defiance of Italy's World War I allies.

May I remind you of Hitler's German Army marching into several small European countries, with them capitulating without the firing of a single shot.

Had it not been for the fighting sons of America and our allies who collaborated in World War II, in stopping the ruthless German march toward world conquest Russia, today would not be afflicted with that same ridiculous and impracticable idea.

It was the intoxication of victory that caused them all to lose even what they thought they had.

Those brief historical facts are reviewed least we as a race be overtaken by the same costly mistake.

We fully agree with T. J. Sellers, editor of the Charlottesville Tribune, in his editorial of December 8, 1950, when he says:

"We have always been opposed to every form of segregation . . . and not because we favor intermarriage either . . . , but because segregation has meant discrimination, oppression and double standard of justice." Mr. Sellers continues by saying, "Segregation has meant slums and dives for Negro housing."

"Segregation has means clean, sanitary hospital wards for one group of citizens, and dark, damp smelly quarters for another group of citizens."

Segregation has meant that one group of children would be taught to look down on another group of children and grow into adulthood frustrated with hatred, distrust, and utter misunderstanding."

Every red-blooded American agrees with Mr. Sellers when he says, "No self-respecting Negro could approve of segregation and most decent white Americans are against it whether they admit it or not."

Despite the aforementioned evils of segregation, and they do not even scratch the surface of the many, the fact remains that segregation has been ingrained in the hearts of both races for many generations past and it is nonsensical to think that it can be totally abolished simply by the twist of the wrist or even by the stroke of a pen.

When one racial group exposed to all the contact and culture of modern civilization and the other group (with ? denied those opportunities, how can they be equal, at least in that respect?

In a recent meeting the speaker of the evening said, "I am for immediate abolition of every form of racial segregation." The speaker continued by saying, "start today that the infants may not know the curse of racial segregation." To some that may have been good oratory. But to others it was very poor logic.

If the speaker could reduce all that American peoples to the stage of infants, his theory might work. But how would he change overnight the opinions of all who have passed the infancy age? Certainly he would find it far more difficult than talking about it.

It might be well to abolish segregation within our own race and then we could see more clearly how to abolish segregation between the races.

There are circles within our race which move in an orbit that completely isolates them from the masses. They know about the life of the masses as they do about what goes on behind the Russian iron curtain, and that's only what they hear.

The masses are not admitted into their circle because they are not wanted. It would help the racial situation a lot for us to so deport ourselves that the opposite group would want our association. After all, to force by law or any other means the abolition of racial segregation would not solve the problem. Until an amicable relationship exists between the two groups the problem will remain the same.

We need to lift the level of our masses and not expose and embarrass them. We need to get them out of the slums before we open to them the doors of palaces. We need to secure for them better educational and economic opportunities. Our people need social development and a deeper sense of race pride, self restraint and self-respect. Above all they need a sane, sober, and deeper respect for womanhood, and particularly the womanhood of our own race.

A total and abrupt reversal of our racial segregation at this time would simply be playing in the hand of our enemies. It is coming. Its coming is inevitable. We may have but little time in which to prepare our people for the change. So let us spend our energy in that direction, so that when the change comes, it will be permanent.

F.E.A.

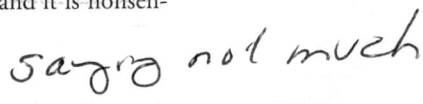

147. ANNE MOODY, *COMING OF AGE IN MISSISSIPPI*

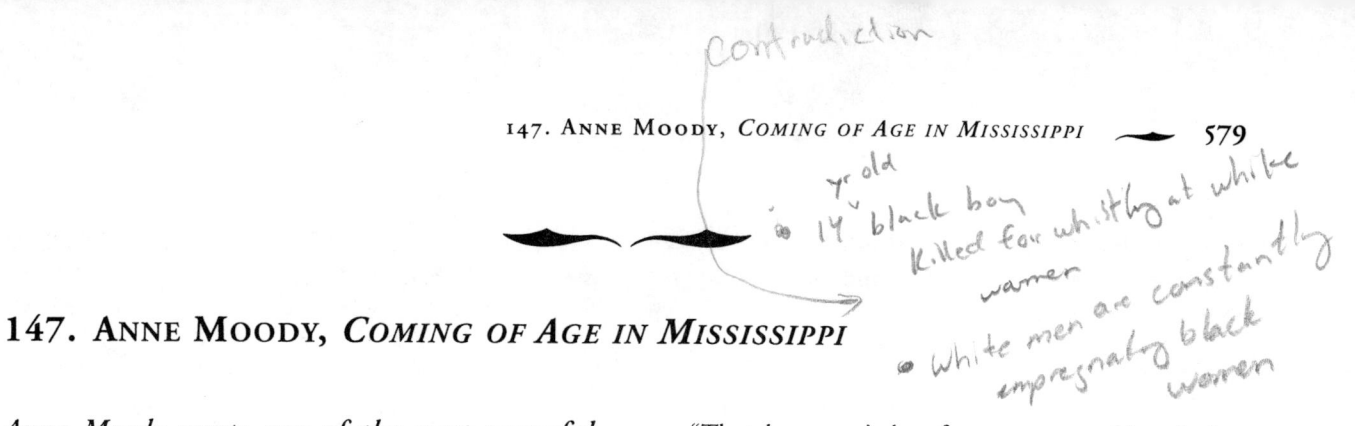

Anne Moody wrote one of the most powerful accounts of what it meant to grow up black in the 1950s in her enduring autobiography, Coming of Age in Mississippi.

Chapter 10

Not only did I enter high school with a new name, but also with a completely new insight into the life of Negroes in Mississippi. I was now working for one of the meanest white women in town, and a week before school started Emmett Till was killed.

Up until his death, I had heard of Negroes found floating in a river or dead somewhere with their bodies riddled with bullets. But I didn't know the mystery behind these killings then. I remember once when I was only seven I heard Mama and one of my aunts talking about some Negro who had been beaten to death. "Just like them lowdown skunks killed him they will do the same to us," Mama had said. When I asked her who killed the man and why, she said, "An Evil Spirit killed him. You gotta be a good girl or it will kill you too." So since I was seven, I had lived in fear of that "Evil Spirit." It took me eight years to learn what that spirit was.

I was coming from school the evening I heard about Emmett Till's death. There was a whole group of us, girls and boys, walking down the road headed home. A group of about six high school boys were walking a few paces ahead of me and several other girls. We were laughing and talking about something that had happened in school that day. However, the six boys in front of us weren't talking very loud. Usually they kept up so much noise. But today they were just walking and talking among themselves. All of a sudden they began to shout at each other.

"Man, what in the hell do you mean?"

"What I mean is these goddamned white folks is gonna start some shit here you just watch!"

"That boy wasn't but fourteen years old and they killed him. Now what kin a fourteen-year-old boy do with a white woman? What if he did whistle at her, he might have thought the whore was pretty."

"Look at all these white men here that's fucking over our women. Everybody knows it too and what's done about that? Look how many white babies we got walking around in our neighborhoods. Their mama's ain't white either. That boy was from Chicago, shit, everybody fuck everybody up there. He probably didn't even think of the bitch as white."

What they were saying shocked me. I knew all of those boys and I had never heard them talk like that. We walked on behind them for a while listening. Questions about who was killed, where, and why started running through my mind. I walked up to one of the boys.

"Eddie, what boy was killed?"

"Moody, where've you been?" he asked me. "Everybody talking about that fourteen-year-old boy who was killed in Greenwood by some white men. You don't know nothing that's going on besides what's in them books of yours, huh?"

Standing there before the rest of the girls, I felt so stupid. It was then that I realized I really didn't know what was going on all around me. It wasn't that I was dumb. It was just that ever since I was nine, I'd had to work after school and do my lessons on lunch hour. I never had time to learn anything, to hang around with people my own age. And you never were told anything by adults.

That evening when I stopped off at the house on my way to Mrs. Burke's Mama was singing. Any other day she would have been yelling at Adline and Junior them to take off their school clothes. I wondered if she knew about Emmett Till. The way she was singing she had something on her mind and it wasn't pleasant either.

> I got a shoe, you got a shoe,
> All of God's chillun got shoes;
> When I get to hebben, I'm gonna put on my shoes,
> And gonna tromp all over God's hebben.
> When I get to hebben I'm gonna put on my shoes,
> And gonna walk all over God's hebben.

Mama was dishing up beans like she didn't know anyone was home. Adline, Junior, and James had just thrown their books down and sat themselves at the table. I didn't

---

Source: Ann Moody, *Coming of Age in Mississippi.* pp. 121–138. Copyright 1980 Doubleday. Reprinted by permission.

usually eat before I went to work. But I wanted to ask Mama about Emmett Till. So I ate and thought of some way of asking her.

"These beans are some good, Mama," I said, trying to sense her mood.

"Why is you eating anyway? You gonna be late for work. You know how Miss Burke is," she said to me.

"I don't have much to do this evening. I kin get it done before I leave work," I said.

The conversation stopped after that. Then Mama started humming that song again.

When I get to hebben, I'm gonna put on my shoes,
And gonna tromp all over God's hebben.

She put a plate on the floor for Jennie Ann and Jerry.

"Jennie Ann! you and Jerry sit down here and eat and don't put beans all over this floor."

Ralph, the baby, started crying, and she went in the bedroom to give him his bottle. I got up and followed her.

"Mama, did you hear about that fourteen-year-old Negro boy who was killed a little over a week ago by some white men?" I asked her.

"Where did you hear that?" she said angrily.

"Boy, everybody really thinks I am dumb or deaf or something. I heard Eddie them talking about it this evening coming from school."

"Eddie them better watch how they go around here talking. These white folks git a hold of it they gonna be in trouble," she said.

"What are they gonna be in trouble about, Mama? People got a right to talk, ain't they?"

"You go on to work before you is late. And don't you let on like you know nothing about that boy being killed before Miss Burke them. Just do your work like you don't know nothing," she said. "That boy's a lot better off in heaven than he is here," she continued and then started singing again.

On my way to Mrs. Burke's that evening, Mama's words kept running through my mind. "Just do your work like you don't know nothing." "Why is Mama acting so scared?" I thought. "And what if Mrs. Burke knew we knew? Why must I pretend I don't know? Why are these people killing Negroes? What did Emmett Till do besides whistle at that woman?"

By the time I got to work, I had worked my nerves up some. I was shaking as I walked up on the porch. "Do your work like you don't know nothing." But once I got inside, I couldn't have acted normal if Mrs. Burke were paying me to be myself.

I was so nervous, I spent most of the evening avoiding them going about the house dusting and sweeping. Everything went along fairly well until dinner was served.

"Don, Wayne, and Mama, y'all come on to dinner. Essie, you can wash up the pots and dishes in the sink now. Then after dinner you won't have as many," Mrs. Burke called to me.

If I had the power to mysteriously disappear at that moment, I would have. They used the breakfast table in the kitchen for most of their meals. The dining room was only used for Sunday dinner or when they had company. I wished they had company tonight so they could eat in the dining room while I was at the kitchen sink.

"I forgot the bread," Mrs. Burke said when they were all seated. "Essie, will you cut it and put it on the table for me?"

I took the cornbread, cut it in squares, and put it on a small round dish. Just as I was about to set it on the table, Wayne yelled at the cat. I dropped the plate and the bread went all over the floor.

"Never mind, Essie." Mrs. Burke said angrily as she got up and got some white bread from the breadbox.

I didn't say anything. I picked up the cornbread from around the table and went back to the dishes. As soon as I got to the sink, I dropped a saucer on the floor and broke it. Didn't anyone say a word until I had picked up the pieces.

"Essie, I bought some new cleanser today. It's setting on the bathroom shelf. See if it will remove the stains in the tub," Mrs. Burke said.

I went to the bathroom to clean the tub. By the time I got through with it, it was snow white. I spent a whole hour scrubbing it. I had removed the stains in no time but I kept scrubbing until they finished dinner.

When they had finished and gone into the living room as usual to watch TV, Mrs. Burke called me to eat. I took a clean plate out of the cabinet and sat down. Just as I was putting the first forkful of food in my mouth, Mrs. Burke entered the kitchen.

"Essie, did you hear about that fourteen-year-old boy who was killed in Greenwood?" she asked me, sitting down in one of the chairs opposite me.

"No, I didn't hear that," I answered, almost choking on the food.

"Do you know why he was killed?" she asked me and I didn't answer.

"He was killed because he got out of his place with a white woman. A boy from Mississippi would have known better than that. This boy was from Chicago. Negroes up North have no respect for people. They think they can get away with anything. He just came to Mississippi and put a whole lot of actions in the boys' heads here and stirred up a lot of trouble," she said passionately.

"How old are you, Essie?" she asked me after a pause.

"Fourteen. I will soon be fifteen though," I said.

"See, that boy was just fourteen too. It's a shame he had to die so soon." She was so red in the face, she looked as if she was on fire.

When she left the kitchen I sat there with my mouth open and my food untouched. I couldn't have eaten now if I were starving. "Just do your work like you don't know nothing" ran through my mind again and I began washing the dishes.

I went home shaking like a leaf on a tree. For the first time out of all her trying, Mrs. Burke had made me feel like rotten garbage. Many times she had tried to instill fear within me and subdue me and had given up. But when she talked about Emmett Till there was something in her voice that sent chills and fear all over me.

Before Emmett Till's murder, I had known the fear of hunger, hell, and the Devil. But now there was a new fear known to me—the fear of being killed just because I was black. This was the worst of my fears. I knew once I got food, the fear of starving to death would leave. I also was told that if I were a good girl, I wouldn't have to fear the Devil or hell. But I didn't know what one had to do or not do as a Negro not to be killed. Probably just being a Negro period was enough, I thought.

A few days later, I went to work and Mrs. Burke had about eight women over for tea. They were all sitting around in the living room when I got there. She told me she was having a "guild meeting," and asked me to help her serve the cookies and tea.

After helping her, I started cleaning the house. I always swept the hallway and porch first. As I was sweeping the hall, I could hear them talking. When I heard the word "nigger," I stopped sweeping and listened. Mrs. Burke must have sensed this, because she suddenly came to the door.

"Essie, finish the hall and clean the bathroom," she said hesitantly. "Then you can go for today. I am not making dinner tonight." Then she went back in the living room with the rest of the ladies.

Before she interrupted my listening, I had picked up the words "NAACP" and "that organization." Because they were talking about niggers, I knew NAACP had something to do with Negroes. All that night I kept wondering what could that NAACP mean?

Later when I was sitting in the kitchen at home doing my lessons, I decided to ask Mama. It was about twelve-thirty. Everyone was in bed but me. When Mama came in to put some milk in Ralph's bottle, I said, "Mama, what do NAACP mean?"

"Where did you git that from?" she asked me, spilling milk all over the floor.

"Mrs. Burke had a meeting tonight—"

"What kind of meeting?" she asked, cutting me off.

"I don't know. She had some women over—she said it was a guild meeting," I said.

"A guild meeting," she repeated.

"Yes, they were talking bout Negroes and I heard some woman say 'that NAACP' and another 'that organization,'" meaning the same thing.

"What else did they say?" she asked me.

"That's all I heard. Mrs. Burke must have thought I was listening, so she told me to clean the bathroom and leave."

"Don't you ever mention that word around Mrs. Burke or no other white person, you heah! Finish your lesson and cut that light out and go to bed," Mama said angrily and left the kitchen.

"With a Mama like that you'll never learn anything," I thought as I got into bed. All night long I thought about Emmett Till and the NAACP. I even got up to look up NAACP in my little concise dictionary. But I didn't find it.

The next day at school, I decided to ask my homeroom teacher Mrs. Rice the meaning of NAACP. When the bell sounded for lunch, I remained in my seat as the other students left the room.

"Are you going to spend your lunch hour studying again today, Moody?" Mrs. Rice asked me.

"Can I ask you a question, Mrs. Rice?" I asked her.

"You *may* ask me a question, yes, but I don't know if you *can* or not," she said.

"What does the word NAACP mean?" I asked.

"Why do you want to know?"

"The lady I worked for had a meeting and I overheard the word mentioned."

"What else did you hear?"

"Nothing. I didn't know what NAACP meant, that's all." I felt like I was on the witness stand or something.

"Well, next time your boss has another meeting you listen more carefully. NAACP is a Negro organization that was established a long time ago to help Negroes gain a few basic rights," she said.

"What's it gotta do with the Emmett Till murder?" I asked.

"They are trying to get a conviction in Emmett Till's case. You see the NAACP is trying to do a lot for the Negroes and get the right to vote for Negroes in the South. I shouldn't be telling you all this. And don't you dare breathe a word of what I said. It could cost me my job if word got out I was teaching my students such. I gotta go to lunch and you should go outside too because it's nice and sunny out today," she said leaving the room. "We'll talk more when I have time."

About a week later, Mrs. Rice had me over for Sunday dinner, and I spent about five hours with her. Within that time, I digested a good meal and accumulated a whole new pool of knowledge about Negroes being butchered and slaughtered by whites in the South. After Mrs. Rice had told me all this, I felt like the lowest animal on earth. At least when other animals (hogs, cows, etc.) were killed by man, they were used as food. But when a man was butchered or killed by men, in the case of Negroes by whites, they were left lying on a road or found floating in a river or something.

Mrs. Rice got to be something like a mother to me. She told me anything I wanted to know. And made me promise that I would keep all this information she was passing on to me to myself. She said she couldn't, rather didn't, want to talk about these things to the other teachers, that they would tell Mr. Willis and she would be fired. At the end of that year she was fired. I never found out why. I haven't seen her since then.

Chapter 11

I was fifteen years old when I began to hate people. I hated the white men who murdered Emmett Till and I hated all the other whites who were responsible for the countless murders Mrs. Rice had told me about and those I vaguely remembered from childhood. But I also hated Negroes. I hated them for not standing up and doing something about the murders. In fact, I think I had a stronger resentment toward Negroes for letting the whites kill them than toward the whites. Anyway, it was at this stage of my life that I began to look upon Negro men as cowards. I could not respect them for smiling in a white man's face, addressing him as Mr. So-an-So, saying yessuh and nossuh when after they were home behind closed doors that same white man was a son of a bitch, a bastard, or any other name more suitable than mister.

Emmett Till's murder provoked a lot of anger and excitement among whites in Centreville. Now just about every evening when I got to work, Mrs. Burke had to attend a guild meeting. She had more women coming over now than ever. She and her friends had organized canvassing teams and a telephone campaign, to solicit for new members. Within a couple of months most of the whites in Centreville where taking part in the Guild. The meetings were initially held in the various houses. There were lawn parties and church gatherings. Then when it began to get cold, they were held in the high school auditorium.

After the Guild had organized about two-thirds of the whites in Centreville, all kinds of happenings were unveiled. The talk was on. White housewives began firing their maids and scolding their husbands and the Negro communities were full of whispered gossip.

The most talked-about subject was a love affair Mr. Fox, the deputy sheriff, and one of my classmates were carrying on. Bess was one of the oldest girls on my class. She was a shapely, high brown girl of about seventeen. She did general housekeeping and nursing for Fox and his wife.

It was general policy that most young white couples in Centreville hired only older Negro women as helpers. However, when they were two or more children in the family, it was more advantageous to hire a young Negro girl. That way, they always had someone to baby-sit when there was a need for a baby-sitter. My job with Linda Jean had been this kind. I kept Donna and Johnny on Sundays and baby-sat on night when they needed me.

Even though the teen-age Negro girls were more desirable for such jobs, very few if any were trusted in the homes of the young couples. The young white housewife didn't dare leave one alone in the house with her loyal and obedient husband. She was afraid that the Negro girl would seduce him, never the contrary.

There had been whispering in the Negro communities about Bess and Fox for some time. Just about every young white man in Centreville had a Negro lover. Therefore Fox, even though he was the deputy sheriff, wasn't doing anything worse than the rest of the men. At least that's the way the Negroes looked at the situation. Fox wasn't anyone special to them. But the whites didn't see it that way. The sheriff and all of his deputies were, in the eyes of their white compatriots, honorable men. And these honorable men were not put into office because they loved Negroes. So when the white community caught on about Fox and Bess, naturally they were out to expose the affair. Such exposure would discourage other officers from similar misbehavior.

Mrs. Fox was completely devoted to her husband. She too thought he was an honest man and she was willing to do anything that would prove him innocent. Soon a scheme was under way. Mrs. Fox was to leave home every so often. It had been reported that every time she was out and Bess was left there alone, Fox found his way home for one reason or another. Mrs. Fox left home purposely a couple of times while the neighbors kept watch. They confirmed the report that Fox would always return home. So one day Mrs. Fox decided to take the children and visit her mother—but she only went as far as the house next door. Bess was to come and give the house a thorough cleaning on the same day.

Mrs. Fox waited almost an hour at her neighbors' and nothing happened. It was said that she was ready to go home and apologize to Bess and call her husband and do likewise. But just as she was about to do so, Fox drove up and went inside. She waited about thirty minutes more, then went home.

When she walked into her bedroom there they were, her husband and Bess, lying in her bed all curled up together. Poor Bess was so frightened that she ran out of the house clothed only in her slip with her panties in her hands. She never set foot in Mrs. Fox's house again. Neither did she return to school afterward. She took a job in the quarters where we lived, in a Negro café. It was said that she didn't need the job, though. Because after her embarrassing episode with Fox, her reputation was beyond repair, and he felt obligated to take care of her. Last I heard of Bess, she was still in Centreville, wearing fine clothes and carrying on as usual. Fox is no longer deputy, I understand, but he and his wife are still together.

It appeared after a while that the much talked about maids raids were only a means of diverting attention from what was really taking place in those guild meetings. In the midst of all the talk about what white man was screwing which Negro woman, new gossip emerged—about what Negro man was screwing which white woman. This gossip created so much tension, every Negro man in Centreville became afraid to walk the streets. They knew too well that they would not get off as easily as the white man who was caught screwing a Negro woman. They had only to look at a white woman and be hanged for it. Emmett Till's murder had proved it was a crime, punishable by death, for a Negro man to even whistle at a white woman in Mississippi.

I had never heard of a single affair in Centreville between a Negro man and a white woman. It was almost impossible for such an affair to take place. Negro men did not have access to white women. Whereas almost every white man in town had a Negro woman in his kitchen or nursing his babies.

The tension lasted for about a month before anything happened. Then one day, a rumor was spread throughout town that a Negro had been making telephone calls to a white operator and threatening to molest her. It was also said that the calls had been traced to a certain phone that was now under watch.

Next thing we heard in the Negro community was that they had caught and nearly beaten to death a boy who, they said, had made the calls to the white operator. All the Negroes went around saying "Y'all know that boy didn't do that." "That boy" was my classmate Jerry. A few months later I got a chance to talk to him and he told me what happened.

He said he had used the telephone at Billups and Fillups service station and was on his way home when Sheriff Ed Cassidy came along in his pickup truck.

"Hey, buddy," Cassidy called, "you on your way home?"

"Yes," Jerry answered.

"Jump in, I'm goin' your way, I'll give you a lift."

Then Jerry told me that when they got out there by the scales where the big trucks weigh at the old camp intersection, Cassidy let him out, telling him that he had forgotten something in town and had to go back and pick it up. At that point, Jerry told me, he didn't suspect anything. He just got out of the truck and told Cassidy thanks. But as soon as the sheriff pulled away, a car came along and stopped. There were four men in it. A deep voice ordered Jerry to get into the car. When he saw that two of the men were Jim Dixon and Nat Withers, whom he had often seen hanging around town with Cassidy, he started to run. But the two in the back jumped out and grabbed him. They forced him into the car and drove out into the camp area. When they got about five miles out, they turned down a little dark dirt road, heavily shaded with trees. They pushed Jerry out of the car onto the ground. He got up and dashed into the woods but they caught up with him and dragged him farther into the woods. Then they tied him to a tree and beat him with a big thick leather strap and a piece of hose pipe.

I asked him if they told him why they were beating him.

"No, not at first," Jerry said, "but when I started screamin' and cryin' and askin' them why they were beatin' me Dixon told me I was tryin' to be smart and they just kept on beatin' me. Then one of the men I didn't know asked me, 'Did you make that phone call, boy?' I said no. I think he kinda believed me 'cause he stopped beatin' me but the others didn't. The rest of them beat me until I passed out. When I came out of it I was lying on the ground, untied, naked and bleeding. I tried to get up but I was hurtin' all over and it was hard to move. Finally I got my clothes on that them sonofabitches had tore offa me and I made it out to the main highway, but I fainted again. When I woke up I was home in bed.

"Daddy them was scared to take me to the hospital in Centreville. I didn't even see a doctor 'cause they were scared to take me to them white doctors. Wasn't any bones or anything broken. I was swollen all over, though. And you can see I still have bruises and cuts from the strap, but otherwise I guess I'm O.K."

When I asked him whether they were going to do anything about it, he said that his daddy had gotten a white lawyer from Baton Rouge. But after the lawyer pried around in Centreville for a few days, he suddenly disappeared.

Jerry's beating shook up all the Negroes in town. But the most shocking and unjust crime of all occurred a few months later, about two weeks before school ended.

One night, about one o'clock, I was awakened by what I thought was a terrible nightmare. It was an empty dream that consisted only of hollering and screaming voices. It seemed as though I was in an empty valley screaming. And the sounds of my voice were reflected in a million echoes that were so loud I was being lifted in mid-air by the sound waves. I found myself standing trembling in the middle of the floor reaching for the light string. Then I saw Mama running to the kitchen, in her nightgown.

"Mama! Mama! What's all them voices? Where're all those people? What's happening?"

"I don't know," she said, coming to my bedroom door.

"Listen! Listen!" I said, almost screaming.

"Stop all that loud talking fo' you wake up the rest of them chaps. It must be a house on fire or somethin' 'cause of all the screamin'. Somebody must be hurt in it or somethin' too. Ray is getting the car, we gonna go see what it is," she said and headed for the back door.

"You going in your gown?" I asked her.

"We ain't gonna get out of the car. Come you, you can go," she said. "But don't slam the door and wake them chaps up."

I followed her out of the back door in my pajamas. Raymond was just backing the car out of the driveway.

When we turned the corner leaving the quarters, Raymond drove slowly alongside hundreds of people running down the road. They were all headed in the direction of the blaze that reddened the sky.

The crowd of people began to swell until driving was utterly impossible. Finally the long line of cars stopped.

We were about two blocks away from the burning house now. The air was so hot that water was running down the faces of the people who ran past the car. The burning house was on the rock road, leading to the school, adjacent to the street we stopped on. So we couldn't tell which house it was. From where we sat, it seemed as though it could have been two or three of them burning. I knew every Negro living in the houses that lined that rock road. I passed them every day on my way to and from school.

I sat there in my pajamas, wishing I had thrown on a dress or something so I could get out of the car.

"Ray, ask somebody who house it is," Mama said to Raymond.

"Hi! Excuse me." Raymond leaned out of the car and spoke to a Negro man. "Do you know who house is on fire?"

"I heard it was the Taplin family. They say the whole family is still in the house. Look like they are done for, so they say."

Didn't any one of us say anything after that. We just sat in the car silently. I couldn't believe what the man had just said. "A whole family burned to death—impossible!" I thought.

"What do you think happened, Ray?" Mama finally said to Raymond.

"I don't know. You never kin tell," Raymond said. "It seems mighty strange though."

Soon people started walking back down the road. The screams and hollering had stopped. People were almost whispering now. They were all Negroes, although I was almost sure I had seen some whites pass before. "I guess not," I thought, sitting there sick inside. Some of the ladies passing the car had tears running down their faces, as they whispered to each other.

"Didn't you smell that gasoline?" I heard a lady who lived in the quarters say.

"That house didn't just catch on fire. And just think them bastard burned up a whole family," another lady said. Then they were quiet again.

Soon their husbands neared the car.

"Heh, Jones," Raymond said to one of the men. "How many was killed?"

"About eight or nine of them, Ray. They say the old lady and one of the children got out. I didn't see her nowhere, though."

"You think the house was set on fire," Raymond asked.

"It sho' looks like it, Ray. It burned down like nothing. When I got there that house was burning on every side. If it had started on the inside of the house at some one place then it wouldn't burn down like it did. All the walls fell in together. Too many strange things are happening round here these days."

Now most of the people and cars were gone. Raymond drove up to the little rock road and parked. I almost vomited when I caught a whiff of the odor of burned bodies mixed with the gasoline. The wooden frame house had been burned to ashes. All that was left were some iron bedposts and springs, a blackened refrigerator, a stove, and some kitchen equipment.

We sat in the car for about an hour, silently looking at this debris and the ashes that covered the nine charcoal-burned bodies. A hundred or more also stood around—Negroes from the neighborhood in their pajamas, nightgowns, and housecoats and even a few whites, with their eyes fixed on that dreadful scene. I shall never forget the expressions on the faces of the Negroes. There was almost unanimous hopelessness in them. The still, sad faces watched the smoke rising from the remains until the smoke died down to practically nothing. There was something strange about that smoke. It was the thickest and blackest smoke I had ever seen.

Raymond finally drove away, but it was impossible for him to take me away from that nightmare. Those screams, those faces, that smoke, would never leave me.

The next day I took the long, roundabout way to school. I didn't want to go by the scene that was so fixed in my mind. I tried to convince myself that nothing had happened in the night. And I wanted so much to believe that, to believe anything but the dream itself. However, at school, everybody was talking about it. All during each class there was whispering from student to student. Hadn't many of my classmates witnessed the burning last night. I wished they had. If so, they wouldn't be talking so much, I thought. Because I had seen it, and *I* couldn't talk about it. I just couldn't.

I was so glad when the bell sounded for the lunch hour. I picked up my books and headed home. I couldn't endure another minute of that torture. I was in such a hurry to get away from the talk at school I forgot to take the roundabout way home. Before I realized it, I was standing there where the Taplins' house had been. It looked quite different by day that it had at night. The ashes and junk had been scattered as if someone had looked for the remains of the bodies. The heavy black smoke had disappeared completely. But I stood there looking at the spot where I had seen it rising and I saw it again, slowly drifting away, disappearing before my eyes. I tore myself away and ran almost all the way home.

When I walked in the house Mama didn't even ask me why I came home. She just looked at me. And for the first time I realized she understood what was going on within me, or was trying to anyway. I took two aspirins and went to bed. I stayed there all afternoon. When it was time for me to go to work after school, Mama didn't come in. She must have known I wasn't in the mood for Mrs. Burke that evening. I wasn't in the mood for anything. I was just there inside of myself, inflicting pain with every thought that ran through my mind.

That night Centreville was like a ghost town. It was so quiet and still. The quietness almost drove me crazy. It was too quiet for sleeping that night, yet it was too restless for dreams and too dry for weeping.

A few days later, it was reported that the fire had started from the kerosene lamp used by Mrs. Taplin as a light for the new baby. Nobody bought that story. At least none of those who witnessed that fire and smelled all that gasoline. They were sure that more than a lampful of kerosene caused that house to burn that fast.

There was so much doubt and dissension about the Taplin burning that finally FBI agents arrived on the scene and quietly conducted an investigation. But as usual in this sort of case, the investigation was dropped as soon as public interest died down.

Months later the story behind the burning was whispered throughout the Negro community. Some of the Taplins' neighbors who had been questioned put their scraps of information together and came up with an answer that made sense.

Living next door to the Taplin family was a Mr. Banks, a high yellow mulatto man of much wealth. He was a bachelor with land and cattle galore. He had for some time discreetly taken care of a white woman, the mother of three whose husband had deserted her, leaving her to care for the children the best way she knew how. She lived in a bottom where a few other poor whites lived. The Guild during one of its investigations discovered the children at home alone one night—and many other nights after that. Naturally, they wondered whether the mother was spending her nights. A few days' observation of the bottom proved she was leaving home, after putting the children to bed, and being picked up by Mr. Banks in inconspicuous places.

When the Taplin family was burned, Mr. Banks escaped his punishment. Very soon afterward he locked his house and disappeared. And so did the white lady from the bottom.

I could barely wait until school was out. I was so sick of Centreville. I made up my mind to tell Mama I had to get away, if only for the summer. I had thought of going to Baton Rouge to live with my Uncle Ed who was now married and living there with his family.

A few days before school ended I sat in the midst of about six of my classmates who insisted on discussing the Taplin family. By the time I got home, my nerves were in shreds from thinking of some of the things they had said. I put my books down, took two aspirins, and got into bed. I didn't think I could go to work that evening because I was too nervous to be around Mrs. Burke. I had not been myself at work since the Emmett Till murder, especially after the way Mrs. Burke had talked to me about the Taplin family. But she had become more observant of my reactions.

"What's wrong with you? Is you sick?" Mama asked me. I didn't answer her.

"Take your shoes off that spread. You better git up and go to work. Mrs. Burke gonna fire you."

"I got a headache and I don't feel like going," I said.

"What's wrong with you, getting so many headaches around here?"

I decided not to wait any longer to tell Mama my plan.

"Mama, I am gonna write Ed and see can I stay with him this summer and get a job in Baton Rouge. I am just tired of working for Mrs. Burke for a dollar a day. I can make five dollars a day in Baton Rouge and I make only six dollars a week here."

"Ed them ain't got enough room for you to live with them. Take your shoes off," Mama said, and left me lying in bed.

As soon as she left, I got up and wrote my letter. About five days later I received an answer from Ed. He said I was welcome, so I started packing to leave the next day. Mama looked at me as if she didn't want me to go. But she knew better than to ask me.

I was fifteen years old and leaving home for the first time. I wasn't even sure I could get a job at that age. But I had to go anyway, if only to breathe a slightly different atmosphere. I was choking to death in Centreville. I couldn't go on working for Mrs. Burke pretending I was dumb and innocent, pretending I didn't know what was going on in all her guild meetings, or about Jerry's beating, or about the Taplin burning, and everything else that was going on. I was sick of pretending, sick of selling my feelings for a dollar a day.

---

148. Lillian Hellman, *Scoundrel Time*

"I cannot and will not cut my conscience to fit this year's fashions," playwright Lillian Hellman wrote to the chairman of the House Committee on Un-American Activities when called to testify in 1952. Her refusal to imitate the behavior of the "scoundrels" of the title of her book, who ruined the lives of others in their groveling appearances before the Committee, came at a particularly grim moment in the Second Red Scare. Alger Hiss had been sent to jail and the Rosenbergs condemned to death. With impunity, Joe McCarthy implicated Democratic officials for every manner of infamous behavior. And the stalemated war in Korea ground on with little hope for victory. Fear and hatred of communism were paramount. In an ugly mood, the American people apparently would brook no interference with the congressional search for spies and scapegoats. Thus, Hellman's offer to answer all questions about herself but refusal to name others—"to bring bad trouble to people"—had an extraordinary impact at the time. Her moral courage in choosing not to hurt innocent people to save herself made it easier for others to deny the demand to name names and inspired still others to speak out

Source: Lillian Hellman, *Scoundrel Time* excerpt. Copyright 1976 Lillian Hellman by Little, Brown and Company. Reprinted by permission.

148. Lillian Hellman, *Scoundrel Time*

for freedom of speech and thought. Although Congress, to the surprise of many, did not cite Hellman for contempt, the author paid dearly for her defiance, as her autobiographical account, Scoundrel Time, *makes painfully clear.*

Dear Mr. Wood:

As you know, I am under subpoena to appear before your Committee on May 21, 1952.

I am most willing to answer all questions about myself. I have nothing to hide from your Committee and there is nothing in my life of which I am ashamed. I have been advised by counsel that under the Fifth Amendment I have a constitutional privilege to decline to answer any questions about my political opinions, activities, and associations, on the grounds of self-incrimination. I do not wish to claim this privilege. I am ready and willing to testify before the representatives of our Government as to my own opinions and my own actions, regardless of any risks of consequences to myself.

But I am advised by counsel that if I answer the Committee's questions about myself, I must also answer questions about other people and that if I refuse to do so, I can be cited for contempt. My counsel tells me that if I answer questions about myself, I will have waived my rights under the Fifth Amendment and could be forced legally to answer questions about others. This is very difficult for a layman to understand. But there is one principle that I do understand: I am not willing, now or in the future, to bring bad trouble to people who, in my past association with them, were completely innocent of any talk or any action that was disloyal or subversive. I do not like subversion or disloyalty in any form, and if I had ever seen any, I would have considered it my duty to have reported it to the proper authorities. But to hurt innocent people whom I knew many years ago in order to save myself is, to me, inhuman and indecent and dishonorable. I cannot and will not cut my conscience to fit this year's fashions, even though I long ago came to the conclusion that I was not a political person and could have no comfortable place in any political group.

I was raised in an old-fashioned American tradition and there were certain homely things that were taught to me: to try to tell the truth, not to bear false witness, not to harm my neighbor, to be loyal to my country, and so on. In general, I respected these ideals of Christian honor and did as well with them as I knew how. It is my belief that you will agree with these simple rules of human decency and will not expect me to violate the good American tradition from which they spring. I would, therefore, like to come before you and speak of myself.

I am prepared to waive the privilege against self-incrimination and to tell you everything you wish to know about my views or actions if your Committee will agree to refrain from asking me to name other people. If the Committee is unwilling to give me this assurance, I will be forced to plead the privilege of the Fifth Amendment at the hearing.

A reply to this letter would be appreciated.

Sincerely,
Lillian Hellman

The answer to the letter is as follows:

Dear Miss Hellman:

Reference is made to your letter dated May 19, 1952, wherein you indicate that in the event the Committee asks you questions regarding your association with other individuals you will be compelled to rely upon the Fifth Amendment in giving your answers to the Committee questions.

In this connection, please be advised that the Committee cannot permit witnesses to set forth the terms under which they will testify.

We have in the past secured a great deal of information from persons in the entertainment profession who cooperated wholeheartedly with the Committee. The Committee appreciates any information furnished it by persons who have been members of the Communist Party. The Committee, of course, realizes that a great number of persons who were members of the Communist Party at one time honestly felt that it was not a subversive organization. However, on the other hand, it should be pointed out that the contributions made to the Communist Party as a whole by persons who are not themselves subversive made it possible for those members of the Communist Party who were and still are subversives to carry on their work.

The Committee has endeavored to furnish a hearing to each person identified as a Communist engaged in work in the entertainment field in order that the record could be made clear as to whether they were still members of the Communist Party. Any persons identified by your during the course of Committee hearings will be afforded the opportunity of appearing before the Committee in accordance with the policy of the Committee.

Sincerely yours,
John S. Wood, *Chairman*

... The room suddenly began to fill up behind me and the press people began to push toward their section and were still piling in when Representative Wood began to pound his gavel. I hadn't seen the Committee come in, don't think I had realized that they were to sit on a raised platform, the government having learned from the stage, or maybe the other way around. I was glad I hadn't seen them come in—they made a gloomy picture. Through the noise of the gavel I heard one of the ladies in the rear cough very loudly. She was to cough all through the hearing. Later I heard one of her friends say loudly, "Irma, take your good cough drops."

The opening questions were standard: what was my name, where was I born, what was my occupation, what were the titles of my plays. It didn't take long to get to what really interested them: my time in Hollywood, which studios had I worked for, what periods of what years, with some mysterious emphasis on 1937. (My time in Spain, I thought, but I was wrong.)

Had I met a writer called Martin Berkeley? (I had never, still have never, met Martin Berkeley, although Hammett told me later that I had once sat at a lunch table of sixteen or seventeen people with him at the old Metro-Goldwyn-Mayer commissary.) I said I must refuse to answer that question. Mr. Tavenner said he'd like to ask me again whether I had stated I was abroad in the summer of 1937. I said yes, explained that I had been in New York for several weeks before going to Europe, and got myself ready for what I knew was coming: Martin Berkeley, one of the Committee's most lavish witnesses on the subject of Hollywood, was now going to be put to work. Mr. Tavenner read Berkeley's testimony. Perhaps he is worth quoting, the small details are nicely formed, even about his "old friend Hammett," who had no more than a bowing acquaintance with him.

MR. TAVENNER: . . . I would like to tell the committee when and where the Hollywood section of the Communist people was first organized.
MR. BERKELEY: Well, sir, by a very large coincidence the section was organized in my house. . . . In June of 1937, the middle of June, the meeting was held in my house. My house was picked because I had a large living room and ample parking facilities. . . . And it was a pretty good meeting. We were honored by the presence of many functionaries from downtown, and the spirit was swell. . . . Well, in addition to Jerome and the others I have mentioned before, and there is no sense in going over the list again and again. . . . Also present was Harry Carlisle, who is now in the process of being deported, for which I am very grateful. He was an English subject. After Stanley Lawrence had stolen what funds there were from the party out here, and to make amends had gone to Spain and gotten himself killed, they sent Harry Carlisle here to conduct Marxist classes. . . . Also at the meeting was Donald Ogden Stewart. His name is spelled Donald Ogden S-t-e-w-a-r-t. Dorothy Parker, also a writer. Her husband Allen Campbell, C-a-m-p-b-e-l-l; my old friend Dashiell Hammett, who is now in jail in New York for his activities; that very excellent playwright, Lillian Hellman . . .

And so on.

When this nonsense was finished, Mr. Tavenner asked me if it was true. I said that I wanted to refer to the letter I had sent. I would like the Committee to reconsider my offer in the letter.

MR. TAVENNER: In other words, you are asking the committee not to ask you any questions regarding the participation of other persons in the Communist Party activities?

I said I hadn't said that.

Mr. Wood said that in order to clarify the record Mr. Tavenner should put into the record the correspondence between me and the Committee. Mr. Tavenner did just that, and when he had finished Rauh sprang to his feet, picked up a stack of mimeographed copies of my letter, and handed them out to the press section. I was puzzled by this—I hadn't noticed he had the copies—but I did notice that Rauh was looking happy.

Mr. Tavenner was upset, far more than the printed words of my hearing show. Rauh said that Tavenner himself had put the letters in the record, and thus he thought passing out copies was proper. The polite words of each as they read on the page were not polite as spoken. I am convinced that in this section of the testimony, as in several other sections—certainly in Hammett's later testimony before the Senate Internal Security Subcommittee—either the court stenographer missed some of what was said and filled it in later, or the documents were, in part, edited. Having read many examples of the work of court stenographers, I have never once seen a completely accurate report.

Mr. Wood told Mr. Tavenner that the Committee could not be "placed in the attitude of trading witnesses as to what they will testify to" and that thus he thought both letters should be read aloud.

Mr. Tavenner did just this, and there was talk I couldn't hear, a kind of rustle, from the press-section. Then Mr. Tavenner asked me if I had attended the meeting described by Berkeley, and one of the hardest things I ever did in my life was to swallow the words, "I don't know him, and a little investigation into the time and place would have proved to you that I could not have been at the meeting he talks about." Instead, I said that I must refuse to answer the question. The "must" in that sentence annoyed Mr. Wood—it was to annoy him again and again—and he corrected me: "You might refuse to answer, the question is asked, do you refuse?"

But Wood's correction of me the irritation in his voice, was making me nervous, and I began to move my right hand as if I had a tic, unexpected, and couldn't stop it. I told myself that if a word irritated him, the insults would begin to come very soon. So I sat up straight, made my left hand hold my right hand, and hoped it would work. But I felt the sweat on my face and arms and knew that something was going to happen to me, something out of control, and I turned to Joe, remembering the suggested toilet intermissions. But the clock said we had only been there sixteen minutes, and if it was going to come, the bad time, I had better hang on for a while.

Was I a member of the Communist Party, had I been, what year had I stopped being? How could I harm such people as Martin Berkeley by admitting I had known them, and so on. At times I couldn't follow the reasoning, at times I understood full well that in refusing to answer questions about membership in the Party I had, of course, trapped myself into a seeming admission that I once had been.

But in the middle of one of the questions about my past, something so remarkable happened that I am to this day convinced that the unknown gentleman who spoke had a great deal to do with the rest of my life. A voice from the press gallery had been for at least three or four minutes louder than the other voices. (By this time, I think, the press had finished reading my letter to the committee and were discussing it.) The loud voice had been answered by a less loud voice, but no words could be distinguished. Suddenly a clear voice said, "Thank God somebody finally had the guts to do it."

It is never wise to say that something is the best minute of your life, you must be forgetting, but I still think that unknown voice made the words that helped to save me. (I had been sure that not only did the elderly ladies in the room disapprove of me, but the press would be antagonistic.) Wood rapped his gavel and said angrily, "If that occurs again, I will clear the press from these chambers."

"You do that sir," said the same voice.

Mr. Wood spoke to somebody over his shoulder and the somebody moved around to the press section, but that is all that happened. To this day I don't know the name of the man who spoke, but for months later, almost every day I would say to myself, I wish I could tell him that I had really wanted to say to Mr. Wood: "There is no Communist menace in this country and you know it. You have made cowards into liars, an ugly business, and you made me write a letter in which I acknowledged your power. I should have gone into your Committee room, given my name and address, and walked out." Many people have said that they liked what I did, but I don't much, and if I hadn't worried about rats in jail, and such.... Ah, the bravery you tell yourself was possible when it's all over, the bravery of the staircase.

In the Committee room I heard Mr. Wood say, "Mr. Walter does not desire to ask the witness any further questions. Is there any reason why this witness should not be excused from further attendance before the Committee?"

Mr. Tavenner said, "No, sir."

My hearing was over an hour and seven minutes after it began. I don't think I understood that it was over, but Joe was whispering so loudly and so happily that I jumped from the noise in my ear.

He said, *"Get up. Get up.* Get out of here immediately. Pollitt will take you. Don't stop for any reason, to answer any question from anybody. Don't run, but walk as fast as you can and just shake your head and keep moving if anybody comes near you."

Life had changed and there were many people who did not call me. But there were others, a few friends, a few half-strangers, who made a point of asking me for dinner or who sent letters. That was kind, because I knew that some of them were worried about the consequences of seeing me.

But the mishmash of those years, beginning before my congressional debut and for years after, took a heavy penalty. My belief in liberalism was mostly gone. I think I have substituted for it something private called, for want of something that should be more accurate, decency. And yet certain connecting strings have outworn many knives, perhaps because the liberal connection has been there for thirty years and that's a long time. There was nothing strange about my problem, it is naive to our time; but it is painful for a nature that no longer accept liberalism not to be able to accept radicalism. One sits uncomfortably on a too comfortable cushion. Many of us now endlessly jump from one side to another and endlessly fall in space. The American creative world is not only equal but superior in talent to their colleagues in other countries, but they have given no leadership, written no words of new theory in a country that cries out for belief and, because it has none, finds too many people acting in strange and aimless violence.

But there were other penalties in that year of 1952: life was to change sharply in ordinary ways. We were to have enough money for a few years and then we didn't have any, and that was to last for a while, with occasional windfalls. I saw that coming the day the subpoena was first served. It was obvious, as I have said, the farm had to be sold. I knew I would now be banned from writing movies, that the theatre was as uncertain as it always has been, and I was slow and usually took two years to write a play. Hammett's radio, television and book money was gone forever. I could have broken up the farm in small pieces and made a fortune—I had had an offer that made that possible—and I might have accepted it except for Hammett, who said—"No, I won't have it that way. Let everybody else mess up the land. Why don't you and I leave it alone?", a fine sentiment with which I agree and have forever regretting listening to. More important than the sale of the farm, I knew that a time of my life had ended and the faster I put it away the easier would be an altered way of living, although I think the sale of the farm was the most painful loss of my life. It was, perhaps, more painful to Hammett, although to compare the pains of the loss of beloved land one has worked oneself, a house that fits because you have made it fit thinking you would live in it forever, is a foolish guess-game.

Chapter XXVIII

The Eisenhower Years, 1953–1960

149. Dwight D. Eisenhower, Eisenhower Explains the Domino Theory, 1954

Q. *Robert Richards. Copley Press:* Mr. President, would you mind commenting on the strategic importance of Indochina to the free world? I think there has been, across the country, some lack of understanding on just what it means to us.

The President: You have, of course, both the specific and the general when you talk about such things.

First of all, you have the specific value of a locality in its production of materials that the world needs.

Then you have the possibility that many human beings pass under a dictatorship that is inimical to the free world.

Finally, you have broader considerations that might follow what you would call the "falling domino" principle. You have a row of dominoes set up, you know over the first one, and what will happen to the last one is the certainty that it will go over very quickly. So you could have a beginning of a disintegration that would have the most profound influences.

Now, with respect to the first one, two of the items from this particular area that the world uses are tin and tungsten. They are very important. There are others, of course, the rubber plantations and so on.

Then with respect to more people passing under this domination, Asia, after all, has already lost some 450 million of its peoples to the Communist dictatorship, and we simply can't afford greater losses.

But when we come to the possible sequence of events, the loss of Indochina, of Burma, of Thailand, of the Peninsula, and Indonesia following, now you begin to talk about areas that not only multiply the disadvantages that you would suffer through loss of materials, sources of materials, but now you are talking about millions and millions and millions of people.

Finally, the geographical position achieved hereby does many things. It turns the so-called island defensive chain of Japan. Formosa, of the Philippines and to the southward; it moves in to threaten Australia and New Zealand.

It takes away, in its economic aspects, that region that Japan must have as a trading area or Japan, in turn, will have only one place in the world to go — that is, toward the Communist areas in order to live.

So, the possible consequences of the loss are just incalculable to the free world.

Source: President Eisenhower Responding to Media Question, 1954. Public Domain Reprint.

150. CHIEF JUSTICE EARL WARREN, *BROWN V. BOARD OF EDUCATION*, 1954

Brown v. Board of Education *was the landmark decision that started the desegregation of Southern schools.*

MAY 17, 1954[1]

MR. CHIEF JUSTICE WARREN delivered the opinion of the Court.

These cases come to us from the states of Kansas, South Carolina, Virginia, and Delaware. They are premised on different facts and different local conditions, but a common legal question justifies their consideration together in this consolidated opinion.[2]

In each of the cases, minors of the Negro race, through their legal representatives, seek the aid of the courts in obtaining admission to the public schools of their community on a nonsegregated basis. In each instance, they had been denied admission to schools attended by white children under laws requiring or permitting segregation according to race. This segregation was alleged to deprive the plaintiffs of the equal protection of the laws under the Fourteenth Amendment. In each of the cases other than the Delaware case, a three-judge federal district court denied relief to the plaintiffs on the socalled "separate but equal" doctrine announced by this Court in *Plessy v. Ferguson*, 163 U.S. 537. Under that doctrine, equality of treatment is accorded when the races are provided substantially equal facilities, even though these facilities be separate. In the equal case, the Supreme Court of Delaware adhered to that doctrine, but ordered that the plaintiffs be admitted to the white schools because of their superiority to the Negro schools.

The plaintiffs contend that segregated public schools are not "equal" and cannot be made "equal," and hence they are deprived of the equal protection of the laws. Because of the obvious importance of the question presented, the Court took jurisdiction. Argument was heard in the 1852 Term, and reargument was heard this Term on certain questions propounded by the Court.

Reargument was largely devoted to the circumstances surrounding the adoption of the Fourteenth Amendment in 1868. It covered exhaustively consideration of the Amendment in Congress, ratification by the states, then-existing practices in racial segregation, and the views of proponents and opponents of the Amendment. This discussion and our own investigations convince us that, although these sources cast some light, it is not enough to resolve the problem with which we are faced. At best, they are inconclusive. The most avid proponents of the post-War Amendments undoubtedly intended them to remove all legal distinctions among "all persons born or naturalized in the United States." Their opponents, just as certainly, were antagonistic to both the letter and the spirit of the Amendment and wished them to have the most limited effect. What others in Congress and the state legislatures had in mind cannot be determined with any degree of certainty.

An additional reason for the inconclusive nature of the Amendment's history, with respect to segregated schools, is the status of public education at that time. In the South, the movement toward free common schools, supported by general taxation, had not yet taken hold. Education of white children was largely in the hands of private groups. Education of Negroes was almost nonexistent, and practically all of the race were illiterate. In fact, any education of Negroes was forbidden by law in some states. Today, in contrast, many Negroes have achieved outstanding success in the arts and sciences as well as in the business and professional world. It is true that public school education at the time of the Amendment had advanced further in the North, but the effect of the Amendment on Northern States was generally ignored in the congressional debates. Even in the North, the conditions of public education did not approximate those existing today. The curriculum was usually rudimentary; ungraded schools were common in rural areas; the school term was but three months a year in many states; and compulsory school attendance was virtually unknown. As a consequence, it is not surprising that there should be so little in the history of the

---

Source: "Brown v. Board of Education." Reprinted from Hubert Humphrey, ed., *School Desegregation: Documents and Commentaries.* Thos. Y. Crowell Co., 1964.

Fourteenth Amendment relating to its intended effect on public education.

In the first cases in this Court construing the Fourteenth Amendment, decided shortly after its adoption, the Court interpreted it as proscribing all state-imposed discriminations against the Negro race. The doctrine of "separate but equal" did not make its appearance in this Court until 1896 in the case of *Plessy v. Ferguson, supra,* involving not education but transportation. American courts have since labored with the doctrine for over half a century. In this Court, there have been six cases involving the "separate but equal" doctrine in the field of public education. In *Cumming v. County Board of Education,* 175 U.S. 528, and *Cong Lum v. Rice,* 275 U.S. 78, the validity of the doctrine itself was not challenged. In more recent cases, all on the graduate school level, inequality was found in that specific benefits enjoyed by white students were denied to Negro students of the same educational qualifications. *Missouri ex rel. Gaines v. Canada,* 305 U.S. 337; *Sipuel v. Oklahoma,* 332 U.S. 631; *Sweatt v. Painter,* 339 U.S. 629; *McLaurin v. Oklahoma State Regents,* 339 U.S. 637. In none of these cases was it necessary to re-examine the doctrine to grant relief to the Negro plaintiff. And in *Sweatt v. Painter, supra,* the Court expressly reserved decision on the question whether *Plessy v. Ferguson* should be held inapplicable to public education.

In the instant cases, that question is directly presented. Here, unlike *Sweatt v. Painter,* there are findings below that the Negro and white schools have been equalized, or are being equalized, with respect to buildings, curricula, qualifications and salaries of teachers, and other "tangible" factors. Our decision, therefore, cannot turn on merely a comparison of these tangible factors in the Negro and white schools involved in each of the cases. We must look instead to the effect of segregation itself on public education.

In approaching this problem, we cannot turn the clock back to 1868 when the Amendment was adopted, or even to 1896 when *Plessy v. Ferguson* was written. We must consider public education in the light of its full development and its present place in American life throughout the Nation. Only in this way can it be determined if segregation in public schools deprives these plaintiffs of the equal protection of the laws.

Today, education is perhaps the most important function of state and local government. Compulsory school attendance laws and the great expenditures for education both demonstrate our recognition of the importance of education to our democratic society. It is required in the performance of our most basic public responsibilities, even service in the armed forces. It is the very foundation of good citizenship. Today it is a principal instrument in awakening the child to cultural values, in preparing him for later professional training, and in helping him to adjust normally to his environment. In these days, it is doubtful that any child may reasonably be expected to succeed in life if he is denied the opportunity of an education. Such an opportunity, where the state has undertaken to provide it is a right which must be made available to all on equal terms.

We come then to the question presented: Does segregation of children in public school solely on the basis of race, even though the physical facilities and other "tangible" factors may be equal, deprive the children of the minority group of equal educational opportunities. We believe that it does.

In *Sweatt v. Painter, supra,* in finding that a segregated law school for Negroes could not provide them equal educational opportunities, this Court relied in large part on "those qualities which are incapable of objective measurement but which make for greatness in a law school." In *McLaurin v. Oklahoma State Regents, supra,* the Court, in requiring that a Negro admitted to white graduate school be treated like all other students, again resorted to intangible considerations: ". . . his ability to study, to engage in discussions and exchange views with other students, and, in general, to learn his profession." Such considerations apply with added force to children in grade and high schools. To separate them from others of similar age and qualifications solely because of their race generates a feeling of inferiority as to their status in the community that may affect their hearts and minds in a way unlikely ever to be undone. The effect of this separation on their educational opportunities was well stated by a finding in the Kansas case by a court which nevertheless felt compelled to rule against the Negro plaintiffs:

> "Segregation of white and colored children in public schools has a detrimental effect upon the colored children. The impact is greater when it has the sanction of the law; for the policy of separating the races is usually interpreted as denoting the inferiority of the negro group. A sense of inferiority affects the motivation of a child to learn. Segregation with the sanction of law, therefore, has a tendency to [retard] the educational and mental development of negro children and to deprive them of some of the benefits they would receive in a racial[ly] integrated school system."

Whatever may have been the extent of psychological knowledge at the time of *Plessy v. Ferguson,* this finding is amply supported by modern authority.³ Any language in *Plessy v. Ferguson* contrary to this finding is rejected.

We conclude that in the field of public education the doctrine of "separate but equal" has no place. Separate educational facilities are inherently unequal. Therefore, we hold that the plaintiffs and other similarly situated for whom the actions have been brought are, by reason of the segregation complained of, deprived of the equal protection of the laws guaranteed by the Fourteenth Amendment. This disposition makes unnecessary any discussion whether such segregation also violates the Due Process Clause of the Fourteenth Amendment.

Because there are class actions, because of the wide applicability of this decision, and because of the great variety of local conditions, the formulation of decrees in these cases presents problems of considerable complexity. On reargument, the consideration of appropriate relief was necessarily subordinated to the primary question—the constitutionality of segregation in public education. We have now announced that such segregation is a denial of the equal protection of the laws. In order that we may have the full assistance of the parties in formulating decrees, the cases will be restored to the docket, and the parties are requested to present further argument on Questions 4 and 5 previously propounded by the Court for the reargument of this Term. The Attorney General of the United States is again invited to participate. The Attorney General of the states requiring or permitting segregation in public education will also be permitted to appear as *amici curiae* upon request to do so by September 15, 1954, and submission of briefs by October 1, 1954.

It is so ordered.

MAY 31, 1955.⁴

MR. CHIEF JUSTICE WARREN delivered the opinion of the court.

These cases were decided on May 17, 1954. The opinions of that date, declaring the fundamental principle that racial discrimination in public education is unconstitutional, are incorporated herein by reference. All provisions of federal, state, or local law requiring or permitting such discrimination must yield to this principle. There remains for consideration the manner in which relief is to be accorded.

Because these cases arose under different local conditions and their disposition will involve a variety of local problems, we requested further argument on the question of relief. In view of the nationwide importance of the decision, we invited the Attorney General of the United States and the Attorney General of all states requiring or permitting racial discrimination in public education to present their views on that question. The parties, the United States, and the States of Florida, North Carolina, Arkansas, Oklahoma, Maryland, and Texas filed briefs and participated in the oral argument.

These presentations were informative and helpful to the Court in its consideration of the complexities arising from the transition to a system of public education freed of racial discrimination. The presentations also demonstrated that substantial steps to eliminate racial discrimination in public schools have already been taken, not only in some of the communities in which these cases arose, but in some of the states appearing as *amici curiae,* and in other states as well. Substantial progress has been made in the District of Columbia and in the communities in Kansas and Delaware involved in this litigation. The defendants in the cases coming to us from South Carolina and Virginia are awaiting the decision of this Court concerning relief.

Full implementation of these constitutional principles may require solution of varied local school problems. School authorities have the primary responsibility for elucidating, assessing, and solving these problems; courts will have to consider whether the action of school authorities constitutes good faith implementation of the governing constitutional principles. Because of their proximity to local conditions and the possible need for further hearings, the courts which originally heard these cases can best perform this judicial appraisal. Accordingly, we believe it appropriate to remand the cases to those courts.

In fashioning and effectuating the decree, the Courts will be guided by equitable principles. Traditionally, equity has been characterized by a practical flexibility in shaping its remedies and by a facility for adjusting and reconciling public and private needs. These cases call for the exercise of these traditional attributes of equity power. At stake is the personal interest of the plaintiffs in admission to public schools as soon as practicable on a nondiscriminatory basis. To effectuate this interest may call for elimination of a variety of obstacles in making the transition to school systems operated in accordance with the constitutional principles set forth in our May 17, 1954, decision. Courts of equity may properly take into account the public interest in the elimination of such obstacles in a systematic and effective manner. But it should go without saying that the vitality of these constitutional principles cannot be allowed to yield simply because of disagreement with them.

While giving weight to these public and private considerations, the courts will require that the defendants make a prompt and reasonable start toward full compliance with our May 17, 1954, ruling. Once such a start had been made, the courts may find that additional time is necessary to carry out the ruling in an effective manner. The burden rests upon the defendants to establish that such time is necessary in the public interest and is consistent with good faith compliance at the earliest practicable date. To that end, the courts may consider problems related to the administration, arising from the physical condition of the school plant, the school transportation system, personnel, revision of school districts and attendance areas into compact units to achieve a system of determining admission to the public schools on a nonracial basis, and revision of local laws and regulations which may be necessary in solving the foregoing problems. They will also consider the adequacy of any plans the defendants may propose to meet these problems and to effectuate a transition to a racially nondiscriminatory school system. Drawing this period of transition, the courts will retain jurisdiction of these cases.

The judgments below, except that in the Delaware case, are accordingly reversed and the cases are remanded to the District Courts to take such proceedings and enter such orders and decrees consistent with this opinion as are necessary and proper to admit to public schools on a racially nondiscriminatory basis with all deliberated speed the parties to these cases. The judgment in the Delaware case—ordering the immediate admission of the plaintiffs to schools previously attended only by white children—is affirmed on the basis of the principles stated in our May 17, 1954, opinion, but the case is remanded to the Supreme Court of Delaware for such further proceedings as that Court may deem necessary in light of this opinion.

It is so ordered.

NOTES

[1] This is the date on which the consolidated opinion was given for the four following cases: No. 1, *Brown et al. v. Board of Education of Topeka et al.,* on appeal from the United States District Court for the District of Kansas, argued December 9, 1952, reargued December 8, 1953; together with No. 2, *Briggs et al. v. Elliott et al.,* on appeal from the United States District Court for the Eastern District of South Carolina, argued December 9–10, 1952, reargued December 7–8, 1953; No. 4, *Davis et al. v. County School Board of Prince Edward County, Virginia, et al.,* on appeal from the United States District Court for the Eastern District of Virginia, argued December 10, 1952, reargued December 7–8, 1953; and No. 10, *Gebhart et al. v. Belton et al.,* on certiorari to the Supreme Court of Delaware, argued December 11, 1952; reargued December 9, 1953. ED.

[2] In the Kansas case, *Brown v. Board of Education,* the plaintiffs are Negro children of elementary school age residing in Topeka. They brought this action in the United States District Court for the District of Kansas to enjoin enforcement of a Kansas statute which permits, but does not require, cities of more than 15,000 population to maintain separate school facilities for Negro and white students. Kan. Gen. Stat. § 72-1724 (1949). Pursuant to that authority, the Topeka Board of Education elected to establish segregated elementary schools. Other public schools in the community, however, are operated on a nonsegregated basis. The three-judge District Court, convened under 28 U.S.C. §§ 2281 and 2284, found that segregation in public education has a detrimental effect upon Negro children, but denied relief on the ground that the Negro and white schools were substantially equal with respect to buildings, transportation, curricula, and educational qualifications of teachers. 98 F. Supp. 797. The case is here on direct appeal under 28 U.S.C. § 1253.

In the South Carolina case, *Briggs v. Elliott,* the plaintiffs are Negro children of both elementary and high school age residing in Clarendon County. They brought this action in the United States District Court for the Eastern District of South Carolina to enjoin enforcement of provisions in the state constitution and statutory code which require the segregation of Negroes and whites in public schools. S.C. Const., Art. XI, §7; S.C. Code § 5377 (1942). The three-judge District Court, convened under 28 U.S.C. §§ 2281 and 2284, denied the requested relief. The court found that the Negro schools were inferior to the white schools and ordered the defendants to begin immediately to equalize the facilities. But the court sustained the validity of the contested provisions and denied the plaintiffs admission to the white schools during the equalization program. 98 F. Supp. 529. This Court vacated the District Court's judgment and remanded the case for the purpose of obtaining the court's views on a report filed by the defendants concerning the progress made in the equalization program. 342 U.S. 350. On remand, the District Court found that substantial equality had been achieved except for buildings and that the defendants were proceeding to rectify this inequality as well. 103 F. Supp. 920. The case is again here on direct appeal under 28 U.S.C. § 1253.

In the Virginia case, *District v. County School Board,* the plaintiffs are Negro children of high school age residing in Prince Edward County. They brought this action in the United States District Court for the Eastern District of Virginia to enjoin enforcement of provisions in the state constitution and statutory code which require the segregation of Negroes and whites in public schools. Va. Const. § 140; Va. Code § 22-221 (1950). The three-judge District Court, convened under 28 U.S.C. §§ 2281 and 2284, denied the requested relief. The court found the Negro school inferior in physical plant, curricula, and transportation, and ordered the defendants forthwith to provide substantially equal curricula and transportation and to "proceed with all reasonable diligence and dispatch to remove" the inequality in physical plant. But, as in the South Carolina case, the court sustained the validity of the contested provisions and denied the plaintiffs admission to the white schools during the equalization program. 103 F. Supp. 337. The case is here on direct appeal under 28 U.S.C. § 1253.

In the Delaware case, *Gebhart v. Belton,* the plaintiffs are Negro children of both elementary and high school age residing in New Castle County. They brought this action in the Delaware Court of Chancery to enjoin enforcement of provisions in the state constitution and statutory code which require the segregation of Negroes and whites in public schools. Del. Const., Art. X, § 2; Del. Rev. Code. § 2631 (1935). The Chancellor gave judgment for the plaintiffs and ordered their immediate admission to schools previously attended only by white children, on the ground that the Negro schools were inferior with respect to teacher training, pupil-teacher ratio, extracurricular activities, physical plant, and time and distance involved in travel. 87 A. 2d 862. The Chancellor also found that segregation itself results in an inferior education for Negro children (see note 10, *infra*), but did not rest his decision on that ground. *Id.,* at 865. The Chancellor's decree was affirmed by the Supreme Court of Delaware, which intimated, however, that the defendants might be able to obtain a modification of the decree after equalization of the Negro and white schools had been accomplished. 91 A.2d 137, 152. The defendants, contending only that the Delaware courts had erred in ordering the immediate admission of the Negro plaintiffs to the white schools, applied to this Court for certiorari. The writ was granted, 344 U.S. 891. The plaintiffs, who were successful below, did not submit a cross-petition.

[3] K. B. Clark, Effect of Prejudice and Discrimination on Personality Development (Midcentury White House Conference on Children and Youth, 1950); Witmer and Kotinsky, Personality in the Making (1952), c. VI; Deutscher and Chein, The Psychological Effects of Enforced Segregation: A Survey of Social Science Opinion, 26 J. Psychol. 259 (1948); Chein, What are the Psychological Effects of Segregation Under Conditions of Equal Facilities?, 3 Int. J. Opinion and Attitude Res. 229 (1949); Brament, Educational Costs, in Discrimination and National Welfare (MacIver, ed., 1949), 44–48; Frazier, The Negro in the United States (1949), 674–681. And see generally Myrdal, An American Dilemma (1944).

[4] The court cases decided in the May 17, 1954, opinion were reargued on the question of relief on April 11–14, 1955, with the opinion and judgments announced on May 31, 1955. An additional case in this opinion was *Bolling et al. v. Sharpe et al.,* on certiorari to the United States Court of Appeals for the District of Columbia Circuit. ED.

151. *Newsweek*, "The Big Surge. . . . The New America," 1955

The 1950s witnessed the multifaceted transformation of the United States, detailed in somewhat breathless fashion by this cover article from Newsweek *in 1955.*

Greatest—So Far

"America is a land of wonders, in which everything is in constant motion and every change seems an improvement . . . No natural boundaries seems to be set to the efforts of man; and in his eyes what is not yet done is only what he has not yet attempted to do."

Since the sharp-eyed visiting Frenchman Alexis de Tocqueville wrote those words 120 years ago, Americans have become accustomed to change—so accustomed that they hardly notice it.

A skyline is transformed; a dread disease is conquered; a war is won.

It is all in a day's work—or a decade's.

For change is America's way of life.

And never has change been so rapid or far-reaching as in the past ten years.

It is a change that affects every man, woman, and child in the nation's burgeoning 165 million population, perhaps everyone in the world.

What has happened in the past ten years is that a new America has been created—new in so many ways that even Americans do not comprehend it.

Of what stuff is the new nation made?

It is made of wealth, and the things that wealth has brought. By and large these are mostly pleasant things: The millions of new homes dotting the countryside, and the tangle of TV antennas atop them the ribbons of superhighways and the relentless stream of flashy new autos flowing down them; the rising birth rate and the dropping death rate; the huge scientific strides that have brought distant horizons close; the greatest splurge of industrial building and expansion ever seen—and the most extensive church-building job in history.

The new prosperity has changed the nature of U.S. politics. It has changed the way people spend their time, the way they act, the way they think. Due largely to the strength of the U.S., the free world found a way to rebuild itself from the rubble of war.

But wealth has also brought problems.

Some of the U.S. farm population is feeling a pinch for the simple, if odd, reason that its segment of the economy has been too productive. Great needs still exist for more schools, more doctors, more roads, and better housing for the millions that still live in sub-par dwellings.

Perhaps the greatest need, in such a time of change, is a little time to think about the change. Time perhaps to relocate some of the values that may have been lost or misplaced.

Never has a nation been so prosperous, never so powerful. Yet the world balances on a knife edge. Seldom has a people lived in less security than do Americans in their day of greatest wealth.

Perhaps great nations are made by challenge, or perhaps they are made to be challenged. The U.S. has met new challenges by changing vastly in the decade past; to meet the still newer ones, it must keep changing.

In this Special Section, NEWSWEEK tells the amazing story of the new America—its people, its politics, its culture, its business, its impact abroad.

Will it prove true, as de Tocqueville said, that what the new American has not yet done "is only what he has not yet attempted to do?"

The Holly Mood

In Los Angeles, "Little Tokyo," this week, gift shops were doing a brisk business selling replicas of the ancient Buddhist Daruma, who never worried about good fortune but to whom it invariably came. Daruma is a symbol of "persisting optimism."

That seemed to be the mood of most of the U.S. as Americans set off on what promised to be the biggest Christmas-shopping binge in history. It was a fitting climax to the country's wealthiest year.

This is how the nation looked:

In Boston, a huge star glittered atop the gold-leaf dome of the red brick State House looking down on

---

Source: *Newsweek*, December 12, 1955, Newsweek Inc. All rights reserved. Reprinted by permission.

Boston Common, where the city's 50-foot Christmas tree had been raised. The air was cold and brisk and the bare trees of the Common were festooned with thousands of electric bulbs that transformed the small park, at night, into a great blaze of color. In the harbor the fishing trawlers back from the Grand Banks were a foot thick in ice. The narrow streets were crowded with shoppers.

It was hog-killing time on the farms of the South ("Never kill a hog till the wind is from the North") and plumes of steam rose from the black scalding pots in the farmers' yards. In the mountains, the leaves were about gone, except for the red oaks, and the mountain folk were stringing up snap-beans pods in their kitchens. The last of the cotton was coming in around Atlanta; wild geese were landing on the Louisiana lakes, and the first of the winter tourists were on the sunny beaches of the South. "Sure is cold," said an attendant at a New England filling station, "but I'm going to Florida next month." He had the money.

In Chicago, 1 million shoppers—a record for one day—jammed the Loop. In New York, stores were filled to overflowing, and the State Employment Service warned store owners that "hammer and tongs" recruiting would be necessary to get the 12,000 to 16,000 extra workers they normally put on for Christmas.

The citizens of Detroit gave nearly $16 million to the United Foundation. Never in the city's history had so much money been given to charity in a single drive. Having given to others, Detroiters went out to shop for themselves in such numbers that the Police Department canceled leaves of 125 men and put them on traffic duty. In Wichita (see page 60), any cop could make an extra $50 a week by spending his spare time wrestling traffic around suburban shopping centers.

An Atlanta shopper drove around for two hours looking for a parking space. He finally ran out of gasoline.

Merchants in Dallas were running a special bus line for their customers. At the border city of Tijuana there were half-hour waits at customs as shoppers poured back from Mexico with duty-free cashmeres, perfumes, and silver knick-knacks. A Washington, D.C., department-store official said: "Business is absolutely sensational, far beyond anybody's expectations."

Nevertheless, there were Americans—and many of them—for whom the year-end was not an unalloyed success.

Homer Thayer, a ruddy-faced livestock farmer of Storm Lake, Iowa, said:

"I'm not hurtin', but I don't think I can make much money. I expect to pay some cattle notes in 60 or 90 days. It's all going to depend on how much money the cattle bring. I plan to sell 35 this year to pay taxes and some notes and carry 10 over to next year when I hope prices won't be as low."

Crime was up for the eighth successive year (an estimated 2,000,000 major crimes). More Americans than ever before were going to psychiatrists, more were in mental hospitals. And underneath the "persisting optimism" was a nagging current of worry.

Theologian Reinhold Niebuhr said:

"We live in a paradise of comfort and prosperity, but this paradise is suspended in a hell of global insecurity. This . . . is a parable of the entire human situation: Suffering from ultimate insecurity, whatever its immediate securities . . ."

POCKETBOOK POLITICS

The nation's great prosperity has created a fundamental change in the character of U.S. politics. For twenty years or more, American politics basically was "the politics of depression." The stock-market crash of 1919 and the economic derangement that followed it overshadowed every political campaign. There were twenty years of Democratic victories, largely because millions of voters automatically identified the Republican Party with the crash.

Nineteen fifty-two was the turning point. During the campaign that year, the Democrats did attempt to revive memories of the depression, but they failed. A whole new generation had come of voting age; they considered the story of 1929 a tedious legend. Since '51, the Eisenhower Administration has completely demolished the notion that a Republican Administration means depression. The Republican Party has now become "the party of prosperity."

This development has created what might be called "the politics of prosperity." In the 1956 campaign, the Republican slogan will be: "Everything is booming but the guns." And the Democrats will not attempt to conjure up fears of depression, as they did from 1929 on; instead, they will take prosperity for granted, as the voters do, and simply insist that "not quite everything is booming." There was an attempt by some Democrats to stir up the "depression" issue in the 1954 Congressional campaign, but their forecasts of bad times ahead proved groundless.

The Republicans believe the boom ensures a Republican victory in '56. Secretary of Commerce Sinclair Week's attitude is typical. Speaking in Chicago last week, the Secretary said:

"As the 1956 Presidential election gets under way, I think . . . that to the average voter the decisive argument boils down to one short, sensible question:

"Why change?

"I predict that Republicans will sweep the country again next November because most people—regardless of local political background—appreciate that they never had it so good and are in no mood to change."

Issue for Democrats

History is with the Republicans, for the voters have never turned a party out of power during a period of prosperity, except in 1952, when corruption in the Truman Administration and the bloody stalemate in Korea became overriding issues. Nevertheless, Democrats are now just as confident of victory as the GOP.

Sen. John J. Sparkman of Alabama, the Democratic candidate for Vice President in 1952, explained why last week:

"If prosperity were a reality across the board—if all segments of the population were enjoying it—then we could say it would remove the economic issue from the campaign picture next year. However, we must remember that we've got certain segments of the economy that are not enjoying this prosperity—for instance, the farmer and many people in economically depressed areas. And there are over 100 of these areas in the U.S.

"Another thing we must remember is that there are 9 million families in the United States with incomes under $2,000 a year. . . .

"This is bound to be discussed in the campaign and bound to have an impact on the election—a favorable impact for the Democrats, needless to say."

LOOKING TO '56

What's ahead for '56?

There has always been one big psychological danger in being at the top: The fear that there is no place to go but down. Not too long ago, this troubled some who thought about the economic outlook. They have since learned that there seem to still be more rungs on the ladder. And while without question 1955 will go down as the nation's best year to date, the record promises to stand only until the 1956 returns are in.

Barring a war, the U.S. should turn out more than $400 billion worth of goods and services next year. (Estimates for the gross national product range from $404 billion to $410 billion compared with the current rate of $391.5 billion and an average of $387 billion for all of 1955). That means that the boom's growth should slow down a bit. This year's gains amounts to 7 per cent. If all goes as indicated, next year should yield a more modest—but still comfortable—4 to 6 per cent.

It has become a vogue among economists to predict no more than six months ahead. The tools for short-range analysis have been highly refined, but for periods beyond that, they are still comparatively crude. "And after all," said one leading economist last week, "we've got our jobs to think of." Those who are willing to go out on a limb for all of 1956 have produced estimates as far apart as: (1) A continued climb, (2) a leveling off, which is the majority view, and (3) a dip, which is decidedly a minority opinion.

A likely rundown on some of the key 1956 figures:
▶ Industrial output (Federal Reserve Board index) at 144 per cent of the 1947–49 average vs. this year's 138.
▶ Consumer income, after taxes, of $280 billion vs. $269 billion. Individuals probably will save a smaller portion of their incomes—around $5\frac{1}{2}$ per cent compared with 6 per cent in 1955.
▶ Corporate income, before taxes, of $49 billion against $44 billion.
▶ Business investment totaling $63.5 billion vs. $59 billion. An estimated $33 billion of this total will be spent on new plants and equipment, 10 per cent above this year.
▶ Federal, state, and local government spending of $78 billion, compared with $75.6 billion.
▶ Unemployment down to an average of only 2.1 million, compared with 2.5 million in 1955.

GOLDEN GUSHER

Harry Karl, a millionaire Los Angeles shoe dealer, gold-plated his car this year. Not the whole thing, of course. Just items like the hub caps, bumpers, and grille. Then he installed a TV set, hi-fi equipment, telephone, tape recorder, a complete bar, a souped-up, 350 horsepower engine. To Karl, whose estranged wife is Marie (The Body) McDonald, it was just like home.

Not every American could afford the $52,000 it cost Karl to indulge his taste. But most were willing to spend almost to the limit of their means—and some beyond—to have things the way they liked them in 1955. And those means have grown considerably. With more than 65 million jobs and factory take-home pay averaging $72 a week, a whole new middle class has been created, with an estimated 14 million families in the $5,000 income bracket or better. After-tax personal income this year probably will hit a record $269 billion, up about 6 per cent from 1954. Of that amount, $253 billion will be spent on everything from honeymoons to new homes to baby shoes.

(Aided by 3 million births through September, baby-shoe sales should pass the 1953 peak of 38 million pairs.)

This willingness to lay out cash amounted, in the opinion of one influential Washington official, to a "consumer spending revolution." It was one of the keys to the 1955 boom, and a strong reason for believing the momentum will carry over well into 1956.

In spending his money, the average individual's wants have gradually been upgraded. He has also started to yearn for something just a little bit different. American industry this year has been ready to fill these wants—ordinary or bizarre—and to expand capacity if need be. This combination points up the most significant fact in this greatest of all prosperities: It has not been spoon-fed by government outlays. In fact, Federal expenditures have declined $3.5 billion in the private year. Private spending more than made up for that by growing $27 billion.

The great American consumer spent a good portion of his 1955 dollar on automobiles; he bought about 7.6 million of this year's record-busting 8 million-car output. While competition was stiff, in some cases, price was no object. When Ford brought out its $10,000 Continental Mark II, officials figured on a quote of twenty for the entire Houston area. They promptly received orders for thirteen from a place called Pampa, Texas, which they needed an atlas to locate. Some clothing makers latched onto the huge auto market with "clothes to match your car."

Outlook for '56: *Automakers say they will make and sell as many cars next year as in 1955. Outsiders doubt this, predict at least a moderate decline. But if sales lag, the industry may well bring out the completely new '57 models earlier than usual as a stimulus.*

If he wasn't interested in clothes to match his car, perhaps the consumer wanted a house to match his personality. Palmer-Krisel, a Los Angeles firm, last week announced "personalized" houses for "introvert" and "extrovert" families. There were dwellings to match every taste—from a $180,000 castle in Ireland (the castle market is "very sticky right now," says New York's Previews, Inc. real estate broker), to a modest Cape Cod-style home for a few thousand dollars. Some 1.3 million buyers found houses to suit their taste this year.

Outlook for '56: *Continuing restrictions on credit probably will help cut 1956 housing starts to about 1,235,000 units. Over-all construction spending, however, should rise from $42 billion to $44 billion.*

It seemed that almost everything consumers touched in 1955 turned to gold for some manufacturer. They spent almost $2 billion for a record 7.9 million TV receivers, another $1.3 billion on servicing and repairs. Color-set sales grew from 5,000 to almost ten times that amount.

Outlook for '56: *More than 7 million black and white and at least 250,000 color sets should be marketed.*

Americans moved about more and spent when they went. Honeymooners spent an average of $428 on wedding trip, 19 per cent over a year ago. American tourists left about $1 billion in foreign countries, provided Europe's biggest single private source of dollars. Airline operating revenues totaled a record $1.6 billion.

Outlook for '56: *There's no reason to expect a letdown.*

And if the girls in 1955 were jaded with the same old diamonds,[1] they could always buy themselves a bit of stardust. An Arizona firm offered "Jewelry from out of this world"—brooches, earrings, and the like made from meteorites and "stardust from out of space and time."

Admittedly, the consumer spent freely in 1955. Did he also spend wildly?

Some alarmed observers thought so, pointing to the rapid growth in consumer debt. Individuals shouldered an additional $20 billion burden. They were in hock on mortgages and installment paper to the tune of $111 billion. There was as yet no evidence, though, that they couldn't support this burden. Losses on consumer loans this year probably will average no greater than last year's 1.18 per cent. But in a declining economy, it is widely agreed, the load could easily become crushing.

There was a great deal more worry about the farmer, who collectively was not benefiting from the general prosperity. Farm prices were 25 per cent below postwar peaks, and still dropping. Only last week, the Agriculture Department's economic director, Frederick V. Waugh, predicted: "We again expect agricultural prices and income to lag behind . . . In other words, we expect the 'cost-price squeeze' to continue." Another Agriculture official, Sherman E. Johnson, remarked gloomily that farm surpluses would "continue to press heavily" on the nation's glutted markets for the next four or five years.

Vanishing Supplies

As the boom picked up speed, the basic industries throbbed (see box following). Materials shortages became a problem. Steel, copper, nickel, aluminum, paper, and many other items were hard to find. One of the country's top economists now fears this might mean that industry may not be able "to bring into being all the new plant and equipment planned for '56."

Prices, which had been remarkably stable in the nation's greatest boom, began to inch up. Last week some grades of steel were boosted $2 a ton; copper rose $1\frac{1}{2}$ cents, to 48 cents a pound, at custom smelters. Earlier, prices of autos, TV sets, and paper were raised. The cost of living very likely will continue to inch up in the months ahead. Among the coming price hikes: Carpets, cement, shoes, appliances, houses. But few experts think this is the beginning of an inflationary spiral. One estimate (Prudential Life's) of the probable cost-of-living a year from now is 115.6 per cent of the 1947–49 average, vs. the latest reading of 114.9. For a fast-growing economy, that would be practically no increase at all.

With the economy's greatest year fast drawing to a close, businessmen and consumers are nevertheless cautious about the future. And that may be the best evidence yet that success has not gone dangerously to their heads.

THE STOCK MARKET: ONWARD AND UPWARD?

One heart faltered, and a million skipped a beat. When the news of President Eisenhower's seizure clicked out that Saturday in September, a thousand kinds of worry gripped the world. But to many U.S. investors, the worry took a single form: Would the confidence that had sent the economy—and the stock market—to new peaks suddenly vanish?

Stocks had climbed since 1949. But only since Mr. Eisenhower took office had they caught up with the economy. The Dow-Jones industrials had risen about 55 per cent since 1952, leaving the old 1929 record far behind, vs. a 10 per cent rise for the gross national product. The bull had grown old. It was vulnerable to the slightest push.

The push, when it came, was a big one. For a while, it looked as if the greatest bull market in history might turn into the greatest collapse. In one day, industrials plummeted about 32 points.

But by last week, industrials had surged to 482.72, just 4.73 points below September's all-time high.

Faith: Basic to the upsurge was investor faith in the overwhelming strength of the economy—and the fact that corporations are cashing in on this prosperity. Pretax earnings in 1955 should reach $44 billion and dividends $11 billion, both records. Dividend yields, which had slipped below 4 per cent for the first time in nine years, were back up to 4.33 per cent. More and more it is being demonstrated that while political developments can cause a jiggle in the market, it is the economy which determines the underlying trend.

Certainly, this has been true in recent years. Nothing—including the Korean war, peace "scares," or Congressional probes—has been able to upset the market.

But was the market moving ahead too fast, and was speculation getting out of hand? The Federal Reserve Board began to apply the brakes, just in case. Margin requirements were raised twice, to 70 per cent. (In the unhealthy 1929 market, margins—set by brokers and not by government—were as low as 10 per cent.) Instead of breaking the market these restrictive measures confirmed its basic strength. Prices held firm.

New Capitalism: Many financial men like to think that the nation has developed a "new capitalism" with an ever-broadening base. Some 7.5 million people hold stock in publicly owned corporations, compared with 6.5 million three years ago. Assets of mutual funds, which give the small investor a chance to spread his risk, have soared from $1.3 billion in 1946 to $7.2 billion. Thousands of workers have become owners of the firms they work for via employee stock-purchase plans.

All of this may not add up to an absolute guarantee against another '29, but most experts are confident that it goes a long way. What about 1956? The economy looked strong. But few thought that the market would rise at its 1955 pace, particularly in an uncertain election year.

BOOM AND A CITY

What has the postwar boom done to change America's representative towns and families?
    To find out, Peter Wyden of NEWSWEEK'S Washington bureau returned to Wichita, Kans., where he lived and worked during the 1940s.
    This is his report:

One morning ten years ago, Dr. Cecil B. Read, head of the mathematics department at the University of Wichita, told his class in statistics: "Please take out all the money you have in your pockets."

As the startled students complied, Dr. Read listed each amount and demonstrated the day's lesson: How to compute averages. That year, near the climax of Wichita's big aircraft-building boom of the second world war, the average came to about $12 a student. With each new class since then, always without warning, Dr. Read repeated his maneuver. Each year the average leaped upward. Last year, according to Dr. Read, boys who had just cashed paychecks from their jobs carried wallets bulging with $400, $500, and more. The average hit $208.23. At that point Dr. Read decided that his students should no longer be compelled to disclose their affluence.

"It was getting to be embarrassing," the professor says.

The last decade has given birth to quite a few galloping statistics in Wichita. Population is up from 203,000 to 296,000 for the metropolitan area. The birth rate has doubled. So has employment. So has the number of cars. Some 30,000 new homes have made the town spill out over 44 square miles, twice its 1945 size. Deposits in savings and loan associations have increased more than fivefold—yet retail sales have tripled.

While there are still some Wichitans having trouble making ends meet, they are hard to find. The police reporter for *The Wichita Beacon* made enough money in oil to buy a Jaguar roadster for himself and a Jaguar sedan for his wife. A potato-chip manufacturer who has long piloted his own plane just bought a second one for his 17-year-old son. And the new $6.5 million court house will have seven spare, unfinished court rooms. They are not needed now, but Wichita feels sure that it will grow into them.

Last week, Ted Cash, who runs a one-man sign-painting business, surveyed his realm and arrived at a conclusion shared by some other Wichitans. Ted moved into a $32,000 ranch house with a 25- by 50-foot swimming pool not long ago. He pilots his own $5,500 plane on week-end hunting and fishing trips. Last year he took his wife on a five-week tour of Europe and North Africa.

"I don't know of anything that I really want and can't have," he said.

What are the ingredients of Wichita's sizzling postwar surge?

Once celebrated as the railhead for the Chisholm cattle trail from Texas, Wichita used to be a cow town. It still is: A million head of livestock a year stomp through its stockyards. Its location at the heart of the wheat belt (and the nation)[2] made it a farmer's town. It still is: Despite drought, 10 million bushels of wheat flowed into its towering grain elevators last year. But it was industry that made the boom.

Planes are on top:

▶ Boeing Airplane Co., idling along with just 1,402 workers a few years ago, employs 25,855 (annual payroll: $126 million) who commute up to 160 miles daily from as far away as Blackwell, Okla. Last year they turned out 300 B-47 stratojet bombers and production continues at the rate of one B-47 per workday. This week the first eight-jet Stratofortress (cost, $8 million) comes off the assembly line and production of the Bomarc guided missile is coming up. "There'll always be a big Air Force," says a Boeing executive confidently.

▶ Cessna Aircraft Co.'s sales were $7.1 million five years ago. Its working force was 807. This year, there are 4,800 employees. Sales volume will be about $50 million, almost half of it from production of 1,700 commercial aircraft and other non-military items. Output of Cessna's model 310 (retail price: $54,950) is sold out through next April and the company is working on a Model 620 ("pressurized for Mr. Businessman") to sell for about $300,000.

▶ Beech Aircraft Corp. sales are up from $19 to $77 million in ten years. The company makes Air Force and Navy trainers and pilotless target drones. Its commercial plane sales ($27 million) are up 40 per cent over last year.

Old and new companies are prospering alike. The 55-year-old Coleman Co., Inc. (stoves, lanterns, portable picnic refrigerators) has ridden with the trend to outdoor living. The Kansas Gas and Electric Co. has a new $2.7 million building. Sears, Roebuck and Co. has a new suburban store with an 800-car parking lot. Southwestern Bell Telephone Co. is starting a $3.5 million addition. Cudahy Packing Co. is expanding for $1.7 million, which includes a new sausage plant. The Union National Bank has put up a new $2.5 million office building. The Fourth National Bank is spending $4.5 million for expansion.

Then there are newcomers like super-charged, Louisiana-born O. A. Sutton, 49, who used to work on a road-paving gang and ran an ice-cream parlor. Fourteen years ago he arrived in Wichita to start a welding shop with $3,000. He hired three employees. After the war, he switched to make a new type of electric fan. The first year he had 200 employees and sales were $1.8 million. Today, the O. A. Sutton Corp.'s 2,000 workers make some $40 million worth of fans and air-conditioners. As a hobby, Al Sutton went into oil, which accounts for part of his personal worth, estimated at $30 million.

His other hobby: A $250,000 yacht.

The same sort of thing has happened to former Mayor Walt Keeler, 48. Not too long ago, Keeler worked at a filling station, drove a truck for a biscuit company and, as a cement finisher ("that's my trade") scuffed about on hands and knees repairing sidewalks. Today he has a $3 million-a-year ready-mix concrete business with 32 mixing trucks (average value, $20,000 each), four mixing plants and a fifth on the way.

The Big Ones and '56 Prospects

Here is the 1956 outlook for a few of the nations' basic industries:

	1955 results	1956 prospects
Steel	115 mil. tons	About the same
Aluminum	1.5 mil. tons	Higher
Coal	407 mil. tons	Higher
Chemicals	$23.5 bil. sales	Higher
Railroads	$10 bil. revenues	Same to higher

Scrambled Streets

Growing pains hurt: More than 275 miles of streets have been paved in a decade but 125 miles still lack hard surfaces. In new neighborhoods expensive ranch houses are sold with private water wells (it takes up to a year and a half to get city water) and the city has had to haul water to some areas in tank wagons. Delivery men live a nightmare: Hundreds of blocks are without street signs and owners of new homes who impatiently numbered their own residences have created such confusion that there are identical addresses miles apart.

The city plans to spend $105 million in the next six years on streets, sewers, and other improvements. Traffic pile-ups may ease next year with a $130 million turnpike (236 no-speed-limit miles from Kansas City to the Oklahoma state line) will take some through traffic off the streets. The city plans to replace Wichita's 65-year-old City Hall; the library where windows have been lined with book shelves; and the barn-like auditorium which the city outgrew twenty years ago. There just isn't enough money to do it all right away, even in Wichita.

The schools have tried to keep pace by rising $3 million for new buildings in the last ten years. One new high school was finished four years ago and has already been enlarged. Another is going up now. Sites for four more have been purchased, some far beyond present city limits. Ingenuity helped: There is no serious teacher shortage because Wichita recruiters travel through three states to sign up help. And while waiting for new buildings, pupils attend classes in 179 "portables"—flat-roofed, one-room

units in blue, pink, gray, and green, which cost $7,000 each and are rolled through town wherever needed.

Much of the city's social life has always taken Wichitans to their churches and the pattern remains unchanged. There are 285 churches (161 of them postwar) and almost every congregation has chipped in for more space. Ten years ago, the First Church of the Nazarene had 250 members. Today it has more than 2,000. "We had 'standing room only' for years," says the pastor, the Rev. G. A. Gough. "We've had to turn them away by the droves." Now there is an almost debt-free, 1,500-seat, $350,000 church right next to the old one (which is being used as an educational building and a nursery with cribs, phonographs, toys, and paid help who segregate their charges by three categories: "Sleepers," "Creepers," and "Leapers."

Merry Melody

Music is booming, too. Competition for vacancies in the two new 100-piece "Youth Symphony" orchestras has lured 4,000 school children into voluntary study of instruments. The 85-piece Wichita Symphony has a new conductor and just sold 4,700 season tickets. Last week, it did Debussy's "La Mer" for the first time. "Ten years ago, people here wouldn't have listened to it," says manager Alan Watrous, "and the orchestra couldn't have played it."

One of the symphony's conscientious first violinists (he practices daily from ? to 8 a.m.) is Frank M. Kessler, former president of the Chamber of Commerce. Kessler, 45, who has a penchant for cowboy string ties, ran a neighborhood lumber yard after he got out of the Navy. He lived in a $40-a-month apartment and drove an Army surplus jeep. Now he is president or an influential figure in eleven corporations, including one that built 2,000 homes and four which build and rent 600 apartments. Kessler also controls large shopping centers, "the biggest bowling alley between here and the West Coast," and about a dozen producing oil wells. What's Kessler worth? "I've never taken time to stop and figure it out," he says.

Wichita was birthplace of 267 corporations last year and the town teems with new entrepreneurs like Kessler. Gene Friedman, 33, had never written a check when he left the field artillery in 1945. He cashed $1,500 worth of war bonds and set up a scrap yard in a garage. Now he bosses a chain of seven clothing stores and a discount house (total sales: $2.2 million this year). The Frontier Chemical Co., started up in 1951, does a $6 million-a-year business and is tripling its capacity. Cornell Smith, former president of the D. A. Schulte, Inc., stores, just opened the new East Side State Bank near the edge of town. Among its features: A "Young Banker's Room" with a teller's window low enough to be reached by small fry and a playroom where a hostess baby-sits and entertains the youngest customers with balloons and comic books. More than 200 accounts were opened during the bank's first week in business.

Second Jobs

Almost everybody who works for a salary seems to be in business, too. A factory car dispatcher owns and rents a string of homes. A typewriter shop owner made a killing in suburban land. A teacher runs a wheat custom-combining outfit in summer. Three cops, during off-duty hours, run a well-guarded money transfer service for payrolls and bank deposits of businesses that didn't, until recently handle enough cash to be worth protecting. A detective makes more than his salary by selling real estate in his spare time. A police captain runs a barbershop and raises rabbits for pregnancy tests.

Despite its quickened pulse, Wichita remains remarkably serene. Wichitans know what transpires in the world beyond their horizons, but it does not worry them unduly. They remain unfailingly friendly ("you scoot right in and get out of that wind," says the airport limousine driver) and even the downtown money-makers who work the hardest—several well-known men had had heart attacks lately—do not appear hurried. There is time for coffee breaks and leisurely lunches at Innes' Team Room. At night, Wichitans cluster about their TV sets (there are 86,040 sets in the county), gripe about the take-off noises of the B-47s at nearby McConnell Air Force Base and the political noises at City Hall. They retire early, secure in the knowledge that all is reasonably well.

Managing the Boom

Besides Secretary Humphrey, there are hundreds in Washington who watch every jiggle of every statistics for possible flaws in the economy.

With the key men lies great power, and their task is delicate. Credit must be tightened when inflation threatens, and loosened again when business slows. Unemployment insurance, farm supports, and other built-in "stabilizers" must be adjusted and improved. The effects of tax policy and government spending must be carefully gauged.

Conservatives once damned nearly all government controls over business as "meddling." In recent years, these cries have noticeably subsided. One reason is that while the current Administration's policies have much in common with the "planned economy" theories of such economists as John Maynard Keynes, there is an important difference. Keynes' ideal was to preserve a static economy. But the U.S. Government regards today's economy as a growing one and bases its plans on encouraging growth while thwarting inflation.

Newsweek here examines the personalities and the economic philosophies of four key men most directly involving in the job of "managing the boom."

Burns

Job: Chairman, Council of Economic Advisors

Few men in Washington have more to do with shaping the nation's top-level economic policies than Arthur Burns, the brilliant, bushy-haired economics professor who is literally President Eisenhower's chief of staff for economic affairs.

Officially, Burns is head of the three-man Council of Economic Advisors, a Presidential advisory group which was nearly disbanded when Congress charged that under the Truman Administration it had been politicking. Since Burns took a leave of absence from Columbia University and the National Bureau of Economic Research to accept the chairmanship in 1953, he has restored the Council's reputation—and made it look like a one-man operation.

The President depends heavily on Burns' interpretations of business developments; before his heart attack, he met with Burns every Monday morning for a briefing on the status of the economy. Burns has been studying business cycles for most of his 51 years, and he is generally considered the world's leading authority on the subject.

His record of predictions belies his own claim that "I know no way to deduce the future with certainty." He accurately forecast the exact extent of the 1953–54 recession, assuring the President that a depression was unlikely but urging a reduction of taxes and an easing of credit. He forecast a rosy year for 1955, and stood his ground when a majority of private economists contradicted him at a Senate hearing on the Economic Report. He was content, he told friends, to "say nothing and see what would develop."

Burns believes that government has the responsibility to prevent depressions by "moderating" the business cycle. And he prefers to play his own part in the background, impartially gathering and analyzing information. He shuns publicity, partly because of shyness but mainly because of a kind of professional integrity. Burns has already turned down at least one White House request for a council report that might have been considered political (the White House had to put out the data it chose over a White House label).

Hague

Job: Administrative Assistant for Economic Affairs

If Arthur Burns is the President's chief economic adviser, people often ask, what does economist Gabe Hague do as "administrative assistant?"

It's a good question, because Hague, at 41, has responsibilities that might immerse a lesser man. His job, which has no counterpart in prior Administrations, is to serve as the President's link with government agencies and with Congress on economic matters. Where Burns deals with broad policy, Hague concentrates on specifics—today it may be farm problems, tomorrow consumer credit, and the next day tariffs.

But Hague in some ways is chief architect of the Administration's economy policy. It was he who got Burns his appointment; he has done more than any man to sell other members of the Eisenhower team on the "bold conservative" approach to economics.

As a professional economist and business magazine writer, Hague has a gift for pulling together complex facts and presenting them in simple, effective language. He wrote most of Eisenhower's whistle-stop speeches in 1952—on all subjects, not just economics.

Hague's meteoric rise in Washington stems mainly from his academic brilliance. Son of a Minnesota Lutheran minister (he keeps a Bible on his desktop at all times), he taught economics at Harvard and Princeton; his Harvard doctorate thesis on Federal debt management led to a job with the New York State banking department and a post in the "brain trust" of Thomas E. Dewey's 1948 campaign. He edited *Business Week's* editorial page before joining the Eisenhower team in '52.

Personally, Hague is a warm, friendly man with a quick sense of humor (despite a somewhat somber appearance), and today is one of the President's closest friends in government. On occasion, he has used his 200 pounds to advantage to play Santa Claus for Ike's grandchildren.

Burgess

Job: Under Secretary of the Treasury for Monetary Affairs

When the Treasury borrows money, the loan runs into billions. The interest rate has a powerful impact on all commercial money markets, and the economy in general.

This complicates the task of Randolph Burgess, the man in direct charge of managing the U.S. debt. He has to judge the market carefully to pay rates high enough for the Treasury to sell its bonds, notes, and other obligations yet not so high that it cost needless millions in interest. At the same time, he must weigh the effect of his borrowing on the whole business picture.

A tall, angular Rhode Islander who looks younger than his 66 years, Burgess has had exhaustive preparation for his job. After his education at Brown and McGill Universities (and a Ph.D. from Columbia), he spent eighteen years with the Federal Reserve Bank of New York, where he took charge of government securities trading. He has held down top jobs in two other banks; his 1927 book, "The Reserve Banks and the Money Markets" is probably *the* book in its field.

Burgess always had a hankering to apply his ideas in public service. When he came to Washington in 1953 as one of Secretary Humphrey's top aides, it was with the firm conviction that a balanced budget should be the first and major goal. This, of course, didn't quite jibe with the Administration's tax-cut policies. But Burgess did set out to convert the Treasury's short-term obligations into longer ones, and thus remove some of the national debt from the hands of banks where it was an inflationary force.

Since he began his "stretch-out" program, the average maturity of the national debt has risen from 3.8 to 4.3 years. Some claim that this policy, plus a stiff government bond rate, helped touch off the 1953–54 slowdown. But Burgess believes it actually helped avoid an inflationary boom-bust cycle that might have followed the '53 boom.

Burgess, a reserved but warm man, has learned much about the practicalities of politics. Washington, says he, is a place for "the wise pursuit of the 'art of the possible.'"

Martin

Job: Chairman, Board of Governors, Federal Reserve System

Businessmen who have to pay higher interest for a bank loan this week than they did the week before can thank (or blame) Bill Martin.

Martin and his six fellow governors[4] of the Federal Reserve Board have the ticklish job of regulating the U.S. money supply. Their tools: Power to control the amount of credit and reserves available to the nation's banks through the Federal Reserve system, and thus make it harder or easier for the banks to lend money profitably. Their aim: To see that the money supply is neither so large that it produces inflation nor so small that it stifles initiative.

Chairman Martin, who may be fretting about inflated stock-market credit on one day and casting a wary eye at consumer or business borrowing the next, is an outspoken foe of the theory that a little bit of inflation is a good thing. But he believes that FRB money management should work for an expanding economy and a rising standard of living.

At 48, he is one of the few top officials in golf-conscious Washington who is still spry enough for tennis. Son of a St. Louis Federal Reserve Bank president, Yale graduate Bill Martin became president of the New York Stock Exchange as a mere youth (31). After a hitch in the service (he rose from private to colonel), he worked with the Import-Export Bank and the World Bank and served as an Assistant Secretary of the Treasury; in the latter post, he helped patch up a rancorous policy dispute between the Treasury and the FRB during the Truman Administration.

Named FRB chairman by President Truman in 1951, Martin is a Democrat, but serves as a staunchly independent nonpartisan. Martin's simple, unchanging definition of the FRB job: "To worry."

On the Crest

What's it like to ride a boom?

Thousands of businessmen have watched their own fortunes rise along with the general economy in the prosperous decade just past. But nearly all would testify that it was neither a free "ride" nor a particularly effortless one. None can testify better than three pre-war college friends named David Lilly, Robert Gibson, and Whitney Miller, who got together just after their discharge from the service and tried to chart their postwar careers.

Since then they have shown how with energy, intelligence—and luck—a small business can still grow along with its markets.

The ten-year story of a company that has fed on America's big surge while helping feed it began when the three men met in Minneapolis in 1945. They already had much in common. All had been Psi U's together at Dartmouth. Lilly, a dark, serious type, had majored in economics and worked in a bank before going into the Army; Gibson, a compact man, who had been an English major and a star football center at college, had also put in a brief hitch with a bank before joining the Navy; Miller had studied geology, but had spent the five years since college as an Air Force instructor. The three were in firm agreement on one thing: They wanted to go into business for themselves.

The business they picked was the Toro Manufacturing Corp., which made tractors and "gang" grass-mowing machines used by golf courses, parks, and cemeteries. Set up in 1914, Toro had never been more than a small business; its plant and machines were worn-out from wartime production of naval ordnance parts, and the management was ready to sell.

Lilly, Gibson, and Miller pooled their savings and formed a stockholder group of friends and relatives (Lilly's father was a bank president, Gibson's father-in-law a wealthy contractor). They raised $537,000 to buy a 51 per cent interest in the company. The real future of Toro, they convinced investors, was not so much in cemeteries or golf courses as in the home lawns that would sprout as Americans populated suburbia.

Mowers by Millions

In the ten years since then, the annual sales of the power-mower industry have grown from 100,000 units to 2.5 million, principally on the strength of consumer sales sparked by the mass trek to the suburbs. In the process, Toro's own sales have risen steadily from 1.4 million to $11.5 million a year; its earnings, from $42,000 to $500,000. Its payroll has grown from 60 to 700 employees; it has 34 products against ten in 1945; the value of its stock has more than doubled.

For Toro it was not simply a matter of growing like Topsy. Of the 130-odd manufacturers who got into the power-mower field just after the war, only a few have really gotten off the ground (seven companies now do 60 per cent of the business). The rest found that problems of overhead, distribution, and changing consumer tastes could be fatal even in a boom.

Toro's postwar management came smack up against these problems in its first weeks. It found a badly disorganized plant; some Toro workers were casually assembling lawn mowers in various corners of the building, rummaging for parts as they needed them. Materials experts were called in to correct this state of affairs with flow plans, index systems, and other efficiency moves.

To help spread production more evenly over the year (mowers can be sold only in late winter and spring), Toro led the industry in producing such "off-season" items as leaf mulchers and snowplows; later, with the same object, it bought out a manufacturer of woodworking tools and plunged full tilt into the do-it-yourself power-tool business. When "rotary"-type mowers (with a single high-speed blade) started to gain ground on the standard reel type, Toro invested $400,000 to buy out the Whirlwind Corp., a specialist in rotaries. As Lilly explains: "The quickest way to get into something new is to buy a company in the field."

Plowing back 70 per cent of its profits into the business and borrowing a total of $13.5 million over the ten-year period, Toro modernized its main plant in Minneapolis, consolidated its small mower production in another plant at Windom, Minn. In suburban Bloomington, the "Toro Research and Development Center" went up in 1952 amid a patchwork of 30 different kinds of grasses (for testing mowers); the research center has already produced a major innovation in its Toro "Power Handle," which can be used to drive mowers, snowplows, or a half dozen other machines (NEWSWEEK, Aug. 1). Toro was the first company to hire a full-time stylist. Today, the leading mower firms are as chrome and color-happy as the automobile industry.

The New Markets

Where most mower makers sell to any retailers, Toro set up its own wholesale distributing organization of gardening specialists; this group passes on its knowledge of grass care and mower servicing to selected retail dealers. "A power tool is a sort of personal thing with a man," explains Gibson. "Having a well-kept lawn is an expression of financial well-being. The home owner wants expert help in that field."

Toro sales have kept climbing. They climbed even in the recession year of 1949, when the pent-up wartime demand for power mowers was finally exhausted. In the new market of the '50s, spurred by the house-building boom, Toro has gained more ground than any competitor. Last year it took the lead in the industry for the first time (with some 10 per cent of sales).

President Lilly (Miller is no longer active in management) doesn't expect any let-up in the next decade. He is already looking forward to the early 1960s, when the big crop of war babies will become lawn-mowing, woodworking homeowners. Some 60 per cent of Toro's sales in the next decade, he figures, will come from products yet to be introduced.

Money for Fun

Cicero might have been talking about today's American (though he was not) when he quoted Scipio on somebody or other: "He was never less at leisure than when at leisure."

Here is how people are spending their spare time in the U.S.—and creating a huge new leisure-time industry in the greatest prosperity the world has ever known.

Never have Americans devoted themselves to play in quite such numbers or in quite such earnest or in quite so many ways as now. The big spenders of yore may be mostly gone; but the little spenders, with bulging pocketbooks, are spending as never before.

The fun-seeking and money-spending take many forms. But whether it be whacking holes in the local golf course, or sitting slack-jawed before a color TV set, or barreling down an icy slope to possible annihilation, or bucking traffic to get out of the city (or into it), the goal is the same: To have a good time.

The most notable method of American fun-seeking, of course, is travel, which this year made the noted tourist invasion of Europe in the '20s look like a convention of living ex-Presidents. More than half a million Americans saw Europe last summer (an estimated 10 per cent increase over the year before), and found ways to spend some $400 million there. More Americans than ever (some 80 million) went out and sight-saw their own country, too[5]—and more were whipping around the countryside in road-hugging sports cars. Most of the sport-car cultists were just having fun, but many of them felt they were accomplishing more than that—they were "doing something" for the sports car in this country. The U.S. now has some 200 car clubs; the biggest of these, the Sports Car Club of America, had 3,000 members the year before last, 5,000 last year, and 7,000 last week.

And where do all these car lovers find themselves when they get there? More and more find themselves under the water (with goggles and a spear) or on top of it (there are 5,537,000 pleasure craft afloat this year—

10 per cent more than in 1953), or somewhere else in the great outdoors. There are, to take one bunch, 165,000 more golfers—for a total of 3,500,000—than there were in 1953 (counting only people who play at least ten rounds a year).

Fine Arts

For the stay-at-homes, there were more ways to spend money for relaxation than ever before. Amateur musicians are buying 20 per cent more pianos this year than last, and nobody in the industry laughs with 19 million sit down at the piano. Some 4 million others are plucking away at guitars.

Many heavy hi-fi investors, who are now as the sands of the desert, are not above classifying their preoccupations as fun. Yet, in a roomful of hi-fi buffs, it is probably best to affect a rather grave air when the discussion turns to tweeters and woofers. It is wise, too, not to make light of the amateur camera bug; after all, he is spending close to $500 million on his hobby this year. The week-end artist, or "Sunday painter," is another dedicated man. (Like the amateur in many other fields, he may spend more on the materials of his craft than the professional does. Art-supply stores have done a $230 million business this year, one third of it with amateurs, whose numbers American Artist magazine sets between 4 and 5 million.

Among the most dedicated of all are the do-it-yourself people who are, of course, engaged in something very necessary; they simply manage to have fun incidentally. No one knows just how many Americans are doing it themselves, in some form or another—but it is known that some 11 million of them are operating power tools. Their number is so great, in fact, that their collective fiddling with dangerous materials was only recently described before the American Public Health Association as "a public health problem of major importance."

Neighbors to the North: Boom of Their Own

"Boom" is not a new word to Canadians: They've been living in the middle of one, almost without interruption, since the second world war. This winter promises to be one of the most prosperous in the nation's history. And tomorrow. "The underlying trend in Canada is decidedly upward," forecasts economist Douglas Gibson of the Bank of Nova Scotia.

The boom is based solidly on the almost incredible richness of the Canadian soil, forests, and mines. Its superstructure is the industrial edifice which has been built up in the past ten years.

Before the war Canada prospered from the steady demand for Canadian oil and newsprint, iron ore and gold, base metals and farm products. Wartime demands stimulated industrial growth as well. Population and markets grew, production speeded up. By war's end Canada had come of age industrially. "In the second world war we learned to do big things in a big way," Prime Minister Louis St. Laurent said last week. Since 1939, Canada's gross national product has risen from $5.7 billion to some $26 billion.

The portents of prosperity are everywhere. The average output of the Canadian worker has just about doubled in the past ten years; wages and salaries have risen more than five times; in terms of goods and services consumed, the standard of living is twice what it was before the war. Investment, employment, labor income, imports, exports are all on the rise. Exports have increased from $3.5 billion in 1935 to $17.5 billion today.

And Canada is only starting on some new wealth-producing projects. The uranium boom has added another valuable metal to Canada's already great store. New deposits of nickel and copper, both in heavy demand, are turning up all over the country. New oil finds in Alberta add to the fabulous natural wealth of the province, and the other prairie provinces are getting in on the oil boom. Tapping the 2 billion-ton iron-ore reserves of Labrador is well under way; Canada's shipments of iron ore for the first eight months of 1955 were more than $50 million compared with $15 million for the same period of 1954. The Aluminum Co. of Canada's $300 million smelter at Kitimat, B.C., is working toward its preliminary 91,500-ton annual production goal. Work is in progress on the St. Lawrence Seaway, which will open Canada's interior to shipping from all the world's ports.

There are some soft spots in the economy. The Canadian farmer, for instance, has the same market woes as his U.S. counterpart. Canadian industrial growth is still restricted by the small domestic market (with an area larger than the U.S., Canada has about the same population as New York State).

But the Canadians are a buoyant bouncy people who are just as confident of the future as they are unconcerned with the past. They have gained a proud sense of nationality which is backed by more than statistics.

Canadians are living better today than they ever did—better than any people in the world, in fact, except their American neighbors.

The Changing Map of Enterprise

The glistening Prudential Insurance Building, newest landmark along Chicago's Lake Michigan skyline, is a 41-story symbol of the mighty boom that has changed the face of the Midwest's biggest city and redrawn the industrial topography of all America. Since 1945, the 40-mile area centered on Chicago has seen 1,133 new plants erected—300 of them within the city limits, the rest sprawling out through the suburbs into what was once prairie farm land.

The story is the same from Boston to Los Angeles, from Seattle to Atlanta. A 22-story, air-conditioned skyscraper is going up on Cleveland's Public Square, the first major office structure in the downtown area in 25 years. Along Travis Street in Houston, $60 million worth of new construction is under way. In New York City, where the hammering never stops, the old conservative apartments along Park Avenue are giving way to glass-fronted office buildings. On the site of the old Sherry's, where the Four Hundred once sipped champagne, hundreds of stenographers now drink coffee at their desks in the spanking-new Colgate building. Even the stone face of Wall Street is changing—the Chase Manhattan Bank plans to erect a Rockefeller Center style headquarters in the financial district's canyons.

All over the U.S. last week, old and new industries were jostling for room. Northwest of Chicago, the brand new Ekco-Alcoa Containers, Inc., was set to build the biggest aluminum-foil plant in the U.S. on a 24-acre tract. W. W. Kimball Co., a 98-year-old piano maker, was building a $2 million factory in another suburb, and International Harvester had already grabbed off Kimball's nearby Chicago plant. When A. B. Dick Co. moved north to Skokie two clothing firms moved into its Chicago plants.

This ceaseless drive has cost industry a staggering $233 billion in the last decade. For that money, the country got twice the manufacturing capacity it had on V-J Day, half again as much as it had when the Korean war started. Even without the spur of defense spending and fast tax write-offs, industry could not have stood still. The forces driving it were irresistible. Some, of course, were war-born: The pent-up demand built up during the years of ration stamps and manufacturing quotas; the natural growth of population; the wear and tear of the war, which made industrial re-building a life-and-death matter.

Population shifts—to new jobs, better climates, new homes—have changed the map of the U.S. The moving industry, for instance, geared for a postwar drop, instead, according to Louis Schramm, Jr., president of Allied Van Lines, long-haul movers, did 382 per cent more business last year than they did in 1945.

The New Geography

Nowhere has the new geography made itself more evident than in the South. On an average of once every working day for three years after Japan's surrender, ground was broken for a new multimillion dollar plant in Dixie. Five Southern states—Texas, Louisiana, Mississippi, Alabama, Florida—have accounted for a sixth of all postwar industrial building. Only this week, Kaiser Aluminum & Chemical Corp. announced it would break ground next spring for a $120 million aluminum-reduction plant in West Virginia and a $60 million aluminum plant in the bayou country of Louisiana, as part of its new $280 million expansion program.

The statistics on the South ring like a rebel yell. In nine years, the number of telephones in nine Southeastern cities jumped from 2.3 million to almost 5.8 million; Southern Bell alone has spent $1.5 billion for new construction since 1945, plans to spend another $250 million next year. "The end," says President Fred J. Turner, "isn't yet in sight."

The piney woods of William Faulkner's Yawknapatawpha County have proved "green gold" to Southern business—a cheap and readily available source of resin, turpentine, and cellulose. Last year more than 70 per cent of the nation's cellulose fibers—750 million pounds—came from nineteen plants in eight Southern states. Counting in Texas, the South has black gold to match the green—70 per cent of the U.S. petroleum reserves, a fifth of its coal.

Industrial relocation, of course, has been a factor in Southern industrial growth. Du Pont now has more than half its operation below the Mason and Dixon Line. General Electric has sunk about $250 million into nineteen new plants in ten Southern states. Nor is this any branch-plant operation. Board chairman Philip Reed figures that GE will double its business in the South during the next ten years. Yet, for all the talk of raiding the North, most of the South's wild growth has represented new industry; less than 1 per cent of its expansion represents industry lured from other parts of the country.

Even the hardheaded realists in the South think this is just the beginning. D. J. Haughton, who runs Lockheed's Marietta, Ga., division, sees aviation putting wings on the Dixie boom, notes the roll call of Douglas, Chance Vought, Fairchild, Martin, Bell, and Convair, "to name the largest." Robert Ingalls Jr., boss of the Ingalls iron works and shipyards, estimates that "Southern industrial expansion will triple in the next ten years as compared with the past decade."

In Atlanta, the superlatives roll in a way that would make Darryl Zanuck blink. Its seaboard rival, Savannah, has a crack that if "Atlanta could suck as hard as it could blow, it'd be a seaport." Actually, Atlanta businessmen talk confidently of a canal and disagree only on what route it should take to the sea.

From Denver to the West Coast, similar dreams are turning into plans, and the plans are become realities. Houston, Texas, has more than doubled since 1945—from 73 to 164 square miles—and people keep growing out into its suburbs. ("Growing, growing, growing, that's Houston," is the way its leading citizen, Jesse Jones, puts it.)

California's sun-kissed prosperity is already a cliché. Los Angeles, with 166 miles of superhighway already packed with traffic, has plans to stretch the network to 535 miles. In the twelve counties around San Francisco Bay, $1.5 billion has been spent since 1945 on new plants and to expand old ones. Yet president T. S. Petersen of Standard Oil of California (whose firm has pumped about $350 million into postwar expansion). "It is almost axiomatic that we will have to expand again and again."

In wintry New England, over which the doomsayers have been clucking for years, Boston alone had $130 million worth of new plants and shopping centers, in a great arc along the new highway that swings around the city from Gloucester to Dedham.

The Industrial Map

All across the nation, raw materials—and the routes to them—have had powerful effects on industrial geography. The iron strikes in Labrador and the final realization of the St. Lawrence Seaway dream gave new impetus to Midwestern steelmakers. Inland Steel, which has already spent $282 million to boost its capacity from 3.4 million tons to more than 5 million, last month announced plans to push it still further, to 5 million tons, at a cost of another $260 million.

Like the steelmakers, the electric-power producers have also been turning themselves inside out to keep up with demand. Ohio Edison has spent better than $300 million since 1945 to more than double its capacity. Cleveland Electric Illuminating has laid out $272 million to build up its facilities along the Lake Erie shore. Even at that, a CEI official says, it can't replace obsolete plant and equipment "because today's high production demands necessitate the use of virtually all operable facilities."

While even outdated machinery can't be decently retired, the utilities have been ticketing fresh money for the newest source of power—the atom. Chicago's Commonwealth Edison is breaking ground for a 180,000 kilowatt nuclear plant. Up the Hudson from New York City, Consolidated Edison has blueprinted a $55 million, 236,000-kilowatt atomic station.

While the atom and the electron are the tools of tomorrow, it has been the old, basic industries that have carried the burden of the biggest spending. Steel men have spent nearly $7 billion since the war to increase capacity to 125.8 million tons a year and customers are waiting in line. The railroads have rebuilt themselves from the roadbed up, to the tune of over $10 billion. And prophets like William T. Faricy, president of the Association of American Railroads, say they will have to spend $6 billion in the next five years.

Even the automakers, to whom manufacturing miracles are routine, are hard-pressed to keep rolling. New models have to come off the line bumper to bumper with last year's—and the retooling has to be sandwiched in. As one General Motors plant manager put it: "We maintain production—we have to. But sometimes we get our legs pretty badly crossed."

Probably the only answer to these harassed industrialists will be faster footwork. For while the production line chiefs are battling to keep next year's models from emerging with last year's grilles, their bosses—in any industry you can name—are being forced to think years ahead. By 1960, jet transports—$625 million worth are already on order for U.S. airlines—will have changed the nation's geography in another way, but pulling its ocean coasts three hours closer to each other. The St. Lawrence Seaway will have opened a fourth coast.

In short, as the classic vaudeville gag goes: "This will be a hell of a country if they ever get it finished."

Machines at Work

In Corning Glass plants scattered from England to Kentucky, there stand fourteen giant glass-blowing machines. While there are only fourteen of them, and each is operated by but a single worker, the machines, in effect, form an entire industry. From them each year flow 90 per cent of the glass light bulbs used in the U.S., plus all the glass tubes used in the nation's radio and TV sets (picture tubes excepted). Out of every ten bulbs that sparkle in the galaxies of Christmas lights going up this week from New York's Fifth Avenue to Wilshire Boulevard in Los Angeles, Corning's handful of behemoths produced nine.

Corning's glass-blowing monsters, while dramatic, are just one example of a trend that has caused the old argument over man vs. machine to rage even louder than ever before. For under the spur of boom times, the business of multiplying the power of the human hand—and now of the brain—has speeded up to unbelievable rates. Pontiac now has a no-hands production one that grids out 2,000 pistons an hour. Chicago's Commonwealth Edison has started billing its 1.8 million customers with an electronic computing system manned by 270 people, that does in two days what a few months ago took nearly 500 clerks a full week. Only last week, the New Haven Railroad demonstrated a self-propelled, crewless passenger car, stopped, started, and slowed by remote control.

The whir of all this amazing new gadgetry has been drowned out by the hubbub of the debate over "automation." Will electronic brains and inhumanly efficient robot factories throw men into the streets? Some labor leaders fear they will. Or will this "second industrial revolution," as its proponents insist, mean more jobs, more leisure, and a higher standard of living?

The Optimists' Case

So far, the arguments for optimism look potent. For one thing, skilled labor is at a premium—and many industrialists can see no chance of a surplus of labor for years to come. During the next ten years, said General Electric president Ralph Cordiner recently, industry will have to meet demand for at least 50 per cent more goods and services—while manpower will increase by only 14 per cent. "Faster progress in the newer field of automation," Cordiner added, "seems to us to be the only available solution."

The big fear is that the robots will come too fast. Labor leader Walter Reuther thinks that without careful planning and readjustment—in the form of shorter hours, higher wages, and lower prices—the new revolution will turn the boom into a "catastrophic" bust. Secretary of Labor James P. Mitchell is also on record as expecting "considerable displacement of workers due to technological advances" in the next ten years.

The displacement has, of course, already started but so far without disaster. The Ford Motor Co., with its automatic engine-making machines, had 1,800 fewer men working directly on engines last year than it did in 1950. But according to vice president D. J. Davis, all of the 1,800 were absorbed in other operations. The long-haul figures are encouraging, too. Henry Ford's Model T wiped out 800 buggy and carriage shops—but the Ford payroll alone is now more than twice as big as that of the vanished industry. Sixteen years ago, when du Pont brought out nylon—which, like most chemical products, is readymade for automatic processing—the silk-stocking weavers went to the wall. But du Pont not only added 13,000 workers for nylon production, it opened up more than 100,000 jobs for nylon fabricators.

The odds, however, are against any headlong rush toward an all-automatic America. Almost half of today's machine tools are no more than ten years old. Few of these are robot-run, yet they are a long way from the scrap heap.

Another factor is that the new machines are not cheap. The Chesapeake and Ohio Railroad, for example, will spend $30,000 a month to rent one of Sperry Rand's Univac computers to handle its paper work. The petroleum industry, which has been using automatic controls for 30 years, now sinks an estimated 15 per cent of its capital investment in oil processing each year into the myriad dials, gauges, and instrument panels that run its refineries.

The days of open warfare by labor against new production methods have vanished, although, as Reuther made clear, labor will insist on sharing in the benefits. And benefits there are sure to be, as evidenced by what has happened in the glass industry, for example. At the end of the first world war, U.S. glass producers paid $101 million to fewer than 84,000 workers. By now—despite machines like Corning's bulb-producing giants—there are 127,000 glass workers, with earnings many times greater.

Multiplying Muscle

The marriage of two of the country's top shoe firms was halted, practically at the altar, by the U.S. Justice Department last week. A Federal judge in St. Louis issued orders temporarily stopping the planned merger of the Brown Shoe Co. and the G. R. Kinney Co.

This court action mirrored Washington's concern over the wave of mergers that has followed in the wake of the postwar boom. (This year the Federal Trade Commission expects more than 500 such "acquisitions and mergers"—a 25-year high.) These industrial combinations, in turn, reflect primarily a huge diversification effort to keep growing, to bring out new products, to level off seasonal production and sales curves—and, always, to make more money.

Practically every company that diversifies does it to get bigger. After a point, the big company can then diversify within itself. Thus General Electric, originally a combine of several small firms, now grows on new products like jet engines and chemicals. General Motors, originally an amalgam of a few auto firms, has branched out into lines like refrigerators and Diesel locomotives.

Eight years ago, John Jay Hopkins, boss of General Dynamics, started to build up Electric Boat, the submarine builder. Hopkins decided to diversify, but to stay primarily in the weapons business. After three mergers, his company now makes atomic subs, jet planes, radio and TV sets, guided missiles—and volume has soared from $45 million in 1945 to $649 million last year.

Merging for Money

Sometimes, a company tires of riding the roller coaster with a seasonal product. McGraw Edison was doing a $21 million business in 1948 with its Toastmaster line, when it branched out into heavy electrical equipment. McGraw's volume now is around $140 million and about a third is in home appliances.

General Tire & Rubber quite frankly diversified to improve volume and profits. General got into chemicals through its wartime work with synthetic rubber. Plastics was a logical next step. Along the way, president William O'Neil bought five TV stations, the nation's biggest radio network (Mutual), and the RKO studio (complete with 800 vintage films that will bring in TV rentals for years). This year, General expects its profits to hit $13.5 million, up 129 per cent from 1954.

Kingpin among the merge-for-money stylists is probably Royal Little of Textron American. Little spent more than a year wrestling an unwilling American Woolen Co. into a merger, though he called the company a "Godawful mess." It did put more working capital into Little's hands, however. Now, armed with a tax-loss credit of $38 million, Little expects Textron's volume to hit $200 million next year—and net better than $20 million vs. $8 million in 1955.

The chances are that the diversification-by-merger will go on as the economy keeps expanding. Pittsburgh's W. F. Rockwell Jr., whose Rockwell Manufacturing Co. (meters, conduits, and hundreds of related items) has acquired fifteen firms since 1940 (and stepped up sales from $9.3 million to $76 million in the process), puts it this way: "It is our belief that a company tied to one industry or operating in one plant is too vulnerable to too many factors."

Riches of Curiosity

"You get into research," said a Texas industrial chemist last week, "or you get out of business."

So many businessmen have recently had the same thought—with reason—that scientific research has sprouted from an academic midget to a perplexing industrial colossus in less than a generation. This year, the incredible giant contributes some $65 billion to the nation's total output of goods and services. It inundates the American consumer with a rising flood of new products and services, creates whole new industries and job opportunities. In the span of one fantastic decade, research has opened up the Atomic Age, and made jet travel an imminent reality. The field is so broad, and the momentum so swift, that the products of research would continue to pour forth from industry for another decade even if every laboratory were shut down tomorrow.

Thanks to science, Americans are clothed and defended, fed and air-conditioned, propelled and medicated by things that simply did not exist a generation ago. Nine out of ten prescriptions filled in today's drugstore were unheard of in 1940; four out of five present-day farm chemicals were unknown in 1945. Passenger aircraft routinely carry six times the weight at twice the speed over double the range of fifteen years ago. Television, a true creature of research, has become as commonplace as a doormat. Those remarkable research chemists, whose recent efforts now account for some 500 new products a year, have made the auto blowout a subject for nostalgic conversation, have rivaled the sheep, the cotton plant, the silkworm, and perhaps even the mink at their own game.

Most significantly, researchers have made it possible for almost every product, from hatpins to locomotives, to be produced with an efficiency quite inconceivable a decade or two ago.

Behind the dazzling parade of new things and new processes is a zooming expenditure for research and development unique in all history. In the past seven years alone, the U.S. has spent as much on its laboratories and their denizens as it did between 1776 and 1948. What is more, since 1920 the rate of research expenditure has gone up much faster (10 per cent a year) than the national output (3 per cent a year).

At the moment, the total tab for research and development is probably about $5 billion annually. Of this the government puts up $2.2 billion, almost all of it for the development of weapons. Industry finances most of the rest, with a relatively minor assist (not more than $200 million) coming from universities, state governments, and foundations.[6]

Although an estimated 15,000 companies have some sort of R&D activity, nearly 70 per cent of the job is handled by 375 large concerns. The two giants of industrial research are the aircraft and electrical-electronics industries. Together they spend approximately $1.5 billion of the research pie (and also get the heftiest government support). Among the other major research spenders: The chemical, nonelectrical machinery, instrument, and petroleum industries.

The result of all this bustling activity is that the U.S. now produces at least half of the world's goods with only 7 per cent of the world's population. But is the U.S. doing enough of the right kind of research? Many experts think not.

For all its apparent health and vigor, U.S. research has two festering sore spots. The first concerns the tenor of research. More and more, some top scientists warn, technology is eating up fundamental scientific concepts far more rapidly than it is growing them. Radar, jet planes, synthetics, and atomic power represent the exploitation of scientific discoveries made twenty, 30, even 50 years ago.

Brains Wanted

Most industrial research is, understandably, inspired by the desire to meet current competition or make an actual profit within the lifetime of the average stockholder. Inevitably, many projects get nudged toward the gadget or gimmick area, tying up top scientific talent that ought to be working far into the future. The sad fact is that industrial laboratories on the average devote a mere 4 per cent of their funds to "pure" research. Government "pure" allocations have risen to about 8 per cent. But the experts guess that no ratio under 10 per cent, as a general rule, will insure a healthy stream of new concepts into the technological river.

The other sore spot is even more distressing. Put simply, it is that the Russians are building an even faster technological escalator. Without regard for the ground rules of education in a few society, they are grinding out scientists, engineers, skilled technicians, and, last, but not least, science teachers, on an academic assembly line. This cadre not only swells in quantity (682,000 professional engineers graduated since 1928 vs. 480,000 in this country), but its technical proficiency keeps winning more respect in U.S. scientific and military circles. The new generation of Russian scientists has shown brisk competence in developing nuclear weapons and jet aircraft. It is currently demonstrating great strength in the arsenal of economic warfare as well—the design of nuclear power plants, for example, and the training of agricultural scientists at double the U.S. rate.

In the U.S., meanwhile, the pinch on personnel for industrial research and for running the machines thus created fills more columns of help-wanted ads by the month. Laboratory recruiters now resort to radio spots and even lure students in British universities, offering, among other things, a free round trip to look over the prospective employer.

The full U.S. answer to the Russian technological spurt has yet to be spelled out by the educators, industrialists, scientists, and government administrators now wrestling with the problem. Rear Adm. H. G. Rickover, chief of the Navy's nuclear-reactor program, is a man who is fully aware that the atomic age is no cinch. "We are faced," he said, "with a fateful challenge."

OUR RUDDY HEALTH

Thousands of American citizens who would hardly have had a prayer of surviving a mere ten years ago are alive and well today.

That simple fact tells the wondrous story of how medical progress has helped shape a new America since the second world war. During four wartime years, American medicine advanced 25 years. More startling still, in the postwar decade of great prosperity, medical research has brought about the greatest progress in health ever encompassed into such a span of time.

The result is that most of the onetime killers have been robbed of their terror. Any hour, any day, a new solution may be found for a problem that has baffled centuries of scientists. It is literally true as a famous medical man said last week, that "the longer you live, the better your chance to live longer." A child born in the U.S. today will live twenty years longer than he would have at the turn of the century. Infant mortality in the first year, for example, has been reduced to less than one quarter of its rate in 1900, and maternal mortality to an even smaller fraction. Life expectancy of 68.9 years in the U.S. outranks most other large nations in the world.

The most spectacular medical advance of recent years, of course, has been the developing victory over paralytic poliomyelitis with the Salk vaccine. But that is only one of medicine's recent happy-ending stories. Some of the others:

▶ Typhoid fever, scarlet fever, whooping cough, diphtheria, smallpox, measles, and malaria have been virtually eliminated as causes of death.
▶ Diabetes can be controlled with insulin; tuberculosis with streptomycin and isoniazid; ACTH, cortisone, and Meticorten relieve acute rheumatoid arthritis.
▶ A whole new vocabulary of antibiotic drugs, ranging from penicillin to the tetracycline group, and representing a $1 billion industry, are hard at work fighting scores of diseases; scientists are even on the threshold of practical immunization against the common cold.
▶ The new tranquilizing drugs, notably Thorazine and Serpasil, soothe disturbed mental patients so that they can accept and profit by practical psychotherapy.
▶ Large quantities of radioactive isotopes are working for peacetime medicine, both as tracers and as treatments, and have already lengthened and saved countless American lives.

"The greatest single medical development in the U.S. since the second world war is the use of antibiotics, as preventive as well as cures," Surgeon General Leonard A. Scheele of the U.S. Public Health Service said last week. And the widespread use of "wonder drugs" has been made possible by cost cutting such as has seldom been seen in any industry. As late as 1943, 100,000 units of penicillin cost $20 wholesale, and the entire world population was sufficient to treat only 400 patients. Today, with production on a mass basis, 100,000 units of penicillin cost less than 1 cent wholesale, and there is enough for every sick person in the world.

Despite such high strides, however, and the big killers—cardiovascular diseases and cancer—have not yet been conquered. Because Americans are living longer, they are more vulnerable to these degenerative diseases, which now account for almost 70 per cent of all deaths, as compared with only 41 per cent twenty years ago. As things stand now, surgery, radiation, chemotherapy, and X-ray therapy still are the only scientifically approved treatments for cancer. But surgical techniques have advanced tremendously in the last ten years: Patients once sent home to die as "inoperable" are now few in numbers, and surgical fatalities have been reduced to a minimum. With prompt treatment and cooperation, victims of heart disease and high blood pressure now have every chance for a long and useful life.

Peak prosperity has brought more and better hospitals and doctors than ever before—yet still there are shortages.

The 1945 total of 6,125 approved hospitals has risen in 1955 to 6,970 for a net gain of 141,183 beds. The ten-year cost of hospital construction: $6.1 billion. But in spite of these gains, says Dr. John W. Cronin of the Department of Health, Education, and Welfare, "we are barely keeping up with the need."

In 1945, there were 191,689 doctors in the United States; today, there are 221,779, or a ratio of one doctor for 730 people. With current medical-school enrollments rising, an improvement is expected in the next few years. In 1955, 6,977 doctors were graduated from 75 approved four-year medical schools.[7] By 1960, seven new, approved four-year schools will be turning out doctors at the universities of Miami, Mississippi, Missouri, West Virginia, and Florida, the Albert Einstein College of Medicine of Yeshiva University, and the Seton Hall College of Medicine and Dentistry.

Insurance

While doctors and nurses are nonetheless still in short supply, the voluntary prepaid medical- and hospital-care programs have played a significant role in preserving American health. More than 100 million people have some sort of health-insurance coverage, and the pioneer Blue Cross and the Blue Shield organizations have signed up almost one third of the nation's population.

For all the progress, big medical problems still remain. Significantly, one of the biggest is a direct result of prosperity. Some 40 million Americans, says Dr. Horace L. Sipple of the Nutrition Foundation, Inc., are "heavier than they should be," and the entire population is 11 per cent heavier than "normal" weight.

"If we continue our present rate of obesity, we cannot avoid the definite health hazards of overweight," said Dr. James M. Hundley of the National Institutes of Health. These include not one, but a combination of serious chronic diseases—diabetes, heart and high blood-pressure ailments, arthritis, and gallbladder infections. The over-all mortality rates for "markedly overweight" people jump by 79 per cent for men and 61 per cent for women.

The paradox of 155, in short, is that many Americans may be digging their graves with their teeth. For all its medical advances, the new America is so prosperous that it is eating too high on the hog for its own health.

THE IMPACT ABROAD

Europeans have had cause to keep an anxious eye on business portents in the United States. In the depression of the late 1920s and 1930s, two thirds of the world's entire trade was wiped out. The U.S. retreated into isolationism, Europe into jittery nationalism.

The second world war shattered what patterns of trade survived. In July 1947, a committee of European economic advisors warned: "If nothing is done, a catastrophe will develop . . ." In 1948, the United States launched its now historic Marshall plan. Total U.S. Government foreign aid since the war, both economic and military: $51.3 billion. Private investments: More than $10 billion.

As this unprecedented transfusion of dollars poured new life into the free world's economy, a total of 28,000 technicians and students streamed to the U.S. from almost all corners of the earth. The gospel they took home was that of mass production and high individual productivity. U.S. techniques were applied to mining and railroads, milk separation, packaging, and sales, to laundromats and the grocery retail business, to poultry farming and seed testing.

From Casablanca to Tokyo, the bustling American way of life wrought other startling changes. Young Japanese women swapped kimonos for sweaters and skirts, now walk arm-in-arm with their boyfriends instead of the traditional three paces behind. In the villages and deserts of the Middle East, Arab chiefs now greet visitors with trays of Cokes served from American-made refrigerators installed proudly in the dining room. Some tribal princes sport palaces replete with neon lights, air conditioning, elevators, and juke boxes.

Astounding Recovery

In the immediate postwar years, Europeans spoke hopefully of struggling back to prewar economic levels. What has happened has astounded the most optimistic.

West Europe's industrial output today is 70 per cent greater than before the war, outstripping even the U.S. rate of climb (one third since 1948). Production of steel since 1948 has doubled, that of cement has nearly tripled. Electric power output is up by 90 per cent; agricultural products by 25 per cent.

U.S. aid gave tremendous impetus to free world trade and released new productive resources not only in Europe but in Asia and Africa. The so-called dollar gap—the nondollar world's unfavorable trade balance, which had reached a calamitous $9 billion in 1947—has all but disappeared.

But figures tell only half the story. Most important of all, the Marshall plan and its successors, in the words of Britain's economist, Barbara Ward, "made good [America's] . . . claim to world leadership and hence held together the unity of free men." Capitalism American style, had indeed redeemed itself.

Europeans generally never had it better. Wages—and purchasing power—were the highest ever, jobs were plentiful, and modern conveniences (including cars and TV sets) were more readily purchasable than ever before. Some of the boom's high spots:

▶ **Britain:** People are finally eating well, concentrating especially on the once-rationed butter, eggs, and meat. They are turning out three times as many cars as they were before the second world war—an estimated 1,250,000 this year. One household in every four boasts a television set.

▶ **West Germany:** The country's industrial production has hit an astonishing rate that is nearly twice that of prewar. Steel output this year—an expected 21 million tons—will top Britain's. West German industrialists have invested $166.5 million in Asia, the Middle East, Africa, and Latin America—chiefly in steel mills, coal and ore mines, chemical plants, and auto-assembly works.

▶ **France:** The average Frenchman's income is up $1 a day since 1952. The birth rate is now on the increase, for the first time since the war. Building activity has climbed to 61 per cent over prewar. Steel production has hit a record 14 million tons.

▶ **Italy:** Rice, sulphur, and perhaps wheat will be stockpiled from surplus production for the first time in Italy's history. Italian shipbuilders have a three-year backlog of orders. There are now 1.5 million motor-scooters on the road compared with only 80,000 in 1948.

Elsewhere, Denmark's cement production has doubled and electricity output tripled since the war. Swedish steel output has doubled, and Premier Tage Erlander says that Sweden's uranium reserves will be sufficient for domestic needs for "several thousand years." Norway is producing twice as much aluminum as it did before the war; its merchant fleet is now the third largest in the world.

In the Middle East, Western investment in the oil industry has risen from $1 billion in 1945 to $2.2 billion in 1954. Oil reserves have grown 240 per cent. Revenues to local governments will total $1.4 billion yearly by 1960.

Even Africa has felt boom tremors. In the past four years, exports have climbed from $3.2 billion to $4.6 billion; agricultural output is up 10 per cent, electric energy 30 per cent.

In Japan, where the economy has been largely dependent on U.S. aid plus the presence of free-spending American troops, there are signs of big new markets on the domestic front as well. Sales of washing machines have increased from 364 in 1949 to an expected 400,000 this year. There are more than 100,000 registered TV sets, and six new theaters are being built in Tokyo.

As the free world's economy has gained ground, so have the inevitable pressures of inflation. Many thousands of workers in many countries have gone on buying sprees, eating into vital dollar-earning exports. As the demand for goods has soared, so have prices—faster in many cases than production. Thus far, ten Western countries have adopted anti-inflation measures.

Another problem is being posed by the gradual reduction of U.S. economic aid, which has tapered from a high of $6.4 billion in 1949 to $1.6 billion. However, counting in direct U.S. military aid plus the spending of 300,000 U.S. troops and 750,000 American tourists, Europe's economy still benefits by some $3.2 billion a year.

With Europe now booming, J. H. Hollister, head of the International Cooperation Administration (ICA), sees "very little need" for further U.S. economic aid there. America's attention now will center on the Middle East and Asia Communist Russia and its satellites, who claim their basic industrial outputs have doubled since the war, are currently pressing an economic war to win Egypt, India, and other neutral nations to the Red orbit. In point of fact, the Reds are so far waging a war primarily of promises. Concrete Communist-bloc aid to the underdeveloped areas this year has come to no more than $127 million, plus some $80 million worth of arms to Egypt.

The Wife Market

Inflation has crept into the jungles of black Africa.

Time was when tribesmen of British Nigeria could buy a bride for $14 to $28. Back in Biblical times, it took only a week's work or a few old goats. Now, bridegrooms have to fork out $280 in pound sterling as dowries to their fathers-in-law. And that's for uneducated wives. Certified teachers, mid-wives, and nurses bring as much as $840.

Nigerian authorities and local chiefs are pondering possible price controls. But, comments the solemn Manchester Guardian: "British experience [in commodities other than brides] throws some doubt on the effectiveness of price controls as a counter to inflation. . . ."

QUESTION: BUT IS IT CULTURE?

If culture were merely something that could be weighed, measured, or counted, there is enough evidence around to prove that the United States is now enjoying a vigorous renaissance. Optimists point to the rosy statistics: The increase in book sales, the attendance at art museums, even the number of musical instruments which are scraped, tootled, and banged by millions around the country.

On the other hand, pessimists still decry the present state of American culture and see no good omen for the future. They deplore the level of popular taste; they are saddened by the absence of new ideas in arts and letters.

There is much to be said on both sides, because of the dual nature of culture itself. It refers to both appreciation and creation, quantity as well as quality.

U.S. book publishers, for example, are having one of their best years; in October, more books were published than in any other October in the history of the nation. Yet a recent study showed that the yearly average per capita expenditure for books in a number of representative cities was a dismal $2. Despite the awesome figure of some 10,000 new titles published last year, many books go unread, except by the author and a few loyal friends. Were it not for the secondary rights—the reprints, movie sales, condensations, and book clubs—most publishers would probably go out of business.

New Look: If books have never been held in high esteem in this country, painting and sculpture have fared even worse. Only recently have things begun to change on a nationwide scale. In the '30s, the great collections built up by the giants of industry returned, by a quirk of history and taxes, to the public domain. They needed museums to house them and the art museum had become a center of artistic activity throughout the country. Almost 3 million visited New York's Metropolitan last year.

Obviously, a great many people drop into the art museum for social or other reasons which have little to do with art. The fact that they come is hopeful. But the habit of spending money for a painting is still so rare that there is no more than a handful of good and serious artists who live from their work alone.

On the brighter side, there is no question that American taste has shown remarkable improvement. Architecture has been transformed by the work of a few experimenters, and even the simplest kitchen objects now often please the eye instead of offending it.

The hi-fi vogue, and soaring sales of classical records are signs of an improving musical taste. The nation supports more than 1,000 symphony orchestras, several of them the equal of any in the world. But while these orchestras flourish, both opera and the solo performer languish. And the composer is apt to spend a couple of thousand dollars in time and material for a negligible return.

The prosperity of the theater these days is even more ambiguous. Since production costs are so high, every show must be a hit to stay on Broadway. This discourages a gamble on new talent, as well as on the play which may be something more than an evening's amusement. Luckily the off-Broadway and community theaters are flourishing as places for the unusual. It is in these and in the far-flung artistic activities in every part of this country that one can see how wrong Oscar Wilde was when he quipped: "The discovery of America was the beginning of the death of art."

The Periscope

BUSINESS TRENDS

The Next Ten Years
Can the economy keep growing as fast or faster than it has in the last decade? Where will we be in 1966?

The U.S. boom has already proved that business forecasting is a risky business by outstripping the most optimistic predictions of a decade ago. It's still doing it. Just a year ago, for example, the Committee on the Economic Report estimated that residential (nonfarm) construction would top the $16 billion level by 1965. It has already passed that mark this year.

Here, in any case, is what businessmen, economists, and government experts now predict for 1966—barring only wars and other catastrophes or a '56 boom that might call for a whole new set of ten-year forecasts.

The nation's total output of goods and services should reach $600 billion, against $387 billion this year (a bigger jump than that of the last ten years, although smaller in percentage).

Most of this increase should be real, productive gain, not just the result of inflation. The population will top 190 million, and there will be some 56 million families.

Bigger Industry
The great industrial developments of the next decade will be the growing use of atomic energy and automatic processes—and expansion.

Industry should be spending $90 billion a year on plants, equipment, and inventories by 1966 (compared to some $60 billion forecast for next year).

Businessmen should be able to afford it. Corporate profits should rise from $44 billion to $65 billion, with a smaller tax bite. Workers' output per man hour will be much higher, and the average work week will be much higher, and the average work week will probably be down to 36 hours. There should be at least 75 million jobs for a total work force of 80 million, although shortages of key scientific personnel and young executives will continue to be acute, particularly in electronics and the newer industries.

For all the business expansion, the huge needs of the population will almost certainly exceed the ability of industry to meet them. Yet businessmen in 1966 will likely be spending some $6 billion or more a year on research and development of new products (against about $3 billion now) to stimulate still more demand.

Better Consumers
By 1966, if the economy follows this pattern, the American consumer will be accustomed to "luxury" living (by today's standards). He will spend far more on personal services, recreation, labor-saving gadgets, gadget repairs, and medical and dental care (whether he's healthier or not). The average house will be considerably larger and two-car families will be commonplace.

Total consumer spending should jump $100 billion or so to more than $360 billion a year—more than the gross national product of 1964. The average family will probably have $3,000 to $3,500 more real buying power, and the head of the family will have more time to enjoy it. The average man on salary will spend 200 fewer hours—25 hours—in the office each year.

Lower Taxes

The U.S. Government will spend more money, but take relatively less out of the economy. Federal taxes should be 15 to 20% lower.

Tax cuts by state and local governments are less likely. They will have to spend some $200 billion in the next ten years for badly needed schools, highways, and other public works.

Parts of the Sum

Here is the 1966 outlook, as of now, in a few vital branches of the economy:

Steel: The industry will have boosted capacity by nearly 40 million tons, the equivalent of adding one giant new steel mill each year.

Electric Power: Annual consumption will have more than doubled, from 476 billion kilowatt hours to well over 1 trillion.

Housing: At least 1.5 million new homes will be built (vs. 1.2 million this year).

Automobiles: At least 10 million cars will be sold each year.

This Week's Newsmaker

MR. NATIONAL ECONOMY

In Washington next month, President Eisenhower will deliver two messages to Congress—a State of the Union address describing the U.S. economy at its all-time high-water mark, and a Budget Report announcing the first balanced Federal budget since the Administration took office. One man—George Magoffin Humphrey—can take more than a small share of the credit on both these cheerful counts.

As Secretary of the Treasury, George Humphrey's part in any government project is to ask: "What's it cost?" He has been a hard man with a dollar where the dollar belonged to Uncle Sam. When a Treasury aide left recently for a series of money discussions in South America with a parting "hasta la vista," Humphrey grumbled good-naturedly: "You better not forget how to say 'no' in English."

But the Secretary is no mere gainsayer of others' billion-dollar plans, nor a man who thinks only in terms of budgets. He has a keen and informed interest in all government programs and their objectives; he is an astute politician who is fully aware that basic policies (including his own) must sometimes be tailored to fit emergency situations. Next to the President, he is probably the most influential man in the Administration, and on financial matters he is virtually Ike's alter ego.

Prototype: Humphrey is the type of man people just naturally listen to. Relaxed, warmly genial, with an air of competence, Humphrey at 65 is the prototype of a businessman's businessman. Raised in Cheboygan, Mich., he studied engineering and law in college, was general counsel for the M.A. Hanna Co. at 28 and president at 39. Under his daring management, the Hanna industrial complex rose from a $2 million deficit in 1925 to a $23 million profit in 1952.

Since he resigned from Hanna to join the Cabinet in 1953, Humphrey has stuck by the conservative business principles which first brought him to the President's attention. He believes that the economy is on a sound footing today mainly because the Administration has had the courage to halt inflation.

Humphrey's own contributions to helping to "manage" the economic boom are most directly concerned with Federal spending and taxes. Riding herd on expenditures, he has guided the nation from a $10 billion deficit in 1952 to an almost certain surplus in 1956—and at the same time put through the biggest tax cuts in U.S. history.

Without the tax cuts, of course, the budget might have been balanced sooner; Humphrey would not have been forced to ask for (and get) an increase in the national debt limit, as he did last year. He has been roundly criticized by some conservatives for what appeared to be tolerance of "deficit financing."

But where other Administrations tried to oil the wheels of the economy by spending more money Humphrey's "deficit financing" reversed the process. He collected less, believing tax cuts would encourage private (as opposed to government) spending and investment.

"Investment creates jobs" the Secretary is fond of saying. The fact is, his tax-relief policies have been one of the biggest factors in boosting production, raising wages, and generally fueling the boom.

He is what one government official terms a "hard-boiled optimist." Sitting in shirt sleeves in his high-ceilinged office, he exudes an unbounded confidence in the future of the economy which is the more impressive because he is a realist talking from experience. "The best that government can do to strengthen our economy," says Humphrey, "is to provide a fertile field in which millions of Americans can work."

NOTES

[1] Which seemed unlikely. World diamond sales this year promise to top the 1952 record of $195 million.

[2] The geographical center of the U.S. is at Lebanon near Smith Center, Kans., 232 miles north and slightly west of Wichita.

[3] Other members of the council: Joseph S. Davis and Raymond J. Saulnier.

[4] C. Canby Balderston, Abbot L. Mills Jr., James L. Robertson, Charles N. Shepardson, Menc S. Szymezac and James K. Vardaman Jr.

[5] A change in the travelers' roadside tastes is reflected in a recent trade show, where the machines for making pizza pies for the drive-in trade considerably outnumbered the wienie heaters on display.

[6] Actually the 160,000 research men employed by industry perform nearly three fourths of all U.S. research and development, since more than half of government R&D funds are spent under contract with industrial labs.

[7] Last week, the Commonwealth Fund, which supports various health and medical education projects, granted $7.1 million to ten university medical schools. The ten: Harvard, Western Reserve, Columbia, Cornell, New York University, Tulane, Yale, Emory, Chicago, and Southern California.

152. WILLIAM H. WHYTE, JR., *The Organization Man:* "A Generation of Bureaucrats," 1956

No sooner had the prosperity of the fifties begun than critics began to worry about its negative effects. William Whyte offered one of the most influential critiques in his book, The Organization Man.

When I was a college senior in 1939, we used to sing a plaintive song about going out into the "cold, cold world." It wasn't really so very cold then, but we did enjoy meditating on the fraughtness of it all. It was a big break we were facing, we told ourselves, and those of us who were going to try our luck in the commercial world would be patronizing toward those who were going on to graduate work or academic life. We were taking the leap.

Seniors still sing the song, but somehow the old note of portent is gone. There is no leap left to take. The union between the world of organization and the college has been so cemented that today's seniors can see a continuity between the college and the life thereafter that we never did. Come graduation, they do not go outside to a hostile world; they transfer.

For the senior who is headed for the corporation it is almost as if it were part of one master scheme. The locale shifts; the training continues, for at the same time that the colleges have been changing their curriculum to suit the corporation, the corporation has responded by setting up its own campuses and classrooms. By now the two have been so well molded that it's difficult to tell where one leaves off and the other begins.

The descent, every spring, of the corporations' recruiters has now become a built-in feature of campus life. If the college is large and its placement director efficient, the processing operation is visibly impressive. I have never been able to erase from my mind the memory of an ordinary day at Purdue's placement center. It is probably the largest and most efficient placement operation in the country, yet, much as in a well-run group clinic, there seemed hardly any activity. In the main room some students were quietly studying company literature arranged on the tables for them; others were checking the interview timetables to find what recruiter they would see and to which cubicle he was assigned; at the central filing desk college employees were sorting the hundreds of names of men who had registered for placement. Except

Source: William Whyte. *The Organization Man.* "A Generation of Bureaucrats." Copyright 1956 Simon and Schuster. Reprinted by permission.

for murmurs from the row of cubicles there was little to indicate that scores of young men were, every hour on the half hour, making the decisions that would determine their whole future life.

Someone from a less organized era might conclude that the standardization of this machinery—and the standardized future it portends—would repel students. It does not. For the median senior this is the optimum future; it meshes so closely with his own aspirations that it is almost as if the corporation was planned in response to an attitude poll.

Because they are the largest single group, the corporation-bound seniors are the most visible manifestation of their generation's values. But in essential their contemporaries headed for other occupations respond to the same urges. The lawyers, the doctors, the scientists—their occupations are also subject to the same centralization, the same trend to group work and to bureaucratization. And so are the young men who will enter them. Whatever their many differences, in one great respect they are all of a piece: more than any generation in memory, theirs will be a generation of bureaucrats.

They are, above all, conservative. Their inclination to accept the status quo does not necessarily mean that in the historic sweep of ideas they are conservative—in the more classical sense of conservatism, it could be argued that the seniors will be, in effect if not by design, agents of revolution. But this is a matter we must leave to late historians. For the immediate present, at any rate, what ideological ferment college men exhibit is not in the direction of basic change.

This shows most clearly in their attitude toward politics. It used to be axiomatic that young men moved to the left end of the spectrum in revolt against their fathers and then, as the years went on, moved slowly to the right. A lot of people still believe this is true, and many businessmen fear that twenty years of the New Deal hopelessly corrupted our youth into radicalism. After the election of 1952 businessmen became somewhat more cheerful, but many are still apprehensive, and whenever a poll indicates that students don't realize that business makes only about 6 per cent profit, there is a flurry of demands for some new crusade to rescue our youth from socialistic tendencies.

If the seniors do any moving, however, it will be from dead center. Liberal groups have almost disappeared from the campus, and what few remain are anemic. There has been no noticeable activity at the other end of the spectrum either. When William Buckely, Jr., produced *Good and Man at Yale,* some people thought this signaled the emergence of a strong right-wing movement among the young men. The militancy, however, has not proved particularly contagious; when the McCarthy issue roused and divided their elders, undergraduates seemed somewhat bored with it all.

Their conservatism is passive. No cause seizes them, and nothing so exuberant or willfully iconoclastic as the Veterans of Future Wars has reappeared. There are Democrats and Republicans, and at election time there is the usual flurry of rallies, but in comparison with the agitation of the thirties no one seems to care too much one way or the other. There has been personal unrest—the suspense over the prospect of military service assures this—but it rarely gets resolved into a thought-out protest. Come spring and students may start whacking each other over the head or roughing up the townees and thereby cause a rush of concern over the wild younger generation. But there is no real revolution in them, and the next day they likely as not will be found with their feet firmly on the ground in the recruiters' cubicles.

Some observers attribute the disinterest to fear. I heard one instructor tell his colleagues that in his politics classes he warned students to keep their noses clean. "I tell them," he said, "that they'd better realize that what they say might be held against them, especially when we get to the part about Marx and Engels. Someday in the future they might find their comments bounced back at them in an investigation."

The advice, as his colleagues retorted, was outrageously unnecessary. The last thing students can be accused of now is dangerous discussion; they are not interested in the kind of big questions that stimulate heresy and whether the subject—the corporation, government, religion—students grow restive if the talk tarries on the philosophical. Most are interested in the philosophical only to the extent of finding out what the accepted view is in order that they may accept it and get on to the practical matters. This spares the bystander from the lofty bulling and the elaborate pose of unorthodoxy that my contemporaries often used to affect, but it does make for a rather stringent utilitarianism.

Even in theological seminaries, this impatience to be on with the job has been evident. Writes Norman Pittenger, professor at General Theological Seminar:

> It is a kind of authoritarianism in reverse. Theological students today, in contrast to their fellows of twenty years ago, want "to be told." I have gone out of my way to ask friends who teach in seminaries of other denominations whether they have recognized the new tendency. Without exception they have told me that they

152. W. H. Whyte, Jr., *The Organization Man:* "A Generation of Bureaucrats," 1956

find the present generation of students less inquiring of mind, more ready to accept an authority, and indeed most anxious to have it "laid on the line."

In the seminary this means that the lecturer must be unusually careful lest his opinion, or what "the Bible says" or "the church teaches," shall be taken as the last word.... What troubles many of us is that students today are not willing enough to think things through for themselves. If this is what the Bible says, then how does it say it and why, and how do we know that this is indeed the teaching of Scripture? If this is what the church teaches, why does it teach it, what evidence can be given for the teaching and what right has the church to teach at all? Or if a professor says that such-and-such a view is correct, why does he say it and what real evidence can he produce that his statement is true? It would be better and healthier if the new respect for authority were more frequently found in combination with a spirit of inquiry, a ready willingness to think through what is authoritatively declared, and a refusal to accept anything simply because some reputable expert makes the statement.

In judging a college generation, one usually bases his judgment on how much it varies from one's own, and presumably superior, class, and I must confess that I find myself tempted to do so. Yet I do not think my generation has any license to damn the acquiescence of seniors as a weakening of intellectual fiber. It is easy for us to forget that if earlier generations were less content with society, there was a great deal less to be contented about. In the intervening years the economy has changed enormously, and even in retrospect the senior can hardly be expected to share former discontents. Society is not out of joint for him, and if he acquiesces it is not out of fear that he does so. He does not want to rebel against the status quo because he really likes it—and his elders, it might be added, are not suggesting anything bold and new to rebel *for*.

Perhaps contemporaryism would be a better word than conservatism to describe their posture. The present, more than the past, is their model; while they share the characteristic American faith in the future also, they see it as more of same. As they paraphrase what they are now reading about America, they argue that at last we have got it. The big questions are all settled; we know the direction, and while many minor details remain to be cleared up, we can be pretty sure of enjoying a wonderful upward rise.

While the degree of their optimism is peculiarly American, the spirit of acquiescence, it should be noted, is by no means confined to the youth of this country. In an Oxford magazine, called, aptly enough, *Couth*, one student writes this of his generation:

It is true that over the last thirty years it has been elementary good manners to be depressed.... But, ... we are not, really, in the least worried by our impending, and other people's present, disasters. This is not the Age of Anxiety. What distinguishes the comfortable young men of today from the uncomfortable young men of the last hundred years ... is that for once the younger generation is not in revolt against anything. ... We don't want to rebel against our elders. They are much too nice to be rebellable-against. Old revolutionaries as they are, they get rather cross with us and tell us we are stuffy and prudish, but even this can't provoke us into hostility.... Our fathers ... brought us up to see them not as the representatives of ancient authority and unalterable law but as rebels against our grandfathers. So naturally we have grown up to be on their side, even if we feel on occasion that they were a wee bit hard on their fathers, or even a little naive.

More than before, there is a tremendous interest in techniques. Having no quarrel with society, they prefer to table the subject of ends and concentrate instead on means. Not what or why but *how* interests them, and any evangelical strain they have they can sublimate; once they have equated the common weal with organization—a task the curriculum makes easy—they will let the organization worry about goals. "These men do not question the system" an economics professor says of them, approvingly. "They want to get in there and lubricate and make them run better. They will be technicians of the society, not innovators."

The attitude of men majoring in social science is particularly revealing on this score. Not so very long ago, the younger social scientist was apt to see his discipline as a vehicle for protest about society as well as the study of it. The seniors that set the fashion for him were frequently angry men, and many of the big studies of the twenties and thirties—Robert and Helen Lynd's *Middletown,* for example—did not conceal strong opinions about the inequities in the social structure. But this is now old hat: it is the "bleeding-heart" school to the younger men (and to some not so young, too), for they do not wish to protest; they wish to collaborate. Reflecting the growing reconciliation with middle-class values that has affected all types of intellectuals, they are turning more and more to an interest in methodology, particularly the techniques of measurement. Older social scientists who have done studies on broad social problems find that the younger men are comparatively uninterested in the problems themselves. When the discussion period comes, the questions the younger men ask are on the technical points; not the what, or why, but the how.

The urge to be a technician, a collaborator, shows most markedly in the kind of jobs seniors prefer. They want to work for somebody else. Paradoxically, the old dream of independence through a business of one's own is held almost exclusively by factory workers—the one group, as a number of sociologists have reported, least able to fulfill it. Even at the bull-session level college seniors do not affect it, and when recruiting time comes around they make the preference clear. Consistently, placement officers find that of the men who intend to go into business—roughly one half of the class—less than 5 per cent express any desire to be an entrepreneur.

---

153. Southern Representatives and Senators, "The Southern Manifesto: Declaration of Constitutional Principles"[1]

The Southern Manifesto was the response of Southern Representatives and Senators to the Brown Decision.

The unwarranted decision of the Supreme Court in the public school cases is now bearing the fruit always produced when men substitute naked power for established law.

The Founding Fathers gave us a Constitution of checks and balances because they realized the inescapable lesson of history that no man or group of men can be safely entrusted with unlimited power. They framed this Constitution with its provisions for change by amendment in order to secure the fundamentals of government against the dangers of temporary popular passion or the personal predilections of public officeholders.

We regard the decision of the Supreme Court in the school cases as a clear abuse of judicial power. It climaxes a trend in the Federal Judiciary undertaking to legislate, in derogation of the authority of Congress, and to encroach upon the reserved rights of the States and the people.

The original Constitution does not mention United States. Neither does the 14th amendment nor any other amendment. The debates preceding the submission of the 14th amendment clearly show that there was no intent that it should affect the system of United States maintained by the States.

The very Congress which proposed the amendment subsequently provided for segregated schools in the District of Columbia.

When the amendment was adopted in 1868, there were 37 States of the Union. Every one of the 26 States that had any substantial racial differences among its people, either approved the operation of segregated schools already in existence or subsequently established such schools by action of the same lawmaking body which considered the 14th amendment.

As admitted by the Supreme Court in the public school case *(Brown v. Board of Education)*, the doctrine of separate but equal schools "apparently originated in *Roberts v. City of Boston* (1849), upholding school segregation against attack as being violative of a State constitutional guarantee of equality." The constitutional doctrine began in the North, not in the South, and it was followed not only in Massachusetts, but in Connecticut, New York, Illinois, Indiana, Michigan, Minnesota, New Jersey, Ohio, Pennsylvania and other northern States until they, exercising their rights as States through the constitutional processes of local self-government, changed their school systems.

In the case of *Plessy v. Ferguson* in 1896 the Supreme Court expressly declared that under the 14th amendment no person was denied any of his rights if the States provided separate but equal public facilities. This decision has been followed in many other cases. It is notable that the Supreme Court, speaking through Chief Justice Taft, a former President of the United States, unanimously declared in 1927 in *Lum v. Rice* that the "separate but equal" principle is "within the discretion of the State in regulating its public schools and does not conflict with the 14th amendment."

Source: The Southern Manifesto reprinted from Hubert Humphrey, ed., *School Desegregation: Documents and Commentaries.* Thos. Y. Crowell Co., 1964.

This interpretation, restated time and again, became a part of the life of the people of many of the States and confirmed their habits, customs, traditions, and way of life. It is founded on elemental humanity and common sense, for parents should not be deprived by Government of the right to direct the lives and education of their own children.

Though there has been no constitutional amendment or act of Congress changing this established legal principle almost a century old the Supreme Court of the United States, with no legal basis for such action, undertook to exercise their naked judicial power and substituted their personal political and social ideas for the established law of the land.

This unwarranted exercise of power by the Court, contrary to the Constitution, is creating chaos and confusion in the States principally affected. It is destroying the amicable relations between the white and constitution races that have been created through 90 years of patient effort by the good people of both races. It has planted hatred and suspicion where there has been heretofore friendship and understanding.

Without regard to the consent of the governed, outside agitators are threatening immediate and revolutionary changes in our public school system. If done, this is certain to destroy the system of public education in some of the States.

With the gravest concern for the explosive and dangerous condition created by this decision and inflamed by outside meddlers:

We reaffirm our reliance on the Constitution as the fundamental law of the land.

We decry the Supreme Court's encroachments on rights reserved to the States and to the people, contrary to established law, and to the Constitution.

We commend the motives of those States which have declared the intention to resist forced integration by any lawful means.

We appeal to the States and people who are not directly affected by these decisions to consider the constitutional principles involved against the time when they too, on issues vital to them, may be the victims of judicial encroachment.

Even though we constitute a minority in the present Congress, we have full faith that a majority of the American people believe in the dual system of government which has enabled us to achieve our greatness and will in time demand that the reserved rights of the States and of the people be made secure against judicial usurpation.

We pledge ourselves to use all lawful means to bring about a reversal of this decision which is contrary to the Constitution and to prevent the use of force in its implementation.

In this trying period, as we all seek to right this wrong, we appeal to our people not to be provoked by the agitators and troublemakers invading our States and to scrupulously refrain from disorder and lawless acts.

Signed by:

MEMBERS OF THE UNITED STATES SENATE

Walter F. George, Richard B. Russell, John Stennis, Sam J. Ervin, Jr., Strom Thurmond, Harry F. Byrd, AAAA. Willis Robertson, John L. McClellan, Allen J. Ellender, Russell B. Long, Lister Hill, James O. Eastland, W. Kerr Scott, John Sparkman, Olin D. Johnston, Price Daniel, J. W. Fulbright, George A. Smathers, Spessard L. Holland.

MEMBERS OF THE UNITED STATES HOUSE OF REPRESENTATIVES

Alabama: Frank W. Boykin, George M. Grant, George W. Andrews, Kenneth A. Roberts, Albert Rains, Armistead I. Selden, Jr., Carl Elliott, Robert E. Jones, George Huddleston, Jr.

Arkansas: E. C. Caathings, Wilburt D. Mills, James W. Trimble, Oren Harris, Brooks Hays, W. F. Norrell.

Florida: Charles E. Bennett, Robert L. F. Sikes, A. S. Herlong, Jr., Paul G. Rogers, James A. Haley, D. R. Matthews, William Cramer.

Georgia: Prince H. Preston, John L. Pilcher, E. L. Forrester, John James Flynt, Jr., James C. Davis, Carl Vinson, Henderson Lanham, Iris F. Blitch, Phil M. Landrum, Paul Brown.

Louisiana: F. Edward Hebert, Hale Boggs, Edwin E. Willis, Overton Brooks, Otto E. Passman, James H. Morrison, T. Ashton Thompson, George S. Long.

Mississippi: Thomas G. Abernethy, Jamie L. Whitten, Frank E. Smith, John Bell Williams, Arthur Winstead, William M. Colmer.

North Carolina: Herbert C. Bonner, L. H. Fountain, Graham A. Barden, Carl T. Durham, F. Ertel Carlyle, Hugh Q. Alexander, Woodrow W. Jones, George A. Shuford, Charles R. Jonas.

South Carolina: L. Mendel Rivers, John J. Riley, W. J. Bryan Dorn, Robert T. Ashmore, James P. Richards, John L. McMillan.

Tennessee: James B. Frazier, Jr., Tom Murray, Jere Cooper, Clifford Davis, Ross Bass.

Texas: Wright Patman, John Dowdy, Walter Rogers, O. C. Fisher, Martin Dies.

Virginia: Edward J. Robeson, Jr., Porter Hardy, Jr., J. Vaughan Gary, Watkins M. Abbitt, William M. Tuck, Richard H. Poff, Burr P. Harrison, Howard W. Smith, W. Pat Jennings, Joel T. Broyhill.

Notes

[1] On March 12, 1956, a group of senators and representatives from eleven southern states presented to Congress the following statement criticizing the Supreme Court for its 1954 ruling on the desegregation of schools. Requiring no Congressional action, the Manifesto, as it came to be called, had no legal standing. It expressed the sentiments of the 101 signers about the Court's decision and also, according to Senatory Harry F. Byrd of Virginia, served as "part of the plan of massive resistance we've been working on." ED

CHAPTER XXIX

Turbulent Years, 1960–1968

154. MICHAEL HARRINGTON, *THE OTHER AMERICA: POVERTY IN THE UNITED STATES*, 1962

Michael Harrington deeply influenced national public policy in the 1960s with his eloquent plea for those who had been left out of the apparently universal prosperity of the preceding decade.

One: The Invisible Land

There is a familiar America. It is celebrated in speeches and advertised on television and in the magazines. It has the highest mass standard of living the world has ever known.

In the 1950's this America worried about itself, yet even its anxieties were products of abundance. The title of a brilliant book was widely misinterpreted, and familiar America began to call itself "the affluent society." There was introspection about Madison Avenue and tail fins; there was discussion of the emotional suffering taking place in the suburbs. In all this, there was an implicit assumption that the basic grinding economic problems had been solved in the United States. In this theory the nation's problems were no longer a matter of basic human needs, of food, shelter, and clothing. Now they were seen as qualitative, a question of learning to live decently amid luxury.

While this discussion was carried on, there existed another America. In it dwelt somewhere between 40,000,000 and 50,000,000 citizens of this land. They were poor. They still are.

To be sure, the other America is not impoverished in the same sense as those poor nations where millions cling to hunger as a defense against starvation. This country has escaped such extremes. That does not change the fact that tens of millions of Americans are, at this very moment, maimed in body and spirit, existing at levels beneath those necessary for human decency. If these people are not starving, they are hungry, and sometimes fat with hunger, for that is what cheap foods do. They are without adequate housing and education and medical care.

The Government has documented what this means to the bodies of the poor, and the figures will be cited throughout this book. But even more basic, this poverty twists and deforms the spirit. The American poor are pessimistic and defeated, and they are victimized by mental suffering to a degree unknown in Suburbia.

This book is a description of the world in which these people live; it is about the other America. Here are the unskilled workers, the migrant farm workers, the aged, the minorities, and all the others who live in the economic underworld of American life. In all this, there will be statistics, and that offers the opportunity for disagreement among honest and sincere men. I would ask the reader to respond critically to every assertion, but not to allow statistical quibbling to obscure the huge, enormous, and intolerable fact of poverty in America. For, when all is said and done, that fact is unmistakable, whatever its exact dimensions, and the truly human reaction can only be outrage. As W. H. Auden wrote:

> Hunger allows no choice
> To the citizen or the police;
> We must love one another or die.

Source: Michael Harrington, *The Other America: Poverty in the United States.* Reprinted by permission of Macmillan Publishing Company. Copyright 1962, 1969 by Michael Harrington.

I

The millions who are poor in the United States tend to become increasingly invisible. Here is a great mass of people, yet it takes an effort of the intellect and will even to see them.

I discovered this personally in a curious way. After I wrote my first article on poverty in America, I had all the statistics down on paper. I had proved to my satisfaction that there were around 50,000,000 poor in this country. Yet, I realized I did not believe my own figures. The poor existed in the Government reports; they were percentages and numbers in long, close columns, but they were not part of my experience. I could prove that the other America existed, but I had never been there.

My response was not accidental. It was typical of what is happening to an entire society, and it reflects profound social changes in this nation. The other America, the America of poverty, is hidden today in a way that it never was before. Its millions are socially invisible to the rest of us. No wonder that so many misinterpreted Galbraith's title and assumed that "the affluent society" meant that everyone had a decent standard of life. The misinterpretation was true as far as the actual day-to-day lives of two-thirds of the nation were concerned. Thus, one must begin a description of the other America by understanding why we do not see it.

There are perennial reasons that make the other America an invisible land.

Poverty is often off the beaten track. It always has been. The ordinary tourist never left the main highway, and today he rides interstate turnpikes. He does not go into the valleys of Pennsylvania where the towns look like movie sets of Wales in the thirties. He does not see the company houses in rows, the rutted roads (the poor always have bad roads whether they live in the city, in towns, or on farms), and everything is black and dirty. And even if he were to pass through such a place by accident, the tourist would not meet the unemployed men in the bar or the women coming home from a runaway sweatshop.

Then, too, beauty and myths are perennial masks of poverty. The traveler comes to the Appalachians in the lovely season. He sees the hills, the streams, the foliage— but not the poor. Or perhaps he looks at a rundown mountain house and, remembering Rousseau rather than seeing with his eyes, decides that "those people" are truly fortunate to be living the way they are and that they are lucky to be exempt from the strains and tensions of the middle class. The only problem is that "those people," the quaint inhabitants of those hills, are undereducated, underprivileged, lack medical care, and are in the process of being forced from the land into a life in the cities, where they are misfits.

These are normal and obvious causes of the invisibility of the poor. It is more important to understand that the very development of American society is creating a new kind of blindness about poverty. The poor are increasingly slipping out of the very experienced and consciousness of the nation.

If the middle class never did like ugliness and poverty, it was at least aware of them. "Across the tracks" was not a very long way to go. There were forays into the slums at Christmas time; there were charitable organizations that brought contact with the poor. Occasionally, almost everyone passed through the Negro ghetto or the blocks of tenements, if only to get downtown to work or to entertainment.

Now the American city has been transformed. The poor still inhabit the miserable housing in the central area, but they are increasingly isolated from contact with, or sight of, anybody else. Middle-class women coming in from Suburbia on a rare trip may catch the merest glimpse of the other America on the way to an evening at the theater, but their children are segregated in suburban schools. The business of professional man may drive along the fringes of slums in a car or bus, but it is not an important experience to him. The failures, the unskilled, the disabled, the aged, and the minorities are right there, across the tracks, where they have always been. But hardly anyone else is.

In short, the very development of the American city has removed poverty from the living, emotional experience of millions upon millions of middle-class Americans. Living out in the suburbs, it is easy to assume that ours is, indeed, an affluent society.

This new segregation of poverty is compounded by a well-meaning ignorance. A good many concerned and sympathetic Americans are aware that there is much discussion of urban renewal. Suddenly, driving through the city, they notice that a familiar slum has been torn down and that there are towering, modern buildings where once there has been tenements or hovels. There is a warm feeling of satisfaction, of pride in the way things are working out: the poor, it is obvious, are being taken care of.

The irony in this (as the chapter on housing will document) is that the truth is nearly the exact opposite to the impression. The total impact of the various housing programs in postwar America has been to squeeze more and more people into existing slums. More often than not, the modern apartment in a towering building rent at $40 a room or more. For during the past decade and a half, there has been more subsidization of middle- and upper-middle housing than there has been of housing for the poor.

Clothes make the poor invisible too: America has the best-dressed poverty the world has ever known. For a variety of reasons, the benefits of mass production have been spread much more evenly in this area than in many others. It is much easier in the United States to be decently dressed than it is to be decently housed, fed, or doctored. Even people with terribly depressed incomes can look prosperous.

This is an extremely important factor in defining our emotional and existential ignorance of poverty. In Detroit the existence of social classes became much more difficult to discern the day the companies put lockers in the plants. From that moment on, one did not see men in work clothes on the way to the factory, but citizens in slacks and white shirts. This process has been magnified with the poor throughout the country. There are tens of thousands of Americans in the big cities who are wearing shoes, perhaps even a stylishly cut suit or dress and yet are hungry. It is not a matter of planning, though it seems as if the affluent society had given out costumes to the poor so that they would not offend the rest of society with the sight of rags.

Then, many of the poor are the wrong age to be seen. A good number of them (over 8,000,000) are sixty-five years of age or better; an even larger number are under eighteen. The aged members of the other America are often sick, and they cannot move. Another group of them live out their lives in loneliness and frustration: they sit in rented rooms, or else they stay close to a house in a neighborhood that has completely changed from the old days. Indeed, one of the worst aspects of poverty among the aged is that these people are out of sight and out of mind, and alone.

The young are somewhat more visible, yet they too stay close to their neighborhoods. Sometimes they advertise their poverty through a lurid tabloid story about a gang killing. But generally they do not disturb the quiet streets of the middle class.

And finally, the poor are politically invisible. It is one of the cruelest ironies of social life in advanced countries that the dispossessed at the bottom of society are unable to speak for themselves. The people of the other America do not, by far and large, belong to unions, to fraternal organizations, or to political parties. They are without lobbies of their own; they put forward no legislative program. As a group, they are atomized. They have no face; they have no voice.

Thus, there is not even a cynical political motive for caring about the poor, as in the old days. Because the slums are no longer centers of powerful political organizations, the politicians need not really care about their inhabitants. The slums are no longer visible to the middle class, so much of the idealistic urge to fight for those who need help is gone. Only the social agencies have a really direct involvement with the other America, and they are without any great political power.

To the extent that the poor have a spokesman in American life, that role is played by the labor movement. The unions have their own particular idealism, an ideology of concern. More than that, they realize that the existence of a reservoir of cheap, unorganized labor is a menace to wages and working conditions throughout the entire economy. Thus, many union legislate proposals — to extend the coverage of minimum wage and social security, to organize migrant farm laborers — articulate the needs of the poor.

That the poor are invisible is one of the most important things about them. They are not simply neglected and forgotten as in the old rhetoric of reform; what is much worse, they are not seen.

One might take a remark from George Eliot's *Felix Holt* as a basic statement of what this book is about:

> . . . there is no private life which has not been determined by a wider public life, from the time when the primeval milkmaid had to wander with the wanderings of her clan, because the cow she milked was one of a herd which had made the pasture bare. Even in the conservatory existence where the fair Camellia is sighed for by the noble Pineapple, neither of them needing to care about the frost or rain outside, there is a nether apparatus of hot water pipes liable to cool down on a strike of the gardeners or a scarcity of coal.
> And the lives we are about to look back upon do not belong to those conservatory species; they are noted in the common earth, having to endure all the ordinary chances of past and present weather.

Forty to 50,000,000 people are becoming increasingly invisible. That is a shocking fact. But there is a second basic irony of poverty that is equally important: if one is to make the mistake of being born poor, he should choose a time when the majority of the people are miserable too.

J. K. Galbraith develops this idea in *The Affluent Society*, and in doing so defines the "newness" of the kind of poverty in contemporary America. The old poverty, Galbraith notes, was general. It was the condition of life of an entire society, or at least of that huge majority who were without special skills or the luck of birth. When the entire economy advanced, a good many of these people gained higher standards of living. Unlike the poor today, the majority poor of a generation ago were an immediate (if cynical) concern of political leaders. The old sums of the immigrants had the votes; they provided the basis for labor organizations; their very numbers could be a powerful force in political conflict. At the same time the new technology required higher skills, more education, and stimulated an upward movement for millions.

Perhaps the most dramatic case of the power of the majority poor took place in the 1930s. The Congress of Industrial Organizations literally organized millions in a matter of years. A labor movement that had been declining and confined to a thin stratum of the highly skilled suddenly embraced masses of men and women in basic industry. At the same time this acted as a pressure upon the Government, and the New Deal codified some of the social giants in laws like the Wagner Act. The result was not a basic transformation of the American system, but it did transform the lives of an entire section of the population.

In the thirties one of the reasons for these advances was that misery was general. There was no need then to write books about unemployment and poverty. That was the decisive social experience of the entire society, and the apple sellers even invaded Wall Street. There was political sympathy from middle-class reformers; there was an élan and spirit that grew out of a deep crisis.

Some of those who advanced in the thirties did so because they had unique and individual personal talents. But for the great mass, it was a question of being at the right point in the economy at the right time in history, and utilizing that position for common struggle. Some of those who failed did so because they did not have the will to take advantage of new opportunities. But for the most part the poor who were left behind had been at the wrong place in the economy at the wrong moment in history.

These were the people in the unorganizable jobs, in the South, in the minority groups, in the fly-by-night factories that were low on capital and high on labor. When some of them did break into the economic mainstream—when, for instance, the CIO opened up the way for some Negroes to find good industrial jobs—they proved to as resourceful as anyone else. As a group, the other Americans who stayed behind were not originally composed primarily of individual failures. Rather, they were victims of an impersonal process that selected some for progress and discriminated against others.

Out of the thirties came the welfare state. Its creation had been stimulated by mass impoverishment and misery, yet it helped the poor least of all. Laws like unemployment compensation, the Wagner Act, the various farm programs, all these were designed for the middle third in the cities, for the organized workers, and for the upper third in the country, for the big market farmers. If a man works in an extremely low-paying job, he may not even be covered by social security or other welfare programs. If he receives unemployment compensation, the payment is scaled down according to his low earnings.

One of the major laws that was designed to cover everyone, rich and poor, was social security. But even here the other Americans suffered discrimination. Over the years social security payments have not even provided a subsistence level of life. The middle third have been able to supplement the Federal pension through private plans negotiated by unions, through joining medical insurance schemes like Blue Cross, and so on. The poor have not been able to do so. They lead a bitter life, and then have to pay for that fact in old age.

Indeed, the paradox that the welfare state benefits those least who need help most is but a single instance of a persistent irony in the other America. Even when the money finally trickles down, even when a school is built in a poor neighborhood, for instance, the poor are still deprived. Their entire environment, their values, do not prepare them to take advantage of the new opportunity. The parents are anxious for the children to go to work; the pupils are pent up, waiting for the moment when their education has complied with the law.

Today's poor, in short, missed the political and social gains of the thirties. They are, as Galbraith rightly points out, the first minority poor in history, the first poor not to be seen, the first poor whom the politicians could leave alone.

The first step toward the new poverty was taken when millions of people proved immune to progress. When that happened, the failure was not individual and personal, but a social product. But once the historic accident takes place, it begins to become a personal fate.

The new poor of the other America saw the rest of society move ahead. They went on living in depressed areas, and often they tended to become depressed human beings. In some of the West Virginia towns, for instance, an entire community will become shabby and defeated. The young and the adventurous go to the city, leaving behind those who cannot move and those who lack the will to do so. The entire area becomes permeated with failure, and that is one more reason the big corporations shy away.

Indeed, one of the most important things about the new poverty is that it cannot be defined in simple, statistical terms. Throughout this book a crucial term is used: aspiration. If a group has internal vitality, a will—if it has aspiration—it may live in dilapidated housing, it may eat an inadequate diet, and it may suffer poverty, but it is not impoverished. So it was in those ethnic slums of the immigrants that played such a dramatic role in the unfolding of the American dream. The people found themselves in slums, but they were not slumdwellers.

But the new poverty is constructed so as to destroy aspiration; it is a system designed to be impervious to hope. The other America does not contain the adventurous seeking a new life and land. It is populated by the failures, by those driven from the land and bewildered by the city, by old people suddenly confronted with the torments of loneliness and poverty, and by minorities facing a wall of prejudice.

In the past, when poverty was general in the unskilled and semi-skilled work force, the poor were all mixed together. The bright and the dull, those who were going to escape into the great society and whose who were to stay behind, all of them lived on the same street. When the middle third rose, the community was destroyed. And the entire invisible land of the other Americans became a ghetto, a modern poor farm for the rejects of society and of the economy.

It is a blow to reform and the political hopes of the poor that the middle class no longer understands that poverty exists. But, perhaps more important, the poor are losing their links with the great world. If statistics and sociology can measure a feeling as delicate as loneliness (and some of the attempts to do so will be cited later on), the other America is becoming increasingly populated by those who do not belong to anybody or anything. They are no longer participants in an ethnic culture from the old country; they are less and less religious; they do not belong to unions or clubs. They are not seen, and because of that they themselves cannot see. Their horizon has become more and more restricted; they see one another, and that means they see little reason to hope.

Galbraith was one of the first writers to begin to describe the newness of contemporary poverty, and that is to his credit. Yet because even he underestimates the problem, it is important to put his definition into perspective.

For Galbraith, there are two main components of the new poverty: case poverty and insular poverty. Case poverty is the plight of those who suffer from some physical or mental disability that is personal and individual and excludes them from the general advance. Insular poverty exists in areas like the Appalachians or the West Virginia coal fields, where an entire section of the country becomes economically obsolete.

Physical and mental disabilities are, to be sure, an important part of poverty in America. the poor are sick in body and in spirit. But this is not an isolated fact about them, an individual "case," a stroke of bad luck. Disease, alcoholism, low IQ's, these express a whole way of life. They are, in the main, the effects of an environment, not the biographies of unlucky individuals. Because of this, the new poverty is something that cannot be dealt with by first aid. If there is to be a lasting assault on the shame of the other America, it must seek to root out of this society an entire environment, and not just the relief of individuals.

But perhaps the idea of "insular" poverty is even more dangerous. To speak of "islands" of the people (or, in the more popular term, "pockets of poverty") is to imply that one is confronted by a serious, but relatively minor problem. This is hardly a description of a misery that extends to 40,000,000 or 50,000,000 people in the United States. They have remained impoverished in spite of increasing productivity and the creation of a welfare state. That fact alone should suggest the dimensions of a serious and basic situation.

And yet, even given these disagreements with Galbraith, his achievement is considerable. He was one of the first to understand that there are enough poor people in the United States to constitute a subculture of misery, but not enough of them to challenge the conscience and the imagination of the nation.

Finally, one might summarize the newness of contemporary poverty by saying: These are the people who are immune to progress. But then the facts are even more cruel. The other Americans are the victims of the very inventions and machines that have provided a higher living standard for the rest of society. They are upside down in the economy, and for them greater productivity often means worse jobs; agricultural advance becomes hunger.

In the optimistic theory, technology is an undisguised blessing. A general increase in productivity, the argument goes, generates a higher standard of living for the whole people. And indeed, this has been true for the middle and upper thirds of American society, the people who made such striking gains in the last two decades. It tends to overstate the automatic character of the process, to omit the role of human struggle. (The CIO was organized by men in conflict, not by economic trends.) Yet it states a certain truth—for those who are lucky enough to participate in it.

But the poor, if they were given to theory, might argue the exact opposite. They might say: Progress is misery.

As the society becomes more technological, more skilled, those who learn to work the machines, who get the expanding education, move up. Those who miss out at the very start find themselves at a new disadvantage. A generation ago in American life the majority of the working people did not have high-school educations. But at that time industry was organized on a lower level of skill and competence. And there was a sort of continuum in the shop: the youth who left school at sixteen could begin as a laborer, and generally pick up skill as he went along.

Today the situation is quite different. The good jobs require much more skill from the very outset. Those who lack a high-school education tend to be condemned to the economic underworld—to low-paying service industries, to backward factories, to sweeping and janitorial duties. If the fathers and mothers of the contemporary poor were penalized a generation ago for their lack of schooling, their children will suffer all the more. The very rise in productivity that created more money and better working conditions for the rest of the society can be a menace to the poor.

But then this technological revolution might have an even more disastrous consequence: it could increase the ranks of the poor as well as intensify the disabilities of poverty. At this point it is too early to make any final judgment, yet there are obvious danger signals. There are millions of Americans who live just the other side of poverty. When a recession comes, they are pushed onto the relief rolls. (Welfare payments in New York respond almost immediately to any economic decline.) If automation continues to inflict more and more penalties on the unskilled and the semiskilled, it could have the impact of permanently increasing the population of the other America.

Even more explosive is the possibility that people who participated in the gains of the thirties and the forties will be pulled back down into poverty. Today the mass-production industries where unionization made such a difference are contracting. Jobs are being destroyed. In the process, workers who had achieved a certain level of wages, who had won working conditions in the shop, are suddenly confronted with impoverishment. This is particularly true for anyone over forty years of age and for members of minority groups. Once their job is abolished, their chances of ever getting similar work are very slim.

It is too early to say whether or not this phenomenon is temporary, or whether it represents a massive retrogression that will swell the numbers of the poor. To a large extent, the answer to this question will be determined by the political response of the United States in the sixties. If serious and massive action is not undertaken, it may be necessary for statisticians to add some old-fashioned, pre-welfare-state poverty to the misery of the other America.

Poverty in the 1960's is invisible and it is new, and both these factors make it more tenacious. It is more isolated and politically powerless than ever before. It is laced with ironies, not the least of which is that many of the people view progress upside-down, as a menace and a threat to their lives. And if the nation does not measure up to the challenge of automation, poverty in the 1960's might be on the increase.

II

There are mighty historical and economic forces that keep the poor down; and there are human beings who help out in this grim business, many of them unwittingly. There are sociological and political reasons why poverty is not seen; and there are misconceptions and prejudices that literally blind the eyes. The latter must be understood if anyone is to make the necessary act of intellect and will so that the people can be noticed.

Here is the most familiar version of social blindness: "The poor are that way because they are afraid of work. And anyway they all have big cars. If they were like me (or my father or my grandfather), they could pay my own. But they prefer to live on the dole and cheat the taxpayers."

This theory, usually thought of as a virtuous and moral statement, is one of the means of making it impossible for the poor ever to pay their way. There are, one must assume, citizens of the other America who choose impoverishment out of fear of work (though, writing it down, I really do not believe it). But the real explanation of why the poor are where they are is that they made the mistake of being born to the wrong parents, in the wrong section of the country, in the wrong industry, or in the wrong racial or ethnic group. Once that mistake has been made, they could have been paragons of will and morality, but most of them would never even have had a chance to get out of the other America.

There are two important ways of saying this: The poor are caught in a vicious cycle; or, The poor live in a culture of poverty.

In a sense, one might define the contemporary poor in the United States as those who, for reasons beyond their control, cannot help themselves. All the most decisive factors making for opportunity and advance are against them. They are born going downward, and most of them stay down. They are victims whose lives are endlessly blown round and round the other America.

Here is one of the most familiar forms of the vicious circle of poverty. The poor get sick more than anyone else in the society. That is because they live in slums, jammed together under unhygienic conditions; they have inadequate diets, and cannot get decent medical care. When they become sick, they are sick longer than any other group in society. Because they are sick more often and longer than anyone else, they lose wages and work, and find it difficult to hold a steady job. And because of this, they cannot pay for good housing, for a nutritious diet, for doctors. At any given point in the circle, particularly when there is a major illness, their prospect is to move to an even lower level and to begin the cycle, round and round, toward even more suffering.

This is only one example of the vicious circle. Each group in the other America has its own particular version of the experience, and these will be detailed throughout this book. But the pattern, whatever its variations, is basic to the other America.

The individual cannot usually break out of this vicious circle. Neither can the group, for it lacks the social energy and political strength to turn its misery into a cause. Only the larger society, with its help and resources, can really make it possible for these people to help themselves. Yet those who could make the difference too often refuse to act because of their ignorant, smug moralisms. They view the effects of poverty—above all, the warping of the will and spirit that is a consequence of being poor—as choices. Understanding the vicious cycle is an important step in breaking down this prejudice.

There is an even richer way of describing this same, general idea: Poverty in the United States is a culture, an institution, a way of life.

There is a famous anecdote about Ernest F. Hemingway and F. Scott Fitzgerald. Fitzgerald is reported to have remarked to Hemingway, "The rich are different." And Hemingway replied, "Yes, they have money." Fitzgerald had much the better of the exchange. He understood that being rich was not a simple fact, like a large bank account, but way of looking at reality, a series of attitudes, a special type of life. If this is true of the rich, it is ten times truer of the poor. Everything about them, from the condition of their teeth to the way in which they love, is suffused and permeated by the fact of their poverty. And this is sometimes a hard idea for a Hemingway-like middle-class America to comprehend.

The family structure of the poor, for instance, is different from that of the rest of society. There are more homes without a father, there are less marriages, more early pregnancy and, if Kinsey's statistical findings can be used, markedly different attitudes toward sex. As a result of this, to take but one consequence of the fact, hundreds of thousands, and perhaps millions, of children in the other America never know stability and "normal" affection.

Or perhaps the policeman is an even better example. For the middle class, the police protect property, give directions, and help old ladies. For the urban poor, the police are those who arrest you. In almost any slum there is a vast conspiracy against the forces of law and order. If someone approaches asking for a person, no one there will have heard of him, even if he lives next door. The outsider is "cop," bill collector, investigator (and, in the Negro ghetto, most dramatically, he is the "Man").

While writing this book, I was arrested for participation in a civil-rights demonstration. A brief experience of a night in a cell made an abstraction personal and immediate: the city jail is one of the basic institutions of the other America. Almost everyone whom I encountered in the "tank" was poor: skid-row whites, Negroes, Puerto Ricans. Their poverty was an incitement to arrest in the first place. (A policeman will be much more careful with a well-dressed, obviously educated man who might have political connections than he will with someone who is poor.) They did not have money for bail or for lawyers. And, perhaps most important, they waited their arraignment with stolidity, in a mood of passive acceptance. They expected the worst, and they probably got it.

There is, in short, a language of the poor, a psychology of the poor, a world view of the poor. To be impoverished is to be an internal alien, to grow up in a culture that is radically different from the one that dominates the society. The poor can be described statistically; they can be analyzed as a group. But they need a novelist as well as a sociologist if we are to see them. They need an American Dickens to record the smell and texture and quality of their lives. The cycles and trends, the massive forces, must be seen as affecting persons who talk and think differently.

I am not that novelist. Yet in this book I have attempted to describe the faces behind the statistics, to tell a little of the "thickness" of personal life in the other America. Of necessity, I have begun with large groups: the dispossessed workers, the minorities, the farm poor, and the aged. Then there are three cases of less massive types of poverty, including the only single humorous component in the other America. And finally, there the slums, and the psychology of the poor.

Throughout, I work on an assumption that cannot be proved by Government figures or even documented by impressions of the other America. It is an ethical proposition, and it can be simply stated: In a nation with a technology that could provide every citizen with a decent life, it is an outrage and scandal that there should be such social misery. Only if one begins with this assumption is it possible to pierce through the invisibility of 40,000,000 to 50,000,000 human beings and to see the other America. We must perceive passionately, if this blindness is to be lifted from us. A fact can be rationalized and explained away; an indignity cannot.

What shall we tell the American poor, once we have seen them? Shall we say to them that they are better off than the Indian poor, the Italian poor, the Russian poor? That is one answer, but it is heartless. I should put it another way. I want to tell every well-fed and optimistic American that it is intolerable that so many millions should be maimed in body and in spirit when it is not necessary that they should be. My standard of comparison is not how much worse things used to be. It is how much better they could be if only we were stirred.

155. RACHEL CARSON, *SILENT SPRING*, 1962

Rachel Carson helped bring national attention to environmental concerns with her best-selling book from 1962, Silent Spring.

I. A Fable for Tomorrow

There was once a town in the heart of America where all life seemed to live in harmony with its surroundings. The town lay in the midst of a checkerboard of prosperous farms, with fields of grain and hillsides of orchards where, in spring, white clouds of bloom drifted above the green fields. In autumn, oak and maple and birch set up a blaze of color that flamed and flickered across a backdrop of pines. Then foxes barked in the hills and deer silently crossed the fields, half hidden in the mists of the fall mornings.

Along the road, laurel, viburnum and alder, great ferns and wildflowers delighted the traveler's eye through much of the year. Even in winter the roadsides were places of beauty, where countless birds came to feed on the berries and on the seed heads of the dried weeds rising above the snow. The countryside was, in fact, famous for the abundance and variety of its bird life, and when the flood of migrants was pouring through in spring and fall people traveled from great distances to observe them. Others came to fish the streams, which flowed clear and cold out of the hills and contained shady pools where trout lay. So it had been from the days many years ago when the first settlers raised their houses, sank their wells, and built their barns.

Then a strange blight crept over the area and everything began to change. Some evil spell had settled on the community: mysterious maladies swept the flocks of chickens; the cattle and sheep sickened and died. Everywhere was a shadow of death. The farmers spoke of much illness among their families. In the town the doctors had become more and more puzzled by new kinds of sickness appearing among their patients. There had been several sudden and unexplained deaths, not only among adults but even among children, who would be stricken suddenly while at play and die within a few hours.

There was a strange stillness. The birds, for example—where had they gone? Many people spoke of them, puzzled and disturbed. The feeding stations in the backyards were deserted. The few birds seen anywhere were moribund; they trembled violently and could not fly. It

---

Source: Rachel Carson, *The Silent Spring.* Copyright 1962 by Rachel Carson, copyright renewed 1990 by Roger Christie. Reprinted by permission of Houghton Mifflin Co. All Rights Reserved.

was a spring without voices. On the mornings that had once throbbed with the dawn chorus of robins, catbirds, doves, jays, wrens, and scores of other bird voices there was now no sound; only silence lay over the fields and woods and marsh.

On the farms the hens brooded, but no chicks hatched. The farmers complained that they were unable to raise any pigs—the litters were small and the young survived only a few days. The apple trees were coming into bloom but no bees droned among the blossoms, so there was no pollination and there would be no fruit.

The roadsides, once so attractive, were now lined with browned and withered vegetation as though swept by fire. These, too, were silent, deserted by all living things. Even the streams were now lifeless. Anglers no longer visited them, for all the fish had died.

In the gutters under the eaves and between the shingles of the roofs, a white granular powder still showed a few patches; some weeks before it had fallen like snow upon the roofs and the lawns, the fields and streams.

No witchcraft, no enemy action had silenced the rebirth of new life in this striken world. The people had done it themselves.

This town does not actually exist, but it might easily have a thousand counterparts in America or elsewhere in the world. I know of no community that has experienced all the misfortunes I describe. Yet every one of these disasters has actually happened somewhere, and many real communities have already suffered a substantial number of them. A grim specter has crept upon us almost unnoticed, and this imagined tragedy may easily become a stark reality we all shall know.

What has already silenced the voices of spring in countless towns in America? This book is an attempt to answer.

2. The Obligation to Endure

The history of life on earth has been a history of interaction between living things and their surroundings. To a large extent, the physical form and the habits of the earth's vegetation and its animal life have been molded by the environment. Considering the whole span of earthly time, the opposite effect, in which life actually modified its surroundings, has been relatively slight. Only within the movement of time represented by the present century has one species—man—acquired significant power to alter the nature of this world.

During the past quarter century this power has not only increased to one of disturbing magnitude but it has changed in character. The most alarming of all man's assaults upon the environment is the contamination of air, earth, rivers, and sea with dangerous and even lethal materials. This pollution is for the most part irrecoverable; the chain of evil it initiates not only in the world that must support life but in living tissues is for the most part irreversible. In this now universal contamination of the environment, chemicals are the sinister and little-recognized partners of radiation in changing the very nature of the world—the very nature of its life. Strontium 90, released through nuclear explosions into the air, comes to earth in rain or drifts down as fallout, lodges in soil, enters into the grass or corn or wheat grown there, and in time takes up its abode in the bones of a human being, there to remain until his death. Similarly, chemicals sprayed on croplands or forests or gardens lie long in soil, entering into living organisms, passing from one to another in a chain of poisoning and death. Or they pass mysteriously by underground streams until they emerge and, through the alchemy of air and sunlight, combine into new forms that kill vegetation, sicken cattle, and work unknown harm on those who drink from once pure wells. As Albert Schweitzer has said, "Man can hardly even recognize the devils of his own creation."

It took hundreds of millions of years to produce the life that now inhabits the earth—eons of time in which that developing and evolving and diversifying life reached a state of adjustment and balance with its surroundings. The environment, rigorously shaping and directing the life it supported, contained elements that were hostile as well as supporting. Certain rocks gave out dangerous radiation; even within the light of the sun, from which all life draws its energy, there were short-wave radiations with power to injure. Given time—time not in years but in millennia—life adjusts, and a balance has been reached. For time is the essential ingredient; but in the modern world there is no time.

The rapidity of change and the speed with which new situations are created follow the impetuous and heedless pace of man rather than the deliberate pace of nature. Radiation is no longer merely the background radiation of rocks, the bombardment of cosmic rays, the ultraviolet of the sun that have existed before there was any life on earth; radiation is now the unnatural creation of man's tampering with the atom. The chemicals to which life is asked to make its adjustment are no longer merely the calcium and silica and copper and all the rest of the minerals washed out of the rocks and carried in rivers to the sea; they are the synthetic creations of man's inventive mind, brewed in his laboratories, and having no counterparts in nature.

To adjust to these chemicals would require time on the scale that is nature's; it would require not merely the years of a man's life but the life of generations. And even this, were it by some miracle possible, would be futile, for the new chemicals come from our laboratories in an endless stream; almost five hundred annually find their way into actual use in the United States alone. The figure is staggering and its implications are not easily grasped—500 new chemicals to which the bodies of men and animals are required somehow to adapt each year, chemicals totally outside the limits of biologic experience.

Among them are many that are used in man's war against nature. Since the mid-1940s over 200 basic chemicals have been created for use in killing insects, weeds, rodents, and other organisms described in the modern vernacular as "pests"; and they are sold under several thousand different brand names.

These sprays, dusts, and aerosols are now applied almost universally to farms, gardens, forests, and homes—nonselective chemicals that have the power to kill every insect, the "good" and the "bad," to still the song of birds and the leaping of fish in the streams, to coat the leaves with a deadly film, and to linger on in soil—all this though the intended target may be only a few weeds or insects. Can anyone believe it is possible to lay down such a barrage of poisons on the surface of the earth without making it unfit for all life? They should not be called "insecticides," but "biocides."

The whole process of spraying seems caught up in an endless spiral. Since DDT was released for civilian use, a process of escalation has been going on in which ever more toxic materials must be found. This has happened because insects, in a triumphant vindication of Darwin's principle of the survival of the fittest, have evolved super races immune to the particular insecticide used, hence a deadlier one has always to be developed—and then a deadlier one than that. It has happened also because, for reasons to be described later, destructive insects often undergo a "flareback," or resurgence, after spraying, in numbers greater than before. Thus the chemical war is never won, and all life is caught in its violent crossfire.

Along with the possibility of the extinction of mankind by nuclear war, the central problem of our age has heretofore become the contamination of man's total environment with such substances of incredible potential for harm—substances that accumulate in the tissues of plants and animals and even penetrate the germ cell to shatter or alter the very material of heredity upon which the shape of the future depends.

Some would-be architects of our future look toward a time when it will be possible to alter the human gene plasm by design. But we may easily be doing so now by inadvertence, for many chemicals, like radiation, bring about gene mutations. It is ironic to think that man might determine his own future by something so seemingly trivial as the choice of an insect spray.

All this has been risked—for what? Future historians may well be amazed by our distorted sense of proportion. How could intelligent beings seek to control a few unwanted species by a method that contaminated the entire environment and brought the threat of disease and death even to their own kind? Yet this is precisely what we have done. We have done it, moreover, for reasons that collapse the moment we examine them. We are told that the enormous and expanding use of pesticides is necessary to maintain farm production. Yet is our real problem not one of *overproduction?* Our farms, despite measures to remove acreages from production and to pay farmers *not* to produce, have yielded such a staggering excess of crops that the American taxpayer in 1962 is paying out more than one billion dollars a year as the total carrying cost of the surplus-food storage program. And is the situation helped when one branch of the Agriculture Department tries to reduce production while another states, as it did in 1958, "It is believed generally that reduction of crop acreages under provisions of the Soil Bank will stimulate interest in use of chemicals to obtain maximum production on the land retained in crops."

All this is not to say there is no insect problem and no need of control. I am saying, rather, that control must be geared to realities, not to mythical situations, and that the method employed must be such that they do not destroy us along with the insects.

The problem whose attempted solution is brought such a train of disaster in its wake is an accompaniment of our modern way of life. Long before the age of man, insects inhabited the earth—a group of extraordinarily varied and adaptable beings. Over the course of time since man's advent, a small percentage of the more than half a million species of insects have come into conflict with human welfare in two principal ways: as competitors for the food supply and as carriers of human disease.

Disease-carrying insects become important where human beings are crowded together, especially under conditions where sanitation is poor, as in time of natural disaster or war or in situations of extreme poverty and deprivation. Then control of some sort becomes necessary. It is a sobering fact, however, as we shall presently see, that the method of massive chemical control has had only limited success, and also threatens to worsen the very conditions it is intended to curb.

Under primitive agricultural conditions the farmer had few insect problems. These arose with the intensification of agriculture—the devotion of immense acreages to a single crop. Such a system set the stage for explosive increases in specific insect populations. Single-crop farming does not take advantage of the principles by which nature works; it is agriculture as an engineer might conceive it to be. Nature has introduced great variety into the landscape, but man has displayed a passion for simplifying it. Thus he undoes the built-in checks and balances by which nature holds the species within bounds. One important natural check is a limit on the amount of suitable habitat for each species. Obviously then, an insect that lives on wheat can build up its population to much higher levels on a farm devoted to wheat than on one in which wheat is intermingled with other crops to which the insect is not adapted.

The same thing happens in other situations. A generation or more ago, the towns of large areas of the United States lined their streets with the noble elm tree. Now the beauty they hopefully created is threatened with complete destruction as disease sweeps through the elms, carried by a beetle that would have only limited chance to build up large populations and to spread from tree to tree if the elms were only occasional trees in a richly diversified planting.

Another factor in the modern insect problem is one that must be viewed against a background of geologic and human history: the spreading of thousands of different kinds of organisms from their native homes to invade new territories. This worldwide migration has been studied and graphically described by the British ecologist Charles Elton in his recent book *The Ecology of Invasions*. During the Cretaceous Period, some hundred million years ago, flooding seas cut many land bridges between continents and living things found themselves confined in what Elton calls "colossal separate nature reserves." There, isolated from others of their kind, they developed many new species. When some of the land masses were joined again, about 15 million years ago, these species began to move out into new territories—a movement that is not only still in progress but is now receiving considerable assistance from man.

The importation of plants is the primary agent in the modern spread of species, for animals have almost invariably gone along with the plants, quarantine being a comparatively recent and not completely effective innovation. The United States Office of Plant Introduction alone has introduced almost 200,000 species and varieties of plants from all over the world. Nearly half of the 180 or so major insect enemies of plants in the United States are accidental imports from abroad, and most of them have come as hitchhikers on plants.

In new territory, out of reach of the restraining hand of the natural enemies that kept down its numbers in its native land, an invading plant or animal is able to become enormously abundant. Thus it is no accident that our most troublesome insects are introduced species.

These invasions, both the naturally occurring and those dependent on human assistance, are likely to continue indefinitely. Quarantine and massive chemical campaigns are only extremely expensive ways of buying time. We are faced, according to Dr. Elton, "with a life-and-death need not just to find new technological means of suppressing this plant or that animal"; instead we need the basic knowledge of animal populations and their relations to their surroundings that will "promote an even balance and damp down the explosive power of outbreaks and new invasions."

Much of the necessary knowledge is now available but we do not use it. We train ecologists in our universities and even employ them in our governmental agencies but we seldom take their advice. We allow the chemical death rain to fall as though there were no alternative, whereas in fact there are many, and our ingenuity could soon discover many more if given opportunity.

Have we fallen into a mesmerized state that makes us accept as inevitable that which is inferior or detrimental, as though having lost the will or the vision to demand that which is good? Such thinking, in the words of the ecologist Paul Shepard, "idealizes life with only its head out of water, inches above the limits of toleration of the corruption of its own environment . . . Why should we tolerate a diet of weak poisons, a home in insipid surroundings, a circle of acquaintances who are not quite our enemies, the noise of motors with just enough relief to prevent insanity? Who would want to live in a world which is just not quite fatal?"

Yet such a world is pressed upon us. The crusade to create a chemically sterile, insect-free world seems to have engendered a fanatic zeal on the part of many specialists and most of the so-called control agencies. On every hand there is evidence that those engaged in spraying operations exercise a ruthless power. "The regulatory entomologists . . . function as prosecutor, judge and jury, tax assessor and collector and sheriff to enforce their own orders," said

Connecticut entomologist Neely Turner. The most flagrant abuses go unchecked in both state and federal agencies.

It is not my contention that chemical insecticides must never be used. I do contend that we have put poisons and biologically potent chemicals indiscriminately into the hands of persons largely or wholly ignorant of their potentials for harm. We have subjected enormous numbers of people to contact with these poisons, without their consent and often without their knowledge. If the Bill of Rights contain no guarantee that a citizen shall be secure against lethal poisons distributed either by private individuals or by public officials, it is surely only because our forefathers, despite their considerable wisdom and foresight, could conceive of no such problem.

I contend, furthermore, that we have allowed these chemicals to be used with little or no advance investigation of their effect on soil, water, wildlife, and man himself. Future generations are unlikely to condone our lack of prudent concern for the integrity of the natural world that supports all life.

There is still very limited awareness of the nature of the threat. This is an era of specialists, each of whom sees his own problem and is unaware of or intolerant of the larger frame into which it fits. It is also an era dominated by industry, in which the right to make a dollar at whatever cost is seldom challenged. When the public protests, confronted with some obvious evidence of damaging results of pesticide applications, it is fed little tranquilizing pills of half truth. We urgently need an end to these false assurances, to the sugar coating of unpalatable facts. It is the public that is being asked to assume the risks that the insect controllers calculate. The public must decide whether it wishes to continue on the present road, and it can do so only when in full possession of the facts. In the words of Jean Rostand, "The obligation to endure gives us the right to know."

156. STUDENTS FOR A DEMOCRATIC SOCIETY, "THE PORT HURON STATEMENT," 1962

The Port Huron statement was the opening salvo in the student revolt.

We are people of this generation, bred in at least modest comfort, housed in universities, looking uncomfortably to the world we inherit.

. . .

Our work is guided by the sense that we may be the last generation in the experiment with living. But we are a minority—the vast majority of our people regard the temporary equilibriums of our society and the world as eternally-functional parts. In this is perhaps the outstanding paradox: We ourselves are imbued with urgency, yet the message of our society is that there is no viable alternative to the present. Beneath the reassuring tones of the politicians, beneath the common opinion that America will "muddle through," beneath the stagnation of those who have closed their minds to the future, is the pervading feeling that there simply are no alternatives, that our times have witnessed the exhaustion not only of Utopias, but of any new departures as well. Feeling the press of complexity upon the emptiness of life, people are fearful of the thought that at any moment things might thrust out of control. They fear change itself, since change might smash whatever invisible framework seems to hold back chaos for them now. For most Americans, all crusades are suspect, threatening. The fact that each individual sees apathy in his fellows perpetuates the common reluctance to organize for changes. The dominant institutions are complex enough to blunt the minds of their potential critics, and entrenched enough to swiftly dissipate or entirely repel the energies of protest and reform, thus limiting human expectancies. Then, too, we are a materially improved society, and by our own improvements we seem to have weakened the case for change.

Some would have us believe that Americans feel contentment amidst prosperity—but might it not better be called a glaze above deeply-felt anxieties about their role

Source: Students for a Democratic Society, "The Port Huron Statement," Port Huron, Michigan Convention, 1962. Reprinted by permission.

in the new world? And if these anxieties produce a developed indifference to human affairs, do they not as well produce a yearning to believe there *is* an alternative to the present, that something *can* be done to change circumstances in the school, the workplaces, the bureaucracies, the government? It is to this latter yearning, at once the spark and engine of change, that we direct our present appeal. The search for truly democratic alternatives to the present, and a commitment to social experimentation with them, is a worthy and fulfilling human enterprise, one which moves us and, we hope, others today. . . .

Values

Making values explicit—an initial task in establishing alternatives—is an activity that has been devalued and corrupted. The conventional moral terms of the age, the politician moralities ("free world," "peoples democracies") reflect realities poorly, if at all, and seem to function more as ruling myths than as descriptive principles. but neither has our experience in the universities brought us moral enlightenment. Our professors and administrators sacrifice controversy to public relations; their curriculums change more slowly than the living events of the world; their skills and silence are purchased by investors in the arms race; passion is called unscholastic. The questions we might want raised—what is really important? can we live in a different and better way? if we wanted to change society, how would we do it?—are not thought to be questions of a "fruitful, empirical nature," and thus are brushed aside.

Unlike youth in other countries we are used to moral leadership being exercised and moral dimensions being clarified by our elders. But today, for us, not even the liberal and socialist preachments of the past seem adequate to the forms of the present. Consider the old slogans: Capitalism Cannot Reform Itself, United Front Against Fascism, General Strike, All Out on May Day. Or, more recently, No Cooperation with Commies and Fellow Travelers, Ideologies Are Exhausted, Bipartisanship, No Utopias. These are incomplete, and there are few new prophets. It has been said that our liberal and socialist predecessors were plagued by vision without program, while our own generation is plagued by program without vision. All around there is astute grasp of method, technique—the committee, the *ad hoc* group, the lobbyist, the hard and soft sell, the make, the projected image—but, if pressed critically, such expertise is incompetent to explain its implicit ideals. It is highly fashionable to identify oneself by old categories, or by naming a respected political figure, or by explaining "how we would vote" on various issues.

Theoretic chaos has replaced the idealistic thinking of old—and, unable to constitute theoretic order, men have condemned idealism itself. Doubt has replaced hopefulness, and men act out a defeatism that is labelled realistic. The decline of utopia and hope is in fact one of the defining features of social life today. The reasons are various: the dreams of the older left were perverted by Stalinism and never recreated; the congressional stalemate makes men narrow their view of the possible; the specialization of human activity leaves little room for sweeping thought; the horrors of the twentieth century, symbolized in the gas ovens and concentration camps and atom bombs, have blasted hopefulness. To be idealistic is to be considered apocalyptic, deluded. To have no serious aspirations, on the contrary, is to be "toughminded."

In suggesting social goals and values, therefore, we are aware of entering a sphere of some disrepute. Perhaps matured by the past, we have no sure formulas, no closed theories—but that does not mean values are beyond discussion and tentative determination. A search for orienting theories and the creation of human values is complex but worthwhile. We are aware that to avoid platitudes we must analyze the concrete conditions of social order. But to direct such an analysis we must use the guideposts of basic principles. Our own social values involve conceptions of human beings, human relationships, and social systems.

We regard *men* as infinitely precious and possessed of unfulfilled capacities for reason, freedom, and love. In affirming these principles we are aware of countering perhaps the dominant conceptions of man in the twentieth century: that he is a thing to be manipulated, and that he is inherently incapable of directing his own affairs. We oppose the depersonalization that reduces human beings to the status of things. If anything, brutalities of the twentieth century teach that means and ends are intimately related, that vague appeals to "posterity" cannot justify the mutilations of the present. We oppose, too, the doctrine of human incompetence because it rests essentially on the modern fact that men have been "competently" manipulated into incompetence. We see little reason why men cannot meet with increasing skill the complexities and responsibilities of their situation, if society is organized not for minority participation but for majority participation in decision-making.

Men have unrealized potential for self-cultivation, self-direction, self-understanding, and creativity. It is this potential that we regard as crucial and to which we appeal—not to the human potentiality for violence, unreason, and submission to authority. The goal of man and society should be human independence: a concern not with image or popularity but with finding a meaning in life that is personally authentic; a quality of mind not compulsively driven by a sense of powerlessness, nor one which unthinkingly adopts status values, nor one which represses all threats to its habits, but one which has full, spontaneous access to present and past experiences, one which easily unites the fragmented parts of personal history, one which openly faces problems which are troubling and unresolved—one with an intuitive awareness of possibilities, an active sense of curiosity, an ability and willingness to learn.

This kind of independence does not mean egoistic individualism; the object is not to have one's way so much as it is to have a way that is one's own. Nor do we deify man—we merely have faith in his potential.

Human relationships should involve fraternity and honesty. Human interdependence is contemporary fact; human brotherhood must be willed, however, as a condition of future survival and as the most appropriate form of social relations. Personal links between man and man are needed, especially to go beyond the partial and fragmentary bonds of function that bind men only as worker to worker, employer to employer, teacher to student, American to Russian.

Loneliness, estrangement, isolation describe the vast distance between man and man today. These dominant tendencies cannot be overcome by better personnel management, nor by improved gadgets, but only when a love of man overcomes the idolatrous worship of things by man.

As the individualism we affirm is not egoism, the selflessness we affirm is not self-elimination. On the contrary, we believe in generosity of a kind that imprints one's unique individual qualities in the relation to other men, and to all human activity. Further, to dislike isolation is not to favor the abolition of privacy; the latter differs from isolation in that it occurs or is abolished according to individual will.

. . .

In the last few years, thousands of American students demonstrated that they at least felt the urgency of the times. They moved actively and directly against racial injustices, the threat of war, violations of individual rights of conscience and, less frequently, against economic manipulation. They succeeded in restoring a small measure of controversy to the campuses after the stillness of the McCarthy period. They succeeded, too, in gaining some concessions from the people and institutions they opposed, especially in the fight against racial bigotry.

The significance of these scattered movements lies not in their success or failure in gaining objectives—at least not yet. Nor does the significance lie in the intellectual "competence" or "maturity" of the students involved—as some pedantic elders allege. The significance is in the fact that the students are breaking the crust of apathy and overcoming the inner alienation—facts that remain the defining characteristics of American college life.

If student movements for change are rarities still on the campus scene, what is commonplace there? The real campus, the familiar campus, is a place of private people, engaged in their notorious "inner emigration." It is a place of commitment to business-as-usual, getting ahead, playing it cool. It is a place of mass affirmation of the Twist, but mass reluctance toward the controversial public stance. Rules are accepted as "inevitable," bureaucracy as "just circumstances," irrelevance as "scholarship," selflessness as "martyrdom," politics as "just another way to make people, and an unprofitable one, too."

Almost no students value activity as a citizen. Passive in public, they are hardly more idealistic in arranging their private lives; Gallup concludes they will settle for "low success, and won't risk high failure." There is not much willingness to take risks (not even in business), no setting of dangerous goals, no real conception of personal identity except one manufactured in the image of others, no real urge for personal fulfillment except to be almost as successful as the very successful people. Attention is being paid to social status (the quality of shirt collars, meeting people, getting wives or husbands, making solid contacts for later on); much, too, is paid to academic status (grades, honors, the med school rat-race). But neglected generally is real intellectual status, the personal cultivation of the mind.

. . .

Look beyond the campus, to America itself. That student life is more intellectual, and perhaps more comfortable, does not obscure the fact that the fundamental qualities of life on the campus reflect the habits of society at large. The fraternity president is seen at the junior manager levels; the sorority queen has gone to Grosse Pointe; the serious poet burns for a place, any place, to work; the once serious and never serious poets work at the advertising agencies. The desperation of people threatened by forces about which they know little and of which they can say less, the cheerful emptiness of people giving up all hope of changing things, and faceless ones polled by Gallup who listed "international affairs" fourteenth on their list of problems but who also expected thermonuclear war in the next few years—in these and other forms, Americans are in withdrawal from public life, from any collective effort at directing their own affairs.

Some regard these national doldrums as a sign of healthy approval of the established order, but is it approval by consent or by manipulated acquiescence? Others declare that the people are withdrawn because compelling issues are fast disappearing; perhaps there are fewer breadlines in America, but is Jim Crow gone, is there enough work and is work more fulfilling, is world war a diminishing threat, and what of the revolutionary new peoples? Still others think the national quietude is a necessary consequence of the need for elites to resolve complex and specialized problems of modern industrial society. But, then, why should business elites help decide foreign policy, and who controls the elites anyway, and are they solving mankind's problems? Others finally shrug knowingly and announce that full democracy never worked anywhere in the past—but why lump qualitatively different civilizations together, and how can a social order work well if its best thinkers are skeptics, and is man really doomed forever to the domination of today?

There are no convincing apologies for the contemporary malaise. . . . The apathy is, first, subjective—the felt powerlessness of ordinary people, the resignation before the enormity of events. But subjective apathy is encouraged by the objective American situation—the actual separation of people from power, from relevant knowledge, from pinnacles of decision-making. Just as the university influences the student way of life, so do major social institutions create the circumstances in which the isolated citizen will try hopelessly to understand his world and himself.

The very isolation of the individual—from power and community and ability to aspire—means the rise of a democracy without publics. With the great mass of people structurally remote and psychologically hesitant with respect to democratic institutions, those institutions themselves attenuate and become, in a fashion of the vicious circle, progressively less accessible to those few who aspire to serious participation in social affairs. The vital democratic connection between community and leadership, between the mass and the several elites, has been so wrenched and perverted that disastrous policies go unchallenged time and again. . . .

The first effort, then, should be to state a vision: What is the perimeter of human possibility in this epoch? . . . The second effort, if we are to be politically responsible, is to evaluate the prospects for obtaining at least a substantial part of that vision in our epoch: What are the social forces that exist, or that must exist, if we are to be successful? And what role have we ourselves to play as a social force?

157. BETTY FRIEDAN, *THE FEMININE MYSTIQUE*, 1963

Betty Friedan helped inaugurate the modern women's movement with her enormously successful book, The Feminine Mystique. *These chapters detail her discovery of the problem and sketch her proposed solutions.*

The problem lay buried, unspoken, for many years in the minds of American women. It was a strange stirring, a sense of dissatisfaction, a yearning that women suffered in the middle of the twentieth century in the United States. Each suburban wife struggled with it alone. As she made the beds, shopped for groceries, matched slipcover material, ate peanut butter sandwiches with her children, chauffeured Cub Scouts and Brownies, lay beside her husband at night—she was afraid to ask even of herself the silent question—"Is this all?"

For over fifteen years there was no word of this yearning in the millions of words written about women, for women, in all the columns, books and articles by experts telling women their role was to seek fulfillment as wives and mothers. Over and over women heard in voices of tradition and of Freudian sophistication that they could

Source: Betty Friedan, *The Feminine Mystique.* "The problem that has no name," pp. 11–27. Copyright Doubleday 1984. Reprinted by permission.

desire no greater destiny than to glory in their own femininity. Experts told them how to catch a man and keep him, how to breastfeed children and handle their toilet training, how to cope with sibling rivalry and adolescent rebellion; how to buy a dishwasher, bake bread, cook gourmet snails, and build a swimming pool with their own hands; how to dress, look, and act more feminine and make marriage more exciting; how to keep their husbands from dying young and their sons from growing into delinquents. They were taught to pity the neurotic, unfeminine, unhappy women who wanted to be poets or physicists or presidents. They learned that truly feminine women do not want careers, higher education, political rights—the independence and the opportunities that the old-fashioned feminists fought for. Some women, in their forties and fifties still remembered painfully giving up those dreams, but most of the younger women no longer even thought about them. A thousand expert voices applauded their femininity, their adjustment, their new maturity. All they had to do was devote their lives from earliest girlhood to finding a husband and bearing children.

By the end of the nineteen-fifties, the average marriage age of women in America dropped to 20, and was still dropping, into the teens. Fourteen million girls were engaged by 17. The proportion of women attending college in comparison with men dropping from 47 per cent in 1920 to 35 per cent in 1958. A century earlier, women had fought for a higher education; now girls went to college to get a husband. By the mid-fifties, 60 per cent dropped out of college to marry, or because they were afraid too much education would be a marriage bar. Colleges built dormitories for "married students," but the students were almost always the husbands. (A new degree was instituted for wives—"Ph.T." (Putting Husband Through).

Then American girls began getting married in high school. And the women's magazines, deploring the unhappy statistics about these young marriages, urged that courses on marriage, and marriage counselors, be installed in the high schools. Girls started going steady at twelve and thirteen, in junior high. Manufacturers put out brassieres with false bosoms of foam rubber for little girls of ten. And an advertisement for a child's dress, sizes 3-6x, in *The New York Times* in the fall of 1960, said: "She Too Can Join the Man-Trap Set."

By the end of the fifties, the United States birthrate was overtaking India's. The birth-control movement, renamed Planned Parenthood, was asked to find a method whereby women who had been advised that a third or fourth baby would be born dead or defective might have it anyhow. Statisticians were especially astounded at the fantastic increase in the number of babies among college women. Where once they had two children, now they had four, five, six. Women who had once wanted careers were now making careers out of having babies. So rejoiced *Life* magazine in a 1956 paean to the movement of American women back to the home.

In a New York hospital, a woman had a nervous breakdown when she found she could not breastfeed her baby. In other hospitals, women dying of cancer refused a drug which research had proved might save their lives: its side effects were said to be unfeminine. "If I have only one life, let me live it as a blonde," a larger-than-life-sized picture of a pretty, vacuous woman proclaimed from the newspaper, magazine, and drugstore ads. And across America, three out of every ten women dyed their hair blonde. They ate a chalk called Metrecal, instead of food, to shrink to the size of the thin young models. Department-store buyers reported that American women, since 1939, had become three and four sizes smaller. "Women are out to fit the clothes, instead of vice-versa," one buyer said.

Interior decorators were designing kitchens with mosaic murals and original paintings, for kitchens were once again the center of women's lives. Home sewing became a million-dollar industry. Many women no longer left their homes, except to shop, chauffeur their children, or attend a social engagement with their husbands. Girls were growing up in America without ever having jobs outside the home. In the late fifties, a sociological phenomenon was suddenly remarked: a third of American women now worked, but most were no longer young and very few were pursuing careers. They were married women who held part-time jobs, selling or secretarial, to put their husbands through school, their sons through college, or to help pay the mortgage. Or they were widows supporting families. Fewer and fewer women were entering professional work. The shortages in the nursing, social work, and teaching professions caused crises in almost every American city. Concerned over the Soviet Union's lead in the space race, scientists noted that America's greatest source of unused brain-power was women. But girls would not study physics: it was "unfeminine." A girl refused a science fellowship at Johns Hopkins to take a job in a real-estate office. All she wanted, she said, was what every other American girl wanted—to get married, have four children and live in a nice house in a nice suburb.

The suburban housewife—she was the dream image of the young American women and the envy, it was said, of women all over the world. The American housewife—

freed by science and labor-saving appliances from the drudgery, the dangers of childbirth and the illnesses of her grandmother. She was healthy, beautiful, educated, concerned only about her husband, her children, her home. She had found true feminine fulfillment. As a housewife and mother, she was respected as a full and equal partner to man in his world. She was free to choose automobiles, clothes, appliances, supermarkets; she had everything that women ever dreamed of.

In the fifteen years after World War II, this mystique of feminine fulfillment became the cherished and self-perpetuating core of contemporary American culture. Millions of women lived their lives in the image of those pretty pictures of the American suburban housewife, kissing their husbands goodbye in front of the picture window, depositing their stationwagonsful of children at school, and smiling as they ran the new electric waxer over the spotless kitchen floor. They baked their own bread, sewed their own and their children's clothes, kept their new washing machines and dryers running all day. They changed the sheets on the beds twice a week instead of once, took the rug-hooking class in adult education, and pitied their poor frustrated mothers, who had dreamed of having a career. Their only dream was to be perfect wives and mothers; their highest ambition to have five children and a beautiful house, their only fight to get and keep their husbands. They had no thought for the unfeminine problems of the world outside the home; they wanted the men to make the major decisions. They gloried in their role as women, and wrote proudly on the census blank: "Occupation: housewife."

For over fifteen years, the words written for women, and the words women used when they talked to each other, while their husbands sat on the other side of the room and talked shop or politics or septic tanks, were about problems with their children, or how to keep their husbands happy, or improve their children's school, or cook chicken or make slipcovers. Nobody argued whether women were inferior or superior to men; they were simply different. Words like "emancipation" and "career" sounded strange and embarrassing; no one had used them for years. When a Frenchwoman named Simone de Beauvoir wrote a book called *The Second Sex,* an American critic commented that she obviously "didn't know what life was all about," and besides she was talking about French women. The "woman problem" in America no longer existed.

If a woman had a problem in the 1950's and 1960's, she knew that something must be wrong with her marriage, or with herself. Other women were satisfied with their lives, she thought. What kind of a woman was she if she did not feel this mysterious fulfillment waxing the kitchen floor? She was so ashamed to admit her dissatisfaction that she never knew how many other women shared it. If she tried to tell her husband, he didn't understand what she was talking about. She did not really understand it herself. For over fifteen years women in America found it harder to talk about this problem than about sex. Even the psychoanalysts had no name for it. When a woman went to a psychiatrist for help, as many women did, she would say, "I'm so ashamed," or "I must be hopelessly neurotic." "I don't know what's wrong with women today," a suburban psychiatrist said uneasily. "I only know something is wrong because most of my patients happen to be women. And their problem isn't sexual." Most women with this problem did not go to see a psychoanalyst, however. "There's nothing wrong really," they kept telling themselves. "There's isn't any problem."

But on an April morning in 1959, I heard a mother of four, having coffee with four other mothers in a suburban development fifteen miles from New York, say in a tone of quiet desperation, "the problem." And the others knew, without words, that she was not talking about a problem with her husband, or her children, or her home. Suddenly they realized they all shared the same problem, the problem that has no name. They began, hesitantly, to talk about it. Later, after they had picked up their children at nursery school and taken them home to nap, two of the women cried, in sheer relief, just to know they were not alone.

Gradually I came to realize that the problem that has no name was shared by countless women in America. As a magazine writer I often interviewed women about problems with their children, or their marriages, or their houses, or their communities. But after a while I began to recognize the telltale signs of this other problem. I saw the same signs in suburban ranch houses and split-levels on Long Island and in New Jersey and Westchester County; in colonial houses in a small Massachusetts town; on patios in Memphis; in suburban and city apartments; in living rooms in the Midwest. Sometimes I sensed the problem, not as a reporter, but as a suburban housewife, for during this time I was also bringing up my own three children in Rockland County, New York. I heard echoes of the problem in college dormitories and semi-private maternity wards, at PTA meetings and luncheons of the League of Women Voters, at suburban cocktail parties, in station wagons waiting for trains, and in snatches of conversation overheard at Schrafft's. The groping words I heard from other women, on quiet afternoons when children were at school or on quiet evenings when husbands worked late, I think I understood first as a woman long before I understood their larger social and psychological implications.

Just what was this problem that has no name? What were the words women used when they tried to express it? Sometimes a woman would say "I feel empty somehow . . . incomplete." Or she would say, "I feel as if I don't exist." Sometimes she blotted out the feeling with a tranquilizer. Sometimes she thought the problem was with her husband, or her children, or that what she really needed was to redecorate her house, or move to a better neighborhood, or have an affair, or another baby. Sometimes, she went to a doctor with symptoms she could hardly describe: "A tired feeling . . . I get so angry with the children it scares me . . . I feel like crying without any reason." (A Cleveland doctor called it "the housewife's syndrome.") A number of women told me about great bleeding blisters that break out on their hands and arms. "I call it the housewife's blight," said a family doctor in Pennsylvania. "I see it so often lately in these young women with four, five and six children who bury themselves in their dishpans. But it isn't caused by detergent and it isn't cured by cortisone."

Sometimes a woman would tell me that the finding gets so strong she runs out of the house and walks through the streets. Or she stays inside her house and cries. Or her children tell her a joke, and she doesn't laugh because she doesn't hear it. I talked to women who had spent years on the analyst's couch, working out their "adjustment to the feminine role," their blocks to "fulfillment as a wife and mother." But the desperate tone in these women's voices, and the look in their eyes, was the same as the tone and the look of other women, who were sure they had no problem, even though they did have a strange feeling of desperation.

A mother of four who left college at nineteen to get married told me:

> I've tried everything women are supposed to do—hobbies, gardening, pickling, canning, being very social with my neighbors, joining committees, running PTA teas. I can do it all, and I like it, but it doesn't leave you anything to think about—any feeling of who you are. I never had any career ambitions. All I wanted was to get married and have four children. I love the kids and Bob and my home. There's no problem you can even put a name to. But I'm desperate. I begin to feel I have no personality. I'm a server of food and putter-on of pants and a bedmaker, somebody who can be called on when you want something. But who am I?

A twenty-three-year-old mother in blue jeans said:

> I ask myself why I'm so dissatisfied. I've got my health, fine children, a lovely new home, enough money. My husband has a real future as an electronics engineer. He doesn't have any of these feelings. He says maybe I need a vacation, let's go to New York for a weekend. But that isn't it. I always had this idea we should do everything together. I can't sit down and read a book alone. If the children are napping and I have one hour to myself I just walk through the house waiting for them to wake up. I don't make a move until I know where the rest of the crowd is going. It's as if ever since you were a little girl, there's always been somebody or something that will take care of your life: your parents, or college, or falling in love, or having a child, or moving to a new house. Then you wake up one morning and there's nothing to look forward to.

A young wife in a Long Island development said:

> I seem to sleep so much. I don't know why I should be so tired. This house isn't nearly so hard to clean as the cold-water flat we had when I was working. The children are at school all day. It's not the work. I just don't feel alive.

In 1960, the problem that has no name burst like a boil through the image of the happy American housewife. In the television commercials the pretty housewives still beamed over their foaming dishpans and *Time*'s cover story on "The Suburban Wife, an American Phenomenon" protested: "Having too good a time . . . to believe that they should be unhappy." But the actual unhappiness of the American housewife was suddenly being reported from the *New York Times* and *Newsweek* to *Good Housekeeping* and CBS Television ("The Trapped Housewife"), although almost everybody who talked about it found some superficial reason to dismiss it. It was attributed to incompetent appliance repairmen (*New York Times*), or the distances children must be chauffeured in the suburbs (*Time*), or too much PTA (*Redbook*). Some said it was the old problem—education: more and more women had education, which naturally made them unhappy in their role as housewives. "The road from Freud to Frigidaire, from Sophocles to Spock, has turned out to be a bumpy one," reported the *New York Times* (June 28, 1960). "Many young women—certainly not all—whose education plunged them into a world of ideas feel stifled in the homes. They find their routine lives out of joint with their training. Like shut-ins, they feel left out. In the last year, the problem of the educated housewife has provided the meat of dozens of speeches made by troubled presidents of women's colleges who maintain, in the face of complaints, that sixteen years of academic training is realistic preparation for wifehood and motherhood."

There was much sympathy for the educated housewife. ("Like a two-headed schizophrenic . . . once she wrote a paper on the Graveyard poets; now she writes notes to the milkman. Once she determined the boiling point of sulphuric acid; now she determines her boiling point with the overdue repairman. . . . The housewife often is reduced to screams and tears. . . . No one, it seems, is appreciative, least of all herself, of the kind of person she becomes in the process of turning from poetess into a shrew.")

Home economists suggested more realistic preparation for housewives, such as high-school workshops in home appliances. College educators suggested more discussion groups on home management and the family, to prepare women for the adjustment to domestic life. A spate of articles appeared in the mass magazines offering "Fifty-eight Ways to Make Your Marriage More Exciting." No month went by without a new book by a psychiatrist or sexologist offering technical advice of finding career fulfillment through sex.

A male humorist joked in *Harper's Bazaar* (July, 1960) that the problem could be solved by taking away woman's right to vote. ("In the pre-19th Amendment era, the American woman was placid, sheltered and sure of her role in American society. She left all the political decisions to her husband and he, in turn, left all the family decisions to her. Today a woman has to make both the family *and* the political decisions, and it's too much for her.")

A number of educators suggested seriously that women no longer be admitted to the four-year colleges and universities; in the growing college crisis, the education which girls could not use as housewives was more urgently needed than ever by boys to do the work of the atomic age.

The problem was also dismissed with drastic solutions no one could take seriously. (A woman writer proposed in *Harper's* that women be drafted for compulsory service as nurses' aides and baby-sitters.) And it was smoothed over with the age-old panaceas: "love is their answer," "the only answer is inner help." "the secret of completeness—children," "a private means of intellectual fulfillment," "to cure this toothache of the spirit—the simple formula of handling one's self and one's will over to God."

The problem was dismissed by telling the housewife she doesn't realize how lucky she is—her own boss, no time clock, no junior executive gunning for her job. What if she isn't happy—does she think men are happy in this world? Does she really, secretly, still want to be a man? Doesn't she know yet how lucky she is to be a woman?

The problem was also, and finally, dismissed by shrugging that there are no solutions: this is what being a woman means, and what is wrong with American women that they can't accept their role gracefully? As *Newsweek* put it (March 7, 1960):

> She is dissatisfied with a lot of women of other hands can only dream of. Her discontent is deep, pervasive, and impervious to the superficial remedies which are offered at every hand. . . . An army of professional explorers have already charted the major sources of trouble. . . . From the beginning of time, the female cycle has defined and confined woman's role. As Freud was credited with saying: "Anatomy is destiny." Though no group of women has ever pushed these natural restrictions as far as the American wife, it seems that she still cannot accept them with good grace. . . . A young mother with a beautiful family, charm, talent and brains is apt to dismiss her role apologetically. "What do I do?" you hear her say. "Why nothing. I'm just a housewife." A good education, it seems, has given this paragon among women an understanding of the value of everything except her own worth. . . .

And so she must accept the fact that "American women's unhappiness is merely the most recently won of women's rights," and adjust and say with the happy housewife found by *Newsweek:* "We ought to salute the wonderful freedom we all have and be proud of our lives today. I have had college and I've worked, but being a housewife is the most rewarding and satisfying role. . . . My mother was never included in my father's business affairs . . . she couldn't get out of the house and away from us children. But I am an equal to my husband; I can go along with him on business trips and to social business affairs."

The alternative offered was a choice that few women would contemplate. In the sympathetic words of the *New York Times:* "All admit to being deeply frustrated at times by the lack of privacy, the physical burden, the routine of family life, the confinement of it. However, none would give up her home and family if she had the choice to make again." *Redbook* commented: "Few women would want to thumb their noses at husbands, children and community and go off on their own. Those who do may be talented individuals, but they rarely are successful women."

The year American women's discontent boiled over, it was also reported (*Look*) that the more 21,000,000 American women who are single, widowed or divorced do not cease even after fifty their frenzied, desperate search for a man. And the search begins early—for seventy per cent of all American women now marry before they are twenty-four. A pretty twenty-five year-old secretary took thirty-five different jobs in six months in the futile hope of finding a husband. Women were moving from one political club to another, taking evening courses in accounting or sailing, learning to play golf or ski, joining a number of churches in succession, going to bars alone, in their ceaseless search for a man.

Of the growing thousands of women currently getting private psychiatric help in the United States, the married ones were reported dissatisfied with their marriages, the unmarried ones suffering from anxiety and, finally, depression. Strangely, a number of psychiatrists stated that, in their experience, unmarried women patients were happier than married ones. So the door of all those pretty suburban houses opened a crack to permit a glimpse of uncounted thousands of American housewives who suffered alone from a problem that suddenly everyone was talking about, and beginning to take for granted, as one of those unreal problems in American life that can never be solved—like the hydrogen bomb. By 1962 the plight of the trapped American housewife had become a national parlor game. Whole issues of magazines, newspaper columns, books learned and frivolous, educational conferences and television panels were devoted to the problem.

Even so, most men, and some women, still did not know that this problem was real. But those who had faced it honestly knew that all the superficial remedies, the sympathetic advice, the scolding words and the cheering words were somehow drowning the problem in unreality. A bitter laugh was beginning to be heard from American women. They were admired, envied, pitied, theorized over until they were sick of it, offered drastic solutions or silly choices that no one could take seriously. They got all kinds of advice from the growing armies of marriage and child-guidance counselors, psychotherapists, and armchair psychologists, on how to adjust to their role as housewives. No other road to fulfillment was offered to American women in the middle of the twentieth century. Most adjusted to their role and suffered or ignored the problem that has no name. It can be less painful for a woman, not to hear the strange, dissatisfied voice stirring within her.

It is no longer possible to ignore that voice, to dismiss the desperation of so many American women. This is not what being a woman means, no matter what the experts say. For human suffering there is a reason; perhaps the reason has not been found because the right questions have not been asked, or pressed far enough. I do not accept the answer that there is no problem because American women have luxuries that women in other times and lands never dreamed of; part of the strange newness of the problem is that it cannot be understood in terms of the age-old material problems of man: poverty, sickness, hunger, cold. The women who suffer this problem have a hunger that food cannot fill. It persists in women whose husbands are struggling internes and law clerks, or prosperous doctors and lawyers; in wives of workers and executives who make $5,000 a year or $50,000. It is not caused by lack of material advantages; it may not even be felt by women preoccupied with desperate problems of hunger, poverty or illness. And women who think it will be solved by more money, a bigger house, a second car, moving to a better suburb, often discover it gets worse.

It is no longer possible today to blame the problem on loss of femininity: to say that education and independence and equality with men have made American woman unfeminine. I have heard so many women try to deny this dissatisfied voice within themselves because it does not fit the pretty picture of femininity the experts have given them. I think, in fact, that this is the first clue to the mystery: the problem cannot be understood in the generally accepted terms by which scientists have studied women, doctors have treated them, counselors have advised them, and writers have written about them. Women who suffer this problem, in whom this voice is stirring, have lived their whole lives in the pursuit of feminine fulfillment. They are not career women (although career women may have other problems); they are women whose greatest ambition has been marriage and children. For the oldest of these women, these daughters of the American middle class, no other dream was possible. The ones in their forties and fifties who once had other dreams gave them up and threw themselves joyously into life as housewives. For the youngest, the new wives and mothers, this was the only dream. They are the ones who quit high school and college to marry, or marked time in some job in which they had no real interest until they married. These women are very "feminine" in the usual sense, and yet they still suffer the problem.

Are the women who finished college, the women who once had dreams beyond housewifery, the ones who suffer the most? According to the experts they are, but listen to these four women:

> My days are all busy, and dull, too. All I ever do is mess around. I get up at eight—I make breakfast, so I do the dishes, have lunch, do some more dishes, and some laundry and cleaning in the afternoon. Then it's supper dishes and I get to sit down a few minutes, before the children have to be sent to bed. . . . There's all there is to my day. It's just like my other wife's day. Humdrum. The biggest time, I am chasing kids.
>
> Ye Gods, what do I do with my time? Well, I get up at six. I get my son dressed and then give him breakfast. After that I wash dishes and bathe and feed the baby. Then I get lunch and while the children nap, I sew or mend or iron and do all the other things I can't get done before noon. Then I cook supper for the family and my husband watches TV while I do the dishes. After I get the children to bed, I set my hair and then I go to bed.

The problem is always being the children's mommy, or the minister's wife and never being myself.

> A film made of any typical morning in my house would look like an old Marx Brothers' comedy. I wash the dishes, rush the older children off to school, dash out in the yard to cultivate the chrysanthemums, run back in to make a phone call about a committee meeting, help the youngest child build a blockhouse, spend fifteen minutes skimming the newspapers so I can be well-informed, then scamper down to the washing machines where my thrice-weekly laundry includes enough clothes to keep a primitive village going for an entire year. By noon I'm ready for a padded cell. Very little of what I've done has been really necessary or important. Outside pressures lash me through the day. Yet I look upon myself as one of the more relaxed housewives in the neighborhood. Many of my friends are even more frantic. In the past sixty years we have come full circle and the American housewife is once again trapped in a squirrel cage. If the cage is now a modern plate-glass-and-broadloom ranch house or a convenient modern apartment, the situation is no less painful than when her grandmother sat over an embroidery hoop in her gilt-and-plush parlor and muttered angrily about women's rights.

The first two women never went to college. They live in developments in Levittown, New Jersey, and Tacoma, Washington, and were interviewed by a team of sociologists studying workingmen's wives. The third, a minister's wife, wrote on the fifteenth reunion questionnaire of her college that she never had any career ambitions, but wishes now she had. The fourth, who has a Ph.D. in anthropology, is today a Nebraska housewife with three children. Their words seem to indicate that housewives of all educational levels suffer the same feeling of desperation.

The fact is that no one today is muttering angrily about "women's rights," even though more and more women have gone to college. In a recent study of all the classes that have graduated from Barnard College, a significant minority of earlier graduates blamed their education for making them want "rights," later classes blamed their education for giving them career dreams, but recent graduates blamed the college for making them feel it was not enough simply to be a housewife and mother; they did not want to feel guilty if they did not read books or take part in community activities. But if education is not the cause of the problem, the fact that education somehow festers in these women may be a clue.

If the secret of feminine fulfillment is having children, never have so many women, with the freedom to choose, had so many children, in so few years, so willingly. If the answer is love, never have women searched for love with such determination. And yet there is a growing suspicion that the problem may not be sexual, though it must somehow be related to sex. I have heard from many doctors evidence of new sexual problems between man and wife—sexual hunger in wives so great their husbands cannot satisfy it. "We have made women a sex creature," said a psychiatrist at the Margaret Sanger marriage counseling clinic. "She has no identity except as a wife and mother. She does not know who she is herself. She waits all day for her husband to come home at night to make her feel alive. And now it is the husband who is not interested. It is terrible for the women, to lie there, night after night, waiting for her husband to make her feel alive." Why is there such a market for books and articles offering sexual advice? The kind of sexual orgasm which Kinsey found in statistical plenitude in the recent generation of American women does not seem to make this problem go away.

On the contrary, new neuroses are being seen among women—and problems as yet unnamed as neuroses—which Freud and his followers did not predict, with physical symptoms, anxieties, and defense mechanisms equal to those caused by sexual repression. And strange new problems are being reported in the growing generations of children whose mothers were always there, driving them around, helping them with their homework—an inability to endure pain or discipline or pursue any self-sustained goal of any sort, a devastating boredom with life. Educators are increasingly uneasy about the dependence, the lack of self-reliance, of the boys and girls who are entering college today. "We fight a continual battle to make our students assume manhood," said a Columbia dean.

A White House conference was held on the physical and muscular deterioration of American children: were they being over-nurtured? Sociologists noted the astounding organization of suburban children's lives: the lessons, parties, entertainments, play and study groups organized for them. A suburban housewife in Portland, Oregon, wondered why the children "need" Brownies and Boy Scouts out here. "This is not the slums. The kids out here have the great outdoors. I think people are so bored, they organize the children, and then try to hook everyone else on it. And the poor kids have no time left just to lie on their beds and daydream."

Can the problem that has no name be somehow related to the domestic routine of the housewife? When a woman tries to put the problem into words, she often merely describes the daily life she leads. What is there in this recital of comfortable domestic detail that could possibly cause such a feeling of desperation? Is she trapped simply by the enormous demands of her role as modern housewife: wife, mistress, mother, nurse, consumer, cook, chauffeur; expert on interior decoration, child care, appliance repair, furniture refinishing, nutrition, and education? Her day is fragmented as she rushes from dishwasher to washing machine to telephone to dryer to station wagon to supermarket, and delivers Johnny to the Little League field, takes Janey to dancing class, gets the lawnmower fixed and meets the 6:45. She can never spend more than 15 minutes on any one thing; she has no time to read books, only magazines; even if she had time, she has lost the power to concentrate. At the end of the day, she is so terribly tired that sometimes her husband has to take over and put the children to bed.

Thus terrible tiredness took so many women to doctors in the 1950's that one decided to investigate it. He found, surprisingly, that his patients suffering from "housewife's fatigue" slept more than an adult needed to sleep—as much as ten hours a day—and that the actual energy they expended on housework did not tax their capacity. The real problem must be something else, he decided—perhaps boredom. Some doctors told their women patients they must get out of the house for a day, treat themselves to a movie in town. Others prescribed tranquilizers. Many suburban housewives were taking tranquilizers like cough drops. "You wake up in the morning, and you feel as if there's no point in going on another day like this. So you take a tranquilizer because it makes you not care so much that it's pointless."

It is easy to see the concrete details that trap the suburban housewife, the continual demands of her time. But the chains that bind her in her trap are chains in her own mind and spirit. They are chains made up of mistaken ideas and misinterpreted facts, of incomplete truths and unreal choices. They are not easily seen and not easily shaken off.

How can any women see the whole truth within the bounds of her own life? How can she believe that voice inside herself, when it denies the conventional, accepted truths by which she has been living? And yet the women I have talked to, who are finally listening to that inner voice, seem in some incredible way to be groping through to a truth that has defied the experts.

I think the experts in a great many fields have been holding pieces of that truth under their microscopes for a long time without realizing it. I found pieces of it in certain new research and theoretical developments in psychological, social and biological science whose implications for women seem never to have been examined. I found many clues by talking to suburban doctors, gynecologists, obstetricians, child-guidance clinicians, pediatricians, high-school guidance counselors, college professors, marriage counselors, psychiatrists and ministers—questioning them not on their theories, but on their actual experience in treating American women. I became aware of a growing body of evidence, much of which has not been reported publicly because it does not fit current modes of thought about women—evidence which throws into question the standards of feminine morality, feminine adjustment, feminine fulfillment, and feminine maturity by which most women are still trying to live.

I began to see in a strange new light the American return to early marriage and the large families that are causing the population explosion; the recent movement to natural childbirth and breastfeeding; suburban conformity, and the new neuroses, character pathologies and sexual problems being reported by the doctors. I began to see new dimensions to old problems that have long been taken for granted among women: menstrual difficulties, sexual frigidity, promiscuity, pregnancy fears, childbirth depression, the high incidence of emotional breakdown and suicide among women in their twenties and thirties, the menopause crises, the so-called passivity and immaturity of American men, the discrepancy between women's tested intellectual abilities in childhood and their adult achievement, the changing incidence of adult sexual orgasm in American women, and persistent problems in psychotherapy and in women's education.

If I am right, the problem that has no name stirring in the minds of so many American women today is not a matter of loss of femininity or too much education, or the demands of domesticity. It is far more important than anyone recognizes. It is the key to these other new and old problems which have been torturing women and their husbands and children, and puzzling their doctors and educators for years. It may well be the key to our future as a nation and a culture. We can no longer ignore that voice within women that says: "I want something more than my husband and my children and my home."

158. Malcolm X, Malcolm X Explains His Ideas, 1964

On his way home from Africa, Malcolm X stopped off in Paris, where he spoke at the Salle de la Mutualité on November 23, 1964, at a meeting sponsored by "Présence Africaine," the African cultural organization. The only report of the meeting in the American press, by Ruth Porter, began as follows:

"There wasn't a square inch of unoccupied space in the meeting room. The seats were filled an hour before the lecture was scheduled to begin. The 'late' arrivals stood or sat on the floor. When not another human being could be jammed into the hall, the crowd spilled into the corridors, hoping to stand within earshot. Those who arrived on time could not find standing room in the corridors and had to leave. The speaker himself could barely push into the room over the assorted legs of those on the floor. Africans, Americans black and white, European leftists of all persuasions, representatives of the press, all were intensely interested in what Malcolm X would say."

(The Militant, December 7, 1964)

Malcolm's opening remarks, printed under the title of "The Black Struggle in the United States" in the English-language edition of Présence Africaine, No. 2, 1965, are omitted here because they repeat material found elsewhere in this book, but the full text of his answers of twenty-four questions follows. In this chapter, three periods (. . .) represent gaps in the tape recording as transcribed by Présence Africaine.

Question 1: How is it possible that some people are still preaching nonviolence?

Malcolm X: That's easy to understand—shows you the power of dollarism. The dollar makes anything possible. In nineteen-sixt—(I forget what year it was when the Sharpeville massacre took place in South Africa) if you read the testimony of Mandela in court, he brought out the fact that at that point the brothers in South Africa had begun to realize that they had to go into action, that nonviolence had become outdated: it only helped the enemy. But at the same time the enemy knows that once eleven million people stop being confined to a nonviolent approach against three million, you're going to have a different situation. They had to use their new modern tricks, so they ran down and got one of the Africans and gave him a glorious peace prize for being nonviolent, and it lent strength to the nonviolent image, to try and keep them a little nonviolent a little while longer. And it's the same way in the States. The black man in the States has begun to see that nonviolence is a trick that is put upon him to keep him from even being able to defend himself.

And so there's an increasing number of black people in America who are absolutely ready and willing to do whatever is necessary to see that their lives and their own property are protected by them.

So you have again your imperialists, and whatever else you call them, come along and give out another peace prize to again try and strengthen the image of

---

Source: Malcolm X, *By Any Means Necessary.* "At a Meeting in Paris," pp. 113–119. Copyright 1970 and 1992 by Betty Shabazz and Pathfinder Press. Reprinted by permission.

nonviolence. This is their way of doing things, but everybody doesn't always accept those peace prizes.

Question 2: I should like to ask Mr. Malcolm X two questions. The first, what is his opinion of the Jewish problem and the solidarity of Jews and Negroes against racism? The second, if he knows the names of Lincoln, Wilberforce, Garrison, John Brown and others, and what is his opinion of these gentlemen?

Malcolm: Most white people who profess to be for the Negro struggle are usually with it as long as they are nonviolent. And they're the ones who encourage them to be nonviolent, to love their enemies, and turn the other cheek. But those who are genuinely for the freedom of the black man—as far as we're concerned, they're all right. Now in regards to what is my opinion of the Jews. I don't think that a man can be intelligent when he's in the frying pan and he becomes wrapped up or involved in trying to solve someone else's problems or cry for someone else. The American Negroes especially have been maneuvered into doing more crying for the Jews than they cry for themselves.

In America the Jews used to be segregated. They never were "Freedom Riders." They didn't use this tactic to solve their problem—begging in, walking in, wading in. Whenever they were barred from an neighborhood they pooled their economic power and purchased that neighborhood. If they were barred from hotels, they bought the hotel. But when they join us, they don't show us how to solve our problem that way. They show us how to wade in and crawl in and beg in. So I'm for the Jew when he shows me how to solve my problem like he has solved his problem.

Question 3: May I ask you if you were a Muslim before joining the "Black Muslims" or if you chose that religion after, and, if so—why?

Malcolm: A man's choice of religion is his personal business, but I might add to your question. Christianity was used in America on us, on our people, not to take us to Heaven but to make us good slaves, primarily—by robbing us of our right to defend ourselves in the name of Jesus.

Question 4: Many black Americans are hoping you will be their leader. Do you have a determined political program and I would like to know, if you do have a political program which has already been set up, would you join this with a new organization which is called "Freedom Now"?

Malcolm: First, I don't profess to be anybody's leader. I'm one of 22 million Afro-Americans, all of whom have suffered the same things. And I probably cry out a little louder against the suffering than most others and therefore, perhaps, I'm better known.

I don't profess to have a political, economic, or social solution to a problem as complicated as the one which our people face in the States, but I am one of those who is willing to try *any means necessary* to bring an end to the injustices our people suffer.

One of the reasons why I say it's difficult to come up and say "this is the solution" or "that is the solution" is that a chicken cannot produce a duck egg, and it can't produce a duck egg because the system itself was produced by a chicken egg and can only reproduce what produced it.

The American system was produced from the enslavement of the black man. This political, economic, and social system of America was produced from the enslavement of the black man and that particular system is capable only of reproducing that out of which itself was produced. The only way a chicken can produce a duck egg [is] you have to revolutionize the system.

Question 5: The history of the United States has clearly proved that none of the previous presidents has been able to solve integration. Now I'd like to know, Mr. Malcolm, your position in so far as the last election is concerned and what do you think in particular of developments in the future under President Johnson?

Malcolm: It's the same system. It's not the President who can help or hurt. And this system is not only ruling us in America—it's ruling the world.

Nowadays when a man is running for president of the United States he's not running for the president of the United States alone, but he has to be acceptable to every area of the world where the influence of the United States reaches. If Johnson had been running all by himself he wouldn't have been acceptable by himself. The only thing that made him acceptable to the world was the shrewd capitalists. The shrewd imperialists knew that the only way that you will voluntarily run to the fox is to show you a wolf. So they created a ghastly alternative and had the whole world, even the so-called intellectuals who call themselves Marxists and other things, hoping that Johnson would beat Goldwater.

I have to say this. Those who claim to be enemies of the system were on their hands and knees waiting for Johnson to get elected because he's supposed to be a man of peace; and he has troops invading the Congo right now and invading Saigon and places where other countries have pulled their troops out. Johnson is sending his troops in. I'm just telling you what I think of him. He sends Peace Corps to Nigeria and mercenaries to the Congo.

Question 6: As a solution to this problem can one envisage the creation of an independent black state in the United States?

Malcolm: No! I wouldn't say "No, No." I wouldn't close the door to any solution. Our problem in the States is so deplorable we are justified to try anything—*anything*. Other independent states have been set up. They set up Israel and they weren't called separationists. But when we start talking about setting up something wherein we can rule ourselves, we're labeled separationists. But we are not separationists, nor are we integrationists. We're human beings.

Question 7: Brother Malcolm, can you foresee the day when the Negro race and culture will be respected in the world and even be predominant?

Malcolm: If I understand your question, brother, I have to say "Yes." I see the time when the black culture will be the dominant culture and when the black man will be the dominant man. And nobody should be against the black man being the dominant man. He's been dominated. I don't think that if we allow ourselves to be dominated it's wrong to pass the ball around once in a while. We've served everyone else, probably more so than anyone else has. We've permitted our continent to be raped and ravaged. We're permitted over 100 million human souls to be uprooted from the mother continent and shipped abroad, many of whom lost their lives at the bottom of the sea or were eaten by sharks. We've contributed to the economy of every country on the face of this earth with our slave labor. So if there's any kind of justice, if there's any kind of judgment, if there's any kind of God—then if he's coming to execute judgment or give some kind of justice—we have some bills that we haven't collected yet.

Question 8: Are you against the love between a black person and a white person?

Malcolm: How can anyone be against love? Whoever a person wants to love that's their business—that's like their religion.

Question 9 (same questioner): But you say "hate the tree."

Malcolm: I haven't said anything about "hate the tree." I said you can't help hating the roots and you hate the roots—not hating the tree—and I said it in reference to the way that they have taught us to hate our roots, which means the African continent. Only many Negroes don't know their roots—they think when you talk about roots you're talking about Europe.

Question 10 (same questioner): Most Negroes in America are "sooners."

Malcolm: Mixed?

Questioner: Just as soon be one thing as another.

Malcolm: That's all through indoctrination, brainwashing and training, but you'll find the Afro-American is getting away from that now. There was a time—I'll comment on that—when you would find the American Negroes who'd be so proud of their white blood—and not only American Negroes, but all over. But this was only because Europe was in a position of power and it served as a status symbol. But, if you notice, Europe is losing its power. When Europe lost its grip in Asia and Africa it upset the economy of these European countries, so that today they face a crisis—not only an economic crisis—they face a political crisis, a social crisis, a moral crisis, and even a military crisis. And so it's not a status symbol any more to be running around bragging about your Scotch blood or your German blood or this other kind of blood. Now the pendulum is changing in the other direction. You've got Europeans talking about that other kind of blood.

Question 11: Do you foresee a total assimilation with equal rights of the Afro-American into the white community of the United States in many, many years to come?

Malcolm: No! Nobody! Who's going to wait many years? I'm glad you asked the question like that because, you see, the oppressed never uses the same yardstick as the oppressor.

And this is what the oppressor doesn't realize. In his position of power he takes things for granted and he takes it for granted that everybody uses his yardstick. Well, today for a long time, we, the oppressed people, not only in America but in Africa, Asia and elsewhere, had to use someone else's yardstick. When they said "fast," what was "fast" to them was "fast" to us, but nowadays the yardstick has changed. We got our own yardstick. And when you say a long time this assimilation, or a long time this solution, the thing you don't realize is that other generations used a different yardstick. They had patience and you could tell them a long time and they would sit around a long time, but the young ones that's coming up now are asking "Why should he wait? Why should he have to wait for what other people have when they're born? Why should he have to go to a Supreme Court or to a Congress, or to a Senate, or to some kind of legislative body to be told he's a man when other people don't have to go through that process to be told that they're a man?" So you have a new generation coming up . . . necessary to let the world know right now that they're going to be men or there just won't be a human being anywhere else.

159. Lyndon B. Johnson, "Why Americans Fight in Vietnam," 1965

President Lyndon Johnson explains the American involvement in the Vietnam War to the American people.

Why must this nation hazard its ease, its interest, and its power for the sake of a people so far away?

We fight because we must fight if we are to live in a world where "every country can shape its own destiny," and only in such a world will our own freedom be finally secure.

This kind of world will never be built by bombs or bullets. Yet the infirmities of man are such that force must often precede reason and the waste of war, the works of peace.

We wish that this were not so. But we must deal with the world as it is, if it is ever to be as we wish.

The world as it is in Asia is not a serene or peaceful place.

The first reality is that North Viet-Nam has attacked the independent nation of South Viet-Nam. Its object is total conquest.

Of course, some of the people of South Viet-Nam are participating in attack on their own government. But trained men and supplies, orders and arms, flow in a constant stream from North to South.

This support is the heartbeat of the war.

And it is a war of unparalleled brutality. Simple farmers are the targets of assassination and kidnapping. Women and children are strangled in the night because their men are loyal to their government. And helpless villages are ravaged by sneak attacks. Large-scale raids are conducted on towns, and terror strikes in the heart of cities.

The confused nature of this conflict cannot mask the fact that it is the new face of an old enemy.

Over this war—and all Asia—is another reality: the deepening shadow of Communist China. The rulers in Hanoi are urged on by Peking. This is a regime which has destroyed freedom in Tibet, which has attacked India and has been condemned by the United Nations for aggression in Korea. It is a nation which is helping the forces of violence is almost every continent. The contest in Viet-Nam is part of a wider pattern of aggressive purposes.

"Why are these realities our concern? Why are we in South Viet-Nam?"

We are there because we have a promise to keep. Since 1954 every American President has offered support to the people of South Viet-Nam. We have helped to build, and we have helped to defend. Thus, over many years, we have made a national pledge to help South Viet-Nam defend its independence.

And I intend to keep that promise.

To dishonor that pledge, to abandon this small and brave nation to its enemies, and to the terror that must follow, would be an unforgivable wrong.

We are also there to strengthen world order. Around the globe from Berlin to Thailand are people whose well being rests in part on the belief that they can count on us if they are attacked. To leave Viet-Nam to its fate would shake the confidence of all these people in the value of an American commitment and in the value of America's word. The result would be increased unrest and instability, and even wider war.

We are also there because there are great stakes in the balance. Let no one think for a moment that retreat from Viet-Nam would bring an end to conflict. The battle would be renewed in one country and then another. The central lesson of our time is that the appetite of aggression is never satisfied. To withdraw from one battlefield means only to prepare for the next. We must say in Southeast Asia—as we did in Europe—in the words of the Bible: "Hitherto shalt thou come, but no further."

There are those who say that all our effort there will be futile—that China's power is such that it is bound to dominate all Southeast Asia. But there is no end to that argument until all of the nations of Asia are swallowed up.

There are those who wonder why we have a responsibility there. Well, we have it there for the same reason that we have a responsibility for the defense of Europe. World War II was fought in both Europe and Asia and

---

Source: Speech by Lyndon Johnson. "Why Americans Fight in Vietnam," 1965. Public Domain Reprint.

when it ended we found ourselves with continued responsibility for the defense of freedom.

Our objective is the independence of South Viet-Nam and its freedom from attack. We want nothing for ourselves—only that the people of South Viet-Nam be allowed to guide their own country in their own way.

We will do everything necessary to reach that objective and we will do only what is absolutely necessary.

In recent months attacks on South Viet-Nam were stepped up. Thus, it became necessary for us to increase our response and to make attacks by air. This is not a change of purpose. It is a change in what we believe that purpose requires.

We do this in order to slow down aggression.

We do this to increase the confidence of the brave people of South Viet-Nam who have bravely borne this brutal battle for so many years with so many casualties.

And we do this to convince the leaders of North Viet-Nam—and all who seek to share their conquest—of a simple fact:

We will not be defeated.

We will not grow tired.

We will not withdraw, either openly or under the cloak of a meaningless agreement.

We know that air attacks alone will not accomplish all of these purposes. But it is our best and prayerful judgment that they are a necessary part of the surest road to peace.

We hope that peace will come swiftly. But that is in the hands of others besides ourselves. And we must be prepared for a long continued conflict. It will require patience as well as bravery—the will to endure as well as the will to resist.

I wish it were possible to convince others with words of what we now find it necessary to say with guns and planes: armed hostility is futile—our resources are equal to any challenge—because we fight for values and we fight for principle, rather than territory or colonies, our patience and our determination are unending.

Once this is clear, then it should also be clear that the only path for reasonable men is the path of peaceful settlement. . . .

These countries of Southeast Asia are homes for millions of impoverished people. Each day these people rise at dawn and struggle through until the night to wrestle existence from the soil. They are often wracked by diseases, plague by hunger, and death comes at the early age of forty.

Stability and peace do not come easily in such a land. Neither independence nor human dignity will ever be won though by arms alone. It also requires the works of peace. The American people have helped generously in times past in these works, and now there must be a much more massive effort to improve the life of man in that conflict-torn corner of our world.

The first step is for the countries of Southeast Asia to associate themselves in a greatly expanded cooperative effort for development. We would hope that North Viet-Nam would take its place in the common effort just as soon as peaceful co-operation is possible.

The United Nations is already actively engaged in development in this area, and as far back as 1961 I conferred with our authorities in Viet-Nam in connection with their work here. And I would hope tonight that the Secretary General of the United Nations could use the prestige of his great office and his deep knowledge of Asia to initiate, as soon as possible, with the countries of that area, a plan for cooperation in increased development.

For our part I will ask the Congress to join in a billion dollar American investment in this effort as soon as it is underway.

And I would hope that all other industrialized countries, including the Soviet Union, will join in this effort to replace despair with hope and terror with progress.

The task is nothing less than to enrich the hopes and existence of more than a hundred million people. And there is much to be done.

The vast Mekong River can provide food and water and power on a scale to dwarf even our own T.V.A.

The wonders of modern medicine can be spread through villages where thousands die every year from lack of care.

Schools can be established to train people in the skills needed to manage the process of development.

And these objectives, and more, are within the reach of a cooperative and determined effort.

I also intend to expand and speed up a program to make available our farm surpluses to assist in feeding and clothing the needy in Asia. We should not allow people to go hungry and wear rags while our own warehouses overflow with an abundance of wheat and corn and rice and cotton.

So I will very shortly name a special team of outstanding, patriotic, and distinguished Americans to inaugurate our participation in these programs. This team will be headed by Mr. Eugene Black, the very able former president of the World Bank.

This will be a disorderly planet for a long time. In Asia, and elsewhere, the forces of the modern world are shaking old ways and uprooting ancient civilizations.

There will be turbulence and struggle and even violence. Great social change—as we see in our own country—does not always come without conflict.

We must also expect that nations will on occasion be in dispute with us. It may be because we are rich, or powerful, or because we have made some mistakes, or because they honestly fear our intentions. However, no nation need ever fear that we desire their land, or to impose our will, or to dictate their institutions.

But we will always oppose the effort of one nation to conquer another nation.

We will do this because our own security is at stake.

But there is more to it than that. For our generation has a dream. It is a very old dream. But we have the power, and now we have the opportunity to make that dream come true.

For centuries nations have struggled among each other. But we dream of a world where disputes are settled by law and reason. And we will try to make it so.

For most of history men have hated and killed one another in battle. But we dream of an end to war. And we will try to make it so.

For all existence most men have lived in poverty, threatened by hunger. But we dream of a world where all are fed and charged with hope. And we will help to make it so.

160. Ho Chi Minh, President Ho Chi Minh's Reply to U.S. President Lyndon B. Johnson, 1967

In a letter to President Johnson in 1967, Ho Chi Minh, the popular Marxist leader in Vietnam explains to Johnson how he viewed the Vietnam struggle.

Your Excellency,

On February 10, 1967, I received your message. This is my reply.

Vietnam is thousands of miles away from the United States. The Vietnamese people have never done any harm to the United States. But contrary to the pledges made by its representatives at the 1954 Geneva Conference, the U.S. Government has ceaselessly intervened in Vietnam, it has unleashed and intensified the war of aggression in South Vietnam with a view to prolonging the partition of Vietnam and turning South Vietnam into a neo-colony and a military base of the United States. For over two years now, the U.S. Government has, with its air and naval forces, carried the war to the Democratic Republic of Vietnam, an independent and sovereign country.

The U.S. Government has committed war crimes, crimes against peace and against mankind. In South Vietnam, half a million U.S. and satellite troops have resorted to the most inhuman weapons and the most barbarous methods of warfare, such as napalm, toxic chemicals and gases, to massacre our compatriots, destroy crops, and raze villages to the ground. In North Vietnam, thousands of U.S. aircraft have dropped hundreds of thousands of tons of bombs, destroying towns, villages, factories, roads, bridges, dykes, dams, and even churches, pagodas, hospitals, schools. In your message, you apparently deplored the sufferings and destructions in Vietnam. May I ask you: Who has perpetrated these monstrous crimes? It is the U.S. and satellite troops. The U.S. Government is entirely responsible for the extremely serious situation in Vietnam.

The U.S. war of aggression against the Vietnamese people constitutes a challenge to the countries of the socialist camp, a threat to the national independence movement, and a serious danger to peace in Asia and the world.

The Vietnamese people deeply love independence, freedom and peace. But in the face of U.S. aggression, they have risen up, united as one man, fearless of sacrifices and hardships; they are determined to carry on their Resistance until they have won genuine independence and freedom and true peace. Our just cause enjoys strong sympathy and support from the peoples of the whole world including broad sections of the American people.

Source: Ho Chi Minh. "Letter to Lyndon Johnson," 1967. Public Domain Reprint.

The U.S. Government has unleashed the war of aggression in Vietnam. It must cease this aggression. That is the only way to the restoration of peace. The U.S. Government must stop definitely and unconditionally its bombing raids and all other acts of war against the Democratic Republic of Vietnam, withdraw from South Vietnam all U.S. and satellite troops, recognize the South Vietnam National Front for Liberation, and let the Vietnamese people settle themselves their own affairs. Such is the basic content of the four-point stand of the Government of the Democratic Republic of Vietnam, which embodies the essential principles and provisions of the 1954 Geneva Agreements on Vietnam. It is the basis of a correct political solution to the Vietnam problem.

In your message, you suggested direct talks between the Democratic Republic of Vietnam and the United States. If the U.S. Government really wants these talks, it must first of all stop unconditionally its bombing raids and all other acts of war against the Democratic Republic of Vietnam. It is only after the unconditional cessation of the U.S. bombing raids and all other acts of war against the Democratic Republic of Vietnam that the Democratic Republic of Vietnam and the United States could enter into talks and discuss questions concerning the two sides.

The Vietnamese people will never submit to force; they will never accept talks under the threat of bombs.

Our cause is absolutely just. It is to be hoped that the U.S. Government will act in accordance with reason.

Sincerely,
Ho Chi Minh

161. Robert F. Kennedy, Kennedy Attacks Johnson's Policy on Vietnam, 1968

Robert F. Kennedy, brother of assassinated President John F. Kennedy and candidate for President, openly opposed the war and criticized Johnson's policy on Vietnam.

Our enemy, savagely striking at will across all of South Vietnam, has finally shattered the mask of official illusion with what we have concealed our true circumstances, even from ourselves. But a short time ago we were serene in our reports and predictions of progress.

The Vietcong will probably withdraw from the cities, as they were forced to withdraw from the American Embassy. Thousands of them will be dead.

But they will, nevertheless, have demonstrated that no part or person of South Vietnam is secure from their attacks: neither district capitals nor American bases, neither the peasant in his rice paddy nor the commanding general of our own great forces.

Source: Robert F. Kennedy on Vietnam War Policies, 1968. Public Domain Reprint.

No one can predict the exact shape or outcome of the battles now in progress, in Saigon or at Khesanh. Let us pray that we will succeed at the lowest possible cost to our young men.

But whatever their outcome, the events of the last two weeks have taught us something. For the sake of those young Americans who are fighting today, if for no other reason, the time has come to take a new look at the war in Vietnam; not by cursing the past but by using it to illuminate the future.

And the first and necessary step is to face the facts. It is to seek out the austere and painful reality of Vietnam, freed from wishful thinking, false hopes and sentimental dreams. It is to rid ourselves of the "good company," of those illusions which have lured us into the deepening swamp of Vietnam.

We must, first of all, rid ourselves of the illusion that the events of the past two weeks represent some sort of victory. That is not so.

It is said the Vietcong will not be able to hold the cities. This is probably true. But they have demonstrated despite all our reports of progress, of government strength and enemy weakness, that half a million American soldiers with 700,000 Vietnamese allies, with total command of the air, total command of the sea, backed by huge resources and the most modern weapons, are unable to secure even a single city from the attacks of an enemy whose total strength is about 250,000. . . .

For years we have been told that the measure of our success and progress in Vietnam was increasing security and control for the population. Now we have seen that none of the population is secure and no area is under sure control.

Four years ago when we only had about 30,000 troops in Vietnam, the Vietcong were unable to mount the assaults on cities they have now conducted against our enormous forces. At one time a suggestion that we protect enclaves was derided. Now there are no protected enclaves.

This has not happened because our men are not brave or effective, because they are. It is because we have misconceived the nature of the war: It is because we have sought to resolve by military might a conflict whose issue depends upon the will and conviction of the South Vietnamese people. It is like sending a lion to halt an epidemic of jungle rot.

This misconception rests on a second illusion—the illusion that we can win a war which the South Vietnamese cannot win for themselves.

You cannot expect people to risk their lives and endure hardship unless they have a stake in their own society. They must have a clear sense of identification with their own government, a belief they are participating in a cause worth fighting for.

People will not fight to line the pockets of generals or swell the bank accounts of the wealthy. They are far more likely to close their eyes and shut their doors in the face of their government—even as they did last week.

More than any election, more than any proud boast, that single fact reveals the truth. We have an ally in name only. We support a government without supporters. Without the efforts of American arms that government would not last a day.

The third illusion is that the unswerving pursuit of military victory, whatever its cost, is in the interest of either ourselves or the people of Vietnam.

For the people of Vietnam, the last three years have meant little but horror. Their tiny lands has been devastated by a weight of bombs and shells greater than Nazi Germany knew in the Second World War.

We have dropped 12 tons of bombs for every square mile in North and South Vietnam. Whole provinces have been substantially destroyed. More than two million South Vietnamese are now homeless refugees.

Imagine the impact in our own country if an equivalent number—over 25 million Americans—were wandering homeless or interned in refugee camps, and millions more refugees were being created as New York and Chicago, Washington and Boston, were being destroyed by a war raging in the streets.

Whatever the outcome of these battles, it is the people we seek to defend who are the greatest losers.

Nor does it serve the interests of America to fight this war as if moral standards could be subordinated to immediate necessities. Last week, a Vietcong suspect was turned over to the chief of the Vietnamese Security Services, who executed him on the spot—a flat violation of the Geneva Convention on the Rules of War.

The photograph of the execution was on front pages all around the world—leading our best and oldest friends to ask, more in sorrow than in anger, what has happened to America?

The fourth illusion is that the American national interest is identical with—or should be subordinated to—the selfish interest of an incompetent military regime.

We are told, of course, that the battle for South Vietnam is in reality a struggle for 250 million Asians—the beginning of a Great Society for all of Asia. But this is pretension.

We can and should offer reasonable assistance to Asia; but we cannot build a Great Society there if we cannot build one in our country. We cannot speak extravagantly of a struggle for 250 million Asians, when a struggle for 15 million in one Asian country so strains our forces, that another Asian country, a fourth-rate power which we have already once defeated in battle, dares to seize an American ship and hold and humiliate her crew.

The fifth illusion is that his war can be settled in our own way and in our own time on our own terms. Such a settlement is the privilege of the triumphant: of those who crush their enemies in battle or wear away their will to fight.

We have not done this, nor is there any prospect we will achieve such a victory.

Unable to defeat our enemy or break his will—at least without a huge, long, and ever more costly effort—we must actively seek a peaceful settlement. We can no longer harden our terms every time Hanoi indicates it may be prepared to negotiate; and we must be willing to foresee a settlement which will give the Vietcong a chance to participate in the political life of the country.

These are some of the illusions which may be discarded if the events of last week are to prove not simply a tragedy, but a lesson: a lesson which carries with it some basic truths.

First, that a total military victory is not within sight or around the corner; that, in fact, it is probably beyond our grasp; and that the effort to win such a victory will only result in the further slaughter of thousands of innocent and helpless people—a slaughter which will forever rest on our national conscience.

Second, that the pursuit of such a victory is not necessary to our national interest, and is even damaging that interest.

Third, that the progress we have claimed toward increasing our control over the country and the security of the population is largely illusory.

Fourth, that the central battle in this war cannot be measured by body counts or bomb damage, but by the extent to which the people of South Vietnam act on a sense of common purpose and hope with those that govern them.

Fifth, that the current regime in Saigon is unwilling or incapable of being an effective ally in the war against the Communists.

Sixth, that a political compromise is not just the best path to peace, but the only path, and we must show as much willingness to "risk some of our prestige" for peace as to risk the lives of young men in war.

Seventh, that the escalation policy in Vietnam, far from strengthening and consolidating international resistance to aggression, is injuring our country through the world, reducing the faith of other peoples in our wisdom and purpose and weakening the world's resolve to stand together for freedom and peace.

Eighth, that the best way to save our most precious stake in Vietnam—the lives of our soldiers—is to stop the enlargement of the war, and that the best way to end casualties is to end the war.

Ninth, that our nation must be told the truth about this war, in all its terrible reality, both because it is right—and because only in this way can any Administration rally the public confidence and unity for the shadowed days which lie ahead.

No war has ever demanded more bravery from our people and our Government—not just bravery under fire or the bravery to make sacrifices—but the bravery to discard the comfort of illusion—to do away with false hopes and alluring promises.

Reality is grim and painful. But it is only a remote echo of the anguish toward which a policy founded on illusion is surely taking us.

This is a great nation and a strong people. Any who seek to comfort rather than speak plainly, reassure rather than instruct, promise satisfaction rather than reveal frustration—they deny that greatness and drain that strength. For today as it was in the beginning, it is the truth that makes us free.

Chapter XXX

Crisis of Confidence, 1969–1980

162. Michael Smith, "Selling the Moon"

"How could so much power accomplish so little real improvement?" asks Michael Smith in this article which studies the American trip to the moon.

"By golly, we've done it!" were the first words millions of television spectators heard when the Apollo 11 lunar module touched down on the surface of the moon. They were spoken, not by the astronauts, or even by the Mission Control technicians in Houston, but by CBS newscaster Walter Cronkite. The ambiguous scope of his pronoun was apt. Spokespersons for the lunar mission defined that "we" with varying degrees of inclusiveness: the astronauts and technical crew, the nation, humankind. But Cronkite could have meant any of these, including the inner circle of direct participants, for he and the mass media "space coverage" he personified were an indisputable aspect of the event. Arguably, in what Guy Debord has called "the society of the spectacle," media coverage of Apollo before had so ambitious an undertaking depended so thoroughly on its public presentation for significance.

The U.S. manned space program of the 1960s provided a salient chapter in the evolution of consumer culture—not just through its technical accomplishments, but by the forms of display its designers and publicists adopted. The project's social function and presentation techniques approximated those of the most highly developed communication medium in American culture: advertising. In a sense, the twelve-year effort to put Americans on the moon constituted the most elaborate advertising campaign ever devised. Its audience was truly global. Eight hundred million people saw or heard the first men on the moon.

The product of this spectacular "advertisement" was not the hardware of space exploration. Missiles, astronauts, and lunar footprints simply provided a visually dramatic new iconography through which the real product could be conveyed: an image of national purpose that equated technological preeminence with military, ideological, and cultural supremacy.

Conceived in the wake of the Sputnik scare, the project's desired effect appeared to be straightforward enough—a Cold War assertion of superiority over the Soviet Union. The merchants of space emerged from two institutions familiar with that goal: the "military-industrial complex," as President Eisenhower called it, and the news media. The first group included Pentagon strategists, scientists, and engineers involved with defense-related research and development defense and aerospace contractors; and their allies in government—civilian and military agencies, congressmen, and even Presidents—who found support of an aggressive manned space program politically useful. The second group consisted of publishers, editors, and reporters for newspapers, magazines, and the newly developed national television newscasts. The needs and powers of these two groups differed, and dissension between and with them emerged repeatedly. Their shared interest in the manned space program centered on its capacity to generate publicity: The first group sought it, and the second made an industry of supplying it. Their roles seemed simple: The defense establishment would deliver the "payload" for the public

Source: Richard Wightman Fox and T. J. Jackson Lears, editors, *The Culture of Consumption.* Copyright 1983 by Richard Fox and T. J. Lears. Reprinted by permission of Pantheon Books, a division of Random House, Inc.

depiction of Americans in space, while the news media provided the vehicle.

The enterprise, however, quickly expanded in scope as its designers recognized that the project's success depended more on the impression it created than on the engineering feats it accomplished. To differentiate U.S. efforts in space from those of the Soviets, Apollo had to convey more than an extraterrestrial show of force; it must portray American use of technology as benign, elegant, beyond the earthbound concerns of military and diplomatic strategy. To succeed fully, the manned space program had to project an image directly contradicting its origins.

Such a task required compelling methods of presentation — methods previously developed by advertisers. The emblematic application of technology surrounding projects Mercury, Gemini, and Apollo embodied the government's increasing postwar reliance on the image-making techniques of the marketplace. Like the marketing of automobiles, the selling of the moon involved not just the problem-solving capacities of science and engineering, but above all the manufacture of a reassuring social image of technology and expertise.

Mission Control, of course, was not merely a Sunbelt efflorescence of Madison Avenue. To be sure, advertisers appropriated images, rituals, and eventually even astronauts from the manned space program. Conversely, NASA occasionally borrowed directly from the pantheon of names, images, and associations stockpiled by advertising. (As John Noble Wilford notes, the space agency named its first manned project Mercury "because a Greek god had a heroic ring and Mercury was considered to be the most familiar of the Olympians to Americans — thanks more to Detroit than to the god or the planet.")

NASA and the news media, however, did not have to enlist the services of an ad agency in order to apply the techniques of advertising to space. By the 1960s any depiction of a man in a shiny new vehicle dealt with images and techniques already made familiar by advertising. It is in this capacity — as a principal source of public attitudes toward science and technology — that advertising influenced the state's depiction of the space race. The underlying relationship of the manned space program to the advertising industry resembled that of a guest conductor to a resident orchestra. NASA waved an impressive baton, but it was primarily because of advertising's ensemble of instruments and performers that the audience knew the score.

Long before Apollo, merchants and generals had discovered the social impact of parading new and exotic products. But in post-World War II America the display value of technology had attained a new preeminence, often overshadowing the technical specifications for a given product, the managerial decisions leading to its development, and even its actual performance. This elevation of technological display marked the emergence of commodity scientism as the prevailing social idiom of science and technology.

The term "scientism" generally connotes a belief in the power and universal applicability of the scientific method. It represents an apparent fusion of opposites: a superstitious belief in the power of science and technology. One of its key assumptions in the science and technology (often referred to interchangeably) proceed in an inevitable sequence of events. Traditionally, the term has applied to those who equate this sequence with progress. The belief in technological determinism, however, is shared by many who consider the proliferation of science and technology to be as destructive as it is irreversible. Technophiles and technophobes alike tend to discern innovations of science and technology as not only inevitable but incomprehensible, and therefore magical. They simply disagree on whether it is white or black magic.

As the previous essays in this collection have noted, the emergence of a consumer culture in the United States has been marked by the transformation of social and personal attributes into detached, salable commodities. Technology has served both as handmaiden and as object of this process. When science itself is commodified, the products of a market-aimed technology are mistaken for the scientific process, and those products, like science, become invested with the inexorable, magical qualities of an unseen social force. For the consumer, the rise of commodity scientism has meant the eclipse of technological literacy by an endless procession of miracle-promising experts and products. For advertisers and governments, it has meant the capacity to recontextualize technology, to assign to its products social attributes that are largely independent of the products' technical design or function.

Commodity scientism emerged, in part, as a response to the steady removal of technological process from daily life. With each passing decade most twentieth-century Americans found technology to be more vital in their lives and less comprehensible. Not only machines but the decisions to create and apply them escalated in complexity and in public inaccessibility, withdrawing behind what Herbert Marcuse called a "technological veil." As public understanding of the social uses of science blurred, only the products of this mysterious realm of expertise periodically burst forth from behind the veil: a polio vaccine, permanent-press shirts, ballistic missiles. As a result, Americans increasingly identified these commodities, rather than the choices and techniques that produced them, as science itself.

This widening gap between process and product, however, did not develop purely as an autonomous and inevitable effect of industrialization. By the close of the First World War, the advertising industry had begun to recognize that the technological veil could serve as a projecting screen—that the half-discernable silhouettes of technological change could be manipulated into salable images. In the shadow-puppet realm of consumer culture, where images of things often appear more convincing and expressive than the things themselves, advertising has served as the principal social medium for commodity scientism. The arms race and the space race demarcate the steady progress of this manipulation of technological display from the private to the public sector.

Most interpreters of the manned space program have fallen into opposing camps—either celebrating it as a triumph (of science, of nationalism, or of our collective "sense of wonder") or denouncing it as "an extravagant feat of technological exhibitionism." Celebrants point to the exuberant public response—in the U.S. and abroad—to the first moon landing, as evidence of the program's success. Detractors fault national leaders for creating the entire manned space program purely to generate and manipulate that exuberance. Neither of these characterizations tell us much about why the program evolved as it did, or what it signified.

In charting the genesis of the astronaut, historians generally point to the humble, 180-pound Sputnik as the ship that forced a thousand launches. But the social significance of the U.S. manned space program is fully discernible only when examined alongside the changing contexts for viewing technology in an advanced consumer culture: the evolution of technological display in industrializing America; the advertising industry's perfection of commodity scientism; the role of the atom bomb in extending this social definition of science into national defense policy; and the U.S. government's "crisis of national purpose" in the 1960s. Viewed in this light, the flight of Apollo 11 represents the triumph of commodity scientism as an agent of national self-definition.

Technology as Display

Products of technology and science have always been assigned social meanings well beyond their apparent design or function. Americans were not the first to discover this tendency, nor did they have to wait until the twentieth century to do so. By the late nineteenth century, the United States had come to excel in two particularly revealing arenas of display: scientific survey expeditions and the great fairs. Both enterprises familiarized the nation with certain display rituals and associations that remained long after the Grand Canyon or the White City had received from public attention.

From Lewis and Clark's reconnaissance of 1804–1806 to the geological expeditions of Powell, Hayden, and King in the post-Civil War decades, explorer-scientists mapped and inventoried the continent, while—often unintentionally—abetting the acquisition and development of land and natural resources. At the same time they were amassing a collection of artifacts and images that contributed to the expanding nation's public image. Their geological and biological specimens filled the country's multiplying natural history museums. And as written accounts, illustrations, and stereoscopic viewcards of their expeditions drifted from the western mountains and plains into Victorian parlors, Americans learned to identify their growing country—and their scientists—with intrepid explorers, acting as advance scouts along an ever receding horizon of amazing curiosities and unimagined opportunities.

As the nation reached the end of both the continent and the century, however, the need for such expeditions diminished. But the display value of the national explorer-scientist seemed to increase as his opportunities dwindled. The polar expeditions of the early twentieth century did not lead to starting new discoveries, annexations, or gold rushes; they did permit the planting of the flag in new territory, and a symbolic conquest in the names of science and national greatness. By mid-century, the "frontiers" of scientific exploration were no longer geographic; planting a flag on the moon created not the substance but a self-conscious simulation of territorial and scientific conquest.

Fairs, too, performed an emblematic as well as a practical function. The proliferation of industrial exhibits, from local mechanics' fairs to the great expositions, often presented fairgoers with their first glimpse of some recent motivation—electric lights, the telephone, new agricultural or industrial equipment. The dramatic display settings created by the fairs also provided symbols of technological prowess for the manufacturer, the consumer, and the nation. At the 1876 Centennial Exposition in Philadelphia, George Corliss' forty-foot-high steam engine supplied the power for all of Machinery Hall; but it generated much more energy among its spectators, who viewed the Corliss engine as a triumph of man over nature, and as an embodiment of "the national genius." The technical and emblematic functions, though distinct, coexisted in the same double towers of pistons, rods, and cylinders.

In the decades to follow, manufacturers recognized and elaborated upon Corliss's insight: that the display value of a product can be as important as its function. At the 1939 New York World's Fair, the most dramatic technological innovation on exhibit—the television—exemplified a growing emphasis on hidden function, projected image. Technological changes—particularly in electricity and electronics—abetted the disappearance of process from the consumer's view. But the general shift from process to product had less to do with technological change itself than with corporate marketing strategies. The 1939 fair's "theme center," unlike the Corliss engine, was a purely symbolic contrivance: "the Trylon, a slender, graceful spire, taller than the Washington Monument, and the Perisphere, a giant globe as high as an 18-story building." Inside the Perisphere, visitors glided on automated ramps past "Democracity"—a scale-model depiction of the thoroughly engineered city of the future. Everything they saw—Trylon, Perisphere, Democracity—bore the exotic futuristic names and precise white streamlined surfaces of an engineered utopia. Yet unlike the Corliss engine, these splendid new symbols of technocracy completed no tasks, presented no innovations; they embodied the elevation of display value over technical function. Their only industrial use came at the close of the fair, when the government reclaimed the steel girders of the Trylon and Perisphere for the production of bombs and tanks.

The Corliss engine and the Trylon and Perisphere were only brief and unusually self-conscious artifacts in the history of American technological display. But they suggest an important pattern of change in the needs and techniques of display-makers. Fairgoers in 1939 were far more familiar with the products of technological change than their grandparents had been in 1876, but less sure of how or why these products had come into being. By 1939 technological display revealed less about the design of a new device than about its sponsor. The Machinery Hall of earlier fairs had diversified into a shopping center of separate structures, many of them (like the cash-register shaped National Cash Register building) served as a corporate logos for the products on display. As products overshadowed process, the marketplace was overtaking the workplace as the major source of popular attitudes toward science and technology. The 1939 World's Fair, as one of its designers lamented, did not resemble the engineered society of the future so much as a "huge department store."

The changing fairs reflected not just the new technology but a fundamental shift in the culture's way of seeing technology. By 1939 the principal function of technological display was to teach consumers to equate personal and social progress with technology, and technology with new products. The World's Fair attempted to do just that. Since 1876, however, another institution had evolved to replace the fairs: national advertising. What fairs and expositions did sporadically and on specific sites, advertisers learned to do every day, in every community. More than any other institution, advertising by the mid-twentieth century had assembled and reshaped the images through which all mass depictions of technology gained public recognition.

In postwar America, only the federal government possessed the communications resources capable of matching national advertising in scale and sustained impact. Its two most ambitious campaigns of technological display—the nuclear arms race and the space race—applied presentation strategies that advertisers had perfected into a kind of dance of the technological veils. To trace commodity scientism's path to the moon, we must follow the variations on that dance—from Madison Avenue to Los Alamos to Houston.

Advertising and the Rise of Commodity Scientism

Reflecting transformations in the commercial culture it served, advertising since the 1920s gradually redefined technology as a social force engaging consumers rather than producers. Henry Ford's assembly lines might reveal almost nothing to his workers about the automobiles they were constructing, but advertising taught them—and everyone else—what social and economic benefits to expect from a new car. Galvanized by the burst of production following World War II, advertising firms entered a new phase of impression management and market research; they repackaged popular images of technology into a consumers' hall of mirrors, where reflections reversed reality, and a product designed to create needs could appear to satisfy them. Thus modern advertising, as Raymond Williams has indicated, learned to operate socially as a form of "*magic:* a highly organized and professional system of magical inducements and satisfactions, functionally very similar to magical systems in simpler societies, but rather strangely coexistent with a highly developed scientific technology.

The success of the manned space program depended on a very similar kind of "magic." Advertisers and space publicists alike drew upon the culture's shared pool, or "ritual idiom," of technological display images. For Cape Canaveral as well as Madison Avenue, the task was to link certain public expectations of technology with the product or event in question. And as their presentations accumulated, both gradually reshaped the public's perception of technology itself. But ad men preceded astronauts. Viewers might consider ads as trivial, and moonshots as compelling. National advertising, however, had permeated the culture with millions of images and techniques; and the conventions of technological display developed through ads provided the only nonmilitary view of technology and its social uses that remained available to a mass audience.

By the mid-fifties, national advertising firms had evolved several closely related patterns of technology display, three of which particularly influenced public presentation of the space program. Unveiling techniques dramatized the introduction of new products, often obscuring the product itself with lavish backdrops or innovative secret ingredients. Techniques of transitivity fostered the illusion of transferring the purported attributes of the product to the consumer, generally through actors with whom consumers were to identify. Among the variety of character types advertisers have evoked, one of the most pervasive figures is the helmsman, whose mastery over his environment through the products of technology provides a model for consumer aspiration. Together, the technique of unveiling, transitivity, and helmsmanship so thoroughly permeated popular notions of science and engineering that every depiction of technology in postwar America showed signs of their influence. To understand why the manned space program emerged as it did, it is necessary to see what its audience saw—the patterns of technological display that confronted them daily through advertising.

In a culture that has traditionally associated physical mobility with individual autonomy and national destiny, the helmsman always has figured prominently. From sea captains to riverboat pilots to aviators, the appeal seemed to derive less from the helmsman or his craft than from the implied relation between them. The explosive acclaim following Lindbergh's solo transatlantic flight in 1927 celebrated both the man and the machine—as if the explorer-scientist had mounted the Corliss engine and taught it to fly. As Lindbergh himself insisted, neither he nor his plane, but rather the third entity that they formed together—"we"—had performed the feat.

Advertisers soon learned the importance of this mutual legitimation. Each of the helmsman's display qualities conveyed value to the product, which in turn appeared to reinforce precisely those qualities in its owner. Foremost among them was his masculinity. In a male-dominated society in which mechanization has been perceived alternately as a source of power and a threat of independence, advertisers forged an alliance between technological and gender display that proved as inextricable as Lindbergh's "we." Technological sophistication and socially admired masculine traits were conveyed each through stylized versions of the other.

National advertising had portrayed technological literacy as a definitive male characteristic since the turn of the century. Depictions of the helmsman increased dramatically, however, in the fifties—a reflection, in part, of the changing work environment of middle-class "organization men" in the postwar years. "Bureaucratic values," Sara Evans notes, "emphasized 'female' traits of cooperation, passivity, and security," while "the older definitions of masculinity remained." As a result, "what one part of their consciousness valued, another part judged unmanly." The helmsman and his obedient machine offered a comforting escape from these contradictions.

Few images captured this alignment of masculinity and helmsmanship so succinctly as Marlboro cigarette ads. In 1954, when Leo Burnett's advertising agency acquired the account, Marlboros were considered a "woman's cigarette." Reasoning that in a male-dominated culture a masculinized product affects everyone, Burnett decided to create for his client's product "an exclusively male personality." Accordingly, he fashioned the consummate helmsman: the Marlboro Man. Effortlessly steering his way through the world of goods, he was a pilot, or a race-car driver, or a sailor. Invariably, he had an anchor tattooed on his wrist. (Reinforcing the transitivity of the Marlboro Man's helmsmanship, millions of washable anchor tattoos were distributed with the cigarettes.) To insure that he conveyed more than technical competence, in 1972 the Marlboro Man acquired a geographical realm all his own: Marlboro Country, where the helmsman were cowboys. The Marlboro Man thus combined stereotypes of masculine America past and present: suffusing frontier autonomy with machine-age know-how, he was the Lone Ranger recast as Lindbergh.

The helmsman proliferated throughout postwar advertising, but his most articulate portrayal came from car ads. The automobile was at once the most complex piece of machinery and the most symbolically charged social emblem the average consumer was likely ever to buy. As such, it elicited the ad industry's finest examples of technological display. And with the resumption of automobile production after World War II, advertisements developed the techniques of helmsmanship, transitivity, and unveiling to new heights of social ritual. Car ads of the fifties might seem remote from the launchpads of Apollo, but they merit close scrutiny; to a large extent, these ads perfected the images and associations through which manned space flight would reach the American public.

Advertisers' predilection for concealed design and dramatic unveiling reached fruition in auto ads of the fifties. Borrowing from the clandestine image of weapons production (and the major automakers continued to serve as defense contractors after the war), car companies leaked aerial "spy photos" of their new models. The introduction of the ill-fated Edsel during "Sputnik autumn" (1957) featured elaborate unveiling strategies. One advertisement revealed only the dashboard of the new model, another portrayed truckloads of canvas-wrapped Edsels en route to their public "debut." The following year, a two-minute television commercial for Chevrolet permitted only split-second glimpses of the car itself.

Transitivity of power from car to driver was promoted through jargon and gadgetry. Through a deliberately unfamiliar configuration of initials, number, and neologisms, jargon provided what motivational researchers called "the illusion of rationality," conveying "inside-dopester" status to the consumer without requiring the slightest mechanical comprehension. Gadgets supplied the functionally marginal trappings that substituted for efficiency, safety, or durability as criteria for judging a product's design.

Gadgets and jargon were destined to play major roles in the popularization of the manned space program. As advertising features, they flourished in auto ads of the fifties. A Chrysler Corporation ad for its 1959 Dodge—"The Newest of Everything Great! The Greatest of Everything New!"—offered a characteristic profusion of both techniques. Two of the new models' feature innovations were simply new terms: the "HC-HE engine—high compression and high economy"; and "Level-Flite Torsion-Aire"—a "new kind of suspension" that "introduces the first 'three-dimensional' driving—ride control, road control, load control." Here were masterful creations of technojargon, studding the ad copy with hyphens and acronyms while revealing nothing about the actual engine or the suspension. In addition, the '59 Dodge offered an impressive array of gadgets. To facilitate the boarding of female passengers, it featured the "Swing-Out Swivel Seat that says 'Please Come In.'" And sitting at his "new elliptical steering wheel," the proud owner faced the "gleaming instrument panel" of "the first all-push-button car." The '56 Dodge had echoed an earlier, substantive innovation—automatic transmission—with a gratuitous one by replacing the commonplace gear-selection lever with pushbuttons ("The Magic Touch of Tomorrow!"). The '59 model added similar buttons for the windshield wipers and defrosters to create "pushbutton control of driving and weather." Like the elliptical steering wheel, the buttons added nothing more than the impression of innovation and control.

But as "illusions of rationality," gadgets addressed the realm of wishes and fears. As long as they triggered interest in the product, their mechanical function could remain superfluous—even self-contradictory. Thus car gadgets often embodied two conflicting manifestations of technical power: the status conveyed by passive, effortless supervision of "automatic control," and the vicarious sense of technical competence imparted by their manipulation. The problem was not confined to automobiles. As consumers became more removed from decisions regarding technology's social uses, all purveyors of technological display—including publicists for space flight—had to convince the public that the "labor-saving" status of increasingly automated technology (the hardware of transitivity) did not diminish the consumer's sense of control (or helmsmanship).

Perhaps the ultimate example of the gadget's conflicting illusions was the 1959 Cadillac's optional Autronic Eye. Earlier models had offered automatic light sensors to free drivers from manually switching their headlights from bright to dim. But automatic headlights tended to flicker erratically in response to minute fluctuations of light. General Motors solved that problem with a new gadget: "With a *twist of the dial* autronic-eye lets *you* control the automatic dimming of your lights." Thus the American driver could manually control an automatic device designed to eliminate the need for manual control. If buttons on his gear selector and defroster gave him "pushbutton control of driving and weather," the Autronic Eye gave him control of his symbols of control.

The public might dismiss—even ridicule—these stylized conflations of technical and personal power. From the advertiser's point of view, that mattered very little. The persuasive power of the Swing-Out Swivel Seat or the Autronic Eye derived not so much from the gadget itself as from the social context in which it situated the prospective buyer. It triggered anxieties—about sexual prowess, technical competence, or mastery of the environment—while offering symbolic conquest of them.

By the late 1960s, claims for the magical directive capacities of technology permeated not only the world of goods but, increasingly, the world of nations. Government dependence on commodity scientism reached a critical juncture in 1945 with the development of the atomic bomb. With each new phase of the ensuing arms race, U.S. leaders became more concerned with technology display. To be sure, nuclear weapons represented an application of technology very different from automobiles; and Washington did not set out to mimic Detroit. Yet the government's depiction of the bomb, and of the weapons systems it spawned, required persuasion techniques much like those of the car ad designer. The Manhattan Project led to the most dramatic unveiling strategy in human history. Presidents and generals promised the nation new autonomy and global helmsmanship through the mere possession of their new "products." They warned that the country's prestige depended on the transitivity of nuclear power from the testing range to the geopolitical conference table. And like advertisers, they developed a growing reliance on the manipulation of appearances. Advertising provided the paradigm for technological display in American culture; the atomic bomb ushered in the geopolitical arena.

Technopolitics and the Bomb

World War II was not the first occasion for the state's application of marketplace patterns of commodity scientism. The First World War introduced unprecedented opportunities for technological display, as weapons production and national image-making alike reached brief but spectacular levels of productivity. Not until what John McPhee has called the "technological piñata" of World War II, however, did a permanent, modern-scale defense bureaucracy evolve, enlisting both the research capacities and the display value of astronaut in the service of militarism. Techniques that had been developed by advertisers were among the resources that government appropriated for the wartime effort. Among the factors contributing to the defense establishment's postwar policies, and its profound effect on public attitudes toward science and technology, nothing introduced so many changes so suddenly as the development of the atomic bomb.

"America stands at this moment at the summit of the world," Winston Churchill proclaimed in August 1945, Churchill's remark was inspired by the deployment of two top-secret weapons, code-named "Fat Man" and "Little Boy," over two Japanese cities. The flashes that obliterated Hiroshima and Nagasaki etched permanent shadows of their victims onto the walls that remained standing. They inscribed an equally indelible message in the minds of a generation of world leaders: The nation that could claim scientific and technological superiority would dominate the globe.

What is often overlooked in dwelling on the destructive force and strategic weight of the A-bomb is the manner in which it was revealed to the world. Like nothing before it, the bomb exemplified the pattern of concealed development and dramatic unveiling that the advertising industry had perfected. The primary effect of this technique—a heightened capacity to manipulate the symbolic as well as the technical impact of a given product (or weapon)—had been glimpsed in previous wars. But the Manhattan Project constituted the most elaborate secret undertaking, and the most lavish concentration of scientific acumen, in history. As such, it created an unprecedented opportunity to stress the engineering of appearances as a vital attribute of the product itself.

Accordingly, two overriding aspects of U.S. government and military leaders' attitudes toward the atomic bomb determined the manner in which it entered the world: first, their adherence to a myth of inevitability concerning the use of the bomb once it was developed; and second, their preoccupation with the global impact of the new weapon's use in combat. In the summer of 1945, with Germany defeated, the Target Committee debated not whether use of the bomb against Japan was necessary but how many could be dropped, and where. The committee's report to Truman stressed "(1) obtaining the *greatest psychological effect* against Japan and (2) making the initial use *sufficiently spectacular* for the importance of the weapon to be internationally recognized when publicity on it was released."

As the committee's second point suggests, Japan was not the bomb's only target. Secretary of State-designated James Byrnes echoed a view shared by Truman and Secretary of War Stimson when he told nuclear physicist Leo Szilard, in May of 1945, that wartime deployment of the bomb "would make Russia more manageable." He suggested a more immediate audience for its combat demonstration when he added, "How would you get Congress to appropriate money for atomic energy research if you do not show results for the money which has been spent already." As Martin Sherwin has observed, it was not simply the bomb's tactical value in defeating Japan, but the "*impression*—the psychological impact of a single bomb dropped from a lone aircraft causing damage equal to that caused by thousands of bombs dropped from hundreds of aircraft—upon which [Truman, Stimson, and Byrnes] based their policy."

The deployment of the atom bomb marked the accession of commodity scientism to the highest reaches of military and foreign policy. Like the marketplace before it, the state learned in the course of the century that each new product of technology was really two: the device itself, and the image of the device in the mind of the consumer or enemy. This second, symbolic weapon, as advertisers knew and generals had begun to suspect, was often the more powerful of the two. The bomb dramatically accelerated this reliance on the publicity value of military technology. By its unparalleled destructiveness, it forced the nation to rely for the first time on a weapon's image rather than on its use. As the first "atomic nation," the United States looked to its growing nuclear arsenal not just for the military supremacy it promised but for emblems of political and cultural supremacy as well.

Cold War diplomacy thus relied on a kind of nuclear transitivity, with the superpowers linking each new weapon breakthrough to functionally unrelated display attributes: the intelligence of its scientists, the wisdom of its leaders, the superiority of its political system. As the symbolic attributes of nuclear weapons overshadowed their technical function, the government became adept at the techniques by which advertisers invented social attributes for their products. Like the private sector before them, policymakers found themselves acting increasingly as agents of impression management.

This social triumph of engineered appearances is just beginning to be understood. Writing at the outset of the postwar era, David Riesman observed that in the age of mass media the earlier social model of a self-motivated, "inner-directed" personality has been giving way to a more self-absorbed, less confident, "other-directed" type. The prevailing characteristic of this new personality, he noted, is the insatiable need for guidance from external sources—particularly from the bombardment of messages conveyed by the mass media; "[t]he goals toward which the other-directed person strives shifts with that guidance."

More recent scholarship has refined Riesman's notion of an other-directed personality, tracing its origins more directly to the needs and marketing techniques of corporate capitalism. Advertising's "progressive fragmentation of commodities . . . into assortments of attributes and messages" had led, according to William Leiss, to a corresponding "fragmentation of individual needs into smaller and smaller elements." The consumer's task, then, is no longer simply to buy an endlessly expanding array of products, but rather to reassemble a coherent aggregate of needs—that is, an apparently integrated personality—and to match them up with a corresponding assemblage of commodity attributes. When a social system depends for its prosperity on an ever growing supply of such impressionable, other-directed consumers, the result is what Christopher Lasch has called a "culture of narcissism," subordinating "being to having," and "possession itself to appearance."

The arms race and the space race demonstrated that the state as well as the consumer was susceptible to this fragmentation. Spurred on by the culture they governed, and by the immense display value they attached to atomic weaponry, postwar U.S. political leaders acquired a striking resemblance to the other-directed individual: repeatedly calling for recognized goals, but capable of sustaining only the appearance of relentless goal-seeking; so concerned with the "credibility" of their policies that credibility itself became the principal object of policymaking; obsessed with security, yet trapped in a spiral of arms acquisition that only increased the need for security. Just as the narcissistic personality learned to seek fulfillment through acts of consumption that diminished in satisfaction as they escalated in scale, "so a culture of procurement" arose among Cold War politicians, the military establishment, and defense contractors, providing the mass media with a shorthand equation of national purpose with multiple warheads and fallout shelters.

Most nuclear weapons, of course, were intended never to be used. They were touted not for what they did but for what they promised to prevent; their primary attribute was the posture of confidence they inspired in their owners. Publicity, not megatonnage, became the true measure of a weapon's effectiveness, and American military and foreign policy depended increasingly on impressions—at home and abroad—of its unused stockpile of weapons.

The postwar arms race thus became a succession of symbolic deployments, not unlike the annual announcement of new car models. As each new weapon or detection system rendered its still unpaid-for, equally oversophisticated predecessor obsolete, the pressure to develop its replacement redoubled. Generals and contractors clamored for the greater "push-button control" for an increasingly uncontrollable defense environment—all in an effort to recapture the brief, euphoric moment when America alone possessed the bomb. For the nation and the consumer alike, security and identity had become subject to buying and exhibiting an accelerating progression of technical innovations, each more expensive and less discernibly improved than the one before it. "Once the purpose of military spending is to create 'perfection,' and weapons are procured as symbols," Richard J. Barnet warns, "there is never enough." Perhaps what was required was not just new weapons but an entirely new display arena. The time for space was ripe.

Occupying Space

From a technical standpoint, the space race began as a diversion of payloads in the arms race. In conjunction with their developments of nuclear weapons, both the United States and the Soviet Union devoted considerable research to the perfection of missiles to carry them—research spearheaded in both countries by former Third Reich V-2 rocket engineers who had been "liberated" (and divided up) by the Allies at Peenemünde. By the early fifties, both superpowers had begun designing intercontinental ballistic missiles. Unlike the Soviet Union, the U.S. had allies within short-range missile or bomber range of its adversary. Consequently, high-thrust, long-range missiles were far more crucial to the Soviets than to the United States. On August 26, 1957, when the Kremlin announced its first successful ICBM test launch, complaints arose among some U.S. military strategists ("We captured the wrong Germans," one general lamented); but neither the government nor the press sounded a general alarm. The American Atlas missile was well under way; the U.S. enjoyed an undisputed advantage both in number and placement bombers; American military superiority remained intact.

On October 4 the Soviets once again fired one of their new ICBMs, this time extending its trajectory, and—by mounting a 36-inch diameter satellite in place of a dummy warhead—placed Sputnik I in orbit. The idea was not new. As early as August 1955 the United States had announced plans to launch a series of artificial satellites during International Geophysical Year (1957–1958). The Eisenhower Administration therefore expressed little concern over Sputnik. Defense Secretary Charles Wilson called the launch "a neat scientific trick." White House aide Clarence Randall dismissed it as a "silly bauble . . . in the sky."

Elsewhere in the government, however, Sputnik became the subject of agitated warnings. Congressional opponents of the Eisenhower Administration—notably Senate Majority Leader Lyndon Johnson and House Speaker John McCormack—contended that Ike's "sluggish" response to the Russian satellite jeopardized national security. "It is not very reassuring to be told that next year we will put a 'better' satellite into the air," Johnson complained. "Perhaps it will even have chrome trim and automatic windshield wipers."

On December 6 Senator Johnson had just convened hearings on the inadequacy of U.S. space efforts when the first American satellite rocket—the Navy's Vanguard—exploded on the launchpad. Press coverage, featuring headlines like "Kaputnik" and "Stayputnik," interpreted the event as proof that a space race was under way, and that America was losing. On January 31, 1958, the first American satellite—the 31-pound Explorer I—rode an Army Redstone rocket into orbit. The Redstone's chief designer, former Peenemünde rocketeer Werner von Braun, became an instant media hero. Space news of every variety was guaranteed front-page status.

By the spring of 1958 opinion polls indicated that an initially unconcerned public had begun to contract "space fever" from Congress, the Pentagon, and the press. The actual threat posed by Sputnik proved difficult to identify. Strategically, the satellite was far less significant than the missile that carried it up. It was, however, the first "first" for the USSR since the arms race had begun, opening a vast new arena for emblematic display of technology. A growing number of American leaders convinced each other that nothing short of "the national purpose" would ride with the country's entry into space.

Politicians, editors, and social commentators saw in Sputnik a symbol of the postwar drift in American culture. Conservatives feared that the "flabbiness" of an increasingly materialistic and complacent citizenry had slowed the nation's reflexes in confronting the pervasive "Red menace." Liberals shared that concern, adding their lament that the constricted scope of public affairs—Cold War posturing abroad, McCarthyism at home—had diminished the nation's "imaginative vision." While implementing a space program, the nation's leaders also launched an elaborate search for goals. In 1960 President Eisenhower appointed a Commission on National Goals, a Rockefeller-funded Special Studies Project undertook the same task, and Henry Luce commissioned a series of essays for *Life* on "The National Purpose." The other-directed nation had begun to diagnose its malady.

The unanimous conclusion was that America stood in grave peril of losing its "sense of mission." Walter Lippman warned that the Soviet Union, unlike the United States, possessed "a sense of great purpose and of high density." George Kennan castigated Americans for the "overwhelming accent of life on personal comfort and amusement, with . . . a surfeit of privately sold gadgetry" but "no highly developed sense of national purpose." The Rockefeller study linked the "lack of purpose in Americans" with its "fear that our young people have lost youth's immemorial fondness for adventure, far horizons, and the challenge of the unpredictable." And most commentators stressed the global dimensions of this challenge. "Our goals abroad," the President's Commission concluded, "are inseparable from our goals at home."

Stripped of its rhetorical flourishes, this "quest for national purpose" did not depart in substance from prevailing Cold War policies. What it called for was a new mode of presentation for these policies. If not purpose, then an *image* of purposefulness would redeem the nation—while providing banner headlines for the press, rejuvenated careers for "space" politicians, and a richly embellished network of aerospace managers, engineers, and contractors. And in 1960 preparation of that image was well under way—not in the pages of committee reports, but in the flight-simulator labs of Project Mercury. Spacesuits would provide the emperor's new clothes.

From the outset, then, the architects of the space program viewed it as a new source of national iconography. Accordingly, a durable and suggestive vocabulary had to be devised—one that could describe space exploits as well as link them, through analogy and repeated association, to familiar images of the nation's past and anticipated greatness. Foremost among the key words in this vocabulary was "science." Just as American culture had conflated science and technology, now "science" and "space" became synonyms. In the wake of Sputnik, major newspapers and mass-market magazines quickly acquired "science editors" whose columns were devoted almost exclusively to the space race. President Eisenhower appointed MIT president James R. Killian as his first Science Advisory purely in response to the furor over Sputnik. And Killian's Science Advisory Committee soon learned that its principal function would be as a public relations office for space policy. The committee's first assignment was to prepare an "Introduction to Space" for the "nontechnical reader" that could be "widely disseminated by all the news media."

Released in March 1958, the Killian committee's report specified "four factors which give importance, urgency, and *inevitability*" to a vigorous, national space program. These "factors" deserve careful scrutiny, for they encapsulate the justifications, tirelessly repeated over the next dozen years, for sending Americans into space: (1) "the compelling urge of man to explore and to discover, the thrust of curiosity that leads men to go where no one has gone before"; (2) "the defense objective"; (3) "national prestige"; and (4) "scientific observation and experiment which will add to our knowledge and understanding of the earth, the solar system, and the universe." Like an M&M candy, this list of "reasons why" concentrated its primary ingredients—"defense" and "national prestige"—in the center, with an outer shell of science and exploration to provide a smooth, colorful appearance.

Perhaps the best way to compare these two realms of motivation is to think of the discretionary functions of government, such as the manned space program, as a legislative variety of play. Roger Caillois has identified two contrasting varieties of play: "competitive" play, which provides a structured performance environment resembling combat, and "vertiginous" play, in which the participant seeks unfettered discovery or imaginative improvisation, without reference to competitors, stopwatches, or performance evaluation. Callois's terms provide a useful distinction between the two basic varieties of social display rituals. Most forms of play—and of display—are not purely of one variety or the other, but some amalgam of the two.

So it was with space policy. Some space enthusiasts emphasized its vertiginous aspects: "the compelling urge of man to explore and to discover," and disinterested "scientific observation and experiment." Others defended its competitive dimension: "the defense objective" and "national prestige." The key, however, to the public presentation of manned space policy rests in the fact that the overwhelming concern—the only substantive concern—of the political leaders, military strategists, and aerospace engineers and scientists who implemented the manned space program was its propaganda value, abroad and at home. The vertiginous "outer shell" of curiosity and scientific wonders attracted a vigorous following. Indeed, the merchants of space counted on that following. But U.S. space policy did not emerge from the sudden "compelling urge" among the country's political, military, and scientific elite to learn the origins of the solar system by 1969.

That fact was most clearly demonstrated by the decision to implement a *manned* space program in the first place. As most of the non-defense subsidized scientific community repeatedly stressed, nearly every measurable space objective—in communications, weather monitoring, exploration of the planets, even military reconnaissance—could be achieved far more effectively, and at considerably less expense, with automated satellites and probes rather than by manned expeditions. Sending men into space was preferable to unmanned projects for only one reason. It vastly enhanced the dramatic impression created by the nation's space exploits.

The question, then, is not whether the creators of American space policy acted from competitive motives; rather, why did they coat unequivocally competitive policies in elaborately vertiginous rhetoric? Cynics have dismissed these accolades for curiosity and intellectual adventurousness, along with the astronauts themselves, as part of the candy coating that sweetened the nation's real objectives—greater power and prestige.

But perhaps more was at stake than that. The space race was consummately other-directed, revealing a curious mixture of unsurpassed power and deep insecurity among American leaders. In constant doubt of their global technological superiority, and unsure how to apply it, they rushed to outdistance their geopolitical rivals in every measurable contest for prestige. A vertiginous depiction of space policy—exploration, rather than a race—might contribute greatly to that prestige, lending the nation the appearance of a self-assured, mature state seeking knowledge for all humanity among the stars. The more other-directed they became, the more desperately Presidents and Congresses sought the inner-directed images by which to convince the world—and themselves—of their sense of purpose. A self-contradictory rhetoric emerged, as jeremiads on the enemy's impending "control of the universe" alternated with invocations of the "measureless wonders" of space.

Crucial to this appropriation of a vertiginous national image was the social characterization of science and technology. It is significant that Killian's committee grouped science with exploration rather than with defense, in spite of government funding's overwhelming preference for the latter. The congressional hearings leading to the creation of NASA provided the first of many efforts to fashion outer space into an ultimate display context for the nation identity—a task requiring a complete refurbishing of the public image of American science.

On April 2, 1958, Eisenhower asked Congress to create a civilian agency for the implementation of national space policy. On April 15 the new House Select Committee of Astronautics and Space Exploration began four weeks of hearings. On May 6 its counterpart in the Senate, the Special Committee on Space and Astronautics, convened for its own less extensive inquiry. The committees' respective chairmen, House Speaker McCormack and Senate Majority Leader Johnson, each opened their proceedings with warnings that the nation's military and international political prestige were at stake. "The Roman Empire controlled the world because it could build roads," Johnson noted; later "the British Empire was dominant because it had ships. In the air age we were powerful because we had airplanes. Now the Communists have established a foothold in outer space." Nearly all of the House committee's witnesses were selected from among Defense Department officials, the armed services, defense contractors, or scientists and engineers connected with military or nuclear research. Despite the civilian status of the space agency-to-be, the hearings leading to its creation were dominated by men with professional interests in an aggressive space policy—particularly in the military application of space technology.

Yet the transcripts of the hearings contain surprisingly little discussion of the defense objectives informing national space policy. Congressmen and witnesses alike mixed straightforward declarations of the space program's propaganda value with fanciful efforts to formulate a vertiginous rhetoric. "In space exploration, and the scientific breakthrough it implies," McCormack assured his committee, "we are beginning an era of discovery literally as far reaching as the discovery of our own continent." Space, he added, would provide the country with a "new frontier"—"the greatest challenge to dynamic thought and deed that our pioneer spirit has ever received." The actual benefits of the undertaking, he explained, remained "beyond the threshold. What we will learn from the moon . . . no man can rightly say"; but surely "the advances will be literally beyond our present understanding."

In his testimony, von Braun agreed that the impact of an energetic U.S. manned space program "will be comparable to the discovery of America." Like McCormack, he stressed the analogy between the role of territorial expansion in the nation's past and the primacy of scientific inquiry in its future. When asked what significance a national space program might have "from a nonmilitary angle," von Braun replied, "Sir, I think the whole idea of exploration of space began with the same motives that have always triggered scientific progress." He concluded with a glowing endorsement of unfettered curiosity: "People are just curious. . . . What follows in the wake of their discoveries is something for the next generation to worry about." In light of his pioneering work on the

V-2 rocket for Hitler, von Braun might have detected flaws in such a cavalier scenario for the social application of technology. But if the nation's "superspace scientist" had any doubts, he did not air them before the congressional committee.

Von Braun was merely one among a procession of distinguished experts who offered hymns to the unknown in the name of science. California Institute of Technology president Lee DuBridge had directed the MIT radiation lab during World War II; he had served for six years on the Atomic Energy Commission's advisory board, and had been a trustee of the Rand Corporation since 1948. He had witnessed firsthand the swiftly escalating role of the military in scientific research and development in the postwar years. Much of his testimony, however, did not address these pertinent areas of expertise. Instead, DuBridge dwelled on the space program's potential for uncovering "wholly unforeseen phenomena." "It is hardly fruitful to speculate as to what these unknown things might be," he explained, "but the history of science is replete with examples" of unanticipated discoveries. The scientist, like the explorer, might expect to learn as much by accident as by design. "There is no reason to suppose that the other side [of the moon] hides any great or undiscovered phenomena of nature." DuBridge told the committee. "Nor will it add anything to scientific knowledge when a man first travels in space. Yet we are all curious to know." Space generated not just a "pure scientific interest," but also "the explorer's interest—the interest in satisfying human curiosity and human yearning."

As witness followed witness, an eloquent mystification of science emerged. The sheer presence of so many eminent scientists and engineers led the hearings—and the very notion of a full-scaled manned space program—the imprimatur of expertise. Yet by equating space, science, and the unpredictable discoveries of exploration, they advocated a national space policy based on a kind of Columbus Principle: Scientists, like the captain of the *Santa Maria*, have made some of their most startling discoveries by accident; therefore space exploration should proceed not on the basis of stated objectives but on the assumption that the equivalent of a New World will appear, justifying the undertaking in retrospect. Curiosity and purposefulness were the only prerequisites. The committee's witnesses did not conduct their own research in this wide-eyed fashion. Here they spoke not for astronaut but for its display value. As many of them had done before on behalf of defense-related projects, they lent their expertise to the "illusion of rationality" Congress required to legitimatize a vigorous manned space program.

In its final report, the House Select Committee enthusiastically embraced its witnesses' celebration of uncertainty. "The implications of man's entry into outer space," the report admitted, were "disturbingly imprecise." Yet "[d]iscovery is impartial and impersonal. It can be controlled by no blueprint. It can be contained by no laws." The nation, then, should not permit a lack of palpable justifications to deter it from "the most challenging and vital exploration feat of all time."

The committee's report also revealed its low tolerance for criticism of a swift and unrestrained entry into the space race. Hugh Dryden, director of the National Advisory Committee for Aeronautics, had been considered Congress's first choice to head the new space agency. But during his testimony, Dryden was one of the few witnesses who expressed doubts about the wisdom of a "crash program" to put Americans into space. "[T]ossing a man up in the air and letting him come back," Dryden observed, was "like shooting a woman out of a cannon." When the news media highlighted this remark, committee chairman McCormack notified the White House of his disapproval of Dryden as NASA director. He also took him to task in the committee's final report: "Some of our sober scientists may talk with disdain of stunts no more useful, they allege, than shooting a woman out of a cannon. This may be so," the report conceded, "but we need not condemn 'stunting' out of hand. Such stunts, even if proved useless scientifically, can have a disturbing political impact." Policymakers thus spoke of the nation's space effort in two languages. When describing its intended effect, they could point candidly to the "political impact" of "stunting," but when they invoked the unpredictable wonders of science and exploration, they were fashioning the images with which to convey that effect.

In December 1958 President Eisenhower initiated the selection process that would lead to NASA's first team of astronauts. In January 1961, when they completed their training, President Kennedy took the oath of office with much more enthusiasm for the manned space program than his predecessor. "Dramatic achievements in space . . . symbolize the technological power and organizing capacity of the nation," proclaimed a memo drafted by Vice President Lyndon Johnson, Defense Secretary Robert McNamara, and NASA's new administrator, James Webb. And only the inclusion of helmsman could insure the effective impression of that symbol: "It is man, not merely machines, in space that captures the imagination of the world."

On April 12, 1961, Soviet cosmonaut Yuri Gagarin became the first man to orbit the earth. On April 17 a clandestine U.S.-sponsored invasion of Cuba ended in a humiliating rout at the Bay of Pigs. On April 20 President Kennedy sent a memo to Vice President Johnson—now chairman of the new National Aeronautics and Space Council—inquiring about the feasibility of a manned lunar mission, and asking whether there might be "any other space program which promises dramatic results in which we could win?" On May 5 Alan Shepard's seventeen-minute ride on a Jupiter missile brought him tumultuous acclaim as the "first American in space." On May 15, Kennedy called a joint session of Congress to announce "that this nation should commit itself to achieving the goal, before this decade is out, of landing a man on the moon and returning him safely to earth. No single space project in this period will be more impressive to mankind," he proclaimed. "And none will be so difficult or expensive to accomplish." For the next eight years, three Presidents embraced the astronauts as fellow helmsmen. What was the nature of these new seekers of the nation grail?

Inventing the Astronaut

From the moment plans for a manned space program were announced, newspapers, magazines, and television networks recognized it as an unparalleled media event. NASA public affairs officials quickly discovered that their image-making duties would be minimal; what Congress had begun, the media took up with alacrity. Long before the first astronaut left the launchpad, space enthusiasts experiment with the analogies and associations that might be attached to the event. The editors of *Newsweek* saw rejuvenative powers in space travel. "[T]he moral energies that drove America to true greatness lately seem diluted," they warned at the outset of "The Sixties: Decades of Man in Space." For too long no new arenas of conquest awaited at the national horizon. Now, however, "Man is embarking on the supreme adventure; he is heading into the universe."

For those who stressed the restorative powers of this "supreme adventure," the presence of helmsmen in space was an essential aspect of the enterprise. Only when the first "awe-struck pilot" experienced "the giddy buoyancy of weightlessness" would man "break free of his terrestrial bonds." Projection of the national imagination into space required a human emissary so that "all mankind may ride along vicariously." The first astronaut's "epochal adventure," *Newsweek*'s "Space and the Atom" editor asserted, "will signal, as no satellite could, the dawn of the space age." "Machines alone will not suffice if men are able to follow," a columnist observed in *The Nation*. "The difference is that between admiring a woman's photograph and marrying her."

Growing emphasis on manned space exploration as the great "collective adventure" of the sixties reflected a nervous evasion of the inadequacy of the project's scientific justification. Press coverage turned with apparent relief from "Why manned?" to "Which men?" as NASA began to select its astronauts. In spite of the project's purported importance to science, no scientists were to fly a U.S. spacecraft until the final Apollo moonshot in 1972. Instead, NASA began its search exclusively among the NASA's five hundred active military test pilots. Candidates had to meet four requirements: an engineering degree "or its equivalent"; fifteen hundred hours of flight time; age limit forty; height limit five feet eleven inches; weight limit 180 pounds (precisely that of Sputnik I). One hundred ten men qualified; half of them volunteered. An exhaustive battery of physical, psychological, and intelligence tests eliminated all but the "Magnificent Seven." On April 9, 1959, the nation met its first astronauts: Carpenter, Cooper, Glenn, Grissom, Schirra, Shepard, Slayton.

Those who lamented the nation's atrophied "moral energies" found the ideal restorative talisman in the ethos of the astronaut. Stress-seeking, uniformly white Protestant, primarily of small-town or rural origins, they seemed to personify the legendary traits of an imagined earlier America. And the astronauts quickly learned to speak of themselves in frontier terms. Alan Shepard attributed his interest in Project Mercury "to an urge to pioneer." Gus Grissom acknowledged a similar "spirit of pioneering and adventure," adding that "I think if I had been alive 150 years ago, I might have wanted to go out and help open up the West."

In 1959, however, the "pioneer spirit" required revision. The appeal of the astronauts, like that of the Marlboro Man, rested in their capacity to combine the pioneering image of "150 years ago" with a forward-looking mastery of technological change. NASA's tendency to equate engineering with science helped to transform the astronauts into "space scientists." Their briefcases bulging with operation manuals, they were depicted as scouts on the technology as well as the physical frontier. Their contributions to engineering and design problems, however minimal, received emphasis in NASA press kits. (John Glenn, for example, suggested the addition of a window to future Mercury capsules.) "Fearless, but not reckless," they combined the youthful panache of a Lindbergh with the sobriety of the seasoned expert. "Here Are the U.S. Spacemen," *U.S. News and World Report* announced, "—Married, Mature, Fathers."

NASA's unveiling strategy evolved with the project. Unmanned test launches were planned—and sometimes executed—in secrecy. Then in February 1961 the agency focused national attention on Alan Shepard, Gus Grissom, and John Glenn when it named them as pilots for the first Mercury flights. Torn between security precautions and a desire to maximize publicity, NASA chose not to reveal which of the three would "command" the first flight until just before lift-off. After Shepard's success as America's first man in space, press restrictions were dropped. Unlike the Manhattan Project, or the Soviet space program, the U.S. manned space project would occur before the eyes of the world. If this apparently unrestricted media coverage tended to obscure more than it revealed about the justifications and strategies of the space program, it nevertheless increased the display value of each flight dramatically.

As publicity exceeded even NASA's expectations, the personalities of the helmsmen became an obsession of the national press. Shepard's "driving urge to get into space," *Time* explained grew out of a lifelong "personal flair" with fast machines. "Particularly fond of his white, high-powered Corvette sports car," *Life* reported, "he would love dearly to drive just as fast and hard as it would go." Through Shepard's eyes the awesome hardware of the launchpad acquired the familiarity of his Corvette: "A capsule is quite a bit like an automobile," he observed. Inspecting the Redstone rocket poised for his flight, America's first space hero "sort of wanted to kick the tires."

Shepard's suborbital flight on May 5, 1961, yielded most of its anticipated prestige to cosmonaut Yuri Gargarin's orbital flight of April 12. Nevertheless, as *Time* observed, the "voluntary hero-making mechanisms of the U.S. worked at full blast." Central to the adulation Shepard received was the news media's determination to depict him as an autonomously self-sufficient pilot—despite a wealth of facts to the contrary. Editors and television reporters effervesced over his "liberation from gravitational force" in a vast "playground of the imagination," "totally free of boundaries." *Time*'s cover illustration of Shepard's flight depicted him free-floating in space. In an otherwise ground-controlled flight, Shepard briefly deflected the capsule's pitch and yaw in a manual operation experiment—not unlike the Cadillac's Autronic Eye. Press coverage seized upon this incident as the key to the flight. "He did not fly as far, fast, or high as Russia's Yuri Gargarin," *Life* conceded; but "he controlled the flight of his capsule—which Gargarin did not." Felix Morley proclaimed Shepard a new Lindbergh who had revived the nations' traditional strengths by asserting "the individual's control over his destiny."

The distance between Lindbergh's "we" and the Mercury astronauts' "we seven," however, was marked by the emergency of a dizzying bureaucratic network of government agencies, committees, and aerospace contractors, with NASA personnel serving as coordinators. As Tom Wolfe has observed, the Mercury astronauts were so superfluous to the piloting of their capsules that many test pilots were unwilling to give up the likes of an X-15 to volunteer for a ride in a mere "tin can." Confined to a space suit, strapped to a form-fitting chair, Shepard viewed the "measureless horizons of space" by squinting through a periscope. His functional role in the flight was not unlike that of a rather elaborate hood ornament. The imaginative leaps by which publicity freed the astronaut's image from the facts of his flight experience borrowed as much from Walter Mitty as from Lindbergh.

Coverage of Shepard's flight, and of Gus Grissom's follow-up suborbital flight, frequently implied a direct link between the astronaut's mission and "national purpose." With John Glenn's orbital flight the following year, the transitivity of achievement from the astronaut to the nation reached its zenith. In the months of preparation and delay preceding his flight, Glenn's personality became the paramount feature of the Mercury program. Raised in New Concord, Ohio, "a quiet shirt-sleeves-and-overalls-town," he read Buck Rogers, studied chemical engineering at the hometown college, married a hometown dentist's daughter. Like Shepard, he followed "the bent I always had for mechanical things" to become an ace pilot. A member of his World War II combat squadron recalled how Glenn "would fly up alongside you and slip his wing right under yours, then tap it gently against your wing tip." But for Glenn, the technological sublime and national destiny were inseparable. To him, *Life* reported, the astronauts carried a mandate "not to just make the flights work out well but also to become symbols of the nation's future." "Purposeful Glenn" represented a purposeful America."

And Americans welcomed the message. On February 20, 1962, 130 million television viewers watched Glenn's Friendship 7 launch into its three-orbital flight. A commemorative stamp appeared the moment he stepped on board the recovery carrier. Its jubilant crew marked Glenn's footprints with white paint "just as the touchdown spot of the Spirit of St. Louis was marked at Paris'

Le Bourget Field." Hundreds of babies born on the day of the flight received Glenn's name. (One helpless infant in Ogden, Utah, was christened "Orbit.") The new hero's exclamation of wonder—"I've never seen anything like it!"—referred not to his flight but to the week of celebration marking his return. Writing in *Newsweek,* Raymond Moley cheered the flight as a reaffirmation of "the copybook maxims which in earlier years sustained [our] forefathers." *Time* portrayed him as "a latter-day Apollo, flashing through the unknown, sending his cool observations and random comments to earth in radio thunderbolts, acting as though orbiting the earth were his everyday occupation." And *America* dubbed Glenn "The Marine Magellan," "a Frank Meriwell of the cosmos."

Like Shepard, Glenn encountered irrepressible adulation of his helmsmanship. Toward the end of his first orbit, the automatic pilot system in the Friendship 7 capsule began to malfunction; Mission Control considered aborting. But Glenn corrected the craft's yaw, axis, prompting journals as diverse as *Aviation Week* and *The New Republic* to hail his flight as proof of "the primacy of man in space," a "human triumph over impersonal technology." However impressive the image of pathbreaking new technology, it was also vaguely threatening; the importance of "the man in command" remained. "Now we can get rid of some of that automatic equipment," Glenn exulted after splashdown, "and let man take over."

As Project Mercury gave way to Gemini and Gemini to Apollo, the lone helmsman was joined by a crewmate, then by another. Space publicists found that the simple elegance of the Lindbergh display format—one pilot, one craft—suffering from overcrowding and personalities. Moreover, as the decade's civil rights and antiwar activities gained momentum, the appeal of a John Glenn, brimming with self-assured piety and patriotism, proved more difficult to evoke.

Not until the first lunar landing approached did the lionization of the astronaut return so exuberantly; and in the intervening years, the tone of presentation shifted. Publicity for Apollo 11 depicted the crew in more "professional," less all-encompassing terms. Their credentials as helmsmen remained prominent: Neil Armstrong, the nation learned, "had his pilot's license before his driver's license," and had "always wanted to do something daring and different." He had gone on to become "the hottest pilot ever to wear the wings of an astronaut"—"the kind of man virtually every father dreams his son will be—Eagle Scout, war hero, aeronautical engineer, test pilot and astronaut." Both he and Buzz Aldrin served as fighter pilots in Korea; he and Michael Collins were test pilots at Edwards Air Force Base, where Armstrong flew the X-15 to an altitude of 200,000 feet."

But compared with their Mercury predecessors, they were more "cosmopolitan" (Collins was "born in Rome," the son of a military attaché to the U.S. embassy; Aldrin's father, a former Air Corps aviator, had been a close friend of Orville Wright, Charles Lindbergh, and rocket pioneer Robert Goddard). And their educational background received more emphasis (Aldrin held a doctorate in astronautics from MIT and had "the best scientific mind we have sent into space"; Armstrong had done postgraduate work in aeronautical engineering). "A new breed of cosmic explorer has emerged," one newsmagazine wrote of the Apollo generation. "Gone is the earliest image of the rocket-riding daredevil, the superman of the 'wild blue yonder.' The astronaut now is seen as a dedicated scientist concerned more with discovery than with setting orbiting records."

For the most part, Apollo coverage focused less on individual astronauts and more on the gadgetry of space flight. Like car salesmen, reporters found that the size, speed, and special features of the spacecraft provided a welcome substitute for discussions of the mission's long-range value. Diagrams of each flight's itinerary covered the nation's newspapers, demonstrating the precision with which Houston could determine its direction. The Saturn 5 rocket that carried Apollo astronaut aloft was acclaimed as the "largest, most powerful machine ever built," with enough power ("150 million horsepower") to carry its payload "ten times faster than a bullet." At 363 feet, it stood "higher than a football field"—or, as the Chicago *Tribune* calculated, "equivalent [in length] to six Santa Marias or four Mayflowers," weighing as much as "four Santa Marias, five Mayflowers, and the United States frigate Constitution."

It was through jargon, however, that space flight became most accessible to its audience. The Mercury flights had established "A-OK" and "lift-off" as passwords for national well-being and determination. Apollo generated an inexhaustible array of technojargon, fusing the telegraphic abruptness of bureaucratese with Pentagon-style obfuscation. If advertisers had been the first to discover the recontextualizing capacity of jargon, Vietnam-era military strategists and arms industries became, in Anthony Sampson's words, the "new masters of news-speak," transforming weapons into "capabilities" and "systems," arms exports into "defence transfers," and the strafing of peasant villages into an agenda of "conflict configurations" wherein helicopters with high "fire growth capability" pursued "objectives" of "optimum interface." Not simply new terms but a new descriptive mode was emerging, insulating operator from technical function, and function from social impact.

Apollo propelled this value-neutral, elegantly opaque language into the vacuum of space—an uncontested field in which to recite the catechism of American technological superiority. Space illiterates might still speak the archaic language of "rockets to the moon"; Houston spoke of "deploying Lem [the lunar module] on the lurain [lunar terrain]." For the uninitiated, Walter Cronkite patiently explained the meaning of "apolune" and "perilune." Like the Marlboro Man's tatoo, the language of Apollo provided an illusory transitivity of expertise. Only three men would make each flight; the rest of us could be jargonauts, vicariously participating in Mission Control's ethos of competence.

That ethos was never articulated directly. The Apollo 11 press kit issued to reporters by nation offered 250 pages of acronyms and charts, but no mention of the project's purpose or social significance. Encoded into this elaborate terminology, however, was an ideology of "systems analysis"—a managerial vision of control, the very terms of which ("systems stabilization and control," "attitude control," "thrust vector control") implied the Marlboro Man's ability to command his social environment as well as his ship. Apollo 11 astronaut, the press kit explained, would launch into EPO (Earth Parking Orbit), from which a lengthy interval of TLC (Translunar Coast) would carry them to the critical LOI (Lunar Orbit Insertion). Having made lunar contact, they would engage in EVA (Extravehicular Activity), culminating in deployment of their SRCs (Sample Rock Collectors). Their mission completed, they could look forward to a Transearth Coast before final Re-entry and Splashdown would bring them back to earth. Once home, they would don their BIGs (Biological Isolation Garments) to insure against contamination.

The detached, problem-solving specificity of nation jargon served a further purpose. As the crew of Apollo 11 made clear at a pre-launch press conference, their mission was to convey a sense of mission. Self-contained details of the flight's agenda insulated them from awkward questions concerning substantive goals or justifications for the enterprise. "The objective of this flight," Neil Armstrong announced, "is precisely to take men to the moon, make a landing there, and return. That is the objective. There are a number of secondary objectives," he added; "[b]ut the primary objective is the ability to demonstrate that man, in fact, can do this kind of job. How we'll use that information in the centuries to come," he concluded on a familiar note, "only history will tell."

As the Apollo program replicated its moon landings, their display value began to diminish. As they grew in scale, they lost immediacy. Loudon Wainwright, who had covered the manned space program for *Life* since the first Mercury launches, attributed his "growing sense of nonexcitement" at the moon launch to "the attrition of 10 years," adding that "precision has a way of dehumanizing adventure." But the major difficulty with the display value of the moonshot was its sponsors' inability to keep the technology of spaceflight apace with the overriding demands of technological display. What advertising had that Apollo lacked was the fathomless resilience of the quack. The actor in the doctor's smock could—and must—change his pitch to match the moment. That was precisely how his sponsor achieved a predictable market, the product could stay the same because its image was free to change.

For example, in 1958, when national space policy was first coalescing, Vought Aircraft portrayed its Crusader III carrier fighter planes ("Cru-SAD-er") streaking across a two-page ad in national newsmagazines ("Automated, missile-armed, missile-fast, it will extend the Nuclear Navy's knockout power to the edge of space"). By 1969 Vought—now Ling-Temco-Vought—was one of the nation's primary defense contractors. At the height of an unpopular war, it still placed ads in national newsmagazines. Now, however, a typical ad depicted a thoughtful young man with stars and spinning electrons in his head. "We're in the business of extending man's sense," the caption declared. ("We can turn a mission concept into sophisticated hardware faster, better, at lower cost than just about anyone." "Our mission: Extending man's senses. What's yours?") For its part, presentation of the man-in-space program proceeded as though the intervening decade had never happened.

Were the merchants of space, then, simply less adept at display modification than a good advertising agency? Or was Apollo's lag in image more willful? In an earlier culture's mythology, Mercury fashioned and delivered to Apollo a harp so beautifully executed that when Apollo played it all Olympus fell into a dream. In many respects the Apollo space capsule was also a time capsule, allowing the nation's Space van Winkles to carry a vision of the fifties intact through My Lai and Watts, assassinations and campus riots, and the Tet offensive. For many commentators, both friend and foe, the social function of Apollo was to sustain a pre-Vietnam dream of conquest.

As late as October 1968 Werner von Braun warned readers of *U.S. News and World Report* that preoccupations with the Vietnam War, the "riots in the cities, and so forth" had "distracted from interest in space" to the point that the nation may have "settled for no. 2 in space." Of recent cuts in NASA's budget, he lamented, "It is like being ordered to disarm while the war is still on."

The following summer *U.S. News and World Report* proclaimed the first moon landing to be above all "a symbolic 'conquest'": By "harnessing natural resources on a wartime scale," and by designating private industry rather than the state to construct the project, America "has emerged, after a decade of self-doubt, as the most technologically and scientifically advanced of all nations." In the years to come, *U.S. News* predicted, Americans would lead the conquest of space, mining and colonizing the moon and planets. Interplanetary military bases, it conceded, seemed less likely than the early Sputnik days; missiles from the moon, for example, would require two or three days' travel time, as opposed to fifteen minutes for earthbound missiles. "Nevertheless weapons on the moon . . . might be *psychologically intimidating*."

Both supporters and critics of Apollo agreed that the Eagle flew like a hawk. William F. Buckley declared the moon landing an "unmitigatedly glorious" "aristocratic venture." His *National Review* blasted "Flat-Earth Liberals" for "ignor[ing] realities of national competition for the sake of abstract UN-type pieties." Carey McWilliams, editor of *The Nation,* agreed that Cold War competition dominated the confusion of motives surrounding the project, but found nothing "glorious" in that fact. Asking "What Price Moondust?," McWilliams noted with trepidation that NASA director Thomas O. Paine had "defended NASA's budget by saying that the technology involved would be helpful in 'winning the next war,' a comment that somewhat tarnishes the 'Space Olympics' image of the moon race."

A few of Apollo's interpreters located the object of its "conquest" closer to home. Eric Hoffer called the landing "the triumph of the squares"—a reaffirmation of traditional middle-class values that had recently endured pervasive denunciation and ridicule. Writing from a different perspective, Peter Collier agreed, "Of, by, and for middle-class America," he wrote in *Ramparts,* "the astronauts were its revenge against all the scruffy third-worlders and long-haired deviants who had stolen arrogantly onto the center stage." The first men on the moon "were to be our Aeneas, removing America's household gods—a flag and a television—to a foreign clime." No need to defoliate or tear-gas the moon; no guerrillas crouched behind those craters, no noisy demonstrators could march into the Sea of Tranquility.

Such visions of vicarious conquest often melted into dreams of escape. Some scientists and science fiction writers (who occupied nearly interchangeable positions of authority in the mass media) argued that moonflight signaled an evolutionary leap forward. Isaac Asimov exulted in the *New York Magazine:* "The Moon Could Answer the Riddle of Life." Apollo's objectives might be unclear at the moment, but he provided "the answer (or anyway, *an* answer) to those who ask why we are spending billions to reach the moon, when it is so much more important to cure cancer on earth. All science is one. If we push back the boundaries of the darkness in any direction, the added light illuminates all places, and not merely the immediate area uncovered." The Columbus Principle still reigned in the form of the "spin-off." Space men were hailed as deliverers of a storehouse of unanticipated wonders, from Teflon to improved electrocardiographs—as if the way to develop a better electrocardiography were to send men to the moon.

For some of Apollo's defenders, the sense of discovery and escape was more generalized. Louis J. Halle proclaimed the Apollo flights to be "man's liberation from this earthly prison"—a vicarious release from "intellectual claustrophobia." "Our position is simply that of the intelligent creatures confined to the ocean deeps," he asserted in *The New Republic.* "Now, however, that we are at last beginning to escape from our native confines, there is no telling what light we may find in the larger universe to dissipate the darkness in our minds."

Several of the manned space project's more outspoken critics agreed that the lunar landing constituted an "escape," but of a less laudable variety. *Ebony* wondered what the astronauts might say to any extraterrestrials they might encounter: "Are they going to say, 'We have millions of people starving to death back home so we thought we'd drop by to see how you're faring'?" Novelist Kurt Vonnegut held a similar view. "Earth is such a pretty blue and pink and white pearl in the pictures NASA sent me," he wrote in the *New York Times Magazine.* "It looks so *clean.* You can't see all hungry, angry earthlings down there—and the smoke and the sewage and trash and sophisticated weaponry."

Mission Control, once an overarching emblem of American use of technology, appeared to many by 1969 to be an arcade of evasions. "The moon is an escape from our earthly responsibilities," Anthony Lewis concluded in the *New York Times,* "and like other escapes, it leaves a troubled conscience." Our discomfort did not stem simply from the discovery of poverty and ugliness in a nation of unprecedented wealth; these problems we had the "technical apparatus" to solve, if we so desired. "What we lack is any agreed moral basis for their solution, a common vision of the good society. Perhaps we are the twentieth century Vikings," Lewis mused, "driven, conquering without humanizing qualities. We would know the stars but we do not know ourselves."

The lunar landings were a triumph of engineering. They also signified the victory of impression management over substantive policy in American government. The manned space program demonstrated that the nation purpose had joined the other commodities of consumer culture as something that could be televised and sold. One widely reprinted photograph featured Apollo's Saturn 5 rocket poised alongside the rising moon, suggesting a lavish reincarnation of the Trylon and Perisphere beautiful, richly evocative, but rather useless once the exposition was concluded.

And if Apollo proved far less disappointing and destructive than the war in Vietnam, these two campaigns of state-sponsored technological display had more in common than crater-pocked terrain. Whether in the hills of Khe Sanh or on the Sea of Tranquility, the deployment of American technology evoked similar questions of home and abroad: How could so much power accomplish so little real improvement? Faith in appearances and the impression of "credibility" might sell millions of oversized, inefficient automobiles; but the lunar module—and the ship of state—could not be so quickly traded in. The years following "moon summer" brought the "credibility crisis" of Watergate, the "energy crisis," new awareness of the environmental and health hazards of industrial technology, an accelerated arms race, and a depressed economy. Decisions concerning the social use of technology, and the masking of those decisions through commodity scientism, were no longer—as Werner von Braun had hoped—"something for the next generation to worry about."

---

163. William Sullivan, "Was the Vietnam War Inevitable?"

William Sullivan offers a recent, iconoclastic view of the Vietnam war in an oral history of the conflict.

This may sound Panglossian, but a Vietnam had to happen to us sometime. This was a very tragic event. It tore the country apart. It had consequences politically, socially, and economically from which we are still suffering. But it did draw a line under the prevailing sense of omnipotence and omniscience that the United States postwar generation had developed. When we came out of World War II we were artificially strong. We had a monopoly on nuclear weapons, the strongest conventional military forces, the most resilient economy, a vibrant political system. The rest of the world was in ruins, but it was bound to come back.

Source: Kem Willenson et al., *The Bad War: An Oral History of the Vietnam War*, pp. 385–387. Copyright 1987, Newsweek, Inc. Reprinted with permission.

And, of course, this is the thing that is so hard to explain to the rednecks. I sometimes do lectures for the Council on Foreign Relations in places like Wichita. Why, they want to know. "Why can't it be like it was then? Goddamnit, we could snap shit and people would pay attention!" A lot of yahoos in this country never accepted that things had inevitably changed. And eventually, just by sheer force of decibels, they got us around to the point that we were prepared to behave like John Wayne and sort of knock their teeth out, knock 'em back, put 'em back in their box, blow 'em back to the Stone Age, whatever phrase you want to use. Sooner or later we were going to run into a place where we tried to do that and it didn't work.

So the Panglossian part is that just in terms of not having suffered the ruination of the country, we were damned lucky it happened in a place that didn't really matter all that much, like Indochina. Had we taken a stand in a place like Hungary, it could have blown up the world, including the United States. Fifty-eight thousand lives is too many to pay for a lesson, but it's probably smaller than we might have paid had we gone into

Czechoslovakia in '68, or done something else that would have led to a direct confrontation with the Soviets or with the Chinese. So Vietnam was a tragedy but it may have been the tragic price that American hubris needed somewhere along the line to get back to reality.

Looking back on Vietnam, the supreme irony of it is that four Presidents took the United States into combat in Vietnam because they were convinced that the strategic balance in Asia was shifting against us and our friend. It was just the Lao Dong [Vietnam Workers' party] moving down into South Vietnam; it was also the Chinese operations in Thailand and Malaysia and the Philippines and above all in Indonesia. What they saw was a vise tightening across the sea-lanes connecting Japan to its energy sources, isolating Australia and New Zealand, and the whole of Southeast Asia becoming Communist.

Now, that didn't happen, but I think the point that all the commentaries that were written on the tenth anniversary missed is that while we didn't win the war, had we won, we would have had to keep troops in South Vietnam. And had we kept troops in South Vietnam, the North Vietnamese and the Chinese would have had to patch up their differences to some extent, and the Soviets and the Chinese would have had to give them logistic support. The whole thing would have stayed glued together even though it was palpably inconsistent. Once we pulled out, everything changed. The Chinese were able then to vent their true feelings about the Vietnamese. The Soviets moved in with the Vietnamese in a way that's concerned the hell out of the Chinese. And what you got was the Chinese making this enormous change and reaching an accommodation with the United States.

And the consequence was a cosmic shift in the geostrategic position. Although the Chinese are not our allies, they act in concert with us, in intelligence and other things. We've changed our whole outlook as a result. WE no longer think in terms of fighting two and a half wars; we think in terms of one and a half wars. The *Soviets* have to think about two and a half wars. It's the Chinese who keep pounding on the Soviets and the Vietnamese in Southeast Asia, and it's the Vietnamese and Soviets who keep the Chinese in check. Had we plotted it and planned it this way as Machiavellians, it couldn't have come out better.

The fact is, we stumbled into it by what turned out to be an enormously, costly, traumatic national experience for the United States — not only fifty-eight thousand people killed, but also the disruption in our own society. Now I think that disruption in some milder form would have come anyway. Vietnam was not a catalyst so much as an accelerator of changes that were inevitable in our society: the civil rights movement in the South, the women's revolution, the youth revolution, the black revolution. Because it all came at once it was somehow or other in our minds associated with Vietnam. But all those things, it seems to have, have obscured the fact that in its own unintended way, the Vietnam operation turned out to be one of the master strategic strokes of the century. Lyndon Johnson would never believe it in his grave but this is so. And when the historians finally get around to it, I think a lot of the pain and the trauma that went with the sixties will be put in another perspective.

It's very easy, particularly for those who philosophically oppose these changes, to attribute them all to Vietnam and to, essentially, a failure of American will. The great right-wing myth is that the military had that war won, but the damn civilians and the press and the fuzzy intellectuals snatched defeat from the jaws of victory. You know damn well we didn't have that war won and the supreme irony is, aren't we lucky we didn't, because we've now got an equilibrium in the Pacific which is probably the best that has prevailed there since the sixteenth century.

164. 93RD CONGRESS, "THE IMPEACHMENT OF RICHARD M. NIXON," AUGUST 20, 1974

The House Judiciary Committee drafted this resolution of impeachment against Richard M. Nixon, listing the charges the committee felt had been substantiated against the President.

August 20, 1974—Referred to the House Calendar and ordered to be printed

Mr. Rodino, from the Committee on the Judiciary, submitted the following

REPORT

together with

SUPPLEMENTAL, ADDITIONAL, SEPARATE, DISSENTING, MINORITY, INDIVIDUAL AND CONCURRING VIEWS

The Committee on the Judiciary, to whom was referred the consideration of recommendations concerning the exercise of the constitutional power to impeach Richard M. Nixon, President of the United States, having considered the same, reports thereon pursuant to H. Res. 803 as follows and recommends that the House exercise its constitutional power to impeach Richard M. Nixon, President of the United States, and that articles of impeachment be exhibited to the Senate as follows:

Resolution

Impeaching Richard M. Nixon, President of the United States, of high crimes and misdemeanors.

Resolved, that Richard M. Nixon, President of the United States, is impeached for high crimes and misdemeanors, and that the following articles of impeachment be exhibited to the Senate:

Articles of impeachment exhibited by the House of Representatives of the United States of America in the name of itself and of all of the people of the United States of America, against Richard M. Nixon, President of the United States of America, in maintenance and support of its impeachment against him for high crimes and misdemeanors.

ARTICLE I

In his conduct of the office of President of the United States, Richard M. Nixon, in violation of his constitutional oath faithfully to execute the office of President of the United States and, to the best of his ability, preserve, protect, and defend the Constitution of the United States, and in violation of his constitutional duty to take care that the laws be faithfully executed, has prevented, obstructed, and impeded the administration of justice, in that:

On June 17, 1972, and prior thereto, agents of the Committee for the Re-election of the President committed unlawful entry of the headquarters of the Democratic National Committee in Washington, District of Columbia, for the purpose of securing political intelligence. Subsequent thereto, Richard M. Nixon, using the powers of his high office, engaged personally and through his subordinates and agents, in a course of conduct or plan designed to delay, impede, and obstruct the investigation of such unlawful entry; to cover up, conceal and protect those responsible; and to conceal the existence and scope of other unlawful covert activities.

The means used to implement this course of conduct or plan included one or more of the following:

1. making or causing to be made false or misleading statements to lawfully authorized investigative officers and employees of the United States;
2. withholding relevant and material evidence or information from lawfully authorized inves-

---

Source: Impeachment of Richard Nixon, House Calendar #426, House of Representatives, 93rd Congress, 2nd Session. Public Domain Reprint.

tigative officers and employees of the United States;
3. approving, condoning, acquiescing in, and counseling witnesses with respect to the giving of false or misleading statements to lawfully authorized investigative officers and employees of the United States and false or misleading testimony in duly instituted judicial and congressional proceedings;
4. interfering or endeavoring to interfere with the conduct of investigations by the Department of Justice of the United States, the Federal Bureau of Investigation, the Office of Watergate Special Prosecution Force, and Congressional Committees;
5. approving, condoning, and acquiescing in the surreptitious payment of substantial sums of money for the purpose of obtaining the silence or influencing the testimony of witnesses, potential witnesses or individuals who participated in such unlawful entry and other illegal activities.
6. endeavoring to misuse the Central Intelligence Agency, an agency of the United States;
7. disseminating information received from officers of the Department of Justice of the United States to subjects of investigation conducted by lawfully authorized investigative officers and employees of the United States, for the purpose of aiding and assisting such subjects in their attempts to avoid criminal liability;
8. making false or misleading public statements for the purpose of deceiving the people of the United States into believing that a thorough and complete investigation had been conducted with respect to allegations of misconduct on the part of personnel of the executive branch of the United States and personnel of the Committee for the Re-election of the President, and that there was no involvement of such personnel in such misconduct; or
9. endeavoring to cause prospective defendants, and individuals duly tried and convicted, to expect favored treatment and consideration in return for their silence or false testimony, or rewarding individuals for their silence or false testimony.

In all of this, Richard M. Nixon has acted in a manner contrary to his trust as President and subversive of constitutional government, to the great prejudice of the cause of law and justice and to the manifest injury of the people of the United States.

Wherefore Richard M. Nixon, by such conduct, warrants impeachment and trial, and removal from office.

Article II

Using the powers of the office of President of the United States, Richard M. Nixon, in violation of his constitutional oath faithfully to execute the office of President of the United States and, to the best of his ability, preserve, protect, and defend the Constitution of the United States, and in disregard of his constitutional duty to take care that the laws be faithfully executed, has repeatedly engaged in conduct violating the constitutional rights of citizens, impairing the due and proper administration of justice and the conduct of lawful inquiries, or contravening the laws governing agencies of the executive branch and the purposes of these agencies.

This conduct has included one or more of the following:

1. He has, acting personally and through his subordinates and agents, endeavored to obtain from the Internal Revenue Service, in violation of the constitutional rights of citizens, confidential information contained in income tax returns for purposes not authorized by law, and to cause, in violation of the constitutional rights of citizens, income tax audits or other income tax investigations to be initiated or conducted in a discriminatory manner.
2. He misused the Federal Bureau of Investigation, the Secret Service, and other executive personnel, in violation or disregard of the constitutional rights of citizens, by directing or authorizing such agencies or personnel to conduct or continue electronic surveillance or other investigations for purposes unrelated to national security, the enforcement of laws, or any other lawful function of his office; he did direct, authorize, or permit the use of information obtained thereby for purposes unrelated to national security, the enforcement of laws, or any other lawful function of his office; and he did direct the concealment of certain records made by the Federal Bureau of Investigation of electronic surveillance.

3. He has, acting personally and through his subordinates and agents, in violation or disregard of the constitutional rights of citizens, authorized and permitted to be maintained a secret investigative unit within the office of the President, financed in part with money derived from campaign contributions, which unlawfully utilized the resources of the Central Intelligence Agency, engaged in covert and unlawful activities, and attempted to prejudice the constitutional right of an accused to a fair trial.

4. He has failed to take care that the laws were faithfully executed by failing to act when he knew or had reason to know that his close subordinates endeavored to impede and frustrate lawful inquiries by duly constituted executive, judicial, and legislative entities concerning the unlawful entry into the headquarters of the Democratic National Committee, and the cover-up thereof, and concerning other unlawful activities, including those relating to the confirmation of Richard Kleindienst as Attorney General of the United States, the electronic surveillance of private citizens, the break-in into the offices of Dr. Lewis Fielding, and the campaign financing practices of the Committee to Re-elect the President.

5. In disregard of the rule of law, he knowingly misused the executive power by interfering with agencies of the executive branch, including the Federal Bureau of Investigation, the Criminal Division, and the Office of Watergate Special Prosecution Force, of the Department of Justice, and the Central Intelligence Agency, in violation of his duty to take care that the laws be faithfully executed.

In all of this, Richard M. Nixon has acted in a manner contrary to his trust as President and subversive of constitutional government, to the great prejudice of the cause of law and justice and to the manifest injury of the people of the United States.

Wherefore, Richard M. Nixon, by such conduct, warrants impeachment and trial, and removal from office.

Article III

In his conduct of the office of the President of the United States, Richard M. Nixon, contrary to his oath faithfully to execute the office of President of the United States and, to the best of his ability, preserve, protect, and defend the Constitution of the United States, and in violation of his constitutional duty to take care that the laws be faithfully executed, has failed without lawful cause or excuse to produce papers and things as directed by duly authorized subpoenas issued by the Committee on the Judiciary of the House of Representatives on April 11, 1974, May 15, 1974, May 30, 1974, and June 24, 1974, and willfully disobeyed such subpoenas. The subpoenaed papers and things were deemed necessary by the Committee in order to resolve by direct evidence fundamental, factual questions relating to Presidential direction, knowledge, or approval of actions demonstrated by other evidence to be substantial grounds for impeachment of the President. In refusing to produce these papers and things, Richard M. Nixon, substituting his judgment as to what materials were necessary for the inquiry, interposed the powers of the Presidency against the lawful subpoenas of the House of Representatives, thereby assuming to himself functions and judgments necessary to the exercise of the sole power of impeachment vested by the Constitution in the House of Representatives.

In all of this, Richard M. Nixon has acted in a manner contrary to his trust as President and subversive of constitutional government, to the great prejudice of the cause of law and justice and to the manifest injury of the people of the United States.

Wherefore, Richard M. Nixon, by such conduct, warrants impeachment and trial, and removal from office.

165. NBC, Richard M. Nixon on "Meet the Press"

In a brief excerpt from a later interview on NBC's "Meet the Press," Nixon summarizes his views of Watergate's origins and effects.

[*The conclusion of NBC's program of April 10, 1988*]

TOM BROKAW: What about when you are self-critical of your personal style or how you treat people or how you look at the world? Do you see anything that you might have done differently?

RICHARD NIXON: Well, I suppose I could have treated the press better.

TOM BROKAW: Well, I wasn't looking for that necessarily.

RICHARD NIXON: But then they might have treated me better. No, I think under the circumstances it's very difficult for one to psychoanalyze himself. You know I don't go much for this psycho-history. I don't go much for psycho-TV shows, either. I think they're rather revolting. And as far as sitting down and psychoanalyzing myself and saying, now, how could I have been a better person, it's just not my bag.

JOHN CHANCELLOR: . . . Write me a paragraph that might be written about the turn of the century or the next century about Richard Nixon.

RICHARD NIXON: . . . History will treat me fairly. Historians probably won't because most historians are on the left, and I understand that. I would say as people look back on the Nixon administration they're probably most likely to remember 50 years from now, 100 years from now, that it made a difference on a very major issue. We changed the world. If it had not been for the China initiative, which only I could do at that point, we would be in a terrible situation today with China aligned with the Soviet Union and with the Soviet Union's power. The China initiative hasn't brought peace to the world. We can't be sure that will happen. But without it, would be in terrible shape.

CHRIS WALLACE: . . . Do you have thoughts about what you could have accomplished in the rest of the second term, and how, flowing from that, America would have been so different?

RICHARD NIXON: My priorities were these. One, interestingly enough, one of the first ones, was the Mideast. I talked about it over and over again with Henry Kissinger in February and March of 1973. Second was [that] we would not have lost the war in Vietnam. I would have seen to it that we would have forced the North Vietnamese to keep the Paris peace agreement. And that would have meant that we wouldn't have had basically what happened in all the places around the world, Cambodia, Laos, even what happened in Africa and even in Nicaragua. The other part is that we—I think we would have done something at home. There was an area particularly I was interested in, and that was to have a real welfare program. I am concerned about the fact that when you look at blacks, they are worse off today, generally speaking, on an average, than they were in 1966 when the Great Society program started, and the problem is the family. We've got to do something about that, and our family assistance program was the right way to go . . .

Source: "Meet the Press" Interview. NBC Program of April 10, 1988.

Chapter XXXI

The Reagan-Bush Years, 1981–1992

166. Jerry Falwell, "Can We Forget the Little Ones?" 1986

Jerry Falwell of Lynchburg tells how he came to direct the energies of evangelical Christians against abortion in the 1970s.

I will never forget the morning of January 23, 1973. I picked up our newspaper from the front porch of my home in Lynchburg, Virginia, and glanced over it on my way into the kitchen for breakfast. I scanned the headlines telling of Lyndon Johnson's death and for a moment I thought his obituary would be the only newsworthy story of the day. Then I saw the smaller headlines announcing a Supreme Court decision on the controversial matter of abortion.

I don't usually read the paper during breakfast. I glance at the headlines to be sure the world is still in orbit before getting down to the serious business of eggs and bacon and raisin toast. That morning was different. I could not stop reading the story of *Roe v. Wade*. The Supreme Court had just made a seven of two decision that would legalize the killing of a generation of unborn children. I couldn't believe that seven justices on that Court could be so callous about the dignity of human life. Were they misinformed? Had they been misled? Were the plunging the nation into a time of darkness and shame without even knowing what they were doing?

My breakfast remained uneaten on my plate. My coffee grew cold as I read and reread the unbelievable story of the Court's decision. I had followed the debate on abortion with growing interest. I had read articles by Dr. Francis Schaeffer and Dr. Jack Willke discussing the implications for a society that condones the mass killings of its unborn children. I had talked to doctors and social workers about the physical and psychological effects on the women who choose abortion to end an unwanted pregnancy. I had preached on abortion and its meaning to my people and had used abortion as an example in several sermons over the past ten years. But, as I read the paper that day, I knew something more had to be done, and I felt a growing conviction that I would have to take my stand among the people who were doing it.

I knew immediately that the nation would be painfully divided by this issue. President Nixon had just been sworn into his second term of office by Chief Justice Burger. The president was against abortion, but the chief justice had sided with the pro-abortion majority of the Court. The church, too, would be divided with the pro-life opposition led by the Roman Catholic Church.

"How many millions of children prior to their birth will never live to see the light of day because of the shocking action of the majority of the United States Supreme Court today?" asked New York's Terence Cardinal Cook.

"It is hard to think of any decision in the two hundred years of our history which has had more disastrous implications for our stability as a civilized society," warned John Joseph Cardinal Krol, the president of the National Conference of Catholic Bishops.

I felt confident that most traditionally conservative churchmen, lay and clergy alike, would agree with the Catholics, while most traditionally liberal churchmen, lay and clergy alike, would applaud the court's decision on behalf of the rights of pregnant women.

Immediately, response began to flow into the Supreme Court building from around the country. Court guards

---

Source: Jerry Falwell, *If I Should Die Before I Wake,* "Can We Forget the Little Ones?," pp. 31–47. Copyright Thomas Nelson Publishers, 1986. Reprinted by permission.

had to set up large bins in the basement to sort the letters, telegrams, and petitions to each justice condemning the Court's decision. Those who saw the letters remember critics comparing the justices "to the butchers of Dachau, to child killers, to immoral beasts, and to Communists." Some people even threatened the justices' lives or sent letter bombs to the Supreme Court Building. Hysteria, I knew, would not bring meaningful or lasting change; rash words and actions would only dishonor the cause. But something had to be said to save the millions of unborn children who would die. Something had to be done on their behalf.

Again I began to preach against abortion, sincerely hoping that words would be enough. I called abortion "America's national sin." I compared abortion to Hitler's "final solution" for the Jews and the Court's decision to setting loose "a biological holocaust" on our nation. Almost immediately I knew in my heart that preaching would not be enough. Opponents of the Court's decision were taking their protest to the streets. For the first time in my life I wanted to be there with them, taking my stand on behalf of this life-and-death issue.

But becoming politically active was not easy for this Baptist preacher. I had always tried to be a responsible citizen in the privacy of the voting booth. My school teachers had taught me the concept of the separation of church and state and I had faithfully practiced that belief. In fact, during the 1960s when liberal churchmen were marching in front lines for every causes imaginable, I had been stunned and appalled by their behavior. In 1965 I preached a sermon entitled "Ministers and Marches." In that sermon I expressed my honest feelings that government could be trusted to correct its own ills. People were descending on Washington by the hundreds of thousands to march for every kind of issue from legalizing marijuana to ending the war in Vietnam. Some of the issues I favored. Others I opposed. However, I believe then that the Christian's best contribution to social change was his or her faithfulness to our primary goals: studying the Word, preaching the gospel, winning souls, building churches and Christian schools, and praying for the eventual healing of the nation.

At ministers' meetings I had preached against the clergy's taking an active role in political cause. Again, I told my fellow pastors across the country that they could trust government to correct itself. "Our role as pastors and Christian leaders," I had said, "is to attend to the spiritual needs of our people." Serving the church and letting government take care of itself had been my lifelong policy.

I had begun the Thomas Road Baptist Church in Lynchburg, Virginia, in 1956, when I was only twenty-two years old. We started our little church with thirty-five members, and I had done almost nothing else but serve that growing congregation for seventeen years. Practically, there hadn't been time to do anything else. Over the years, our Christian education ministry had expanded to include an academy, a college, and a program of continuing education for thousands of students. Our evangelism program had grown to include a worldwide television and radio ministry, along with the publication of books, pamphlets, and study guides. By the time of the *Roe v. Wade* decision, I was preacher, teacher, chief executive officer, and pastor to a congregation of over fifteen thousand members. At first I was convinced that there was no time in the day to do more than preach or teach against abortion and pray that someone else would risk his life and vocation on behalf of millions of unborn babies whose lives were in jeopardy.

Also, I reminded myself, when fundamentalist Christians finally get involved in political issues, they often betray their own ignorance about the problems and their naivete about the political processes that lead to solutions. This Supreme Court decision was no exception. In the immediate outpouring of public sentiment against the legalization of abortion, more than one thousand Baptists and similar religious groups sent angry letters and telegrams to Justice Hugo Black condemning his participation in the Court's decision. Justice Black had been dead for sixteen months. The writers of those letters had their hearts in the right place but they were uninformed and thus ineffective. If I were to become involved, I knew I would have to understand the legal process and the complex issues. There would be books and pamphlets and legal briefs to read. There would be experts and authorities to interview.

There was another good reason to stay away from the complex and explosive abortion issue. I believe in a pluralistic nation. I pastored a church where people could hold various political views and still be one in Christ. Already the nation was being divided over the issue. Would that also happen to my congregation?

There were plenty of reasons to let this issue pass, but the more I thought about the killing of the unborn child, the more I knew my reasons were not reasons at all, but excuses, excuses to save me from the extra work, from the risk, from the pressures and the embarrassment of taking a stand in an arena where I had not taken a stand before.

One day not long after the Supreme Court's decision, I saw a full-color picture of an unborn child approximately sixteen to eighteen weeks old. The child's eyes were closed. She was sound asleep, sucking her thumb, floating in a silken sack, waiting for that moment when she would decide that her time inside had ended and her time outside would begin. She had delicate, graceful fingers and toes. Her skin was shiny and transparent. You could see her vital organs shadowed in shades of pink and red. Her heart, already beating 120 to 160 times a minute, was pumping blood that she herself had made to her perfectly shaped arms and legs and torso and then back through her heart again through a weblike maze of microscopic veins.

In that picture I saw a tiny, trusting child whom God had created. Regardless of the human reasons behind this child's conception, God loved her. It didn't matter if her human parents wanted her to live or die. God wanted her to live. The Supreme Court of the United States of America had made a terrible mistake. Because of their decision that tiny, unborn miracle of God's creation could be killed with the consent of her mother, the medical profession, and the highest court of the land. Now I was certain my position was valid, but I still hesitated to take a public stand.

It was my family who finally helped me decide to become active in the pro-life movement. During the winter of 1974, almost a year after the Supreme Court decision, we were sitting around a roaring fireplace in the living room of our home in Lynchburg. My older son, twelve-year-old Jerry, had just read a passage from the book of Revelation describing the final return of Christ to earth. My ten-year-old daughter, Jennie, sat in my wife's lap. And my youngest son, Jonathan, an eight-year-old redhead, was lying on the floor looking up at me.

During the course of that night's family altar time I shared, a bit too freely, my own skepticism regarding our nation's health. I must have been tired that night for I said dark, gloomy things about the future. Frankly, I was concerned, perhaps more than I ever had been before. The country had so deteriorated during that last decade that feared for my children's future. I honestly believed that what my wife and I had known of the greatness and the goodness of this country, our children might never know.

The laundry list of America's ills was long and disheartening. While abortion was at the top of my list of priorities that needed attention, there were others: pornography, drugs, the 40 percent divorce rate, sex without commitment, children without marriage, and the growing hostility of our young people toward the family, the church, free enterprise, and the nation. The country seemed doomed. The trends toward liberalism and hedonism seemed irreversible. We were entering a new age of secular humanism, and I was afraid for my country and for my children who were growing up just as my country seemed to be falling apart.

Throughout my tired-father confession that night I used the legal murder of millions of America's unborn children as a primary example of the terrible condition in which the country found itself.

"Why don't you do something about it, Dad?" my spunky red-headed son finally interrupted, rising up on one elbow and looking me in the eye.

"Yeah," chimed in my daughter. "Do something for the babies."

I tried to explain to them that there was little I could do. We lived in a small town in the Blue Ridge Mountains of Virginia. We had no great financial resources. We had no political power or influence on people with that power. I was already working twenty-five hour days even though I wanted to spend more time with my family. I made a list of excuses that silenced but did not seem to convince them.

Twenty-four hours passed. The next night the three children came to our family altar prepared to blast my excuses out of the water. Apparently they had been thinking about my words. They didn't want to face a bleak, frightening future. They told me in no uncertain terms that it was my responsibility as their father to get off my chair and go out into the world and do what I could to make a difference.

"Dad, you know those babies you were talking about last night," said my twelve-year-old, "those babies that are getting killed? You ought to try to stop it."

My children hounded me those next few weeks. They never stopped reminding me about the babies who were dying. I began to pray and think seriously about this task and the others. Honestly, I didn't have the foggiest idea what I as one insignificant Baptist preacher in Lynchburg, Virginia, could do to influence a nation. But as I thought and prayed and argued with my own kids, convictions began to grow. My nation had made some wrong choices. At the top of the list was the legalization of abortion. What would they legalize next? The killing of the handicapped? The killing of the aged? The killing of the ill? Something needed to be done. There was only one way I knew to do it, and I could delay that task no longer.

One day I was a Baptist preacher who had managed to stay out of the political arena for twenty years of ministry. The next day I jumped into that same political arena feet first. At the heart of my decision was a story from the New Testament. Jesus' enemies, the Pharisees, had gathered to trick and trap Him in a public debate.

"Is it lawful to pay taxes to Caesar, or not?" the Pharisees asked, looking around at the crowd, knowing that either way Jesus answered He would be in trouble. If He answered, "No, don't pay taxes to the government," the soldiers would arrest Him and throw Him in jail. If He answers, "Yes, pay your taxes," He would offend the people who hated the government and wanted to see it overthrown. Jesus didn't answer immediately. Instead, He called for a Pharisee to hold up a coin used in paying the tax.

"Whose image and inscription is this?" Jesus asked.

"Caesar's," answered the Pharisees.

"Then render to Caesar the things that are Caesar's and to God the things that are God's."

It was a clever answer. Both sides were satisfied. But it wasn't only clever. Jesus' answer cut to the heart of our human predicament. We live in two different worlds simultaneously. The world that God is building in the hearts of men and women is an invisible world based on eternal values that will last forever. The world that man is building is a world of cement and steel and glass based on human values that will not last. The trouble is that we live in both worlds simultaneously. We who are committed to the invisible world of God and to His values cannot simply stand aside while the other world destroys itself and the world we share. In that confrontation with the Pharisees, Jesus reminded us that through our first allegiance to God and His goals for this planet, we must still be responsible citizens, willing to play our part in maintaining the world of man.

There was a second important reminder for me in that story. When Jesus said, "Render to Caesar the things that are Caesar's, and to God the things that are God's," He was not just telling us to be responsible in both worlds, He was also reminding us to keep the worlds apart. Each world works differently. What we do in God's world and with His people has different rules from what we do in the world of government with elected officials and volunteers. America is not a theocracy, a government with God as its commander-in-chief. America is a democratic republic with a man (perhaps one day, a woman) as its chief executive officer. In God's world, we decide by God's rules. In a democratic republic, we work together, governed by the will of the majority. In God's world, we submit to Him. In man's world we submit to the law of man.

But a third, unwritten truth of this story, which Jesus made clear by His life and by His death, kept me from ignoring the Supreme Court's decision. Although we live in two worlds simultaneously and although both worlds are to be kept separate, when there is a conflict between the worlds, the world of God takes precedence over the world of man. When we feel the law of man is unjust or contrary to the law of God, we work to change man's law. And if the law of man actually comes into conflict with the law of God, we disobey man's law and pay the penalty.

We cannot forget God's laws as we live in man's world. We must live by God's law in both worlds, whatever it may cost us. We must work to convince others that God's law is right and will bring health and long life to the nation. We do not insist on others' believing as we believe, or worshiping as we worship. We protect the freedom of every person in the land. But if we feel a law is wrong or harmful for the nation, we work tirelessly to change it. And we use every legal tool to accomplish that end.

During my first years of ministry, I had given to God what was God's and had almost eliminated my responsibility to Caesar (government) altogether. I had paid my taxes, of course. I had voted. I had occasionally made a call or written a letter or carried on a conversation to influence public policy. From time to time my sermons commented on issues of significance to the nation. But to work hard to change public policy or to dedicate time and energy to influence government was a new experience for me. I had spent my lifetime working in the context of the church, God's world. I knew how to bring change in that world, but to bring change in the world of city, state, and national government was new.

It didn't happen overnight. First, I began to read everything I could get my hands on concerning the issues that were high on my priority list. My reading habits had been fairly limited to the Bible, biblical reference books, commentaries, church history, ethics, theology, psychology, and philosophy. There were books, journals, magazines, and articles that helped me in sermon preparation and in the development of my spiritual life. To round out the other side, the secular side, I had just read the newspaper and various newsmagazines. I had watched television news, public broadcasting, and various documentaries on the subjects of special interest to me and to my people at the Thomas Road Baptist Church.

Once I entered the political arena, I realized my study habits would have to be enlarged. The news magazines gave short, encapsulated, often one-sided reviews of current events. I had to read papers, journals, and special reports that gave fuller, deeper coverage. I began to read both sides of the complex abortion issue. I read the *Congressional Record,* medical and scientific studies, journals of the pro-life and pro-choice groups, summaries of the court decisions, and papers, books, and articles from many points of view.

I traced the Supreme Court's decision back to the beginning of the legal battle. I learned that early in 1971, a young woman in Texas, not unlike our own Jennifer, found herself pregnant and wanted to abort her child. The laws of the state of Texas said, "No! Although we respect your right of choice, we are also committed to protecting the rights of the unborn child living within you." In Texas, as in a majority of states, abortion was illegal unless the mother's life was threatened. The young woman, named "Jane Roe" by the United States District Court for the Northern District of Texas, used the state to have the law revoked. The court decided in Jane Roe's favor.

According to the court, Jane Roe's right to choose whether to have a child or to abort it was "protected by the 9th through the 14th Amendments of the U.S. Constitution." The federal court declared that the Texas laws against abortion were void because they were "unconstitutionally vague and overbroad." Texas appealed the court's decision to the United States Court of Appeals for the Fifth Circuit. Eventually, the case was heard by the United States Supreme Court.

The abortion issue was a hot potato thrown back and forth by the nine justices for more than two years between the opening arguments heard December 13, 1971, and the Court's final decision, January 22, 1973. Chief Justice Burger assigned Justice Blackmun, a fellow Minnesotan, the difficult task of writing the majority opinion. The justices, their clerks, and secretaries prepared memo after memo, rough draft after rough draft, trying to reach a conclusion that would properly interpret the Constitution on this important matter.

But the Constitution itself provided no specific guidelines on the abortion issue. The 14th Amendment to the United States Constitution had been quoted in Jane Roe's trial by her lawyers to protect the young woman's right to abort her baby. But it was also quoted by lawyers for the state of Texas to protect Jane Roe's unborn child from abortion. The 14th Amendment simply states:

> Nor shall any state deprive any person of life, liberty or property within the due process of law, nor deny to any person within its jurisdiction to equal protection of the laws.

Both sides, those who favor the legalization of abortion (sometimes called "pro-choice") and those who oppose abortion (sometimes called "pro-life") quote the 14th Amendment when making their cases. However, in 1868 when the 14th Amendment was adopted, at least thirty-six states or territories had laws on the books limiting abortion. Those anti-abortion laws were not changed when the 14th Amendment was ratified, making it clear that the framers of the 14th Amendment did not originally intend to use it to keep the states from regulating abortions.

As Justice Rehnquist and White pointed out later in their dissenting opinions, nothing in the language or history of the Constitution supported the Court's judgment to legalize abortion. Justice Blackmun, formerly a legal advisor to the Mayo Clinic in Rochester, Minnesota, turned to medical and social policy, not to the law, to guide him in writing the Court's decision. Wearing a cardigan sweater and working at an isolated mahogany table hidden in the second floor library of the Supreme Court Building, Justice Blackmun read hundreds of legal briefs, medical books, and memos from his fellow justices and their clerks in his honest struggle to do justice to the millions of people born and unborn who would be affected by the Court's decision. His clerks, secretaries, and messengers were warned not to interrupt the justice as he puzzled over the complex and confounding materials. Even Chief Justice Burger and the other seven justices of the Court knew not to bother him there.

Justice Blackmun decided that his major responsibility was to protect the rights of choice and privacy of the pregnant woman guaranteed her by the United States Constitution. Here, medical science misled the Court in advising the justices that the fetus was not a person and had no rights to be protected, at least not in the first three months after conception. During the first trimester, the fetus was seen as tissue, a nonperson without Constitutional rights or privileges. Most medical authorities saw the unborn child as "not very much a person" up through the second three months of pregnancy. Many medical experts even claimed the fetus was a nonperson through the entire pregnancy. To these authorities, the fetus only became a "viable" person when delivered out of the mother and into the world, free from the mother's life support system and able to survive on its own.

If Justice Blackmun had regarded the fetus as a person, then that person, though unborn, would be protected by the Constitution. He did not. But to avoid the controversy he knew would follow, the justice left out any direct discussion of the viability of the fetus and tried to dodge the issue in a complex discussion of the three trimesters of pregnancy. However, before Justice Stewart would add his signature to the majority decision, he insisted that Justice Blackmun say more clearly that the fetus wasn't a person. Justice Blackmun consented to his colleague's request. "A fetus," wrote Justice Blackmun, "is not a person under the Constitution and thus has no legal right to life."

During the first three months of pregnancy, the Supreme Court instructed the courts in every state that, "the abortion decision and its effectuation must be left to the medical judgment of the pregnant woman's attending physician." After the first trimester, a state may "regulate the abortion procedure in ways that are reasonably related to maternal health," for example, by requiring hospitalization. Only after the fetus has developed enough to have a chance of survival on its own — usually during the seventh month — may a state "regulate and even proscribe abortion except where it is necessary . . . for the preservation or health of the mother."

The state of Texas, after losing its appeal, petitioned for rehearing, comparing Blackmun's decision (that a fetus was not a person) to the Court's decision in 1957, which stated that Dred Scot, a black slave, was not a citizen or person under the Constitution.

Once I understood the judicial history of the abortion decision, I began to study government and how it works. I learned that the wall of separation that my school teachers had said divided church and state was not even mentioned in the United States Constitution. In fact, the words *church* and *state* were not part of the First Amendment, as some people suggested. Thomas Jefferson wrote these words in a letter in 1802 to a group of Baptists and Congregationalists in Danbury, Connecticut. During Jefferson's campaign for president, the group attacked him, calling him an infidel, an atheist, and a few other uncomplimentary names. Jefferson told them they should stay in their place. There should be "a wall of separation between church and state," he had said. The principle I had been taught so long ago was not a part of the Constitution, as I had always believed.

I also learned the principles of changing and affecting government policies. There were babies to be saved and in order to save them, I had to learn about voter registration, district door-to-door campaign, legislative lobbying, and power politics. My library looked like a battle zone. Every room in our home was loaded with reading materials. I kept notes on the important findings in my study. I copied quotations that were meaningful or carried emotional clout. In my brain a plan was beginning to take shape.

Next, I began to associate with people who knew about the issues and who could help me understand them better, even if I didn't agree with them. I began to make regular calls to congressmen and senators. I called and telegraphed and visited with leaders on the abortion issue from around the country. I visited pro-life group meetings and talked to pro-life leaders. I visited pro-choice groups and talked to their leaders as well. I met Christians, Jews, Moslems, agnostics, and atheists who were all Americans and who all had something to teach me about the issue. I listened. I talked. I argued. And I learned.

Already, critics were condemning me for entering the political world. They were even quoting my old sermon from 1965, "Ministers and Marches," in which I had clearly called pastors away from what I was now doing. I received nasty letters and telegrams from Christian friends and allies chastising me for associating with "worldly people," warning me to get out of politics and back into religion where I belonged. And from a third and more frightening group, hidden behind unsigned letters and mysterious phone calls in the night, I began to get ugly threats against my life and the lives of my family. But I had committed myself to helping save the babies and their mothers, both victims of the Court's decision on abortion, and there was no turning back.

Whatever small risks we take to save a Jennifer and her baby are worth it; Jennifer is only one example of the millions of young women who have recently chosen to abort their unwanted babies. As she shared with us her own private memories of the abortionist and his clinic, try to feel how she felt that awful day her baby died.

167. David Stockman, *The Triumph of Politics: How the Reagan Revolution Failed*, 1986

David Stockman was the Director of the Office of Management & Budget under Ronald Reagan and the author of many of Reagan's supply-side strategies. Here, he tells why he changed his mind.

Epilogue

"You ain't seen nothing yet." The White House made that its official campaign slogan for 1984. When it did, I knew that my own days were numbered, and that even the reluctant loyalty I had maintained during the long battle to reverse the President's tax policy was no longer defensible. Now I had to resort to out-and-out subversion—scheming with the congressional leaders during the first half of 1985 to force a tax hike. But that failed too, leaving me with no choice but to resign in the knowledge that my original ideological excesses had given rise to a fiscal and political disorder that was probably beyond correction.

Politics had triumphed: first by blocking spending cuts and then by stopping revenue increases. There was nothing left to do but follow former Governor Hugh Carey's example and head out of town, whupped.

That the politics of American democracy made a shambles of my anti-welfare state theory I can now understand. Whatever its substantive merit, it rested on the illusion that the will of the people was at drastic variance with the actions of the politicians.

But the political history of the past five years mostly invalidates that proposition. We have had a tumultuous national referendum on everything in our half-trillion-dollars welfare state budget. By virtue of experiencing the battle day after day in the legislative and bureaucratic trenches, I am as qualified as anyone to discern the verdict. Lavish Social Security benefits, wasteful dairy subsidies, futile UDAG grants, and all the remainder of the federal subventions do not persist solely due to weak-kneed politicians or the nefarious graspings of special-interest groups.

Despite their often fuzzy rhetoric and twisted rationalizations, congressmen and senators ultimately deliver what their constituencies demand. The notion that Washington amounts to a puzzle palace on the Potomac, divorced from the genuine desires of the voters, thus constitutes more myth than truth. So does the related proposition eloquently expressed in the editorial pages of *The Wall Street Journal*. Somehow it manages to divine a great unwashed mass of the citizenry demanding the opposite of the spending agendas presented by the Claude Peppers, the homebuilders' lobby, and the other hired guns of K Street.

But those who suggest the existence of an anti-statist electorate are in fact demanding that national policy be harnessed to their own particular doctrine of the public good. The actual electorate, however, is not interested in this doctrine; when it is interested at all, it is interested in getting help from the government to compensate for a perceived disadvantage. Consequently, the spending politics of Washington do reflect the heterogeneous and parochial demands that arise from the diverse, activated fragments of the electorate scattered across the land. What you see done in the halls of the politicians may not be wise, but it is the only real and viable definition of what the electorate wants.

I cannot be so patient with the White House. By 1984 it had become a dreamland. It was holding the American economy hostage to a reckless, unstable fiscal policy based on the politics of high spending and the doctrine of low taxes. Yet rather than acknowledge that the resulting massive buildup of public debt would eventually generate serious economic troubles, the White House proclaimed a roaring economic success. It bragged that its policies had worked as never before when, in fact, they had produced fiscal excesses that had never before been imagined.

The brash phrasemakers of the White House had given George Orwell a new resonance—and right on

---

Source: David Stockman, *The Triumph of Politics: How the Reagan Revolution Failed.* pp. 376–394. Copyright 1986 by David Stockman. Reprinted by permission of Harper Collins Publishers, Inc.

schedule. In 1984 we were plainly drifting into unprecedented economic peril. But they had the audacity to proclaim a golden age of prosperity.

What economic success there was had almost nothing to do with our original supply-side doctrine. Instead, Paul Volcker and the business cycle had brought inflation down and economic activity surging back. But there was nothing new, revolutionary, or sustainable about this favorable turn of events. The cycle of economic boom and bust had been going on for decades, and by election day its oscillations had reached the high end of the charts. That was all.

To be sure, credit is due where it is deserved. Paul Volcker will surely go down as the Federal Reserve Chairman in history for the masterful and courageous manner in which he purged the American and world economy of runaway inflation. This success turned out to require the traditional, painful, costly cure of a deep recession, but it took all that Volcker brought to the task — a strong will, an incisive mind, and a towering personal credibility — to see it through.

There is also little doubt that Volcker's feat would not have been possible without Ronald Reagan's unwavering support during the dark days of 1982. The President stands almost alone among Washington's current politicians in his instinctive comprehension that inflation is a profoundly destructive phenomenon. He has often been misled by the mumbo-jumbo of his advisers. But when it counted, the President gave Volcker the political latitude to do what had to be done. It was a genuine achievement.

Unfortunately, Volcker's hard-won victory was not what the White House media men had in mind when they proclaimed that "America is back." They were boasting of something far more grand: that the business cycle itself had been vanquished and that the nation had entered an era of unprecedented economic growth and wealth creation. As they had it, profound new possibilities for economic performance and social progress over the long haul had now been guaranteed by the policies in place. It sounded too good to be true and it was.

"You ain't seen nothing yet" was to have unintended, ironic meaning. It pointed to a frightful day of reckoning, a day that will reveal just how arrogant, superficial, and willfully ignorant the White House phrasemakers really were.

By the end of 1985 the economic expansion was three years old and the numbers demonstrated no miracle. Real GNP growth had averaged 4.1 percent — an utterly unexceptional, prosaic business cycle recovery by historical standards, and especially so in light of the extraordinary depth of the 1981–82 recession. The glowing pre-election GNP and employment numbers, therefore, had manifested only the truism that when the business cycle turns down, it will inevitably bounce back for a while.

Still, the White House breastbeating had to do with the future, and that depends upon the fundamental health of the economy and the soundness of policy. Yet how can economic growth remain high and inflation low for the long run when the administration's de facto policy is to consume two thirds of the nation's net private savings to fund the federal deficit?

The fundamental reality of 1984 was not the advent of a new day, but a lapse into fiscal indiscipline on a scale never before experienced in peacetime. There is no basis in economic history or theory for believing that from this wobbly foundation a lasting era of prosperity can actually emerge.

Indeed, just beneath the surface the American economy was already being twisted and weakened by Washington's free lunch joy ride. Thanks to the half-revolution adopted in July 1981, more than a trillion dollars has already been needlessly added to our national debt — a burden that will plague us indefinitely. Our national savings has been squandered to pay for a tax cut we could not afford. We have consequently borrowed enormous amounts of foreign capital to make up for the shortfall between our national production and our national spending. Now, the U.S. economy will almost surely grow much more slowly than its potential in the decade ahead. By turning ourselves into a debtor nation for the first time since World War I, we have sacrificed future living standards in order to service the debts we have already incurred.

Borrowing these hundreds of billions of dollars has also distorted the whole warp and woof of the U.S. economy. The high dollar exchange rate that has been required to attract so much foreign capital has devastated our industries of agriculture, mining, and manufacturing. Jobs, capital, and production have been permanently lost.

All of this was evident in 1984, and so was its implication for the future. We had prosperity of a sort — but it rested on easy money and borrowed time. To lift the economy out of recession against the weight of massive deficits and unprecedented real interest rates, the Fed has had to throw open the money spigots as never before. This in turn has stimulated an orgy of debt creation the balance sheets of American consumers and corporations that is still gathering momentum today. Its magnitude is numbing. When the government sector's own massive debt is included, the nation will shortly owe $10 trillion — three times more than just a dozen years ago.

One thing is certain. At some point global investors will lose confidence in our easy dollars and debt-financed prosperity, and then the chickens will come home to roost. In the short run, we will be absolutely dependent upon a $100 billion per year inflow of foreign capital to finance our twin deficits—trade and the federal budget. Faced with a sinking dollar, the Fed will have no choice but to suddenly and dramatically tighten monetary policy, forcing up interest rates to attract the foreign savings needed to underwrite our lavish current spending.

This action will cause a recession, but this time neither Paul Volcker nor Ronald Reagan will have the wherewithal to stay the course. American politics will resound with the pleas of debtors demanding relief in the form of out-and-out reflation. Since our balance sheets already reflect the highest ratios of debt in peacetime history, there will be no margin at all to weather an interruption of cash flow: not at the federal level, where we are borrowing three times more relative to GNP than at the comparable stage of any previous cycle; nor at the corporate and household level, where debt service to income has soared off the charts.

The clock is thus ticking away inexorably toward another bout of inflationary excess. If we stay the course we are now on, the decade will end with a worse hyperinflation than the one with which it began. Indeed, the increased fragility and instability of the global economy, along with still fresh memories of the debauched financial assets of the 1970s, will make this inflationary cycle even more violent and destructive.

One reason I plotted to raise taxes in 1985, then, was to help correct an economic policy course that was leading to long-run disaster.

But there was also another, more compelling reason. As the original architect of the fiscal policy error now threatening so much grief, I was appalled by the false promises of the 1984 campaign. Ronald Reagan had been induced by his advisers and his own illusions to embrace one of the more irresponsible platforms of modern times. He had promised, as it were, to alter the laws of arithmetic. No program that had a name or line in the budget would be cut; no taxes would be raised. Yet the deficit was pronounced intolerable and it was pledged to be eliminated.

This was the essence of the unreality. The President and his retainers promised to eliminate the monster deficit with spending cuts when for all practical purposes they had already embraced or endorsed 95 percent of all the spending there was to cut.

The White House itself had surrendered to the political necessities of the welfare state early on. By 1985, only the White House speechwriters carried on a lonely war of words, hurling a stream of presidential rhetoric at a ghostly abstraction called Big Government.

The White House's claim to be serious about cutting the budget had, in fact, become an institutionalized fantasy. I had tried diplomatically and delicately to convey the facts that made this so, but the only response I got was a new whispering campaign led by Ed Meese: Stockman is too pessimistic; he's been on the Hill too long; he's one of *them!*

Maybe so. Ever since September 1981 I'd been reduced to making one-sided spending deals. The politicians got what their constituents wanted, but here and there we trimmed the edges. But my relentless dealmaking inherently yielded savings that amounted to rounding errors in a trillion-dollar budget because it was based on bluff and searching out for obscure tidbits of spending that could be exercised without arousing massive political resistance. Thus, for example, we did get the second-tier COLA in the railroad retirement program capped below the inflation rate. This reduced overall spending by 0.0001 percent!

But nothing meaningful could be done about federal spending because even the President no longer had a plausible program to do anything about it. The White House had thrown in the towel on all the big spending components that could make a difference on the deficit. And it had abandoned nearly every policy principle that could have been the basis for organizing a renewed anti-spending coalition.

The domestic budget is huge, but nearly 90 percent of it is accounted for by a handful of big programs: Social Security and other social insurance; Medicare; the safety net, veterans, agriculture and transportation.

By 1984, the White House had explicitly decided not to challenge these big components of the welfare state budget in any significant way. Jim Baker had been proven correct about the political consequences of attacking the basic entitlement and COLA of the 36 million citizens receiving Social Security and Medicare. So I had eventually been reduced to trying to get Congress to modestly trim the Medicare entitlement. But in the election/budget year of 1984 even the President rejected proposal for increased patient cost sharing, and then went on to plant his feet in concrete against any cuts in Social Security at all.

These two programs accounted for half of the welfare state budget, yet by 1985 the only option we had left was to squeeze a few percent of their massive $270 billion cost from the doctors and hospitals that delivered the services the old folks were now guaranteed to receive. Right then and there the fiscal arithmetic of coping with a $200 billion deficit through spending cuts alone had become prohibitive.

The President had also inadvertently safeguarded the civil service retirement system from cuts, too. The administration budget carried a proposal to cap civil service COLAs and penalize early retirement (before age sixty-two), but its legislative prospects depending crucially on applying the same concept to the even more generous military retirement program. Both proposals were put in the President's budget, but the Joint Chiefs of Staff soon complained loudly. The President then cancelled the military reforms, buttressing the $25 billion civil service retirement programs as he did so.

Likewise, the $27 billion complex of veterans' programs was also given immunity in a curious way. The White House appointed a VA administrator, by the name of Harry Waters, who spent a large part of his time denouncing the President's budget director at American Legion conventions. Whatever tiny veterans' cuts I managed to stuff into the budget were made instantly non-operative by Mr. Waters's ability to claim with impunity that he spoke for the President. No one at the White House ever said he didn't.

After the first round of cuts in the $75 billion complex of welfare, food stamp, and safety net programs, the White House raised the white flag there, too. The President promised the governors not to tamper seriously with Medicaid — the largest program — and appointed a task force which recommended that we repeal some of the nutrition program reforms we had already made. While we continued to send up to the Hill small, technical proposals to nick a billion or two, the clear White House message was that the safety net was now inviolate.

That position reflected the overwhelming sentiment of the public, and in that sense was justifiable. But it also constituted another big block of evidence that the President's anti-spending rhetoric amounted to an illusion.

By the mid-1980s the Reagan transportation budget in constant dollars topped Jimmy Carter's best year by 15 percent, Johnson's by about 40 percent, and Kennedy's by about 50 percent. Big Government? That was something for the speechwriters to fight as long as they didn't mention any names. The problem with all these local roads and buses was that other politicians had an equally strong case for aiding local projects — classrooms, public libraries, day care centers, alcoholism clinics and jailhouses. Spending continues largely unabated in all cases.

Indeed, the White House record was nearly bereft of any consistent anti-spending policy principles by 1984, and that fact had not escaped the notice of all the other politicians on Capitol Hill. Early on we had demonstrated that even in the politically easiest cases there was no consistent standard for what constituted appropriate federal spending.

That's why we ended up giving several billion dollars to Exxon, Union Oil and some gas pipelines to build synthetic fuel plants. When Meese chimed in with the point that these corporations had already invested a small fraction of one percent of their own equity in these projects, the President had an answer.

"We can't cause an honest business to lose money," he said. All these projects turned out to be total white elephants, but the lesson was clear. If Exxon couldn't be permitted to drill a dry hole right in the Roosevelt Room where the decision was made, what other business subsidy had a chance of being eliminated?

Nor was this an aberration. Right before the 1984 election, the giant timber companies sought an economic bailout that would cost $1.5 billion over several years. We had fought this proposal since 1982, but now it was alleged to make the crucial difference that would put Oregon in the President's electoral column, possibly along with the other forty-nine states. I protested that the bill would hand over $15 to $30 million each to seven Fortune 500 companies, including poverty cases like Boise Cascade. "No," replied the President, "we can't veto. The companies wouldn't really pay us that money, anyway. They would just pass it on to consumers."

If there was any thin sliver of the welfare state where the Reagan Administration might have raised the free enterprise and anti-spending banner, it was against the socialistic enterprises of U.S. Agriculture. But by 1984 we had accommodated to the political facts of life here, too. As I contemplated the task of formulating a strategy to deal with the nation's massive deficit after the election, two White House episodes regarding agriculture stood out in my mind vividly. They were the smoking gun which proved that the White House couldn't even tackle the fabulous excesses of the farm pork barrel, and that was the very bottom of the whole spending barrel.[1]

The first episode had occurred in the summer of 1982. The issue was agriculture marketing orders, an out-and-out socialist relic from the New Deal that tells every California orange and lemon grower how many of these little fruits can be marketed each week.

The established growers like this kind of lemon socialism because it keeps prices up, supplies down, and new competition out of the market.

By then I knew better than to argue on behalf of "market-place efficiency," "consumer welfare," and the supposed right of free Americans to produce and sell whatever kind of fruits, nuts, and widgets they want.

So I'd located some photographs of this lemon socialism at work. They showed guarantuan mountains— bigger than the White House—of California oranges rotting in the field. The reason for all this deliberate garbage creation was that the USDA orange commissar had cut back the weekly marketing quota, fearing that a bumper crop would drop the price and give consumers too good a deal on oranges.

Since we'd also just talked about a free food program for the homeless, my pictures did seem to suggest something rather ludicrous, and everyone around the cabinet table began to laugh. But then the California politicians swung into action.

Dick Lyng, an old California Reaganaut and Under Secretary of Agriculture, said I was fibbing. "The USDA had nothing to do with this. The growers elect their own committees to stabilize the market.

"You remember, Mr. President," he added, "that a lot of our friends out there depend on these marketing orders."

Well, okay. Some of our friends are members of the Navel Orange Growers Soviet. It wasn't a compelling argument.

Meese then glanced at his Adam Smith tie and took his turn. "We need to study the possibility of long-range reform," he said, "but remember these are businessmen. It would be wrong for government to suddenly disrupt their market."

Disruption thus had a new definition. Every week the growers rig the market in what would be a violation of the anti-trust law, and now, if the Agriculture Department didn't use its power to exempt them from federal prosecution, well, that was "disruption." But never mind Meese's deputy, Jim Jenkins, who was the White House welcome mat for special interest groups, had a better idea.

"Without marketing orders you would never get the multi-million-dollar investments in refrigeration equipment and storage facilities necessary for a year-round supply. A competitive market would be too risky."

I asked him how about year-round Florida oranges that come right off the free market, with no supply control by a Florida Orange Grower Soviet at all. He said my point wasn't valid because I was mixing oranges and oranges.

Jim Lake, the Reagan campaign press secretary and paid lobbyist in that off season, had another point. He just went up to the Hill and got a law passed making it illegal for the director of OMB even to read the marketing orders before they were stamped out by USDA. That was that for free enterprise in California. Needless to say, there remained equally compelling cases for other variations of Big Government in the other forty-nine states.

It was the handful of dairy states which in fact brought the second episode to a head. In late 1983 Ed Meese had called me to his office to deliver some truly stunning news.

"I thought you would want to know," he said crisply, "the President just signed the dairy bill."

"Ed, I'm so shocked I don't know what to say," I muttered in response, "except that you're turning this whole thing into a bad joke." I then huffed out of his office.

It was shocking. Ronald Reagan had just signed a bill paying dairy farmers $1,300 per head *not to milk their cows!* It also contained a hidden tax on consumers which would be used to pay farmers to slaughter their whole herd for the equivalent of $5 *per pound of hamburger.*

I'd been fighting this $2 billion per year rip-off for fifteen months. Time after time I had brought the dairy bill up at LSG meetings. Everybody's on board for a veto, right? Nobody's going to pull the rug on me, right?

Each and every time Meese had earnestly bobbed his head in the affirmative, so I had spread the word high and low on Capitol Hill that the bill was a goner.

Now I was the fool, and the reasons revealed the final answer as to why the Reagan White House's anti-spending rhetoric could not be taken seriously. The Reaganites were, in the final analysis, just plain welfare state politicians like everybody else.

In this case the three culprits were Ed Meese, Dick Lyng, and Jesse Helms. You hardly needed to know any more.

Meese always came to the lick log with his Adam Smith tie on and usually left without his shirt. The political consequences of the Reagan Revolution's free market and anti-spending principles were just too unsettling for him to tolerate.

Dick Lyng believed in free markets but had also learned all about farm park politics in Sacramento. While Jack Block, a decent and well-intended hog farmer from Illinois, was the nominal Department Secretary, there was never any doubt that Lyng was the political engineer who ran up the USDA budget.

Jesse Helms was, well, tobacco, and he couldn't get re-elected at all without bringing home the socialist bacon from Washington.

And the bacon of politics didn't come one slice at a time. It was always maddeningly interlinked. That's what this dairy bill fiasco exemplified perfectly.

I had anticipated the dairy bill because I had originally thought it was an exception to the rule. Rather than being protected in an omnibus farm bill with all the wheat, corn, cotton, sugar, peanuts, rice, and mohair constituencies locked together arm in arm, the 1983 dairy bill was going to have to roll down Pennsylvania Avenue all by its lonesome. Then: *zap!*

But at the eleventh hour Jesse Helms got desperate about tobacco. An earlier so-called allotment reform bill had decreed that by December 1983 certain absentee allotment holders had to sell their state-granted licenses. This turned out to include churches, YMCAs, 4-H Clubs, and Boy Scout chapters. What all these presumably God-fearing adults and children were doing owning tobacco allotments, I never did find out. But I quickly learned that Jesse Helms was determined to postpone the statutory deadline.

So he did what every politician does when he wants something bad enough. Helms added his tiny little amendment to rescue the Boy Scouts' tobacco allotment to the dairy bill. He then put his shoulder down to the log and started rolling it toward the White House.

By the time the dairy bill reached the President's desk bedecked with the tobacco rider, it had a new informal title: "The Jesse Helms Re-election Act of 1984." That transformed the whole character of the bill, causing a strange chorus to arise from the anti-socialist New Right: *This bill's for Jesse, no other bill will do.*

There's where Meese suddenly entered the picture. Helms and the New Right pulled his political chain and in a flash he was in the Oval Office pushing the President's official pen toward the signature line.

In the same flash something else happened: the singlest, cleanest, easiest and most justified shot at budget cutting during the entire Reagan presidency was kicked in the ditch. If this one couldn't be done, then nothing, but nothing, could be done about federal spending.

Needless to say, news that the President had signed the bill after several months of heated veto threats from his budget director brought an instantaneous response on the Hill: unadulterated guffaws, hilarity, and belly laughs. The politicians now knew without a doubt what had been true since June 1981. The only thing the Reagan Administration could do about federal spending was: fake.

As I prepared to make one last run at the deficit monster in late 1984, I soon found myself impaled upon an awful dilemma. Given the fiscal facts of life, I somehow believed that the White House would be prepared to wriggle out of its militant no-tax increase campaign pledges. With everyone for the welfare state and no one against it, the only thing left to do was to pay for it. But I was mistaken once again. Ed Meese made that crystal clear at the first post-election meeting of the cabinet.

"We have three goals for the second term," he said, "but the first and highest is to keep our pledge not to raise taxes."

So now our goal was *"Don't pay a red cent of Big Government, just blame 'them' for all the red ink of it."* After four years in office the Reaganites had no more sense that governance involved making unpalatable choices than they had in the Wexford garage way back at the beginning.

So I attempted to stimulate one more round of Ping-Pong. The final play *had* to yield a tax increase. It was vital.

The first step was easy and involved the establishment of a $50 billion target for deficit reduction in the President's 1985 budget—the minimum credible goal under the circumstances.

I next got out my supply-side catechism book and scrounged for spending cuts that would not poison the political environment or violate iron-clad presidential commitments. This eliminated most of the budget—Social Security, the safety net, veterans' benefits—but there was still one small corner to work in.

Dozens of small economic subsidies and state and local grants could be attacked on principle, even if there was little hope of prevailing on Capitol Hill. I thus targeted Amtrak, EDA, the Ex-Im Bank, federally owner power marketing authorities, student aid, the Small Business Administration, mass transit subsidies, REA, and many more. These savings barely added up to $35 billion, but with a small defense trim, the usual quota of smoke and mirrors, and debt service savings, the President's 1986 spending-cut total was gussied up to match the $50 billion target.

But now without a struggle because the relevant cabinet officers fought to the last drop of blood against even these minor cuts. Jim Sanders, the SBA administrator, was soon even visibly campaigning on the Hill to defeat my proposal to eliminate subsidized loans for used-car dealers.

The next step was to get the Senate GOP leadership on board. The College of Cardinals was more than willing to get the disagreeable business of raising taxes over with. Dole, Domenici, Hatfield, Laxalt, Packwood, Simpson, Danford, Heinz, Chafee, Boschwitz, Gordon, even Armstrong and McClure, were ready. To a man, they knew you weren't going to meaningfully reduce the deficit without additional revenue.

But the responsible leaders of the Senate were now in a quandary. If they came right out for higher taxes, they would soon be on a collision course with the White House, inviting renewed stalemate.

Finally we came up with a long shot: We would try to cobble together the largest spending-cut package possible in the Senate. All those who knew we also needed to raise taxes agreed to bite their tongues for a while. The Senate spending-cut-only package would be the final housekeeping of the welfare state. Anything we could persuade fifty-one senators to cut or throw overboard would be included in it.

Then we would bounce it over to the House side. Since the Democratic majority wanted to cut no spending at all, they would bounce back a budget package with taxes in it. The politicians of Capitol Hill would next compromise between the two and then bounce a decent-sized deficit and reduction package which included both tax increases and spending cuts down Pennsylvania Avenue. Then we would find out if it was Clint Eastwood—"make my day"—or a modicum of reason that would determine the nation's economic and fiscal future.

Dole and Domenici worked the strategy all spring. Day after day we round-tabled in Dole's office, and this time it was the real thing. We marched through one program at a time, one Republican faction at a time, until we had gotten through the whole trillion-dollar budget. Never before had the game of fiscal governance been played so seriously, so completely, or so broadly as it was in Bob Dole's office in the spring of 1985. Rarely before have two political leaders displayed such patience, determination, and ability as did Bob Dole and Pete Domenici.

By May it was time for the Senate to start voting on its package designed to reduce the deficit by $55 billion in 1986, and by rising amounts in the out-years. One by one the Republican politicians came with their final demands as to what *couldn't* be cut if we were to have their vote. And we needed nearly every single vote among the fifty-three Republicans because no Democrats would play this lousy game of having to tiptoe around the President in public.

As the long, final day of the Republican budget round-tabling passed into the middle of the night in Bob Dole's office, I finally saw, as the politicians circled the budget one last time, the awesome staying power of the Second Republic.

We had killed impact aid in February 1981 in the Cutting Room, but it has been resurrected repeatedly in the interim until the Dole-Domenici budget abolished it again. Now along came Senator Jim Abdnor of South Dakota, who stood to lose $300,000 at a single Air Force base school district out yonder in the badlands. In the end his vote went in the yes column and $100 billion in impact aid when back into the budget.

The Johnson War on Poverty was long dead, and what remained was only a $300 million echo in the federal budget. The Dole-Domenici budget silenced this echo, but only until ultra-conservative Senator Charles Grassley of Iowa came along and traded his vote for LBJ's tattered legacy.

Senator Bob Kasten was a Kempite anti-taxer, so he visited Dole's Cutting Room too. He wanted to make sure that we were not planning to raise a tax in a recovery year. He also wanted to make sure that we were not planning to cut any spending for farm subsidies and UDAG in an election year. He left satisfied on all counts, for, like all the others, he was the last vote that added up to fifty.

Bill Cohen from Maine was justifiably mad because the northwestern senators had prevailed in overriding my plan to make the Bonneville Power Administration pay back its debt to Uncle Sam. I had pleaded until I was blue in the face with Senators Gorton, Evans, and Hatfield for even a token $100 million per year in repayment on its $8 billion debt. But they had three votes, I had none, and so we had saved no money.

Bill Cohen said rural housing was just as important to his state, but unlike them he would compromise rather than insist on rule or ruin. After $4 billion in spending had been haggled back into the budget, he pronounced the remaining cut reasonable.

We had come up with a $5,000 annual cap on college student aid that saved billions, but Bob Stafford, chairman of the Higher Education Subcommittee, regretted that he couldn't go along. Someone might need $8,000 or $10,000 from Uncle Sam to go to Harvard or Middlebury College in Vermont. We gratefully took his vote and a token cut in lieu of real reform and moved on.

We ended up adding money back for the Ex-Im Bank, soil conservation, Medicare, mass transit, Amtrak, child nutrition, education for the handicapped, National Institutes of Health, vocational rehabilitation, and the Small Business Administration, too.

The latter four programs had gotten about $1 billion in added funding when Senator Lowell Weicker had glared my way and bellowed, "How long are we going to allow this little pissant to dictate around here? He's had his head up his ass from day one."

If it hadn't been for the difficulty of speaking from that position, I might have called him a name too. But I had some quick figuring to do because the vote was coming shortly.

We had cut about $54 billion from the 1986 budget. That consisted of $24 billion in defense and about $10 billion in debt service and smoke and mirrors. So after all the round-tabling in Bob Dole's Cutting Room, we had picked through the half-trillion-dollar welfare state budget and come up with $20 billion that Republican senators were willing to cut.

Ninety-six percent stays, 4 percent goes. That's what we had come to in Bob Dole's Cutting Room after the most thorough, inspired, and detailed attempt ever made by the collectivity of the nation's Republican politicians to decide what it was wanted from Big Government and what they could do without.

Just the same, the Senate Republicans were heroes that night when they walked the plank and passed the Dole-Domenici budget. They had put a cap on the COLAs of 40 million voters. They had cut, nicked, and squeezed wherever their collective politics permitted. It was utterly the best that could be done.

But it was all for naught. In rapid order the remainder of the Republican politicians weighed in, blowing the Dole budget and the Ping-Pong game to smithereens.

Jack Kemp joined Claude Pepper in leading the charge to save the COLAs of the old folks. The Merrill Lynch bull charged in again and agreed with Kemp and the House Republicans. Nobody was going to walk the plank on Social Security.

Dole and Domenici then came up with an oil tax to fill up the hole left by the COLAs' demise. The President said absolutely not. He would wait for the pony.

There was not a rational possibility left to deal with the irrationality that had descended upon the nation.

I gathered up my black books, knowing that what I had started four years before had come to a dismal end.

I could not help recalling what my father had said about that mess out in the tomato field twenty-seven years before.

"What counts around here is what you do, not what you intend."

What I had done was helped make another mess.

"One of these days you will learn," he had said.

Maybe at last I had.

Some will be tempted to read into the failure of the Reagan Revolution more than is warranted. It represents the triumph of politics over a particular doctrine of economic governance and that is all. It does not mean American democracy is fatally flawed: special interest groups do wield great power, but their influence is deeply rooted in local popular support. Certainly, it does not mechanically guarantee the inevitability of permanent massive budget deficits or economic doom.

Its implications are deeply pessimistic only for the small and politically insignificant set of anti-statist conservatives who inhabit niches in the world of government, academia, business, and journalism. For us, there is no room for equivocation. The Reagan Revolution amounted to the clearest test of doctrine ever likely to occur in a heterogeneous democracy like our own. And the anti-statist position was utterly repudiated by the combined forces of the politicians—Republican and Democrat, those in the executive branch as well as the legislative.

This verdict has implications, however, which go well beyond the invalidation of anti-statist doctrine. The triumphant welfare state principle means that economic governance must consist of a fundamental trade-off between capitalist prosperity and social security. As a nation we have chosen to have less of the former in order to have more of the latter.

Social Security, trade protectionism, safety net programs, UDAG, and farm price supports all have one thing in common. They seek to bolster the lot of less productive industries, regions, and citizens by taxing the wealth and income of everyone else.

The case for all this redistributionism is lodged in the modern tradition of social democracy. In America we have seldom explicitly acknowledged this principle of governance, but it is in fact what we have. And to some degree it works. On the basis of private cash income alone, more than 55 million Americans would end up below the so-called poverty line. But after the welfare state's cash and in-kind benefits are paid and taxes are collected, the number of statistically poor drops by nearly two-thirds. So although it is riddled with inefficiency and injustice, the American welfare state does fulfill at least some of its promises.

But it does so at the expense of a less dynamic and productive capitalism. The kind of high growth and constant economic change envisioned by the supply-side doctrine is not possible if government taxes away economic rewards, blocks capital and labor reallocations, and funds a high safety net.

Social democracy also encourages the electorate to fragment into narrow interest groups designed to thwart and override market outcomes. That these pressure groups prevail most of the time should not be surprising. The essential welfare state principle of modern American governance sanctions both their role and their claims.

Viewed in this light, our political system performs its intended function fairly well. Its search to balance and calibrate the requisites of capitalism with social democracy's quest for stability and security has produced a surprising result. By any comparative standard, American politicians have created a more favorable balance between the two than in any other advanced industrial democracy.

Local, state, and federal spending in the United States now amounts to slightly over 33 percent of GNP. Ten percentage points of that are consumed in servicing our governmental debts and paying for our national security. So under the broadest measure possible, the American welfare state costs about 22 to 23 percent of GNP. By contrast, while the Japanese are frugal, they spend nearly 30 percent of their GNP for domestic welfare. The cradle of social democracy—Great Britain—still spends nearly 40 percent of GNP on its welfare state, the valiant efforts of Prime Minister Thatcher notwithstanding.

The Germans spend nearly as much as Great Britain, and the fading socialists of France spend even more. Sweden is in a class by itself, spending over half of its GNP on its vast, debilitating welfare state, or more than double what we do.

So we can afford to be the arsenal of the free world and have our modest welfare state, too. The only thing we cannot afford is to continue pretending we do not have to finance it out of current taxation.

This observation brings us to the true crossroads of the future. Our budget is now drastically out of balance not because this condition is endemic to our politics. Rather, it is the consequence of an accident of governance which occurred in 1981. That it persists is due to the untenable anti-tax position of the White House. After five years of presidential intransigence, all of the normal mechanisms of economic governance have become ensnared in a web of folly. But this condition can be remedied whenever the White House decides to face the facts of life.

Meanwhile, the economic danger mounts and the fiscal folly of the Reagan Revolution's aftermath reaches new heights. The recently enacted Gramm-Rudman deficit reduction law stands as testimony to that proposition. It is truly difficult to conceive of a more mischievous, unworkable blunderbuss than this alleged automatic budget-cutting device.

Gramm-Rudman will never reduce the nation's giant and dangerous budget deficit by any significant amount. After one or two years, its mechanical formula for across-the-board expenditure reductions in the 50 percent of the budget not exempted or protected would produce havoc. The defense cuts would be so draconian as to amount to unilateral disarmament; a large portion of the IRS staff would be fired and we would collect no revenue at all; life-saving new drug applications would pile up at the Food and Drug Administration unreviewed; our airports would become a parking lot for cars, people, and planes because the FAA would be too short-handed to manage even a fraction of the normal traffic.

All of this chaos and much, much more is inherent in the arithmetic of Gramm-Rudman, and is the reason it will be eventually repealed or drastically amended. Hopefully, the Supreme Court will spare us much trouble by ruling it unconstitutional.

Still, extricating ourselves from the fiscal folly now upon the nation by means of an alternative legislative solution will test our institutions of governance and our political leaders as rarely before. Folly has begotten folly, and the web has become hopelessly entangled in a five-year history of action and reaction. But the politicians of both parties still have a sound and valid reason for disengaging from the Reagan Revolution's destructive aftermath. A radical change in national economic policy was not their idea; economic utopia was not their conception of what was possible in 1981 when the policies of the past collapsed. Republican and Democratic politicians together can tell the American people that a few ideologues made a giant mistake, and that the government the public wants will require greater sacrifices in the future in the form of the new taxes which must be levied.

The politicians can tell the American people that a dangerous experiment has been tried and an old lesson has been demonstrated once again. Economic governance of the world's greatest democracy has been shown to be a deadly serious business. There is no room in its equation for scribblers, dreamers, ideologues, and passionate young men bent upon remaking the world according to their own grand prescription. The truth to be remembered is that history in a democracy does not live to be rewritten and rerouted; it just lives for another day, finding its way into the future along the trajectory of its well-worn and palpable past.

Since repudiating the debt through inflation will soon be revealed as the inevitable consequence of the course we are now set on, there remains a slim hope that we will turn back before its too late. Despite all his illusions, Ronald Reagan is still our President, and he instinctively understands and abhors the evils of inflation. When the choice between raising taxes and debauching our money finally comes to him, I somehow believe that he will yet do the right thing to save his presidency and the nation's economy. It is still not too late for the nation's most imposing politician to join with the other politicians and do what together they must: Trim a little more spending where the democratic consensus will permit it, and raise a lot of new taxes to pay for the government the nation has decided it wants.

This solution will not bring about economic perfection by a long shot. Taxes will end up too high and government will end up too big. But catastrophe will have been avoided, and that is the main thing now.

These prescriptions do not add up to a shining City on The Hill. But what is attainable—a return to a modicum of national fiscal solvency and economic stability—is far preferable to the dangerous course we are now on.

In a way, the big tax increase we need will confirm the triumph of politics. But in a democracy the politicians must have the last word once it is clear that their course is consistent with the preferences of the electorate. The abortive Reagan Revolution proved that the American electorate wants a moderate social democracy to shield it from capitalism's rougher edges. Recognition of this in the Oval Office is all that stands between a tolerable economic future and one fraught with unpredecented perils.

NOTES

[1] This was verified in December 1985 when the President signed the most expensive farm bill in history. It would cost $50–75 billion over three years, exceeding even the bill he signed in 1981 that had established the previous record.

168. STEPHEN L. CARTER, "RACIAL PREFERENCES? SO WHAT?", 1991

Stephen L. Carter teaches law at Yale University. His book, Reflections of an Affirmative Action Baby, *has attracted much attention.*

I got into law school because I am black. As many black professionals think they must, I have long suppressed this truth, insisting instead that I got where I am the same way everybody else did. Today I am a professor at Yale Law School. I like to think that I am a good one, but I am hardly the most objective judge. What I am fairly sure of, and can now say without trepidation, is that were my skin not the color that it is, I would not have had the chance to try.

For many, perhaps most, black professionals of my generation, the matter of who got where and how is left in a studied and, I think, purposeful ambiguity. Some of us, as they say, would have made it into an elite college or professional school anyway. (But, in my generation, many fewer than we like to pretend, even though one might question the much-publicized claim by Derek Bok, the president of Harvard University, that in the absence of preferences, only 1 percent of Harvard's entering class would be black.) Most of us, perhaps nearly all of us, have learned to bury the matter far back in our minds. We are who we are and where we are, we have records of accomplishment or failure, and there is no rational reason that anybody—employer, client, whoever—should care any longer whether racial preference played any role in our admission to a top professional school.

When people in positions to help or hurt our careers *do* seem to care, we tend to react with fury. Those of us who have graduated professional school over the past fifteen to twenty years, and are not white, travel career paths that are frequently bumpy with suspicions that we

---

Source: Stephen Carter, *Reflections of an Affirmative Action Baby,* "Racial Preferences? So What?," pp. 11–27. Copyright Basic Books, 1991. Reprinted by permission.

did not earn the right to be where we are. We bristle when others raise what might be called the qualification question—"Did you get into school or get hired because of a special program?"—and that prickly sensitivity is the best evidence, if any is needed, of one of the principal costs of racial preferences. Scratch a black professional with the qualification question, and you're likely to get a caustic response, such as this one from a senior executive at a major airline: "Some whites think I've made it because I'm black. Some blacks think I've made it only because I'm an Uncle Tom. The fact is, I've made it because I'm good."

Given the way that so many Americans seem to treat receipt of the benefits of affirmative action as a badge of shame, answers of this sort are both predictable and sensible. In the professional world, moreover, they are very often true: relatively few corporations are in a position to hand out charity. The peculiar aspect of the routine denial, however, is that so many of those who will bristle at the suggestion that they themselves have gained from racial preferences will try simultaneously to insist that racial preferences be preserved and to force the world to pretend that no one benefits from them. That awkward balancing of fact and fiction explains the frequent but generally groundless cry that it is racist to suggest that some individual's professional accomplishments would be fewer but for affirmative action and therein hangs a tale.

For students at the leading law schools, autumn brings the recruiting season, the idyllic weeks when law firms from around the country compete to lavish upon them lunches and dinners and other attentions, all with the professed goal of obtaining the students' services—perhaps for the summer, perhaps for a longer term. The autumn of 1989 was different, however, because the nation's largest firm, Baker & McKenzie, was banned from interviewing students at the University of Chicago Law School, and on probation—that is, enjoined to be on its best behavior—at some others.

The immediate source of Baker & McKenzie's problems was a racially charged interview that a partner in the firm had conducted the previous fall with a black third-year student at the school. The interviewer evidently suggested that other lawyers might call her "nigger" or "black bitch" and wanted to know how she felt about that. Perhaps out of surprise that she played golf, he observed that "there aren't too many golf courses in the ghetto." He also suggested that the school was admitting "foreigners" and excluding "qualified" Americans.

The law school reacted swiftly, and the firm was banned from interviewing on campus. Other schools contemplated taking action against the firm, and some of them did. Because I am black myself, and teach in a law school, I suppose the easiest thing for me to have done would have been to clamor in solidarity for punishment. Yet I found myself strangely reluctant to applaud the school's action. Instead, I was disturbed rather than excited by this vision of law schools circling the wagons, as it were, to defend their beleaguered minority students against racially insensitive remarks. It is emphatically not my intention to defend the interviewer, most of whose reported questions and comments were inexplicable and inexcusable. I am troubled, however, by my suspicion that there would still have been an outrage—not as much, but some—had the interviewer asked only what I called at the beginning of the chapter the qualification question.

I suspect this because in my own students days, something over a decade ago, an interviewer from a prominent law firm addressed this very question to a Yale student who was not white, and the student voices—including my own—howled in protest. "Racism!" we insisted. "Ban them!" But with the passing years, I have come to wonder whether our anger might have been misplaced.

To be sure, the Yale interviewer had a grade record and résumé right in front of him, it was probably irrelevant as well. (It is useful here to dispose of one common but rather silly anti-affirmative action bromide: the old question, "Do you really wanted to be treated by a doctor who got into medical school because of his skin color?" The answer is, or ought to be, that the patient doesn't particularly care how the doctor got *into* school; what matters is how the doctor got *out*. The right question, the sensible question is not "What medical school performance did your grades and test scores predict?" but "What was your medical school performance?") But irrelevance and boorishness cannot explain our rage at the qualification questions that meet the tests of boorishness and irrelevance.

The controversy is not limited to outsiders who come onto campus to recruit. In the spring of 1991, for example, students at Georgetown Law School demanded punishment for a classmate who argued in the school newspaper that affirmative action is unfair because students of color are often admitted to law school on the basis of grades and test scores that would cause white applicants to be rejected. Several universities have considered proposals that would deem it "racial harassment" for a (white?) student to question the qualifications of nonwhite classmates. But we can't change either the truths or the myths about racial preferences by punishing those who speak them.

This clamor for protection from the qualification question is powerful evidence of the terrible psychological pressure that racial preference often put on their beneficiaries. Indeed, it sometimes seems as though the programs are not supposed to have any beneficiaries—or, at least, that no one is permitted to suggest that they have any.

And that's ridiculous. If one supports racial preferences in professional school admissions, for example, one must be prepared to treat them like any other preference in admission and believe that they make a difference, that some students would not be admitted if the preferences did not exist. This is not a racist observation. It is not normative in any sense. It is simply a fact. A good deal of emotional underbrush might be cleared away were the fact simply conceded, and made the beginning, not the end, of any discussion of preferences. For once it is conceded that the programs have beneficiaries, it follows that some of us who are professionals and are not white must be among them. Supporters of preferences must stop pretending otherwise. Rather, some large segment of us must be willing to meet the qualification question head-on, to say, "Yes, I got into law school because of racial preferences. So what?"—and having said it, must be ready with a list of what we have made of the opportunities the preferences provided.

Now, this is a costly concession, because it carries with it all the baggage of the bitter rhetorical battle over the relationship between preferences and merit. But bristling at the question suggests a deep-seated fear that the dichotomy might be real. Indeed, if admitting that racial preferences make a difference leaves a funny aftertaste in the mouths of proponents, they might be more comfortable fighting against preferences rather than for them.

So let us bring some honesty as well as rigor to the debate, and begin at the beginning. I have already made clear my starting point: I got into a top law school because I am black. Not only am I unashamed of this fact, but I can prove its truth.

As a senior at Stanford back in the mid-1970s, I applied to about half a dozen law schools. Yale, where I would ultimately enroll, came through fairly early with an acceptance. So did all but one of the others. The last school, Harvard, dawdled and dawdled. Finally, toward the end of the admission season, I received a letter of rejection. Then, within days, two different Harvard officials and a professor contacted me by telephone to apologize. They were quite frank in their explanation for the "error." I was told by one official that the school had initially rejected me because "we assumed from your record that you were white." (The words have always stuck in my mind, a tantalizing reminder of what is expected of me.) Suddenly coy, he went on to say that the school had obtained "additional information that should have been counted in your favor"—that is, Harvard had discovered the color of my skin. And if I had already made a deposit to confirm my decision to go elsewhere, well, that, I was told, would "not be allowed" to stand in my way should I enroll at Harvard.

Naturally, I was insulted by this miracle. Stephen Carter, the white male, was not good enough for the Harvard Law School; Stephen Carter, the black male, not only was good enough but rated agonized telephone calls urging him to attend. And Stephen Carter, color unknown, must have been white. How else could he have achieved what he did in college? Except that my college achievements were obviously not sufficiently spectacular to merit acceptance had I been white. In other words, my academic record was too good for a black Stanford University undergraduate, but not good enough for a white Harvard law student. Because I turned out to be black, however, Harvard was quite happy to scrape me from what it apparently considered somewhere nearer the bottom of the barrel.

My objective is not to single out Harvard for special criticism; on the contrary, although my ego insists otherwise, I make no claim that a white student with my academic record would have been admitted to any of the leading law schools. The insult I felt came from the pain of being reminded so forcefully that in the judgment of those with the power to dispose, I was good enough for a top law school only because I happened to be black.

Naturally, I should not have been insulted at all; that is what racial preferences are for—racial preference. But I was insulted and went off to Yale instead, even though I had then and have now absolutely no reason to imagine that Yale's judgment was based on different criteria than Harvard's. Hardly anyone granted admission at Yale is denied admission at Harvard, which admits a far larger class; but several hundreds of students who are admitted at Harvard are denied admission at Yale. Because Yale is far more selective, the chances are good that I was admitted at Yale for essentially the same reason I was admitted at Harvard—the color of my skin made up for what were evidently considered other deficiencies in my academic record. I may embrace this truth as a matter of simple justice or rail against it as one of life's great evils, but being a member of the affirmative action generation means that the one thing I cannot do is deny it. I will say it again: I got into law school because I am black. So what?

II

One answer to the "So what?" question is that someone more deserving than I—someone white—may have been turned away. I hardly know what to make of this argument, for I doubt that the mythical white student on the cusp, the one who almost made it to Yale but for my rude intervention, would have done better than I did in law school.[1] Nor am I some peculiar case: the Yale Law School of my youth trained any number of affirmative action babies who went on to fine academic performances and are now in the midst of stellar careers in the law.

Even in the abstract, what I call the "fairness story" has never struck me as one of the more convincing arguments against preferential policies. The costs of affirmative action differ from the costs of taxation only in degree, not in kind. People are routinely taxed for services they do not receive that are deemed by their government necessary to right social wrongs they did not commit. The taxpayer-financed "bailout" of the weak or collapsed savings-and-loan institutions is one example. Another is the provision of tax dollars for emergency disaster assistance after a hurricane devastates a coastal community. The people who bear the costs of these programs are not the people who caused the damage, but they still have to pay.

Like many, perhaps most, of America's domestic policies, affirmative action programs are essentially redistributive in nature. They transfer resources from their allocation in the market to other recipients favored for social policy reasons. Much of the attack on affirmative action is fueled by the same instinct—the same American dream—that stands as a bulwark against any substantial redistribution of wealth. In America, most people like to think, it is possible for anyone to make it, and those who do not have been victims principally of their own sloth or lack of talent or perhaps plain bad luck—but not of anybody else's sinister plottings. Seymour Martin Lipset, among others, has arguably plausibly that a stable democracy is possible only when an economically secure middle class exists to battle against radical economic reforms that the wealthier classes would otherwise resist by using means outside the system. In America, that middle class plainly exists, and racial preferences are among the radical reforms it is willing to resist.

Sometimes the fervent opposition of the great majority of white Americans to affirmative action is put down to racism, or at least resentment, and I do not want to argue that neither motivation is *ever* present. But affirmative action programs are different from other social transfers, and the way they differ is in the basis on which the favored and disfavored groups are identified. The basis is rare, and sometimes sex—and that makes all the difference.

I say that race is different not because I favor the ideal of a color-blind society; indeed, for reasons I discuss in chapter 9, I fear that the rhetoric of color blindness conflates values that are best kept separate. Race is different for obvious historical reasons: the world is general, and this nation in particular, should know well the risks of encouraging powerful institutions to categorize by such immutable characteristics as race. Besides, even were race as a category less controversial, there is still the further fairness argument, that the sins for which the programs purportedly offer compensation are not sins of the current generation.

Many proponents of preferential policies, however, insist that the current generation of white males deserves to bear the costs of affirmative action. "White males," we are told, "have had exclusive access to certain information, education, experience, and contacts through which they have gained unfair advantage." In the words of a leading scholar, "[W]e have to say to whites, 'Listen, you have benefitted in countless ways from racism, from its notions of beauty [and] its exclusion of minorities in jobs and schools.'" The argument has a second step, too: "For most of this country's history," wrote one commentator, "the nation's top universities practiced the most effective form of affirmative action ever; the quota was for 100 percent white males." The analogy is fair—indeed, it is so fair that it wins the endorsement of opponents as well as supporters of affirmative action—but what does it imply? For proponents of preferences, the answer is clear: if white males have been for centuries the beneficiaries of a vast and all-encompassing program of affirmative action, today's more limited programs can be defended as simply trying to undo the most pernicious effects of that one. That is how, in the contemporary rhetoric of affirmative action, white males turn out to deserve the disfavored treatment that the programs accord.

But there is risk in this rhetoric. To make race the determining factor not simply of the favored group but of the disfavored one encourages an analytical structure that seeks and assigns reasons in the present world for disfavoring one group. The simplest structure—and the one that has come, with mysterious force, to dominate the terms of intellectual campus debate—is what Thomas Sowell has called "social irredentism," an insistence that all members of the disfavored dominant group bear the mantle of oppressor. Affirmative action, then, becomes a punishment for the sin of being born the wrong color and the wrong sex.

All of this carries a neat historical irony. The personalization of affirmative action, the specification of white males as the villains, has diluted the message of the black left of the 1960s and early 1970s, which often (but by no means always) joined forces with the white left to insist that the problems were systemic, not individual. In those halcyon days of campus radicalism, the race struggle was widely described as hand-in-glove with the class struggle. Racial justice was said to be impossible under capitalism, and the principal debate among radical students was over what form of socialism was best for black people—a separate society or an integrated one, central planning or local communities?

As for affirmative action, well, sophisticated nationalists understood that it was part of the problem. By funneling the best and brightest young black men and women into the white-dominated system of higher education, the critics argued, the programs would simply skim the cream from our community, co-opting into the (white) mainstream those who should have been our leaders. An attack on efforts to substitute enhanced educational opportunities for racial justice was a principal focus of Robert Allen's provocative 1969 book *Black Awakening in Capitalist America.* "The black student," Allen warned, "is crucial to corporate America's neocolonial plans." The best and brightest among black youth, he argued, instead of criticizing capitalism from the outside, would be trained to serve it from the inside. Nationalist reviewers agreed. For example, Anne Kelley, wrote in *The Black Scholar* that "the emphasis on higher education for black students" was part of a "neocolonist scheme" that was "designed to stabilize the masses."

But the language of protest is quite different now, and the success of affirmative action is one of the reasons; to paraphrase John Le Carré, it is hard to criticize the system when it has brought you inside at its own expense. Affirmative action programs in education are designed to move people of color into productive roles in capitalist society, and the best sign that they are working is the way the argument has shifted. While males have replaced "the society" or "the system" or "the establishment" in the rhetoric of racial justice, perhaps because the rhetoric of justice is no longer under the control of genuine radicals. The modern proponents of preferences rarely plan to spend their lives in community organizing as they await the revolutionary moment, and there is no particular reason that they should. They are liberal reformers, not radical revolutionaries; with the collapse of communism as a force in the world, nobody seems to think any longer that the solution is to burn everything down and start over. On campuses nowadays, especially in the professional schools, the students of color seem about as likely as their white classmates to be capitalists to their very fingertips; they have no desire to kill the golden goose that the (white male) establishment has created. Or, to switch metaphors, today's affirmative action advocates want mainly to share in the pie, not to see it divided up in some scientific socialist redistribution.

III

Which helps explain, I think, why the "So what?" that I advocate is not easy to utter. Students of color are in the professional schools for the same reason white students are there: to get a good education and a good job. Because so many people seem to assume that the beneficiaries of affirmative action programs are necessarily bound for failure, or at least for inferiority, there is an understandable tendency for people of color to resist being thought of as beneficiaries. After all, who wants to be bound for failure? (Especially when so many beneficiaries of racial preferences really *don't* succeed as they would like.) Better not to think about it; better to make sure nobody else thinks about it either. Rather than saying, "So what?" better to say, "How dare you?"

I understand perfectly this temptation to try to make the world shut up, to pursue the fantasy that doubts that are not expressed do not exist. When I listen to the labored but heartfelt arguments on why potential employers (and, for that matter, other students) should not be permitted to question the admission qualifications of students of color, I am reminded uneasily of another incident from my own student days, a shining moment when we too, thought, that if we could only stifle debate on the question, we could make it go away.

The incident I have in mind occurred during the fall of 1978, my third year in law school, a few months after the Supreme Court's decision in *Regents of the University of California v. Bakke,* which placed what seemed to many of us unnecessarily severe restrictions on the operation of racially conscious admission programs. The air was thick with swirling critiques of racial preferences, most of them couched in the language of merit versus qualification. Everywhere we turned, someone seemed to be pointing at us and saying, "You don't belong here."

We looked around and saw an academic world that seemed to be doing its best to get rid of us.

So we struck back. We called the critics racist. We tried to paint the question of our qualifications as a racist one. And one evening, when the Yale Political Union, a student organization, had scheduled a debate on the matter (the title, as I recall, was "The Future of Affirmative Action"), we demonstrated. All of us.

Our unanimity was astonishing. Then as now, the black students at the law school were divided, politically, socially, and in dozens of other ways. But on this issue, we were suddenly united. We picketed the Political Union meeting, roaring our slogan (*"We are not debatable! We are not debatable!"*) in tones of righteous outrage. We made so much noise that at last they threw wide the doors and invited us in. In exchange for our promise to end the demonstration so that the debate could be conducted, we were offered, and we accepted, the chance to have one of our number address the assembly. That task, for some reason, fell to me.

I remember my rising excitement as I stood before the audience of immaculately attired undergraduates, many of them still in their teens. There was something sweet and naive and appealing about the Political Union members as they sat nervously but politely in their tidy rows, secure (or, perhaps, momentarily insecure) in their faith that a commitment to openness and debate would lead to moral truth. But I set my face against the smile that was twitching there, and tried to work up in its stead a glower sufficient to convey the image of the retributive fury of the radical black left. (Having missed those days in college, I thought perhaps to rekindle them briefly.) And while some of the kids seemed annoyed at the intrusion, others looked frightened, even intimidated, which I suppose was our goal. I spoke briefly, pointing out that it was easy for white people to call for color-blind admissions when they understood perfectly well that none of the costs would fall on them. I carefully avoided the word *racism,* but I let the implication hang in the air anyway, lest I be misunderstood.

And then we marched out again, triumphantly, clapping and chanting rhythmically as though in solemn reminder that should the Political Union folks get up to any more nonsense, we might return and drown them out again. (A few of the undergraduates and one of the speakers joined us in our clapping.) We were, for a shining moment, in our glory; the reporters were there, tapes rolling, cameras clicking; in our minds, we had turned back the calendar by a decade and the campuses were in flames (or at least awash with megaphones and boycotts and banners and an administration ready to compromise); the school would meet us with a promise of justice or we would tear it down!

Then all at once it was over. We dispersed, returning to our dormitory rooms and apartments, our law review and moot court activities, our long nights in the library to prepare for class and our freshly cleaned suits for job interviews, our political differences and our social cliques. We returned to the humdrum interests of law school life, and suddenly we were just like everybody else again. Absolutely nothing had changed. *Bakke* was still the law of the land. There was no magic, the campus was not in flames, and there had never been a shining moment. There was only the uneasy tension of our dual existence. The peculiar uncertainty provoked by affirmative action was still with us, and our outrage at being reminded of its reality was undiminished. And as for the eager young minds of the Political Union, I suppose they held their debate and I suppose somebody won.

IV

The demonstration at the Political Union seems very long ago now, not only in time but in place: Could that really have been Yale? Could that really have been *us?* (I look around at the chanting faces in my memory and pick out their subsequent histories: this one a partner in an elite law firm, that one an investment banker, this one a leading public interest lawyer, that one another partner, this one in the State Department, that one a professor at a leading law school, this one a prosecuting attorney, that one in the legal department of a Fortune 100 corporations, and so on.) We are not the people we were then, but the fact that the debate was held over our boisterous objections seems not to have diverted our careers. We are a successful generation of lawyers, walking advertisements, it might seem, for the bright side of affirmative action. Our doubts, seen from this end of the tunnel, seem vague and insubstantial.

At the time, however, the doubts, and the anger, were painfully real. I do not want to suggest that the doubts have persisted into our careers or those of other black professionals—I am as irritated as anybody else by the frequent suggestion that there lurks inside each black professional a confused and uncertain ego, desperately seeking reassurance—but that it is certainly true that as long as racial preference exist, the one thing that cannot be proved in which people of color in my generation would have achieved what they have in their absence.

At this point in the argument many of us are told, as though in reassurance, "Oh, don't worry, you're not here because affirmative action—you're here on merit." But it is not easy to take this as quite the compliment it is presumably meant to be. In the first place, it continues the opposition of merit to preference that has brought about the pain and anger to begin with. More important, and perhaps more devastating, it places the judgment on how good we are just where we do not want it to be: in the minds and mouths of white colleagues, whose arrogant "assurances" serve as eloquent reminders of how fragile a trophy is our hardwon professional status.

Very well, perhaps we were wrong in our youthful enthusiasm to try to stifle debate, but that is not the point of the story. The point, rather, is that our outrage was misdirected. Even at the time of my glowering diatribe, I realized that not all of what I said was fair. Looking back, I have come to understand even better how much of my message—our message—was driven by our pain over *Bakke* and the nation's changing mood. "Don't you understand?" we were crying. "We have fought hard to get here, and we will not be pushed back!"

Our anguish was not less real for being misdirected. Whether one wants to blame racial preferences or white racism or the pressures of professional school or some combination of them all, our pain was too great for us to consider for an instant the possibility that victory in the battle to "get here" did not logically entail affirmative action. We were not prepared to discuss or even to imagine life without preferences, a world in which we would be challenged to meet and beat whatever standards for admission and advancement were placed before us. We wanted no discussion at all, only capitulation. All we saw was that the Supreme Court had given us the back of its hand in *Bakke* (we wore little buttons: FIGHT RACISM, OVERTURN BAKKE) and the forces of reaction were closing in.

Now that I am a law professor, one of my more delicate tasks is convincing my students, whatever their color, to consider the possibility that perhaps the forces of reaction are *not* closing in. Perhaps what seems to them (and to many other people) a backlash against affirmative action is instead (or in addition) a signal that the programs, at least in their current expansive form, have run their course. Or perhaps, if the programs are to be preserved, they should move closer to their roots: the provision of opportunities for people of color who might not otherwise have the advanced training that will allow them to prove what they can do.

My students tend to disagree, sometimes vehemently. The bad guys are out there, they tell me, and they are winning. And one of the reasons they are winning, as I understand it, is that they get to set the rules. A couple of years ago, for example, a student complained to me that people of color are forced to disguise their true voices and write like white males in order to survive the writing competition for membership on the *Yale Law Journal*. One critic has argued that university faculties employ a "hierarchical majoritarian" standard for judging academic work—a standard that is not sensitive to the special perspective people of color can bring to scholarship. And all over the corporate world, I am led to believe, the standards of what counts as merit are designed, perhaps intentionally, to keep us out.

Nowadays, racial preferences are said to be our tool for forcing those bad guys—the white males who run the place, the purveyors, so I am told, of so much misery and the inheritors of so much unearned privilege—to acknowledge that theirs is only one way of looking at the world. Anyone who can't see the force of this argument is evidently a part of the problem. White people who ask whether the quest for diversity contemplates a lowering of standards of excellence are still charged with racism, just as in the old days. (The forces of reaction *are* closing in.) People of color who venture similar thoughts are labeled turncoats and worse, just as they always have been. (Don't they *know* that academic standard are a white male invention aimed at maintaining a eurocentric hegemony?) And through it all, the devotion to numbers that has long characterized the affirmative action debate continues.

Certainly the proportions of black people in the various professions are nothing to shout about. In my own field of law teaching, for example, a study prepared for the Society of American Law Teachers shows that only 3.7 percent of faculty members are black at law schools that are, as the report puts it in an unfortunate bit of jargon, "majority-run." In other professions, too, although the numbers have generally improved in recent years, the percentages of black folk remain small. On medical school faculties, for example, 1.9 percent of the professors are black. On university faculties generally, just 4 percent of the faculty members are black. For lawyers and judges, the figure is 2.3 percent. For physicians, 3.3 percent. Financial managers, 4.3 percent. (And, as long as we're at it, for authors, 0.4 percent, about 1 out of 250.)

But while we might agree on the desirability of raising these numbers, the question of strategy continues to divide us. To try to argue (as I do elsewhere in this book) that purported racism in professional standards is not a plausible explanation for most of the data is to risk being dismissed for one's naïveté. And as to my oft-stated preference for returning to the roots of affirmative action: well, the roots, as it turns out, had the matter all wrong. My generation, with its obsessive concern with proving itself in the white man's world, pressed an argument that was beside the point. Had we but understood the ways in which our experiences differ from those of the dominant majority, it seems, we would have insisted on an affirmative action that rewrites the standards for excellence, rather than one that trains us to meet them.

Notes

[1] It had always struck me as quite bizarre that so many otherwise thoughtful people on both sides of the affirmative action controversy seem to think so much turns on the question of how the beneficiaries perform. I would not dismiss the inquiry as irrelevant, but I am reluctant to say that it is the whole ball game. It may be the case, as many critics have argued, that the affirmative action beneficiary who fails at Harvard College might have performed quite well at a less competitive school and gone on to an excellent and productive career that will almost surely be lost because of the shattering experience of academic failure; but one must weigh this cost (and personal choice) against the tale of the student who would not have attended Harvard without affirmative action and who succeeds brilliantly there. It may be that those who do less well in school because of preferences outnumber those who do better, but such statistics are only the edge of the canvas, a tiny part of a much larger and more complex picture, and that is why I think the energy devoted to the qualification question is largely wasted.

Even accepting this dubious rhetorical construct, it is easy to see that racial preferences call for sacrifices not from white males as a group but from the subgroups of white males most likely to be excluded by a preference benefitting someone else—that is, the most disadvantaged white males, those who, by hypothesis, have gained the least from racism.

169. John Tenula, "Voices from Southeast Asia, 1991"

In the 1970s and 1980s refugees from southeast Asia came to the United States, including Virginia, in large numbers. These oral histories give their view of what America has meant for them and their children.

Ho Xuan Tam

Dreams of Stanford

He is wearing a three-piece blue business suit. There is a great deal of self-confidence in the way he presents himself.

Source: John Tenula, *Voices from Southeast Asia,* pp. 121–129. Copyright Holmes and Meier, 1991. Reprinted by permission.

I would like to study math at Stanford University when I finish high school next year. I have been in the United States seven years this fall. Sometimes, I wish I could just skip my senior year and go to Stanford; I've learned enough—I'm bored and I've learned all I am going to learn from high school.

My mother and father were very educated people from Saigon, and there was always pressure to study. I can remember my father helping me with my studies when I was first in this country; he had difficulty with the language, but somehow he always understood my assignments. It was always a big ritual after dinner to study with him; I knew he looked forward to it. The higher math I had was difficult for him, but he kept at it until trig, and then he said I could complete that assignment without his assistance. My mother played hardly any place in this homework help.

My father was a famous lawyer in Vietnam; he had a great love for books. He always told me that a book was like a beautiful bird—the more you read of it the more beautiful it becomes. He was very, very proud when my older sister got a scholarship to study premed last year at Stanford. It was as if he got the scholarship. So this is pretty much what I'm going to do—go to Stanford.

We have always lived in the Tenderloin section in San Francisco, and I go to Galileo High School—which isn't so bad. Most of the students are okay, but your friends are always from your people—your own nationality.

Tell me about your friends.

I have two Vietnamese friends. It is difficult to break into any new group, people stick to themselves. My one Vietnamese friend knows a few Chinese, but it's more that they are polite to her rather than they are friends.

Scholastically, Galileo is not the best high school in San Francisco. Most Asians do pretty well in school, and there is always some jealousy by the black and Spanish students, but I don't care. If they are jealous, I can't do anything about it. I work hard, they can too. Besides, the Vietnamese are supposed to raise the math and science scores in all of the San Francisco schools, so we help improve the system for everybody.

I think one of the big problems in the school is all this wasted time in lunch and study halls, and most of the teachers are not so good. They just keep repeating what they've already said. Me, I'd changed the whole system and speed it up—let you get out of there earlier.

To get a full scholarship to Stanford is very difficult. They want to see somebody with everything going for them. I don't think my guidance counselor at Galileo understands how important this is to me. All he talks about are the second and third choices of schools. I want the best and he doesn't know my father. In some ways, I'm following in my sister's shadow. So everyone thinks I will do the same. I wish my parents could see that.

Do you attend school sports events?

No, and I don't go to school dances; there are more important things to do. I want to be able to get a higher SAT score than my sister had. It's not impossible, but it's not very realistic because I'm still weak in my verbal scores. I need to practice more. For me, math is the purest of all sciences. It is the most powerful language, and you can learn to speak it even if your English is not perfect.

Heng Mui

CITIZENSHIP

She has very expressive eyes, and has brought me a collection of photographs of herself, mostly from her life in this country.

I became a citizen last year; I am now an American. I do not especially feel like an American, but I don't know if there is any special way I should feel. There are lots of stereotypes about how Americans look and how they act; I don't fall into any of those categories.

For some refugees, becoming an American is not an easy thing to do. It means you give up that final thing that is yours, your nationality. To take away your nationality is to deprive you of an important piece of your identity. We have lost so much, so many of us arrived with nothing. To give up our nationality is just too much to ask. I know people who are not ready to do this; it's too painful, too embarrassing.

I remember when my sister suddenly died in France, and I went to the immigration office and applied for a travel document. When the woman at the desk asked me to write my nationality, which was question three, I wrote South Vietnam. When she saw the application, she took a pencil and put two lines through the word Vietnam and wrote "stateless." Those two pencil lines scratched through my heart. In a few minutes she took away my nationality. There was nothing I could do.

When I took my oath, I thought, "Oh my God! Everything is gone!" But after it happened, I never thought about it. The most painful part was just thinking about it. There is something exciting about holding my new blue passport and knowing that I will vote next year for the president.

Phyllis and Toan Nguyen

BRIDGING TWO CULTURES

I first met Phyllis and Toan in Houston where she was a social worker and he was in his last year of dental school. They both have a great sense of humor, including practical jokes I observed they played on each other. They seem to understand each other's background and culture and are very comfortable talking about their own likes and dislikes. Doing the right thing in an ethically tough or questionable situation is very important to them. They have survived together, as they say, in spite of their families. They are both very much involved with their church work.

Phyllis: I was not what my mother-in-law expected when she thought of a daughter-in-law. I guess I never will be, but that doesn't worry me now. She had an image of how I should be. You know, it's that Pearl Buck type daughter-in-law image, which is the traditional, subservient, and above all else obedient daughter-in-law. But I think it's the same with my mother-in-law and daughter-in-law relationship—there are the good times and the bad times. I like talking about the good times.

My in-laws live in Midland, Texas, which is a safe distance. I think it's real important that married people respect their mates first and not parents; that's a real twist from the Vietnamese relationships. Mind you, there is a great deal of room for misunderstandings in all of these issues. I don't mean to criticize or be unfair, but that's just the way it is.

I spent two years in Vietnam, 1972 to 1974. There were a lot of political changes going on in the country—right under my nose—and I missed most of them. I was a journeyman for the Southern Baptist Convention; which meant I was a support person to the Baptist mission. Vietnam was not my choice; I really wanted to go to Africa or Israel. But it proved to be a great choice and I fell in love with Vietnamese culture and the Vietnamese people. There was no way that I could get enough of the language, the traditions. There I was, this small-town Texas Baptist girl headed for all of these new experiences with Asian culture. It was a great thing. My eyes couldn't get bigger.

Toan: I am an example of that very ambitious Vietnamese who wants to get ahead here. You see, I always have to prove myself. I do very well in the educational systems here. I like the way you can study and are able to excel. You either know the answer or you do not. I like that, the exactness.

I got my mechanical engineering degree from the university of Texas and worked for a year for Atlantic Richfield. It was a good job and good money; but I got bored so I applied to dental school; in part because my dentist made it sound so good and encouraged me, and I thought it would be a good job. Well, I graduated top in my class. But I was restless and after two years I wanted something more. I was very good at surgery *[he shows me his hands]* and I wanted a more challenging outlet, you know, something more creative. I want to be a plastic surgeon so here I am in my first year of medical school in Lubbock.

Did your families agree to the marriage?

Phyllis: Both of our families were opposed from the start to our marriage—and I mean dead opposed. We met at the University of Texas and were married in 1978. Toan has seven brothers and sisters. They all have Vietnamese spouses. So for us the families were the difficult hurdle.

I don't think my mom ever really accepted the marriage. Although she was what you call a "concerned Christian," I was her daughter and there are limitations to these things. Anyway, she died six months after we were married. My father accepts Toan and they get along very well. The kids help the situation—we have two boys, Jesse, who is six, and Mark, who is four. The kids bring us together. A large part of it is seeing that we are happy, but the fact that Toan is a professional, ambitious, and successful person helps.

What does education mean to Vietnamese?

Education is God. That is how the Vietnamese looks at it. You want to talk about success stories, well, Toan's family is a perfect example. Every one of his brothers and sisters is a professional. The youngest brother is trying to find himself right now, but he'll work it out. I have enormous respect for my father-in-law. He was very wealthy in Vietnam, a high-placed minister in the government, and then he lost everything and now he is a machinist. He had to learn how to work. I'm serious—it's a different kind of work style.

The main difference between the American and Vietnamese families is, I guess, the discipline aspect. The father's role is to monitor and control and help the kids keep focus. It's that focus that always impresses me. It's real direction, no deviation. You just look straight ahead. For example, Toan's father was aware of all the kids' university exam schedules and would call the kids before the test and after it to find out the results. Talk about pressure! And what's more, they were expecting his calls.

Have you experienced racism?

Toan: Racism—sure, I've experienced it, but I don't like talking about it. You sense it—it has never been direct. It's sort of a feeling. You know the stereotypes, so when they push me to the wall, I show them my degrees. Sure,

I am a minority person but this is what I really am and this is what I really do. It's a weapon, a defense; I know that, so what? As a minority person with your degrees, you get power in this country. You better your position in society. I never think of myself in terms of being a minority.

As a D.D.S., you are kind of a second-class citizen; the M.D.s run the hospital. There are only two hundred D.D.S./M.D.s in this country. It's a prestigious combination and I will soon have it.

I've gotten a lot of teasing mostly when other Vietnamese get angry about me having an American wife. I don't think it's really malicious or evil. They joke and tell me I have betrayed Vietnamese culture, that my wife is a capitalist. Can you believe it—who could be better capitalists than the Vietnamese?

What makes a successful marriage between people from two different cultures?

Phyllis: For me, the success key to my intercultural marriage is having lived there on his soil. You have to know the society—that speaks directly to the way the person will react with you in your marriage. If I didn't have that, I'd be in deep trouble. I have seen other couples in that trouble. You've got to know the likes and dislikes of these people, how they play and work—all that sort of stuff.

Toan: I understand American reactions to Vietnam. First, no one really understands the war and the loss of the war; second, no one really understands the culture and history of Vietnam. A lot of people came here and they can't adapt like I did. An American wife helps. But for me the language is the most important thing—you've simply got to get the language. You know, I know many Vietnamese people who deal only with Vietnamese; like they are still in Vietnam. These people left with preconceived notions and aren't about to change. They like to ghettoize and I don't like it at all.

Let me say that there is also a negative aspect to these Vietnamese-American communities and that is the way some do business; many people cheat on their taxes, and a lot of dentists cheat on insurance forms. It happens. Why not? In Vietnam, it was part of the system and it was the way you did business. Getting away with something was the way it was. Okay, these are just a few, but they are the greedy ones who make a bad name for all of us. They want to beat a system they do not yet know. Boy, I get angry.

Phyllis: I suppose there is cultural snobbishness by some of the Vietnamese. They get Americanized to a degree and then they stop. They want to keep their identity. I understand a lot of this, but most Americans would be really critical of this, like: "Who do they think they are?" Some of it is a survival technique. They want the enclaves just to hear the language, to remind them that not all is lost, and they strive real hard to hold on to something. But for some it is just too much and they refuse to participate.

You know, I lost the thrill of the Vietnamese culture when I married. The fascination went out the door. I don't know why, it just went. We never speak Vietnamese and I don't want to. Funny, isn't it? It is like something in the past that I accomplished and now I can't go back. I speak English with Toan's family. All of their English is getting better, except his mother's—who refuses to learn it and uses an interpreter. She may always need one, but that's okay.

How is your marriage different here than it would be in Vietnam?

Toan: What America gives us as husband and wife is more freedom from the family—I mean the in-laws. The wife in Vietnam is more submissive, the mother-in-law more powerful. Parents control more there. For me, all of the events in my life were planned. You see, I am very much involved with my church here. God planned all of this for me. I really believe that. Funny, in Vietnam you don't believe in many things. I mean you know all about war, bombs, and death; you get used to anything. But here, your life is organized and you can believe in a future. You see that's what America is all about—the future.

Sokhoa Gioi

DOMESTIC WORK

She is a diminutive person wearing a black turtleneck sweater and pearls. Her conversation is punctuated by French expressions when she is excited. We are sitting in a room with oil paintings of birds and flowers that she has painted. There are certain things she doesn't want to discuss, and I feel her past is frozen. Somehow you can tell she came from a wealthy family.

I was a schoolteacher in Cambodia. I taught grade four for eight years, then the war came and my husband and two children and I went to Thailand. Here in Washington, D.C., I clean people's homes. I am a maid.

My first, my husband would not let me leave the house and the children, but I put the children in a Cambodian day-care center where there were other children with mothers who work like me. We very much needed the money because very often my husband does not work and it is easier for a woman to get a job than it is for a man. My husband was a teacher when he was in Cambodia.

I have worked for this one woman for almost one year, and she still keeps talking to me about Vietnam and Vietnamese boat people. I know that she does not know I am Cambodian, not Vietnamese. I like to work better for men. The American woman demands too much for the money she pays me and the more I do, that much more she will want done.

In Cambodia, I had two servants. I remember them very well; they were older women and they worked for us for many years. I knew their families. Here, no one cares about me except to say that I come on Tuesday and Friday. I don't know if ever I would be able to teach again. I just keep working and trying to help the family maybe buy a house in Maryland.

There is nothing more for me to say. I just go to work and come home on the Metro and then work for my family. No, I try not to think about what my life was before Pol Pot, before we left Cambodia.

Mong Pang

A Soldier without a Country

He is wearing green, institutional work clothes, probably from Sears; a red checked bandanna is tied around his neck. He is graying at the temples, bespectacled, probably five feet tall. We sit on a bench, talking in English, and drink coffee.

I am a janitor for the Baptist church in Atlanta near Ponce de Leon. This is the job that I have had since I came to the U.S. and Atlanta in December 1980. I don't think about this fact too much. It is a job for us and we do not live on welfare.

Sometime when the work gets too much because they have a wedding or some celebration, my wife Duong helps. She never worked for another person before she came here, and she does not mind too much. I have four children. The oldest has just finished high school and wants to study computers. We all live in the same house that was given to us by the church here. The rent is good and it is close so I can walk to work. It is a simple house and often many of our friends are there. You see, Laotians do not mind many people in a house. The Americans do not like this. Here, everyone has his own room; this is not so with Laotian culture.

With I was in Laos I was in the army. I was a colonel in the north and worked for some years with the Americans. I never got to know the Americans but I worked with them and some seemed nice. They drank too much beer . . .

It was a good life in Laos and I miss my country very much. I want to go back if the Communists get out. I look to that day all of the time. We left so quickly. We just locked the door and left. We don't know about our possessions or our house. I hope it is still there. I think about relatives and friend. Every time the news talks about the war and the Thai/Laos border problems, I worry about my brother left there. I am sure others do the same. I fought very hard for my country, and now all of that is gone and it will not come back. It is very sad, very sad.

There is nothing I wish to do here. Why should I? I do not have my heart here. My family soon will become U.S. citizens and they have new lives here. All of that is good and they start new lives. I will be happy for them.

When I first started this work, the tears went into the toilet. I was so sad. There is not much else I can do here in America. What do they do with a soldier who has no country? What could they educate me to be? I don't know. All of these years that I clean the church, I just do it. No one bothers me—I am my own boss. They are good to me, these Christian people. They gave me my first station wagon and they always invited me to church, but I just went to hear the music. Every Christmas they give us food and money.

Lao Hospitality

Come and take rice.
That is the Lao greeting of welcome.
Take rice with Pa Dek and we will talk.
I remember Vietiane and my family that for so long
I know nothing about.
I live here in Fresno with other lowland people,
but I dream of my city that as a child
I knew from darkness to light.
I miss the familiar streets that were always filled
with the people that my family knew for many, many

generations. Now, all that is only dust and my dreams become distant.
I work on a farm here in Fresno. It is very hard work. There are many men here who live like I do—with memories and the dust of their dreams is what we work with in the fields each day. Dust that fills the fields with all of our secrets and memories of a life we no longer will know.
Now come and take rice.

Laotian farmer, Fresno, California
[translated from French]

170. *U.S. News and World Report*, "Triumph Without Victory: The Unreported History of the Persian Gulf War, 1991"

U.S. News and World Report compiled this "unwritten history" of the war in the Persian Gulf.

At 11:30 a.m. on March 3, General H. Norman Schwarzkopf and his Saudi counterpart, Lieutenant General Khalid ibn Sultan, took their seats in the center of a long table beneath a large tent that had been erected at a remote air base in southern Iraq. The Safwan airfield was occupied by Major General Ronald Griffith's U.S. 1st Infantry Division. Across the table from Schwarzkopf and Khalid were Iraqi Lieutenant General Sultan Hashim Ahmad and his aide, Lieutenant General Salah Abud Mahmud. Schwarzkopf calmly instructed the Iraqi generals in the terms of the cease-fire.

Within hours after the talks ended, Iraqi Shiites in Basra rose up against Baghdad's rule. In northern Iraq, Kurds too began to rebel violently, driving Iraqi garrison forces first out of small mountain villages and ultimately out of the city of Kirkuk.

It would require several days, but eventually, Saddam Hussein would redeploy the very same Republican Guard forces that had not been disarmed in the Basra pocket to quell the twin rebellions. Refugees from both areas would tell tales of atrocities, of Shiite rebels hung from the big guns of T-72 tanks, of tanks and mortar fire on apartment houses and private residents, of Iraqi helicopter gunships slaughtering thousands of defenseless Kurds on frozen mountainsides. Many infants and children were among the victims.

Just miles away, in their bases in southern Iraq, and later at emergency relief camps established on Iraq's northern border with Turkey, American soldiers would stand by, angry and helpless. For the tank crews in Colonel Montgomery Meigs's brigade of the U.S. 1st Armored Division, the cease-fire was falling frustration. Iraqis defiantly strode in front of them, and taunted them. "We could see them out there at 600 and 700 meters, waving at us, waving their weapons, and just walking away. These were the guys who had been shooting at us earlier," said Sergeant Anthony Widner. "They came back and right in front of us. They went to their bunkers and got food. They dismounted, [they numbered approximately] 120 men. They could have given us a lot of trouble. So we got the order to move forward and take them. They were real smart-ass, they had a bad attitude. That's when everybody said, 'We should have finished those bastards.'"

For a military operation that had been born of such extraordinary deft and successful diplomacy and then prosecuted with such skill and vision, it was a tragic conclusion, one that no amount of postwar celebration could disguise. There could be no doubt that America and its allies had triumphed over Iraq's army on the battlefield. But inasmuch as victory suggests the decisive defeat of an opponent, there was none. This triumph without victory was perhaps the most striking irony of the entire conflict.

Before the war began, and during the forty-two days of hostilities, President Bush had refused to second-guess General Schwarzkopf and his battlefield commanders. He had issued no orders from the Oval Office instructing them to strike specific targets. Virtually to a man, every American commander in the Gulf conflict expressed gratitude and satisfaction over the fact that their President and commander-in-chief had allowed them to fight the war as they saw fit. Toward the end of the conflict, how-

---

Source: U. S. News and World Report, "Triumph Without Victory." Copyright Random House.

ever, because of the pressure brought to bear on the Bush administration by Saudi Arabia and Egypt, the two most important members of the American-led coalition, the President had begun pushing his military advisers for an answer as to how soon offensive operations against the Iraqis could be ended. Aides to the President said he would not have ordered the cessation of hostilities when he did if he had received strong objections from Schwarzkopf. Bush himself was adamant on the point. "I was very careful in being sure that the military supported the cessation of fighting," he told *U.S. News.* "It was stated to me clearly by General Powell, who indeed talked on the phone to General Schwarzkopf from my office, that the time had come to stop the fighting. The goal was to kick Iraq out of Kuwait, and the goal, in the opinion of our top fighters, had been achieved. There were no pressures brought upon the President of the United States to stop hostilities before our top command recommended that hostilities be stopped."

Aides stated further that Bush could have resisted pressure from Saudi Arabia and Egypt if it meant extending the period of hostilities another twenty-four hours or so. "At that point," said a senior adviser, "we could have stiff-armed them." Still other advisers provided another explanation for the timing of the cease-fire. In Moscow, Mikhail Gorbachev was under increasing pressure from Kremlin hard-liners as the war continued. Some advisers worried that if all of central Baghdad were reduced to rubble, it might be enough of an excuse for Gorbachev's opponents in the military and the KGB to move against him. With no strong dissent from Schwarzkopf on the timing of the cease-fire, these aids said, the real reason for Bush's decision to quit early might have been to protect Gorbachev.

While it may be true that no one had ordered Schwarzkopf to stop fighting, aides to Schwarzkopf said that the general wanted at least several more hours to prosecute the war, to clarify the situation on the battlefield, and to disarm the forces of the Republican Guard that Lieutenant General Fred Franks and his other battlefield commanders nearly had surrounded. On the battlefield itself, brigade commanders and their superiors were still confused about the location of key enemy units when they received word of an impending cease-fire. No provisions had been made for a demilitarized zone or *cordon sanitaire,* an area of the desert recognized by both the Iraqis and the Allied forces where conflict should not occur.

After the war, it was easy to argue that the allies should have further pursued the Republican Guard, destroyed them, and occupied southern Iraq if necessary to prevent Saddam's crushing of the Shiites. But it is difficult to see how such efforts would have succeeded militarily. Neither the U.S. military nor America's political leaders wanted to occupy large chunks of Iraq indefinitely. None of the commanders, including Franks, wanted to follow the Iraqis into Basra itself and risk engaging in street battles to pry them out, fighting that would have cost many American soldiers and Iraqi citizens their lives. Some high-level Army officers also said that if they had continued with Frank's double envelopment and trapped the Iraqis in the Basra pocket the ensuing slaughter would have been inimical to American interests and morale. But several commanders did believe that had the Republican Guard been trapped in the Basra pocket, they might have been forced to surrender and give up their tanks and weapons.

Indeed, the cease-fire agreed to by President Bush had left the battlefield situation so confused that two days afterward, on March 2, General Barry McCaffery's 24th Infantry Division (Mechanized) found itself in one of the largest tank battles of the war. Elements of the Hammurabi division of the Republican Guard had attempted to escape through the Rumaila oil field with hundreds of vehicles and heavy transporters, many of them carrying undamaged T-72 heavy tanks. After Iraqi soldiers fired at Colonel John LeMoyne's 1st Brigade, General McCaffery ordered LeMoyne and his other commanders to respond in kind. "It wasn't a gaggle running for it," LeMoyne said. "This was tanks and BMPs lined up in a combat-movement profile, with tanks forward and thin-skinned vehicles to the rear. As far as we knew at that point, all the bridges over the Euphrates were down and the only way out of that oil field would be to drive right through us."

At the end of nearly two hours of attack, McCaffery reported destroying 30 Iraqi tanks, 65 armored personnel carriers, and 400 trucks. The Hammurabi division, however, was estimated to have had 350 tanks at the start of the war. Days later, the Hammurabi's remaining tanks rolled through town after town in southern Iraq, their guns smashing the Shiite rebellions.

The terms of the cease-fire had also allowed the Iraqi army to fly helicopters. General Schwarzkopf insisted that the Iraqis fly no fixed-wing aircraft, but he assented to the use of helicopters when the Iraqi general said they needed them to transport wounded soldiers and for other tasks Schwarzkopf said days afterward that he was "suckered" by the Iraqis. By then, Saddam Hussein's soldiers were firing from the helicopters at the hapless Kurds in the mountains of northern Iraq. It is certain that Saddam's Republican Guard would have quelled the Kurdish uprising ultimately. But in the difficult terrain of the mountains, the helicopters turned what might have been a negotiated truce into a massacre. While the Bush administration send aid to the Kurdish refugees (after an embarrassing international outcry), it never raised a finger to prevent the slaughter by soldiers in helicopters.

On several occasions prior to and during the war, Bush made it plain that the quarrel of the international community was not with the people of Iraq, but with Saddam Hussein. Rise up and remove him, Bush said, and Iraq will be at peace with the world. During the course of the slaughter of the Shiites and Kurds in the aftermath of the war, Iraqi opposition figures reminded the Bush administration of the President's words of encouragement.

Aides to the President pointed out that Bush had said that if the Iraq people "and the army" rose up, the international community would support them. Because the Iraqi army never rose up and rebelled, these presidential aides explained, the United States was unable to come to the aid of the Kurds and the Shiites. It was a weak excuse. It was also the case that the administration was unwilling to deal directly with any Iraqi opposition figures not specifically approved by King Fahd and, to a lesser extent, Egyptian President Hosni Mubarak. Fear of radical Shiite fundamentalism and Kurdish separatism may well have stayed Washington's hand. In addition, there was little sentiment among the American public for having U.S. troops become embroiled in a centuries-old ethnic conflict.

The sentiment was shared by President Bush. "The battles between the Kurds and the Baath Party have been going for a long, long time," Bush told *U.S. News.* "To solve that problem forever was not part of the United Nations' goals, nor was it the goal of the United States. We deplore killings, of course. But to tie the Kurdish or Shiite problem into the handling of the aggression of Iraq is simply a bit revisionistic. It is disappointing that Saddam Hussein remains in power and is still brutal and powerful. But that in no way diminishes the highly successful effort to stop the aggression against Kuwait."

An examination of the forty-two days of Desert Storm yields some surprising conclusions. One week before the commencement of the air campaign on January 16, 1991, a Pentagon spokesman stated that Allied soldiers would face an estimated force of 540,000 Iraqi troops in the Kuwait Theater of Operations (KTO), a zone defined by the Pentagon as the area south of the 31st parallel of latitude and east of the 45th line of longitude. The KTO encompassed all of Kuwait and a portion of southeastern Iraq three times larger than Kuwait itself. After the war, General Schwarzkopf would testify to two committees of Congress that his army had confronted forty-three Iraqi divisions. Those divisions, Schwarzkopf said, boasted 623,000 Iraqi soldiers. Of these the General Command estimated that 65,000 were taken prisoner during the conflict. The Pentagon further asserted that about four divisions, or 60,000 soldiers, had escaped. The CIA said the number was even greater. The Defense Intelligence Agency estimated that another 100,000 Iraqi soldiers perished in the war, but it conceded that the number might be wrong by as much as 50 percent in either direction. In other words, there could have been as few as 50,000 or as many as 150,000 Iraqis killed.

Given the rapidity and confusion of the Gulf War and the fact that Allied forces did not engage in Vietnam-style "body counts," such uncertainty is understandable. But even allowing for those factors, it is difficult to make sense of the Pentagon's estimates of the number of Iraqi soldiers present in the KTO and those killed there. Several respected analysts believe that the number of Iraqi soldiers present on the battlefield in the KTO at the time the ground war began was well below both the Pentagon's estimate of 540,000 and 623,000 claimed by General Schwarzkopf.

American estimates of the Iraqi order of battle were derived from satellite photographs and intercepts of electronic communication between Iraqi units in the KTO. The aerial photos were most useful for determining the disposition of Iraqi equipment and defensive barriers. The satellite imagery could not count soldiers, however. Nevertheless, U.S. intelligence analysts concluded that there were 142 separate "brigades." This amounted to 43 divisions, of which approximately 25 were infantry divisions assigned to the front lines of defense in southern Kuwait. The analysts, however, ascribed to the Iraqi forces the manpower of their American counterparts, a practice that overestimated the fighting strength of the Iraqis.

Sources familiar with Iraqi force levels said that almost without exception the Iraqi front-line units were poorly trained and poorly led, made up of the least educated men from the countryside and the cities. Many of these divisions were created for the war as the army was mobilized; the units were provisional, and at least fifteen were disbanded after the war ended. "A lot of those divisions were under strength, called up rapidly, and not filled up," said Ahmed Hashim, a Washington-based consultant on Middle Eastern affairs. Egyptian by birth, Hashim is a U.S. citizen who spent five years studying the Iraqi army for a doctoral dissertation on the Iran-Iraq war at the Massachusetts Institute of Technology that was completed two months before Iraq invaded Kuwait. His assessment of the strength of the Iraqi army was derived from Middle Eastern sources, from publications, and from relatives and acquaintances who fought in the Iraqi army. Hashim convincingly argued that about 70 percent of Saddam's front-line forces were Shiites, 20 percent Kurds. He called these forces Saddam Hussein's "throwaway divisions."

At peak levels, Iraqi infantry divisions were significantly smaller than the typical divisions of Western armies. An American division ordinarily comprises three combat brigades totaling about 16,000 soldiers. A fully manned Iraqi infantry division had just two brigades of between 6,000 and 8,000 men. It was likely, moreover, that many of the rapidly formed Iraqi "divisions" were really only brigades made up of between 1,000 and 5,000 soldiers. By Hashim's estimates, Kuwait's border defenses at their greatest strength were manned by 75,000 to 150,000 soldiers. According to U.S. intelligence estimates, the Iraqis had arrayed eight armored divisions plus three brigades behind their defensive lines, an army of about 120,000 men. Behind these divisions were eight Republican Guard divisions, a force of 100,000 well-armed and well-trained soldiers. The Republican Guard divisions were more likely to be manned at full levels. Thus, the peak number of soldiers in the Kuwait Theater of Operators, according to Hashim, was somewhere between 300,000 and 370,000—a significant difference from the numbers estimated by the Pentagon and by Schwarzkopf.

On the eve of the war, it was likely that the number of Iraqi soldiers on the battlefield was smaller still. During the Iran-Iraq war, front-line soldiers enjoyed a liberal leave policy. They were allowed to spend one week at home for each three on the front. Documents captured at the conclusion of the Gulf War indicated that a similar leave policy had been in effect for front-line units. But interviews with Iraqi prisoners of war and defectors suggested that many Iraqi soldiers who left the front on leave never returned. It was likely, according to U.S. intelligence officials, that, as a result of desertion, some front-line Iraqi units suffered attrition rates of between 20 and 50 percent before and during the Allied air campaign. If true, that would have reduced the front-line forces to as few as 50,000 soldiers on the eve of the commencement of the ground campaign. On February 24, then, when the ground war began, Saddam Hussein may well have had as few as 300,000 soldiers in the Kuwait Theater of Operations. Citing the information provided by his own sources, Hashim believed the number was even smaller, and that perhaps as few as 200,000 soldiers remained in the KTO by the time the ground war began.

Such low estimates of the size of the Iraqi force appear to jibe with other facts known about the war. It appeared that about $4\frac{1}{2}$ of Saddam Hussein's eight Republican Guard divisions—the Adnan, the Nebuchadnezzar, the Al Faw, the 8th Special Forces, and part of the Hammurabi—escaped the Allied onslaught. This amounted to a force of well over 60,000 men. Many of these were the forces that Lieutenant General Fred Franks had intended to trap in the Basra pocket. All were integral elements of the "center of gravity" that General Schwarzkopf and his commanders had targeted prior to the war.

Postwar reconstructions and interviews suggested that at least half of the soldiers from Iraq's eight to ten armored and mechanized divisions escaped. This would amount to a total of perhaps 50,000 men. When added to the 60,000 soldiers from the Republican Guard divisions who are believed to have escaped, the number of escaped Iraqi forces jumps to 110,000. The Pentagon's count of 65,000 captured Iraqis seems reasonable. Hashim and other analysts suggested that perhaps another 25,000 to 50,000 Iraqi soldiers were killed and wounded. Those numbers would bring the total Iraqi force level on the eve of the ground war to somewhere between 200,000 and 225,000 soldiers.

The Central Command and the Pentagon have been reluctant to estimate the numbers of Iraqi military casualties. They note correctly that the Allied forces never engaged in a "body count." The Allied air campaign targeted only Iraqi strategic centers and airfields, logistics sites, and war equipment—never soldiers. But the estimate by the Central Command and the Pentagon that 100,000 Iraqi soldiers perished in the war is difficult to countenance. The first and most obvious problem with the estimate is the historical ratio of dead to wounded in modern battles. Typically in modern warfare, military historians have found that the wounded have outnumbered the dead by ratios of between 3:1 and 4:1. If 100,000 Iraqis died, another 300,000 to 400,000 Iraqis would likely have been wounded. Evidence, however, from postwar interviews with Iraqi soldiers, Allied medics, and other sources indicated that the number of Iraqi wounded on the battlefield was probably in the tens of thousands.

Military analysts have long known that average daily personnel-casualty rates for ground forces have declined significantly over the past 300 years for forces of roughly comparable size. According to George W. S. Kuhn, a Washington, D.C., defense analyst, improvements in the effectiveness of battlefield weapons have been more than offset by other improvements. For example, better communications have allowed soldiers to disperse widely over the battlefield. Movement across larger battle areas is increasingly rapid because of improved vehicles. Soldiers are better protected by both vehicle armor and body armor.

During the prosecution of Operation Desert Storm, Kuhn completed a detailed four-year study for the Defense Department on the patterns of battle-casualty rates associated with patterns of modern ground operations. His study encompassed campaigns of the Second World War, the Korean War, the Arab-Israeli wars, and hundreds of mock battles fought at the U.S. Army's National Training Center. After finishing this study, Kuhn independently examined the numbers released by the Pentagon and other public records on the conduct of Operation Desert Storm. He scrutinized the figures released on Iraqi tanks, artillery, and armored personnel carriers that had been destroyed by air and ground forces during the forty-two days of conflict in January and February. He allowed for the character and numbers of other types of targets, such as command and logistics sites and headquarters. He noted reports of the character of the bombing campaign, of Iraqi shelters, and of the fighting on the Iraqi defensive lines and the armored engagements in the ground war. He also considered the count of prisoners of war, and the range of possible sizes for the Iraqi force in the KTO.

Given the extraordinarily mobile and rapid nature of the ground campaign, Kuhn concluded that the maximum probable rate of Iraqi wounded during the four-day ground campaign was almost certainly no more than 10 percent; a more realistic figure would be around 5 percent. If Kuhn is correct and if there were 540,000 Iraqis in the KTO, as the Pentagon asserted, the maximum probable number of wounded would be 54,000, but a more reasonable maximum would be 27,000. Using the historical ratio of wounded to killed in modern wars of 3:1 to 4:1, that yields a maximum number of killed ranging from 6,500 to 18,000 during the ground campaign.

If there were 250,000 Iraqis in the Kuwait Theater of Operations, as Ahmed Hashim estimated, Kuhn's patterns of rates for this type of ground operation suggest that there would have been 12,500 to 25,000 Iraqi soldiers wounded and another 3,000 to 8,000 killed during the ground campaign. Those numbers correlate with a separate approach Kuhn took in his analysis. Kuhn calculated the probable number of casualties from the number of weapons, vehicles, and other targets the Pentagon has said were destroyed in the air and ground campaigns. Working from the Pentagon counts, the air campaign in the KTO may have killed some 5,000 to 10,000 Iraqis, while the four-day ground campaign added perhaps another 3,000 to 7,000 dead. Combining the two analyses, and assuming Hashim's figure of 250,000 Iraqi troops in the KTO, the air and ground campaigns against the Iraqi forces in the Kuwait Theater of Operations may have accounted for a maximum total of perhaps 8,000 to 18,000 Iraqi dead. Kuhn suspected that the numbers may be lower.

Anthony H. Cordesman, a highly regarded defense analyst and the co-author of two authoritative books on the Iran-Iraq war, placed the number of Iraqi casualties from the war at a maximum of 25,000 killed and 50,000 wounded. Cordesman insisted that these were only guesstimates, and he conceded that they were probably "on the high side." Cordesman's estimate is somewhat higher than George Kuhn's but significantly lower than that of the Pentagon. Cordesman concludes that the ratio of dead to injured in the Iraqi army may have been higher than in other wars because the Iraqi medical services in the rear broke down, contributing to a higher-than-usual number of Iraqi fatalities on the front lines. In any event, Cordesman also does not believe there were 540,000 of 623,000 Iraqi soldiers in the KTO. Cordesman noted that those force-size numbers were nominal ones associated with fully manned divisions—a worst-case Pentagon planning estimate. "Those are the numbers that were cited," he said, "but it becomes more and more difficult to support them."

Anecdotal evidence from postwar interviews with Iraqi soldiers supports a conclusion that there were not as many killed as the Pentagon has suggested. Iraqi prisoners talked of being terrified by bombing attacks, but not of being slaughtered by them. They told how they protected themselves by hiding in ditches next to their tanks or in their bunkers. Convoy drivers spoke of running from their vehicles when they came under air attack. Historically, bombing attacks against dug-in infantry have rarely produced high casualty rates. In this case, however, they prompted wholesale desertion.

On the Allied side, soldiers spoke of seeing dead Iraqis, but most admitted to seeing tens or scores of corpses—not thousands. In the biggest tank battle of the war, in which the U.S. 1st Armored Division destroyed about 100 Iraqi tanks and armored personnel carriers, an intelligence officer from the division estimated that about 340 Iraqis had died. In fact, there were few other heavy force-on-force battles. The Tawakalna division was largely overrun by the U.S. 1st and 3rd Armored Divisions after several sharp skirmishes with cavalry; the Marines made short work of a battalion of Iraq's 5th Mechanized Division in the al-Burgan oil field fight. In several other fights, the anecdotal evidence suggested that hundreds of Iraqis died in each, but not thousands. As soldiers from the U.S. 1st and 2nd Marine Divisions swept through the heavily defended southeastern quarter of Kuwait, for instance, officers reported that their units had destroyed 2,080 tanks, armored personnel carriers, and artillery pieces. Their count after four days of fighting was 1,510 Iraqi soldiers killed in those battles. Even the so-called highway of death west of Kuwait City was really more of a highway of destruction and panic, Anthony Cordesman concluded. He walked the highway through the Mutlah pass after the war. "It was an incredibly impressive achievement of air power," Cordesman said, "but it was not a highway of death." When the lead and rear vehicles came under attack, most of the drivers and passengers fled the scene. Cordesman said that most of the vehicles he saw were intact and abandoned. "There weren't that many bodies, and on the other vehicles, there certainly wasn't any blood."

These numbers, if true, reveal the genuine triumph of American and Allied soldiers and airmen, their battlefield commanders, and the generals and their aides who planned and directed the war effort against Iraq. The goal of the Jedi Knights, with their doctrine of maneuver, was to confuse and terrorize the Iraqis and to force them to surrender or flee, but to avoid battles where possible. In conception and execution, the Allied war plan did just that. A devastating air campaign took away the enemy's intelligence sources, leaving him bewildered and fearful, and exhausted from relentless bombing. Feints and deception kept the Iraqis pinned in place, while the ground forces swept around their defense and rolled them up from behind. Only the Republican Guard stood and fought, and they were stunned and ultimately destroyed by the range and accuracy of superior American weaponry, which allowed soldiers to kill their opposition from long distances, before the enemy was even in a position to fix his sights on a target and fire on it.

In its emphasis on high technology, the Pentagon has been amply vindicated by the Gulf War. The performance of the F-117A Stealth fighter appears to have silenced its critics. Although Baghdad's air-defense radars were formidable, the F-117A defeated them with ease, delivering its ordinance with extraordinary accuracy. Postwar examination of the destruction wrought by the Stealth fighters in central Baghdad confirmed that so-called collateral damage—damage to structures in the immediate vicinity of bombing targets—was remarkably light. A team of reporters sent to Baghdad after the war published an account of their visit in *The Nation* magazine. They concluded that the injuries from such damage were remarkably light. At the worst, reporters found, the bombing might have killed 3,000 civilians, but the number probably was much smaller.

There has nevertheless been some thought criticism of target selection in Baghdad, both from inside the Pentagon and from without. Analysts concluded that at the end of the war on February 28, only 15 percent of Iraq's electricity-delivery grid remained functional; by contrast, at the conclusion of the Second World War, Germany had *lost* only 15 percent of its electrical grid. Some civilian engineering analysts have estimated that the war cost the Iraqi people some fifteen to twenty years of industrial and infrastructural development. More immediately, it left the Iraqi people susceptible to the rapid spread of cholera, typhoid, and other diseases.

Air Force officials said that they had to target the Iraqi electrical grid because of its critical importance to the facilities in which Saddam Hussein continued to develop his weapons of mass destruction. American intelligence officials confirmed that, because there was so little certainty about the location and even the existence of several nuclear-development and chemical-weapons facilities, the Iraqi electrical grid had to be virtually destroyed. The secret nuclear-weapons complex at al-Atheer forty miles south of Baghdad is perhaps the best example of the problems the United States and its allies had in identifying such facilities; its existence was never confirmed until long after hostilities were concluded.

Indeed, inspectors from the United Nations and the International Atomic Energy Agency (IAEA) were started to discover in their postwar inspections just how advanced the Iraqis were in their efforts to develop both nuclear and hydrogen bombs. By the early 1980s, the Iraqis were fully engaged in what one analyst called the equivalent of the Manhattan Project, the mammoth American effort during the Second World War to build an atomic bomb. David Kay, one of the two chief inspectors on the U.N. team, said the Iraqi program employed 15,000 to 20,000 scientists and engineers and technicians and cost Iraq billions of dollars while it was fighting its war with Iran. By August 1990, on the eve of Saddam Hussein's invasion of Kuwait, Iraq was only twelve to eighteen months away from producing its first nuclear bomb—not five to ten years, as some experts had previously thought.

Among the 45,000 pages of documents the U.N. team found was one linking an unspecified surface-to-surface missile program with the nuclear program. It was a memo from the Ministry of Defense to the Iraqi Atomic Energy Commission that spoke of using a concrete warhead device to test the missile. "The people who ought to be scared about this are not the Israelis," Kay said. "It's the other Arab states. This was a long-term program to provide regional dominance, and a deterrence to keep the superpowers out."

Since the end of the war, Saddam Hussein has taken steps to quickly rebuild his army. Of the sixty to seventy divisions he had prior to the war, twenty to twenty-five never were engaged in the Kuwait Theater of Operations. Besides the $4\frac{1}{2}$ Republican Guard divisions that escaped virtually unharmed, one—the four-brigade Baghdad Division—saw almost no action. An estimated 700 Iraqi tanks escaped destruction. They became the nucleus of a new army.

At the end of the war, Saddam abolished his 800,000-man Popular Army, a ragtag militia that many Iraqis had taken to calling "the unpopular army." He has since set about reconstructing his army of sixty to seventy divisions into a leaner but more capable and mobile force of approximately forty divisions, with 300,000 to 400,000 men. He has eliminated the twenty-five infantry divisions that were overrun on the front lines in southern Kuwait. The Republican Guard is being rebuilt and enlarged, probably to a force of between twelve and fourteen divisions. Other armored and mechanized forces will be kept at their former level of between six and eight divisions. These forces will all be supplied with tanks, including at least 500 T-72s and thousands of armored personnel carriers.

One of the mysteries of the ground war was the whereabouts of the Iraqi army's armored personnel carriers (APCs) and infantry fighting vehicles (IFVs). For desert warfare, these tracked and wheeled armored vehicles with large-caliber rapid-firing guns are second only to the tank in fearsomeness. Iraq was said to have some 6,000 APCs and IFVs, but Allied intelligence counted only 2,800 in the KTO, of which an estimated 1,400 escaped. The Central Command estimates defy logic, since most mechanized armies travel with roughly an equal number of tanks and APCs. Central Command also claimed to have counted 4,500 tanks in the KTO, of which 3,800 were destroyed and 700 escaped. One explanation would be that many APCs and IFS were counted as tanks. If so, that would mean there were fewer tanks and more APCs in the theater, and fewer tanks and more APCs were destroyed. But the answer may never be known.

The International Institute for Strategic Studies in London estimated that as of October 1991 the Iraqi army had about 2,300 tanks and 4,400 armored vehicles. Ahmed Hashim disagreed, putting the number of tanks at between 1,700 and 2,600. What is certain is that, less than a year after the war had ended, Iraq already had rebuilt its army to a size more potent than that of any of its neighboring countries.

If anyone lost the war besides the Iraqi army, it was the American and international press. Disorganized, anarchic by nature, and chronically competitive among themselves, the news reporters assigned to cover Desert Storm were no match for the machine of the U.S. Central Command and the Pentagon. The mismatch was compounded by the fact that Saudi Arabia was openly hostile to the press. There was thus virtually no way to circumvent the restrictions imposed by the military. Reporters were forced to cover the war in "combat pools," small groups of reporters sent to Pentagon-approved sites where they reported and wrote stories for all reporters in the country.

As a result, the news that came from the Persian Gulf War was the news the military wanted presented. It was not that reporters did not want to do a better job or were not willing to risk their lives to get better stories; indeed, many reporters in the Gulf seethed with the knowledge that their coverage was inadequate. But they simply could not get to the story to cover it.

One consequence of this was that the press as an institution fell still further in the public's esteem. Journalists poorly prepared to cover war, high technology, and international diplomacy were assigned to cover the conflict in the Gulf. A great many embarrassed the profession. By contrast, briefers provided to the press by the military seemed, more often than not, professional, knowledgeable, and worthy of trust. The situation became so bad that "Saturday Night Live" aired a skit satirizing the performance of the press corps assigned to cover Desert Storm and lauding the military.

More seriously, the American public, because of the shackling of the press, learned little of the heroics of soldiers like those in Captain Gerald Davie's cavalry troops or Colonel Randolph House's brigade who defended and rescued their comrades during vicious firefights. The taxpayers who bore the burden of the cost of Desert Storm were told of virtually none of the battles of the war, where they were fought, or how tough they were. The combined cost of Desert Storm is estimated at somewhere between $60 billion and $70 billion, budget analysts and government officials said. Cash contributions from other countries were expected to cover roughly $42 billion of that amount, though other "in kind" contributions of fuel, food, and other goods will defray that further. Whatever the final cost, it is clear that the American taxpayer had a substantial investment in the war. And yet for all of the air time and newsprint and magazine coverage devoted to the war, only an extremely incomplete and limited picture of the war was conveyed to the people on whose support the effort relied.

Perhaps the most troubling aspects of the conflict was the Bush administrations' desire to circumvent Congress by seeking United Nations approval for intervention in the Middle East. The decision to secure the approval of the U.N. Security Council before moving against Iraq was at least partly rooted in the calculations of domestic politics, according to several advisers to President Bush. While there was nothing improper in that, Bush and his advisers have since attempted to cloak their motives in rhetoric about their lofty aspirations for a rejuvenated world body. In fact, the Bush administration's reliance on the United Nations has been highly selective. In its postwar diplomacy in the Middle East and in its attempts to broker a conclusion to the Ethiopian civil war, to cite just two examples, the administration all but ignored the United Nations.

When the administration moved closer to a showdown with Saddam Hussein, as the United Nations' January 15 deadline approached, there was virtual hostility on the part of the President and his men toward the constitutional requirements that govern the nation's conduct of foreign policy, especially as it may lead to war. Like each of his predecessors since Richard Nixon, George Bush believed that the War Powers Resolution passed by Congress in 1973 was unconstitutional. Also like his predecessors, Bush refused to test the resolution's constitutionality in the courts. The problem with the War Powers Resolution was that it was so riddled with loopholes that the executive branch has found it a simple matter to ignore its strictures. The White House was convinced that it could proceed toward war with Iraq without the consent of Congress, with or without the resolution. Indeed, the resolution has served as a smokescreen, obscuring the true state of relations between the executive and legislative branches. There is virtually no meaningful debate among constitutional scholars about the fact that it is Congress alone that has the authority to put the nation into war. That Congress has virtually abdicated its constitutional responsibilities in so many areas does not mean that its war-making authority is thereby conferred upon the executive branch. The President is authorized by the Constitution to commit military forces only where the defense of the nation is at issue. Where offensive military operations are contemplated, the Constitutional clearly requires the consent of Congress.

George Bush's remarkable success in constructing the international coalition against Iraq should not obscure this point. Although he ultimately sought and received the approval of Congress, Bush has stated that he believed such approval was not needed. In the twentieth century, wars begun by Presidents have been responsible for most of the armed conflicts in which the United States has been engaged; since the Second World War, Presidents have led the United States into every armed conflict. On this crucial matter, the genesis and manner of American intervention in the Persian Gulf have only deepened the debate over how the United States ought to properly and democratically decide whether or not to commit the republic to war.

Chapter XXXII

From Prosperity to Terrorism, 1992–2003

171. The Republican Party, "The Contract with America," 1994

Led by Georgia representative Newt Gingrich, the Republican Party gained control of both the Senate and the House of Representatives in the 1994 congressional elections. Gingrich proclaimed the victory a revolution, a full and final rejection of liberal public policy that Gingrich said had dominated American politics since the 1960s. The Republican Party promoted its cause in the Contract with America, a set of pledges, principles, and policy initiatives designed to be sure winners with voters. Reprinted here, the Contract with America lays out a libertarian agenda that included tax cuts, a balanced federal budget, and smaller government on the national level.

As Republican Members of the House of Representatives and as citizens seeking to join that body we propose not just to change its policies, but even more important, to restore the bonds of trust between the people and their elected representatives. That is why, in this era of official evasion and posturing, we offer instead a detailed agenda for national renewal, a written commitment with no fine print.

This year's election offers the chance, after four decades of one-party control, to bring to the House a new majority that will transform the way Congress works. That historic change would be the end of government that is too big, too intrusive, and too easy with the public's money. It can be the beginning of a Congress that respects the values and shares the faith of the American family.

Like Lincoln, our first Republican president, we intend to act "with firmness in the right, as God gives us to see the right." To restore accountability to Congress. To end its cycle of scandal and disgrace. To make us all proud again of the way free people govern themselves.

On the first day of the 104th Congress, the new Republican majority will immediately pass the following major reforms, aimed at restoring the faith and trust of the American people in their government:

First, require all laws that apply to the rest of the country also apply equally to the Congress;
Second, select a major independent auditing firm to conduct a comprehensive audit of Congress for waste, fraud, or abuse;
Third, cut the number of House committees, and cut committee staff by one-third;
Fourth, limit the terms of all committee chairs;
Fifth, ban the casting of proxy votes in committee;
Sixth, require committee meetings to be open to the public;
Seventh, require a three-fifths majority vote to pass a tax increase;
Eighth, guarantee an honest accounting of our federal budget by implementing zero baseline budgeting.

Thereafter, within the first hundred days of the 104th Congress, we shall bring to the House Floor the following bills, each to be given full and open debate, each to

Source: Ed Gillespie and Bob Schellhas, eds. *Contract With America: The Bold Plan by Rep. Newt Gingrich, Rep. Dick Armey and the House Republicans to Change the Nation* (New York: Times Books, 1994), 7–19.

be given a clear and fair vote, and each to be immediately available this day for public inspection and scrutiny.

THE FISCAL RESPONSIBILITY ACT

• A balanced budget/tax limitation amendment and a legislative line-item veto to restore fiscal responsibility to an out-of-control Congress, requiring them to live under the same budget constraints as families and businesses.

THE TAKING BACK OUR STREETS ACT

• An anti-crime package including stronger truth in sentencing, "good faith" exclusionary rule exemptions, effective death penalty provisions, and cuts in social spending from this summer's crime bill to fund prison construction and additional law enforcement to keep people secure in their neighborhoods and kids safe in their schools.

THE PERSONAL RESPONSIBILITY ACT

• Discourage illegitimacy and teen pregnancy by prohibiting welfare to minor mothers and denying increased AFDC for additional children while on welfare, cut spending for welfare programs, and enact a tough two-years-and-out provision with work requirements to promote individual responsibility.

THE FAMILY REINFORCEMENT ACT

• Child support enforcement, tax incentives for adoption, strengthening rights of parents in their children's education, stronger child pornography laws, and an elderly dependent care tax credit to reinforce the central role of families in American society.

THE AMERICAN DREAM RESTORATION ACT

• A $500-per-child tax credit, begin repeal of the marriage tax penalty, and creation of American Dream Savings Accounts to provide middle-class tax relief.

THE NATIONAL SECURITY RESTORATION ACT

• No U.S. troops under UN command and restoration of the essential parts of our national security funding to strengthen our national defense and maintain our credibility around the world.

THE SENIOR CITIZENS FAIRNESS ACT

• Raise the Social Security earnings limit, which currently forces seniors out of the workforce, repeal the 1993 tax hikes on Social Security benefits, and provide tax incentives for private long-term care insurance to let older Americans keep more of what they have earned over the years.

THE JOB CREATION AND WAGE ENHANCEMENT ACT

• Small business incentives, capital gains cut and indexation, neutral cost recovery, risk assessment/cost-benefit analysis, strengthening of the Regulatory Flexibility Act and unfunded mandate reform to create jobs and raise worker wages.

THE COMMON SENSE LEGAL REFORMS ACT

• "Loser pays" laws, reasonable limits on punitive damages, and reform of product liability laws to stem the endless tide of litigation.

THE CITIZEN LEGISLATURE ACT

• A first-ever vote on term limits to replace career politicians with citizen legislators.

TEN BILLS: SIGNED PROMISES, SPECIFIC GOALS

1. *Balanced budget amendment/line-item veto.*
2. *Stop violent criminals:*
   —effective death penalty provisions;
   —greater emphasis on prison funding and law enforcement.
3. *Welfare reform:*
   —discourages illegitimacy and teen pregnancy by prohibiting welfare to minor mothers and denying increased AFDC for additional children while on welfare;
   —cuts spending for welfare programs;
   —ends welfare for families collecting AFDC for five years and for noncitizens;
   —requires welfare recipients to work.
4. *Protect our kids:*
   —child support enforcement;
   —tax incentives for adoption;
   —strengthening rights of parents in their children's education;

- stronger child pornography laws;
- an elderly dependent care tax credit.
5. *Tax cuts for families:*
   - a $500-per-child family tax credit;
   - reforming the anti-marriage bias in the tax code;
   - an "American Dream Savings Accounts" in the form of individual retirement accounts (IRAs) for first-time home buyers, education expenses, and retirement.
6. *Strong national defense:*
   - no U.S. troops under UN command;
   - building budget firewalls between defense and nondefense spending to prevent raids on the defense budget;
   - creating a missile defense system against rogue dictatorships like North Korea.
7. *Raise the senior citizens' earning limit:*
   - increases the earnings limit to at least $30,000;
   - repeals the Clinton tax hikes on Social Security benefits;
   - provides tax incentives for private long-term care insurance.
8. *Economic growth and regulatory reform:*
   - capital gains cut and indexation;
   - neutral cost recovery;
   - risk assessment/cost-benefit analysis;
   - strengthening the Regulatory Flexibility Act;
   - unfunded mandates reforms.
9. *Common sense legal reforms:*
   - "loser pays" to stop frivolous lawsuits;
   - limits on punitive damages;
   - honesty in evidence to exclude "junk science."
10. *Congressional term limits:*
    - a first-ever vote on term limits for members of Congress to replace career politicians with citizen legislators, including six-year and twelve-year term limits.

172. Brent Schlender, "Microsoft: First America, Now the World," 1997

The American economy boomed in the 1990s. It sustained strong growth year after year, even surviving virtually unscathed a deep recession in Asian markets. Computer and communications technology drove much of American economic growth, and Bill Gates's Microsoft Corporation led the way in that sector. Gates was the richest person in the world in the 1990s and the envy of millions. Here, Fortune *magazine looks at Microsoft's moves to dominate the global computer market.*

For a fellow with a net worth of $42 billion, Bill Gates stays awfully hungry. Every year he makes a point of visiting China at least once. He makes grueling, whistle-stop tours, like the one in India in March to talk to customers, government officials, and employees. Why? "That's where we'll get a lot of our growth in the coming years," he replies. "These countries are only just getting started buying PCs in big numbers. And because they usually don't have lots of legacy systems already in place—you know, mainframes and minicomputers—we have a chance to have an even bigger share of the overall computer business than we do in the U.S. or Europe or Japan. You bet I think it's important."

As infotech booms around the world, companies like Microsoft can't help but take note. During the past fiscal year, which ended in June, more than half of the company's $11.4 billion or so in total software sales came from its overseas operation. Most of that derives from Europe and Japan. But the developing economies of Latin America, Eastern Europe, Africa, and Asia—countries that heretofore have been both technological backwaters and hotbeds of software piracy—now account for nearly 10% of Microsoft's overseas sales and are by far the company's fastest-expanding markets.

Source: Brent Schlender, "Microsoft: First America, Now the World," *Fortune* 136:4 (August 18, 1997), 214–217.

To best tap these markets, Gates has mapped out a blueprint for making Microsoft a globetrotting multinational. The Microsoft approach, like its software, is fast, lean, and smart. Gates hires mostly local managers to run operations. Microsoft's sales offices and wholly owned subsidiaries are spread throughout nearly 60 countries and are staffed by 6,200 employees, among whom—believe it or not—only five are expats.

These managers, knowledgeable about their home markets, create partnerships with small companies that peddle Microsoft products like Windows, Microsoft Office, and Windows NT. This allows Gates to keep his foreign staff small. Each overseas employee generates more than $1 *million* of revenue. (For the entire 22,000-person company, the figure is about $500,000 per employee.)

In fact, Microsoft's go-go globalism in many ways resembles a pyramid scheme, much like the symbiotic, multilevel marketing and direct-sales structures employed by Avon or Mary Kay Cosmetics. Its small local "partner" companies do most of the grunt work of actually flogging software and supporting customers. These partners in turn train other partners, and the sales network grows.

More than simply attempting to build its own aggressive overseas sales force, Microsoft's real goal is to foster miniature local software industries to exploit nascent markets on the company's behalf. For instance, Microsoft helps bankroll independent software distributors, which are openly encouraged to handle competitors' products as well. And it prods still other local companies to write their own commercial software programs that, of course, complement its flagship Windows operating systems but also often compete directly with Microsoft's word processors, spreadsheets, and other applications. The most extreme example is China, where Microsoft's staff of 70 works with hundreds of budding software companies and a legion of 15,000 certified resellers (not people but companies), whose ranks could easily double in the coming year.

There are a couple of big reasons Microsoft is able to do so much overseas with so little. First, because software products are so easy to manufacture and a snap to ship, Gates doesn't have to worry about building and operating factories. Instead Microsoft, as it does in the U.S., contracts out to others to duplicate and package much of its software. Just as important, PCs are so cheap and easy to set up, unlike mainframes and minicomputers, that businesses and governments in even the poorest and most backward nations can afford them. In fact they are the perfect technology to enable small-scale—or even rustic—enterprises to break into the Information Age.

Of course, there are big impediments too. Microsoft must adapt its products to support dozens of different languages and writing schemes, but that's another task it is increasingly farming out to local contractors. Distribution systems are a joke in many developing regions, as are transportation and telecommunications infrastructures. Also, software, like computers, faces stiff tariffs in many developing countries—until recently, for example, India imposed 112% duties on imported high-tech goods, though it's moving to eliminate them.

But by far the biggest bugaboo is piracy. In Eastern Europe, China, and much of the rest of Asia, more than 90% of the copies of software in use are ripped-off versions. In some countries the government is the worst offender. Even in Western Europe the figure tops 50% in many markets. According to Orlando Ayala, the dapper 40-year-old Colombian who manages Microsoft's efforts in Latin America, Southeast Asia, the South Pacific, India, Africa, and the Middle East, the market value of illicit software worldwide runs in the tens of *billions* of dollars each year. Says he: "I drool more than I cry about it, though, because if we can take back even a fraction of those lost sales, it's pure upside."

One of the best places to observe how Microsoft's global formula all fits together is in India, a country where Gates was feted like royalty when he visited earlier this year. On the Microsoft org chart, India is part of what is called the "intercontinental region," that enormous territory supervised by Ayala. It's a diverse cultural quilt that reflects the entire spectrum of economic development, from industrialized countries like Australia and South Africa, to stirring giants like Brazil, Mexico, and Indonesia, to outposts in Africa that have one-person sales offices.

While India, with its billion-plus population, is by far the biggest country in the territory, it contributed only about $30 million, or 4% of the intercontinental region's $740 million in sales, this fiscal year. Despite its mind-boggling poverty, Gates and Ayala still think India is one of the most promising emerging markets on the globe because it also harbors a thriving middle class of more than 50 million people, many of whom are well educated and speak and read English. The country also can boast some of the best computer programmers on the planet.

When Microsoft first opened an office in Bombay in 1990, it didn't parachute in an expat to get things started. ("That's key," says Gates. "It sends the wrong message to have a foreigner come in to run things.") Instead it hired Rajiv Nair, a gregarious, 34-year-old U.S.-educated Indian who worked for computer maker Unisys.

Nair's initial goal was rather modest—to make sure that the hundreds of thousands of PCs made in India each year were loaded with legitimate copies of Microsoft's operating systems and applications. In those early days virtually every Indian computer maker bundled pirated software not only because it was easy to copy but because import duties made the real thing prohibitively expensive. Recalls Nair: "Back then a basic PC with a monochrome monitor cost $7,000. Nobody wanted to pay for the software too."

It was slow going those first few years—not until 1993 did Microsoft surpass $1 million in annual sales, even though Indians had embraced PCs with a vengeance. Besides lobbying the government to reduce tariffs and enforce anti-counterfeiting laws, and cajoling PC makers to come clean, Nair also had to build a distribution channel from scratch. He and a handful of associates traveled from city to city trying to find small businesses willing to risk becoming distributors of products that retailers didn't want to carry and that customers didn't want to pay for. At first there were few takers.

But Nair stuck with it. By 1995 annual sales were only about $7 million but were more than doubling every year. More important, the government had finally begun phasing out tariffs on high-tech imports, which would dramatically lower software prices. That combination of news caught the attention of Steve Ballmer, Microsoft's executive vice president for sales and marketing. Intrigued, Ballmer, who is also Gates' right-hand man, went to India in 1995 for a whirlwind weeklong look-see. His conclusion: India was potentially a huge opportunity, and time was a-wasting. Shortly after he got back to headquarters in Redmond, Wash., he authorized turning the Indian operation into a full-blown subsidiary. He also convinced Sanjay Parthasarathy, 32, one of Microsoft's most respected computer scientists at headquarters, to go back to his homeland to become the director of a newly created region that includes India, Nepal, Bhutan, and Sri Lanka.

By the end of this year Parthasarathy and Nair, who is now the general manager of the subsidiary, will have quadrupled the size of the Indian staff to 100, opened liaison offices in five cities, and set up reseller training centers that have certified 1,500 new resellers. Many of those resellers in turn were also certified to train still others. By the end of 1997, Nair's goal is to have 10,000 certified resellers, all capable of advising various kinds of enterprises and institutions on how to use Microsoft software to automate their businesses.

Meanwhile, the company also set up a special office in Bangalore—a city that many call India's Silicon Valley—to help local software developers build more Windows-compatible programs. For instance, after Gates learned during his recent visit that India is a land of more than a dozen different languages, he asked Nair and Parthasarathy to contract with local software developers to quickly adapt Windows to as many of them as possible. (Gates is also contemplating establishing a software research and development center in Bangalore to tap into the rich vein of Indian programming talent.)

All this effort is paying off handsomely. The piracy rate in India is down to 75% from 90% two years ago, and needless to say, sales are accelerating. That's not good enough for Parthasarathy, who is as intense as Nair is cheerful. (They make a great good-cop/bad-cop team.) Says he: "I think we were a couple of years late really getting going here, but on the other hand, I don't think anybody else recognized India's enormous potential either. It's too easy to overlook that there are as many people in India's middle and upper classes as there are in most European countries. I'd be extremely disappointed if we didn't surpass $100 million in sales by the end of the decade."

That's not chump change, and the same scenario is playing out in Brazil, Russia, Indonesia, and, of course, China. Ayala thinks his region alone—which doesn't include either Russia or China—will ring up more than $3 billion in sales by 2000. Okay, but before Microsoft gets there, it faces a big challenge.

Some observers wonder whether Microsoft is delegating too much responsibility to its partner companies around the globe, many of which are tiny three- or five-person outfits getting into business for the first time. The worry is: Does this approach remove Microsoft too far from its ultimate customers? Gates and Ayala contend that the same model has worked for years in the U.S., Japan, and Europe, so why shouldn't it in developing countries too? Says Ayala: "The idea is simple: If you spread the wealth among your partners, they will be just as entrepreneurial as we would be. Besides, when you have a lot of partners, if one isn't doing a good job, it will get squeezed out by one that does."

In the larger developing countries, Microsoft helps its partners professionalize their operations by offering management and sales training. Also, in China and Eastern

Europe the company offers exchange programs in which it invites promising people from key resellers and software developers to come to work for Microsoft for a year or so to pick up more worldly ways.

Microsoft has one more not-so-secret weapon going for it that nobody else has: namely Bill Gates. He may be an icon in the U.S., but in the developing world he's the apotheosis of success, the ultimate entrepreneurial role model, who gives Microsoft a cachet no other company can boast. When he visited India last March, literally thousands of businessmen dropped everything to go hear him speak and find out what opportunities he saw for India.

"I've never seen anything like it," said an exhausted Nair as he sipped a Scotch during the final banquet of Gates' pilgrimage. "He may be the richest man in the world, but you can't begin to put a value on what he means to our business."

Try $42 billion and counting.

---

173. Debra Dickerson, "Crazy as They Wanna Be," 1999

On April 21, 1999, two students at Columbine High School in suburban Littleton, Colorado, brought guns to school and opened fire on their classmates. An hour later, one teacher and fourteen students, including the two gunmen, lay dead. The Littleton tragedy was the most deadly of a nationwide string of school shootings perpetrated by students. Consequently, Littleton provoked a national, media-induced soul-searching in an attempt to discover the causes of teen violence. In this essay, Debra Dickerson looks at race and a sense of white entitlement to throw new light on the subject.

Blacks have always known that white folks are crazy. Whenever news breaks of yet another bizarre massacre or hideous chain-saw-and-cannibalism-type crime, we call each other from our cubicles and whisper conspiratorially something like, "You know that was somebody white. A brother will shoot you for stepping on his new Nikes or to steal a nice jacket. But white folks—they kill people they don't even know, for no apparent reason, on purpose!"

Blacks routinely characterize certain types of crime as white (and insane) just as whites characterize certain types as black (and animalistic). There was never much doubt among blacks that the Littleton killers were white and male. Someday, maybe, we'll all see that crime and craziness have no race. They do, however, have socioeconomic types. People can only commit crimes or go crazy in the ways that are available to them, logistically and psychologically.

First, let's look at crime and economics. How many blacks (or women, for that matter) were involved in the savings and loan debacle, a bazillion-dollar fiscal rape of America that our grandchildren will still be paying for? I will go out on a limb and guess: few. How many blacks were involved in stupid, intra-ghetto, macho-man gunplay over trivialities? Again, it's just a guess, but I'll go with it: lots.

It is willfully stupid and hateful to think this discrepancy is genetic. It's not that whites are nonviolent by nature, and accordingly choose to express their criminality in kinder, gentler ways, or that blacks are bell-curved at birth with the Willie Horton gene. As more blacks matriculate at the Wharton School, rest assured, more will also sticky-finger their way into Club Med prisons where they can ride around in those cute little golf carts and water peonies for punishment. There's a reason why stockbrokers and insurance agents commit few violent or property crimes and it isn't DNA. The only people who have to fear for their physical safety around a middle-class man (of any race) are his wife, children, mistress and business partners. He can commit crimes from the comfort of his home office and car phone; the illiterate crimi-

---

Source: Debra Dickerson, "Crazy as they Wanna Be," salon.com>News. May 4, 1999. URL: http://www.salon.com/news/feature/1999/05/04/crazy

nal has little choice but to draw blood. More blacks are poor and poorly educated so more blacks commit crimes that don't require special training. Educate them and watch those embezzlement rates soar.

With senseless, non-economic violent crime, the issue is one of societal entitlement and what each strata of society sees as coming to it—that's the "socio" half of the equation. The Littleton killers felt robbed. As white, middle-class males, they understood that they had a certain amount of societal deference coming to them—but where was it? They took their comfort, nice neighborhood and (until their rampage) safe school for granted; those things weren't enough. That couldn't give them the sense of specialness they so clearly craved and felt entitled to. Angry white men in the making, they didn't feel powerful, they didn't feel respected. They felt insignificant, weak, unsure and angry.

They felt like teenagers, in other words, but they were so insulated by their atomized, suburban lives (and no doubt hands-off parenting), they didn't know it would pass. Because they were so incredibly immature, they didn't know that they were incredibly immature, that they could eventually learn to share their sense of entitlement to full citizenship. Being white and well-off, they just knew that attention must be paid and, being children, the only way they could imagine to get some was childish. The result was fiendishly adult, but the underlying impulse was an angry 8-year-old's (the plan to crash a plane into New York City is pure video game).

It's true: Being white, male and well-off doesn't mean what it used to. Most accept it. A few join the black-helicopter brigades and issue pathetic manifestos. Others rant and rave at city council meetings about minorities' special privileges. Eric Harris and Dylan Klebold murdered their way onto the front pages, a place only disturbed children could consider one of glory. But they got their wish. Attention was paid.

Blacks lose their minds on a much smaller, much more self-destructive scale. We burn down our own neighborhoods, disable our own elevators and smash the only grocery store for miles. We graffiti the walls we have to look at every day and we make our own mothers wade through broken malt liquor bottles to get to the bus stop. We're like the teenage girls who slash themselves; feeling pain is feeling something, causing pain is having control over something. We hate our cage but because we neither believe we can leave it or view it as valuable, we make it worse. We blame whites but we punish ourselves. Defeatist blacks who defile their own communities, that all too visible minority, implicitly accept the short leashes of poverty and ignorance and strike back by trashing the jail cell they believe they have to live in. Violent blacks have no belief that they can, let alone should, affect the world; all they want is not to be disrespected on their own patch of turf.

A Def Jam comedian once offered a summary of the difference between whites' and blacks' worldviews. I don't understand white folks, he said. They get depressed. So they spend $5,000 on a psychiatrist. A black man got $5,000? He ain't depressed. Whites think criminals are disproportionately black; blacks think neurotics are disproportionately white. Blacks routinely dismiss suicide, incest, sexual fetishes and any freaky, taboo behavior in general as afflicting only whites. These beliefs extend to the ridiculous. As a hairdresser worked on me once, I asked her about head lice, and she cut me off saying that only whites got them. They don't live in *our* hair. The next day a doctor confirmed my suspicions: I'd had head lice even as the hairdresser worked on me, but her racism blinded her to the little squigglers.

Suicide rates are climbing in the black community, especially among young men, but we refuse to see that either. Sexual abuse and depression debilitate millions of black women but we deny that, too. Poor mental health abounds in the black community, but it's a silent agony. It can't be acknowledged because that's weak and that's white. I'm not white, some harried black woman will quip, I can't afford a nervous breakdown. So we come home from a day in a hairnet and spank our children mercilessly for minor infractions. I'm never sure if it's better or worse that it's almost all inwardly directed.

Even black artistic expression reflects that limited sense of entitlement. I've been so struck by the self-contained worldview of black comedians that I once categorized most of a TV season's-worth of their jokes. Of 45 Def Jam-type comics (extremely popular with the black working and poverty class), exactly one made reference to the world outside of the black community (she made rather sophisticated fun of Jesse Helms and the Republicans). The Clintons' bimbo problems, the two-party system, the economy, war, the collapse of Communism? Nothing. Except for ruminating endlessly about the differences between blacks and whites (and in these jokes, too, whites often came out ahead), it was all about the 'hood. Popular black movies tend to be the same. They're simplistic takes on white racism, drug dealer melodramas or How to be a Player While Making a Booty Call. It's as if the totality of the American reality is off-limits to blacks.

In their own minds, the deranged Littleton killers saw themselves as glorious heroes, something most blacks are still a long way from daring to imagine. Hollywood helps reinforce this exclusion. Virtually no black soldiers were depicted in "Saving Private Ryan," for instance. Spielberg said he chose his soldiers to closely resemble the immigrants of that era, thus automatically excluding blacks though many, like my father, served. It may be that few blacks actually served in the units he depicted, but neither did Tom Hanks. It's all about who gets to portray real Americans.

In comedy, as in killing, for black folks it's still about one powerless individual adrift in a cruel world doing what he has to in order to hold on to his few crumbs and look good doing it. It was inside out for the unhappy white boys Eric and Dylan—they demanded acknowledgement. When societal change made them feel powerless and impotent (in other words, black), they snapped. Unhappy black boys kill for a pair of sneakers. Unhappy white boys kill to be noticed. What's the difference, really?